T0192096

Lecture Notes in Computer Science

Lecture Notes in Artificial Intelligence   13925

Founding Editor

Jörg Siekmann

Series Editors

Randy Goebel, *University of Alberta, Edmonton, Canada*
Wolfgang Wahlster, *DFKI, Berlin, Germany*
Zhi-Hua Zhou, *Nanjing University, Nanjing, China*

The series Lecture Notes in Artificial Intelligence (LNAI) was established in 1988 as a topical subseries of LNCS devoted to artificial intelligence.

The series publishes state-of-the-art research results at a high level. As with the LNCS mother series, the mission of the series is to serve the international R & D community by providing an invaluable service, mainly focused on the publication of conference and workshop proceedings and postproceedings.

Hamido Fujita · Yinglin Wang · Yanghua Xiao ·
Ali Moonis
Editors

Advances and Trends in Artificial Intelligence

Theory and Applications

36th International Conference
on Industrial, Engineering and Other Applications
of Applied Intelligent Systems, IEA/AIE 2023
Shanghai, China, July 19–22, 2023
Proceedings, Part I

 Springer

Editors
Hamido Fujita [iD]
Universiti Teknologi Malaysia
Kuala Lumpur, Malaysia

Yanghua Xiao
Fudan University
Shanghai, China

Yinglin Wang
Shanghai University of Finance
and Economics
Shanghai, China

Ali Moonis
Texas State University
San Marcos, TX, USA

ISSN 0302-9743 ISSN 1611-3349 (electronic)
Lecture Notes in Artificial Intelligence
ISBN 978-3-031-36818-9 ISBN 978-3-031-36819-6 (eBook)
https://doi.org/10.1007/978-3-031-36819-6

LNCS Sublibrary: SL7 – Artificial Intelligence

This Springer imprint is published by the registered company Springer Nature Switzerland AG
The registered company address is: Gewerbestrasse 11, 6330 Cham, Switzerland

Preface

In the last few years, significant progress has been made in computing infrastructures, deep learning, and big foundation models, catalyzing the rapid advancement of artificial intelligence. Computing infrastructures have witnessed remarkable improvements, with the popularity of cloud computing and graphical processing units providing researchers and practitioners with immense computational resources to train and deploy complex AI models. Deep learning enables machines to automatically learn intricate patterns and representations from vast amounts of data. Additionally, big foundation models, such as transformer architectures, have emerged as building blocks for natural language processing and computer vision, empowering AI systems with enhanced understanding and decision-making capabilities. These developments have accelerated the development of more effective intelligent systems to solve real-world complex problems. Moreover, innovative applications of artificial intelligence are continually emerging.

This volume contains the proceedings of the 36th edition of the International Conference on Industrial, Engineering, and other Applications of Applied Intelligent Systems (IEA/AIE 2023), which was held on July 19–22, 2023, in Shanghai, China. IEA/AIE is a yearly conference that focuses on applications of applied intelligent systems to solve real-life problems in all areas including business and finance, science, engineering, industry, cyberspace, bioinformatics, automation, robotics, medicine and biomedicine, and human-machine interactions. IEA/AIE 2023 was organized in cooperation with the ACM Special Interest Group on Artificial Intelligence (SIGAI). This year, 129 submissions were received. Each paper was evaluated using double-blind peer review by at least three reviewers from an international Program Committee consisting of 174 members from 25 countries. Based on the evaluation, a total of 50 papers were selected as full papers and 20 as short papers, which are presented in the two volumes of this book. The acceptance rate was 54%. We would like to thank all the reviewers for the time spent on writing detailed and constructive comments for the authors, and to the latter for the proposal of many high-quality papers.

In the program of IEA/AIE 2023, four special sessions were organized: Collective Intelligence in Social Media (CISM 2023), Intelligent Knowledge Engineering in Decision Making Systems (IKEDMS 2023), Intelligent Systems and e-Applications (iSeA 2023) and Causal Inference and Machine Learning (CIML 2023). In addition, two keynote talks were given by two distinguished researchers, one by Michael Sheng from Macquarie University (Australia) and the other by Cewu Lu from Shanghai Jiaotong University (China). We would like to thank everyone who has contributed to the success of this year's edition of IEA/AIE, that is the authors, reviewers, keynote speakers, Program Committee members and organizers. We would like thank all the sponsors and institutions that have provided strong support for the conference, including Association for the Advancement of Artificial Intelligence (AAAI), Association for Computing Machinery (ACM), Shanghai Computer Society, i-SOMET Incorporated Association, Springer and the Conference Management Toolkit. We are particularly grateful to the organizers of this year's event, including Shanghai University of Finance and Economics, Fudan University and Shanghai Business School. Their support was crucial for the success of this year's conference.

May 2023

Hamido Fujita
Yinglin Wang
Yanghua Xiao
Ali Moonis

Organization

Honorary Chair

Tao Wu   Shanghai University of Medicine and Health Sciences, China

General Chairs

Hamido Fujita   Universiti Teknologi Malaysia, Kuala Lumpur, Malaysia

Ali Moonis   Texas State University, USA

Program Committee Chairs

Yinglin Wang   Shanghai University of Finance and Economics, China

Yanghua Xiao   Fudan University, China

Organizing Chairs

Jun Sasaki   i-SOMET Inc., Japan

Duoqian Miao   Tongji University, China

Liang Zhou   Shanghai University of Medicine and Health Sciences, China

Xing Wu   Shanghai University, China

Bo Huang   Shanghai University of Engineering Science, China

Special Session Chairs

Ali Selamat   Universiti Teknologi Malaysia, Malaysia

Ngoc Thanh Nguyen   Wroclaw University of Technology, Poland

Xiaodong Yue   Shanghai University, China

Xin Xu	Wuhan University of Science and Technology, China
Yufei Chen	Tongji University, China

Program Committee

Alban Grastien	Australian National University, Australia
Alberto Cano	Virginia Commonwealth University, USA
Andreas Speck	Kiel University, Germany
Andrew Tzer-Yeu Chen	University of Auckland, New Zealand
Arkadiusz Liber	Wroclaw University of Science and Technology, Poland
Ayahiko Niimi	Future University Hakodate, Japan
Azri Azmi	Universiti Teknologi Malaysia, Malaysia
Bilel Marzouki	National School of Computer Science, Tunisia
Bin Zhou	National University of Defense Technology, China
Bing Liu	Harbin Institute of Technology, China
Binh Nguyen	University of Science, VNUHCM, Vietnam
Bo Huang	Shanghai University of Engineering Science, China
Bo Xu	Donghua University, China
Chao Shi	Shanghai University of Finance and Economics, China
Chao Tong	Beihang University, China
Chen Chen	Huawei HK, China
Chenkai Guo	Nankai University, China
Chenxu Wang	Xi'an Jiaotong University, China
Claudio Tomazzoli	University of Verona, Italy
Danyang Chen	Guangxi University, China
Dongbo Li	Harbin Institute of Technology, China
Dongdong Zhao	Lanzhou University, China
Dosam Hwang	Yeungnam University, South Korea
Du Nguyen	Nong Lam University, Vietnam
Duc Nguyen	Vietnam Maritime University, Vietnam
Dung Hoang	HCMC University of Technology and Education, Vietnam
Erlei Zhang	Northwest A&F University, China
Erping Zhao	Xizang Minzu University, China
Fan Liu	Hohai University, China
Fei Wang	Xi'an Jiaotong University, China

Francisco Javier Cabrerizo	University of Granada, Spain
Frederick Maier	University of Georgia, USA
Gang Pan	Tianjin University, China
Gautram Srivastava	Brandon University, Canada
Guanghui Zhu	Nanjing University, China
Guoqing Chao	Harbin Institue of Technology at Weihai, China
Hafiza Ayesha Hoor Chaudhry	University of Turin, Italy
Hai Tran	Ho Chi Minh City University of Pedagogy, Vietnam
Han Ding	Xi'an Jiaotong University, China
Hao Sun	Central China Normal University, China
Hao Zhang	Harbin Institute of Technology, China
Haopeng Chen	Shanghai Jiao Tong University, China
Hau Pham	Quang Binh University, Vietnam
Heeryon Cho	Chung-Ang University, South Korea
Hien Nguyen	University of Information Technology, VNU-HCM, Vietnam
Hongming Cai	Shanghai Jiao Tong University, China
Hongping Gan	Northwestern Polytechnical University, China
Hongwei Feng	Fudan University, China
Hua Huang	Guizhou University, China
Huafeng Li	Kunming University of Science and Technology, China
Huiyan Wang	Nanjing University, China
Iman Dehzangi	Rutgers University, USA
Jerry Chun-Wei Lin	Western Norway University of Applied Sciences, Norway
Jia Wei	South China University of Technology, China
Jianming Zhang	Changsha University of Science and Technology, China
Jianqiang Huang	Qinghai University, China
Jiapeng Xiu	Beijing University of Posts and Telecommunications, China
Jiaqing Liang	Fudan University, China
Jing Huo	Nanjing University, China
Jingping Liu	East China University of Science and Technology, China
Jinsong Bao	Donghua University, China
Jixiang Guo	Sichuan University, China
Jukka Ruohonen	University of Turku, Finland
Jun Zhou	East China Normal University, China
Junwei Zhou	Wuhan University of Technology, China
Jyrki Nummenmaa	Tampere University, Finland

Kejia Chen	Nanjing University of Posts and Telecommunications, China
Krishna Reddy P.	International Institute of Information Technology, Hyderabad, India
Lei Huang	Ocean University of China, China
Liang Hu	Tongji University, China
Liang Li	Tianjin University, China
Liang Tao	Hong Kong Metropolitan University, China
Liang Wang	Nanjing University, China
Liangyu Chen	East China Normal University, China
Li-Fang Zhou	Chongqing University of Posts and Telecommunications, China
Liming Zhang	University of Macau, China
Lingyan Ran	Northwestern Polytechnical University, China
Lingyun Song	Northwestern Polytechnical University, China
Lizong Zhang	University of Electronic Science and Technology of China, China
M. Saqib Nawaz	Shenzhen University, China
Marcin Pietranik	Wroclaw University of Science and Technology, Poland
Masaki Kurematsu	Iwate Prefectural University, Japan
Ming Dong	Central China Normal University, China
Mingxi Zhang	University of Shanghai for Science and Technology, China
Min-Ling Zhang	Southeast University, China
Miroslav Hudec	University of Economics in Bratislava, Slovakia
Miroslav Velev	Aries Design Automation, LLC, USA
Mohammad Rashedur Rahman	North South University, Bangladesh
Moulay A. Akhloufi	Université de Moncton, Canada
Mourad Nouioua	Mohamed El Bachir El Ibrahimi University of Bordj Bou Arréridj, Algeria
Nannan Wu	Tianjin University, China
Ngoc-Thanh Nguyen	Wroclaw University of Technology, Poland
Ning Xu	Southeast University, China
Nurulhuda Zainuddin	Universiti Teknologi Malaysia, Malaysia
Pengpeng Zhao	Soochow University, China
Phi Le Nguyen	Hanoi University of Science and Technology, Vietnam
Pingpeng Yuan	Huazhong University of Science & Technology, China
Qian Huang	Hohai University, China
Qian Jiang	Yunnan University, China
Qidong Liu	Zhengzhou University, China

Qingsong Guo	University of Helsinki, Finland
Qiuzhen Lin	Shenzhen University, China
Qiyang Zhao	Beihang University, China
Senyue Zhang	Shenyang Aerospace University, China
Sergei Gorlatch	Münster University, Germany
Shangce Gao	University of Toyama, Japan
Sheng Fang	Shandong University of Science and Technology, China
Shengdong Du	Southwest Jiaotong University, China
Stefania Tomasiello	University of Tartu, Estonia
Tai Dinh	Kyoto College of Graduate Studies for Informatics, Japan
Takeru Yokoi	Tokyo Metropolitan College of Industrial Technology, Japan
Tao Lian	Taiyuan University of Technology, China
Tao Shen	Kunming University of Science and Technology, China
Tao Wang	Northwestern Polytechnical University, China
Tat-Bao-Thien Nguyen	Thuyloi University, Vietnam
Tauheed Khan Mohd	Augustana College, USA
Teeradaj Racharak	Japan Advanced Institute of Science and Technology, Japan
Thi Huyen Trang Phan	Yeungnam University, South Korea
Thomas Lacombe	University of Auckland, New Zealand
Tianxing Wu	Southeast University, China
Tieyun Qian	Wuhan University, China
Ting Liu	Northwestern Polytechnical University, China
Tong Liu	Shandong University of Science and Technology, China
Uday Rage	University of Aizu, Japan
Wai Khuen Cheng	Universiti Tunku Abdul Rahman, Malaysia
Wang Yunlan	Northwestern Polytechnical University, China
Wanyuan Wang	Southeast Univerity, China
Wanyun Cui	Shanghai University of Finance and Economics, China
Wei Ke	Xi'an Jiaotong University, China
Wei Wang	Wuhan University of Science and Technology, China
Wei Zhang	Harbin Institute of Technology, China
Weiguo Zheng	Fudan University, China
Weihao Zheng	Lanzhou University, China
Weixin Jiang	Northwestern University, USA
Wu Yirui	Hohai University, China

Xiao Wang	Shanghai University of Finance and Economics, China
Xiaofang Xia	Xidian University, China
Xiaofeng Ding	Huazhong University of Science and Technology, China
Xiaojun Zhou	Central South University, China
Xiaolin Han	Northwestern Polytechnical University, China
Xiaoxia Zhang	Chongqing University of Posts and Telecommunications, China
Xiaoyan Jiang	Shanghai University of Engineering Science, China
Xiaozhi Du	Xi'an Jiaotong University, China
Xin Jin	Yunnan University, China
Xin Xu	Wuhan University of Science and Technology, China
Xing Wu	Shanghai University, China
Xingpeng Zhang	Southwest Petroleum University, China
Xinshan Zhu	Tianjin University, China
Xizi Chen	Huazhong Agricultural University, China
Xue Rui	China Academy of Railway Sciences, China
Yang Li	East China Normal University, China
Yang Zou	Hohai University, China
Yanyan Xu	Shanghai Jiao Tong University, China
Yasser Mohammed	Assiut University, Egypt
Yong Wang	Ocean University of China, China
Yonghong Song	Xi'an Jiaotong University, China
Youcef Djenouri	University of Southern Denmark, Denmark
Youshan Zhang	Yeshiva University, USA
Yu Liu	Huazhong University of Science and Technology, China
Yufei Chen	Tongji University, China
Yu-Jie Xiong	Shanghai University of Engineering Science, China
Yun Chen	Shanghai University of Finance and Economics, China
Yun Liu	Southwest University, China
Yunhai Wang	Shandong University, China
Yupeng Hu	Hunan University, China
Yutaka Watanobe	University of Aizu, Japan
Yuwei Peng	Wuhan University, China
Zaki Brahmi	University of Sousse, Tunisia
Zalán Bodó	Babeş-Bolyai University, Romania

Keynote Speech

Smart IoT Sensing for Aging Well: Research Activities and Future Directions

Michael Sheng

School of Computing, Faculty of Science and Engineering, Macquarie University, Sydney, Australia
michael.sheng@mq.edu.au

Abstract. Worldwide, the population is aging due to increasing life expectancy and decreasing fertility. The significant growth in older population presents many challenges to health and aged care services. Over the past two decades, the Internet of Things (IoT) has gained significant momentum and is widely regarded as an important technology to change the world in the coming decade. Indeed, IoT will play a critical role to improve productivity, operational effectiveness, decision making, and to identify new business service models for social and economic opportunities. Indeed, with the development of low-cost, unobtrusive IoT sensors, along with data analytics and artificial intelligence (AI) technologies, there is now a significant opportunity to improve the wellbeing and quality of life particularly of our older population. In this talk, we will overview some related research projects and also discuss several research directions.

Biography: Michael Sheng is a full Professor and Head of School of Computing at Macquarie University, Sydney, Australia. Before moving to Macquarie University, he spent 10 years at School of Computer Science, the University of Adelaide. Michael Sheng's research interests include the Internet of Things (IoT), service computing, big data analytics, machine learning, and Web technologies. He is ranked by Microsoft Academic as one of the Most Impactful Authors in Services Computing (ranked Top 5 All Time) and in Web of Things (ranked Top 20 All Time). Michael Sheng is the recipient of AMiner Most Influential Scholar in IoT (2018), ARC (Australian Research Council) Future Fellowship (2014), Chris Wallace Award for Outstanding Research Contribution (2012), and Microsoft Research Fellowship (2003). He is the Vice Chair of the Executive Committee of the IEEE Technical Community on Services Computing

(IEEE TCSVC), the Associate Director of Macquarie University Smart Green Cities Research Center, and a member of the ACS (Australian Computer Society) Technical Advisory Board on IoT.

Behavior Understanding and Embodied Intelligence

Cewu Lu

Department of Computer Science and Engineering, Shanghai Jiao Tong University,
Shanghai, China
lu-cw@cs.sjtu.edu.cn

Abstract. This talk discusses the problem of behavior understanding of intelligent agents. From the perspective of machine cognition, how to make the machine understand the behavior? We introduce the work of human behavior knowledge engine and behavior semantic unification under Poincaré space. From the perspective of neurocognition, what is the inner relationship between machine semantic understanding and brain neurocognition? We introduce how to explain the intrinsic relationship between visual behavior understanding and brain nerves, and establish a stable mapping model. From the perspective of embodied cognition, how to make the robot have the first-person behavior ability? We introduce the proposed PIE (perception-imagination-execution) scheme, in which the representative work grassNet reaches the human level for the first time in grasping unknown objects.

Biography: Cewu Lu is a professor of Shanghai Jiao Tong University. In 2016, he was selected under the National "1000 Youth Talents Plan". In 2018, he was selected as one of 35 Innovators Under 35 (MIT TR35) by MIT Technology Review. In 2019, he was awarded Qiu Shi Outstanding Young Scholar. In 2020, he was awarded the Special Prize of Shanghai Science and Technology Progress Award (ranked third). In 2021, he won the title of Highly Cited Scholar in China. In 2022, he was awarded one of the best papers in IROS (6/3579). he, as the corresponding author or the first author, has published 100 papers in high-level journals and conferences. He has served as reviewer for Science main issue, Nature sub-journal, Cell sub-journal and other journals, area chair of NeurIPS, CVPR, ICCV, ECCV, IROS, ICRA. His research interests fall mainly in Computer Vision and Robot Learning.

Contents – Part I

Decision Making

E-Learning

Machine Learning Theory

Pattern Recognition

Contents – Part II

Optimization

Prediction

Reinforcement Learning

Security

Classification and Case-Based Reasoning

Reducing Reliance on Domain Knowledge in Case-Based Reasoning

Fateh Boulmaiz[1(✉)], Patrick Reignier[1], and Stephane Ploix[2]

[1] Univ. Grenoble Alpes, CNRS, Grenoble INP, LIG, 38000 Grenoble, France
`fateh.boulmaiz@univ-grenoble-alpes.fr`
[2] Univ. Grenoble Alpes, CNRS, Grenoble INP, G-SCOP, 38000 Grenoble, France

Abstract. Case-based reasoning is an intuitive approach to problem-solving in artificial intelligence that involves reusing existing experience, including solutions to problems or mechanisms to derive them. However, current Case-based reasoning systems suffer from a lack of generality due to their heavy reliance on domain-specific knowledge, and they often struggle with the adaptation process, which is driven by the application domain. In addition, these systems often perform poorly as they treat each step of the Case-based reasoning methodology separately and independently. To address these limitations, this work proposes a domain-independent Case-based reasoning framework that integrates each step of the reasoning process to support other stages of the process. The framework is evaluated in an experimental setting on a sober consumption energy system in buildings, demonstrating its effectiveness.

Keywords: Case-based reasoning · Similarity · Compositional adaptation · Local model · Genetic algorithm

1 Introduction

Case-based reasoning (CBR) is an area of artificial intelligence that has gained popularity across a wide range of domains, including engineering, medicine, and finance. It involves using past problem-solving experiences to address new problems, similar to how humans reason. CBR has been favored over traditional rule-based and neural network approaches due to its ability to reduce knowledge acquisition bottlenecks, facilitate system maintenance, and provide reasonable solutions even with incomplete data sets.

However, the adoption of CBR has also introduced new challenges, including the acquisition of different types of knowledge, such as domain description, similarity knowledge, and adaptation knowledge. Each type of knowledge requires dedicated learning processes, and mechanisms must be put in place to support the acquisition, refinement, and evolution of this knowledge. Managing these knowledge bases from their design through to maintenance is a challenging task, as the knowledge is closely related and should not be considered independently.

H. Fujita et al. (Eds.): IEA/AIE 2023, LNAI 13925, pp. 3–13, 2023.
https://doi.org/10.1007/978-3-031-36819-6_1

To address these challenges, we propose a holistic methodology for the CBR approach. Our framework includes a refined formalism for representing cases, an approach based on genetic algorithms for feature weighting, a method for identifying similar cases using appropriate metrics, and a novel adaptation strategy for developing an efficient reuse process that is as independent as possible from the application domain. Our contributions aim to enhance the effectiveness and efficiency of the CBR approach in solving diverse problems in various domains.

Our CBR methodology is presented in Sect. 2. Section 3 reports on an evaluation of our approach by considering a case study with real-world data. Section 4 provides conclusion and future improvements.

2 A More Domain Knowledge Independent Approach

This section presents a new methodology to address the findings outlined in the introduction. Particularly, we present a new formalism to represent a case, followed by a description of a novel method to evaluate the similarity and finally we develop a new domain-independent approach for the adaptation process.

2.1 Case Structure

Existing studies on case-based reasoning (CBR) follow the case structure proposed in [5], which separates case knowledge into a problem specification and a solution description. The problem part outlines the objectives to be achieved, while the solution part provides a description of the reasoning process that led to the solution. In contrast to earlier CBR systems, our approach proposes a new case structure that classifies application domain phenomena more finely. These phenomena are assumed to be described using a language $\mathcal{L}_D = \mathcal{L}_C \cup \mathcal{L}_A \cup \mathcal{L}_E$. Our new structure includes:

- *Context variables (features)*, which model the environmental phenomena of the application domain that are not under control. These are defined using the language $\mathcal{L}_C$. For example, weather conditions in an energy management system (EMS).
- *Action variables*, which represent controllable phenomena and are defined using the language $\mathcal{L}_A$. For example, adjusting the set-point of a heating system in an EMS.
- *Effect variables*, which model the system state after applying actions and are defined using the language $\mathcal{L}_E$. For example, the temperature inside a room after opening the windows in an EMS.

Definition 1 (Case). *A case is a tuple of three components* $(\mathcal{C}, \mathcal{A}, \mathcal{E}) \in \mathcal{L}_C \times \mathcal{L}_A \times \mathcal{L}_E$ *which assumes the existence of a relation* $\mathcal{R} : \mathcal{C} \times \mathcal{A} \to \mathcal{E}$, *meaning that* $\mathcal{E}$ *is the consequence of application of* $\mathcal{A}$ *to* $\mathcal{C}$.

The revised structure of a case introduced in Definition 1 leads to a reformulation of the guiding hypothesis of the CBR approach (i.e., "Similar problems produce similar solutions") as stated in Hypothesis 1.

Hypothesis 1 (Consistency). *Carrying out the same actions in similar contexts generates similar effects.*

We assume that each variable $Q \in \{context, action, effect\}$, is represented by a descriptor $d_Q = (v_Q, R_Q)$. The descriptor contains a unique attribute v_Q associated with a sub-language $R_Q \in \{\mathcal{L}_C, \mathcal{L}_A, \mathcal{L}_E\}$ which could take several forms, such as an atomic value, constraints, or a vector. We use the vector representation because it is suitable for weak theory domains.

2.2   Retrieving Similar Cases

The main purpose of the retrieval stage in CBR is to identify relevant cases for the process of current problem resolution. In the following, we first introduce some definitions and notations for the notions that will be employed throughout the presentation of our approach, followed by a description of the proposed method for estimating the weights of the variables, and we close this section by a presentation of the similar cases retrieving approach.

Definitions and Notations

Definition 2 (Sensitivity distance). *The sensitivity distance d_{sen}^Q for a variable Q is the maximum distance determined by a domain expert, above which two values of Q are considered dissimilar.*

Sensitivity distance helps overcome the limitation of finding exact matching feature values in practice. For example, humans can perceive a temperature change of $1\,°C$, so we use sensitivity distance to compare effect variables between cases.

Definition 3 (Effect-based similarity). *Two cases are similarly based on their effects if the maximum distance between the values of each effect variable does not exceed the corresponding sensitivity distance: $\forall(C1, C2) \in CB, \forall \mathcal{E}_i \in \mathcal{L}_E, \mathcal{E}_i^{C1} - \mathcal{E}_i^{C2} \leq d_{sen}^{\mathcal{E}_i}$, With $d_{sen}^{\mathcal{E}_i}$ – the sensitivity distance for effect variable $\mathcal{E}_i$.*

Definition 4 (Performance). *The performance $\mathcal{P}_{C_i}(\mathcal{C}_i, \mathcal{A}_i)$ of a case $C_i(\mathcal{C}_i, \mathcal{A}_i, \mathcal{E}_i)$ models the quality of the effects following the application of an action plan to a particular context,*

Note that thereafter no assumption is made regarding the distance metrics used. Any distance metric can be used so far as it can deal with the formalism introduced in the Sect. 2.1.

Literature [4] emphasizes the importance of incorporating weight variables in distance calculation for better accuracy. Our proposal is to use a metric that considers variable weights. We introduce a relevant method that employs a genetic algorithm (GA) with a clustering strategy to estimate variable weights.

Features Weighting. Our weighting approach finds weights that group similar cases with close context-action distances ($\mathcal{D}_{CA}$), which leads to close effect distances ($\mathcal{D}_E$). Context and action variables are associated through $\mathcal{D}_{CA}$ because action effects depend on the context and vice versa. For example, in EMS, sunlight importance for warming a room depends on blind opening/closing. The main steps of the GA process are described shortly as follows:

1. Create a random population of individuals consisting of real values corresponding to requested weights.
2. Group similar cases in the case base using K-means clustering based on $\mathcal{D}_{CA}$ distance weighted with chromosome values.
3. Evaluate fitness value of each individual using the fitness function which is the average of $\mathcal{D}_E$ distances between cases of the same cluster. Optimization criteria are to minimize average $\mathcal{D}_E$ distance and number of formed clusters.
4. Generate a new population by applying evolution operators (selection, crossover, mutation).
5. Repeat steps 2–4 until termination criteria are met, which is either no improvement in optimization criterion after 10 consecutive iterations or reaching 500 iterations for computational efficiency.

Similar Cases Retrieving. We introduce a novel approach that adapts the number of similar source cases based on a similarity distance threshold, unlike traditional distance-based methods that use a fixed KNN-like approach. Similarity evaluation is based on $\mathcal{D}_{CA}$ distance, as explained in Sect. 2.2. The objective is to determine similar source cases using a similarity metric that only considers cases within a threshold distance, disregarding cases beyond this limit.

Equation (1) presents a similarity measure that addresses this need. It defines μ as the highest acceptable $\mathcal{D}_{CA}$ between two cases for them to be considered similar. To determine the threshold distance μ_* for the target case C_*, two steps are involved in the learning process:

– *Learn a distance threshold for each source case:* Learning a threshold distance for each source case is not a one-size-fits-all approach. The optimal distance threshold to identify similar cases varies depending on the domain and context of each case. Therefore, we propose Property 1 based on Hypothesis 1, which defines a specific distance threshold μ_{C_i} for each source case C_i in the case base CB. These distance thresholds are denoted by the set $\Pi = \{\mu_{C_i}\}, \forall\, C_i \in CB$.
– *Learn a distance threshold for target case:* The aim is to estimate the distance threshold μ_* for the target case C_* by utilizing the threshold distances computed in the previous step. At most, the number of distance thresholds would be equal to the number of source cases ($|\Pi| = |BC|$). To find the optimal distance threshold μ_*, we search within the set Π for the distance that balances recall (the ratio of extracted relevant similar cases to the total number of relevant similar cases) and precision (the number of extracted relevant similar cases to the total number of extracted cases). This is achieved

using the F1-score, which is a statistically optimal decision method. Thus, the distance threshold μ_* corresponds to the distance $\mu \in \Pi$ that maximizes the F1-score as expressed in Eq. (2)

$$\forall C_i, C_j \in CB, \mathcal{S}(C_i, C_j) = \begin{cases} \left(1 - \frac{\mathcal{D}_{CA}(C_i, C_j)}{\mu}\right), & \text{if } \mathcal{D}_{CA}(C_i, C_j) \leq \mu \\ 0, & \text{otherwise.} \end{cases} \tag{1}$$

Property 1. The distance threshold μ_{C_i} for each case C_i should satisfy the condition that, $\forall C_j \in CB, \mathcal{D}_{CA}(C_i, C_j) \leq \mu_{C_i} \Rightarrow C$ and C_i are similarly based on their effects (see Definition 3).

$$\mu_* = \underset{\mu_{C_i}}{\operatorname{argmax}}(F1 - score(\mu_{C_i})) \tag{2}$$

However, applying the context-action threshold is not straightforward because the actions of the target case C_* are unknown, and only the context data is available. Therefore, the similarity assessment between C_* and the cases in the case base is based solely on context variables. As a result, the retrieval function profile is defined as $F_{\mathcal{S}} : \mathcal{C}_* \mapsto (\mathcal{C}_i, \mathcal{A}_i, \mathcal{E}_i) \triangleq C_i \in CB$.

The task at hand is to determine the threshold $\overline{\mu}_*$ that defines the maximum context distance for the similar neighborhoods $\mathcal{S}_{C_*}$ of the case C_*, where $\forall C_i \in \mathcal{S}_{C_*}, \mathcal{D}_C(C_*, C_i) \leq \overline{\mu}_*$. To overcome this challenge, one approach is to use a projection function ϕ that maps the feature space $\mathcal{L}_C^n \times \mathcal{L}_A^m$ to an n-dimensional feature subspace $\phi(\mathcal{L}_C^n \times \mathcal{L}_A^m) \in \mathcal{L}_C^n$, where n is the number of context features and m is the number of action features. The goal of the projection function ϕ is to maintain the data structure between the original data set and the transformed data set. The data structure is captured by the distances between cases. Due to space limitations, we do not present the projection process here, but interested readers can refer to [3] for more information.

2.3 An Optimization Approach for Adaptation

The adaptation process modifies similar source actions to produce target effects that meet the constraints of the target context. It consists of two functions, $F_{\mathcal{S}}$ and F_A, where $F_{\mathcal{S}}$ retrieves relevant information from source cases, and F_A transforms this information to produce a potential solution that satisfies the target context. The profile of F_A is given by Formula (3).

$$\begin{aligned} F_A : (\mathcal{L}_C \times \mathcal{L}_A \times \mathcal{L}_E)^k \times \mathcal{L}_C &\longrightarrow \mathcal{L}_A \\ ((\mathcal{C}_i, \mathcal{A}_i, \mathcal{E}_i)_{i \in [1,k]}, \mathcal{C}_*) &\longmapsto \mathcal{A}_*, \forall (\mathcal{C}_i, \mathcal{A}_i, \mathcal{E}_i) \triangleq C_i \in \mathcal{S}_{C_*} \end{aligned} \tag{3}$$

Where $k = |\mathcal{S}_{C_*}|$ – the number of similar source cases to case C_*.

Formula (3) allows for any number of similar cases to be used in the adaptation process, as long as it is not zero. Our proposed approach is compositional adaptation, where multiple source cases are efficiently combined to produce a target solution. Previous studies [2] have shown that compositional adaptation is more accurate than single-case adaptation, which can struggle when only a part of the source problem is relevant to the target problem. The adaptation strategy proposed here is assumes a two-phase approach to adaptation:

– *Hybrid learning model*: Machine learning systems often suffer from poor performance due to an overemphasis on either local or global learning approaches. A fully local strategy tends to overemphasize local irregularities and fails to capture the structure of the data, while a strictly global strategy may have inadequate complexity for certain parts of the input data. A hybrid approach that reconciles the dichotomy between global and local learning is needed to take advantage of the benefits of both strategies. We propose a local model learning approach that captures the global structure of the data through weighted features. The literature provides various model learning approaches, including artificial neural networks, decision trees, support vector machines, etc., but there are no clear guidelines for choosing an effective model. However, learning a model on similar cases is typically simpler and more accurate than a global model of the system. More information on learning models can be found in [6].

More formally, this step consists in learning a model $\mathcal{M}_{C_*}$ of the local behaviour of the effects according to the context and the actions:

$$\mathcal{M}_{C_*} : \mathcal{E}_i = g(\mathcal{C}_i, \mathcal{A}_i), \forall (\mathcal{C}_i, \mathcal{A}_i, \mathcal{E}_i) \triangleq C_i \in \mathcal{S}_{C_*} \qquad (4)$$

With g – the modelling function, $\mathcal{S}_{C_*}$ – the set of similar cases.

– *Model optimization*: The solution to be proposed (the actions) consists in solving an optimization problem with an objective function representing the performances $\mathcal{P}(\mathcal{C}_*, \mathcal{A}_*)$ of the proposed actions (cf. Definition 4). We outline below the mathematical foundations behind this optimisation:
  • The objective function is to maximize the performance $\mathcal{P}_{C_*}$ of the case C_* to solve.
  • The decision variables which represent the variables that can be changed to influence the objective function value; consist of actions variables.
  • The constraints require that the decision variables satisfy the local model specified by Formula (4) in order for the solution to be accepted.

So, the optimization problem for determining the suggested actions $\mathcal{A}_*$ to solve the given case C_* can be formulated as follows: $\mathcal{E}_* = \text{argmax}_{\mathcal{A}_*} \mathcal{P}(\mathcal{C}_*, \mathcal{A}_*)$, subject to the learned model $\mathcal{M}_{C_*} : \mathcal{E}_* = g(\mathcal{C}_*, \mathcal{A}_*)$.

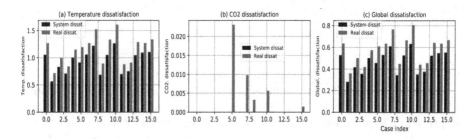

Fig. 1. Performance evaluation

3 Experimental Evaluation

3.1 Case Study

A case study evaluated the use of CBR to improve energy efficiency in buildings while maintaining or enhancing occupant comfort. The approach aimed to guide occupants' actions, which can significantly impact energy usage [7], rather than implementing demand-side management strategies that are often rejected by occupants. An EMS was developed based on this approach, which proposed an optimal action schedule to enhance occupant comfort without increasing energy costs.

The performance function used in the adaptation process consists in evaluating the user dissatisfaction with the generated effects following the application of the actions proposed by the EMS. The user dissatisfaction with the thermal comfort $S_T^h(T)$ and the air quality $S_C^h(C)$ at the hth hour are modelled by the Formula (5). The global dissatisfaction S^h is defined as the average of $S_T^h(T)$ and $S_C^h(C)$.

$$S_T^h(T) = \begin{cases} 0 & \text{if } T \in [21, 23] \\ \frac{T-23}{26-23} & \text{if } T > 23 \\ \frac{21-T}{21-18} & \text{if } T < 21 \end{cases} \quad , \quad S_C^h(C) = \begin{cases} 0 & \text{if } C \leq 500 \\ \frac{C-500}{1500-1000} & \text{if } C > 500 \end{cases} \tag{5}$$

3.2 Dataset Description

Real data collected from an office at the University of Grenoble Alpes, France, equipped with 18 sensors, was used to experimentally evaluate our approach. Data was recorded from April 1, 2015, to October 30, 2016, and meteorological data was provided by a service provider for the same period. Hourly averages were taken for all measurements except for the variables Windows opening (v_{13}) and Door opening (v_{14}), which were represented as fractions of the hour during which they were open. For example, if a window was open for 15 min during the kth hour of the day, then $v_{13} = 60/15 = 0.25$. The different variables that model the features considered in this experimentation are:

- *Effect variables:* indoor temperature (v_1), indoor CO_2 concentration (v_2).
- *Context variables:* corridor temperature (v_3), illuminance (v_4), solar radiation (v_5), wind speed (v_6), corridor CO_2 concentration (v_7), electricity power (v_8), heater temperature (v_9), occupancy (v_{10}), nebulosity (v_{11}), outdoor temperature (v_{12}).
- *Action variables:* window opening (v_{13}), door opening (v_{14}).

Preprocessing. The performance and accuracy of our approach, like any data-driven approach, rely heavily on the quality of available data used during the learning phase. To ensure optimal data quality, a three-step preprocessing phase was performed in this case study, including:

- *Data cleaning*: The data cleaning process aims to replace missing values, remove noise, and identify and correct outliers. Any detected outlier or missing value is replaced by the average value of its left and right neighbors in the feature's value vector
- *Data normalization*: To reduce the effects of dominant features, we have opted for the MinMax method to rescale the features' values between 0 and 1.
- *Data filtering*: The data are collected continuously. For efficiency reasons, we filter out the days on which there are no people in the office (e.g., closed days and weekends) since there are no actions recorded on these days.

Structure of a Case. The case base used in this study organizes the daily data from the database into cases, where each feature vector is represented as a 24-dimensional vector, with each element representing the feature value for each hour of the day (from 0:00 to 23:00). Since the building under study is a university building, the analysis is restricted to office hours only (08:00 to 20:00), and action plans are presented to occupants during this time range only. There are no actions proposed during other hours since there are no occupants present in the office.

3.3   Simulation and Model Validation

Following the data processing phase, 98 days were retained for the experimentation. The case base is randomly split into disjoint training (74 days) and validation (24 days) sets (i.e. 75% and 25% respectively).

To evaluate the accuracy of our approach, we need to reproduce the behaviour of the office following the application of the proposed action plan. The simulation is performed using the physical model of the office proposed in [1]. To ensure consistency with the results generated by the physical model, the effect variable values in the database presented in Sect. 3.2 are replaced with values simulated by the physical model. The local behaviour of the data is predicted using a regressive approach through the use of a Generalized Linear Model (GLM).

3.4   Empirical Evaluation

Features Weighting and Context-Distance Threshold. The genetic algorithm described in Sect. 2.2 was used to assign weights to the features. The algorithm converged to the optimal weights for the variables in the 11th generation. As shown in Table 1, the results indicate that the variable v_3 (corridor temperature) has the highest weight. This finding is consistent with the results obtained from the physical model of the office, which confirms the effectiveness of our algorithm in accurately estimating the weights of the features.

The similarity evaluation approach proposed in this study enabled the definition of a threshold for the context distance of $\overline{\mu}_* = 1.2$. However, it is unfortunate that due to a lack of data, this threshold only allows for the identification of neighbors for 16 out of the 24 validation cases.

Table 1. Features weights.

Feature	V_3	V_4	V_5	V_6	V_7	V_8	V_9	V_{10}	V_{11}	V_12	V_13	V_{14}
Weight	0.211	0.102	0.026	0.042	0.040	0.088	0.108	0.039	0.004	0.029	0.016	0.094

Model Accuracy. The accuracy of the model was estimated using two commonly used statistical indicators, namely root mean square error (RMSE) and coefficient of determination (R^2) between the model output value (estimated temperature and estimated CO_2 concentration) and the real value from the case base. In particular, we study the impact of the number of nearest neighbours to be considered on the accuracy of the learned local model. We experiment the influence of several values for the number of neighbours K from the lowest value ($K = 2$) to the whole case base ($K = 74$) including the particular case $K = K(\overline{\mu}_*)$ corresponding to the threshold distance $\overline{\mu}_*$. The results are summarized in Table 2. The indicators values presented in Table 2 consider the average of the corresponding indicators values for the retained validation cases (16 cases).

Upon examining the RMSE and R^2 values presented in Table 2, it is apparent that there exists a correlation between the number of K and the RMSE and R^2 values. Specifically, it can be observed that as the value of K moves away from the threshold value $\overline{\mu}_*$, there is a clear trend of increasing R^2 and decreasing RMSE. This suggests that the CBR process is better suited to considering fewer, but more similar cases rather than a large number of less similar cases.

Table 2. Model accuracy.

K	Temperature		CO_2 concentration	
	RMSE	$R^2(\%)$	RMSE	$R^2(\%)$
all cases	0.659	76.21	18.85	74.09
60	0.619	76.84	15.14	76.28
50	0.602	78.02	14.35	81.92
40	0.559	78.51	12.63	83.78
30	0.553	79.02	9.04	86.97
20	0.531	82.17	8.76	88.64
10	0.315	85.42	5.28	90.96
2	0.273	89.67	4.44	91.66
$K(\overline{\mu}_*)$	0.103	91.85	4.02	92.97

Adaptation Performance. The efficiency of the adaptation approach is evaluated by comparing, for each test case, the performance (using Formulas (5)) of the proposed actions and the performance of the actions already recorded in the case base. The average of the performances of all effect variables is used to estimate the overall performance.

Figures 1(a) and, 1(b) show the performance of the system regarding variable v_1 and variable v_2. For both variables, the system (red bars) outperforms the recorded actions (grey bars) for all 16 validation cases. Specifically, the system outperforms by 13.58% to 24.83% for v_1 and up to 100% for v_2. We observe that for the variable v_2, the actions recorded for the cases 0,1,2,3,4,6,9,11,12,13 and 14 are already optimal, the system is as good as these actions. For the five remaining cases, the results of the system are better. Figure 1(c) depicts the overall performance of the system. The results show that the system improves the performance in 100% of the cases. The enhancement is between 13.28% and 31.46%.

4   Conclusion

We presented a novel approach to the case-based reasoning system conception with more generic methodologies. In particular, we proposed a refined case formalism. The latter is used to define a new method for estimating similarity using a genetic algorithm as a feature weighting mechanism. Furthermore, we introduced a domain-independent strategy for adaptation by combining machine learning and optimization methods. We illustrated the effectiveness of this approach through a detailed application example in the context of an energy management system. One potential limitation of our approach is that the retrieval process requires some minimal domain knowledge to define the similarity threshold of the effect variables. Our immediate focus for future work is to validate the proposed approach using more extensive datasets. As for our medium-term goals, we aim to create efficient methods for indexing and integrating new cases into the case base during the retention phase, utilizing the knowledge acquired from the retrieval and adaptation stages. Moreover, we plan to investigate the feasibility of an adaptation approach based on optimization that takes into account the context distance and performance of similar cases. Specifically, we will evaluate the efficacy of an operator that not only avoids poorly performing neighbors but also moves away from them.

References

1. Alyafi, A.A., Pal, M., Ploix, S., Reignier, P.: Differential explanations for energy management in buildings. In: 2017 Computing Conference, pp. 507–516 (2017)
2. Chedrawy, Z., Raza Abidi, S.S.: Case based reasoning for information personalization: using a context-sensitive compositional case adaptation approach. In: IEEE International Conference on Engineering of Intelligent Systems (2006)
3. Espadoto, M., Martins, R.M., Kerren, A., Hirata, N.S.T.: Toward a quantitative survey of dimension reduction techniques. IEEE Trans. Vis. Comput. Graph. **27**(3), 2153–2173 (2021)
4. Keyvanpour, M., Tavoli, R.: Feature weighting for improving document image retrieval system performance. IJCSI J. **9**, 125–130 (2012)
5. Kolodner, J.: Case-Based Reasoning. Morgan Kaufmann Publishers, Burlington (1993)

6. Shalev-Shwartz, S., Ben-David, S.: Understanding Machine Learning: From Theory to Algorithms. Cambridge University Press, Cambridge (2014)
7. Uddin, M.N., Wei, H.-H., Chi, H.L.: Influence of occupant behavior for building energy conservation: a systematic review study of diverse modeling and simulation approach. Buildings **11**(2), 41 (2021)

Feature Selection on Imbalanced Domains: A Stability-Based Analysis

Paolo Orrù and Barbara Pes$^{(\boxtimes)}$

Dipartimento di Matematica e Informatica, Università degli Studi di Cagliari, Via Ospedale 72, 09124 Cagliari, Italy
pes@unica.it

Abstract. A large body of literature has shown the beneficial impact of feature selection on the efficiency, interpretability, and generalization ability of machine learning models. Most of the existing studies, however, focus on the effectiveness of feature selection algorithms in identifying small subsets of predictive features, often neglecting the stability of the selection process, i.e., its robustness with respect to sample variation, which can be crucial for the actual exploitation of the results. In particular, little research has so far investigated the stability of feature selection methods in class-imbalanced domains, where some classes are under-represented and any perturbation in the set of training records can strongly affect the final selection outcome. This work aims to investigate this important issue by studying the stability of different selection algorithms across high-dimensional datasets that present different levels of class imbalance. To this end, a methodological pipeline is discussed which allows a joint evaluation of the selection outcome both in terms of stability and final predictive performance. Although not exhaustive, our experiments provide very useful insight into which methods can be more stable on imbalanced data while still ensuring good generalization results.

Keywords: Machine Learning · Feature Selection · Selection Stability · High-dimensional Data · Genomic Data · Class Imbalance

1 Introduction

High dimensionality is a major issue in several real-world domains, including biomedicine, text mining, and image analysis, where relevant data is characterized by a large number of attributes (or *features*). In similar contexts, most machine learning algorithms can strongly benefit from a preliminary dimensionality reduction [1], performed through proper techniques such as *feature extraction* or *feature selection*: indeed, the former creates new features that are meaningful combinations of the original ones, while the latter selects a subset of the original features by removing irrelevant or redundant information. Feature selection methods are particularly suitable when the interpretability of the results is a primary concern as they allow to gain useful knowledge about the domain of interest [2].

H. Fujita et al. (Eds.): IEA/AIE 2023, LNAI 13925, pp. 14–27, 2023.
https://doi.org/10.1007/978-3-031-36819-6_2

A large corpus of machine learning literature has compared the available selection algorithms across multiple application contexts, examining their strengths and weaknesses from different points of view [3–6]. Most of the studies so far conducted, however, evaluate the extent to which the different methods are effective in selecting small subsets of predictive features but do not consider the overall robustness of the selection process with respect to changes in the input data [7]. Specifically, the term robustness or *stability* refers to the capacity of an algorithm of producing similar outcomes on different versions of a given dataset, thus leading to results that are not highly dependent on a specific set of training instances. While often overlooked, this is a crucial aspect in the context of feature selection: indeed, interpreting the selected feature subsets can be very difficult if they are too sensitive to variations in the set of input instances. Furthermore, the instability of the selection process can reduce the confidence of final users, making them less likely to actually exploit the results of the overall analysis.

This important issue has received attention only in recent years and there is still a lack of systematic studies investigating the degree of robustness of different selection algorithms in multiple problem settings [8]. In particular, little research has studied the stability of feature selection algorithms in connection with the class imbalance problem [9], i.e., in the presence of underrepresented classes that may be quite difficult to discriminate. As recognized by recent literature, the correct classification of minority instances can be particularly challenging when the data representation space involves a large number of features. Indeed, the interaction of class imbalance and high dimensionality may complicate the analysis and cause overlapping among the classes [10]. In such a scenario, reducing the data dimensionality in a robust way is of paramount importance to obtain models that can better separate majority and minority instances [11] and are, at the same time, more understandable and interpretable [7].

To the best of our knowledge, no comparative studies exist that comprehensively investigate the behaviour of feature selection algorithms in this respect. To give a contribution in such a direction, this work presents a methodology that allows a joint evaluation of the feature selection process along two dimensions: *(i)* the predictive power of the selected feature subsets and *(ii)* their stability with respect to perturbations of the training data. A stratified sub-sampling procedure is embedded in the methodology to properly deal with imbalanced class distributions. Furthermore, the approach can be easily tuned to evaluate feature subsets of different cardinalities and is general enough to be applied to different feature selection methods and different learning algorithms.

A wide comparative study involving ten selection methods, three learning algorithms, and five high-dimensional datasets has been conducted across different levels of dimensionality reduction. Specifically, the considered datasets come from the genomic domain and represent quite challenging benchmarks due to the low instances-to-features ratio. They also present different levels of class imbalance, from a moderate (22% of minority instances) to a severe imbalance level (3% of minority instances).

Overall, the results of our experiments provide interesting insight into the intrinsic stability of the considered selection methods, as well as into their stability pattern for different numbers of selected features, showing which methods can achieve the best trade-off between selection stability and predictive performance on high-dimensional, imbalanced problems such as those examined here.

The remainder of this paper is structured as follows. Section 2 briefly introduces some related works in this field. Section 3 describes the methodology adopted for the stability analysis and Sect. 4 presents all the materials and methods relevant to our study, i.e., the datasets, the selection algorithms considered, and the specific settings adopted for the experiments. A summary of the experimental results is presented and discussed in Sect. 5. Finally, Sect. 6 gives the concluding remarks and outlines future research directions.

2   Related Work

Over the past two decades, a large amount of research has been devoted to investigating suitable approaches to deal with high-dimensional datasets [12], focusing both on learning methods that scale well on high-dimensional spaces and on adequate dimensionality reduction techniques, such as feature selection. Similarly, a lot of research work has been done in the field of imbalance learning [13], and several strategies have been proposed to deal with imbalanced class distributions, including sampling-based approaches, cost-sensitive approaches, and ensemble approaches. Although the two issues, namely high dimensionality and class imbalance, often coexist, they have mostly been studied independently, as separate problems, without considering their joint effects.

The importance of devising suitable learning strategies to handle datasets that are, at the same time, high-dimensional and imbalanced has been highlighted recently [14], with a number of proposals focused on modifying existing selection algorithms to better cope with imbalanced class distributions [15, 16] as well as on combining feature selection with data-balancing or cost-sensitive approaches [17]. It has also been observed that, in small sample size settings, feature selection alone can actually contribute to combatting the class imbalance problem, without any specific correction [11]. Few studies, however, have systematically compared the behaviour of different selection algorithms in imbalanced settings [18, 19] and only partial indications are available on which selection algorithms can produce more stable results on imbalanced data [20, 21].

From a methodological point of view, no consolidated protocols exist to jointly evaluate both the predictive performance and the stability of the selected feature subsets [7], although an increasing amount of research has been conducted to define proper metrics to reliably quantify the sensitivity of the feature selection process to variations in the input data. Different approaches have been proposed in this regard [8, 22], which mostly focus on measuring the average degree of similarity among the feature subsets obtained by applying the same selection algorithm to differently sampled versions of the original data. Recent research has also investigated the causes of feature selection instability [23], but the definition of suitable methodologies that can ensure a better trade-off between selection stability and predictive performance is still an open question [24, 25].

3   Methodology for Stability Evaluation

As anticipated in Sect. 1, our methodological approach is meant to be general enough to be implemented with different selection algorithms. Indeed, regardless of the specific method used to identify a subset of relevant features, we adopt a stratified subsampling approach to produce different reduced versions of the input dataset, each with a level of class imbalance that reflects the original class distribution. The resulting data samples are used to evaluate, in a joint manner, both the stability of the selection method and its effectiveness in terms of predictive performance, as schematized in Fig. 1.

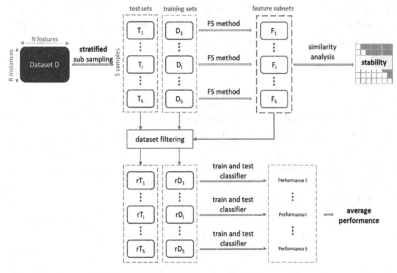

Fig. 1. The adopted methodology.

More in detail, given a dataset D with N features and R instances, we create S different training sets D_i, $i = 1, ..., S$, each containing a fraction X of the R input instances. A test set T_i, $i = 1, ..., S$, is also built for each training set, using the remaining fraction (i.e., $1 - X$) of instances. A feature selection (*FS*) method is then applied to each D_i to obtain a subset F_i of relevant features, for a total of S different subsets that are evaluated along two dimensions:

- *Stability evaluation.* A proper consistency index [26] is used to assess the pair-wise similarity between the subsets F_i ($i = 1, ..., S$), which results in an $S \times S$ similarity matrix [27]. An average similarity is computed from this matrix to obtain an overall estimate of stability: the higher the average similarity, the more stable the selection process.
- *Performance evaluation.* Each training set D_i, filtered to retain only the features in F_i, is used to train a classifier whose performance is then evaluated (through appropriate metrics such as the F-measure and the G-mean [17]) on the corresponding test set T_i, itself filtered to include only the features in F_i. The average performance across the S training/test sets provides a measure of the extent to which the selected feature subsets are predictive in conjunction with a given classifier.

As detailed below, our study leverages the above methodology to comparatively evaluate different selection methods, in conjunction with different classifiers, across five high-dimensional datasets that exhibit different levels of class imbalance. The analysis is carried out considering feature subsets of different cardinalities, in order to evaluate how stability and final performance are affected by the level of dimensionality reduction.

4 Materials and Methods

This section summarizes all the materials and methods involved in our study, including the datasets (Subsect. 4.1) and the specific algorithms considered with the settings chosen for the comparative analysis (Subsect. 4.2).

4.1 Datasets

For our study, we chose five genomic benchmarks that exhibit different levels of class imbalance, as shown in Table 1. Specifically, each dataset refers to a binary classification task where the aim is to discriminate the pathological condition of a given biological sample based on the expression level of thousands of genes. Note that the number of features (i.e., the genes) is much higher than the number of instances (i.e., the biological samples), which makes it difficult to obtain an optimal trade-off between selection stability and classification performance.

Table 1. Datasets used in the comparative study.

Dataset Name	Number of features	Number of instances	Percentage of minority instances	Instances-to-features ratio
SRBCT_NB	2308	83	21.7%	0.036
SRBCT_BL	2308	83	13.3%	0.036
LUNG_mich	7129	96	10.4%	0.013
LUNG_squa	12600	203	10.3%	0.016
LUNG_sclc	12600	203	3.0%	0.016

More in detail, the SRBCT_NB dataset contains 83 tumour samples, 18 of which represent patients affected by neuroblastoma (NB); similarly, the SRBCT_BL dataset contains 83 tumour samples, 11 of which represent Burkitt lymphoma (BL) patients. In both cases, the task is to discriminate the minority class against the other based on the expression level of 2308 genes [10]. In the LUNG_mich dataset, gene-expression profiles are used to predict patient survival in early-stage lung adenocarcinomas; 86 primary lung adenocarcinomas samples and 10 non-neoplastic lung samples are included, each described by 7129 genes [28]. Finally, both LUNG_squa and LUNG_sclc datasets contain 12600 genes and 203 instances representing cancerous and normal lung samples [29]. Specifically, 21 samples of squamous cell lung carcinomas (SQUA) are included in the LUNG_squa dataset, while 6 samples of small-cell lung carcinomas (SCLC) are included in the LUNG_sclc dataset. This last benchmark is the most imbalanced, besides having a very low instances-to-features ratio.

4.2 Methods and Settings

The considered selection methods are representative of different heuristics that allow for a proper weighting of the input features based on the strength of their correlation with the target to be predicted. Regardless of the specific method adopted, the weights assigned to the features were used in our experimental investigation to rank the features, i.e., to order them according to their predictive power, and then select feature subsets of different cardinalities, containing the desired number of top-ranked features.

More in detail, we applied the following selection approaches:

- *Statistical methods* such as *ChiSquared*, which derives a weight for the features by measuring their chi-squared statistic with respect to the class, and *Pearson's Correlation*, which assesses the importance of the features by evaluating the extent to which they are linearly related to the class.
- *Entropic methods* that rely on the information-theoretical measure of *entropy*. Specifically, the *Information Gain* criterion estimates how much the entropy of the class (namely the uncertainty in the class prediction) decreases when the value of a given feature is known, which allows quantifying the relevance of that feature for the predictive task at hand. In turn, *Symmetrical Uncertainty* and *Gain Ratio* exploit the *Information Gain* criterion but introduce proper corrections that aim to reduce the bias toward features with more values.
- *Relief-based methods* that assign weights to the features based on their ability to discriminate among data points that are close to each other (neighbours) in the N-dimensional feature space. In particular, the rationale of the *ReliefF* approach is that a "good" feature should have the same value for neighbours of the same class and different values for neighbours of different classes. The distance of neighbours can also be taken into account when assessing the relevance of the features, as in the *ReliefF-Weighted* method.
- *Classifier-based methods* that leverage a suitable learning algorithm to derive the feature weights. Specifically, the *OneR* method measures the worth of every single feature based on the accuracy of a classification rule built on that feature. Proper feature weights can also be obtained by training a linear *Support Vector Machine* classifier and considering the contribution of each feature to the multivariate decision function of the classifier itself (*SVM-AW* approach). This *SVM*-based approach can be implemented in a more sophisticated way, as in the *SVM-RFE* method which iteratively removes a given percentage (50% in our experiments) of the features, those with the lowest weights, and repeats the weighting process on the remaining ones.

A more detailed description of the above-mentioned selection methods can be found for example in [6, 12]. Note that some of them only rely on the intrinsic data characteristics (statistical, entropic, and *Relief*-based approaches) and are typically referred to as *filter* methods. In contrast, the approaches that exploit a suitable classifier to compute the feature weights (*OneR*, *SVM-AW*, and *SVM-RFE*) are generally referred to as *embedded* methods. A different approach (known as the *wrapper* approach) involves using a proper search strategy (e.g., an evolutionary search or a greedy search) to create different candidate feature subsets; each of them is then evaluated by applying the learning algorithm that will ultimately be used to build the final model. However, this may be impractical in the presence of thousands of features due to the high computational cost [4], often requiring a preliminary dimensionality reduction through more efficient methods [30, 31].

It is also important to observe that some of the adopted algorithms perform a univariate evaluation of the features, i.e., they weigh every single feature independently of the others. This is the case for the statistical and entropic methods as well as the rule-based *OneR* approach. On the other hand, the *Relief*-based and the *SVM*-based methods perform a multivariate evaluation that depends on the position of the instances in the attribute space and can also capture, to some extent, the interdependencies among the features.

The comparative evaluation of the different selection methods was carried out, according to the methodology detailed in Sect. 3, in conjunction with different classifiers, namely *Random Forest, Support Vector Machine*, and *k-Nearest Neighbor*, which have been widely employed in several kinds of experiments based on high-dimensional genomic benchmarks such as those considered here [10, 15, 17, 32–34]. For the joint analysis of stability and performance, we employed $S = 20$ training sets, each containing a fraction $X = 0.80$ of the original instances, with the remaining fraction of instances reserved for testing (as shown in Fig. 1). The overall experimental study was conducted by leveraging the *WEKA* machine learning library [35], which contains several functions for data sampling and manipulation, feature ranking and selection, and data classification.

5 Experimental Results and Discussion

The results of our experimental analysis are summarized in what follows by distinguishing the univariate selection methods previously introduced (hereafter, *ChiSquared, Correlation, InfoGain, SymUncert, GainRatio, OneR*) and the multivariate ones (hereafter, *ReliefF, ReliefF-W, SVM-AW, SVM-RFE50*). For each method, the analysis has been conducted for feature subsets containing different numbers of selected features, corresponding to 0.25%, 0.5%, 1%, 2%, 3%, 4%, 5%, 6%, 7%, 8%, 9%, and 10% of the original number N of features (which is reported in Table 1 for each of the benchmarks considered in the study).

For a given percentage of selected features, we measured both the selection stability and the final predictive performance, according to the methodology explained in Sect. 3. In particular, the selection stability does not depend on the adopted classifier as it expresses the average similarity among the feature subsets obtained by applying a given selection method to different training sets randomly drawn (preserving the original class distribution) from the dataset at hand. The resulting stability patterns are shown, for feature subsets of increasing size, in Figs. 2, 3, 4, 5 and 6 that refer to *SRBCT_NB, SRBCT_BL, LUNG_mich, LUNG_squa*, and *LUNG_sclc* datasets respectively. In each figure, the results for the univariate methods are shown on the left, and those for the multivariate methods on the right.

As a general comment, we can see that the stability measured across the five examined datasets is always lower than the maximum value of 1, which confirms that the instability of the selection outcome is a critical, though mostly neglected, issue in high-dimensional and imbalanced problems. We can also observe, across all the datasets considered, that strong differences exist among the stability patterns of the ten selection methods included in our study, with clear evidence of a less robust behaviour of some selection heuristics.

In particular, among the univariate approaches, *OneR* turns out to be, in most cases, the least stable method, followed by *GainRatio*, which turns out to be less robust than the other entropic methods, namely *SymUncert* and *InfoGain*, which often perform very similarly to each other. *SymUncert* and *InfoGain* also produce results quite similar to the *ChiSquared* statistical approach, while the other statistical method, namely *Correlation*, is the one that achieves the highest stability values, especially for small subset sizes.

As regards the multivariate approaches, the *Relief*-based methods, namely *ReliefF* and *ReliefF-W*, turn out to be systematically more robust than the *SVM*-based methods, namely *SVM-AW* and *SVM-RFE50*. The latter approach, in particular, exhibits a very poor stability behaviour, despite having been recognized as one of the most effective selection methods for high-dimensional biomedical data, even in the presence of imbalanced data distributions [36, 37]. Overall, the selection methods of the *embedded* category, i.e., *OneR*, *SVM-AW* and *SVM-RFE50*, which rely on the feature weights computed by some classification algorithm, appear to be much more sensitive to variations in the set of training instances compared to the *filter* methods that only rely on the intrinsic characteristics of the training data.

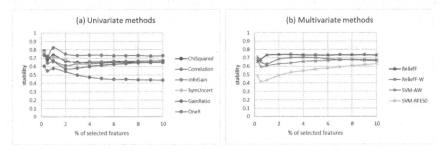

Fig. 2. *SRBCT_NB* dataset: stability of (a) univariate and (b) multivariate selection methods.

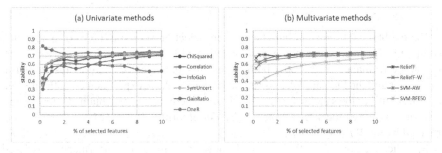

Fig. 3. *SRBCT_BL* dataset: stability of (a) univariate and (b) multivariate selection methods.

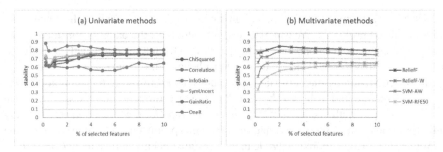

Fig. 4. *LUNG_mich* dataset: stability of (a) univariate and (b) multivariate selection methods.

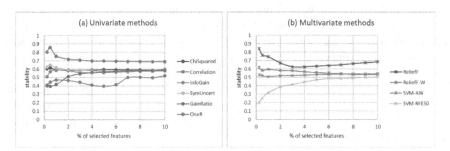

Fig. 5. *LUNG_squa* dataset: stability of (a) univariate and (b) multivariate selection methods.

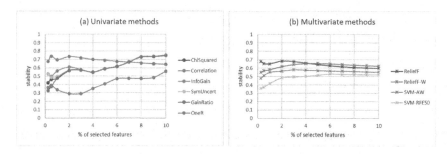

Fig. 6. *LUNG_sclc* dataset: stability of (a) univariate and (b) multivariate selection methods.

But to obtain a full insight into the different selection heuristics here considered, the stability results must be examined in conjunction with the final predictive performance, i.e., the performance of a model built using only the selected features (as shown in Fig. 1). To build the final model, as discussed in Sect. 4.2, we experimented with different classifiers but, for the sake of space, we only show here the results obtained with the best performing one, i.e., the *Support Vector Machine* algorithm (in the *SMO* implementation provided by the *WEKA* library [35]).

Specifically, Figs. 7, 8, 9, 10 and 11 show the F-measure performance, averaged over 20 training/test iterations, obtained respectively on the *SRBCT_NB*, *SRBCT_BL*, *LUNG_mich*, *LUNG_squa*, and *LUNG_sclc* datasets, both on the full set of features (dashed line) as well as in conjunction with the univariate (on the left) and multivariate (on the right) selection methods.

As can be seen, differently from other learning algorithms considered, the *SMO* classifier performs very well on the original high-dimensional space, reaching an excellent average F-measure on the first three benchmarks (Figs. 7, 8 and 9); the F-measure performance on the whole feature set is still quite good on the *LUNG_squa* dataset (Fig. 10) and decreases significantly only on the *LUNG_sclc* dataset (Fig. 11), which is the most imbalanced among the benchmarks included in this study (with only 3% of minority instances).

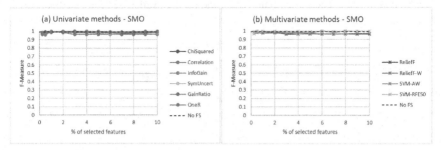

Fig. 7. *SRBCT_NB* dataset: F-measure of the *SMO* classifier, without feature selection (dashed line) as well as in conjunction with (a) univariate and (b) multivariate selection methods.

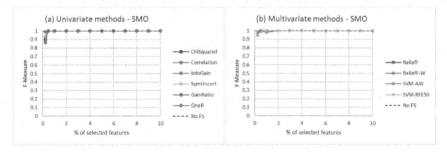

Fig. 8. *SRBCT_BL* dataset: F-measure of the *SMO* classifier, without feature selection (dashed line) as well as in conjunction with (a) univariate and (b) multivariate selection methods.

Interestingly, in this last case, feature selection significantly contributes to alleviating the adverse effects of class imbalance, improving the F-measure performance to a very great extent, especially for small percentages of selected features. Nonetheless, even for the least imbalanced datasets, feature selection can be very helpful as it reduces the data dimensionality without degrading the final performance, thus improving efficiency and leading to a better understanding of which factors are really relevant for prediction.

Another interesting observation is that quite different selection heuristics, though selecting different subsets of features, can lead to very similar results in terms of final performance (measured in terms of F-measure or other suitable metrics). Actually, if we compare the ten selection methods included in the study by jointly considering the

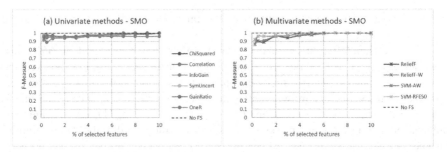

Fig. 9. *LUNG_mich* dataset: F-measure of the *SMO* classifier, without feature selection (dashed line) as well as in conjunction with (a) univariate and (b) multivariate selection methods.

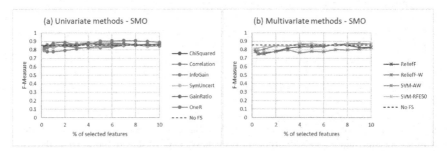

Fig. 10. *LUNG_squa* dataset: F-measure of the *SMO* classifier, without feature selection (dashed line) as well as in conjunction with (a) univariate and (b) multivariate selection methods.

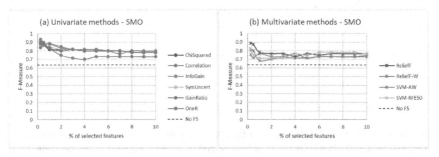

Fig. 11. *LUNG_sclc* dataset: F-measure of the *SMO* classifier, without feature selection (dashed line) as well as in conjunction with (a) univariate and (b) multivariate selection methods.

stability behaviour (Figs. 2, 3, 4, 5 and 6) and the predictive performance (Figs. 7, 8, 9, 10 and 11), it emerges that the differences in stability are often significant, while the corresponding differences in performance are smaller or even negligible.

The selection stability, therefore, can be used as a discriminating criterion when choosing a suitable selection method for a given task: indeed, with equal or comparable predictive capability, a more stable method can ensure more reproducible and reliable results. This is especially important in those domains, such as the one considered here, when the understandability and interpretability of the final models play a crucial role.

6 Conclusions

This work has presented a stability-based analysis of different feature selection methods in the context of high-dimensional and imbalanced data. Focusing on the genomic domain, which is particularly challenging due to the low instances-to-features ratio, our study has shown that some selection methods perform systematically poorly in terms of stability, for different levels of dimensionality reduction (i.e., irrespective of the number of selected features).

In particular, the embedded selection methods, such as the rule-based *OneR* and the *SVM*-based selection approaches, exhibit an unsatisfactory trade-off between stability and predictive performance. Among the filter methods, *Pearson's Correlation* and *ReliefF*, which are representative of the univariate and multivariate approaches respectively, have proved to be the most robust across the different datasets considered, leading to good stability and performance results, especially for small subsets of selected features.

Further research will be conducted to deeply investigate the degree of robustness of state-of-art selection algorithms in multiple application scenarios, considering datasets from different domains and encompassing different problem settings, e.g., in terms of level of imbalance, number of classes, and instances-to-features ratio. Different stability measures will be also considered in order to characterize the stability behaviour of each selection heuristic from multiple and complementary points of view.

Acknowledgements. This research was supported by the ASTRID project (Fondazione di Sardegna, L.R. 7 agosto 2007, n°7, CUP: F75F21001220007).

References

1. Ray, P., Reddy, S.S., Banerjee, T.: Various dimension reduction techniques for high dimensional data analysis: a review. Artif. Intell. Rev. **54**(5), 3473–3515 (2021). https://doi.org/10.1007/s10462-020-09928-0
2. Bolón-Canedo, V., Alonso-Betanzos, A., Morán-Fernández, L., Cancela, B.: Feature selection: from the past to the future. In: Virvou, M., Tsihrintzis, G.A., Jain, L.C. (eds.) Advances in Selected Artificial Intelligence Areas, Learning and Analytics in Intelligent Systems, vol. 24, pp. 11–34. Springer, Cham (2022). https://doi.org/10.1007/978-3-030-93052-3_2
3. Bommert, A., Sun, X., Bischl, B., Rahnenführer, J., Lang, M.: Benchmark for filter methods for feature selection in high-dimensional classification data. Comput. Stat. Data Anal. **143**, 106839 (2020)
4. Hambali, M.A., Oladele, T.O., Adewole, K.S.: Microarray cancer feature selection: review, challenges and research directions. Int. J. Cogn. Comput. Eng. **1**, 78–97 (2020)
5. Bolón-Canedo, V., Rego-Fernández, D., Peteiro-Barral, D., Alonso-Betanzos, A., Guijarro-Berdiñas, B., Sánchez-Maroño, N.: On the scalability of feature selection methods on high-dimensional data. Knowl. Inf. Syst. **56**(2), 395–442 (2017). https://doi.org/10.1007/s10115-017-1140-3
6. Pes, B., Lai, G.: Cost-sensitive learning strategies for high-dimensional and imbalanced data: a comparative study. PeerJ Comput. Sci. **7**, e832 (2021)
7. Khaire, U.M., Dhanalakshmi, R.: Stability of feature selection algorithm: a review. J. King Saud Univ. Comput. Inf. Sci. **34**, 1060–1073 (2022)

8. Nogueira, S., Sechidis, K., Brown, G.: On the stability of feature selection algorithms. J. Mach. Learn. Res. **18**, 1–54 (2018)
9. Haixiang, G., Yijing, L., Shang, J., Mingyun, G., Yuanyue, H., Bing, G.: Learning from class-imbalanced data. Expert Syst. Appl. **73**, 220–239 (2017)
10. Fu, G.H., Wu, Y.J., Zong, M.J., Pan, J.: Hellinger distance-based stable sparse feature selection for high-dimensional class-imbalanced data. BMC Bioinform. **21**, 121 (2020)
11. Wasikowski, M., Chen, X.: Combating the small sample class imbalance problem using feature selection. IEEE Trans. Knowl. Data Eng. **22**(10), 1388–1400 (2010)
12. Bolón-Canedo, V., Sánchez-Maroño, N., Alonso-Betanzos, A.: Feature Selection for High-Dimensional Data, Artificial Intelligence: Foundations, Theory, and Algorithms. Springer, Cham (2015). https://doi.org/10.1007/978-3-319-21858-8
13. Fernández, A., García, S., Galar, M., Prati, R.C., Krawczyk, B., Herrera, F.: Learning from Imbalanced Data Sets. Springer, Cham (2018). https://doi.org/10.1007/978-3-319-98074-4
14. Zhang, C., Zhou, Y., Guo, J., Wang, G., Wang, X.: Research on classification method of high-dimensional class-imbalanced datasets based on SVM. Int. J. Mach. Learn. Cybern. **10**(7), 1765–1778 (2018). https://doi.org/10.1007/s13042-018-0853-2
15. Maldonado, S., Weber, R., Famili, F.: Feature selection for high-dimensional class-imbalanced data sets using Support Vector Machines. Inform. Sci. **286**, 228–246 (2014)
16. Moayedikia, A., Ong, K.L., Boo, Y.L., Yeoh, W.G.S., Jensen, R.: Feature selection for high dimensional imbalanced class data using harmony search. Eng. Appl. Artif. Intell. **57**, 38–49 (2017)
17. Pes, B.: Learning from high-dimensional and class-imbalanced datasets using random forests. Information **12**(8), 286 (2021)
18. Zheng, Z., Wu, X., Srihari, R.: Feature selection for text categorization on imbalanced data. ACM SIGKDD Explor. Newsl. **6**(1), 80–89 (2004)
19. Cho, B.H., Yu, H., Kim, K.W., Kim, T.H., Kim, I.Y., Kim, S.I.: Application of irregular and unbalanced data to predict diabetic nephropathy using visualization and feature selection methods. Artif. Intell. Med. **42**(1), 37–53 (2008)
20. Wang, H., Khoshgoftaar, T.M., Napolitano, A.: An empirical study on the stability of feature selection for imbalanced software engineering data. In: 11th International Conference on Machine Learning and Applications, pp. 317–323 (2012)
21. Li, F., Mi, H., Yang, F.: Exploring the stability of feature selection for imbalanced intrusion detection data. In: 9th IEEE International Conference on Control and Automation, pp. 750–754 (2011)
22. Somol, P., Novovicova, J.: Evaluating stability and comparing output of feature selectors that optimize feature subset cardinality. IEEE Trans. Pattern Anal. Mach. Intell. **32**(11), 1921–1939 (2010)
23. He, Z., Yu, W.: Stable feature selection for biomarker discovery. Comput. Biol. Chem. **34**(4), 215–225 (2010)
24. Dessì, N., Pes, B.: Stability in biomarker discovery: does ensemble feature selection really help? In: Ali, M., Kwon, Y.S., Lee, C.-H., Kim, J., Kim, Y. (eds.) IEA/AIE 2015. LNCS (LNAI), vol. 9101, pp. 191–200. Springer, Cham (2015). https://doi.org/10.1007/978-3-319-19066-2_19
25. Cateni, S., Colla, V., Vannucci, M.: Improving the stability of the variable selection with small datasets in classification and regression tasks. Neural Process. Lett. (2022)
26. Kuncheva, L.I.: A stability index for feature selection. In: 25th IASTED International Multi-Conference: Artificial Intelligence and Applications, pp. 390–395. ACTA Press, Anaheim (2007)
27. Cannas, L.M., Dessì, N., Pes, B.: Assessing similarity of feature selection techniques in high-dimensional domains. Pattern Recogn. Lett. **34**(12), 1446–1453 (2013)

28. GEO Series GSE68571. https://www.ncbi.nlm.nih.gov/geo/query/acc.cgi?acc=GSE68571. Accessed 04 Apr 2023
29. GEO Series GSE83227. https://www.ncbi.nlm.nih.gov/geo/query/acc.cgi?acc=GSE83227. Accessed 04 Apr 2023
30. Almugren, N., Alshamlan, H.: A survey on hybrid feature selection methods in microarray gene expression data for cancer classification. IEEE Access **7**, 78533–78548 (2019)
31. Cannas, L.M., Dessì, N., Pes, B.: A filter-based evolutionary approach for selecting features in high-dimensional micro-array data. In: Shi, Z., Vadera, S., Aamodt, A., Leake, D. (eds.) IIP 2010. IAICT, vol. 340, pp. 297–307. Springer, Heidelberg (2010). https://doi.org/10.1007/978-3-642-16327-2_36
32. Ayyad, S.M., Saleh, A.I., Labib, L.M.: Gene expression cancer classification using modified K-Nearest Neighbors technique. Biosystems **176**, 41–51 (2019)
33. Bosin, A., Dessì, N., Fugini, M.G., Liberati, D., Pes, B.: Applying enterprise models to design cooperative scientific environments. In: Bussler, C.J., Haller, A. (eds.) BPM 2005. LNCS, vol. 3812, pp. 281–292. Springer, Heidelberg (2006). https://doi.org/10.1007/11678564_25
34. Dessì, N., Milia, G., Pes, B.: Enhancing random forests performance in microarray data classification. In: Peek, N., Marín Morales, R., Peleg, M. (eds.) AIME 2013. LNCS (LNAI), vol. 7885, pp. 99–103. Springer, Heidelberg (2013). https://doi.org/10.1007/978-3-642-38326-7_15
35. WEKA. https://www.cs.waikato.ac.nz/ml/weka/. Accessed 04 Apr 2023
36. Guyon, I., Weston, J., Barnhill, S., Vapnik, V.: Gene selection for cancer classification using support vector machines. Mach. Learn. **46**, 389–422 (2002)
37. Li, Z., Xie, W., Liu, T.: Efficient feature selection and classification for microarray data. PLoS ONE **13**(8), e0202167 (2018)

Principal Components Analysis Based Imputation for Logistic Regression

Thuong H. T. Nguyen[2,3], Bao Le[1,2,3], Phuc Nguyen[2,3], Linh G. H. Tran[2,3], Thu Nguyen[4], and Binh T. Nguyen[1,2,3(✉)]

[1] AISIA Research Lab, Ho Chi Minh City, Vietnam
ngtbinh@hcmus.edu.vn
[2] University of Science, Ho Chi Minh City, Vietnam
[3] Vietnam National University, Ho Chi Minh City, Vietnam
[4] Simula Metropolitan, Oslo, Norway

Abstract. The field of AI and machine learning is constantly evolving, and as the size of data continues to grow, so does the need for accurate and efficient methods of data processing. However, the data is not always perfect, and missing data is becoming common and occurs more frequently. Therefore, imputation techniques, aside from precision, needed to be scalable. For that reason, we examine the performance of Principle Components Analysis Imputation (PCAI) [9], an imputation speeding up framework, for logistic regression. Note that the coefficients of a logistic regression model are usually used for interpretation. Therefore, in addition to examining the improvement in the speed of PCAI, we examine how the coefficients of fitted logistic regression models change when using this imputation speeding-up mechanism. To demonstrate the efficiency of the mentioned method, the model's performance is compared against frequently used imputation methods on three popular datasets: Fashion MNIST, Gene, and Parkinson. And achieves lower time and better accuracy in most experiments.

Keywords: Missing data · Data imputation · Logistic Regression · Principle Components Analysis

1 Introduction

Missing data problems have grown and become ubiquitous. In many situations, Data might not be available because it was never collected, got lost, etc. the unknown values should be imputed before the dataset can be used. The reason is that dealing with incomplete information can lead to a loss of necessary information and yield abysmal results when many data points are missing. Therefore, imputation approaches [5, 14] continue to be popular despite recent efforts to deal directly with missing data [7]. This is since managing missing data can be challenging. On the other hand, imputation can be more flexible since it makes the data complete, i.e., there are no longer any missing values. As a result, it is simpler to carry out analyses and data visualizations.

© The Author(s), under exclusive license to Springer Nature Switzerland AG 2023
H. Fujita et al. (Eds.): IEA/AIE 2023, LNAI 13925, pp. 28–36, 2023.
https://doi.org/10.1007/978-3-031-36819-6_3

There are many methods for imputation of missing data [5, 15, 18]; however, most of them are computationally costly for large datasets. For instance, experiments in [11] demonstrate that MICE [14] and missForest [12] are unable to complete the imputation process for Fashion MNIST [17], a dataset with 70,000 samples and 784 features, within three hours for a missing rate of 20%. It is critical to accelerating the currently available imputation approaches since datasets are moving in the direction of greater sizes with hundreds of thousands of features [6]. When resource constraint are considered, a new method must be suggested to deal with the problems related to memory and time complexity.

In this paper me examine PCA Imputation (PCAI), an innovative framework based on Principal Component Analysis (PCA) that can speed up the imputation of many existing approaches on classification task using logistic regression [13] where there are missing values in data. PCAI is used to speed up imputation by partitioning the data into features with complete observations and features with partial observations. The missing component is then reconstructed based on the union of the fully observed portion and the missing part as reduced via PCA.

In summary, the contributions of this paper can be listed as follows:

(a) We examine the improvement in speed that PCAI can help achieve for five popular imputation techniques (softImpute [8], MissForest [12], MICE [14], KNNI [16] and GAIN [18]).
(b) Besides running time, we also maintain comparable accuracy of logistic regression results on three datasets.
(c) We illustrate that in some cases, logistic models fitted by imputation data resulting from PCAI can have coefficients that are closer to the true model.

2 Related Works

There have been various approaches proposed to tackle incomplete data problems. For example, Baligh and [2] presented a new method that applied genetic programming and weighted K-nearest neighbors for symbolic regression. The proposed solution constructs GP-based models using other available features to predict the missing values of incomplete features, their proposed method outweighs multiple state-of-the-art (SOTA) approaches. In the same year, Deep-MVI was presented by Bansal et al. [3], a deep learning method for missing value imputation in multidimensional time-series data. DeepMVI was significantly more accurate, declining error by more than 50% in more than half the cases, compared to the best existing method.

The application of Principal Component Analysis when dealing with missing values was firstly explored in [1], where they used only a single component and a single iteration for imputation. More recently, [4] has put forward for constructing a PCA model while working with missing data. Beside using PCA as imputation methods, Nguyen and colleagues [9] proposed Principal Component Analysis Imputation (PCAI) frameworks and PCA Imputation - Classification (PIC) by using PCA as dimension reduction on fully observed features, it enhances the imputation speed remarkably while achieving competitive MSE and accuracy compared to direct imputation. Other relevant works can be found at [10].

3   Methodology

This section will present the two-form of Principal Component Analysis (PCA) as techniques to reduce the data dimension. Furthermore, we detail Principal Component Analysis Imputation (PCAI) [9], a simple technique based on Principal Component Analysis (PCA) to accelerate and reduce the memory problems of the imputation process. We use similar notations mentioned in [9].

In what follows, we suppose that there is a data set $D = [x_1, x_2, ..., x_n], x_i \in R^p$ with n samples and p features. In addition, the features are centered and scaled.

3.1   Problem Formulation

PCA is a data reduction technique that linearly transforms the data into a new coordinate system with fewer dimensions. Therefore, fewer unnecessary factors make these smaller datasets easier and faster to analyze. This work will present two specific PCA approaches formulated on a covariance matrix and an input matrix.

3.1.1   PCA Based on Covariance Matrix (PCA-Form1)

The first step is to calculate the covariance matrix of the data matrix of n samples and p features. Let Σ represent the estimated covariance matrix of $\mathbf{X}$ based on the data. Next, let $(\lambda_1, \mathbf{v}_1), ..., (\lambda_p, \mathbf{v}_p)$ be the sorted eigenvalue-eigenvector pairs of Σ where $\lambda_1 \geq \lambda_2 \geq ... \geq \lambda_p \geq 0$. Suppose one wants to choose the first r pairs for dimension reduction. Then, the proportion of variance explained by these r pairs is given by:

$$\frac{\lambda_1 + \lambda_2 + ... + \lambda_r}{\lambda_1 + \lambda_2 + ... + \lambda_p} \tag{1}$$

Next, let $\mathbf{V} = [\mathbf{v}_1, \mathbf{v}_2, ..., \mathbf{v}_r]$. After that, one can obtain $\mathbf{XV}$ for the reduced version $R_\mathbf{X}$ of $\mathbf{X}$.

3.1.2   PCA Based on the Input Matrix X (PCA-Form2)

First, we identify a few variables that $\mathbf{U}$ is an $n \times p$ orthogonal matrix, $\mathbf{W}$ is a $p \times p$ orthogonal matrix, and $\mathbf{D}$ is a $p \times p$ diagonal matrix whose diagonal elements are $d_1 \geq d_2 \geq ... \geq d_p \geq 0$. The solution of PCA can also be produced based on the singular value decomposition of $\mathbf{X}$:

$$\mathbf{X} = \mathbf{UDW}^T \tag{2}$$

Suppose that r eigenvalues are used, and $\mathbf{W}_r$ consists of the first r columns of $\mathbf{W}$, then the projection matrix is $\mathbf{V} = \mathbf{W}_r$. Clearly, the reduced version $R_\mathbf{X}$ of $\mathbf{X}$ is also $\mathbf{XV}$.

3.2   PCA Imputation (PCAI)

The approach "PCA Imputation" (PCAI) is described in the below algorithms. Suppose one has a dataset $\mathcal{D} = \mathcal{F} \cup \mathcal{M}$, where $\mathcal{F}$ is the fully observed partition and $\mathcal{M}$ is the partition with missing values. One can first use $pca(A)$ to reduce dimension of $\mathcal{F}$, which return $\mathcal{R_F}$. Then, the imputation process can be done on $\mathcal{R_F} \cup \mathcal{M}$ instead of $\mathcal{F} \cup \mathcal{M}$ like other SOTA imputation methods usually done.

As illustrated in experiments section, PCAI seems to perform slightly better while significantly reduce the running time of every imputation methods.

Algorithm 1. PCAI imputation framework

Require:
   $\mathcal{D} \leftarrow \mathcal{F} \cup \mathcal{M}$
   Imputer I
   PCA algorithm pca
Procedure:
   $(\mathcal{R}, V) \leftarrow pca(\mathcal{F})$
   $\mathcal{M'} \leftarrow I(\mathcal{R} \cup \mathcal{M})$
   Return Imputed version $\mathcal{M'}$ of $\mathcal{M}$

---

4   Experiments

4.1   Evaluation Metrics

In our experiments, we use classification accuracy and running time to evaluate the performance of methods. In addition, we also evaluate L^2 relative error norm r between the coefficients of the model fitted on fully observed data (β_F) and the coefficients of the model fitted on imputed data (β_I).

$$r = \frac{||\beta_F - \beta_I||_2}{||\beta_F||_2} \tag{3}$$

4.2   Datasets

To illustrate the efficiency of the PCAI approach, we experiment on 3 datasets:

1. Gene dataset is extracted by gene expressions of patients with different tumor types: BRCA, KIRC, COAD, LUAD, and PRAD.
2. Parkinson dataset has a range of biomedical voice measurements from 31 people, 23 with Parkinson's disease (PD), It is worth noting that both Gene and Parkinson datasets are taken from the Machine Learning Database Repository at the University.
3. One large dataset, Fashion MNIST [17], including clothing images is also selected in our experiments.

All datasets have significant features to impute. Which makes them computationally expensive to impute in terms of time and memory complexity. The details of each dataset can be listed in Table 1.

Table 1. Description of datasets used in our experiments.

Dataset	# classes	# features	Samples
Fashion MNIST	10	784	70000
Gene	5	20531	801
Parkinson	2	754	756

4.3   Experimental Design

We compare the speed and accuracy of PCAI with Direct Imputation (DI) methods. The imputation methods we use in our experiments are:

(a) **SoftImpute** [8]: The algorithm fills in missing values with random values and then solves an optimization problem by using soft-thresholded SVD.
(b) **MissForest** [12]: Imputes missing values using Random Forests in an iterative fashion.
(c) **MICE** [14]: models each feature with missing values as a function of other features to estimate for imputation in an iterated round-robin fashion.
(d) **kNN Imputation (KNNI)** [16]: Weights each samples using the mean squared difference on features for which two data points both have observed data.
(e) **GAIN** [18]: A deep learning approach for imputing missing data by utilizing Generative Adversarial Network (GAN).

All methods are implemented with default configurations. Here, the default PCA formulation is PCA-form1 for Fashion MNIST and Parkinson and PCA-form2 for Gene due to its large amount of features. For all PCA computations, the number of eigenvectors is chosen so that the total variance explained is at least 95%. We use logistic regression as our classifier in all cases.

Note that any datasets can be rearranged so that the first q features are not missing and the remaining ones are missing. Therefore, we assume that the first q features of each dataset are not missing, and the remaining ones contain missing values. We simulated missing data randomly on the missing partition M with default missing rates of 20%. We ran all experiments on Intel Xeon CPU, except with GAIN, we ran on 2 GPU T4. We terminate an experiment if no result is produced after 20000 s or if a memory allocating issue arises. We denote this as **NA** in the result tables.

4.4   Results and Discussion

The overall results are listed in Table 2. One can see that all PCAI approaches have slightly better accuracy than direct imputation methods while also significantly reduce the imputation time across all datasets.

Table 2. Accuracy (%) and Running time (s) of every imputation method.

Methods	Strategy	Fashion MNIST	Gene	Parkinson
Soft Impute	Direct Impute	(**74.33, 23.05**)	(97.736, 11.864)	(76.055, 0.558)
	PCAI	(74.05, 26.33)	(**98.113, 4.929**)	(**76.852, 0.448**)
GAIN	Direct Impute	(73.87, 145.18)	NA	(76.05, 736.95)
	PCAI	(**74.05, 73.67**)	(**96.226, 750.895**)	(**76.85, 159.5**)
MICE	Direct Impute	(**73.92**, 13086.91)	NA	(76.05, 494.76)
	PCAI	(73.56, **1646.6**)	(**98.86, 536.78**)	(**76.85, 38.9**)
KNNI	Direct Impute	(**74.22**, 5259.756)	(98.491, 11.7)	(76.055, **0.761**)
	PCAI	(74.09, **4317.16**)	(**98.491, 5.08**)	(**76.852**, 1.08)
MissForest	Direct Impute	(73.73, **1623.62**)	(99.245, 5387.13)	(76.05, **33.5**)
	PCAI	(**74.28**, 1690.68)	(**99.875, 2042.01**)	(**76.85**, 45.1)

We observe that all PCAI maintain competitive or even slightly better results than their Direct Imputation methods. This can be explained that PCA only retains the vital information from the data while removing some noise, which helps improve the imputation quality.

In Fashion MNIST, MICE is the slowest method, which takes 13086 s to impute. Still, with PCA Imputation, the running time reduces to 1646 s, which reduces up to 87% running time while maintaining almost the same accuracy.

In datasets with large features like the Gene dataset, the PCAI method stands out. As we can't get the results on this dataset with GAIN and MICE due to memory issues. But with PCAI, we can alleviate this issue and obtain the results.

With the Parkinson dataset, all PCA Imputation methods have a faster imputation process than DI methods. Moreover, especially with GAIN, the running time of the imputation process reduces by up to 50%. Except for MissForest, the PCAI approach takes a longer running time than DI method. We report Relative error norm r logistic regression coefficients of every imputation method in

Table 3. Relative L^2 error norm r of imputation methods

Methods	Strategy	Fashion MNIST	Gene	Parkinson
Soft Impute	Direct Impute	106.9	0.876	10849325
	PCAI	106.9	0.461	1809449
GAIN	Direct Impute	121.584	NA	10748200
	PCAI	121.071	0.457	1812283
MICE	Direct Impute	111.35	NA	10858541
	PCAI	105.8	0.464	1809449
KNNI	Direct Impute	114.6	0.869	10836499
	PCAI	108.5	0.466	1807958
MissForest	Direct Impute	109.86	0.879	10797846
	PCAI	107.05	0.489	3118440

Table 3. In the Fashion MNIST dataset, the relative error is not a significant difference. Still, in other datasets, the relative error of PCAI methods was reduced by almost 50% in Gene and 83% compared to DI. Overall, one can see that the approach has lower r than other Direct Imputation methods.

4.5   Comparision Between PCA-Form1 and PCA-Form1

In this section, we aim to analyze two PCA formulations' performance. As expected, the two formulations have no significant difference in accuracy. In comparing the running time, we observed that PCA-form1 performed better in Fashion MNIST and Parkinson, especially in Fashion MNIST, with MICE taking only 1645 s to impute in PCA-form1 compared to 8878 s in PCA-form2. Other methods also gain benefit from running time with PCA-form1. But in Gene, we could not obtain the results in PCA-form1 due to memory issues.

This can be explained when the sample size is larger than of fully observed features dimension, PCA-form1 should be used since the covariance matrix is much smaller than $\mathcal{F}$, making it faster than PCA-form2. In contrast, when the number of fully observed features is larger than the sample size, PCA-form2 should be preferred (Table 4).

Table 4. The accuracy (%) and Running time (s) of two PCA formulations.

Methods	Formulation	Fashion MNIST	Gene	Parkinson
Soft Impute	PCA-form1	(74.05, **23.05**)	NA	(76.85, **0.448**)
	PCA-form2	(**74.63**, 28.37)	(**98.113**, **4.929**)	(**76.9**, 0.825)
GAIN	PCA-form1	(74.05, **73.67**)	NA	(**76.85**, **159.5**)
	PCA-form2	(**74.52**, 106.24)	(**96.226**, **750.895**)	(75.2, 299.06)
MICE	PCA-form1	(73.56, **1645.6**)	NA	(76.85, **101.7**)
	PCA-form2	(**73.86**, 8878.35	(**99.25**, **536.78**)	(**76.9**, 163.94)
KNNI	PCA-form1	(74.09, **3058.28**)	NA	(**76.852**, 1.08)
	PCA-form2	(**74.27**, 4266.16)	(**98.491**, **5.085**)	(75.2, **0.74**)
MissForest	PCA-form1	(**74.28**, **1690.69**)	NA	(**76.85**, **45.1**)
	PCA-form2	(74.27, 3800.732)	(**99.875**, **2042.01**)	(75.2, 67.24)

5   Conclusion and Future Works

In this paper, we have conducted a variety of experiments applying the PCA imputation framework. As a result, the proposed method has significantly enhanced the imputation process's speed while maintaining competitive accuracy compared to direct imputation, alleviating the memory issue for imputation approaches that require large memory footprints such as KNNI, Mice, and GAIN.

However, if there are not many fully observed features, PCA imputation may not lead to any improvement in speed. In the near future, we aim to explore our framework to solve the issue when the dataset does not have many fully observed features. Moreover, we will study whether applying PCA variants to the missing M partition can improve the efficiency and the imputation time.

Acknowledgments. We want to thank the University of Science, Vietnam National University in Ho Chi Minh City, and AISIA Research Lab in Vietnam for supporting us throughout this paper.

Funding. This research is funded by Vietnam National University Ho Chi Minh City (VNU-HCM) in Ho Chi Minh City, Vietnam under the grant number DS2023-18-01.

References

1. A principal-component missing-data method for multiple regression models. System Development Corporation (1959)
2. Al-helali, B., Chen, Q., Xue, B., Zhang, M.: A new imputation method based on genetic programming and weighted KNN for symbolic regression with incomplete data. Soft Comput. **25**, 1–20 (2021)
3. Bansal, P., Deshpande, P., Sarawagi, S.: Missing value imputation on multidimensional time series. CoRR, abs/2103.01600 (2021)
4. Fortuny-Folch, A., Arteaga, F., Ferrer, A.: PCA model building with missing data: new proposals and a comparative study. System Development Corporation (2015)
5. Garg, A., Naryani, D., Aggarwal, G., Aggarwal, S.: DL-GSA: a deep learning meta-heuristic approach to missing data imputation. In: Tan, Y., Shi, Y., Tang, Q. (eds.) ICSI 2018. LNCS, vol. 10942, pp. 513–521. Springer, Cham (2018). https://doi.org/10.1007/978-3-319-93818-9_49
6. Guyon, I., Li, J., Mader, T., Pletscher, P.A., Schneider, G., Uhr, M.: Competitive baseline methods set new standards for the NIPS 2003 feature selection benchmark. Pattern Recogn. Lett. **28**(12), 1438–1444 (2007)
7. Lipton, Z.C., Kale, D.C., Wetzel, R., et al.: Modeling missing data in clinical time series with RNNs. Mach. Learn. Healthcare **56**, 253–270 (2016)
8. Mazumder, R., Hastie, T., Tibshirani, R.: Spectral regularization algorithms for learning large incomplete matrices. J. Mach. Learn. Res. **11**(80), 2287–2322 (2010)
9. Nguyen, T., Ly, H.T., Riegler, M.A., Halvorsen, P.: Principal component analysis based frameworks for efficient missing data imputation algorithms (2022)
10. Nguyen, T., Nguyen, D.H., Nguyen, H., Nguyen, B.T., Wade, B.A.: EPEM: efficient parameter estimation for multiple class monotone missing data. Inf. Sci. **567**, 1–22 (2021)
11. Nguyen, T., Nguyen-Duy, K.M., Nguyen, D.H.M., Nguyen, B.T., Wade, B.A.: DPER: direct parameter estimation for randomly missing data. Knowl.-Based Syst. **240**, 108082 (2022)
12. Stekhoven, D.J., Bühlmann, P.: MissForest-non-parametric missing value imputation for mixed-type data. Bioinformatics **28**(1), 112–118 (2012)
13. Tolles, J., Meurer, W.J.: Logistic regression: relating patient characteristics to outcomes. JAMA **316**(5), 533–534 (2016)
14. van Buuren, S., Groothuis-Oudshoorn, K.: Mice: multivariate imputation by chained equations in R. J. Stat. Softw. **45**(3), 1–67 (2011)
15. Vu, M.A., et al.: Conditional expectation for missing data imputation. arXiv preprint arXiv:2302.00911 (2023)

16. Woźnica, K., Biecek, P.: Does imputation matter? Benchmark for predictive models (2020)
17. Xiao, H., Rasul, K., Vollgraf, R.: Fashion-MNIST: a novel image dataset for benchmarking machine learning algorithms. arXiv preprint arXiv:1708.07747 (2017)
18. Yoon, J., Jordon, J., van der Schaar, M.: Gain: missing data imputation using generative adversarial nets (2018)

A Selective Supervised Latent Beta-Liouville Allocation for Document Classification

Zhiwen Luo[1]($\boxtimes$), Manar Amayri[1], Wentao Fan[2], and Nizar Bouguila[1]

[1] The Concordia Institute for Information Systems Engineering (CIISE),
Concordia University, Montréal, QC H3H 1M8, Canada
zhiwen.luo@mail.concordia.ca, {manar.amayri,nizar.bouguila}@concordia.ca
[2] Department of Computer Science, Beijing Normal University-Hong Kong Baptist
University United International College (UIC), Zhuhai 519088, Guangdong, China
wentaofan@uic.edu.cn

Abstract. We propose a novel model, selective supervised Latent Beta-Liouville (ssLBLA), that improves the performance and generative process of supervised probabilistic topic models with a more flexible prior and simple framework. ssLBLA model utilizes the "bag-of-selective-words" instead of the "bag-of-words" in the topic modeling by using a Bernoulli distribution to identify the discrimination power of a word for its assigned topic. Indeed, ssLBLA improves and inherits the general framework of selective supervised Latent Dirichlet Allocation (ssLDA) and can predict many types of responses. This paper presents a simple framework that utilizes the collapsed Gibbs sampling inference technique coupled with the flexible Beta-Liouville (BL) distribution prior to achieve more accurate estimations. Experimental results in single-label document classification show the merits of our new approach.

Keywords: Topic model · Beta-Liouville · supervised learning · collapsed Gibbs sampler · classification

1 Introduction

Effectively processing large amounts of data is becoming increasingly important in data analytics. Many researchers have investigated techniques to process data while extracting valuable information efficiently. Probabilistic topic models, which can discover the latent semantics in documents by probabilistic approach, have gained significant attention for analyzing text and image documents [2,12,14,17] based on the Bag of Words (BoW) scheme. Latent Dirichlet Allocation (LDA) [4], as a famous hierarchical Bayesian model, has been widely studied and applied in various fields [5]. As an unsupervised model, LDA can not take advantage of the useful auxiliary information from many real-world document datasets. Therefore, this unsupervised approach only can learn latent representations of documents that are not mainly for making predictions [3]. To enhance

H. Fujita et al. (Eds.): IEA/AIE 2023, LNAI 13925, pp. 37–48, 2023.
https://doi.org/10.1007/978-3-031-36819-6_4

the performance of the LDA model in classification tasks, researchers have developed supervised versions of LDA. However, most existing supervised extensions of LDA only focuses on discovering latent semantics or topic of words in the "bag-of-topics" representation of documents [19]. Those methods consider all words assigned to the topic equally informative, which ignores the fact that different words may have different levels of discrimination power. Selective supervised LDA (ssLDA) [19] tries to take into account the discriminative power of words for topics to construct a more predictive representation of the document under "bag-of-selective-words" (BoSW) assumption, resulting in more robust prediction performance.

On the other hand, most existing supervised topic models rely on the standard LDA model framework with Dirichlet distribution as conjugate prior to multinomial distribution for both document and corpus parameters. The Dirichlet distribution is commonly used in topic modeling because it is simple to calculate [8,10]. However, this distribution has a limitation in that it cannot reflect the correlation across topics due to its limited negative covariance matrix structure [1,11]. Because of this limitation, researchers have developed extensions to LDA that use more flexible priors, such as Latent Beta-Liouville Allocation (LBLA) [1,11,13].

Therefore, to alleviate the above limitations, we present a supervised topic model called the selective supervised Latent Beta-Liouville allocation (ssLBLA) model. The ssLBLA model, as a novel extension of ssLDA, can acquire a more predictive representation of a document by taking into account both the latent semantics underlying the words and the words themselves. Specifically, words are treated as features in the ssLBLA model, and their topic assignments are used to adjust the weights of words under the BoSW assumption. Moreover, ssLBLA overcomes the limitation of the Dirichlet prior and prior knowledge in the ssLDA model by introducing a more flexible prior, Beta-Liouville distribution, for both topic and corpus parameters and adding Beta distribution prior for Bernouill distribution in discrimination value. Moreover, we utilize collapsed Gibbs sampling inference technique for ssLBLA (CGS-ssLBLA) model, which allows the sampling process from the actual posterior distribution rather than the approximate variational distribution in variational Bayesian (VB) inference scheme [15]. Experimental results in document classification show the merits of the new approach. The results show that the method has an accurate and straightforward inference scheme for analyzing topic correlation and word discrimination value, resulting in better performance. The paper is organized as follows. Section 2 reviews the related works in the previous extensions. We present our ssLBLA model and its inference process in Sect. 3. Section 4 is devoted to the experimental results. Section 5 concludes this paper and gives our conclusions and future work.

2   Related Works

Latent Dirichlet Allocation (LDA) model [4] is a complete generative probabilistic topic model which overcomes overfitting and the difficulty in predicting test documents probability problems in previous topic models. To discover predictive representations for unseen documents, the supervised LDA (sLDA) [3] model utilizes the documents' auxiliary information. The maximum entropy discrimination Latent Dirichlet Allocation (MedLDA) model uses the max-margin principle to extend the sLDA model and obtain more accurate predictive topic representations. However, most existing supervised extensions of LDA only focus on finding predictive representations of a document according to the latent topic regardless of the word's discrimination power for its assigned topic [19]. To address this limitation, selective supervised Latent Dirichlet Allocation (ssLDA) [19] takes the discrimination power of words into a model by incorporating it as a model parameter and estimating it. Those supervised topic models above utilize the variational Bayesian (VB) inference technique because it allows for easy convergence. However, VB inference assumes strong independence between parameters and latent variables, which can lead to a bias in the joint posterior distribution and negatively impact the lower bound of log likelihood, likelihood distribution, and overall performance.

Even though those supervised topic models obtain an acceptable result in topic modeling and document classification, numerous studies [1,11,13] have shown that the constraints of Dirichlet prior hamper the LDA and its extensions' performance. Because the Dirichlet distribution has a very restrictive negative covariance structure, it has difficulties performing in a topic correlation analysis [13]. Recent breakthroughs in topic modeling have highlighted the necessity for more flexible priors. Ihou and Bouguila [11] showed that using more flexible priors such as Beta-Liouville (BL) distributions in document and corpus parameters can improve the performance of the original LDA model in text modeling and computer vision applications. In this paper, to solve the problems above, we have implemented a novel and straightforward approach, the collapsed Gibbs sampler scheme for selective supervised Latent Beta-Liouvill allocation (CGS-ssLBLA) model.

3   Selective Supervised Latent Beta-Liouvill Allocation Model

Our new model, selective supervised latent Beta-Liouville allocation (ssLBLA), aims to identify discriminative words across different topics to improve the predictive representations of documents. ssLBLA model integrates ssLDA [19], and LBLA [11] models as a more flexible supervised topic model that takes BL on document and corpus parameters. Similar to the ssLDA framework, we choose a binary indicator to determine the discriminative power of words for their assigned topic. The binary indicator variable is sampled from a Bernoulli distribution. For example, value 1 and 0 corresponds strongly and weakly for words' discriminative power separately. Nevertheless, unlike ssLDA, we employ Beta distribution as a prior for the Bernoulli distribution to improve the model's generative process. For the complete analysis of the ssLBLA model, we will first state the generative process of the ssLBLA model, and then we will develop the inference equations using the collapsed Gibbs sampling for learning (CGS-ssLBLA).

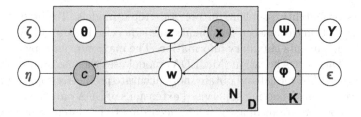

Fig. 1. Graphical representation of selective supervised Latent Beta-Liouvill allocation

We will start with a study of the generative process of the ssLBLA model. The graphical topic model (Fig. 1) is described by a list of variables. Table 1 provides the variables in this paper to allow readers to understand our model and follow the inference steps easily.

Table 1. Model variables and definitions

C - total number of collections
D - total number of documents
W - total number of words in each document
K - total number of topics
$\mathbf{w} = w_{ij}$ - observed words
$\mathbf{z} = z_{ij}$ - latent variables
θ - topic mixing proportions
ϕ_k - corpus parameters
ψ_k - parameter in Bernoulli distribution
$\theta \sim BL(\zeta)$ - Beta-Liouville distribution
$\phi_k \sim BL(\epsilon)$ - Beta-Liouville distribution
$\psi_k \sim Beta(\gamma_0, \gamma_1)$ - Beta distribution
$x_{ck} \sim Bernoulli(\psi_k)$ - Bernoulli distribution
$z_{jk}/\theta_k \sim Mult(\theta_k)$ - multinomial distribution
$w_{jk}/z_{jk}, \phi_k, x = 1 \sim Mult(\phi_k)$ - multinomial distribution

The task of learning topics and the discrimination power of the word for its assigned topic is modeled as the estimation for posterior distributions of Beta-Liouville and Bernoulli variables θ and ψ. Our ssLBLA model is a Bayesian graphical model designed for efficiently computing these values. The word $\mathbf{w}$ and the class label c of the document d can be generated from the following generative process:

– For each document **d**, draw a topic mixture θ from $BL(\zeta)$.
– Draw a word distribution ϕ_k from $BL(\epsilon)$ for each topic $\mathbf{z}$

- Draw a Bernoulli distribution ψ_k from $Beta(\gamma_0, \gamma_1)$ for each topic $\mathbf{z}$
- Then for each word w_i in $\mathbf{d}$:

  • Sample a topic z_i from $Mutl(\theta_d)$
  • Sample a word w_i from $Mutl(\phi_{z_i})$
  • Sample discriminative value x_i from $Bernoulli(\psi_{z_i})$

- Draw class label c_d with the probability

$$p(c_d \mid w_d, x_d, \eta) = \frac{\exp(\sum_{n=1}^{W} \eta_{c_d w_{dn}} s_{dn})}{\sum_{l=1}^{C} \exp(\sum_{n=1}^{W} \eta_{l w_{dn}} s_{dn})} \tag{1}$$

3.1 Inference

Because the estimation of the posterior distribution in Bayesian topic models is intractable, inference methods such as variational inference (VB) [4,19] and MCMC [13] have become the standard choices to estimate the latent topics and the model parameters. For the ssLBLA model, we choose collapsed space representation because it contributes to the performance of batch models [9]. Then, the collapsed Gibbs sampling is used to infer the proposed ssLBLA model because this method provides a more accurate inference than the VB approach. Details about collapsed Gibbs sampling inference will be provided. Specifically, ζ carries the document hyperparameters α and β. In more detail, $\zeta = (\alpha_1, ..., \alpha_{K-1}, \alpha, \beta)$ means the hyperparameter set of a document, and K is the number of topics. The corpus hyperparameter variable ϵ can be extended as $\epsilon = (\lambda_1, ..., \lambda_{W-1}, \lambda, \kappa)$ while W is the size of the vocabulary or codebook. Therefore, in our implementation, ζ is the K dimensional BL hyperparameter $(\alpha_1, ..., \alpha_{K-1}, \alpha, \beta)$ for the document in a K dimensional space. The ϵ is the W dimensional BL hyperparameters for the vocabulary in a W dimensional space.

In collapsed space, the parameters are marginalized, leaving only the latent variables that are conditionally independent [9]. The collapsed space of latent variables is low-dimensional compared with joint space. Estimation in collapsed space is faster than in joint space because the parameters ϕ, σ, and θ are marginalized. The collapsed Gibbs sampling inference approach uses a Bayesian method to estimate the posterior distributions by computing expectations through a sampling process of the latent variables. The CGS is easier to implement and computationally quicker than ordinary Gibbs sampling in the joint space. Because the CGS inference does not need the usage of digamma functions, it increases computational efficiency. As a result, when the Markov chain achieves its stationary distribution, the CGS inference accurately approximates the actual posterior distribution.

Joint Distribution. Based on the generative process of ssLBLA model, the joint distribution of our proposed model can be represented as follows:

$$p(\mathbf{w}, \mathbf{z}, \mathbf{x}, \mathbf{c} \mid \zeta, \epsilon, \eta, \gamma)$$

$$= p(\zeta)p(\epsilon)p(\gamma) \times \prod_{d=1}^{D} p(c_d \mid w_d, x_d, \eta)$$

$$\times \prod_{j=1}^{D} \prod_{i=1}^{W} p(\mathbf{x}_{ij} \mid \psi_{z_{ij}w_{ij}}) \prod_{j=1}^{D} \prod_{i=1}^{W} p(\mathbf{w}_{ij} \mid \phi_{z_{ij}}) \tag{2}$$

$$\times \prod_{j=1}^{D} \prod_{i=1}^{W} p(\mathbf{z}_{ij} \mid \theta_j) \times \prod_{j=1}^{K} p(\psi_j \mid \gamma) \prod_{j=1}^{D} p(\theta_j \mid \zeta) \prod_{j=1}^{K} p(\phi_j \mid \epsilon)$$

Latent Variables. In the CGS-based ssLBLA scheme, the conditional probabilities of latent variable z_{ij} are calculated by the current state of all variables except the particular variable z_{ij} being processed in the marginal joint distribution $p(\mathbf{w}, \mathbf{z}, \mathbf{x} \mid \zeta, \epsilon, \gamma)$. This algorithm applies the collapsed Gibbs sampler for topic assignments. The conditional probability of z_{ij} is $p(z_{ij} = k \mid x_i = 1, \mathbf{z}_{-ij}, \mathbf{w}, \zeta, \epsilon, \gamma)$. The $-ij$ represents the counts with z_{ij} excluded [9,13]. This conditional probability is expressed as:

$$p(z_{ij} = k \mid x_{ij} = 1, \mathbf{z}^{-ij}, \mathbf{w}, \zeta, \epsilon, \gamma) = \frac{p(z_{ij} = k, z^{-ij}, \mathbf{w}, x_{ij} = 1 \mid \zeta, \epsilon, \gamma)}{p(z^{-ij}, \mathbf{w}, x_{ij} = 1 \mid \zeta, \epsilon, \gamma)} \tag{3}$$

Equation 3 can be simplified as follows:

$$p(z_{ij} = k \mid x_{ij} = 1, \mathbf{z}^{-ij}, \mathbf{w}, \zeta, \epsilon, \gamma) \propto p(z_{ij} = k, z^{-ij}, \mathbf{w}, x_{ij} = 1 \mid \zeta, \epsilon, \gamma) \tag{4}$$

To speed up the training process, we marginalize these parameters in the collapsed space because sampling in the collapsed space is much faster than in the joint space of latent variables and parameters [11]. By integrating out the parameters, Gibbs sampler's equations are obtained as expectation expressions:

$$p(z_{ij} = k \mid x_{ij} = 1, \mathbf{z}^{-ij}, \mathbf{w}, \zeta, \epsilon, \gamma)$$
$$= E_{p(z_{ij}=k\mid x_{ij}=1, \mathbf{w}, \zeta, \epsilon, \gamma)}[p(z_{ij} = k \mid x_{ij} = 1, z^{-ij}, \mathbf{w}, \zeta, \epsilon, \gamma)] \tag{5}$$

In the collapsed space, we can integrate out θ, ϕ, σ, and ψ to get Eqs. 6 and 6 according to the conjugacy of the Beta/Binomial and BL/Multinomial distributions. In CGS algorithm iterations, we sample new assignments of $\mathbf{z}$ and $\mathbf{x}$ alternately with the following equations:

$$p(x_{ij} = x \mid x_{-ij}, \mathbf{z}, \mathbf{w}, \gamma, \epsilon) \propto \frac{N_x^{ck} + \gamma_x}{N_{\cdot}^{ck} + \gamma_0 + \gamma_1} \tag{6}$$

$$p(z_i = k \mid x_i = 1, \mathbf{z}_{-i}, \mathbf{w}, \zeta, \epsilon, \gamma) \propto$$

$$\frac{(\alpha_k + N_{jk}^{-ij})}{(\sum_{l=1}^{K-1} \alpha_l + \sum_{l=1}^{K-1} N_{jl}^{-ij})} \times \frac{(\alpha + \sum_{l=1}^{K-1} N_{jl}^{-ij})}{(\alpha + \beta + \sum_{l=1}^{K} N_{jl}^{-ij})}$$

$$\times \frac{(\lambda_v + N_{kv}^{-ij})}{(\sum_{l=1}^{V-1} \lambda_l + \sum_{l=1}^{V-1} N_{kl}^{-ij})} \times \frac{(\lambda + \sum_{l=1}^{V-1} N_{kl}^{-ij})}{(\lambda + \eta + \sum_{l=1}^{V} N_{kl}^{-ij})} \qquad (7)$$

$$\times \frac{N_{x=1}^{ck} + \gamma_1}{N^{ck} + \gamma_0 + \gamma_1}$$

The count N_{jk} is for topics. Specifically, the count N_{jk}^{ij} is the number of words w_i in the document j and topic k. Besides, N_{jk}^{-ij} is the total number of words in document j and topic k except for the word w_i being sampled. The count $N_{kw_{ij}}^{ij}$ is the number of times the word w_{ij} appears in topic k and document j. In addition, $N_{kw_{ij}}^{-ij}$ is the number of times the word w_{ij} appears in document j and topic k except being sampled. $N_x^{k,c}$ is the number of $\mathbf{x}$ in topic k, and class c. $\mathbf{x}$ should be initialized as 1 for all tokens. We initially assume that everything has a strong discrimination power.

Parameters Estimation. Variables θ and ϕ are multinomial distributions with BL priors. ψ is Bernoulli distribution with Beta prior. According to Bayes's rule, these parameters can be computed from the above posteriors. For parameters estimation, the document parameter distribution is:

$$\theta_{jk} = \frac{(\alpha_k + N_{jk})}{(\sum_{l=1}^{K-1} \alpha_l + \sum_{l=1}^{K-1} N_{jl})} \times \frac{(\alpha + \sum_{l=1}^{K-1} N_{jl})}{(\alpha + \beta + \sum_{l=1}^{K} N_{jl})} \qquad (8)$$

The predictive distributions of the words is:

$$\phi_{kw} = \frac{(\lambda_v + N_{kv})}{(\sum_{l=1}^{V-1} \lambda_l + \sum_{l=1}^{V-1} N_{kl})} \times \frac{(\lambda + \sum_{l=1}^{V-1} N_{kl})}{(\lambda + \eta + \sum_{l=1}^{V} N_{kl})} \qquad (9)$$

The posterior of ψ is as follows:

$$\psi_{ck} = \frac{N_{x=1}^{ck} + \gamma_1}{N^{ck} + \gamma_0 + \gamma_1} \qquad (10)$$

Collapsed Gibbs Sampling Algorithm. Algorithm 1 shows the summary of the CGS-ssLBLA model. The procedure has the following three count variables: N_{jk}, N_{kv}, N_{cw}, and N_x^{ck}. There are three stages for the collapsed Gibbs sampling algorithm of CGS-ssLBLA model: initialization, a burn-in period, and a sampling period.

Algorithm 1. Summary of CGS-ssLBLA model

Input : Max iteration T, Prior parameters ζ, ϵ and γ,
          Topic number K, Corpus D, **w**, Class c
Output : Parameters θ, ϕ, and ψ using Eq. 8–10
          //**Initialization**
Initialize **z**, **x**, N_{jk}, N_{kw}, N_x
    Obtain N_{cw} for prediction
    //**Collapsed Gibbs Sampling**
    //**burn − in period and sampling period**
while iter $< T$ **do**
    for $i \in$ document D and $j \in$ in class c **do**
        update x_{ij} using Eq. 6
        update z_{ij} using Eq. 7
        update N_{jk}, N_{kw}, N_x
    end for
end while

3.2 Class Prediction

Classification of an unlabeled document d thus becomes the problem of choosing the c that maximizes the formula:

$$p(c_{d_{new}} \mid w_{d_{new}}, x_{d_{new}}, \eta_{train}) = \frac{\exp(\sum_{n=1}^{W} \eta_{c_{d_{new}} w_{d_{new}} n} s_{d_{new} n})}{\sum_{l=1}^{C} \exp(\sum_{n=1}^{W} \eta_{l w_{d_{new}} n} s_{d_{new} n})} \quad (11)$$

For prediction, given an unlabeled test document, we perform a collapsed Gibbs sampling similar to Algorithm 1 without using the N_{cw} to calculate η from the test document. η is obtained when the model is learned on a training set, except for s_{dn}, which depends on the new document. Specifically, η_c is a W-vector of real values. In Eq. 11, we use a simple approximation from the learned η, which represents the average word mxiture within that class: $\eta_{c_d w_{dn}} \approx \frac{N_{c_d w_{dn}}}{\sum_{n=1}^{W} N_{c_d w_{dn}}}$. Besides, $s_{dn} = \tau_1 x_{dn} + \tau_0 (1 - x_{dn})$ denotes the new weight of the word w_{dn} when the corresponding discriminative x_{dn} is taken into consideration, where the peak weight $0.5 \leq \tau_1 \leq 1$ is the weight of w_{dn} when $x_{dn} = 1$. The vally weight $0 \leq \tau_0 \leq 0.5$ is the weight of the w_{dn} when $x_{dn} = 0$. In this paper, we set a reasonable constraint $\tau_0 + \tau_1 = 1$.

4 Experimental Results

The proposed ssLBLA model is validated in this section using two document classification tasks with a famous real-world dataset, 20Newsgroup.

4.1 Dataset

20Newsgroups[1]. This dataset has been frequently utilized to evaluate the performance of supervised topic models in text classification tasks [7]. Specifically, 20Newsgroups contains approximately 20,000 newsgroup documents grouped into 20 categories. There are approximately 1,000 documents in each category. To test the performance of our model with a different number of categories, we first use 20 categories, such as *comp.graphics*, *rec.autos*, and *sci.space* to do document classification task. After that, the distinct categories of 20 Newsgroups can also be divided into 4 top categories, with several sub-categories for *comp*, *sci*, *rec*, and *talk*. Then, we will evaluate our model's performance of single-label document classification with this 4 top categories.

4.2 Implementation and Baselines

For document classification application, we preprocess the text datasets by first tokenizing words with the Natural Language ToolKit (NLTK) [16], removing punctuation, stop-words and then lemmatizing tokens to derive their common base form. We choose BL priors hyperparameters following the same setting of the asymmetric BL priors in [11]. For the Dirichlet-based model, the topic distribution priors are fixed, and $\alpha = 0.1$. Then, we set β to 0.01; for γ_0 and γ_1, we use the same value, 1.0. To examine the performances of our proposed model on document classification tasks, we compare ssLBLA with four state-of-the-art topic models: ssLDA [19], MedLDA [18], and sLDA [3], LDA+SVM [4] with "bag-of-topic" assumption. For the ssLDA and ssLBLA, we set $\tau_0 = 0.2$. The source codes of LDA, sLDA, and MedLDA are publicly available[2]. The code of SVM is from LIBSVM [6].

4.3 Document Classification Results

Table 2. Classification Accuracies (%) on 20Newsgroups

Task	LDA+SVM	sLDA	MedLDA	ssLDA	ssLBLA
20-class 20Newsgroup	70.72	65.98	79.64	83.46	**89.56**
4-class 20Newsgroup	76.38	73.54	84.23	89.90	**95.33**
average	73.55	69.76	81.93	86.68	**92.45**

Table 2 demonstrates two sets of document classification experiments: 4-class 20Newsgroup and 20-class 20Newsgroup classifications. In two 20Newsgroup classification tasks, we compare our proposed model, ssLBLA, with ssLDA [19],

---

[1] http://qwone.com/~jason/20Newsgroups/.
[2] http://www.cs.columbia.edu/~blei/topicmodeling.html.

MedLDA [18], and sLDA [3], LDA+SVM [4]. Table 2 shows that our ssLBLA model beats all of these approaches on the remaining tasks and improves the classification accuracies by [6%, 7.3%]. Our proposed model improves the accuracy from 86.68% (ssLDA) to 92.45%. Based on Table 2, ssLBLA and ssLDA obtain better results than other topic models with "bag-of-words" or "bag-of-topics" assumption because both can identify the discrimination power of words specified to topics, which contributes to classification performance. Moreover, our ssLBLA consistently achieves the best classification performance among all the topic models. Therefore, we also can conclude that the CGS-ssLBLA approach can provide outstanding results than the other competitors using the variational Bayes (VB) inference because the collapsed Gibbs sampling (CGS) is a more accurate inference scheme.

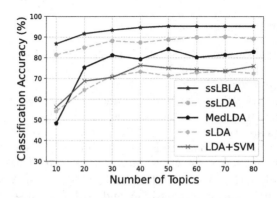

Fig. 2. The average accuracies for "state-of-the-art" topic models and ssLBLA with different topic numbers on 4-class 20Newsgroup dataset

The average accuracy for our ssLBLA and four topic models on both 4-class 20newsgroups and 20-class 20newsgroups datasets with different topics values is shown in Fig. 2 and Fig. 3. Our proposed model, ssLBLA, generally achieves higher accuracy than other topic models in all datasets. Like ssLDA, ssLBLA is also not very sensitive to the number of topics K. Nevertheless, the ssLBLA model achieves better accuracy than the ssLDA model with the same "bag-of-selective-words" assumption. Because our proposed model introduces BL distribution to replace Dirichlet distribution with a strict negative correlative structure [11,13]. Also, our new model provides a complete structure. This result also demonstrates the flexibility of the BL priors with a more general covariance structure compared to the Dirichlet distribution, which is very limited for its inability to perform in the case of positively correlated datasets. Hence, we can conclude that the main reason for our proposed model's (ssLBLA) improvement is that the BL prior has a better topic correlation and modeling capabilities [1,11]. These results demonstrate that the generative schemes with more flexible priors (BL distributions) can enhance the supervised topic model's prediction performance by overcoming the negative covariance structure of the Dirichlet distribution.

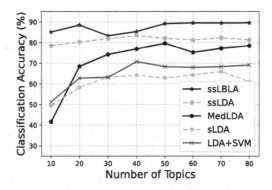

Fig. 3. The average accuracies for "state-of-the-art" topic models and ssLBLA with different topic numbers on 20-class 20Newsgroup dataset

5 Conclusion

In this article, we proposed a selective supervised Beta-Liouville allocation model (ssLBLA) that addresses the limitations of the Dirichlet prior and variational Bayes (VB) inference method. ssLBLA model utilizes the Beta-Liouville (BL) distributions instead of Dirichlet for both topic, and corpus parameters to improve the previous supervised topic models because BL prior has a complete topic representation. Moreover, we use Beta distribution as a prior for the Bernoulli distribution to improve the model's generative process. Experimental results show that our model outperforms four state-of-the-art methods, demonstrating our model's effectiveness. Document classification experiments show that our proposed CGS-ssLBLA scheme is straightforward and efficient because the flexible prior and a more comprehensive structure with collapsed Gibbs sampling inference approach can help the model learn better features for the classification task. For future work, we can naturally extend the proposed model by introducing a more flexible prior to improve the model's performance. Besides, we aim to enhance the efficiency of our proposed model so that it can be used for real-time streaming data.

References

1. Bakhtiari, A.S., Bouguila, N.: A latent Beta-Liouville allocation model. Expert Syst. Appl. **45**, 260–272 (2016)
2. Blei, D.M.: Probabilistic topic models. Commun. ACM **55**(4), 77–84 (2012)
3. Blei, D.M., McAuliffe, J.D.: Supervised topic models. In: Platt, J.C., Koller, D., Singer, Y., Roweis, S.T. (eds.) Advances in Neural Information Processing Systems 20. Proceedings of the Twenty-First Annual Conference on Neural Information Processing Systems, Vancouver, British Columbia, Canada, 3–6 December 2007, pp. 121–128. Curran Associates Inc. (2007)
4. Blei, D.M., Ng, A.Y., Jordan, M.I.: Latent Dirichlet allocation. J. Mach. Learn. Res. **3**, 993–1022 (2003)

5. Boyd-Graber, J.L., Hu, Y., Mimno, D.M.: Applications of topic models. Found. Trends Inf. Retr. **11**(2–3), 143–296 (2017)
6. Chang, C., Lin, C.: LIBSVM: a library for support vector machines. ACM Trans. Intell. Syst. Technol. **2**(3), 27:1–27:27 (2011)
7. Hua, T., Lu, C., Choo, J., Reddy, C.K.: Probabilistic topic modeling for comparative analysis of document collections. ACM Trans. Knowl. Discov. Data **14**(2), 24:1–24:27 (2020)
8. Ihou, K.E., Bouguila, N.: A new latent generalized Dirichlet allocation model for image classification. In: Seventh International Conference on Image Processing Theory. Tools and Applications, IPTA 2017, Montreal, QC, Canada, 28 November–1 December 2017, pp. 1–6. IEEE (2017)
9. Ihou, K.E., Bouguila, N.: A smoothed latent generalized Dirichlet allocation model in the collapsed space. In: IEEE 61st International Midwest Symposium on Circuits and Systems, MWSCAS 2018, Windsor, ON, Canada, Windsor, ON, Canada, 5–8 August 2018, pp. 877–880. IEEE (2018)
10. Ihou, K.E., Bouguila, N.: Variational-based latent generalized Dirichlet allocation model in the collapsed space and applications. Neurocomputing **332**, 372–395 (2019)
11. Ihou, K.E., Bouguila, N.: Stochastic topic models for large scale and nonstationary data. Eng. Appl. Artif. Intell. **88** (2020)
12. Ihou, K.E., Bouguila, N., Bouachir, W.: Efficient integration of generative topic models into discriminative classifiers using robust probabilistic kernels. Pattern Anal. Appl. **24**(1), 217–241 (2021)
13. Luo, Z., Amayri, M., Fan, W., Bouguila, N.: Cross-collection latent Beta-Liouville allocation model training with privacy protection and applications. Appl. Intell. 1–25 (2023)
14. Prasad, K.R., Mohammed, M., Mohammed, N.R.: Visual topic models for healthcare data clustering. Evol. Intell. **14**(2), 545–562 (2021)
15. Teh, Y.W., Newman, D., Welling, M.: A collapsed variational Bayesian inference algorithm for latent Dirichlet allocation. In: Schölkopf, B., Platt, J.C., Hofmann, T. (eds.) Advances in Neural Information Processing Systems 19, Proceedings of the Twentieth Annual Conference on Neural Information Processing Systems, Vancouver, British Columbia, Canada, 4–7 December 2006, pp. 1353–1360. MIT Press (2006)
16. Wagner, W.: Steven bird, Ewan Klein and Edward Loper: natural language processing with python, analyzing text with the natural language toolkit - O'Reilly Media, Beijing, 2009. Lang. Resour. Eval. **44**(4), 421–424 (2010)
17. Yao, F., Wang, Y.: Tracking urban geo-topics based on dynamic topic model. Comput. Environ. Urban Syst. **79** (2020)
18. Zhu, J., Ahmed, A., Xing, E.P.: MedLDA: maximum margin supervised topic models. J. Mach. Learn. Res. **13**, 2237–2278 (2012)
19. Zhuang, Y., Gao, H., Wu, F., Tang, S., Zhang, Y., Zhang, Z.M.: Probabilistic word selection via topic modeling. IEEE Trans. Knowl. Data Eng. **27**(6), 1643–1655 (2015)

A Clustering Strategy-Based Evolutionary Algorithm for Feature Selection in Classification

Baohang Zhang[1], Ziqian Wang[1], Zhenyu Lei[1], Jiatianyi Yu[1],
Ting Jin[2], and Shangce Gao[1](✉)

[1] Faculty of Engineering, University of Toyama, Toyama 930-8555, Japan
gaosc@eng.u-toyama.ac.jp
[2] School of Science, Nanjing Forestry University, Nanjing 210037, China

Abstract. Feature selection is a technique used in data pre-processing to select the most relevant subset of features from a larger set, with the goal of improving classification performance. Evolutionary algorithms have been commonly proposed to solve feature selection problems, but they can suffer from issues originated from diversity reduction and crowding distance decrease, which can lead to suboptimal results. In this study, we propose a new evolutionary algorithm called clustering strategy based evolutionary algorithm (CEA) for feature selection in classification. CEA combines the clustering mechanism to gather individuals into different clusters, and the crossover operation is dominated by the parents in different clusters, thus enhancing the exploration ability of the algorithm and avoiding the population falling into the local optimal solution space. The performance of CEA was evaluated on 13 classification datasets and compared to four mainstream evolutionary algorithms. The experimental results showed that CEA was able to achieve better classification performance using similar or fewer features than the other algorithms.

Keywords: Evolutionary Algorithm · Classification · Feature Selection · Clustering

1 Introduction

Feature selection (FS) plays a crucial role in classification tasks within machine learning [1]. It involves selecting a subset of relevant features from the full feature set to improve classification accuracy and reduce computational cost by eliminating irrelevant or redundant features [2]. However, the complexity of the decision

This research was partially supported by the Japan Society for the Promotion of Science (JSPS) KAKENHI under Grant JP22H03643, Japan Science and Technology Agency (JST) Support for Pioneering Research Initiated by the Next Generation (SPRING) under Grant JPMJSP2145, JST through the Establishment of University Fellowships towards the Creation of Science Technology Innovation under Grant JPMJFS2115, and Natural Science Foundation of Jiangsu Province (No. BK20210605).

H. Fujita et al. (Eds.): IEA/AIE 2023, LNAI 13925, pp. 49–59, 2023.
https://doi.org/10.1007/978-3-031-36819-6_5

space of the FS problems increases exponentially with the number of features. This exponential increase in decision space complexity often results in a limited performance of the classification model due to computational constraints. [3].

Evolutionary algorithms (EAs) have become a popular choice for feature selection because of their ability to effectively find the optimal feature set that maximizes the performance of machine learning applications over the past few decades [4]. EAs are inspired by natural evolution and have been widely used in various fields such as machine learning, artificial intelligence, and engineering [5].

In EAs, a higher diversity of populations helps to achieve global optimization and avoid poor performance due to premature convergence [6]. Despite their effectiveness, EAs are still vulnerable to the challenge of local optima, which can lead to a range of issues such as population crowding, reduced genetic diversity, and increased similarity between individuals. These factors can ultimately hinder the algorithm's ability to explore and exploit the solution space effectively, resulting in suboptimal performance. Therefore, it is critical to develop robust strategies to mitigate the impact of local optima and enhance the algorithm's search capability for optimal solutions [7]. On the other hand, the application scenarios for FS are becoming more complex in tandem with industrial development and social progress, the curse of dimensionality [8] will become unavoidable if EAs are unable to appropriately depart the local optimum. One of the important reasons why EAs are prone to fall into local optima in high-dimensional problems is the low inter-individual variability, i.e., low population diversity.

Based on these considerations, we propose an evolutionary algorithm for feature selection in classification problems, referred to as CEA, which leverages the framework of evolutionary algorithms. CEA offers the following contributions: (1) CEA incorporates a clustering mechanism to filter out diverse parents from the original population, thereby reducing the risk of local optima and improving the overall quality of individuals in the population. Compared to other similar algorithms, CEA demonstrates strong competitiveness in terms of the minimal classification error rate (MCE) and selected feature number (FN) across 13 classical classification problems. (2) The introduced clustering mechanism proves effective in maintaining population diversity within an acceptable range, and outperforms the comparison algorithm without clustering operations. Our experimental results demonstrate the efficacy of CEA and its ability to achieve superior performance in solving classification problems.

The remaining content is organized as follows: Sect. 2 clearly describes the proposed CEA. The diversity analysis of CEA and the comparison of CEA and the other four classical EAs on the metrics of MCE and FN are explained in Sect. 3. Finally, a brief conclusion and outlook are presented in Sect. 4.

2   Related Works

In the domain of feature selection, common approaches can be classified into three main categories: filter, wrapper, and embedded methods. Filter methods assess the correlation between features and labels, without considering the potential loss of classification accuracy caused by redundant features [9]. Embedded methods, on the other hand, typically provide a learning framework and construct a model to adjust the components of the feature subset. However, this approach can suffer from multiple parameters and excessive dependence on the loss function [10]. Wrapper methods, in contrast, do not require a specific loss function and instead evaluate the performance of a feature subset based on its classification accuracy on the classifier. These methods typically have fewer parameters and provide an optimized subset of features at the end of the iteration [11].

EAs are often regarded as a wrapper method in feature selection, as they provide users with a solution or a set of solutions comprising selected features. Several popular EA-based feature selection methods include binary genetic algorithms, which imitate the process of natural selection [12]; whale optimization algorithms, which draw inspiration from whale hunting behavior [13]; differential evolution algorithms, which utilize a population of candidate solutions to find the optimal feature subset [14]; and simulated annealing algorithms, which are based on the physical process of annealing [15].

Clustering algorithms are unsupervised learning methods commonly used in machine learning to combine similar data points together [16]. Although K-means clustering is one of the earliest clustering techniques, it continues to be the most popular clustering method due to its exceptional ability and efficiency in clustering data [17]. It partitions a dataset into K clusters based on the mean of each cluster, and iteratively updates the centroid of each cluster, resulting in the optimal partition of data points into their respective clusters. Consciously preprocessing operations to classify individuals in parental populations according to their distance from each other can be considered a solution to enhance population diversity and improve the ability of populations to jump out of local optima [18].

3   The Proposed CEA

A binary EA framework for feature selection typically comprises a population of candidate feature subsets that are generated randomly or through heuristic methods. When applied to a classification task, the EA designs an appropriate objective function based on the specific task and employs a population iteration and optimization process to identify the optimal feature subset. Subsequently, the optimal feature subset is utilized to train and test the classifier, thereby facilitating the evaluation of the feature selection algorithm's performance. Finally, the optimal feature subset is selected based on the performance metrics and the composition of the feature subset. Each individual in the population can be represented as a solution, which is typically described as:

$$x = (F_1, F_2, ..., F_D) \tag{1}$$

where x represents the individual, D represents the dimension of the dataset. F is a marker indicating whether a feature is selected or not, each $F \in \{0, 1\}$,

---

Algorithm 1: The main procedure of CEA.

Data: initialized population X; population fitness f; population size N;
      dimensionality D; global optimal matrix G.

Result: the new population X and its fitness f.

1 **while** *Not Terminated* **do**

2   Set $K = 2$ and divide X into two sub-population p and q by K-means
     method;

3   I = the number of individuals in p;

4   X' = Rearrange X according to the K-means clustering;

5   **for** $i = 1 : I$ **do**

6   O_i is generated by crossover and muation operators between X_i' and p_i;

7   **end**

8   **for** $i = I{+}1 : N$ **do**

9   O_i is generated by crossover and muation operators between X_i' and
         q_{i-I};

10   **end**

11   f_O = evaluate population O;

12   S = find the index of $(f_O \leq f)$;

13     $X'(S) = O(S)$;

14     $f(S) = f_O(S)$;

15     $X = X'$;

16 **end**

---

when F is equal to 0, it means that the current feature is not selected. While if the value of F is equal to 1, the current feature is selected. Set the population size to N, the population X can be described as:

$$X = (x_1, x_2, ...x_N)' \qquad (2)$$

Before participating in the iteration, population X will be initialized as a binary matrix of size $N * D$. The operation of initializing the population can be represented as:

$$X_i^j = \begin{cases} 1, & if\ i \in t \\ 0, & else \end{cases} \qquad (3)$$

where i denotes the $i - th$ individual of population X and j denotes the $j - th$ dimension of individual X_i. $i \in 1, 2, 3..., N$, and $j \in 1, 2, 3..., D$. t denotes the randomly selected position in X_i^j.

An evaluation function is necessarily applied to each subset in the population to measure its performance, which can be described as:

$$f_i = h(X_i) \qquad (4)$$

where f_i is the fitness of individual X_i, and $h(\cdot)$ the classification accuracy evaluation function.

The steps of the K-means clustering method before the operator of crossover in EA can be summarized as follows:

Algorithm 2: The main procedure of CM.

Data: Individual e_1 and individual e_2 as the parents.
Result: The new individual O_i.
1 Find the different position between e_1 and e_2 as Ind;
2 Randomly select a position from the Ind as the intersection point Cr;
3 $O_i^{1-Cr} = e_1^{1-Cr}$;
4 $O_i^{Cr-D} = e_2^{Cr-D}$;
5 $l_1 =$ the number of selected features in O_i;
6 $l_0 =$ the number of unselected features in O_i;
7 **if** $l_1 \geq l_0$ **then**
8 $\quad |$ Randomly drop a selected feature in O_i;
9 **end**
10 **else if** $l_1 < l_0$ **then**
11 $\quad |$ Randomly select one more feature in O_i;
12 **end**

1: Initialize M as the maximum number of iteration; Initialize K centroids randomly from the population X.
2: Assign each individual to the cluster whose centroid is closest to it.
3: Recalculate the centroid of each cluster by taking the mean of all individuals assigned to that cluster.
4: Repeat 2, 3 until convergence or the number of clustering iterations equals M.

The design of the crossover, mutation, and selection operators of CEA follows the framework of classical EAs. In addition, since CEAs follow a binary encoding approach, the population is initialized by randomly selecting positions in the population to set 1 and the rest to set 0. The procedure of CEA can be represented as shown in Algorithm 1.

In the Algorithm 1, the population X is classified by the K-means clustering into two clusters, denoted as p and q, respectively. Subsequently, X is rearranged into X' according to the cluster to which the individual belongs. Assuming that I is the number of individuals contained in population p, the relationship among population X', p, and q, can be expressed as follows:

$$X' = (p_1, p_2, ...p_I, q_{I+1}, q_{I+2}, ...q_N) \quad (5)$$

And O represents a population state that acts as an intermediary between the old and new populations. The update mechanism for O can be expressed as:

$$O_i \leftarrow \begin{cases} CM(X_i', p_i), & if \ i < I \\ CM(X_i', q_i), & if \ i > I \end{cases} \quad (6)$$

where i is the ith individual in population, $CM(\cdot)$ denote the crossover and the mutation operators in the algorithm. The pseudo code for $CM(\cdot)$ is shown in Algorithm 2.

Table 1. Benchmark Datasets.

No.	Name	Features	Instances	Classes	No.	Name	Features	Instances	Classes
1	Australian	14	690	2	8	Waveform	40	5000	3
2	Vehicle	18	946	4	9	Spect	44	267	2
3	German	24	1000	2	10	Sonar	60	208	2
4	Breast	30	569	2	11	Hillvalley	100	1212	2
5	Ionosphere	34	351	2	12	MUSK1	166	476	2
6	Dermatology	34	366	6	13	Urban Land Cover	147	675	9
7	KrVsKpEW	36	3169	2					

4 Experimental Results and Discussion

4.1 Experimental Design

All experiments were implemented in MATLAB R2021b on a computer with an Intel Core i7-8550U, 1.8 GHz CPU, and 16 GB of memory. Table 1 lists the information of the 13 datasets used in this study, including their names, number of features, number of instances and number of classes. All of the above datasets are publicly available from the UCI machine learning repository and are derived from real-world scenarios, including finance, life, physics, and image analysis [19]. Furthermore, the population size N of five algorithms was set to 30, with a maximum number of iterations of 100. Therefore, the maximum number of evaluations FES is set to N*100. KNN is chosen as the classifier due to its simplicity and low computational cost.

To verify the improvement of population diversity by the K-means clustering algorithm in CEA, it will be divided into CEA-1 and CEA-2 on the basis of the framework of Algorithm 1, where CEA-1 uses K-means clustering operation to preprocess the populations, while CEA-2 does not use any form of preprocessing for the populations.

In order to evaluate the effectiveness of our proposed CEA algorithm, we conducted a comprehensive comparison with four classic evolutionary algorithms, namely the genetic algorithm (GA), differential evolution in combination with the global optimum-based search strategy (DEGoS) [20], whale optimization algorithm (WOA), and simulated annealing (SA), on 13 benchmark classification datasets. The performance of each algorithm was evaluated through 30 independent runs on the 13 datasets, and the results were analyzed using statistical measures such as the mean and standard deviation of MCE and the FN of selected features. To assess these algorithms' generalization performance, the datasets were randomly split into 70% for training and 30% for testing, with 10-fold cross-validation used in the training stage.

4.2 Diversity Analysis

Population diversity has a major impact on the efficiency of evolutionary algorithms. High diversity throughout the course of the iterative process may effec-

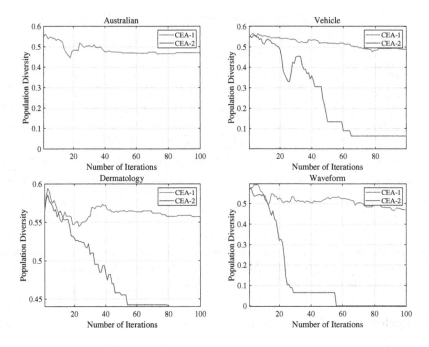

Fig. 1. The population diversity curves.

tively prevent the population from being evaluated again around the local optimal space, allowing the population to search in a wider solution space and escape the local optimal solution zone. Numerous research have shown that a high diversity of population is essential for preventing early convergence and removing local optimization. The population diversity is considered and calculated as follows:

$$Div(X) = \frac{1}{N} \sum_{i=1}^{N} \|X_i - \overline{X}\| / max_{1 \leq i,j \leq N} \|X_i - X_j\| \tag{7}$$

$$\overline{X} = \frac{1}{N} \sum_{i=1}^{N} X_i \tag{8}$$

where N and $\overline{X}$ are the population size and the average point, respectively.

Figure 1 illustrates the variation patterns of population diversity in CEA-1 and CEA-2 on six out of the 13 datasets. The initial populations of CEA-1 and CEA-2 exhibit the same diversity. However, as the iterations progress, the diversity of CEA-2 decreases significantly and falls below 0 in the Australian and Waveform datasets. This indicates that the population has become trapped in a local optimum and has lost its ability to explore the solution space. In contrast, CEA-1 maintains a healthy level of diversity throughout the iterations, providing more opportunities to find the global optimal solution for complex and high-dimensional problems.

Table 2. The Training Mean and Std of MCE.

	CEA		BGA		DEGoS		BSA		WOA	
	Mean	Std	Mean	Std	Mean	Std	Mean	Std	Mean	Std
1	**1.401E−01**	4.188E−03	1.573E−01	5.027E−03 +	1.489E−01	7.362E−03 +	1.661E−01	8.453E−03 +	1.665E−01	5.529E−02 +
2	**2.507E−01**	4.694E−03	2.757E−01	6.857E−03 +	2.588E−01	1.079E−02 +	2.888E−01	9.172E−03 +	2.707E−01	1.208E−02 +
3	**2.289E−01**	4.741E−03	2.479E−01	9.745E−03 +	2.332E−01	8.219E−03 +	2.633E−01	7.450E−03 +	2.449E−01	1.041E−02 +
4	**4.027E−02**	1.305E−03	4.461E−02	1.529E−03 +	4.060E−02	1.665E−03 =	4.612E−02	2.600E−03 +	4.946E−02	1.101E−02 +
5	**6.396E−02**	3.839E−03	8.970E−02	7.076E−03 +	8.076E−02	1.178E−02 +	1.149E−01	9.179E−03 +	9.783E−02	3.338E−02 +
6	**6.744E−03**	2.027E−03	1.323E−02	3.327E−03 +	1.414E−02	8.142E−03 +	2.036E−02	3.639E−03 +	1.038E−02	3.869E−03 +
7	**1.580E−02**	2.623E−03	2.315E−02	2.906E−03 +	3.506E−02	1.132E−02 +	3.667E−02	5.250E−03 +	1.896E−02	6.709E−03 +
8	**1.547E−01**	2.114E−03	1.676E−01	3.829E−03 +	1.727E−01	5.986E−03 +	1.894E−01	5.902E−03 +	1.682E−01	4.821E−03 +
9	**1.403E−01**	1.112E−02	1.786E−01	1.276E−02 +	1.410E−01	1.456E−02 =	2.043E−01	1.082E−02 +	1.820E−01	3.551E−02 +
10	**9.064E−02**	1.059E−02	1.326E−01	1.041E−02 +	1.023E−01	1.526E−02 +	1.557E−01	1.048E−02 +	1.301E−01	2.479E−02 +
11	**4.010E−02**	5.718E−03	4.366E−01	7.068E−03 +	4.124E−01	9.931E−03 +	4.515E−01	7.559E−03 +	4.446E−01	1.232E−02 +
12	**9.032E−02**	7.586E−03	1.182E−01	8.161E−03 +	9.661E−02	8.647E−03 +	1.385E−01	8.539E−03 +	1.196E−01	1.644E−02 +
13	**1.413E−01**	7.932E−03	3.534E−01	7.130E−02 +	2.963E−01	9.943E−02 +	4.798E−01	1.603E−02 +	2.922E−01	1.526E−01 +
W/T/L	-/-/-		13/0/0		11/2/0		13/0/0		13/0/0	

Based on the above, it is evident that CEA with K-means (CEA-1) is more stable and capable of producing higher-quality solutions. We can also conclude that the K-means strategy is effective and efficient.

4.3 Performance Comparison

In this section, we present a comparative analysis of CEA against its counterparts on 13 benchmark problems using two performance metrics, namely the minimum classification error rate (MCE) and the selection feature number (FN). To evaluate the significance of the difference between CEA and its peers, we employed the Wilcoxon rank-sum test for each metric, with a statistical significance of 0.05.

MCE is a metric that reflects the classification error rate, and a lower value of MCE indicates better algorithm performance. On the other hand, FN represents the number of selected features in the feature subset, and fewer selected features can lead to a potential reduction in computational cost. All algorithms were independently validated 30 times on the 13 classification datasets, and each runtime obtained the same number of evaluations. The best MCE and FN value for each dataset are presented in bold in all tables. Additionally, the results of the Wilcoxon rank-sum test are also provided in the table, with the comparison algorithms marked as '+', '=', and '-'. The '+' sign indicates that CEA performs significantly better than its peers on the problem, the '=' sign indicates that there is no significant difference between the two, and the '-' sign indicates that CEA performs weaker than its peers.

Table 2 and 3 show the mean and standard deviation (std) values of MCE obtained the training and test datasets, respectively. From the two tables of MCE, we can find that CEA outperforms its peers on all 13 problems in the training datasets. In the testing datasets, CEA outperforms its peers on nine problems among all problems, and on German (3rd), Spect (9th), and Sonar (10th), it performs second best. Table 4 exhibits the mean and standard deviation values of the FN. In the comparative analysis of FN results, DEGoS exhibits a

Table 3. The Testing Mean and Std of MCE.

	CEA		BGA		DEGoS		BSA		WOA	
	Mean	Std	Mean	Std	Mean	Std	Mean	Std	Mean	Std
1	**1.069E−01**	6.918E−03	1.082E−01	4.503E−03 +	1.325E−01	2.167E−02 +	2.899E−01	2.258E−16 +	1.454E−01	6.069E−02 +
2	2.593E−01	9.203E−03	**2.556E−01**	7.216E−03 =	2.910E−01	2.322E−02 +	3.083E−01	5.646E−17 +	2.783E−01	1.240E−02 +
3	**2.289E−01**	1.512E−02	2.317E−01	1.180E−02 =	2.637E−01	1.805E−02 +	2.600E−01	1.694E−16 +	2.626E−01	1.688E−02 +
4	6.020E−02	2.965E−03	**5.529E−02**	3.656E−03 −	6.706E−02	5.029E−03 +	5.882E−02	1.412E−17 −	6.549E−02	5.929E−03 +
5	**8.762E−02**	1.013E−02	1.070E−01	9.252E−03 +	1.308E−01	1.520E−02 +	1.619E−01	1.412E−16 +	1.346E−01	1.933E−02 +
6	**1.621E−02**	4.624E−03	1.682E−02	6.412E−03 =	4.159E−02	2.308E−02 +	1.468E−01	5.646E−17 +	3.517E−02	1.106E−02 +
7	**1.907E−02**	2.628E−03	2.206E−02	1.771E−03 +	4.276E−02	1.303E−02 +	4.906E−02	2.117E−17 +	2.373E−02	5.164E−03 +
8	**1.472E−01**	4.376E−03	1.540E−01	4.405E−02 +	1.788E−01	1.228E−02 +	1.973E−01	5.646E−17 +	1.751E−01	9.815E−03 +
9	1.183E−01	1.495E−02	**1.150E−01**	1.810E−02 −	1.817E−01	3.768E−02 +	1.625E−01	2.823E−17 +	1.563E−01	2.196E−02 +
10	1.812E−01	2.767E−02	**1.753E−01**	2.231E−02 =	2.478E−01	3.531E−02 +	3.226E−01	0.000E+00 +	2.339E−01	4.123E−02 +
11	**4.165E−01**	1.389E−02	4.406E−01	5.647E−03 +	4.601E−01	1.370E−02 +	4.821E−01	2.258E−16 +	4.644E−01	1.155E−02 +
12	**1.002E−01**	1.380E−02	1.094E−01	1.074E−02 +	1.439E−01	2.380E−02 +	1.479E−01	0.000E+00 +	1.289E−01	1.458E−02 +
13	**1.970E−01**	1.243E−02	3.257E−01	6.119E−02 +	3.295E−01	9.106E−02 +	5.446E−01	4.517E−16 +	3.246E−01	1.349E−01 +
W/T/L	**-/-/-**		**7/5/1**		**13/0/0**		**12/0/1**		**13/0/0**	

Table 4. The Mean and Std of FN.

	CEA		BGA		DEGoS		BSA		WOA	
	Mean	Std	Mean	Std	Mean	Std	Mean	Std	Mean	Std
1	4.000E−01	5.812E−02	3.381E−01	7.944E−02 −	2.729E−01	7.245E−02 −	**1.825E−01**	3.148E−01 −	3.669E−01	9.150E−02 −
2	4.852E−01	4.598E−02	5.611E−01	8.169E−02 +	**4.367E−01**	7.184E−02 −	5.170E−01	2.757E−01 =	7.390E−01	6.271E−01 +
3	4.708E−01	4.397E−02	5.042E−01	8.709E−02 =	**4.103E−01**	7.846E−02 −	4.736E−01	1.903E−01 =	6.177E−01	1.613E−01 +
4	5.167E−01	7.415E−02	4.800E−01	8.514E−02 =	**3.938E−01**	6.389E−02 −	5.001E−01	2.108E−01 =	5.608E−01	3.746E−01 =
5	**1.961E−01**	5.025E−02	2.931E−01	4.265E−02 +	2.769E−01	6.705E−02 +	2.723E−01	1.983E−01 +	3.450E−01	7.687E−02 +
6	6.127E−01	5.243E−02	6.186E−01	6.711E−02 =	**5.028E−01**	5.620E−02 −	6.065E−01	1.544E−01 =	5.735E−01	3.990E−01 =
7	5.500E−01	3.676E−02	5.417E−01	4.988E−02 =	**4.149E−01**	6.322E−02 −	5.808E−01	2.016E−01 =	5.407E−01	1.940E−01 =
8	4.725E−01	5.058E−02	6.100E−01	6.747E−02 +	**4.643E−01**	8.289E−02 −	6.423E−01	2.437E−01 +	7.165E−01	4.306E−01 +
9	4.606E−01	5.167E−02	4.545E−01	6.805E−02 −	**3.833E−01**	6.694E−02 −	4.513E−01	1.506E−01 =	5.522E−01	1.534E−01 +
10	4.561E−01	7.198E−02	4.550E−01	5.291E−02 =	**3.645E−01**	6.488E−02 −	4.293E−01	1.410E−01 =	6.937E−01	5.821E−01 +
11	**3.457E−01**	7.964E−02	4.737E−01	5.282E−02 +	3.840E−01	6.174E−02 +	5.055E−01	1.539E−01 +	5.276E−01	2.453E−01 +
12	4.046E−01	6.294E−02	5.046E−01	2.996E−02 +	**3.956E−01**	3.487E−02 =	5.184E−01	7.377E−02 +	6.373E−01	2.243E−01 +
13	**2.832E−01**	5.571E−02	4.887E−01	3.519E−02 +	3.756E−01	4.611E−02 +	4.785E−01	1.178E−01 +	4.761E−01	2.937E−01 +
W/T/L	**-/-/-**		**6/5/2**		**3/2/8**		**5/7/1**		**9/3/1**	

commendable capability in feature reduction, indicating its streamlined feature selection approach. However, its performance in terms of MEC is comparatively modest. On the other hand, CEA outperforms the other three peer algorithms in FN results, showcasing its superior performance FN outcomes.

In summary, it can be concluded that CEA is a competitive method in terms of feature selection effectiveness and classification performance, and its flexibility in feature selection could also lead to a decrease in computational costs.

5 Conclusion

This study proposed a novel evolutionary algorithm called Clustering Strategy-based Evolutionary Algorithm (CEA) for feature selection in classification. CEA incorporates a clustering mechanism to cluster out diverse parents and allievate the shortcoming of falling into local optimal. The algorithm was tested on 13 classification datasets and compared to four classic evolutionary algorithms. The experimental results showed that the cluster mechanism successfully increased population diversity, and CEA was able to achieve better classification performance using similar or fewer features than the other algorithms. This suggests that CEA is a promising approach for feature selection in classification problems, and its clustering-based strategy can effectively improve search efficiency and accuracy.

Our future work aims to further explore the improvement of clustering methods for evolutionary algorithms for feature selection problems. Besides, we intend to try to improve the performance of evolutionary algorithms for multi-objective domains using clustering methods.

References

1. Frank, E., et al.: WEKA-a machine learning workbench for data mining. In: Maimon, O., Rokach, L. (eds.) Data Mining and Knowledge Discovery Handbook, pp. 1269–1277. Springer, Boston (2010). https://doi.org/10.1007/978-0-387-09823-4_66
2. Wang, Z., Gao, S., Zhou, M., Sato, S., Cheng, J., Wang, J.: Information-theory-based nondominated sorting ant colony optimization for multiobjective feature selection in classification. IEEE Trans. Cybern. (2022)
3. Wang, Z., Gao, S., Zhang, Y., Guo, L.: Symmetric uncertainty-incorporated probabilistic sequence-based ant colony optimization for feature selection in classification. Knowl.-Based Syst. **256**, 109874 (2022)
4. Xue, B., Zhang, M., Browne, W.N., Yao, X.: A survey on evolutionary computation approaches to feature selection. IEEE Trans. Evol. Comput. **20**(4), 606–626 (2015)
5. Zhan, Z.-H., Shi, L., Tan, K.C., Zhang, J.: A survey on evolutionary computation for complex continuous optimization. Artif. Intell. Rev. **55**(1), 59–110 (2021). https://doi.org/10.1007/s10462-021-10042-y
6. Sudholt, D.: The benefits of population diversity in evolutionary algorithms: a survey of rigorous runtime analyses. In: Theory of Evolutionary Computation. NCS, pp. 359–404. Springer, Cham (2020). https://doi.org/10.1007/978-3-030-29414-4_8
7. Wang, Y., Gao, S., Zhou, M., Yu, Y.: A multi-layered gravitational search algorithm for function optimization and real-world problems. IEEE/CAA J. Automatica Sinica **8**(1), 94–109 (2020)
8. Gheyas, I.A., Smith, L.S.: Feature subset selection in large dimensionality domains. Pattern Recogn. **43**(1), 5–13 (2010)
9. Xu, H., Xue, B., Zhang, M.: A duplication analysis-based evolutionary algorithm for biobjective feature selection. IEEE Trans. Evol. Comput. **25**(2), 205–218 (2020)
10. Deng, X., Li, Y., Weng, J., Zhang, J.: Feature selection for text classification: a review. Multimed. Tools Appl. **78**, 3797–3816 (2019)
11. Chandrashekar, G., Sahin, F.: A survey on feature selection methods. Comput. Electr. Eng. **40**(1), 16–28 (2014)
12. Heris, M.K.: Binary and real-coded genetic algorithms in matlab (2015). https://yarpiz.com/23/ypea101-genetic-algorithms
13. Kumar, V., Kumar, D.: Binary whale optimization algorithm and its application to unit commitment problem. Neural Comput. Appl. **32**, 2095–2123 (2020)
14. Price, K.V.: Differential evolution. In: Zelinka, I., Snášel, V., Abraham, A. (eds.) Handbook of Optimization: From Classical to Modern Approach, pp. 187–214. Springer, Heidelberg (2013). https://doi.org/10.1007/978-3-642-30504-7_8
15. Bertsimas, D., Tsitsiklis, J.: Simulated annealing. Stat. Sci. **8**(1), 10–15 (1993)
16. Xu, D., Tian, Y.: A comprehensive survey of clustering algorithms. Ann. Data Sci. **2**, 165–193 (2015)

17. Zeebaree, D.Q., Haron, H., Abdulazeez, A.M., Zeebaree, S.: Combination of k-means clustering with genetic algorithm: a review. Int. J. Appl. Eng. Res. **12**(24), 14238–14245 (2017)
18. Sinha, A., Jana, P.K.: A hybrid mapreduce-based k-means clustering using genetic algorithm for distributed datasets. J. Supercomput. **74**(4), 1562–1579 (2018)
19. Dua, D., Graff, C.: UCI machine learning repository (2017). http://archive.ics.uci.edu/ml
20. Yu, Y., Gao, S., Wang, Y., Todo, Y.: Global optimum-based search differential evolution. IEEE/CAA J. Automatica Sinica **6**(2), 379–394 (2019)

On Completeness-Aware Reasoning in Case-Based Reasoning

Fateh Boulmaiz[1]([✉]), Patrick Reignier[1], and Stephane Ploix[2]

[1] Univ. Grenoble Alpes, CNRS, Grenoble INP, LIG, 38000 Grenoble, France
`fateh.boulmaiz@univ-grenoble-alpes.fr`
[2] Univ. Grenoble Alpes, CNRS, Grenoble INP, G-SCOP, 38000 Grenoble, France

Abstract. Data quality is a critical aspect of machine learning as the performance of a model is directly impacted by the quality of the data used for training and testing. Poor-quality data can result in biased models, overfitting, or suboptimal performance. A range of tools are proposed to evaluate the data quality regarding the most commonly used quality indicators. Unfortunately, current solutions are too generic to effectively deal with the specifics of each machine learning approach. In this study, a first investigation on data quality regarding the completeness dimension in the case-based reasoning paradigm was performed. We introduce an algorithm to check the completeness of data according to the open-world assumption leading to improving the performance of the reasoning process of the case-based reasoning approach.

Keywords: Case based reasoning · Data quality · Data completeness

1 Introduction

In the age of massive digitization and ubiquitous computing, assuring the quality of manipulated data becomes one of the major challenges for both companies and academic research, whatever discipline: database, artificial intelligence, image processing, information systems, etc. Several studies have confirmed the tremendous impact of data quality on the process in which such data are handled. For instance, it has been proven in [14] that the performance of machine learning algorithms is directly influenced by the quality of the data used in the learning process, while the survey conducted in [1] focused on the effect of poor data quality on the economy of countries, in particular, it estimates that poor data quality lost the USA's economy alone more than $3 trillion per year. This financial cost engendered by poor data quality is still increasing [2].

With organizations confronting more and more complex data issues which potentially influence the profitability of their business and with research proposing increasingly data quality-sensitive algorithms, the necessity for precise and trusted data is more crucial than ever before. The different objectives and the multiple ways of using the data have led to different data quality dimensions (requirements). The later ones usually characterize a quality property such as accuracy, completeness, consistency, etc. Albeit the awareness of the need for

H. Fujita et al. (Eds.): IEA/AIE 2023, LNAI 13925, pp. 60–73, 2023.
https://doi.org/10.1007/978-3-031-36819-6_6

acceptable data quality is reflected in the emergence of exhaustive literature devoted to this issue (see [7] for an overview), it is worth highlighting that: 1) Despite a wide range of work and ongoing research on data quality, there is no consensus on the properties that should be considered in defining a data quality norm [13]. For instance, the authors in [18] identify 179 dimensions for data quality, while in another more recent study [11] more than 300 properties to be considered for defining data quality are described; 2) Although some requirements have been unanimously identified to be important, there is no consensus on their precise definitions, i.e., the same requirement name is used with different semantics from one study to another; 3) Data quality assessment is a domain-specific process because of the diversity of data sources, the multiplicity of quality dimensions, and the specificity of the application domain. So, it is not possible to propose a generic data quality assessment approach applicable to all data-intensive applications.

While data quality is extensively studied by the database and data mining communities, it is entirely neglected in the machine learning domain in favor of developing learning algorithms and reasoning approaches, assuming high-quality data to feed learning algorithms. This paper addresses the issue of data quality in the context of machine learning to improve the robustness of learning algorithms in handling data of varying quality and to reduce the impact of poor quality data on the overall result of the machine learning process. However, since the scope of both the data quality and machine learning domains are broad, some limitations were imposed to make this work possible. The machine learning domain is too large to provide a single data quality assessment method that is valid for all machine learning approaches. We, therefore, restrict our scope of research to approaches based on the case-based reasoning paradigm. Concerning data quality, we only investigate the data completeness dimension, which is still widely unexplored, if not never investigated in the context of case-based reasoning.

The remainder of the paper is organized along the following lines: Sect. 2 describes the background of the research. Section 3 outlines the problem statement through an motivating example followed by a formulation of the problem. Section 4 details the proposed approach to address the problem under consideration. Section 5 evaluates the proposed approach through a real case study and discusses the results. Section 6 concludes the paper and presents future work.

2   Background

2.1   Case-Based Reasoning and Data Completeness

Case-based reasoning (CBR) is a reasoning paradigm based on a case base $\mathbb{CB}$ representing a collection of source cases. A case $\mathbb{C}$ represents an experience of problem-solving, usually defined by a couple $(\mathfrak{p}, \mathfrak{s})$ wherein $\mathfrak{p}$ is a problem in the considered application domain and $\mathfrak{s}$ is its solution. In the following, we assume a finer representation of the case $\mathbb{C}$ as a triplet $(\mathsf{C}^C, \mathsf{A}^C, \mathsf{E}^C)$ [5]. Let $\mathbb{C}^S$, $\mathbb{A}^S$, and $\mathbb{E}^S$ be three sets. The context C^C is an element of $\mathbb{C}^S$ representing the phenomena undergone by the application domain. The actions A^C is an element of $\mathbb{A}^S$ modeling controllable phenomena of the application domain. The effects E^C is an element of $\mathbb{E}^S$ describing the consequence of the application of the actions $\mathbf{A}^C$ to the context $\mathbf{A}^C$. The intuition underlying the CBR paradigm is formulated by Hypothesis 1. The process of solving a target case $\mathbb{C}_{tg}$, which is formed initially from the context only, consists in calculating the relevant actions, which once applied will produce effects, generating a new source case in the case base.

Assumption 1 (Consistency). *The effects of applying similar actions to similar contexts are similar.*

Precisely, the reasoning strategy starts by looking for the set $\mathtt{SIM}^{\mathbb{C}_{tg}}$ of source cases $\mathbb{C}_{sr}$ similar to the target case $\mathbb{C}_{tg}$ (retrieval stage), followed by the modification of the actions of the cases $\mathbb{C}_{sr}$ to match the specificity of the context of the case $\mathbb{C}_{tg}$, generating thus the actions $\mathbf{A}^{\mathbb{C}_{tg}}$ (adaptation stage). According to the adopted validation stage, the effects $\mathbf{E}^{\mathbb{C}_{tg}}$ of the application of $\mathbf{A}^{\mathbb{C}_{tg}}$ to the context $\mathbf{C}^{\mathbb{C}_{tg}}$ are generated, and thus the new target case $\mathbb{C}_{tg}(\mathbf{C}^{\mathbb{C}_{tg}}, \mathbf{A}^{\mathbb{C}_{tg}}, \mathbf{E}^{\mathbb{C}_{tg}})$, if approved, is integrated into the case base $\mathbb{CB}$ (memorization stage). This can be formalized as follows:

$$\texttt{CBR system} : \texttt{Memorization} \circ \texttt{Validation} \circ \texttt{Adaptation} \circ \texttt{Retrieval}$$

$$\texttt{Retrieval function} : \mathbf{C}^{\mathbb{C}_{tg}} \longmapsto \mathtt{SIM}^{\mathbb{C}_{tg}} = \{\mathbb{C}_{sr}\} \subseteq \mathbb{CB}$$

$$\texttt{Adaptation function} : \mathtt{SIM}^{\mathbb{C}_{tg}} \cup \mathbf{C}^{\mathbb{C}_{tg}} \longmapsto \mathbf{A}^{\mathbb{C}_{tg}} \cup \{\texttt{failure}\}$$

$$\texttt{Validation function} : \mathbf{A}^{\mathbb{C}_{tg}} \longmapsto \mathbb{C}_{tg}(\mathbf{C}^{\mathbb{C}_{tg}}, \mathbf{A}^{\mathbb{C}_{tg}}, \mathbf{E}^{\mathbb{C}_{tg}})$$

$$\texttt{Memorization function} : (\mathbb{CB}, \mathbf{C}^{\mathbb{C}_{tg}}) \longmapsto \mathbb{CB} \cup \mathbb{C}_{tg}(\mathbf{C}^{\mathbb{C}_{tg}}, \mathbf{A}^{\mathbb{C}_{tg}}, \mathbf{E}^{\mathbb{C}_{tg}})$$

To conduct the different steps of the reasoning process, a CBR system draws on a set of knowledge spread over four containers: domain, case, similarity, and adaptation knowledge [16]. Usually, each stage of the reasoning process is supported by several knowledge containers because of the close connections existing between them.

Completeness. In keeping with existing literature on Knowledge bases [8] and databases [10], we consider completeness through an ideal reference domain knowledge container $\mathtt{K}_R^D$, which captures all the real-world aspects of the application domain. The domain knowledge $\mathtt{K}^D$ of CBR system is complete if the application of any actions (defined in $\mathtt{K}^D$) to any context (likewise defined in $\mathtt{K}^D$) generates the same effects on $\mathtt{K}^D$ as on $\mathtt{K}_R^D$.

Definition 1 *[Completeness]. Completeness refers to the ability of the domain knowledge container of a CBR system to describe every relevant state of the domain application environment.*

The principal barrier to assessing and achieving completeness, as stated in Definition 1, is the Open World Assumption. The latter states that if a given piece of real-world knowledge is not represented in the Knowledge domain $\mathtt{K}^D$, then that knowledge is not necessarily false, it may be real-world true but not included in the $\mathtt{K}^D$.

A plethora of work has been done on data quality assessment, which continues to be an intense research domain in such diverse fields as relational databases, big data, machine learning, data mining, etc. Data quality verification remains a challenging process for several reasons:

- *Data quality verification is a permanent process.* This is due to the data nature (particularly, their velocity) on one side and the different processings performed on the data (e.g., data cleaning) on the other side.
- *Data quality verification is strongly dependent on the application-task domain.* The different dimensions of data quality are evaluated by metrics whose specification strongly depends on the needs of the user/expert, the application domain (the aeronautics domain does not have the same requirements in terms of data quality as the education domain, for example) but also on the task (in the health domain, there are different requirements for the diagnostic phase and the treatment phase).

2.2 Change Point Analysis

Change points in a data set modeling a system are defined by abrupt shifts in the data. These change points can represent transitions that occur between states of the modeled system due to hidden changes in the properties of the data set. Determining the change points in a data set is the objective of the change point analysis approaches, which have sparked an increasing work in statistics [17] as well as in several application domains such as climate [9], medical [19], finance [6], etc.

More formally, consider a system characterized by non-stationary random phenomena and modeled by a multivariate vector $\Omega = \{\omega_1, \ldots, \omega_m\}$ whose values are defined in $\mathbb{R}^{d \geq 1}$ and consisting of m samples. It is further supposed that the vector Ω is piecewise stationary, i.e., certain phenomena of the system change abruptly at unknown instants $t_1, t_2, \ldots, t_m$. The detection of the change points consists in solving a model detection problem whose objective is to determine the optimal segmentation S based on a quantitative criterion to be minimized. Specifically, it consists in identifying the number m of changes and finding the indices $ti_{1 \leq i \leq m}$.

3   Problem Setting

3.1   Motivating Example

We motivate the need to guarantee the completeness of data in a CBR system through a concrete scenario. Let's consider the scenario of a CBR-based energy management system (EMS) that monitors a building equipped with an air-conditioning (AC) system, but the EMS designer has not envisaged any means to discover the AC system function. On two days with a similar context (e.g., the same weather conditions) and the same actions, if the AC system was turned on one day but not on the other (this phenomenon cannot be detected by the system), the two days would have different effects (e.g., different indoor temperatures), which calls into question the founding assumption of the CBR technique.

3.2   Problem Formulation

Existing CBR systems exploit directly the case base to carry out the different steps of the CBR cycle, assuming that the domain knowledge is consistent. Indeed, by adopting the consistency assumption (Assumption 1), it is implicitly admitted that the completeness hypothesis is valid. However, it is arguably not warranted, especially considering the modeling of a complex domain with many dependent variables. The violation of the completeness assumption poses some substantive issues:

- the system has no guarantee that the principle of the CBR approach (Assumption 1) is respected.
- the CBR system cannot identify incomplete data and therefore cannot determine which data reflects reality for use in the reasoning process.
- as a consequence of the previous statements, the performance of the reasoning process may degrade as the case base includes cases that are wrongly judged as similar.

The failure of one of four knowledge containers to be adequately defined (incomplete) can be overwhelming to the whole CBR system unless any of the remaining knowledge containers can fill the missing knowledge. As a result, either the CBR system will fail to respond or provide inaccurate solutions. In particular, it was established that incomplete domain knowledge generates such a critical dysfunction of a CBR system [3]. Incomplete domain knowledge in a CBR system most likely leads to the generation of incomplete cases. Moreover, the retrieval process is burdened by the absence of missing data since the similarity evaluation is biased by the incompleteness of the data. Furthermore, incomplete cases can also degrade the adaptation process when the adaptation knowledge is acquired automatically from the case base.

It is obvious that the problem of incompleteness verification can be reformulated as a hidden variable detection problem. Indeed, an incompleteness situation occurs in a case base when a group of similar cases produces different effects, which is necessarily a consequence of the existence of context and/or action variables that are not considered in the similarity evaluation process.

Formally, consider a case base $\mathbb{CB} = \{\mathbb{C}_i\}_{1 \leq i \leq n}$ consisting of a finite number n of cases $\mathbb{C}_i$. Each element of the latter is described by a set of features:

- the context variables which refer to the current state of the system or the environment in which the system operates. It includes all the relevant factors that can affect the system's behavior. The context $\mathsf{C}^{\mathbb{C}_i}$ of case $\mathbb{C}_i$ is specified by $\mathsf{C}^{\mathbb{C}_i} = \{O_{\mathsf{C}j}^{\mathbb{C}_i}\}_{1 \leq j \leq n_1}$, where the observed features O_{C} are defined on the knowledge domain $\mathsf{K}_{\mathsf{C}}^{\mathbb{D}}$.
- the action variables which are the set of inputs that can be manipulated or controlled by the system. These variables are used to modify the current

state of the system and achieve a desired effect. Actions are typically chosen based on the current context and the system's objectives. The actions $\mathtt{A}^{\mathbb{C}_i}$ are modeled by the observed features $\{O_{Aj}^{\mathbb{C}_i}\}_{1 \leq j \leq n_2}$ which are defined on the knowledge domain $\mathtt{K}_A^D$.

- the effect represents the outcome or result of performing an action on a given context. It is a set of variables or attributes that describe the changes that occur in the context as a result of performing the action. The effect can be immediate or delayed and may include both intended and unintended consequences. The effects are specified on the knowledge domain $\mathtt{K}_E^D$ by the observed features $\{O_{Ej}^{\mathbb{C}_i}\}_{1 \leq j \leq n_3}$.

The knowledge domain $\mathtt{K}^D$ of the CBR system is defined by $\mathtt{K}^D = \mathtt{K}_C^D \cup \mathtt{K}_A^D \cup \mathtt{K}_E^D$. Let's also assume, $\{H_{Cj}\}_{1 \leq j \leq m_1}$, $\{H_{Aj}\}_{1 \leq j \leq m_2}$, and $\{H_{Ej}\}_{1 \leq j \leq m_3}$ are the hidden features of the context, action, and effects elements respectively. We denote the reference knowledge domain by $\mathtt{K}_R^D = \mathtt{K}^D \cup \{H_{Cj}\}_{1 \leq j \leq m_1} \cup \{H_{Aj}\}_{1 \leq j \leq m_2} \cup \{H_{Ej}\}_{1 \leq j \leq m_3}$.

The completeness evaluation problem of a CBR system against $\mathtt{K}_R^D$ consists in identifying eventual incompleteness situations in the case base. An incompleteness situation is formalized as:

$$\text{CBR system} \Leftrightarrow \exists\ \mathbb{C}_1, \mathbb{C}_2 \in \mathbb{CB}/$$
$$(\{O_{Cj}^{\mathbb{C}_1}\} = \{O_{Cj}^{\mathbb{C}_2}\})_{1 \leq j \leq n_1} \wedge (\{O_{Aj}^{\mathbb{C}_1}\} = \{O_{Aj}^{\mathbb{C}_2}\})_{1 \leq j \leq n_2} \wedge (\{O_{Ej}^{\mathbb{C}_1}\} \neq \{O_{Ej}^{\mathbb{C}_2}\})_{1 \leq j \leq n_3}$$
$$\implies \exists f \in \{H_{Cj}\}_{1 \leq j \leq m_1} \cup \{H_{Aj}\}_{1 \leq j \leq m_2}$$

For effectiveness reasons, we argue that is a prerequisite to check the completeness of the data as early as possible in the problem-solving process.

4 Completeness Checking in the CBR System

In this section, we detail the workflow of our 2CCBR (Completeness Checking CBR) algorithm to evaluate data completeness in a CBR system. This section is divided according to the global architecture of the 2CCBR algorithm into two parts. In this workflow, starting from splitting the case base into the best possible segmentation by grouping the cases according to their effects, we exploit the resulting partitions to search for possible incomplete situations by relying on an effective method based on context and action knowledge.

4.1 Case Base Partitioning

The process of partitioning the case base aims to identify possible patterns in the cases' effects, i.e., detecting and estimating changes in the statistical properties of the effects, so that cases having similar effects can be grouped into the same cluster. In this section, a hybrid method based on the change point detection approach is proposed to achieve this objective. This is a mixture of two techniques: the cumulative sum (CUMSUM) technique proposed in [15] and the bootstrapping mechanism introduced in [12]. In short, the detection of change points in the case effects model is an iterative process involving the following two steps:

Step 1: Cumulative Sums. Considering the notation introduced in Sect. 2.1, cumulative sums CS_i of the effect variables are calculated by the recursive formula described in Eq. (1). Note that the cumulative sums do not represent the cumulative sums of the effect variables but rather they represent the cumulative sums of the differences between the values and the average $\overline{\mu}$. Consequently, the last cumulative sum (CS_n) is always null.

By plotting the chart of cumulative sums CS_i, potentials change points in the effect variables could be identified as changes in the direction of the diagram. However, the cumulative sums chart cannot determine with certainty either the existence of these change points or the indices of the cases corresponding to these changes. These two problems are the focus of the second step. For the sake of the second step, it will be necessary to estimate the change magnitude CS_M of cumulative sums CS_i. One way to do so is to apply Formula (2).

$$\forall\, i \le n,\; CS_i = \begin{cases} CS_{i-1} + (E^{C_i} - \overline{\mu}) \\ 0, & \text{if } i = 0 \end{cases} \tag{1}$$

With n – the number of cases, $\overline{\mu}$ – the average of effect variables given as $\overline{\mu} = \frac{1}{n}\sum_{i=1}^{n} E^{C_i}$.

$$CS_M = \max_{0 \le i \le n} CS_i - \min_{0 \le i \le n} CS_i \tag{2}$$

Step 2: Bootstrapping. The first objective of the this step is to determine a confidence level for the observed change points. In the following, this issue is addressed with a bootstrapping approach. The rationale underlying the bootstrapping is to imitate the behavior of the cumulative sums CS_i^b in the case where there is no change in the patterns of effects. The resulting cumulative sums will provide a baseline for comparing the cumulative sums CS_i of the effects of the cases in their original order (as calculated in step 1). The bootstrapping process consists in applying the same process from step 1 to the randomly reorganized case base, which produces the cumulative sums CS_i^b and the change magnitude CS_M^b.

When the plot of the cumulative sums CS_i^b is likely to remain closer to zero than the chart of the original cumulative sums CS_i, a change has probably taken place. The estimation of the index of confidence in the existence of a change point includes conducting a significant k number of bootstraps and determining the number (let l be this number) of situations for which the magnitude of change CS_M^b is smaller than the change magnitude CS_M of the original case base. The confidence index CI that a shift in the pattern of effects is given by Formula (3).

$$\text{CI} = \frac{l}{k} \times 100 \tag{3}$$

Change Point Position. If the confidence level is high enough (typically around 90%) to confirm the existence of a change point, one way to estimate the case index corresponding to the change in the model of effects is to use the mean square error (MSE) metric. The case base is divided into two parts containing z and $n - z$ cases, where z is the index of the last case preceding the change in effect model. The estimation of the index z consists in solving an optimization problem whose objective is to minimize Function 4.

$$\text{MSE} = \sum_{i=1}^{z}(E^{C_1} - \overline{\mu}_1)^2 + \sum_{i=z+1}^{n}(E^{C_1} - \overline{\mu}_2)^2 \tag{4}$$

With $\overline{\mu}_1 = \frac{1}{z}\sum_{i=1}^{z} E^{C_i}$, $\overline{\mu}_2 = \frac{1}{n-z}\sum_{i=z+1}^{n} E^{C_i}$.

Once a change point is identified, the case base is divided into two case bases, a first case base including cases from 1 to z and the remaining cases composing the second case base. The process described in steps 1 and 2 is then iteratively applied on each of the case bases until there are no other change points in the case bases. As a result, more changes, if existing, are detected.

4.2 Incompleteness Detection

Let $m \neq 0$ be the number of change points detected in the case base $\mathbb{CB}$. Let $\mathcal{I}$ denotes the set of indices of the cases whose effects represent a change in the model, such as $|\mathcal{I}| = m$ and $\mathcal{I} = \{I_j\}_{1 \leq j \leq m}$. Precisely, index I_j corresponds to the index of the case preceding the jth change in the model of the effect variables. Then, the case base $\mathbb{CB}$ can be broken into $m + 1$ groups $\mathbb{G}_{1 \leq j \leq m+1}$ Such that constraints (5) are satisfied.

$$\mathbb{CB} = \bigcup_{j=1}^{m+1} \mathbb{G}_j$$
$$\mathbb{G}_j = \begin{cases} \{\mathbb{C}_t\}_{I_{j-1} < t \leq I_j} \\ \{\mathbb{C}_t\}_{0 \leq t \leq I_j}, & \text{if } j = 1 \end{cases} \tag{5}$$

The idea behind the completeness evaluation is to detect situations where two cases with similar actions and similar contexts but different effects. Specifically, the investigation of possible incompleteness situations is performed as follows.

1. given the set of groups $\{\mathbb{G}_j\}$, for each group $\mathbb{G}_j$, which represents the set of cases with similar effects, compute the maximum context-action distance $D_{CA,j}^{max}$ and minimum one $D_{CA,j}^{min}$. Let S_j^{CA} denote the interval $\left[D_{CA,j}^{min}, D_{CA,j}^{max}\right]$. Let $S_j^{E} = \left[E_j^{min}, E_j^{max}\right]$ be the effect variable interval of group $\mathbb{G}_j$.
2. A situation of incompleteness is reliably identified if there exist two cases $\mathbb{C}_1$ and $\mathbb{C}_2$, located respectively in two different groups $\mathbb{G}_1$ and $\mathbb{G}_2$ whose effect models differ, such that the context-action distance between $\mathbb{C}_1$ and $\mathbb{C}_2$ belongs to one of the intervals S_1^{CA}, S_2^{CA}. Formally:

$$\exists\, \mathbb{C}_{i'} \in \mathbb{G}_i, \mathbb{C}_{j'} \in \mathbb{G}_j, k \in \{i, j\}/$$
$$D_{CA}(\mathbb{C}_{i'}, \mathbb{C}_{j'}) \in S_k^{CA} \implies S_i^{E} \cap S_j^{E} = \emptyset \vee (E^{C_1} \notin S_i^{E} \cap S_j^{E} \wedge E^{C_2} \notin S_i^{E} \cap S_j^{E})$$
$$\vee\, (E^{C_m} \notin S_i^{E} \cap S_j^{E}, m \in \{i', j'\} \wedge \mathbb{C}_m \notin \mathbb{G}_k)$$

5   Evaluation

The objective of the experiment is to investigate the reliability and efficiency of the C2CBR algorithm to discover incompleteness in a case base. First, we describe the dataset used in the experimentation, then we present the experimental setup, and finally, we report the results.

Dataset. To investigate the effectiveness of the C2CBR approach, we conducted experiments using real word dataset. We used the real dataset from [4] that resulted from the experiment of the motivation example (see Sect. 3.1) in the context of an academic building. More precisely, the authors proposed a CBR-based approach to improve the energy efficiency of buildings considering the comfort of the occupants. The approach is evaluated through a case study where data are collected from numerous sensors deployed in an academic research office.

Collected data are classified into three categories according to the structure of a case presented in Sect. 2.1. The context data, which besides the meteorological data, includes the number of occupants. The action data model opening/closing of doors/windows. The effect data concern the temperature and the concentration of CO_2 in the office. A case corresponds to one-day measurements. The case base used in the present evaluation consists of 98 cases ordered by their measurements' dates. In this experiment, we are restricted to the incompleteness evaluation regarding the indoor temperature as the only effect variable.

Experimental Setup. To avoid biasing the results of the similarity assessment due to the dominant influence of variables with large values, the context and action data are rescaled between 0 and 1 using the MinMax strategy.

In this experiment, the weighted Euclidean distance is used as a similarity function to evaluate the context-action-based similarity between two cases. It is beyond the scope of this work to detail the process of weighting context and action variables. We adopted the approach developed in [5] to estimate these weights.

The experiments were performed on a 13″ MacBook Pro laptop equipped with an Intel® Core™ i7-8559U CPU 2.70 GHz, 16 GB of RAM, powered by Windows 10 pro 64 bit. The C2CBR algorithm is implemented in Python 3.9. The code was ran in Jupyter Notebook 6.4.

Case Base with Random Incompleteness. At this stage, we do not know whether the case base is complete since the modeling of the building environment is difficult due to the high number and the complex interactions between the phenomena influencing the energetic behavior of a building. To check the efficiency of the C2CBR algorithm, we need a baseline for which it certainly presents incompleteness situations.

We constructed an incomplete case base $\mathbb{CB}^I$ from the case base $\mathbb{CB}$. The process of generating the incompleteness situations is described as follows:

- we introduced incompleteness in $\mathbb{CB}$ by randomly choosing and modifying 5% of the cases (5 cases).
- as the office where the experimentation took place was not equipped with an air-conditioning system, the modification of the chosen cases consists in integrating a new action variable modeling the air conditioning in the office. This variable simulates the presence of a hidden variable in the CBR system. Values of this variable are sampled from a discrete uniform distribution between 18 °C and 23 °C.
- the effects following the application of the new actions (turn on the air conditioner) to the context of the chosen cases are generated using the physical model of the office. For consistency, the real effects of the other cases are simulated by the physical model too.

Empirical Results. Figure 1 plots the average of the real effect variable (temperature) of the 98 cases (blue curve) and the corresponding simulated values (red curve). Note that the simulated effects of cases $\mathbb{C}_6$, $\mathbb{C}_{19}$, $\mathbb{C}_{25}$, $\mathbb{C}_{59}$, and $\mathbb{C}_{71}$ are far from their original ones. The significant discrepancy between the original values and the simulated ones is due to the influence of the hidden variable (modeling air conditioning) on the effects of these cases, i.e., these cases correspond to the five randomly chosen and modified cases. Note also that the two curves overlap almost all along the plot. The Mean Absolute Percentage Error (MAPE) analysis, excluding the modified cases, indicates that the variation of the simulated data from the real data is less than 2.50%, showing the robustness of the physical model used in the simulation of the effect variables.

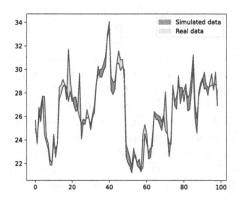

Fig. 1. Real and simulated effect. (Color figure online)

The results of the first step of the C2CBR algorithm, which consists in detecting changes in the model of effects (temperature), are depicted in Figs. 2 and 3. In Fig. 2 plotting the cumulative sums of the effect variable, each color change in the background corresponds to an abrupt change in the direction of the chart

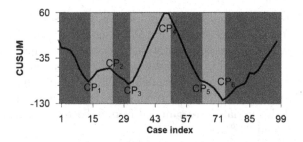

Fig. 2. Change point detection (Color figure online)

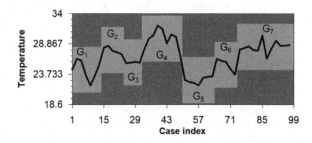

Fig. 3. Identified effect groups (Color figure online)

indicating the occurrence of a pattern change, i.e., each swap between the yellow and turquoise colors models a change point. It emerges that there are 6 permutations of background colors, which correspond to 6 change points. The 6 identified change points serve to split the case base into 7 disjointed groups according to the chronological recording of case effects, as presented in Fig. 3. Each change point is displayed by a shift in the turquoise-colored background and corresponds to a case index in the case base. A turquoise-shaded segment depicts a group containing all cases based on the current effect variable model formed by two successive change points. Each row of Table 1 provides detailed information on each change point. The index of the change case from which a model change is detected is assigned a confidence interval estimated at a 95% probability of being accurate. For instance, with a probability of 95%, the 6th change point is estimated to be between cases 75 and 77. Furthermore, using Formula 3, a confidence index in each detected change point is reported to qualify the quality of the analysis. For instance, the system is 99% confident that the 6th change point took place. Further information is also provided as averages of the groups' effect variables before and after a change point. Table 2 gives the values of the S^{CA} and S^{E} metrics (defined in Sect. 4.2) for each of the seven groups.

After applying the proposed heuristic, The five incompleteness situations that were artificially generated in the previous step have been correctly identified, as shown in Table 3. Each probable incompleteness situation is described by the two cases $\mathbb{C}_1^I$ and $\mathbb{C}_2^I$ generating this situation. Note that the cases in column $\mathbb{C}_1^I$ of Table 3 correspond to the five modified cases. For instance, the incompleteness situation S5 is observed between the cases $\mathbb{C}_{71}$ and $\mathbb{C}_{79}$ since the distance $D_{CA}(\mathbb{C}_{71}, \mathbb{C}_{79})$ is lower than the distance D_{CA}^{max} of the group $\mathbb{G}_7$ to which the case $\mathbb{C}_{79}$ belongs but the effect variable of the case $\mathbb{C}_{71}$ belongs to the group $\mathbb{G}_6$ knowing that $E^{\mathbb{C}_6} = 24.77 \notin S_6^E \cap S_7^E$ and $E^{\mathbb{C}_7} = 28.43 \notin S_6^E \cap S_7^E$.

Table 1. Change points details.

Index	Confidence interval	Confidence index	From	To	Level
15	(11, 15)	96%	24.49	27.814	4
25	(25, 25)	94%	27.814	25.725	5
33	(33, 37)	99%	25.725	29.733	3
51	(51, 51)	100%	29.733	22.745	2
65	(65, 67)	98%	22.745	25.305	3
75	(75, 77)	99%	25.305	28.355	1

Table 2. Groups' properties.

Group	S^{CA}	S^E
$\mathbb{G}_1$	$[0.138, 0.526]$	$[21.88, 27.25]$
$\mathbb{G}_2$	$[0.199, 0.550]$	$[26.61, 28.70]$
$\mathbb{G}_3$	$[0.156, 0.516]$	$[25.26, 26.14]$
$\mathbb{G}_4$	$[0.166, 0.390]$	$[23.65, 33.42]$
$\mathbb{G}_5$	$[0.188, 0.377]$	$[21.35, 24.54]$
$\mathbb{G}_6$	$[0.155, 0.440]$	$[23.64, 26.42]$
$\mathbb{G}_7$	$[0.126, 0.602]$	$[25.79, 31.23]$

Table 3. Incompleteness situation characteristics

Situation	$\mathbb{C}_1^I$	$\mathbb{C}_2^I$	D_{CA}
S1	$\mathbb{C}_6 \in \mathbb{G}_1$	$\mathbb{C}_{85} \in \mathbb{G}_7$	0.531
S2	$\mathbb{C}_{19} \in \mathbb{G}_2$	$\mathbb{C}_{39} \in \mathbb{G}_4$	0.184
S3	$\mathbb{C}_{25} \in \mathbb{G}_3$	$\mathbb{C}_{18} \in \mathbb{G}_2$	0.275
S4	$\mathbb{C}_{59} \in \mathbb{G}_5$	$\mathbb{C}_{69} \in \mathbb{G}_6$	0.369
S5	$\mathbb{C}_{71} \in \mathbb{G}_6$	$\mathbb{C}_{79} \in \mathbb{G}_7$	0.545

6   Conclusion

For the authors' knowledge, this work presents for the first time an attempt to address the problem of data incompleteness in a CBR system under the open-world assumption. The proposed approach C2CBR combines a change point detection method and a heuristic strategy to identify potential incompleteness in the case base.

While the approach shows promising results in the experiments conducted, further validation on a larger dataset is needed to ensure its effectiveness and generalizability. Thus, future work could focus on validating the proposed approach on a larger dataset to evaluate its performance and scalability.

Furthermore, it would be interesting to compare the proposed approach to other state-of-the-art methods for handling missing data in CBR systems to evaluate its effectiveness in comparison to existing techniques. Unfortunately, we were unable to find any methods for evaluating data completeness specifically in the context of CBR systems. Therefore, future work could focus on comparing the proposed approach to methods proposed in data mining and database literature to gain further insights into its performance. Another objective that we plan to pursue to enhance our approach is to investigate the effectiveness of the pairwise comparison process between cases and propose potential improvements to the comparison process.

References

1. Extracting business value from the 4 v's of big data. Techreport, IBM (2016). http://www.ibmbigdatahub.com/infographic/extracting-business-value-4-vs-big-data. Accessed 31 May 2022
2. 2019 Global data management research. Taking control in the digital age. Benchmarkreport, Experian UK&I, February 2019
3. Bergmann, R., Wilke, W., Vollrath, I.: Integrating general knowledge with object-oriented case representation and reasoning. In: 4th German Workshop: Case-Based Reasoning - System Development and Evaluation (1996)
4. Boulmaiz, F., Ploix, S., Reignier, P.: A data-driven approach for guiding the occupant's actions to achieve better comfort in buildings. In: IEEE 33rd International Conference on Tools with Artificial Intelligence (ICTAI) (2021)
5. Boulmaiz, F., Reignier, P., Ploix, S.: An occupant-centered approach to improve both his comfort and the energy efficiency of the building. Knowl.-Based Syst. **249**, 108970 (2022)
6. Charakopoulos, A., Karakasidis, T.: Backward degree a new index for online and offline change point detection based on complex network analysis. Phys. A **604**, 127929 (2022)
7. Cichy, C., Rass, S.: An overview of data quality frameworks. IEEE Access **7**, 24634–24648 (2019)
8. Galárraga, L., Razniewski, S., Amarilli, A., Suchanek, F.M.: Predicting completeness in knowledge bases. In: Proceedings of the Tenth ACM International Conference on Web Search and Data Mining. ACM (2017)
9. Getahun, Y.S., Li, M.-H., Pun, I.-F.: Trend and change-point detection analyses of rainfall and temperature over the awash river basin of Ethiopia. Heliyon **7**(9), e08024 (2021)
10. Grohe, M., Lindner, P.: Probabilistic databases with an infinite open-world assumption. In: Proceedings of the 38th ACM SIGMOD. ACM Press (2019)
11. Haug, A.: Understanding the differences across data quality classifications: a literature review and guidelines for future research. Industr. Manage. Data Syst. **121**(12), 2651–2671 (2021)
12. Hinkley, D.V., Schechtman, E.: Conditional bootstrap methods in the mean-shift model. Biometrika **74**, 85–93 (1987)
13. Liaw, S.-T., et al.: Towards an ontology for data quality in integrated chronic disease management: a realist review of the literature. Int. J. Med. Inform. **82**, 139 (2013)
14. Nguyen, P.T., Di Rocco, J., Iovino, L., Di Ruscio, D., Pierantonio, A.: Evaluation of a machine learning classifier for metamodels. Softw. Syst. Model. **20**(6), 1797–1821 (2021)

15. Pettitt, A.N.: A simple cumulative sum type statistic for the change-point problem with zero-one observations. Biometrika **67**(1), 79–84 (1980)
16. Richter, M.M.: The knowledge contained in similarity measures. In: International Conference on Case-Based Reasoning, ICCBR 1995, Sesimbra, Portugal (1995)
17. Truong, C., Oudre, L., Vayatis, N.: Selective review of offline change point detection methods. Signal Process. **167**, 107299 (2020)
18. Wang, R., Strong, D.: Beyond accuracy: what data quality means to data consumers. J. Manage. Inf. Syst. **12**(4), 5–33 (1996)
19. You, S.-H., Jang, E.J., Kim, M.-S., Lee, M.-T., Kang, Y.-J., Lee, J.-E.: Change point analysis for detecting vaccine safety signals. Vaccines **9**(3), 206 (2021)

Learning from Successes and Failures: An Exploration of a Case-Based Reasoning Technique

Fateh Boulmaiz[1]([✉]), Patrick Reignier[1], and Stephane Ploix[2]

[1] Univ. Grenoble Alpes, CNRS, Grenoble INP, LIG, 38000 Grenoble, France
`fateh.boulmaiz@univ-grenoble-alpes.fr`
[2] Univ. Grenoble Alpes, CNRS, Grenoble INP, G-SCOP, 38000 Grenoble, France

Abstract. Usually, existing works on adaptation in case-based reasoning assume that the case base holds only successful cases, i.e., cases having solutions believed to be appropriate for the corresponding problems. However, in practice, the case base could hold failed cases, resulting from an earlier adaptation process but discarded by the revision process. Not considering failed cases would be missing an interesting opportunity to learn more knowledge for improving the adaptation process. This paper proposes a novel approach to the adaptation process in the case-based reasoning paradigm, based on an improved barycentric approach by considering the failed cases. The experiment performed on real data demonstrates the benefit of the method considering the failed cases in the adaptation process compared to the classical ones that ignore them, thus, improving the performance of the case-based reasoning system.

Keywords: Case-based reasoning · adaptation · successful case · failed case

1 Introduction

Case-based reasoning (CBR) is certainly the most intuitive approach of artificial intelligence to solve a problem since it mimics human behavior in problem-solving. A CBR system looks in its memory represented by a base of previously solved experiments called source cases, for cases having similar problems to the target problem to be solved by adapting their solutions if necessary. The target solution is revised to make sure of its adequacy to solve the target problem and finally the base of cases is enriched following the new experiment of resolution of the target case. Each step of the reasoning process is supported by a process of acquiring the necessary knowledge to perform this step. It is worth highlighting the close connection between the knowledge of the different stages of the CBR approach.

Of the four principal stages of the reasoning process, adaptation is a crucial stage since the quality of the solution heavily depends on its performance. Its focus is on fitting the solutions of similar source cases to meet the specific requirements of the target problem. This is particularly important since the

H. Fujita et al. (Eds.): IEA/AIE 2023, LNAI 13925, pp. 74–87, 2023.
https://doi.org/10.1007/978-3-031-36819-6_7

source problems usually do not match the target problem, and as a consequence, without this step, the CBR system cannot ultimately generate an appropriate solution to the target problem. Awareness of the pivotal role that adaptation plays was noted from the early days of CBR systems, as a result, there is a large number of studies exploring various approaches to acquiring adaptation knowledge to improve its performance.

Existing adaptation approaches focus exclusively on cases whose solutions are deemed relevant to the corresponding problems (hereafter these cases are referred to as successful cases and are denoted by $C+$). The appreciation of success is subjective to the application domain, e.g., in the context of the CBR application in the elaboration of an energy management system in a building, a successful case would correspond to a scenario satisfying the user's comfort while minimizing the energy expenditure. However, there are also failed cases. A failed case (noted hereafter $C-$) is a case having an unsatisfactory solution to the problem to solve, in particular, these are cases proposed by the adaptation process but rejected during the validation phase. Moreover, the adaptation process often involves the acquisition of the knowledge required to generate the adaptation rules. Usually, such knowledge is strongly dependent on the application domain, making the acquisition process complex and challenging to understand and grasp.

Surprisingly, despite a large number of research studies and an increased interest in the adaptation issue (for instance, check out [11] for a comprehensive overview of existing adaptation approaches in CBR in the Medical Domain), few works are concerned with the challenge of proposing a domain-independent adaptation approach. Even less studies consider adaptation from the solution quality perspective, i.e., addressing both failed and successful cases. These cases are seldom used by the CBR systems even though they constitute potentially useful source of knowledge. After conducting an extensive review of the literature, it is known to the authors that only one study [8] has recently investigated the concept of using negative cases in the adaptation process. However, the proposed method in this study presents some limitations. Firstly, the adaptation process is based on the case difference heuristic (CDH) approach. The CDH approach relies on collecting pairs of cases from a case base and creating rules that link the differences in problem descriptions (i.e., problem differences) between the pairs to the differences in their corresponding solution descriptions (i.e., solution differences). As a result, the effectiveness of this approach is highly dependent on the specific domain of application. Secondly, the approach requires a binary representation of the case features, which can limit the expressiveness of the feature space and potentially lead to information loss. Therefore, there is a need for further research to explore alternative approaches for using negative cases in the adaptation process.

In this work, we propose a novel perspective on the adaptation process of the CBR paradigm, based on a fully domain-independent approach and drawing on both successful and failed cases. In particular, the present study proposes a new approach to the acquisition of adaptation knowledge exploiting both successful cases and failed ones. The approach takes its inspiration from studies in the planning of the path of a robot moving towards a destination in an unknown and insecure environment (includes obstacles). The originality of this approach consists in applying artificial forces to the solution to be proposed to move away from failed source solutions and move closer to successful source solutions.

The rest of this paper is arranged as follows. Section 2 introduces an illustration of motivation and the background of this work. Section 3 details the contribution to harnessing failed and successful cases for a new adaptation approach. An evaluation of the proposed approach is presented and discussed in Sect. 4, before drawing conclusions about this work and outlining some guidelines for future work in Sect. 5.

2   Motivating Example and Preliminaries

A CBR-based energy management system (EMS) in a building is a representative case study of the systems relevant to the scope of this study. The objective of an EMS is to fulfill the user's desire for thermal comfort, air quality, etc. while minimizing the energy consumption in the building. Indeed, a building is a complex system whose potential to save energy depends on several factors with dependencies difficult to identify [3], such as climate, building materials, geographical position, and energy rate, but also the occupant of the building exercises a major influence. Findings of earlier work [9] has already highlighted the advantage of acquiring adaptation knowledge in improving the performance of a CBR-based EMS. Furthermore, due to the growing awareness of environmental issues, several studies have focused on the correlation between energy consumption in a building and the comfort of its occupants, leading to the definition of standards [1,2,6] to estimate the comfort of users. Thanks to the norms defined in these standards, the revision process can gauge the quality of the target solution proposed by the adaptation process, allowing the retention process to label this solution as a successful case $C+$ or a failed one $C-$.

In the CBR-based EMS proposed in [3], the objective is to make the user conscious of the influence of his actions on the energy behavior of the building. For this, the system guides the user in his actions by advising him on a set of actions aiming at decreasing the energy waste while considering his comfort. A case describes the energy management scenario of a building for one day. The actions retained in the system case base are the actions effectively carried out by the building occupant, so there is no guarantee that they are actions that generate satisfactory effects for the occupant. For this reason, the system is provided with a function to evaluate the performance of the actions stored in the case base, allowing to label the corresponding cases with the appropriate labels ($C+$ or $C-$).

2.1   Founding Notions and Notations About CBR Approach

The memory of a CBR system is made of a set of source cases C_{sr} which constitute a case base CB.

Case Description. Let $\mathbb{C}$, $\mathbb{A}$, and $\mathbb{E}$ be three mutually disjoint sets. A case is a triplet $(\mathscr{C}, \mathcal{A}, \mathcal{E}) \in \mathbb{C} \times \mathbb{A} \times \mathbb{E}$ where:

- $\mathscr{C}$ is an element of the context domain $\mathbb{C}$, i.e., the imposed elements of the problem over which one cannot exert control. For instance, in a CBR-based disease treatment system, the context data can be the different physiological measures of the patient (blood pressure, glycemic rate, etc.).
- $\mathcal{A}$ is an element of the action domain $\mathbb{A}$, i.e., elements that can be controlled to achieve the relevant outcomes. It represents the solution proposed by the system. For instance, the names and the protocol for administering the drugs prescribed in a CBR-based disease treatment system.
- $\mathcal{E}$ is an element of the effect domain $\mathbb{E}$, i.e., elements describe the state of the system after applying action $\mathcal{A}$ to context $\mathscr{C}$. For instance, the patient's physiological measures after the treatment.

A target context $\mathscr{C}_{tg}$ is a context for which the CBR system tries to predict target actions $\mathcal{A}_{tg}$ to generate target effects $\mathcal{E}_{tg}$ and thus elaborate a target case C_{tg}. Formally, the resolution of a problem in the CBR paradigm is defined by Eq. (1).

$$
\text{CBR system: } (CB, \mathscr{C}_{tg}) \longmapsto \mathcal{A}_{tg}
$$
$$
C_{tg} \triangleq (\mathscr{C}_{tg}, \mathcal{A}_{tg}, \mathcal{E}_{tg}) \tag{1}
$$

Retrieving and Adaptation. A full presentation of the reasoning process is beyond the focus of this paper, but due to the particular connection between adaptation and retrieving knowledge, it is usually necessary to present the adaptation process in conjunction with the retrieval process. Indeed, the reasoning process modeled by Eq. (1) is made up of two main steps.

- *retrieval process*: Given a threshold σ for the distance between the context variables of the source cases and the target context, the retrieval process consists of identifying the source cases having a context similar to the target context. The profile of the retrieval function is given in Eq. (2).

$$
\text{Retrieve: } \quad \mathscr{C}_{tg} \longmapsto \{\forall C_{sr} \in CB / Distance(\mathscr{C}_{tg}, \mathscr{C}_{sr}) \leq \sigma\} = \mathcal{S}_{C_{tg}} \tag{2}
$$

  where $Distance(\mathscr{C}_{tg}, \mathscr{C}_{sr})$ – a metric that computes the distance between the context variable $\mathscr{C}_{tg}$ and the context variable $\mathscr{C}_{sr}$.
  No constraints are imposed on the type of distance to use since it permits handling the context variables. For instance, the Minkowski metric can be used to calculate the context distance in a CBR-based EMS since the context variables are real values.
- *adaptation process*: Since the source contexts usually do not match the target context, it is required to define a function to adapt the source actions to satisfy the requirements of the target context. The profile of the adaptation function is defined by the Formula (3).

$$
\text{Adaptation: } \forall\, C_{sr} \triangleq (\mathscr{C}_{sr}, \mathcal{A}_{sr}, \mathcal{E}_{sr}) \in \mathcal{S}_{C_{tg}},
$$
$$
(\{(\mathscr{C}_{sr}, \mathcal{A}_{sr}, \mathcal{E}_{sr})\}, \mathscr{C}_{tg}) \longmapsto \mathcal{A}_{tg} \tag{3}
$$

where $\mathcal{S}_{\mathcal{C}_{t_g}}$ – the set of similar source cases as defined by Eq. (2).

Note that Eq. (3) does not impose any constraints on the number of similar cases considered in the adaptation process, thus we are dealing with a compositional adaptation (whose single case adaptation is a particular case), where solutions from several source cases are combined to yield a target solution. Indeed, the experiment indicated that retaining a single case often gives less accurate results [12]. This is explained by the fact that frequently only a part of the problem of the similar source case is relevant for the target problem, which makes the task of adaptation complicated (if not impossible).

2.2   Collisionless Path Planning

Robot path planning study focus on the path planning of an autonomous robot moving in an unknown environment, i.e., guide the robot in its movement from an initial position to a target position by calculating the optimal but moreover the safest path to avoid obstacles that can occur along the path towards the target.

Several approaches were proposed to tackle this challenge, in particular, the Artificial Potential Field (APF) approach originally proposed in [7] is extensively adopted in robot guidance. The APF approach can cope with the reality of the current environment of the robot displacement by considering both the objectives to be reached and the obstacles to be avoided while moving. The key idea of this approach is to consider the robot as a point evolving in a 2-dimensional space (in the basic scenario) subject to the field influences of targets to reach and obstacles to avoid. Consequently, the robot is subjected to two kinds of forces, including an attractive one $\mathbb{F}_{at}$ generated by targets and a repulsive one $\mathbb{F}_{rp}$ generated by obstacles to move the robot further away.

Whereas repulsive forces are disproportional to the distance between the robot and the obstacles, i.e. they are strongest close to the obstacles and are less influential at distance, attractive forces are proportional to the distance between the target and the robot. The combined (total) of all the forces $\overrightarrow{\mathbb{F}} = \overrightarrow{\mathbb{F}_{at}} + \overrightarrow{\mathbb{F}_{rp}}$ applied to the robot defines the movement direction of the robot and its speed whilst avoiding collisions with obstacles. For the sake of simplification, the principle of this method for a robot traveling in a 2-dimensions environment is depicted in Fig. 1.

3   Reasoning from Successful and Failed Cases

3.1   Problem Formalization

The adaptation problem considering failed and successful cases can be formalized as follows. Given the following observations:

- the case base CB is divided into two partitions of failed cases $CB\_$ and successful cases CB_+. So, $CB = CB\_ \cup CB_+$.

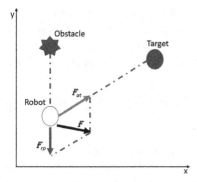

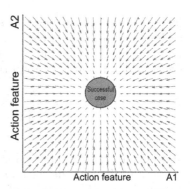

Fig. 1. Artificial potential field.   **Fig. 2.** CBR attractive force

– by misuse of language, we refer to a target case as the elements of a target context for which we are looking for a solution. The case structure is not completely defined as the elements representing the actions and therefore, the effects are unknown.

Find a solution for a target case (thus under construction) is to infer, from source cases having similar context, a set of target actions that best satisfy the target context, which leads to the definition of the target effects, and thus to building an effective case containing the three elements: context, actions, and effects.

Similar source cases should be handled differently depending on whether they are failed (member of $CB\_$) or successful (member of CB_+) and on their degree of similarity to the target case. The method to be proposed should provide mechanisms to move towards the solutions of successful similar source cases and away from failed similar source cases while taking into account that the closer the source case to the target case the more influence its solution has on the target solution.

3.2 Principle

The principle of our approach to considering failed cases in the adaptation process is inspired by navigation algorithms originating from the literature on the programming of autonomous robots, in particular, based on the artificial potential field presented in Sect. 2.2.

Before describing the details of our approach in the next section, to ensure the successful implementation of an artificial potential field-like concept in the context of this work, some assumptions are formulated:

– while the labeling process falls outside the scope of this study, we assume that previous experiences (source cases) are already labeled as successful or failed cases. Furthermore, we suppose that the CBR system is given a quality function Q which scores the efficacy of the actions applied to the context. The highest scores are the best. This implicitly defines a threshold value $\mathcal{P}_s^{\mathcal{E}_i}$ for each effect feature $\mathcal{E}_i$ according to Eq. (4). This approach has already been proposed in [4], where the $\mathcal{P}_s^{\mathcal{E}_i}$ threshold is defined either by an expert or can be learned automatically from the available case knowledge in the case base

$$\forall\, C_i \in CB\ ,\ \mathcal{Q} : \mathcal{E}_i \longmapsto \mathbb{R}$$

$$\mathcal{L}(C_i) = \begin{cases} C_i+ & \text{if } \mathcal{Q}(\mathcal{E}_i) \geq \mathcal{P}_s^{\mathcal{E}_i}\ ,\ \forall \mathcal{E}_i \in \mathbb{E} \\ C_i- & \text{otherwise.} \end{cases} \tag{4}$$

With $\mathcal{L}$ – the labeling function, $\mathcal{E}_i$ – an effect feature of case C_i.

- classical CBR methods retrieve a defined number of neighboring cases from the case base CB regardless of an optimal number of similar ones regarding the target case. This KNN-like approach poses some issues since the target cases do not necessarily have the same number of similar neighbors, while some target cases should have more similar cases, others less. Furthermore, the configuration where much more source cases with equal distance from a target case than the predefined number, must be handled. In this work, we assume the existence of a retrieval approach that adjusts the number of source cases similar to the target case C_{tr} by dynamically defining a similarity threshold $\sigma_{C_{tr}}$ for the context distance between C_{tr} and the neighboring source cases. For instance, the work presented in [3], provides a method to define this threshold by combining a statistical approach and a genetic algorithm.

The key idea of the approach proposed in this work is to map the type of source cases available in the case base, i.e., successful and failed cases, to the type of objects handled in the context of robot moving, i.e., target and obstacles. Therefore, failed cases are assimilated into obstacles and successful cases into targets. While cases $C_i+ \in \mathcal{S}_{C_{tg}}$ with good performances should generate an attractive force $\mathbb{F}_{at}$ that pulls the target solution towards them, the bad cases $C_i- \in \mathcal{S}_{C_{tg}}$ should produce a repulsive force $\mathbb{F}_{rp}$ that pushes away the solution from them.

The successful and failed source cases are considered to be sources for generating a potential field representing the properties of the target solution. As in the robotic potential field method, the CBR potential field is still composed of two fields. For instance, regarding the attractive potential field, an attractive force is produced from the target solution to the source solutions of the successful cases by the configuration of the latter, which allows to pull the target solution towards the solutions of these cases.

To illustrate this concept, let's consider, for the sake of presentation, a system with domain knowledge containing only 2 action variables, the attractive potential field generated by any successful case looks like Fig. 2, where at each point of the context space representing the target context, the force vectors are directed towards the successful source case. Concerning the repulsive potential field, a pushback force is generated by the configuration of the failed case towards the target solution, which allows to pull the target solution away from the solutions of these cases. Figure 3 depicts the CBR repulsive force in a similar configuration to the example illustrating the CBR attractive force.

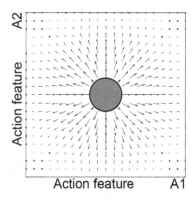

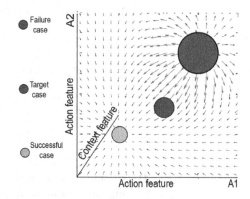

Fig. 3. CBR repulsive force   **Fig. 4.** CBR total potential force

Ultimately, the configuration of the target solution, i.e., the position of the target solution in the space of solutions (actions), is determined by summing all repulsive and attractive forces generated by neighboring failed and successful cases respectively. For the simple case of only two neighbors, a successful case and a failed case, the total potential field has the shape shown in Fig. 4.

3.3   Local Prediction of the Target Solution

Although we are inspired by the potential artificial field method, its application in the context of this work as applied in the robotics context does not permit determining the solution for many reasons:

- the potential total force in the robotic context depends exclusively on the distance between the goal/obstacles and the robot. In the CBR context, the magnitude of the attraction and repulsion forces are not dependent only on the distance between the target context and the neighboring source contexts but also on the performance (quality solution) of the neighboring source contexts.
- within the robotics context, unlike the attractive force, the magnitude of the repulsive force is at its highest value close to the obstacle and decreases proportionally when moving away from it. Within the context of CBR applications, the magnitude of the two forces should be proportional to the performance of the source solutions but disproportional to the distance between the source contexts and the target one.
- there is usually only one goal to reach in robotic applications, but in the case of a multi-goal environment, one looks for a path that goes through all these goals in sequential order by optimizing some criteria. for CBR systems, the aim is to combine the knowledge of all the neighboring source cases to infer the target solution.
- while the purpose of the robotic potential artificial field is to find the safe path to the goal, its purpose in the CBR application is to acquire new knowledge

Table 1. Summery of results on synthetic dataset

APPROACH	TEST SET																	
	S1			S2			S3			S4			S5			GLOBAL		
	METRICS			METRICS			METRICS			METRICS			METRICS			METRICS		
	PER (%)	APR(%)	TIR(%)	PER	APR	TIR	PER	APR	TIR	PER	APR	TIR	PER	APR	TIR	PER	APR	TIR
$CBR-S$	16.73	59.13	59.13	17.85	48.57	48.57	19.53	60.12	60.12	20.48	56.07	56.07	18.79	64.48	64.48	18.68	57.67	57.67
$CBR-B$	18.27	57.51	57.51	15.36	63.90	63.90	22.85	59.69	59.69	24.23	65.52	65.52	21.10	662.71	62.71	20.36	61.87	61.87
$CBR-P$	22.62	42.26	57.10	18.54	48.85	63.71	20.14	50.21	60.10	22.48	52.92	70.19	23.47	39.86	60.09	21.45	46;82	62,24
$CBR-R$	-2.56	32.18	49.75	9.12	29.89	51.19	14.71	43.07	64.24	17.45	39.52	57.74	12.04	41.26	62.84	10.15	37.18	57.15
$CBR-APF$	**34.68**	**100**	**100**	**28.85**	**99.76**	**99.76**	**33.91**	**100**	**100**	**31.27**	**100**	**100**	**38.73**	**99.88**	**99.88**	**33.49**	**99.92**	**99.92**

that guides the adaptation process in the construction of the target solution, i.e., to orient the reasoning process towards the most useful solutions (closest and best-performing cases) and away from the worst cases (farthest away or bad performance).

It is, therefore, necessary to adapt the approach of the artificial potential field to take into consideration the specificities of the CBR adaptation process. To do so, our approach defines the target solution (actions) $\mathcal{A}_{tg}$ by the vectorial sum of all attractive forces ($\mathrm{F}_{at}^{C_i+}, \forall C_i+ \in \mathcal{S}_{\mathcal{C}_{tg}}$) and all repulsive forces ($\mathrm{F}_{rp}^{C_i-}, \forall C_i- \in \mathcal{S}_{\mathcal{C}_{tg}}$) as described in Eq. (5).

$$\forall\, C_i+ \in \mathcal{S}_{\mathcal{C}_{tg}}, \forall\, C_i- \in \mathcal{S}_{\mathcal{C}_{tg}},$$
$$\sum_{C_i} \mathrm{F}^{C_i}\overrightarrow{\mathcal{A}_{tg}\mathcal{A}_i} = \sum_{C_i+} \mathrm{F}_{at}^{C_i+}\overrightarrow{\mathcal{A}_{tg}\mathcal{A}_{C_i+}} + \sum_{C_i-} \mathrm{F}_{rp}^{C_i-}\overrightarrow{\mathcal{A}_{tg}\mathcal{A}_{C_i-}} = 0 \qquad (5)$$

As already mentioned earlier, the magnitude of the repulsion and attraction forces depends both on the distance of the target context from the context of the similar source case and on the performance of the latter. From Eq. (5), the metric F^{C_i} defines the magnitude and direction of the associated force to the case C_i. We propose in Eq. (6) a formula to estimate its value.

$$\forall\, C_i \in \mathcal{S}_{\mathcal{C}_{tg}}, \mathrm{F}^{C_i} = \begin{cases} \left(1 - \dfrac{\mathcal{D}_C(C_{tg}, C_i)}{\sigma_{C_{tg}}}\right) \times (\mathcal{Q}_i - \mathcal{P}_s) & \text{if } \mathcal{Q}_i \neq \mathcal{P}_s \\ 1 - \dfrac{\mathcal{D}_C(C_{tg}, C_i)}{\sigma_{C_{tg}}} & \text{else} \end{cases} \qquad (6)$$

With $\sigma_{C_{tg}}$ – the context distance threshold, $\mathcal{Q}_i$ – the performance of the case C_i, $\mathcal{P}_s$ – the performance threshold, $\mathcal{D}_C(C_{tg}, C_i)$ – the context distance between C_{tg} and its neighbor C_i.

From Eq. (6), one can observe that whatever the type of force, its magnitude progressively decreases at the expense of an increasing context distance until it becomes null when the context distance equals the similarity threshold $\sigma_{C_{tg}}$. Besides defining the magnitude of the force, the operand $\mathcal{Q}_i - \mathcal{P}_s$ specifies the type of the force. When $\mathcal{Q}_i \geq \mathcal{P}_s$, then $\mathrm{F}^{C_i} \geq 0$, and the case C_i generates an attractive force else, it should be a repulsive force.

In this manner, the actions to be proposed $\mathcal{A}_{tg}$ have to satisfy:

$$\mathcal{A}_{tg} = \frac{1}{\sum_{C_i} \mathrm{F}^{C_i}} \sum_{C_i} \mathrm{F}^{C_i} \mathcal{A}_i \, , \ \forall\, C_i \in \mathcal{S}_{\mathcal{C}_{tg}} \qquad (7)$$

4   Evaluation

The present section provides an empirical evaluation of our approach. The objective of the evaluation is twofold, i) study the potential impact of considering both failed and successful cases on improving the performance of the CBR system; ii) assess the performance of the artificial potential field approach, this is referred to as CBR-APF in the following, compared to other adaptation approaches.

4.1   Experimental Setup

As mentioned in Sect. 2, the approach is implemented in an EMS whose objective is to make the user aware of the impact of his actions on the energy use in a building. Concretely, the EMS proposes to the occupant a series of actions to improve the comfort while consuming less energy.

To evaluate our approach, we conducted an experiment using semi-synthetic data generated from real-data presented in [5]. The case base contains 15,948 cases, where each case is composed of: 1) the effect variables which represent the temperature and air quality in the building; 2) the action variables which model the opening of the door and window; 3) the context variables which are weather conditions. Each variable is described by a 24-value vector corresponding to one day. We adopted a 5-fold cross-validation where the original case base is randomly split into five equal-sized subsets: $S1$, $S2$, $S3$, $S4$, and $S5$. A single set is selected as a test set CB^T (target cases) while the remaining four sets are used as a learning set CB^L (source cases). The cross-validation procedure is performed five times, each of the five sets being used once as a test set. The results of the metrics adopted to evaluate the performance are averaged to provide a final estimate.

To evaluate case performance we used functions that assess the user's dissatisfaction with the effects of the actions, as presented by Formula (8). To simulate the effects following the application of the proposed actions, a physical model of the building involved in the experiment was developed.

$$\mathcal{S}_T^h(T) = \begin{cases} 0 & \text{if } T \in [21,23] \\ \frac{T-23}{26-23} & \text{if } T > 23 \\ \frac{21-T}{21-18} & \text{if } T < 21 \end{cases} , \quad \mathcal{S}_C^h(C) = \begin{cases} 0 & \text{if } C \le 500 \\ \frac{C-500}{1500-1000} & \text{if } C > 500 \end{cases} \quad (8)$$

4.2   Baselines and Metrics

Several baselines are considered in the evaluation process:

1. the approach proposed in [5], denoted CBR-S in the following, exploits failed and successful cases but with a null adaptation process as the latter consists in making a vote among the similar cases solutions to select the solution with the best performance (maximizes the quality function) by applying it directly to the target case. The choice of this baseline is to check the relevance of using several source cases to establish the adaptation process.

2. a standard barycentric approach that combines solutions from the set of successful and failed similar source cases without artificial forces, noted CBR-B hereafter. The goal is to validate the efficiency of the artificial forces in improving the adaptation process.
3. a modified variant denoted CBR-P of our approach is tested, it considers only positive cases and thus uses only attractive forces. The objective is to illustrate the advantage of considering both negative and positive cases w.r.t only positive cases.
4. the approach proposed in [10] is used as a further baseline. This approach referred to as CBR-R, is based on a KNN approach to select similar source cases from which a generalized case is generated. Similar cases are used also to train a linear regression model, which is applied to the generalized case to predict the target case solution.

Note that in the experiment, the performance evaluation of all tested approaches is performed by comparison against a reference which is the actions carried out by the user without assistance according to three measures:

– *Performance Enhancement Rate (PER)*: The PER consists of comparing, for each test case C_i, the average of the thermal performances Q_T^*, the air quality performances Q_C^*, and the global performance Q^* of the proposed actions to the corresponding values Q_T^r, Q_C^r, and Q^r of the actions already recorded in the case base. The PER_{C_i} related to the test case C_i, if any, is given by the (9).

$$PER_{C_i} = \frac{Q^* - Q^r}{Q^r} \qquad (9)$$

– *Approach Efficiency Rate (APR)*: The APR is defined as the average of the ratio of the number of test cases whose performance is improved by applying the actions recommended by this approach to the total number of test cases.

$$APR = \frac{Z^+}{Z} \qquad (10)$$

With $Z = |CB^T|$ – the set of test cases, $Z^+ = \{C_i \in CB^T \ / \ PER_{C_i} > 0\}$
– *True Improvement Rate (TIR)*: This measure is the average of the ratio between the number of test cases whose performance is improved by applying the actions recommended by the approach and the total number of the test cases for which the approach successfully proposed a solution (improving or degrading performance compared to the user's actions).

4.3   Results and Analyse

Whatever the adaptation approach applied in a CBR system, its performance depends partially on the retrieval process. Analyze the latter goes beyond the scope of the present paper, We use the approach given in [5] to estimate the similarity and define the similar source cases in the training set. It follows that each target case from the test set has at least one similar source case from the training set.

Table 1 summarizes the results of the 5-fold cross-validation of our approach against the four baselines considered. Some important findings from this experiment are:

- while the value of the TIR metric corresponds to the value of APR for the CBR-S, CBR-B, and CBR-APF approaches, the APR value is less than that of TIR for the CBR-P and CBR-R approaches, this is due to the ability of the first three approaches to computing a solution even with a similar set of cases consisting exclusively of failed cases.
- regardless of the test set, our CBR-APF approach is clearly better in performance than all other baselines with also better APR and TIR.
- the number of similar source cases has a significant influence on the quality of the adaptation process, a compositional adaptation systematically gives a better PER, as illustrated by the comparison between PERs of CBR-APF which is a compositional approach and CBR-S which uses a single similar case.
- attraction and repulsion forces have an important impact on the results of the adaptation process. Given the same number of similar cases, by using these forces, our CBR-APF approach outperforms the CBR-B baseline, which does not use them. CBR-APF is 1.64 times more performing than CBR-B regarding the improvement of the cases performances (global PER= 33.49% versus 20.36%) and 1.61 times more efficient according to the number of cases for which it manages to find a solution (CBR-APF improves the performance of the solutions proposed by the user without assistance for 99.92% of cases against 61.87% for CBR-B).
- using failed cases in case-based reasoning significantly influences the performance of a CBR system. By exploiting both successful and failed cases, the system improves the results of the reasoning process. Comparing the performance of the CBR-APF approach with that of the CBR-P and CBR-R approaches (both do not use failed cases in their reasoning), the TIR results show that the CBR-APF approach outperforms the other baselines. CBR-APF approach is more than three times more efficient than CBR-R and more than 1.5 times more than CBR-P in improving the performance (PER).

5   Conclusion

This paper proposed a new approach to the adaptation process in the CBR paradigm by looking at both failed and successful source cases instead of the traditional practice of considering only successful source case. We found inspiration in the studies on planning safe paths for a robot moving in an unknown environment. The concept is that both successful and failed cases generate attraction and repulsion forces respectively on a likely barycentric solution to drive the reasoning towards the best performing solutions and away from the failed ones.

The experimentation of this approach in the context of an EMS showed a significant improvement in the system performance by considering both successful cases and failed ones.

In this work we have developed and evaluated an approach considering the whole set of successful and failed similar cases, it would be interesting to perform a deeper evaluation taking into account the number of neighboring successful and failed cases considering only the n cases with the best performances and the m cases with the worst performances. Another line of future research for this work would be to explore the possible impact of a failed case on the domain ontology (if any). It could be useful to suggest new necessary conditions to add to the domain ontology that would avoid the reappearance of such a negative case in the future.

References

1. ASHRAE (ed.): ASHRAE Standard Thermal Environmental Conditions for Human Occupancy. American Society of Heating, Refrigerating and Air-Conditioning Engineers, Atlanta, USA (1992)
2. ASHRAE (ed.):. Indoor air quality guide: best practices for design, construction, and commissioning. American Society of Heating, Refrigerating and Air-Conditioning Engineers, Atlanta, USA (2009)
3. Boulmaiz, F., Alyafi, A.A., Ploix, S., Reignier, P.: Optimizing occupant actions to enhance his comfort while reducing energy demand in buildings. In: 11th IEEE IDAACS (2021)
4. Boulmaiz, F., Ploix, S., Reignier, P.: A data-driven approach for guiding the occupant's actions to achieve better comfort in buildings. In: 2021 IEEE 33rd ICTAI, pp. 463–468 (2021)
5. Boulmaiz, F., Reignier, P., Ploix, S.: An occupant-centered approach to improve both his comfort and the energy efficiency of the building. Knowl.-Based Syst. **249**, 108970 (2022)
6. CSA Group. Z412–17 Office ergonomics - An application standard for workplace ergonomics (2017)
7. Khatib, O.: Real-time obstacle avoidance for manipulators and mobile robots. In: Proceedings of IEEE International Conference on Robotics and Automation (1985)
8. Lieber, J., Nauer, E.: Adaptation knowledge discovery using positive and negative cases. In: Sánchez-Ruiz, A.A., Floyd, M.W. (eds.) ICCBR 2021. LNCS (LNAI), vol. 12877, pp. 140–155. Springer, Cham (2021). https://doi.org/10.1007/978-3-030-86957-1_10
9. Minor, M., Marx, L.: Case-based reasoning for inert systems in building energy management. In: Aha, D.W., Lieber, J. (eds.) ICCBR 2017. LNCS (LNAI), vol. 10339, pp. 200–211. Springer, Cham (2017). https://doi.org/10.1007/978-3-319-61030-6_14
10. Patterson, D.W., Rooney, N., Galushka, M.: A regression based adaptation strategy for case-based reasoning. In: AAAI/IAAI (2002)

11. Pusztová, L., Babic, F., Paralic, J., Paralicova, Z.: How to improve the adaptation phase of the CBR in the medical domain. In: Machine Learning and Knowledge Extraction, pp. 168–177 (2019)
12. Sizov, G., Öztürk, P., Marsi, E.: Compositional adaptation of explanations in textual case-based reasoning. In: Goel, A., Díaz-Agudo, M.B., Roth-Berghofer, T. (eds.) ICCBR 2016. LNCS (LNAI), vol. 9969, pp. 387–401. Springer, Cham (2016). https://doi.org/10.1007/978-3-319-47096-2_26

Computer Vision

A Monocular Vision Ranging Method Related to Neural Networks

Xing Wang[1,2], Pengfei Zeng[1,2(✉)], Zhaorui Cao[1,2], Guoliang Bu[3], and Yongping Hao[2]

[1] School of Mechanical Engineering, Shenyang Ligong University, Shenyang 110159, China
pfzeng@163.com
[2] Liaoning Province Key Laboratory of Advanced Manufacturing Technology and Equipment, Shenyang Ligong University, Shenyang 110159, China
yphsit@126.com
[3] Xi'an Sirui Copper Alloy Innovation Center Co., Ltd., Xian 710000, China

Abstract. This paper proposes a neural network-based monocular vision ranging method for the situation of large camera calibration and distance variation in monocular vision ranging. The imaging size of the corresponding target under different distances of the same camera is recorded, and the distance variation is recorded according to the change of the imaging size, and a dataset is made accordingly. The ranging network model is established by referring to the neural network and trained on the dataset. The yolov7 target detection network is combined with the ranging network, and real-time ranging is performed according to the real-time target frame output by the target detection network. The monocular vision ranging method in this paper avoids the complex calibration of the camera's internal parameters, has a simple structure, fast operation speed, low cost and easy implementation. The training results of this paper's ranging method show that the average distance error is 0.1m within 20m range, which meets the accuracy requirements and verifies the feasibility and effectiveness of this method by real-time ranging experiment.

Keywords: Monocular · Visual ranging · YOLOv7 · Neural network · Object detection

1 Introductions

Current vision ranging research mainly falls into two categories: binocular vision ranging and monocular vision ranging [1]. Binocular vision ranging uses multi-directional parallax to obtain depth information [2], but it has slow computation speed, high cost, and difficulty in image registration. Monocular vision uses camera intrinsic parameters and geometric relationships to perform ranging, which has the advantages of simple structure, low computation, high timeliness, and high ranging accuracy compared to binocular vision ranging.

At present, domestic and foreign monocular vision ranging research is divided into two categories: data regression modeling methods and geometric position relationship methods. The advantage of data regression modeling methods [3] is that they are not affected by lens distortion and optical path deviation. This method obtains a large number of sample points and establishes a corresponding relationship with the image plane coordinates, and then uses data regression modeling methods to establish a mapping model. However, for different camera systems, a new model needs to be rebuilt.

Geometric position relationship methods use camera intrinsic parameters and camera placement angles, pitch angles and other auxiliary parameters to perform modeling and coordinate transformation, which are more flexible and have less preliminary work and more portability than data regression methods. Literature [4] proposes a longitudinal distance ranging method based on focal length and pinhole imaging principle, which can achieve good results when the target is in the center, but has large errors when the target deviates from the center. Literature [5] uses the target width ratio relationship to perform ranging, which is easily affected by the diversity of target width and the change of target shooting angle, resulting in poor ranging effect.

At present, using deep learning for object detection has achieved good results. Combining object detection using deep learning with object ranging methods can perform ranging in more scenarios [6]. Monocular vision sensors can obtain depth information of objects, have less interference, but usually need to calibrate the camera, which is relatively complex to use [7, 8] Most of the current monocular vision ranging methods use the calibrated parameters of the camera, introduce the area characteristics of the target for calculation, and obtain the ranging expression [9, 10]. Generally speaking, monocular vision ranging cannot be used for situations where objects undergo lateral position changes and lateral position changes followed by their own posture adjustments, as well as scenarios where object distances vary greatly [11].

This paper proposes a neural network ranging algorithm to avoid complex camera internal parameter calibration, which is simple to calculate and easy to implement. Aiming at the problem of large error and error rate in real-time distance variation situations, this paper proposes a visual ranging method that combines object detection network and neural network-based ranging network to achieve real-time distance calculation. This method has the characteristics of simple structure, clear principle, small environmental influence factors, no need for complex internal calibration of the camera, and suitable for large-range distance measurement of medium-range objects.

2   Ranging System

2.1   Principle of Ranging System

The process of taking an image by a camera can be simplified into a form of aperture imaging, which can be used to derive a mathematical expression of the camera model. Imaging principle of pinhole imaging model [12] as shown in Fig. 1.

The coordinate origin o' of the image coordinate system in Fig. 1. The origin of the camera coordinate system is the light center O point. Any point P in space can be represented by the camera coordinate system and the world coordinate system. The distance between the origin of the camera coordinate system and the origin of the image coordinate system can be expressed as the focal length f of the lens. P is the target under test and P' is the imaging point. X' is the imaging size and Xc is the target size. Ideally, the relationship between focal length f and target size and image size, as well as target

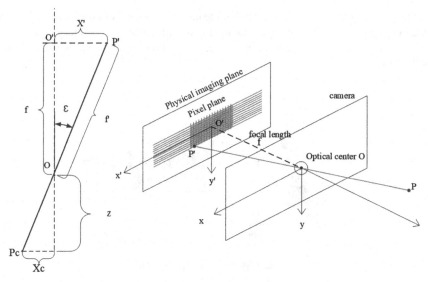

Fig. 1. Small hole imaging model diagram

distance Z, when the target is clearly imaged can be obtained by combining the figure with the triangle similarity principle as shown in Eq. (1):

$$Z = \frac{x_c}{x'} \times f \tag{1}$$

If the target object moves horizontally in the image space and a large posture adjustment occurs during the moving process, the center point coordinates of the target can be obtained by the deep learning target recognition algorithm to get the lateral moving distance of the target in the image space. If X' is the lateral moving distance, o' is the original target location, P' is the current target location, F' is the current location image distance. Formula (2) calculates the yaw angle of the target in image space ε. Formula (3) gives the image distance F of the present position P' in image space. Finally, a trained neural network distance prediction algorithm is used to obtain the target distance of the present location P' in real space. Thus, the distance prediction after the target moves horizontally is achieved.

$$cos\varepsilon = (f^2 + f'^2 - x'^2)/2ff' \tag{2}$$

$$f' = sin(90° - \varepsilon) \times x' \tag{3}$$

2.2 Ranging Procedure

The overall structure is shown in Fig. 2. The real length, width and distance D of the target in the real scene of object space are obtained by camera shooting, then the target recognition frame [13] of the image space recognition image is obtained by deep learning of the target recognition algorithm. Finally, the target distance Z of the object is obtained by the ranging network of the neural network, thus omitting the tedious internal parameter matrix R and external parameter matrix T in camera calibration. The calibration of focal length f [14].

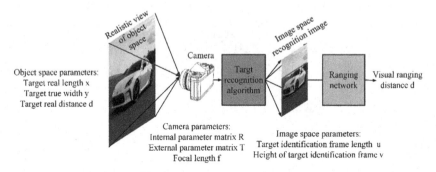

Fig. 2. Overall structure diagram

3 Training Process of Distance Measuring Network Based on Neural Network

3.1 Establishment of Dataset

It is necessary to find some similar relationship between object distance and image size to establish datasets corresponding to object distance, focal length, object size and image size through experiments, but considering that the input data is multidimensional data in the mapping of these two components, it is impossible to fit them with general fitting relationship, so a neural network is used to describe the non-linear relationship between them [15].

Experiments can only determine the position of the clear image, not the corresponding image distance and camera focal length. Because camera calibration is omitted, there is no corresponding camera internal and external parameters, and the object distance cannot be calculated directly using the Gaussian formula. Using a camera range finder, target image sequences are collected at equal distances along a fixed direction, each time moving at a distance of 20 cm, and the corresponding image size and target distance are recorded for each image. Starting at 4m, 86 groups of experiments were performed. The focal length was unchanged. As the object distance increased, the image size of the object in the image space increased. Repeat the above steps. Finally, a dataset corresponding to the object distance, image size and target size is obtained. Ten datasets are shown in Table 1.

Table 1. Ten training datasets

Target Distance/m	Imaging Width/μm	Imaging Height/μm	Imaging Aspect ratio
4.0	120.7708	528	0.305556
6.0	90.578125	363	0.333333333
8.0	65.875	286	0.307692308
9.0	60.38541667	245.6667	0.328358209
10.0	52.15104167	227.3333333	0.306451613
11.0	52.15104167	209	0.333333333
12.0	49.40625	198	0.333333333
13.0	43.91666667	187	0.31372549
14.0	41.171875	168.6666667	0.326086957
15.0	38.42708333	161.3333333	0.318181818

3.2 Training Sample Value of Neural Network

In data fitting, the neural network needs to map from one dataset to another [16]. Pycharm software using Windows11 platform uses Python language and deep learning framework Pytorch to build and write program [17]. The network uses an algorithm to divide 70% of the data into training samples, 15% into validation samples and the remaining 15% into test samples.

The stochastic gradient descent algorithm (SGD [18]) was used as the optimization algorithm to optimize the training process parameters [19]. The training process set the momentum to 0.6, the weight decay to 0.00015, the initial learning rate to 0.001, the learning rate decay to 0.001 per training 10 times, and the total training to 10000 times. The training flowchart is shown in Fig. 3. After network initialization, input training data from the dataset, normalize the data, train the network model with parameters set, test the network model, then normalize the data, and finally do the result analysis error to meet the requirements. If it does not meet the requirements, train again, if it meets the requirements, complete the training.

The model training outputs predicted d by the input image size of long, high and true object distance d, after fitting with multi-layer hidden layer, and optimizes the virtual parameters, such as camera internal parameters R, external parameter matrix T, by optimizing with real D loss and back propagation. The function is fitted by the neural network. Thus, the calibration of ignoring the camera can also complete the ranging task (Fig. 4).

4 Experimental Accuracy Analysis

4.1 Accuracy Analysis of Ranging Network Experiment

In the range of 20 m, 80 groups of distances are selected for experiments, and a series of pictures are obtained by target detection at different distances. Based on the image size of the target on the pictures, the predictions are input into the trained neural network.

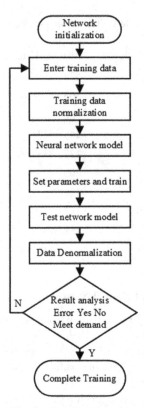

Fig. 3. Training Flowchart

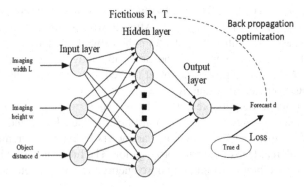

Fig. 4. Model Training Diagram

Finally, the calculated results are compared with the actual object distance to analyze whether the error meets the requirements of ranging accuracy. The test error is 0.1 m as shown in Fig. 5.

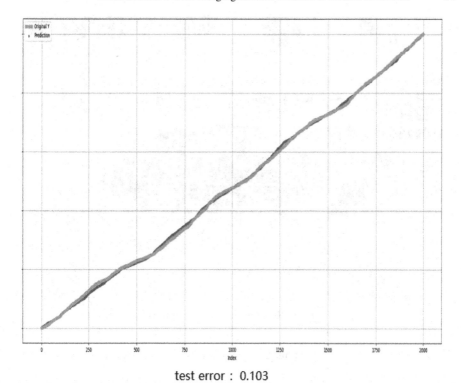

test error : 0.103

Fig. 5. Predict average Error Chart

4.2   Real Time Target Detection and Ranging Experiment

The target detection network uses the YOLOv7 network [20], uses the Pycharm platform and Pytorch library to transfer the target frame size and center point coordinates of the YOLOV7 network output to the visual ranging network, so as to predict the actual distance of the target and display them in the upper left corner of the prediction box.

Figure 6 is an experiment I conducted using a monocular camera, which shows distance measurement under real-time vehicle target detection.

Table 2 lists the predicted results by the neural network and the fitted results by the piecewise function. The piecewise function fits are piecewise according to the proportional relationship between object distance and image size. The multisegment linear relationship is obtained from Table 1. The average error of the fitted results by the multi-segment function is 0.544 m, the relative error is 0.84%, and the data error predicted by the neural network is 0.1m and the relative error is 0.14%. With the increase of object distance, the errors and relative errors do not increase significantly. The system has a good stability at medium and short distance, and is suitable for large changes in object distance. The measurement error mainly lies in the accuracy of target detection network, environmental factors such as illumination of camera acquisition status, and inaccuracy of human operation.

Fig. 6. Real time target ranging map

Table 2. Accuracy test data

Target Distance/m	Neural network prediction			Piecewise function fitting		
	experimental result/m	Error/m	relative error/%	experimental result/m	Error/m	relative error/%
20	20.0998	0.0998	0.498%	19	1	5%
30	29.9686	0.0314	0.104%	26.5637	0.4363	1.454%
40	39.9674	0.0326	0.081%	39.235	0.765	1.912%
50	49.8234	0.1766	0.353%	49.4376	0.5621	1.124%
60	59.8761	0.1239	0.206%	59.5894	0.4106	0.684%
70	70.1354	0.1354	0.193%	69.2698	0.7302	1.043%
80	80.1986	0.1986	0.248%	79.5145	0.4855	0.606%
90	90.1746	0.1746	0.194%	89.6376	0.3624	0.402%
100	100.1846	0.1846	0.184%	99.4518	0.5482	0.548%
110	110.0476	0.0476	0.043%	109.6589	0.3411	0.310%
120	120.0796	0.0796	0.066%	119.5487	0.4513	0.376%
130	130.0562	0.0562	0.043%	129.5412	0.4588	0.352%

(*continued*)

Table 2. (*continued*)

Target Distance/m	Neural network prediction			Piecewise function fitting		
	experimental result/m	Error/m	relative error/%	experimental result/m	Error/m	relative error/%
140	140.0176	0.0176	0.012%	139.8501	0.1499	0.107%
150	149.9976	0.0024	0.001%	149.7303	0.2697	0.179%
160	160.0256	0.0256	0.016%	159.1257	0.8743	0.546%
170	169.5453	0.4547	0.267%	169.013	0.987	0.580%
180	180.1946	0.1946	0.108%	179.5855	0.4145	0.230%
190	190.4579	0.4579	0.240%	189.6791	0.3209	0.168%
200	199.8276	0.1277	0.063%	199.2193	0.7807	0.390%

5 Conclusions

The ranging method described in this paper is a monocular visual ranging based on the relationship between the training distance of the neural network and the imaging size of the target. It does not require complicated camera calibration. Output target imaging size and center store coordinates from the target detection network based on deep learning are transferred to the distance measurement network based on the neural network to output the distance from the camera distance target.

The real-time ranging experiments based on YOLOv7 verify the effectiveness of this method. At the same time, the feasibility of the system is verified. Experiments show that the average distance error is around 0.1 m, and the relative error is less than 0.5%, which meets the accuracy and stability requirements. The ranging system has the features of simple structure, simple principle and little influence by environmental factors. Especially, it has a prominent advantage for measuring stationary objects in a closed environment. By replacing a more accurate camera, a larger ranging range can be achieved, and it can be extended to mechanical manufacturing, coal mining and other industries.

Acknowledgments. Thank you to the anonymous reviewers for their detailed suggestions and the editors for their hard work in this meeting. The research is Partially funded by the Applied Basic Research Program of Liaoning Province (grant no. 2022JH2/101300254) and the Postgraduate Education Reform Project of Liaoning Province (LNYJG2022101). Thank you very much again for the funding from these funds.In addition, the successful completion of this article is inseparable from the guidance and assistance of Professor Zeng Pengfei. Here, I would also like to thank Professor Hao Yongping, brothers Bu Guoliang, and brothers Cao Zhaorui for their guidance and assistance.

References

1. Du, Y., Chen, M.: Research on vehicle distance detection algorithm with single and double camera switching. Control Eng. China **26**(2), 327–335 (2019). https://doi.org/10.14107/j.cnki.kzgc.161359
2. Hu, J., Zhang, F., Li, Z., Huang, H.: Research on indoor 3D measurement algorithm based on binocular technology. Comput. Meas. Control **27**(9), 66–70 (2019). https://doi.org/10.16526/j.cnki.11-4762/tp.2019.09.015
3. Yang, P.: Forward vehicle detection and ranging algorithm based on deep learning. Xi'an University of Electronic Science and Technology, pp. 37–54 (2019). https://doi.org/10.27389/d.cnki.gxadu/2019.002695
4. Yang, W., Wei, L., Gong, J., Zhang, Q.: The research of longitudinal vehicle spacing detection based on monocular vision. Comput. Meas. Control **20**(08), 2039–2041 (2012). https://doi.org/10.16526/j.cnki.11-4762/tp.2012.08.061
5. Ki, P., Sun, H.: Robust range estimation with a monocular camera for vision-based forward collision warning system. Sci. World J. (2014). http://dx.doi.org/10.1155/2014/923632
6. Deng, B., Hao, L.: Survey of target detection based on neural network. J. Phys.: Conf. Ser. **1952**(2) (2021). https://doi.org/10.1088/1742-6596/1952/2/022055
7. Lin, C., Su, F., Wang, H., Gao, J.: A camera calibration method for obstacle distance measurement based on monocular vision. In: 4th International Conference on Communication Systems & Network Technologies, pp. 1148–1151. IEEE Computer Society, India (2014). https://doi.org/10.1109/CSNT.2014.233
8. Chen, X., Zhang, M., Ruan, K., Gong, C., Zhang, Y., Yang, S.: A ranging model based on bp neural network. Intell. Autom. Soft Comput. **22**(2), 325–329 (2015). https://doi.org/10.1080/10798587.2015.1095484
9. Han, Y., Zhang, Z., Dai, M., Gong, C., Zhang, Y., Yang, S.: Monocular vision measurement method for target ranging. Opt. Precis. Eng. **19**(05), 1110–1117 (2011). https://doi.org/10.3788/OPE.20111905.1110
10. Qu, Y., Liu, Z., Jiang, Y., Zhou, D., Wang, Y.: Adaptive variable scale feature point extraction method. Opt. Precis. Eng. **25**(1), 188–197 (2017). https://doi.org/10.3788/OPE.20172501.0188
11. Guo, L., Xu, Y., Li, K., Lian, X.: Research on real-time ranging method based on monocular vision. China J. Image Graph. **1**, 74–81 (2006). https://doi.org/10.3969/j.issn.1006-8961.2006.01.012
12. Kehtarnavaz, N., Oh, H.J.: Development and real-time implementation of a rule-based autofocus algorithm. Real-Time Imaging **9**(3), 197–203 (2015). https://doi.org/10.1016/S1077-2014(03)00037-8
13. Li, Y., Yuan, H., Wang, Y., Xiao, C.: GGT-YOLO: a novel object detection algorithm for drone-based maritime cruising. Drones **6**(11), 335 (2022). https://doi.org/10.3390/drones6110335
14. Jia, S., Peng, W., Qin, Z., Hong, Q.: Overview of camera calibration for computer vision. In: Proceeding of the 11th World Congress on Intelligent Control & Automation, pp. 86–92 IEEE, Shenyang (2015). https://doi.org/10.1109/WCICA.2014.7052692
15. Zhang, Y., Lao, W., Yu, X., Li, J.: Weight and structure determination of forward neural network with two-input power excitation. Comput. Eng. Appl. **48**(15), 102–106+122 (2012). https://doi.org/10.3778/j.issn.1002-8331.2012.15.022
16. Li, Y., Fan, N., Jiang, W., Yang, J., Song, T., Zhao, Q.: Research on intelligent desk area recognition method based on BP neural network. Electr. Meas. Instrum. **54**(3), 25–30 (2017). CNKI:SUN:DCYQ.0.2017-03-005

17. Ketkar, N., Moolayil, J.: Introduction to PyTorch. In: Deep Learning with Python, pp. 27–91. Apress, Berkeley (2021). http://hdl.handle.net/1853/58786
18. Xu, X., Ma, Y., Qian, X.: Scale-aware real-time pedestrian detection in auto-driving scenes. China J. Image Graph. **26**(1), 93–100 (2021)
19. Wu, X.: Research on image labeling algorithm based on convolution neural network. Suzhou University, Suzhou (2019). https://doi.org/10.27351/d.cnki.gszhu.2019.001284
20. Wang, C.Y., Bochkovskiy, A., Liao, H.: YOLOv7: trainable bag-of-freebies sets new state-of-the-art for real-time object detectors. arXiv e-prints (2022). https://doi.org/10.48550/arXiv.2207.02696

PDAN Light: An Improved Attention Network for Action Detection

David Garcia-Retuerta[1(✉)], Besik Dundua[2,3], and Mariam Dedabrishvili[4]

[1] University of Salamanca, Salamanca, Spain
dvid@usal.es
[2] Tbilisi State University, Tbilisi, Georgia
[3] Kutaisi International University, Kutaisi, Georgia
[4] International Black Sea University, Tbilisi, Georgia
mdedabrishvili@ibsu.edu.ge

Abstract. Action detection in densely annotated, untrimmed videos is a challenging and important task, with important implications in practical applications. Not only the right actions must be discovered, but also their start and end times. Recent advances in deep neural networks have pushed forward the action detection capabilities, in particular the I3D network. This paper describes a network with attention, which is based on the I3D features and includes state-of-the-art blocks, namely: MLP-Mixer and Vision Permutator. A light version of the original network is proposed, called *PDAN light*, which has 22.5% fewer parameters than the original PDAN, while improving the accuracy a 1.98% on average; and the MLP-Mixer-based architecture which has 34.5% fewer parameters than the original PDAN, while improving the accuracy a 0.95% on average. All the code is available in https://github.com/dvidgar/PDAN_light.

Keywords: Human Activity Recognition · Multilayer Perceptron · Computer Vision

1 Introduction

Recent advances in human activity recognition (HAR) have enabled a wide range of applications, including the Internet of Things (IoT) [1], healthcare [8] and enhanced manufacturing [5]. Activity recognition is critical to humanity because it records people's behaviors with data that computing systems can use to monitor, analyze, and assist them in their daily lives using input data sources such as sensing devices, including vision sensors and embedded sensors. The improvement of video surveillance or closed-circuit television (CCTV) technology has resulted in improved video quality, easier setup, lower costs, and secure communication. Hence, an increasing number of applications utilizing CCTV systems for security and monitoring purposes have successfully been applied.

The main domains of HAR include surveillance systems, gesture recognition [14], behavior analysis [2], patient monitoring systems [15] and a range of

H. Fujita et al. (Eds.): IEA/AIE 2023, LNAI 13925, pp. 102–114, 2023.
https://doi.org/10.1007/978-3-031-36819-6_9

healthcare systems [16]. As a result, tracking daily activities is required to provide clinicians with up-to-date reports and inform patients with real-time on their progress. For instance, patients with declined mental ability or mental disorders must be continuously monitored in order to detect unusual behavior on time and thus avoid unintended negative consequences.

However, due to the fact that there is no standard procedure for associating the massive volume of collected data with a specific action, HAR is regarded as a difficult research problem. Other challenges of the study area include: feature extraction, class imbalance, data segmentation, computational cost, and privacy. Video action recognition is the first step of video understanding, a critical component of vision-based HAR, and an active research area in recent years.

1.1 Deep Learning

Action detection is an important task in machine learning (ML) that involves recognizing and localizing human actions in videos. It is a challenging problem due to the large variability in human actions, camera viewpoints and lighting conditions. To address this challenge, several traditional ML algorithms have been applied to HAR so far and have demonstrated remarkable performance but under strictly defined learning environments and limited input data.

The mentioned circumstances are related to the requirement of multiple preprocessing steps and heuristic features, which are mostly engineered based on time and frequency domain transformations and statistical measurements. It is noteworthy that these approaches are quite time-consuming and challenging.

Deep learning-based research has demonstrated excellent performance in numerous study domains, including computer vision, object detection and recognition, and natural language processing (NLP). Early studies, such as [6], that investigated the applicability of deep learning in HAR, have inspired researchers to work in this field actively. The main advantage of deep learning over traditional ML algorithms is the minimized effort while picking up the right features by automatically extracting simple to abstract features through several hidden layers. Other preferences include:

- Layer-by-Layer architecture that enables deep models to learn descriptive features from complex and multimodal sensory data and get high accuracy rates using powerful GPUs;
- Neural network structure diversification, which provides flexibility to choose an appropriate model based on the learning environment. For instance, convolutional neural networks (CNNs) are preferred to analyze multimodal sensory data by exploring local connections, while Recurrent neural networks (RNNs) are suitable for streaming sensory data in human activity recognition because they extract temporal connections and incrementally learn information through time intervals.
- Optimization function role in unified network composition, providing that deep neural networks are detachable.

Transfer Learning. Transfer learning is a typical ML approach that allows the classification ability of the learning model to be transferred from the predefined environment to a dynamic setting. Transfer learning is especially useful for resolving problems with distribution discrepancies. It prevents learning model performance from degrading when the distributions of the training and test data differ. This problem emerges in the activity recognition context when activity recognition models are applied to new configurations such as recognition of new activities, involvement of new sensors and users, etc.

The source domain in transfer learning corresponds to domains incorporating vast amounts of annotated data and the main objective is to use the information from the source domain to annotate the samples in the target domain. In activity recognition, the source domain relates to the initial configuration, while the target domain denotes a new deployment that the system has never seen before.

This paper proposes a light version of the PDAN architecture, capable of achieving a better performance while decreasing the number of parameters. It is organized as follows: Sect. 2 describes the most important research works related to the current topic. Section 3 introduces the used data as well as the proposed architectures, and their results. Finally, Sect. 4 draws some conclusions from the research experience.

2   Related Works

The two-Stream Inflated 3D ConvNet (I3D) has become a *de facto* foundation of most modern HAR algorithms. It is based on the inflated Inception-V1 architecture, which is formed by Inception modules as well as convolutions and max-pooling. Several HAR proposals load a pre-trained I3D model, extract the features of the original data and, then, use them as inputs for their customized model [3]. This process is believed to capture spatiotemporal information from the video. [13] makes use of I3D features and their "super-event" to obtain a 36.4% per frame-mAP on the Multi-THUMOS dataset, and [9] make a clever usage of I3D, Bidirectional Gated Recurrent Units (BiGRU) and VS-ST-MPNN to obtain a 23.7% per frame-mAP on the Charades dataset.

Transformers have gained considerable popularity recently, being commonly used in the state-of-the-art proposal for NLP and computer vision. Action Transformers have been proposed by [10] to address the challenges of HAR, outperforming standard models significantly (0.8–10.68% improvement). Their self-attention capabilities are a great leap forward with certain drawbacks, namely: increased complexity and a larger number of parameters.

PDAN [4] is an alternative architecture that includes an attention mechanism for HAR. Its core is the *Dilated Attention Layer (DAL)*, a block capable of processing the information with different dilatations. The original authors propose to apply one convolution, then 5 DAL blocks (dilatation equal to 2^i in the i-th block), and then a convolution. It uses local I3D features as input, thus making indirect use of an Action Transformer trained with the ImageNet dataset and then fine-tuned for the Charades dataset [3]. This iterative process to develop a

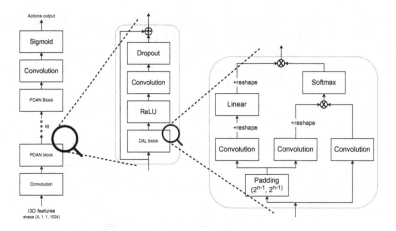

Fig. 1. PDAN deep learning architecture including n DAL blocks.

new model is a current trend in deep learning—instead of developing a model from scratch, re-use parts of previously trained deep models (transfer learning).

A summary of the PDAN architecture can be found in Fig. 1.

PDAN outperforms all other methods for action detection in the Charades dataset challenge, both on the RGB modality and on the RGB+flow modality. Details can be found in Table 1, where PDAN and other architectures [12,13] are compared against a basic classifier trained on top of the extracted I3D features.

Table 1. Accuracy comparison of the different action recognition architectures. They are all based on the extracted I3D features, and compared against a basic classifier trained on top of the segment-level I3D features.

	Modality	Per frame-mAP difference (%)
WSGN (supervised)	RGB	+19.87
Stacked-STGCN	RGB	+22.43
PDAN	**RGB**	**+51.92**
Super event	RGB + Flow	+12.79
3 TGMs	RGB + Flow	+25.00
3 TGMs+Super event	RGB + Flow	+29.65
Dilated-TCN	RGB + Flow	+36.62
MS-TCN	RGB + Flow	+40.69
PDAN	**RGB + Flow**	**+54.06**

Another important deep learning architecture that has gained popularity recently is **MLP-Mixer** [19], or simply Mixer for simplicity. The developers' aim was to propose an alternative to Transformers and convolutions in computer vision, with similar accuracy. Their proposal is based solely on MLPs which are repeatedly applied across the feature channels and the spatial locations. It relies only on matrix multiplications, scalar nonlinearities, reshapes, and transpositions. Figure 2 shows a summary of the architecture.

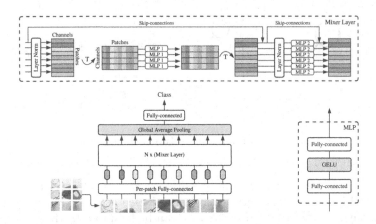

Fig. 2. MLP-Mixer deep learning architecture summary. Extracted from [11].

Let $\mathbf{X} \in \mathbb{R}^{S \times C}$ be a real-valuated two-dimensional table of S non-overlapping patches of the input image, and let C be its *hidden dimension* (non-learnable parameter). The mixer consists of multiple layers of identical size which input is geometrically altered, and each layer consists of two MLP blocks:

- *Token-mixing* layer is applied to the columns of $\mathbf{X}$ and maps $\mathbb{R}^S \to \mathbb{R}^S$.
- *Channel-mixing* layer is applied to the rows of $\mathbf{X}$ and maps $\mathbb{R}^C \to \mathbb{R}^C$.

Omitting layer indices, mixer layers can be described as:

$$
\begin{aligned}
U_{*,i} &= \mathbf{X}_{*,i} + W_2\, \sigma(W_1 \mathrm{LayerNorm}(\mathbf{X})_{*,i}), \quad \text{for } i \in \{1, ..., C\} \\
Y_{j,*} &= \mathbf{X}_{j,*} + W_4\, \sigma(W_3 \mathrm{LayerNorm}(\mathbf{X})_{j,*}), \quad \text{for } j \in \{1, ..., S\}
\end{aligned}
\tag{1}
$$

Two datasets were selected for the experimental phase, and the PDAN architecture is used to set a baseline.

The Charades dataset, introduced by [18], is a densely annotated dataset composed of 9,848 videos of daily indoor activities with an average length of 30 s, involving interactions with 46 objects classes in 15 types of indoor scenes and containing a vocabulary of 30 verbs leading to 157 action classes. Each video is annotated by multiple free-text descriptions, action labels, action intervals, and classes of interacting objects. 267 different users were presented with a sentence, which includes objects and actions from a fixed vocabulary, and they recorded a video acting out the sentence. In total, the dataset contains 66,500 temporal

Fig. 3. Examples of three actions from the Charades dataset: reading a book, opening a refrigerator, drinking from a cup. Extracted from [18].

annotations for 157 action classes, 41,104 labels for 46 object classes, and 27,847 textual descriptions of the videos. In the standard split, there are 7,986 training videos and 1,863 validation videos. Only the actions annotations are used. An example of the dataset videos can be found in Fig. 3.

Another dataset considered is Toyota Smarthome Untrimmed (TSU). It is a dataset for activity detection in long untrimmed videos. It contains 536 videos with an average duration of 21 mins, densely annotated with 51 activities. The dataset poses a unique combination of challenges: high intra-class variation, high-class imbalance, and activities with similar motion and high duration variance. Activities were annotated with both coarse and fine-grained labels.

The dataset has been recorded in an apartment equipped with 7 Kinect v1 cameras. It contains common daily living activities of 18 subjects, with a resolution of 640 × 480. Due to privacy-preserving reasons, the face of the subjects is blurred.

3   Proposed Method: Light Pyramid Dilated Attention Networks with MLP-Mixer and Vision Permutator

It has been found that developing a deep learning network based on I3D features provides state-of-the-art accuracy as well as speed up the training phase [9]. In particular, the combination of I3D features + PDAN obtains the best per frame-mAP accuracy at the moment. As a result, this promising network is the cornerstone of the developed models, which try to adapt it and integrate it with other modern deep learning blocks.

It is necessary to lightweight the PDAN model for several reasons. Firstly, lighter models are easier to deploy on resource-constrained devices such as mobile phones, smart cameras, and embedded systems. This makes it possible to bring action detection to a wider range of applications, including those that require real-time processing or operate in low-power environments. Secondly, lighter models can reduce the cost of computation and storage, making it more practical to scale up the deployment of action detection systems. Finally, by reducing the complexity of the model, it becomes easier to interpret and understand its behavior.

The comparative study of [7] provides a good starting point for discovering state-of-the-art deep learning architectures derived from the classical MLP. In particular, MLP-Mixer and the Vision Permutator were the most interesting for integrating with the PDAN architecture.

The hardware used in this research was a computer with an i7-8700K processor, 16GB RAM memory, and a Nvidia GeForce GTX 1070 GPU.

Note that the available hardware caused limitations in the study as the I3D features could not be extracted as other authors did. The I3D network had to be modified to shrink its GPU memory requirements. Only up to 1,000 frames could be inputted into the network at once, as opposed to the original configuration of up to 16,000 frames. A new baseline with the extracted features was used for the experiments.

The original PDAN architecture was implemented and tested following the authors' indications, and it was also adapted to run with the available computer resources. An evaluation accuracy of **23.1639% per-frame-mAP** was obtained for the Charades dataset, which is set to be the **baseline** of this research work.

Then, it was modified by removing one of the convolutional layers in the DAL block which was found to be redundant and adapting the structure of the new block. Figure 4 shows just the proposed DAL block. The resulting architecture is henceforth called **PDAN light**.

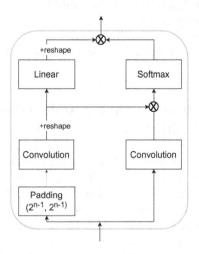

Fig. 4. DAL block in the proposed PDAN light architecture.

The new DAL-light block maintains multiple dilation rates, which inherently makes it learn the attention weights at different temporal scales. The information is processed across the temporal domain to preserve the spatial information. It only contains two learnable 1×1 kernels, resulting in **22.4% fewer parameters** than the original architecture (4547741 and 5858461 parameters respectively).

Let's consider the n-th DAL-light block. Then, the attentional operation (output) $a_n(\cdot)$ of input features vector f_{nt} at time $t \in \{1, ..., T\}$ is:

$$a_n(f_{nt}) = Q_n(f_{nt})[\text{softmax}(Q_n(f_{nt})K_n(f'_{nt}))] \qquad (2)$$

where $f_{nt} \in \mathbb{R}^{1 \times C_2}$ and $f'_{nt} \in \mathbb{R}^{KS \times C_2}$ with KS being the kernel size; $K_n(f'_{nt}) = W_{K_n} f'_{nt}$ and $Q_n(f_{nt}) = W_{Q_n} f_{nt}$ are two independent bottleneck convolutions; and $W_{Q_n}, W_{K_n} \in \mathbb{R}^{C_2 \times C_2} \ \forall n$.

Therefore, the output of the n-th DAL block for the whole video will be:

$$output_n = [a_n(f_{n1}), ..., a_n(f_{nT})] \qquad (3)$$

Note that only the DAL block was modified, the overall structure of the network is unchanged for now. This may act as a regularization mechanism.

In order to further enhance the network, integration of PDAN light was performed with MLP-Mixer and Vision Permutator blocks. In all the cases, the best-performing architecture consisted of having 4 PDAN blocks with dilatations starting in $(i+1)$ and adding the new block as represented in Fig. 5. The network state in the epoch with the higher accuracy is used as the trained network.

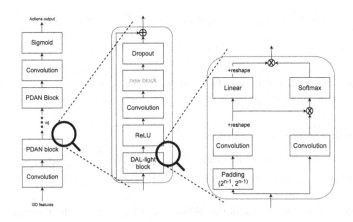

Fig. 5. Integration architecture for new block into PDAN light.

Vision Permutator needed to be specially altered to integrate well and provide good performance. Alterations are described in detail below, and Fig. 6 provides a graphical description.

Let $X \in \mathbb{R}^{H \times W \times C}$ be the block input, with $H \times W \times C$ being the shape of the input. We then apply three independent fully connected layers with weights $W_1, W_2, W_3 \in \mathbb{R}^{C \times C}$. Let X_1, X_2, X_3 be their respective output. Then, a fully connected layer (linear projection) is applied to the addition of all X_i, resulting in:

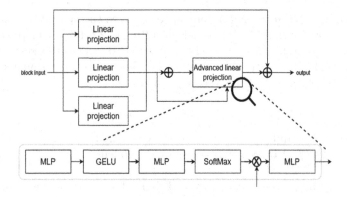

Fig. 6. Proposed weighted vision permutator deep learning block.

$$\hat{X} = \text{proj}(\sum_i X_i) \tag{4}$$

In this case, the projection has a similar structure to the feed-forward layer of Transformers: two fully connected layers with a GELU activation in the middle.

Afterwards, a softmax function is applied, and the components of $\hat{X}$ are multiplied by X_i $\forall i$:

$$Y = \text{softmax}(\hat{X})_x \cdot X_1 + \text{softmax}(\hat{X})_y \cdot X_2 + \text{softmax}(\hat{X})_z \cdot X_3 \tag{5}$$

Lastly:

$$output = X + \text{proj}(Y) \tag{6}$$

The number of training epochs for evaluation is selected using the regularization method *early stopping*.

3.1   Results and Discussion

A summary of the accuracy obtained with the different integrated architectures on the Charades dataset can be found in Table 2.

Table 2. Accuracy comparison of the different architectures on the Charades dataset, with the baseline on in red.

Networks	Parameters (M)	Train size	Test size	Eval. accuracy
PDAN	5.85	7985	1863	23.164
+ MLP-Mixer	4.89	7985	1863	23.664
+ Vision Permutator	10.32	7985	1863	23.965
PDAN light	4.54	7985	1863	23.455
+ MLP-Mixer	3.84	7985	1863	23.595
+ Vision Permutator	9.27	7985	1863	23.617

Let's first consider the Charades dataset. The best-performing architecture, in this case, is the integration of PDAN and Vision permutator, obtaining a **23.965 per-frame mAP**. This represents a **3.34% improvement** compared to the baseline. However, the most balanced architecture is the one including MLP-mixer: it has a reduced number of parameters, which results in fast training; and achieves a 23.595 per-frame mAP accuracy. Results indicate that PDAN light does not adapt well to the modern MLP blocks, as the performance increase is lower than in the integration with the original network. However, the PDAN light architecture has a positive behavior alone, with a 23.455 per-frame mAP, a 22.4% parameter reduction, and a 30.96% decrease in training times.

It is also interesting to analyze the accuracy in each epoch of the different architectures during the training. As it can be seen in Fig. 7, PDAN light behaves very similarly to the original PDAN architectures, despite having significantly fewer parameters. The architecture including Vision Permutator achieves a higher accuracy in the early stages which then decreases fast, an overfitting behavior that is expected due to its high number of parameters. The mixer provides a balanced improvement: it reduces the number of parameters, achieves a higher peak accuracy, and overfits less over time. Lastly, gMLP makes the training slower but more consistent: it starts with lower accuracy than the baseline but then surpasses it and overfits less over time.

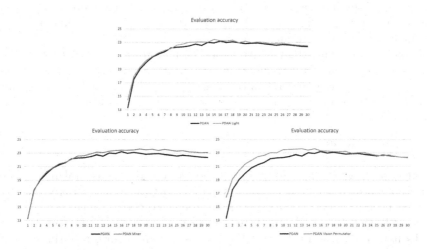

Fig. 7. Evaluation accuracy of the proposed architectures on the Charades dataset. The baseline is always shown in red in all charts. The x-axis shows the epoch number and the y-axis shows the per-frame mAP accuracy. (Color figure online)

Moreover, experiments on the TSU dataset were carried out. Table 3 provides a summary of the accuracy obtained with the different integrated architectures.

In the TSU dataset, PDAN light obtained the best results with a **+2.7% accuracy increase** and a **22.6% reduction of trainable parameters**, compared to the baseline PDAN. This increase accounts for a 32.554 per-frame

Table 3. Accuracy comparison of the different architectures on the TSU dataset, with the baseline on in red.

Networks	Parameters (M)	Train size	Test size	Eval. accuracy
PDAN	5.80	351	185	31.714
+ MLP-Mixer	4.83	351	185	31.929
+ Vision Permutator	10.27	351	185	30.870
PDAN light	4.49	351	185	32.554
+ MLP-Mixer	3.78	351	185	31.715
+ Vision Permutator	9.22	351	185	31.612

mAP. It is also noteworthy that the integration on PDAN light and MLP-Mixer resulted in the greatest reduction in the number of parameters, a -34.8%, while maintaining an accuracy statistically similar to the baseline. The architecture including Vision Permutator performs badly in this dataset, below the baseline; and again PDAN light seems not to integrate well with the modern MLP blocks, as the accuracy of PDAN light alone is the highest.

All in all, results indicate that PDAN light is an improvement of the original architecture regarding both the computational cost and the model performance. Furthermore, the integration of PDAN light and MLP-Mixer provides an outstanding reduction of the computational cost of the architecture while providing a comparatively similar accuracy to the original architecture.

However, combining PDAN with Vision Permutator is not successful. Results seem to indicate that the parameter increase makes the model prone to overfitting, as there is a sharp increase in training accuracy during the first epochs; and also because the good performance does not transfer across different datasets.

4 Conclusions

In this paper, we have explored how to model complex temporal relations in densely annotated video streams. A modified version of the PDAN architecture has been proposed, improving the accuracy and performance, and reducing the overall computational complexity. Moreover, state-of-the-art deep learning blocks have been integrated with the proposed architecture, resulting in even higher accuracy and the capability to better learn the features' representation across time. The method has been evaluated on two densely annotated multi-label datasets: Charades and Toyota Smarthome Untrimmed. The former is a common benchmark for Action Detection in the state of the art, and the latter poses a unique combination of challenges with very long videos. Results indicate that PDAN light outperforms all other state-of-the-art methods.

Acknowledgements. This research has been supported by "Intelligent and sustainable mobility supported by multi-agent systems and edge computing (InEDGE-Mobility): Towards Sustainable Intelligent Mobility: Blockchain-based framework for

IoT Security", Reference: RTI2018-095390-B-C32, financed by the Spanish Ministry of Science, Innovation and Universities, the State Research Agency and the European Regional Development Fund. This research was also partially supported by Shota Rustaveli National Science Foundation of Georgia (SRNSFG) under the grant YS-19-1633. This work is part of the PhD dissertation of David García Retuerta "Deep Learning for Computer Vision in Smart Cities", and can be found under Chapter 4 [17].

References

1. Akbari, A., Wu, J., et al.: Hierarchical signal segmentation and classification for accurate activity recognition. In: 2018 ACM International Joint Conference (2018)
2. Batchuluun, G., Kim, J.H., et al.: Fuzzy system based human behavior recognition by combining behavior prediction and recognition. Expert Syst. Appl. **81**, 108–133 (2017)
3. Carreira, J., Zisserman, A.: Quo vadis, action recognition? A new model and the kinetics dataset. In: proceedings of the IEEE Conference on Computer Vision and Pattern Recognition, pp. 6299–6308 (2017)
4. Dai, R., Das, S., et al.: PDAN: pyramid dilated attention network for action detection. In: CVF Winter Conference on Applications of Computer Vision (2021)
5. Gumaei, A.H., Hassan, M.M., et al.: A hybrid deep learning model for human activity recognition using multimodal body sensing data. IEEE Access **7**, 99152–99160 (2019)
6. Ha, S., Yun, J.M., Choi, S.: Multi-modal convolutional neural networks for activity recognition. In: 2015 IEEE International Conference on Systems, Man, and Cybernetics, pp. 3017–3022 (2015)
7. Liu, R., Li, Y., et al.: Are we ready for a new paradigm shift? A survey on visual deep MLP. Patterns **3**(7), 100520 (2022)
8. Lyu, L., He, X., et al.: Privacy-preserving collaborative deep learning with application to human activity recognition. In: Proceedings of the 2017 ACM on Conference on Information and Knowledge Management (2017)
9. Mavroudi, E., Haro, B.B., Vidal, R.: Representation learning on visual-symbolic graphs for video understanding. In: Vedaldi, A., Bischof, H., Brox, T., Frahm, J.-M. (eds.) ECCV 2020. LNCS, vol. 12374, pp. 71–90. Springer, Cham (2020). https://doi.org/10.1007/978-3-030-58526-6_5
10. Mazzia, V., Angarano, S., et al.: Action transformer: a self-attention model for short-time pose-based human action recognition. Pattern Recognit. 1084–1087 (2021)
11. Moscholidou, I., Pangbourne, K.: A preliminary assessment of regulatory efforts to steer smart mobility in London and Seattle. Transp. Policy **98**, 170–177 (2020)
12. Piergiovanni, A., Ryoo, M.: Temporal gaussian mixture layer for videos. In: International Conference on Machine learning, pp. 5152–5161. PMLR (2019)
13. Piergiovanni, A., Ryoo, M.S.: Learning latent super-events to detect multiple activities in videos. In: Proceedings of the IEEE Conference on Computer Vision and Pattern Recognition, pp. 5304–5313 (2018)
14. Pigou, L., van den Oord, A., et al.: Beyond temporal pooling: recurrence and temporal convolutions for gesture recognition in video. Int. J. Comput. Vision **126**, 430–439 (2016)
15. Prati, A., Shan, C., Wang, K.I.K.: Sensors, vision and networks: from video surveillance to activity recognition and health monitoring. J. Ambient Intell. Smart Environ. **11**, 5–22 (2019)

16. Qi, J., Yang, P., Hanneghan, M., et al.: A hybrid hierarchical framework for gym physical activity recognition and measurement using wearable sensors. IEEE Internet Things J. **6**, 1384–1393 (2019)
17. Retuerta, D.G.: Deep learning for computer vision in smart cities. Ph.D. thesis, Department of Computer Science and Automation, Faculty of Science, the University of Salamanca, Salamanca, Spain (2022)
18. Sigurdsson, G.A., Varol, G., Wang, X., Farhadi, A., Laptev, I., Gupta, A.: Hollywood in homes: crowdsourcing data collection for activity understanding. In: Leibe, B., Matas, J., Sebe, N., Welling, M. (eds.) ECCV 2016. LNCS, vol. 9905, pp. 510–526. Springer, Cham (2016). https://doi.org/10.1007/978-3-319-46448-0_31
19. Tolstikhin, I.O., Houlsby, N., et al.: MLP-mixer: an all-MLP architecture for vision. Adv. Neural. Inf. Process. Syst. **34**, 24261–24272 (2021)

RSHN: Residual Stacked Hourglass Network for Multi-person Pose Estimation

Xing Wu[1,2(✉)], Chengyou Cai[1], and Dong Zhu[3]

[1] School of Computer Engineering and Science, Shanghai University,
Shanghai 200444, China
{xingwu,caicy}@shu.edu.cn

[2] Shanghai Institute for Advanced Communication and Data Science,
Shanghai University, Shanghai 200444, China

[3] School of Wushu (Chinese Martial Arts), Shanghai University of Sport,
Shanghai 200444, China
zhudong@sus.edu.cn

Abstract. Multi-person pose estimation is frequently employed in sports analysis, medical assistance, and virtual reality, which consists of key-point localization and classification. Furthermore, it aims to automatically locate all persons' joints from a single image of visual field. However, multi-object detection and complex interactions between different persons will reduce the accuracy of pose estimation. To meet the challenge, we propose an approach called Residual Stacked Hourglass Network (RSHN). The learning process of the proposed RSHN is divided into two stages. The knowledge extracted by the down-sampling module of the object detector is transferred into the pose estimator. Extensive experiments demonstrate that the proposed RSHN method outperforms state-of-the-art methods, which achieves 91.2 PCKm on the MPII dataset with a competitive computational budget.

Keywords: Pose estimation · Top-down technique · Multi-scale representations · Knowledge transfer · Feature fusion

1 Introduction

Multi-person pose estimation is widely used in various fields, such as sports analysis, medical assistance, and virtual reality. It has recently gained great attention because of the growing need for multiple applications. The goal of multi-person pose estimation is to automatically locate the body joints of all people in a single image. However, the accuracy of pose estimation decreases due to the inherent difficulty of multi-object detection [29,30] and unpredictable interactions between different persons. Therefore, researches about multi-person pose estimation are necessary to meet the need of multiple applications.

Recently, deep learning has significantly advanced researches about multi-person pose estimation. There are two main methods to achieve multi-person

H. Fujita et al. (Eds.): IEA/AIE 2023, LNAI 13925, pp. 115–126, 2023.
https://doi.org/10.1007/978-3-031-36819-6_10

pose estimation: bottom-up methods and top-down methods. Bottom-up methods [3,14,17,20] directly predict all joints and group them into full poses of different persons. Generally, bottom-up methods are more appropriate in multi-person conditions. However, parts of the detection candidates cannot be accurately partitioned into proper person clusters by these methods. Top-down methods [8,12,13,19] interpret the process of detecting joints as a two-stage pipeline: firstly, detect and crop all persons from the image, then estimate the pose of the single person in the cropped image patches. Top-down methods have higher accuracy but lower speed than bottom-up methods. A direct way to improve the performance of top-down methods is to deploy a pre-trained object detection model.

Inspired by the above methods, we propose a novel network architecture termed Residual Stack Hourglass Network (RSHN) to solve the multi-person pose estimation problem. As shown in Fig. 1. It is composed of a multi-person detection module (MPDM), an hourglass residual heatmap generator (HRHG), and a refine inference module (RIM). MPDM aims to extract the single-person patches from the image. HRHG is used to learn the representation of the extracted image patch and generate heat maps of the joints. In RIM, the heat maps are refined in order to infer the final results.

Different from previous works, a feature fusion strategy motivated by transfer learning [15,27,28] is proposed, which divides the optimization process into detection and estimation stages. In the detection stage, the detector employed by our methods is primarily based on Feature Pyramid Network [16] (FPN). A part of the object detector's parameter weights is loaded into HRHG to better initialize the model. In the estimation stage, HRHG is fine-tuned to generate the heat map of joints. Furthermore, several deconvolutional layers are deployed in the backbone network over the last convolution stage to up-sample the feature maps.

Our main contributions can be summarized as follows:

1. The proposed RSHN introduces the transfer learning technique to pose estimation, in which a feature fusion strategy is proposed to reduce the difficulty of parameter optimization.
2. Compared with interpolation methods, the proposed RSHN uses deconvolutional layers to up-sample the feature maps, leading to more delicate representations.
3. The proposed RSHN achieves high performance with fewer computational budgets.

2   Related Works

2.1   Object Detection

Since top-down methods offer superior accuracy, there has been a trend in recent researches to estimate multiple persons' joint positions using a two-stage pipeline. In this case, a human detector, as well as a single-person pose estimator, is essential in order to obtain a satisfactory performance.

The Region-CNN (R-CNN) algorithms [9,10,21] serve as the primary guide for object detection methods. These detection methods consist of two stages in general. First, default anchors are used to construct box proposals. Following that, the box proposals are cropped from the feature map and further refined to obtain the final bounding boxes using the R-CNN network.

2.2 Pose Estimation

Recent methods [2,11,18,24,31] of pose estimation rely on the development of deep learning, falling into two categories: regression-based methods [4,24] and heatmap-based methods [6,7,32]. A cascade of Convolution Neural Network (CNN) pose regressors is first proposed to solve the pose estimation problem in DeepPose [24]. Tompson et al. [23] attempt to solve the problem by generating heat map of joints using a convolutional network and a probabilistic graphical model. Later works [26] show outstanding performance by generating joints' score maps using intense convolutional neural networks.

Generally, the task of pose estimation comprises keypoint localization and classification. Given that semantic information is appropriate for the classification task and spatial information aids the localization task, lots of works has been carried out around a significant problem: how to extract these two kinds of information. Our approach falls into this category.

Current works mainly focus on extracting and aggregating multi-scale features. High-Resolution Network [22,25] (HRNet) keeps spatial information in high-resolution sub-networks and gradually extracts semantic information from low-resolution sub-networks. Hourglass [18] recovers the high resolution through a symmetric up-sampling module. Furthermore, multi-scale features are aggregated by the skip-connections between the same resolution layers of the down-sampling and up-sampling modules. On the contrary, Cascaded Pyramid Network [5] (CPN) deploys a heavy down-sampling module and a light up-sampling module in which a refine network combines the multi-scale features processed through convolutions. Moreover, dilated convolutions are also used to expand the receptive fields of the later layers in a down-sampling network. Bao et al. [1] introduce multi-residual module hourglass sub-networks, in which residual connections are employed to improve performance. However, residual connections are not employed between these sub-networks and other modules.

Inspired by these works, we deploy a sub-network decreasing the resolution of feature maps and a sub-network generating the representations with the exact resolution as its input in the HRHG block of the proposed RSHN model. Moreover, stacked HRHG blocks are followed by a regressor generating the heat maps where the positions of joints are estimated and then transformed to full resolution.

3 Methodology

3.1 Problem Formulation

The overview of proposed RSHN model is illustrated in Fig. 1. The modeling tasks are represented as three components: MPDM, HRHG, and RIM. They are organically linked to improve overall performance.

Given a collection of data maps containing the input image, bounding boxes and joint positions $\{I_{in}^{(m)}, \{B_{gt}^{(n)}, J_{gt}^{(n)}\}^{(m)}\}^{M,N}$ as training data, where M is the size of the dataset, N is the number of bounding boxes in a single image. The goal is to learn an RSHN model that can predict joint positions $\{J_{out}^{(n)}\}^N$ from their corresponding image $\{I_{in}\}$. Therefore, we formulate a new mapping function as follows:

$$J_{out} = RSHN(I_{in}, B_{gt}, J_{gt}) \qquad (1)$$

Specifically, the optimization process is divided into two stages: the detection stage and the estimation stage. In the detection stage, the object detector based on FPN is trained. The intermediate features of overall RSHN are extracted from I_{in} by the object detector. The parameter weights of the object detector's down-sampling module are loaded into HRHG to provide a better initialization. In the estimation stage, the skip-connections between the same-resolution layers of HRHG fuse spatial and semantic information.

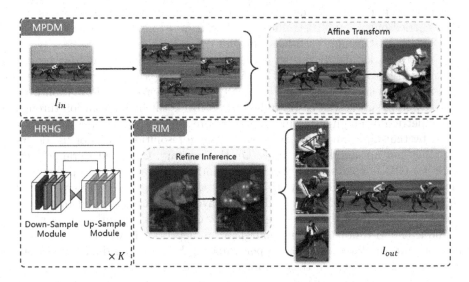

Fig. 1. Overview of the RSHN model architecture.

3.2   Model Architecture

Multi-Person Detection Module (MPDM). An object detector based on FPN is deployed, where ROIAlign from Mask RCNN is adopted to replace the ROIPooling in FPN. After object detection, affine transforms are applied to the bounding areas of the image to obtain sub-images. The overall process of MPDM is formulated as the following:

$$\{B_{out}, I_{sub}\} = Affine(Detector(I_{in}, B_{gt}), I_{in}) \qquad (2)$$

where $\{I_{sub}, B_{out}\}$ is the set of bounding boxes with their corresponding sub-images detected from the input image I_{in}.

Hourglass Residual Heatmap Generator (HRHG). Motivated by the works [18], we propose an effective convolution block termed hourglass residual heat map generator (HRHG) to generate heat maps first and predict joints based on the heat maps. Because of the stacking strategy's effectiveness, several hourglasses consisting of down-sampling and up-sampling modules are stacked to enhance the pose estimation performance. Furthermore, the skip-connections are deployed on not only inter-level layers but also intra-level layers.

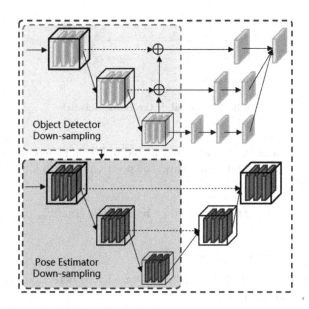

Fig. 2. Transfer knowledge from detector to estimator.

Each HRHG block is provided a better initialization with the parameter weights of the object detector's down-sampling module. The detail of knowledge transfer is depicted in Fig. 2. The process of HRHG is summarized as the following:

$$\{H_{out}\} = Stack(Generator(I_{sub}, Gaussian(J_{gt})), K) \tag{3}$$

where H_{out} is the output heat maps of the stacked generator, K is the number of HRHG blocks.

Refine Inference Module (RIM). In order to keep the integrity of information extracting, we deploy a refine network to explicitly integrates the spatial information and semantic information of the multi-scale representations generated by stacked HRHG through up-sampling and concatenating.

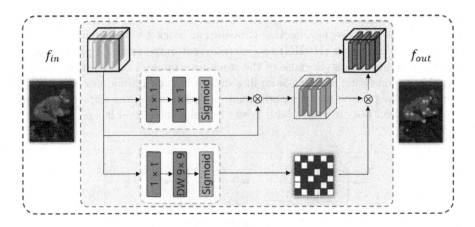

Fig. 3. The detail of the refine network.

The detail of the refine network is depicted in Fig. 3. Based on the heat maps which are generated by a refine network, the positions of each joint are estimated as the following:

$$\{J_{out}\} = InverseAffine(Argmax(Refine(H_{out}))) \tag{4}$$

3.3 Model Training

The training process of RSHN can be separated into detection and estimation stages, as shown in Algorithm 1.

In the detection stage, to train the object detector, all eighty categories from the COCO dataset are used during the training process, but only the boxes of the human category are used for the later pose estimation task.

In the estimation stage, the pre-trained weights of the object detector's down-sampling module are loaded into each HRHG block. The Up-sampling modules of HRHG blocks are randomly initialized. The overall framework is fine-tuned for pose estimation, and the final output is obtained through MPDM, HRHG, and RIM. Since the pixel value in the heat map indicates the keypoint existence probability in that position, the loss function is defined as follows:

$$JointMSELoss = \frac{1}{RC} \sum_{r=1}^{R} \sum_{c=1}^{C} (Gaussian(J_{gt})^{(r,c)} - H_{out}^{(r,c)})^2 \tag{5}$$

where R, C represents the resolutions of the heat map.

Algorithm 1. Training Details

DETECTION

    Input (I_{in}, B_{gt})

    Load the object detector based on FPN

    for i = 0; i<max_epochs **do:**

        Train the object detector

    return (B_{out}, I_{sub})

ESTIMATION

    Input (I_{sub}, J_{gt})

    Calculate the heat maps of $J_{gt} : H_{gt} = Gaussian(J_{gt})$

    Load pre-trained weights of down-sampling module

    Randomly initialize up-sampling moudule

    for i = 0; i<max_epochs **do:**

        Fine-tune the stacked HRHG blocks and RIM with loss calculated by Eq. 5

    return (H_{out}, J_{out})

---

4   Experiments

4.1   Datasets

COCO Dataset. The COCO dataset contains over 200,000 images and 250,000 person instances labeled with 17 joints. Our model is trained on COCO train2017 dataset, which includes 57,000 images and 150,000 person instances. We evaluate our approach on the val2017 set, which contains 5000 images.

MPII Dataset. The MPII dataset consists of images from a wide range of real-world activities with full-body pose annotations. There are around 25,000 images with 40,000 subjects, where there are 28,000 subjects for training and the remaining subjects for the test set.

4.2   Experimental Settings

Implementation Details. All experiments are conducted on two NVIDIA GeForce RTX 3090 GPUs. Pytorch-Lightning is used to develop the overall framework, which we implement. In order to train the RSHN model, we employ the Adam algorithm with a $1e-3$ weight decay for parameter optimization.

The bounding box is cropped from the image and resized to fixed sizes of 256×192 and 25 6×256, respectively, in COCO and MPII. After cropping from images, we apply random flip, random rotation $(-30, 30)$, and random scale $(0.75, 1.25)$.

Evaluation Metrics. Three metrics are used to evaluate the performance of the proposed RSHN model: Object Keypoint Similarity (OKS), Percentage of Correct Keypoints (PCK), and PCKm. The definitions are as follows:

$$OKS_p = \frac{\sum_i \exp\left[\frac{-d_{pi}^2}{2s_p^2 k_i^2} \delta(v_{pi} > 0)\right]}{\sum_i \delta(v_{pi} > 0)} \tag{6a}$$

$$AP@T = \frac{\sum_p OKS_p > T}{\sum_p 1} \tag{6b}$$

where OKS indicates the similarity between the predicted keypoints and the annotation.

$$PCK^{(i)}@T = \frac{\sum_p \delta(\frac{d_{pi}}{d_p^{def}} \leq T)}{\sum_p 1} \tag{7a}$$

$$PCK_m@T = \frac{\sum_p \sum_i \delta(\frac{d_{pi}}{d_p^{def}} \leq T)}{\sum_p \sum_i 1} \tag{7b}$$

where $PCK^{(i)}$ indicates the PCK value of the joint i with threshold T and PCK_m indicates the mean value of $\{PCK^{(i)}\}^N$.

4.3 Comparison Experiments

Results on COCO Dataset. We compare our RSHN model with existing state-of-the-art methods on the COCO2017 dataset. As shown in Table 1, our method achieves favorable results under all the metrics. It achieves 73.1 AP, which outperforms the baseline method (8-stage Hourglass) by 6.2, indicating our model's robustness.

Table 1. Comparison with SOTA Methods on COCO Dataset

Model	AP	AP@0.5	AP@0.75	AR
8-stage Hourglass	66.9	/	/	/
CPN+OHKM	69.4	/	/	/
HRNet-W32	73.4	89.5	80.7	78.9
RSHN (Ours, pretrained)	73.6	91.7	80.9	78.9

Results on MPII Dataset. RSHN is validated on the MPII dataset, a single-person pose estimation benchmark. As shown in Table 2, RSHN outperforms the SOTA performance by 0.7 in PCKm@0.5, which indicates the superiority and generalization ability of our model.

Table 2. Comparison with SOTA Methods on MPII Dataset

Model	Head	Shoulder	Elbow	Wrist	Hip	Knee	Ankle	PCKm@0.5
8-stage Hourglass	97.1	96.1	90.8	86.2	89.9	85.9	83.5	90
FPN	97.4	96.2	91.1	86.9	90.1	86	83.9	90.3
HRNet-W32	97.4	96.2	91	86.9	90.6	86.8	84.5	90.5
RSHN(Ours, pretrained)	97.7	96.2	91.2	87.2	91.4	89.3	86.1	91.2

4.4   Ablation Studies

In this part, we conduct ablation experiments to verify the effectiveness of each component on the COCO dataset and MPII dataset. AP and PCKm is reported for analysis.

Analysis on Pre-training of the Detection Module. As can be seen in Table 3, we provide the results of pre-trained and un-pretrained detection modules on the COCO dataset, which indicate that a pretrained detection module brings a 0.5 improvement in the performance of AP. The results suggest that RSHN with a pretrained detection module is more accurate and efficient.

Table 3. Analysis on Pre-training of the Detection Module

Detection Module	AP	AP@0.5	AP@0.75	AR
Un-pretrained	73.1	89.3	79.8	78.8
Pretrained	73.6	91.7	80.9	78.9

Analysis on Knowledge Transfer of Down-Sampling Module Ablation research is used further to verify the core designs of our RSHN model. As shown in Table 4, we provide the results of transferred RSHN and plain RSHN on the MPII dataset. The first row is the objective results of the RSHN whose HRHG blocks without a loaded down-sampling module from the object detector. The results indicate that an HRHG block with a better initialization brings a progressive performance improvement and a faster convergence, which verifies the effectiveness of knowledge transferred from the object detector.

Table 4. Analysis on Knowledge Transfer of Down-sampling Module

Down-sampling Module of HRHG	Convergence	PCKm@0.5
Random Initialization	110 epochs	90.2
Knowledge Transfer	15 epochs	91.2

Analysis on Skip Connections in RSHN. To prove the effectiveness of more skip connections in RSHN, the output of each HRHG block is added to the final output heat maps, effectively providing a skip connection around the HRHG block. We get a 0.1 improvement in PCKm@0.5 with more skip connections. Since the intermediate results cannot be carried forward independently, RSHN will pass minimal gradients back to the early convolution layers that are furthest from the loss calculation if the output of each HRHG block is directly sent to the next block.

5   Conclusion and Future Works

We investigate a problem known as multi-person estimation and propose a novel approach named Residual Stacked Hourglass Network (RSHN). In order to reduce the difficulty of parameter optimization, transfer learning technique is introduced to achieve knowledge transfer between the object detector and the pose estimator. A multi-scale feature fusion strategy is developped to increase the efficiency of extracting spatial and semantic information. The proposed RSHN achieves 91.2 PCKm on the MPII dataset with a competitive computational budget, indicating our model's superiority. In order to further improve the efficiency of pose estimation tasks. We would focus on the following:

1. Exploring lightweight regression-based models to reduce computational complexity.
2. Exploring knowledge distillation techniques to better reuse the features extracted by the detector.
3. Exploring the self-supervised learning technique to construct a scalable pose estimator.

Acknowledgments. This work is supported by the National Natural Science Foundation of China (Grant No. 62172267), the Natural Science Foundation of Shanghai, China (Grant No. 20ZR1420400), the State Key Program of National Natural Science Foundation of China (Grant No. 61936001), the Shanghai Pujiang Program (Grant No. 21PJ1404200), the Key Research Project of Zhejiang Laboratory (No. 2021PE0AC02).

References

1. Bao, W., Yang, Y., Liang, D., Zhu, M.: Multi-residual module stacked hourglass networks for human pose estimation. J. Beijing Inst. Technol. **29**(1), 10 (2020)
2. Bulat, A., Tzimiropoulos, G.: Human pose estimation via convolutional part heatmap regression. In: Leibe, B., Matas, J., Sebe, N., Welling, M. (eds.) ECCV 2016, Part VII. LNCS, vol. 9911, pp. 717–732. Springer, Cham (2016). https://doi.org/10.1007/978-3-319-46478-7_44
3. Cao, Z., Simon, T., Wei, S.E., Sheikh, Y.: Realtime multi-person 2D pose estimation using part affinity fields. In: Proceedings of the IEEE Conference on Computer Vision and Pattern Recognition, pp. 7291–7299 (2017)

4. Carreira, J., Agrawal, P., Fragkiadaki, K., Malik, J.: Human pose estimation with iterative error feedback. In: Proceedings of the IEEE Conference on Computer Vision and Pattern Recognition, pp. 4733–4742 (2016)
5. Chen, Y., Wang, Z., Peng, Y., Zhang, Z., Yu, G., Sun, J.: Cascaded pyramid network for multi-person pose estimation. In: Proceedings of the IEEE Conference on Computer Vision and Pattern Recognition, pp. 7103–7112 (2018)
6. Chu, X., Ouyang, W., Li, H., Wang, X.: Structured feature learning for pose estimation. In: Proceedings of the IEEE Conference on Computer Vision and Pattern Recognition, pp. 4715–4723 (2016)
7. Chu, X., Yang, W., Ouyang, W., Ma, C., Yuille, A.L., Wang, X.: Multi-context attention for human pose estimation. In: Proceedings of the IEEE Conference on Computer Vision and Pattern Recognition, pp. 1831–1840 (2017)
8. Fang, H.S., Xie, S., Tai, Y.W., Lu, C.: RMPE: regional multi-person pose estimation. In: Proceedings of the IEEE International Conference on Computer Vision, pp. 2334–2343 (2017)
9. Girshick, R.: Fast R-CNN. In: Proceedings of the IEEE International Conference on Computer Vision, pp. 1440–1448 (2015)
10. Girshick, R., Donahue, J., Darrell, T., Malik, J.: Rich feature hierarchies for accurate object detection and semantic segmentation. In: Proceedings of the IEEE Conference on Computer Vision and Pattern Recognition, pp. 580–587 (2014)
11. Gkioxari, G., Toshev, A., Jaitly, N.: Chained predictions using convolutional neural networks. In: Leibe, B., Matas, J., Sebe, N., Welling, M. (eds.) ECCV 2016, Part IV. LNCS, vol. 9908, pp. 728–743. Springer, Cham (2016). https://doi.org/10.1007/978-3-319-46493-0_44
12. He, K., Gkioxari, G., Dollár, P., Girshick, R.: Mask R-CNN. In: Proceedings of the IEEE International Conference on Computer Vision, pp. 2961–2969 (2017)
13. Huang, S., Gong, M., Tao, D.: A coarse-fine network for keypoint localization. In: Proceedings of the IEEE International Conference on Computer Vision, pp. 3028–3037 (2017)
14. Insafutdinov, E., Pishchulin, L., Andres, B., Andriluka, M., Schiele, B.: DeeperCut: a deeper, stronger, and faster multi-person pose estimation model. In: Leibe, B., Matas, J., Sebe, N., Welling, M. (eds.) ECCV 2016, Part VI. LNCS, vol. 9910, pp. 34–50. Springer, Cham (2016). https://doi.org/10.1007/978-3-319-46466-4_3
15. Li, Z., Wu, X., Wang, J., Guo, Y.: Weather-degraded image semantic segmentation with multi-task knowledge distillation. Image Vis. Comput. **127**, 104554 (2022)
16. Lin, T.Y., Dollár, P., Girshick, R., He, K., Hariharan, B., Belongie, S.: Feature pyramid networks for object detection. In: Proceedings of the IEEE Conference on Computer Vision and Pattern Recognition, pp. 2117–2125 (2017)
17. Newell, A., Huang, Z., Deng, J.: Associative embedding: end-to-end learning for joint detection and grouping. Adv. Neural Inf. Process. Syst. **30** (2017)
18. Newell, A., Yang, K., Deng, J.: Stacked hourglass networks for human pose estimation. In: Leibe, B., Matas, J., Sebe, N., Welling, M. (eds.) ECCV 2016, Part VIII. LNCS, vol. 9912, pp. 483–499. Springer, Cham (2016). https://doi.org/10.1007/978-3-319-46484-8_29
19. Papandreou, G., et al.: Towards accurate multi-person pose estimation in the wild. In: Proceedings of the IEEE Conference on Computer Vision and Pattern Recognition, pp. 4903–4911 (2017)
20. Pishchulin, L., et al.: DeepCut: joint subset partition and labeling for multi person pose estimation. In: Proceedings of the IEEE Conference on Computer Vision and Pattern Recognition, pp. 4929–4937 (2016)

21. Ren, S., He, K., Girshick, R., Sun, J.: Faster r-cnn: Towards real-time object detection with region proposal networks. Adv. Neural Inf. Process. Syst. **28** (2015)
22. Sun, K., Xiao, B., Liu, D., Wang, J.: Deep high-resolution representation learning for human pose estimation. In: Proceedings of the IEEE/CVF Conference on Computer Vision and Pattern Recognition, pp. 5693–5703 (2019)
23. Tompson, J.J., Jain, A., LeCun, Y., Bregler, C.: Joint training of a convolutional network and a graphical model for human pose estimation. Adv. Neural Inf. Process. Syst. **27** (2014)
24. Toshev, A., Szegedy, C.: DeepPose: human pose estimation via deep neural networks. In: Proceedings of the IEEE Conference on Computer Vision and Pattern Recognition, pp. 1653–1660 (2014)
25. Wang, J., et al.: Deep high-resolution representation learning for visual recognition. IEEE Trans. Pattern Anal. Mach. Intell. **43**(10), 3349–3364 (2020)
26. Wei, S.E., Ramakrishna, V., Kanade, T., Sheikh, Y.: Convolutional pose machines. In: Proceedings of the IEEE Conference on Computer Vision and Pattern Recognition, pp. 4724–4732 (2016)
27. Wu, X., et al.: FTAP: feature transferring autonomous machine learning pipeline. Inf. Sci. **593**, 385–397 (2022)
28. Wu, X., Jin, Y., Wang, J., Qian, Q., Guo, Y.: MKD: mixup-based knowledge distillation for mandarin end-to-end speech recognition. Algorithms **15**(5), 160 (2022)
29. Wu, X., Qi, Y., Tang, B., Liu, H.: DA-STD: deformable attention-based scene text detection in arbitrary shape. In: 2021 IEEE International Conference on Progress in Informatics and Computing (PIC), pp. 102–106. IEEE (2021)
30. Wu, X., Zhang, Q., Wang, J., Yao, J., Guo, Y.: Multiple detection model fusion framework for printed circuit board defect detection. J. Shanghai Jiaotong Univ. (Sci.) 1–11 (2022)
31. Yang, W., Li, S., Ouyang, W., Li, H., Wang, X.: Learning feature pyramids for human pose estimation. In: proceedings of the IEEE International Conference on Computer Vision, pp. 1281–1290 (2017)
32. Yang, W., Ouyang, W., Li, H., Wang, X.: End-to-end learning of deformable mixture of parts and deep convolutional neural networks for human pose estimation. In: Proceedings of the IEEE Conference on Computer Vision and Pattern Recognition, pp. 3073–3082 (2016)

Clothing Detection and Classification with Fine-Tuned YOLO-Based Models

Hai T. Nguyen[1], Khanh K. Nguyen[2], Pham T.-N.-Diem[1], and Tran T.-Dien[1(✉)]

[1] Can Tho University, Can Tho, Vietnam
{nthai.cit,ptndiem,ttdien}@ctu.edu.vn
[2] FPT University, Can Tho, Vietnam
khanhnk7@fe.edu.vn

Abstract. Clothing helps to enhance the wearer's appearance, so many people pay attention to choosing clothes to suit the events they attend. Nowadays, e-commerce websites are growing strongly, while products are also increasingly diverse and abundant in all areas of life, especially apparel, and clothes with many different types and brands. Therefore, finding appropriate clothes with only an image is challenging. This collected ordinary clothes types in Vietnam, then fine-tuned the model of You Only Look Once (YOLO) version of 5l to provide better accuracy with smaller image size in clothes recognition in the image compared to the original one YOLOv5l with default values of hyper-parameters, and previous YOLO versions. As a result, the method obtains an accuracy of 0.933 in clothes detection on over 10,000 images of 18 clothes types, including popular clothes in Vietnam. The work is expected to provide an image-based useful search for e-commerce systems.

Keywords: e-commerce systems · YOLO · clothes detection

1 Introduction

Nowadays, people are more and more concerned with their self-image. Therefore, clothing is no longer covered and protected but is also a means of communication to reflect people's social position and lifestyle. From how we dress and look, we can judge the personality and habits of the opposite person. Everyone has different personalities and interests. Therefore, today's costumes have become diverse and increasingly rich in meeting people's needs. Fashion brands associated with apparel are also growing. The problem is how to find suitable clothes easily and quickly for users.

Much research on the classification of clothes in images has been presented. The authors in [6] proposed a method to group categories with high visual and semantic similarity and then perform detection to improve the accuracy of costume detection. On the other hand, from the classification of clothes, they oriented fashion and human development as in the study of [1] on the Vintage

© The Author(s), under exclusive license to Springer Nature Switzerland AG 2023
H. Fujita et al. (Eds.): IEA/AIE 2023, LNAI 13925, pp. 127–132, 2023.
https://doi.org/10.1007/978-3-031-36819-6_11

dataset and the text set. The study used ResNet-18 pre-trained ImageNet on DeepFashion and Mask-RCNN to classify clothes, thereby calculating and predicting current and future fashion trends. The result was that 57% of styles performed better when influences were included, with 8% of styles improving over 10%. Warren Jouanneau et al. [3] presented an extensive evaluation of instance segmentation in the context of images containing clothes. They evaluated various levels, quantifying the predicted segmentation masks' contour accuracy and color content. From there, the research shows the performance of the models through the tests. The work in [7] introduced the method Fahsionformer, the object query for segmentation, and the attribute query for attribute prediction. The study was performed on three human fashion datasets and achieved a relative improvement of 10% compared to previous methods in the case of a standard index (APmask IoU + F1). Another study in [5] proposed an attention-driven technique for tackling visual fashion clothes analysis to analyze clothes in images.

Our study collected more than 10,000 images manually bounded boxes with 18 clothes types in the images, then used the YOLO-based models to train and evaluate the model in recognizing and classifying clothes in the image. We leveraged YOLOv5 and [2] created some sets of hyperparameters (namely, Hyp-default, Hyp-med, Hyp-high, Hyp-evolve) that were suitable for the research data set, thereby enhancing the training images through hyperparameter sets. Experimental results on different sets of hyperparameters show some improvements when adjusting the appropriate set. The fine-tuned models are evaluated based on various metrics and compared to baselines YOLOv4 and YOLOv5l using default values of hyper-parameters.

2   Methods

2.1   Data Collection

We collected and extracted 8,400 images from Apparel Classification with Style dataset, including 15 categories of men's and women's clothing (blouses, cloaks, coats, jackets, T-shirts, long dresses, sport shirt, robes, shirts, short dresses, suits, sweater, undergarments, uniform, vest) that can be popular in Vietnam. In addition, the research data set is also supplemented with three types of costumes: traditional Vietnamese custom, ao dai, general pants, and skirts. The Clothes dataset is divided into three parts: The training set (81%) includes 9,000 photos, of which 500 photos are taken for each outfit. The validation set consists of 10%, while the test set (9%) includes 1,000 images (Table 1).

2.2   YOLOv5l and Four Sets of Hyperparameters for Clothing Detection and Classification

YOLOv5 provides a default set of hyperparameters named Hyp-default for model training. In addition, other sets of hyperparameters are adjusted during the training process to fit the research model by using genetic algorithms [8] to develop (evolve) based on a baseline scenario. The study was trained on four

Table 1. Details of Clothes dataset

	Label	Description	#samples
1	ao dai	a type of Vietnamese traditional costume	528
2	blouses	Women's style tops or shirts	925
3	cloak	Sleeveless and open front cape or shawl	570
4	coat	The jacket has the shortest length to the thigh	605
5	jacket	Jacket length from the bottom up	596
6	jersey, T-shirt	T-shirt without buttons and cleavage	793
7	long dress	Knee length dress	599
8	pants	Including: jeans, shorts, khaki, etc.	1499
9	polo shirt, sport shirt	T-shirts with pleats or buttons	607
10	robe	Robe with sleeves and ties at the waist	522
11	shirt	Men's and women's shirts (traditional form)	635
12	short dress	Short dress above the knee	606
13	skirt	Short or long skirt	705
14	suit, suit of clothes	Western clothes	486
15	sweater	Sweaters, hoodies, long-sleeves	638
16	undergarment, upper body	Includes: underwear, swimwear, tank top, sports bra	648
17	uniform	Uniforms: military, students	872
18	vest, waistcoat	Short-sleeve jacket, vest	540

sets of hyperparameters (detailed in Table 2) including **Hyp-default** (default values of hyperparameters of YOLOv5), **Hyp-evolve** (a set of hyperparameters developed using the evolving algorithm based on the Clothes research dataset), **Hyp-med** and **Hyp-high**. **Hyp-med** and **Hyp-high** were developed from the default hyper-parameter trained on COCO dataset [4].

3 Experiments

Research results are evaluated based on accuracy, F1 score, and baseline method. Baseline evaluation is a method that uses a simple model that uses default parameters as a baseline to provide good results for a task and only requires a little expertise and time to build. The distribution of clothing labels in the dataset is relatively balanced. For example, the type of pants has the most significant number with 1,499 photos because it is often combined with a shirt and jacket; the suit class has at least 486 images but is not much different from the rest of the clothes (Table 1).

Table 3 reveals that the two sets of hyperparameters Hyp-high and Hyp-evolve achieve the highest F1 score value of 0.693. In contrast, the Hyp-med hyperparameter set achieved an F1 score of 0.69, and the default hyperparameter set Hyp-default achieved an F1 score of 0.688. The F1 score values do not differ much between sets of hyperparameters. In addition, with an image size of 640, the case of the model using the hyperparameter set Hyp-high achieves the value F1 score of 0.676, which is the highest compared to the remaining three sets of hyperparameters but lower than the other sets of hyperparameters in the case image size of 320. Figure 1 shows that the loss of the training set is quite

Table 2. Four sets of hyperparameters: Hyp-default, Hyp-med, Hyp-high, Hyp-evolve. "*" denotes that we changed from the default value.

	Hyp-default	Hyp-med	Hyp-high	Hyp-evolve
warmup_momentum	0.8	0.8	0.8	0.66975(*)
warmup_bias_lr	0.1	0.1	0.1	0.07364(*)
box	0.05	0.05	0.05	0.05367(*)
cls	0.5	0.3(*)	0.3(*)	0.62242(*)
cls_pw	1	1	1	0.88053(*)
obj	1	0.7(*)	0.7(*)	0.8555(*)
obj_pw	1	1	1	0.94731(*)
anchor_t	4	4	4	3.52487(*)
hsv_h	0.015	0.015	0.015	0.01897(*)
hsv_s	0.7	0.7	0.7	0.58962(*)
hsv_v	0.4	0.4	0.4	0.30388(*)
translate	0.1	0.1	0.1	0.06608(*)
scale	0.5	0.9(*)	0.9(*)	0.53412(*)
mixup	0	0.1(*)	0.1(*)	0
copy_paste	0	0	0.1(*)	0
anchors				2.0(*)
lr0	0.01	0.01	0.01	0.00882(*)
lrf	0.1	0.1	0.2(*)	0.10651(*)
momentum	0.937	0.937	0.937	0.87346(*)
weight_decay	0.0005	0.0005	0.0005	0.00047(*)
warmup_epochs	3	3	3	2,37216(*)

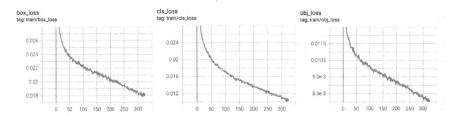

Fig. 1. Various Loss (bounding box, classification, and object detection) in the training set.

good, decreasing steadily over time. On the other hand, the loss value of the validation set was not very good (Fig. 2). It increased from about epoch = 100, so the model stopped at epoch = 300, earlier than the initial epoch value of 500, with the early stopping technique based on evaluating the loss value on the validation set. This technique helps to prevent the model from overfitting. Finally, the model runs experimentally on the test set with a confidence level

Table 3. Experimental results on validation set with various hyper-parameters

	Hyp-default		Hyp-med		Hyp-high		Hyp-evolve	
Image size	320	640	320	640	320	640	320	640
Precision	0.7155	0.7081	0.7353	0.7123	0.7505	0.7411	0.7461	0.6986
Recall	0.6622	0.6193	0.6549	0.6386	0.6385	0.6207	0.6477	0.6267
mAP@0.5	0.6996	0.6684	0.7162	0.6972	0.7228	0.6935	0.6993	0.6570
mAP@0.5:0.95	0.6268	0.5886	0.6391	0.6212	0.6423	0.6243	0.6259	0.5841
F1 score	0.6880	0.6610	0.6930	0.6730	0.6900	0.6760	0.6930	0.6610

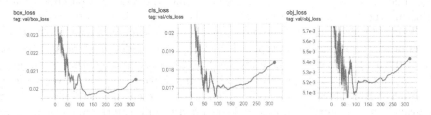

Fig. 2. Various Loss (bounding box, classification, and object detection) in the validation set.

Fig. 3. Some clothes recognition results from the proposed workflow: (a) one type of clothes, (b) two clothes with the same type, (c) three different types.

Table 4. Experimental results on the test set

	Hyp-default		Hyp-med		Hyp-high		Hyp-evolve	
Image size	320	640	320	640	320	640	320	640
Accuracy on objection detection	0.837	0.757	0.888	0.764	0.933	0.799	0.846	0.753
Accuracy classification	0.772	0.633	0.612	0.647	0.687	0.733	0.703	0.522

of 0.25. Figure 3 illustrates the clothes recognition results on images containing one clothes type, two clothes types, and three different clothes. The last one contains three types of coats, sweaters, and pants. Table 4 shows that the Hyp-high model achieves the highest recognition accuracy of 93.3%; The Hyp-default hyperparameter set with the image size of 320 achieved the highest classification accuracy of 77.2%. On the other hand, in these two cases, the hyper-high with

image size has a higher F1 score than the other cases, but the classification accuracy is still relatively low at 68.7%.

4   Conclusion

This study collected a Clothes dataset and trained it based on the YOLOv5l model to recognize and classify the clothes in the image. Through tuning the sets of hyperparameters, we achieve an accuracy of 75.7% for identification and 63.3% for classification on the default set of hyperparameters, a recognition accuracy of 84.6%, and a classification accuracy of 70.3% on the evolve hyperparameter setting. The model also achieved better results than the YOLOv4 baseline without adjusting the hyperparameters. However, the model still needs to recognize the small-size clothes. The classification also confuses some costumes with similar colors or shapes but different types. The model results identified most of the costumes (93.3%). However, some costumes are tiny, obscured by other costumes or objects, and still need to be well recognized. In addition, there are several similar costumes, with only slight differences, leading to the classification needing more accurate (68.7%). Further work can be studied to improve the model's accuracy to be applied in practice on e-commerce sites.

References

1. Hsiao, W.L., Grauman, K.: From culture to clothing: discovering the world events behind a century of fashion images (2021). https://doi.org/10.48550/ARXIV.2102.01690
2. Jocher, G.E.A.: Ultralytics/yolov5: v7.0 - yolov5 sota realtime instance segmentation (2022). https://doi.org/10.5281/ZENODO.3908559, https://zenodo.org/record/3908559
3. Jouanneau, W., Bugeau, A., Palyart, M., Papadakis, N., Vezard, L.: Where are my clothes? a multi-level approach for evaluating deep instance segmentation architectures on fashion images. In: 2021 IEEE/CVF Conference on Computer Vision and Pattern Recognition Workshops (CVPRW). IEEE (2021). https://doi.org/10.1109/cvprw53098.2021.00443
4. Lin, T., et al.: Microsoft COCO: common objects in context. CoRR abs/1405.0312 (2014). abs/1405.0312
5. Shajini, M., Ramanan, A.: An improved landmark-driven and spatial–channel attentive convolutional neural network for fashion clothes classification. Vis. Comput. **37**(6), 1517–1526 (2020). https://doi.org/10.1007/s00371-020-01885-7
6. Tian, Q., Chanda, S., Kumar, K.C.A., Gray, D.: Improving apparel detection with category grouping and multi-grained branches (2021). https://doi.org/10.48550/ARXIV.2101.06770
7. Xu, S., Li, X., Wang, J., Cheng, G., Tong, Y., Tao, D.: Fashionformer: A simple, effective and unified baseline for human fashion segmentation and recognition. In: Avidan, S., Brostow, G., Cissé, M., Farinella, G.M., Hassner, T. (eds.) ECCV 2022. LNCS, vol. 13697, pp. 545–563. Springer, Cham (2022). https://doi.org/10.1007/978-3-031-19836-6_31
8. Yang, X.S.: Nature-inspired optimization algorithms: challenges and open problems. J. Comput. Sci. **46**, 101104 (2020). https://doi.org/10.1016/j.jocs.2020.101104

A Novel Parallel Spatiotemporal Image Fusion Method for Predicting High-Resolution Satellite Images

Vipul Chhabra[1]([✉]), Uday Kiran Rage[2], Abinash Maharana[1], Juan Xiao[3], Krishna Reddy Polepalli[1], Ram Avtar[3], Yoshiko Ogawa[2], and Makiko Ohtake[2]

[1] IIIT-Hyderabad, Hyderabad, Telangana, India
{vipul.chhabra,abinash.maharana}@research.iiit.ac.in, pkreddy@iiit.ac.in
[2] The University of AIZU, Fukushima, Japan
{udayrage,yoshiko,makiko-o}@u-aizu.ac.jp
[3] Hokkaido University, Sapporo, Japan
xiao@eis.hokudai.ac.jp, ram@ees.hokudai.ac.jp

Abstract. High-resolution spatiotemporal image fusion is an important geo-analytical technique with many applications. It involves two steps: (i) understanding the spatial correlation between the high and low-resolution pixels of an area at a particular time across multiple bands and (ii) generating a high-resolution image for the same area from the low-resolution image taken at a later time. HISTIF is the state-of-the-art single CPU-based sequential algorithm to perform image fusion. Unfortunately, due to its sequential nature, this algorithm suffers from scalability while dealing with big imagery data. This paper exploits multi-core architecture and proposes an efficient parallel algorithm, Parallel HISTIF (PHISTIF), to perform image fusion. PHISTIF involves the following four steps: (i) assigning bands to CPU cores using a novel load-balancing technique, (ii) performing cross-scale matching for each band in a CPU core, (iii) executing modulation of changes at the pixel level, and (iv) merging the predicted bands of each core into one final image. The experimental results on the real-world satellite imagery datasets demonstrate that the proposed algorithm is runtime efficient and highly scalable.

Keywords: Satellite images · Monitoring · Image fusion

1 Introduction

Satellite imagery data plays a vital role in understanding, planning and monitoring landscapes at scale. This data contains both spatial and temporal information about the objects, which helps to monitor vegetation seasonality, estimation of crop yields, crop planning etc. The spatial resolution of a satellite defines the surface area of the earth covered by a pixel in an image, and the temporal resolution of a satellite defines the interval between the two subsequent revisits of a satellite over the same area. Due to the tradeoff between the scanning swath and

H. Fujita et al. (Eds.): IEA/AIE 2023, LNAI 13925, pp. 133–144, 2023.
https://doi.org/10.1007/978-3-031-36819-6_12

pixel size, the currently available satellites can be classified into two broad categories based on the resolution of the data they capture (i) high temporal but low spatial resolution and (ii) low temporal but high spatial resolution satellites. For example, MODIS [7] and SeaWiFS [13] capture the data daily, but their spatial resolution is low, ranging from 250 m to 1000 m, while the Sentil-2 [13] has a longer revisit frequency (approximately 10 days) but very high spatial resolution varying from 10 m to 60 m.

With increased automation demands in agriculture, intelligent systems require frequent high-resolution images to gain better insights and create an efficient plan. However, high-resolution images are not abundantly available because of satellites' high operational cost and low revisit frequency [8]. Moreover, abundantly available low spatial resolution images may not be efficient for building intelligent systems. When confronted with this problem in real-world applications, researchers introduced a **high-resolution spatiotemporal image fusion approach** that provides a feasible alternative for generating high-resolution images by blending the information of the course-resolution image, which is widely available. This approach captures the changes in pixel values of coarse images over time and models similar changes over the high-resolution image taken at a particular time to predict high-resolution for a later time.

Example 1. Figure 1(a) displays a low-resolution image of a location captured by a satellite at a specific timestamp, labelled as t_0. Figure 1(b) shows a higher-resolution image of the same location taken by another satellite at nearly the same timestamp, t_0. The high-resolution spatiotemporal image fusion technique involves understanding the correlation between the pixels in both figures and then using this information to predict a higher-resolution image from the low-resolution image taken at a different timestamp, t_1 shown in Fig. 1(c). Intelligent systems utilize this generated image for various decision-making processes, such as fertilizer application and harvesting.

(a) Coarse Image at t0   (b) Fine Image at t0   (c) Coarse Image at t1   (d) Fine Image at t1

Fig. 1. Illustration of high-resolution spatiotemporal image fusion technique

Super-resolution is the process of improving the spatial resolution of an image by generating a higher-resolution image from a lower-resolution one. Several models [1,12] have been discussed in the literature to perform super-resolution.

Please note that these models cannot be directly applied for handling spatiotemporal satellite data as they fail to capture the temporal information of the image. In this context, the supportive move has been made in this paper to improve spatiotemporal image fusion techniques as they capture both spatial and temporal information of the images.

Multiple spatiotemporal image fusion methods have already been described in the literature, such as high resolution spatiotemporal image fusion (HISTIF) [6], IHISTIF [4], STARFM [5], and ESTARFM [14]. The fusion techniques vary from the fusion level depending upon the use case and the extent of changes. Most of the existing techniques focus both on land cover and phenological changes. However, some existing image fusion methods are used explicitly to capture the land's phenological changes, such as the spatial and temporal adaptive reflectance model (STARFM) [5], and Enhanced STARFM (ESTARFM) [14]. These algorithms depend entirely on classification accuracy and are adversely affected by misclassification errors. Also, these algorithms did not consider the cross-scale spatial mismatch due to geo-registration errors and point spread function (PSF). The HISTIF algorithm was proposed to predict phenological changes and account for the geo-registration errors [13]. Unfortunately, HISTIF being a sequential single cpu algorithm, suffers from scalability problems while handling very large imagery datasets.

With this motivation, this paper exploits the multi-core architecture and proposes a novel multi-core parallel algorithm, Parallel HISTIF (PHISTIF). PHISTIF performs the following four steps: (i) introducing a novel load-balancing technique and using it to assign bands to CPU cores, (ii) performing cross-scale matching for each band in a CPU core, (iii) executing modulation of changes at the pixel level, and (iv) merging the predicted bands of each core into one final image. The experimental results on four real-world datasets demonstrate that the proposed algorithm is runtime efficient and scalable.

The remaining study is organized as follows. In Sect. 2, we discuss the literature on spatiotemporal image fusion. Further, in Sect. 3, we describe PHISTIF. Section 4 describes the experimentation and parameters considered for evaluating the model and presents the experimental results. Finally, in Sect. 5, we conclude this study along with future research directions.

2   Related Work

Gao et al. [5] first introduced the STARFM model to perform the spatiotemporal image fusion model. Since then, several models have been described in the literature to perform spatiotemporal image fusion [3]. These models can be broadly classified into three broad categories depending upon the level of operation [11]: (i) the pixel level [6], (ii) feature level [2], and (iii) decision level [9]. Pixel-level fusion combines individual pixels from multiple images to create a new image, while feature-level fusion combines specific features, such as land-cover classes, from multiple images. Decision-level fusion combines the decision or information obtained from multiple images, such as classification results. Each fusion method has its own advantages and disadvantages. As a result, no universally accepted best method exists to perform image fusion for any given dataset. In other words, selecting the suitable fusion method is subjective, depending on the user/application requirements.

Recently, a pixel-based model, HISTIF, has been widely utilized in image fusion tasks as it effectively addresses the problem of fusion errors raised due to cross-scale spatial mismatch. However, HISTIF failed to address one of the critical issues of computational efficiency for processing large datasets at scale.

An improved HISTIF algorithm known as *IHISTIF* has been developed by some of the authors of this paper recently. This algorithm also suffers from scalability issues to its sequential nature. Since IHISTIF is an increment improvement of HISTIF, the techniques suggested in this paper can be extended to the IHISTIF algorithm. Henceforth, this paper focuses on addressing the fundamental problem encountered by the HISTIF algorithm.

3   HISTIF Model and Algorithm

The model of HISITF is shown in Fig. 2 and contains the following three steps: (*i*) Preprocessing, (*ii*) Filtering for Cross-Scale Spatial Mismatch (FCSM) and (*iii*) Modulation of Temporal Changes (MTC). We now briefly explain each of these steps. Please refer to [6] for more details on HISTIF.

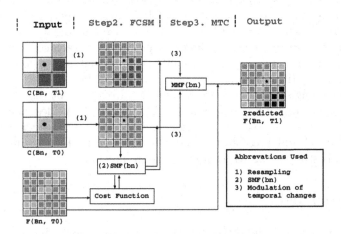

Fig. 2. Illustration of the overall workflow

3.1   Preprocessing

The model takes as input one image pair taken at reference time t_0 and one coarse resolution image taken at time t_1 to predict the high-resolution image at time t_1. Before using the model, it is important to ensure that all input images have been calibrated to surface reflectance and have been reprojected to the same coordinate system. To maintain the spectral integrity of the original images, nearest neighbour interpolation can be used to resample the coarse images to a higher resolution. After the initial processing of the data, let $C(b_n, t_0)$, $F(b_n, t_0)$, $C(b_n, t_1)$ be the coarse image at time t_0, fine image at time t_0, coarse image at time t_1 and b_n signifies, the nth band of the image.

3.2 Filtering for Cross-Scale Spatial Mismatch (FCSM)

Traditional filtering methods assume regular changes within classes from t_0 to t_1 and are prone to classification accuracy errors and geo-registration errors. To overcome these limitations and account for the effect of the sensor's point spread function (PSF), we use FCSM. The PSF of a sensor can consist of multiple components, but we focus on the two critical components: the optical and detector PSF. These can be modelled using a 2-D Gaussian function as described in [10].

$$PSF(x,y) = \frac{G(x) \cdot G(y)}{\sum G(x) \cdot G(y)} \tag{1}$$

where the Gaussian functions used are

$$G(x) = e^{\frac{-X^2}{2\sigma_x^2}} \ and \ G(y) = e^{\frac{-Y^2}{2\sigma_y^2}} \tag{2}$$

To account for the difference in the observation angle by the sensors, the filter can be built by multiplying the PSF by the rotation matrix as follows

$$SMF(FWHM_x, FWHM_y, \theta) = PSF \cdot \begin{bmatrix} \cos\theta & \sin\theta & 0 \\ -\sin\theta & \cos\theta & 0 \\ 0 & 0 & 1 \end{bmatrix} \tag{3}$$

To reduce the geo-registration error, the SMF is convolved with the coarse image as follows

$$\hat{C}_{SMF}(b_n, t_0) = C(b_n, t_0) \otimes SMF(b_n) \tag{4}$$

The convolved image may be shifted in the East-West and North-South dimensions, resulting in the removal of blocky artifacts in $C(b_n, t_0)$ and reducing the cross-scale spatial mismatch between the image pairs. To automate the error optimization process and remove the blocky artifacts, the root mean square error (RMSE) is used as the cost function and considers the size, rotation, and shift as the three sets of parameters determining the SMF.

$$RMSE = \sqrt{\frac{\sum (\hat{C}_{SMF}(b_n, t_0) - F(b_n, t_0))^2}{N}} \tag{5}$$

Particle swarm optimization (PSO) is used to optimize the parameters of an equation to remove blocky artifacts and reduce the cross-scale spatial mismatch between image pairs. In cases where the PSF effect and geometry are constant, the same SMF can be used to obtain a filtered image at time t_1 using an image pair at time t_0.

$$\hat{C}_{SMF}(b_n, t_1) = C(b_n, t_1) \otimes SMF(b_n) \tag{6}$$

where $\hat{C}_{SMF}(b_n, t_1)$ is the filtered coarse image in band n at time t_1.

3.3   Modulation of Temporal Changes (MTC)

To account for changes at the sub-field level over time, changes are measured at the pixel level instead of by class. The changes in the coarse image from t_0 to t_1 can be represented using

$$MMF(b_n) = \frac{\hat{C}_{SMF}(b_n, t_1)}{\hat{C}_{SMF}(b_n, t_0)} \tag{7}$$

The high-resolution image at t_1 can be predicted from the low-resolution image at t_1 as follows

$$F(b_n, t_1) = MMF(b_n) \times F(b_n, t_0) \tag{8}$$

$$F(b_n, t_1) = \frac{\hat{C}(b_n, t_1)}{\hat{C}(b_n, t_0)} \times F(b_n, t_0) \tag{9}$$

3.4   HISTIF Algorithm

Jiang et al. [6] described a single CPU-based sequential algorithm to perform spatiotemporal image fusion. Unfortunately, this algorithm suffers from scalability while dealing with large datasets. We tackle this problem by proposing a multi-core parallel algorithm, PHISTIF, to perform spatiotemporal image fusion. Our algorithm is introduced in the next section.

4   Proposed Algorithm

In this section, we first describe the basic idea of PHISTIF algorithm. Next, we present our novel load-balancing technique. Finally, we present the PHISTIF algorithm.

4.1   Basic Idea

The proposed algorithm initiates a pool of child processes in order to distribute the processing of bands across different cores. The working of the proposed algorithm is shown in Fig. 3 and described in the following four steps:

1. The input satellite images are split into multiple component bands
2. Assign each band from the input images to a process from the pool. The assignment of each band to the process is crucial for achieving proper load balance because the improper assignment of the band can significantly decrease the overall performance.

3. Each process will pass the assigned band to the first FCSM and then the MTC step to predict the band of the high-resolution satellite image.
   – In the FCSM step, the coarse image gets precisely aligned with the fine image, reducing the geo-registration error. For the band obtained at t_0, the PSF is calculated and multiplied with the rotation matrix to align the coarse image with the same band in the fine image at t_0. The cost function used for optimizing the parameters is RSME which optimizes with the same band of the fine image making the estimation of the parameters independent of other bands in the image.
   – In the step of MTC, multiplicative factors for each pixel are calculated by comparing the same band across the coarse image at t_0 and t_1 and further multiplied with the same band in the fine image at t_0, making it also independent of other bands in the image.
   – Since the processes are independent of other bands in the image, it allows us to process each band separately and accelerate the overall process, exploiting multi-core architecture.
4. Predicted band obtained from the child processes are merged to form a single by the parent process

Since step 3 of our algorithm is computationally more expensive than the other steps in the algorithm, it becomes essential to perform appropriate load balancing. To reduce the computational cost efficiently, we describe a novel load-balancing technique in the next section.

4.2   An Efficient Load Balancing Technique

The methodology for assigning bands to the child processes is essential to achieve the appropriate load balance across the available cores. To achieve an equal load on the available cores, we employ the following process.

1. Create a pool of child processes based on the number of available cores in the system. Let N denote the number of cores, and B denote the number of bands in the image.
2. Let $P = \{p_1, p_2, ..., p_x\}$, $x \geq 1$ and $x \leq N$, denotes the pool of child processes available for processing the input bands and predicting the bands in parallel. Assign each band b_m to child process p_k where $p_k \in P$ in a round-robin fashion using the following formula

$$k = (m\%|P|) + 1 \tag{10}$$

   where m is the band number and $|P|$ denotes the number of child processes
3. The round-robin approach of assigning bands to the child processes shows better workload balance across multiple cores rather than the naive approach of randomly assigning the bands to child processes.

The parallel implementation of the overall process can be summarized using Fig. 3 and Algorithm 1.

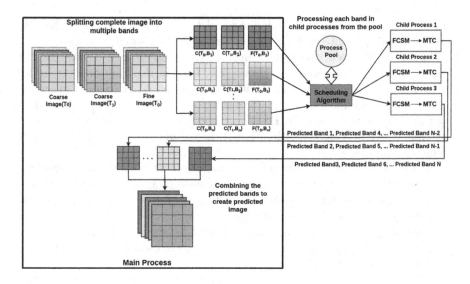

Fig. 3. Illustration of the parallel algorithm

Algorithm 1: Parallel Algorithm

Input: Low resolution satellite image at time t_0 and t_1 and High resolution satellite image at time t_0

Output: Predicted High resolution satellite image at t_1

1 Split the input images into different bands

2 **for** *each band assigned to a child process by scheduling algorithm* **do**

3   **for** *Filtering for cross-scale spatial mismatch (FCMS)* **do**

4   , initialization of 2-D Gaussian with random values

5   Multiplication with the Rotation Matrix

6   PSO for optimization of RMSE and identification of correct parameters

7

8   **for** *Modulation of temporal changes (MTC)* **do**

9   Calculate MMF

10   Multiply MMF with the same band of fine image

11

12 Combine and Merge predictions of each band in a single image

13 **return** *Predicted high-resolution image at time t_1*

4.3 Theoretical Analysis of Acceleration

The parallel version of HISTIF overcomes the computational bottleneck of the sequential algorithm by distributing the workload across multiple processors, resulting in faster computation of each band's fusion. Load-balancing techniques are employed to distribute the workload evenly among processors, minimizing idle time and maximizing throughput.

The acceleration ratio is essential to determine the potential speedup that can be achieved by the algorithm on multiple processors. The acceleration ratio is calculated by dividing the execution time of the sequential algorithm by the execution time of the parallel algorithm.

$$acceleration\text{-}ratio = time(HISTIF)/time(PHISTIF) \tag{11}$$

$$acceleration\text{-}ratio = n * time(b_n)/(\lceil n/p \rceil) * time(b_n) \tag{12}$$

where $time(b_n)$ represents the time required to process n-th band of the satellite image, n is number of bands in the image and p is number of available processors.

To calculate the exact acceleration-ratio obtained, we consider 3 cases

1. if $p \geq n$, each band is assigned to each processor separately, and the acceleration obtained would be n times.
2. if $p < n$ and $n\%p == 0$, each band would be assigned to the available processors in the round-robin fashion by the scheduling algorithm, and the acceleration obtained would be p times.
3. if $p < n$ and $n\%p! = 0$, each processor cannot accommodate the equal number of bands and would result in extra processing time for some processors, and the acceleration obtained would be $(n * p)/(n + (p - (n\%p)))$ times.

5   Experimentation and Results

In this section, we evaluate the performance of HISTIF and the proposed PHIS-TIF algorithms across four real-world datasets and show that PHISTIF algorithm is efficient over varied image sizes and scale factors. The scale factor is a parameter used to define the range of parameters that need to be identified in the FCSM step. The larger the scale factor's value, the larger the search space for the optimization algorithm and vice versa. We also demonstrate the efficiency of the scheduling algorithm by varying the number of cores used. (Please note that we are not comparing the PHISTIF against super-resolution methods [1,12] as they ignore the temporal information of the images.).

In the context of evaluating band-wise predictions against ground truth, **Correlation Coefficient** (CC), **Root Mean Square Error** ($RMSE$), and **Mean Absolute Difference** (MAD) are used as performance metrics. Notably, parallelization of the algorithm did not affect values of performance metrics, as each band was processed identically to the single CPU-based sequential approach.

The algorithms HISTIF and PHISTIF were written in Python3.9. The experiments were conducted on a Gigabyte R282-Z94 2U rack server containing 2 NUMA nodes, 64 physical cores, 128 virtual cores, and 400 GB RAM. Experiments were performed on four datasets (**D1, D2, D3 and D4**), each containing four bands. In each of these datasets, fine and coarse images were obtained from **Planet** and **Landsat** Websites, respectively. The spatial resolution of the fine and coarse images are **3 m** and **30 m**, respectively.

The dimensions of images in the D1 and D3 datasets are 31×31 (before resampling) and 280×280 pixels for coarse and fine images, respectively. The dimensions for the D2 and D4 datasets are 110×110 (before resampling) and 1080×1080 pixels for coarse and fine images, respectively. For D1 and D3

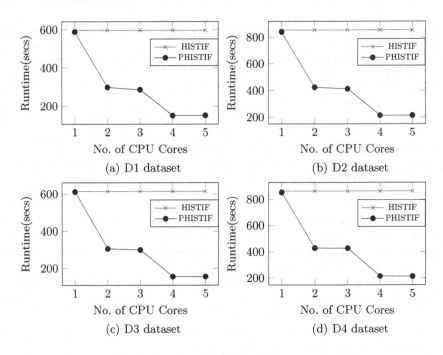

Fig. 4. Runtime vs Number of cores used

datasets, the fine images were obtained on 2021/07/28 and 2021/08/07, and coarse images were obtained on 2021/07/28 and 2021/08/06 for t_0 and t_1, respectively. For the D2 dataset, the pair of fine and coarse images were obtained on 2020/06/02 and the second pair of fine and coarse images on 2020/09/29, for t_0 and t_1, respectively. While, For the D4 dataset, the pair of fine and coarse images were obtained on 2020/09/29 and the second pair of fine and coarse images on 2022/05/17, for t_0 and t_1, respectively. Please note that the number of iterations used for the optimization process in the FCSM step is set to 50 for all the experiments.

Figures 4 (a), (b), (c) and (d) show the runtime requirements of HISTIF and PHSIF algorithms in various datasets varying the numbers of CPU cores keeping the scale factor constant. The following observations can be drawn from these figures: (i) Since HISTIF is a single cpu-based sequential algorithm, it fails to utilize the multiple CPUs available in the server machine. Consequently, the runtime requirements of the HISTIF algorithm remained the same across multiple cores and, thus, been represented with a straight line. (ii) An increase in the number of cores has decreased the runtime requirements of the PHISTIF algorithm. It is because PHISTIF was able to exploit the available cores to perform spatiotemporal image fusion parallel.

Figures 5 (a), (b), (c) and (d) shows the runtime of the D1, D2, D3 and D4 datasets, respectively, at different scale factors. It can be observed that the runtime of PHISTIF drastically reduces when the processes get distributed across multiple cores, especially at higher scale factors.

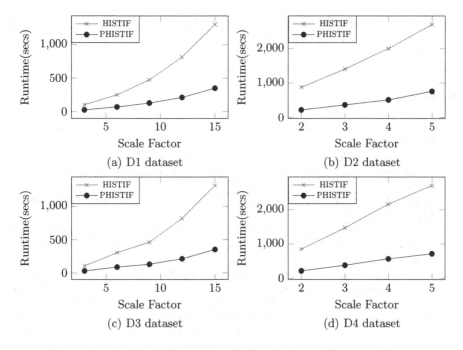

Fig. 5. Runtime vs Scaling factor used

6   Conclusion and Future Work

This article presents a parallel implementation of the HISTIF spatiotemporal fusion algorithm for large-scale sub-field level monitoring. The algorithm predicts the fine-resolution satellite data from the coarse-resolution satellite data at time t_1, given the pair of fine and its corresponding coarse image at time t_0 by the fusion of spatial and temporal features using the multi-core architecture. It addresses the challenge of providing dynamics of a large area in real-time without sacrificing the fusion accuracy. The algorithm consists of two steps FCSM and MTC. The satellite image is split into different bands and processed separately from each other in child processes, and the parent process later combines predictions from each band. The algorithm's performance was evaluated by measuring its runtime against four real datasets from **Planet** and **Landsat**, with varying scale factors, using HISTIF as the baseline and varying the number of cores used. The results show that the parallel implementation, leveraging multi-core architecture, provided prediction approx. **3.9× faster** than the HISTIF and delivered predictions at scale. This method has the potential for sub-field level monitoring at a large scale with low resources, such as crop monitoring and precision agriculture, providing stable and efficient predictions.

As part of future work, we would like to extend the current model by using different ways of applying the Modulation Factor (MF). For example, Kwan et al. [8] observed that the prediction could be more accurate if we divided the image into multiple patches. Also, the proposed model assumes that the temporal changes on different scales do not significantly differ. So further work can be done to remove this assumption.

References

1. Atkinson, P.: Downscaling in remote sensing. Int. J. Appl. Earth Obs. Geoinf. **22**, 106–114 (2013)
2. Bai, X., Liu, C., Ren, P., Zhou, J., Zhao, H., Su, Y.: Object classification via feature fusion based marginalized kernels. IEEE Geosci. Remote Sens. Lett. **12**(1), 8–12 (2014)
3. Belgiu, M., Stein, A.: Spatiotemporal image fusion in remote sensing. Remote Sens. **11**(7), 818 (2019)
4. Chhabra, V., Kiran, R.U., Xiao, J., Reddy, P.K., Avtar, R.: A spatiotemporal image fusion method for predicting high-resolution satellite images. In: Fujita, H., Fournier-Viger, P., Ali, M., Wang, Y. (eds.) IEA/AIE 2022. LNCS, vol. 13343, pp. 470–481. Springer, Cham (2022). https://doi.org/10.1007/978-3-031-08530-7_40
5. Gao, F., Masek, J., Schwaller, M., Hall, F.: On the blending of the landsat and MODIS surface reflectance: predicting daily landsat surface reflectance. IEEE Trans. Geosci. Remote Sens. **44**(8), 2207–2218 (2006)
6. Jiang, J., et al.: HISTIF: a new spatiotemporal image fusion method for high-resolution monitoring of crops at the subfield level. IEEE J. Sel. Top. Appl. Earth Obs. Remote Sens. **13**, 4607–4626 (2020)
7. Justice, C.O., et al.: The moderate resolution imaging spectroradiometer (MODIS): land remote sensing for global change research. IEEE Trans. Geosci. Remote Sens. **36**(4), 1228–1249 (1998)
8. Kwan, C., Budavari, B., Gao, F., Zhu, X.: A hybrid color mapping approach to fusing MODIS and landsat images for forward prediction. Remote Sens. **10**, 520 (2018)
9. Luo, B., Khan, M.M., Bienvenu, T., Chanussot, J., Zhang, L.: Decision-based fusion for pansharpening of remote sensing images. IEEE Geosci. Remote Sens. Lett. **10**(1), 19–23 (2012)
10. Mira, M., et al.: The MODIS (collection v006) BRDF/albedo product MCD43D: temporal course evaluated over agricultural landscape. Remote Sens. Environ. **170**, 216–228 (2015)
11. Pohl, C., Van Genderen, J.L.: Review article multisensor image fusion in remote sensing: concepts, methods and applications. Int. J. Remote Sens. **19**(5), 823–854 (1998)
12. van Genderen, J., Pohl, C.: Image fusion : issues, techniques and applications : a selected bibliography on image fusion. In: EARSeL Workshop On Intelligent Image Fusion, p. 12. 11 September 1994, Strasbourg (1994)
13. Zhu, X., Cai, F., Tian, J., Williams, T.K.A.: Spatiotemporal fusion of multisource remote sensing data: literature survey, taxonomy, principles, applications, and future directions. Remote Sens. **10**(4), 527 (2018)
14. Zhu, X., Chen, J., Gao, F., Chen, X., Masek, J.: An enhanced spatial and temporal adaptive reflectance fusion model for complex heterogeneous regions. Remote Sens. Environ. **114**, 2610–2623 (2010)

A Transfer Learning-Based Approach for Rice Plant Disease Detection

An Cong Tran[✉], Thuy Mong Nguyen-Thi, Nguyen Huu Van Long, and Hai Thanh Nguyen

Can Tho University, Can Tho, Vietnam
{tcan,nhvlong}@cit.ctu.edu.vn, nthai.cit@ctu.edu.vn

Abstract. Vietnam is a significant exporter of agricultural products in the region and the world. However, farmers face the impact of global climate change, which creates conditions for many types of pests through stormy and sunny weather, where rice diseases can develop rapidly. Therefore, early detection and timely treatment of rice diseases are paramount to farmers. Therefore, there is an urgent need to find a method that can quickly and accurately distinguish multiple rice disease images. Machine learning-based methods can be a potential solution for image classification for rice disease detection. They can process a large amount of data and increase the accuracy of disease diagnosis so that farmers can detect the disease to provide treatment solutions promptly. This paper proposes a solution for disease detection in rice leaves using three transfer learning models, including EfficientNetB3, VGG-16, and MobileNetv2. The proposed method achieved 90%, 93%, and 94% accuracy, respectively, in detecting nine types of diseases and normal leaves. These results can be used to predict diseases on rice leaves from images, suggesting appropriate prevention and treatment solutions to help farmers improve rice productivity.

Keywords: agricultural · Rice Plant Disease · transfer learning

1 Introduction

Rice is a product with great benefits for the Mekong Delta. However, the difficulty in rice cultivation is the occurrence of diseases such as rice blast, brown spot disease, leaf blight, and thorn weevil, which affect both production and quality of rice cultivation. Rice cultivation requires consistent monitoring, as various diseases and pests can attack rice plants, resulting in yield losses of up to 70%. Expert supervision is often necessary to minimize these diseases and prevent crop losses. Given the limited availability of crop protection specialists, manual disease diagnosis is tedious and expensive. Therefore, it is becoming increasingly important to automate the disease detection process by leveraging computer vision-based techniques, which have shown promising results in various fields.

Vietnam is a major exporter of agricultural products in the region and the world. For example, the report in [1] stated that the Vietnam Food Association

© The Author(s), under exclusive license to Springer Nature Switzerland AG 2023
H. Fujita et al. (Eds.): IEA/AIE 2023, LNAI 13925, pp. 145–150, 2023.
https://doi.org/10.1007/978-3-031-36819-6_13

announced that Vietnamese rice exports reached about 4.8 million tonnes in the first eight months of 2022, with a turnover of at least 2.3 billion USD. Therefore, it is necessary to build an image classification model whose input is the images of the rice condition and whose output is the name of the predicted disease that the rice plant has in the fastest and most accurate way. Based on the output, farmers can detect diseases as early as possible to develop the most appropriate methods of response and treatment.

Because of the urgency in distinguishing the diseases harmful to rice, the topic has interested many domestic and foreign researchers. The study in [2] centered around precision agriculture for the high formation of rice using Support Vector Machines, Convolutional Neural Networks, and VGG16. GoogleNet was used in [3] with some improvement and could achieve an accuracy of 99.58% and reached a gain of 1.72% over the original GoogLeNet model. A work on [4], feature weighted fuzzy clustering was leveraged to predict rice disease. The study in [5] surveyed the effects of various amendments on As species dynamics in soil porewater, accumulation of As species in rice husks and grains, and the incidence of straight head disease in five field experiments conducted over two years at three sites where the straight head disease was observed in previous seasons. The authors in [6] worked on the public multi-spectral and Red-Green-Blue images dataset and a deep learning pipeline for rice plant disease detection using multi-modal data. The authors in [7] implemented InceptionV3, VGG-16, ResNet, SqueezeNet, and VGG-19 for Leaf classification to diagnose four types of diseases. It shows that classic convolutional neural networks are still feasible and promising for rice leaf disease detection.

This study proposes an approach based on transfer learning techniques with famous architectures, including VGG-16, EfficientNetB3, and MobileNetV2, to detect nine common diseases on rice leaves.

2   Methods

2.1   Dataset

The dataset includes 10,407 (75%) images labeled across ten categories (nine types of disease and normal leaves). Furthermore, we also provide additional metadata for each image, such as rice variety and rice age. Kaggle provided additional metadata for each image, such as rice variety and age. The dataset consists of 9886 images used to train the model. Each labeled disease has the following images as shown in Table 1. We can see that the dataset provides many images of blasts, dead heat, and hispa that commonly appear in rice, as illustrated in Fig. 1.

2.2   Transfer Learning Architectures for Rice Disease on Leaves

VGG-16. VGG16 [8] achieved 92.7% accuracy of the top 5 tests in ImageNet, a dataset of more than 14 million images belonging to 1000 classes. It can improve AlexNet by replacing the filters with large kernel sizes with multiple filters with 3×3 kernel sizes sequence. VGG-16 in this study receives the input of 300×200.

Table 1. Distribution of diseases on the dataset

Class	Number of samples
Normal	1676
Bacterial leaf blight	455
Bacterial leaf streak	361
Bacterial panicle blight	320
Blast	1651
Brown spot	917
Dead heart	1370
Downy mildew	589
Hispa	1514
Tungro	1033

(a) Bacterial Leaf Blight   (b) Bacterial leaf streak   (c)   Bacterial   panicle blight

Fig. 1. An illustration of some types of diseases on rice plants.

EFFICIENTNET-B3. As stated from [8], the network can be expanded by increasing the number of layers or making each layer wider, or the input image has a higher resolution or a combination of all these factors. To understand the impact of scaling the network, the team systematically studied the effect of scaling on different model dimensions. The efficiency of model scaling is also highly dependent on the underlying network. To improve performance further, they also developed a new base network by performing a neural architecture search using the AutoML MNAS framework, which optimizes accuracy and efficiency. The resulting architecture uses mobile reverse bottleneck convolution, similar to MobileNetV2 and MnasNet, but slightly more significant due to the increased FLOP budget. Then the authors scaled the base network to get a group of models called EfficientNets [9].

MobileNetV2. This architecture [10] is one of the most popular architectures when developing AI applications in computer vision. Many architectures use MobileNetV2 backbones, such as SSDLite in object detection and DeepLabV3 in image segmentation. MobileNetV2 has several improvements over MobileNetV1 that give it higher accuracy, fewer parameters, and fewer calculations. MobileNet is one of the most popular and widely used architectures because of its computational accuracy and performance.

3   Experiments

The input images are downsized to 300 × 300 and fetched into the training model running to 80 epochs. This section reveals results from transfer learning techniques based on VGG16, MobileNetV2, and EfficientNetB3 in Table 2.

Table 2. Results of three architectures

	VGG16			mobilenet_v2			EfficientNetB3			
	Recall	Precision	F1-core	Recall	Precision	F1-core	Recall	Precision	F1-core	Support
bacterial_leaf_blight	0.8333	0.9524	0.8889	0.9167	0.9565	0.9362	0.9583	0.8846	0.9200	24
bacterial_leaf_streak	0.8947	0.8095	0.8500	0.8947	0.9444	0.9189	1.0000	0.9500	0.9744	19
bacterial_panicle_blight	0.9412	0.8000	0.8649	0.9412	0.8421	0.8889	1.0000	0.8947	0.9444	17
blast	0.9885	0.9348	0.9609	0.9770	0.9043	0.9392	0.9195	0.9524	0.9357	87
brown_spot	0.8958	0.9773	0.9348	0.7917	0.9268	0.8539	0.8958	0.9773	0.9348	48
dead_heart	0.9583	0.9718	0.9650	0.9306	0.9178	0.9241	1.0000	1.0000	1.0000	72
downy_mildew	0.8710	0.8710	0.8710	0.9032	0.9655	0.9333	0.9355	0.8529	0.8923	31
hispa	0.9625	0.9277	0.9448	0.9375	0.9375	0.9375	0.9000	0.9474	0.9231	80
normal	0.9318	0.9762	0.9535	0.9545	0.9333	0.9438	0.9545	0.9231	0.9385	88
tungro	0.9091	0.9259	0.9174	0.9091	0.9259	0.9174	0.9636	0.9636	0.9636	55
accuracy			0.9347			0.9251			0.9443	521
macro avg	0.9186	0.9147	0.9151	0.9156	0.9254	0.9193	0.9527	0.9346	0.9427	521
weight avg	0.9347	0.9368	0.9349	0.9251	0.9260	0.9246	0.9443	0.9457	0.9444	521

As seen from Table 2, the average result of VGG16 is 93.5% in accuracy. The best trained gives an F1-score of 0.965. In another architecture, MobileNet, the average result is 92.5% accurate. For example, the best-trained Normal disease gives an exact result of f1 = 0.944. Meanwhile, the subclass of Blast disease is not high, f1 = 0.854. The results show that the Mobilenet-v2 model gives low results compared to the VGG-16 and EfficientNet-B3 models. However, for cases where the amount of data is small and the model training time is fast with reasonable accuracy, then Mobilenet is also an option. Observed from Table 2, applying transfer learning models in disease identification on rice leaves is entirely feasible. This application can meet support farmers in detecting rice diseases to take measures for timely prevention. The above results show that the EfficientNetB3 model gives the best prediction results, followed by VGG-16 and MobileNet-v3.

From 3 confusion matrices shown in Fig. 2, for the Vgg-16 model, there are 34 falsely predicted images, in which the normal rice prediction is confused the most with six images. On the other hand, bacterial Panicle Blight and Blast diseases are the least commonly confused diseases, with a misrepresentation count of 1. For Mobilenet-v3, Brow-spot disease was the most confused disease, with ten

	B_L_B	B_L_S	B_P_B	Blast	BrowSpot	DeadHeart	DownyMildew	Hispa	Normal	Tungro
B_L_B	20	0	0	1	0	0	0	2	1	0
B_L_S	0	17	0	0	0	1	1	0	0	0
B_P_B	0	1	16	0	0	0	0	0	0	0
Blast	0	0	0	86	0	0	1	0	0	0
BrowSpot	0	1	1	0	43	1	0	0	0	2
DeadHeart	0	0	1	1	0	69	1	0	0	0
DownyMildew	1	0	0	1	1	0	27	1	0	0
Hispa	0	0	0	1	0	0	0	77	0	2
Normal	0	2	1	1	0	0	0	2	82	0
Tungro	0	0	1	1	0	0	1	1	1	50
VGG-16										

(a) VGG-16

	B_L_B	B_L_S	B_P_B	Blast	BrowSpot	DeadHeart	DownyMildew	Hispa	Normal	Tungro
B_L_B	23	0	0	0	0	0	0	0	1	0
B_L_S	0	19	0	0	0	0	0	0	0	0
B_P_B	0	0	17	0	0	0	0	0	0	0
Blast	0	0	0	80	1	0	2	2	1	1
BrowSpot	2	0	0	2	43	0	0	0	1	0
DeadHeart	0	0	0	0	0	72	0	0	0	0
DownyMildew	1	1	0	0	0	0	29	0	0	0
Hispa	0	0	0	2	0	0	2	72	4	0
Normal	0	0	2	0	0	0	0	1	84	0
Tungro	0	0	0	0	0	0	1	1	0	53
EfficientNetB3										

(b) EfficientNetB3

	B_L_B	B_L_S	B_P_B	Blast	BrowSpot	DeadHeart	DownyMildew	Hispa	Normal	Tungro
B_L_B	22	1	0	0	0	0	0	0	0	1
B_L_S	1	17	0	0	0	1	0	0	0	0
B_P_B	0	0	16	0	0	1	0	0	0	0
Blast	0	0	0	85	1	0	0	0	1	0
BrowSpot	0	0	0	4	38	2	0	0	2	2
DeadHeart	0	0	3	0	1	67	0	0	0	1
DownyMildew	0	0	0	1	1	0	28	1	0	0
Hispa	0	0	0	2	0	0	0	75	3	0
Normal	0	0	0	0	0	2	0	2	84	0
Tungro	0	0	0	2	0	0	1	2	0	50
MOBILENET-V2										

(c) MobileNetV2

Fig. 2. An illustration of classification performance of three considered architectures (B_L_B, B_L_S, B_P_B denote Bacterial leaf blight, Bacterial leaf streak, and Bacterial panicle blight).

falsely predicted images, and Bacterial Panicle Blight had only one mistaken image. And finally, the EfficientnetB3 model has 29 falsely predicted images, of which at most eight are falsely predicted to be Hispa. On the other hand, Deadheart, Bacterial Leaf Blight, and Bacterial Leaf Streak have no images that are mistaken for them.

4   Conclusion

The work has built a model to classify nine types of rice diseases common in Vietnam: leaf blight, stripe spot disease, grain blight disease, rice blast disease, leaf brown spot disease, late blight, rice blast disease, spiny beetle, leafhopper disease, heart disease with more than 90% in accuracy. This result will be a tool to help quickly and accurately detect rice leaf diseases when there are first symptoms, contributing to building and developing intelligent agricultural solutions. In the future, the research can add many other diseases on rice leaves so that the program can expand the identification; further work can implement more augmentation methods to improve the model's accuracy, Perform on a Larger dataset and Perform model training on other Classifications.

References

1. Nam, B.N.N.V.: Vietnam's rice exports in 2022 are expected to surpass 2021 (2022). https://vietnamagriculture.nongnghiep.vn/vietnams-rice-exports-in-2022-are-expected-to-surpass-2021-d333083.html. section: News
2. Verma, A.: SVM, CNN and VGG16 classifiers of artificial intelligence used for the detection of diseases of rice crop: a review. In: Shakya, S., Balas, V.E., Kamol-phiwong, S., Du, K.-L. (eds.) Sentimental Analysis and Deep Learning. AISC, vol. 1408, pp. 917–931. Springer, Singapore (2022). https://doi.org/10.1007/978-981-16-5157-1_71
3. Yang, L., et al.: GoogLeNet based on residual network and attention mechanism identification of rice leaf diseases. Comput. Electron. Agric. **204**, 107543 (2023). https://doi.org/10.1016/j.compag.2022.107543
4. Senthilkumar, T.P., Prabhusundhar, P.: Prediction of rice disease using modified feature weighted fuzzy clustering (MFWFC) based segmentation and hybrid classification model. Int. J. Syst. Assur. Eng. Manag. (2023). https://doi.org/10.1007/s13198-022-01835-7
5. Gao, A., et al.: Multi-site field trials demonstrate the effectiveness of silicon fertilizer on suppressing dimethylarsenate accumulation and mitigating straighthead disease in rice. Environ. Pollut. **316**, 120515 (2023). https://doi.org/10.1016/j.envpol.2022.120515
6. Alnaggar, Y.A., Sebaq, A., Amer, K., Naeem, E., Elhelw, M.: Rice plant disease detection and diagnosis using deep convolutional neural networks and multispectral imaging. In: Fournier-Viger, P., Hassan, A., Bellatreche, L. (eds.) MEDI. LNCS, vol. 13761, pp. 16–25. Springer, Cham (2022). https://doi.org/10.1007/978-3-031-21595-7_2
7. Gautam, V., et al.: A transfer learning-based artificial intelligence model for leaf disease assessment. Sustainability **14**(20), 13610 (2022). https://doi.org/10.3390/su142013610
8. Simonyan, K., Zisserman, A.: Very deep convolutional networks for large-scale image recognition (2014). https://arxiv.org/abs/1409.1556
9. Tan, M., Le, Q.V.: EfficientNet: rethinking model scaling for convolutional neural networks (2019). https://arxiv.org/abs/1905.11946
10. Sandler, M., Howard, A., Zhu, M., Zhmoginov, A., Chen, L.C.: Mobilenetv2: inverted residuals and linear bottlenecks. In: 2018 IEEE/CVF Conference on Computer Vision and Pattern Recognition, pp. 4510–4520 (2018)

Unsupervised Defogging for Rotary Kilns Image

Tao Li$^{(\boxtimes)}$, Yijia Zhou, Na Zhao, and Hongzhe Zhao

College of Computer Science and Electronic Engineering, Hunan University,
Changsha 410082, China
{jt_litao,yijiazhou,nanazhao,volt99}@hnu.edu.cn

Abstract. Image processing of rotary kilns is extremely important for their combustion efficiency. Most of the current image processing on kilns is focused on image classification, but image defogging is also one of the key aspects, which is still a challenging problem. Due to the harsh combustion environment, the large amount of smoke and dust generated during the combustion process leads to poor visualization of rotary kiln images. To solve its combustion uncertainty and real-time, We propose an unsupervised layer-based defogging network that employs a graph decomposition defogging approach, which decomposes images into three layers for defogging. In particular, the proposed UPSCA-Net, which is a U-shaped network combining an attention mechanism and focus loss, uses a long connection, jump fusion of different features for extracting image features and balancing the uncertainty of fogging, and achieves zero-sample kiln image defogging, making the defogging effect closer to the ground truth. In addition to this, flame images do not have a fog-free image for reference and cannot be measured with a referenced baseline, so we have conducted extensive experiments using a reference-free image quality metric based on real-world rotary kiln combustion images. The defogging results show that our proposed method outperforms several different defogging methods in various indicators. Excellent visual effects are also achieved.

Keywords: Unsupervised · zero-sample · rotary kilns · flame image · defogging

1 Introduction

Rotary kilns are widely used in industrial production such as power generation, metallurgy and cement. Their main function is to sinter industrial raw materials to produce clinker. In the rotary kiln production process, the material combustion process is extremely important, and a large number of physicochemical reactions take place in the kiln with great uncertainty. Conventional kilns control the kiln combustion temperature and its state by controlling the amount of coal injected by the operator, and the different combustion states of the material determine the quality of the production results [1]. Therefore, how to discern

H. Fujita et al. (Eds.): IEA/AIE 2023, LNAI 13925, pp. 151–166, 2023.
https://doi.org/10.1007/978-3-031-36819-6_14

and thus control the combustion state to achieve energy savings and emission reduction has become a major existing problem.

Misjudgement of the sintering process in rotary kilns can lead to toxic emissions or energy loss, and is particularly important for image condition determination. Nevertheless, due to the high-temperature combustion coupled with frequent crusting on the kiln wall, the kiln head and kiln tail are sealed, and the lookout hole area returns ash, while the crusted material area falls off; dust and flying sand are serious and there is more dust on the equipment and flying sand in the kiln. Second, coal dust particles are suspended in the pipeline of high-temperature gas. In addition, the brightness of the saturated CCD when shooting, coal dust explosions and other conditions lead to overexposure of the image after imaging, which results in the overall color being white. These factors lead to poor contrast and blurred details, and the picture cannot be distinguished.

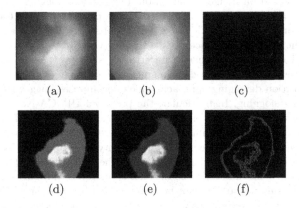

Fig. 1. The edges are compared to the original image and the defogged image. (a) A real foggy image; (b) a grayscale image converted from (a); (c) the edge image extracted by (a); (d) the defogged image; (e) the grayscale image converted from (d); (f) the edge image extracted with (d).

In practice, first, to judge the combustion situation, the visual perception of the flame, such as size, length, and color, is usually observed. However, the images obtained in rotary kilns have blurred shape edges and inconspicuous colors, and it is especially difficult to distinguish the center of the flame. For example, in the case of normal-combustion and over-combustion, errors in judgment can occur based on the above conditions, and this can be assisted by observing the shape of the center of the flame to make more accurate distinctions. Therefore, whether the flame center of the image can be segmented clearly can also be measured, as in Fig. 1. Figure 1(a) is the original image, Fig. 1 (a), (b), and (c), are the original image, the gray image obtained by edge-based blurring measurement, and the edge images, respectively. Figure 1 (d), (e), and (f) are the defogged image, the gray image, and the edge image after defogging, respectively. In the figure, the flame region of the defogged edge image and the flame center edge segmentation are visible, but the original image edge is almost not extracted, which is not conducive to the next step of intelligent classification learning of the flame image.

In the traditional industrial context, the harsh environment of the kiln and the fog generated by combustion, including various particles, can obscure the combustion characteristics of the flame. Moreover, there are many unstable factors for identifying the combustion status, hence it is especially important to take intelligent control of the combustion situation of the rotary kiln. In recent years, image defogging has received much attention [2–8] and can be broadly classified as image enhancement-based, image recovery-based, and deep learning-based. Despite the considerable progress of image restoration-based defogging methods, the simplified atmospheric scattering model leads to a certain error in transmittance and atmospheric light estimation, and the a priori information is not universally applicable and is prone to incomplete fogging and color distortion. However, the simplified atmospheric scattering model leads to some errors in transmittance and atmospheric light estimation, as in [5,9].

For rotary kiln flame images, the visual effect of overexposure is white, with the edges of the flame blurred and the center of the flame indistinguishable. Burning flame images have a single color. In a recent deep learning-based approach, [10] proposed the end-to-end defogging network DCP, which uses an encoder-decoder network structure and a multiscale pooling strategy to aggregate features at different levels to ensure stable performance of the defogging model; however, the color distortion of the defogged image is unnatural. The more concentrated area in flame image defogging is flame color defogging, and extracting the flame center as well as the edge part of the flame screen requires finer feature extraction in different dimensions. We hope to obtain defogged images with natural color and clear segmentation edges, and we only need to focus on the region of interest when performing feature extraction while suppressing the background regions that are not relevant to the segmentation task.

The imaging conditions of flame-burning images and the haze level at the time of shooting are unpredictable, and the situation of the dataset we obtained is beyond our control, so the haze level of each burning image has some variation, and the haze level of each region may be different. [11] proposed a defogging network AOD-Net. AOD-Net is based on multiscale image features to estimate the transmission map and atmospheric light, and it retains the effective image information, but there is still haze in some areas of the haze image. In flame image defogging, there will be a gap between the defogging effect of background and flame layer segmentation defogging due to different haze levels. And we should balance this gap to obtain a comparable defogging effect.

To address the above-mentioned challenges, we propose an unsupervised method to remove haze from kiln flame images. We use a hierarchical method to decompose it into three layers and then compute the clean image layer and estimate the atmospheric light value without the clean image for training, where focal loss is introduced for loss estimation of image reconstruction.

Our main contributions are as follows:

- We design a new network structure UNet-plus spatial and channel attention net (UPSCA-Net), incorporating a pyramidal "spatio-temporal" attention mechanism, where multi-level extraction of features can effectively capture and fuse features at different levels, allowing It can remove the effects of large particles and haze from the flame, extract clearer flame colours and segment more distinct flame shapes.
- We introduce a focal loss that balances the hard and easy samples, equalising the problem of inconsistent haze in different regions, which allows the loss to converge continuously and the fog removal effect to be closer to the ground truth.
- We propose a zero-sample defogging method that does not require training and supervision, and since it is not accompanied by a ground reality of training and does not have a large dataset. It is therefore suitable for flame image processing in industrial applications.

In the remainder of this paper, Sect. 2 describes the related work. Section 3 presents our proposed approach. Section 4 explains our experiments, and finally, Sect. 5 concludes the paper.

2 Related Work

In this section, we present previous researches that are most related to our work. First we review existing methods on kiln image processing, followed by methods for image defogging.

2.1 Image Processing

Rotary kilns have been used for power generation, metallurgy and cement production due to their good thermal conductivity and high mixing capacity, which have contributed to the development of industrial industries. However, due to the complexity of the rotary kiln structure and the non-linearity of combustion, the combustion status of rotary kilns is often 'manually monitored', a method that leads to a waste of human resources and an increased risk of misjudgment.

With the continuous development in the field of computers, Wang Jiesheng et al. proposed a combustion condition recognition method based on generalized learning vector neural network based on the texture features of pulverized coal combustion flame images of rotary kiln oxide pellet sintering process [12], a large number of methods based on flame image feature extraction have been proposed and studied [13,14]. Among them, [14] extracted three luminescent features and four dynamic features from the image flame region using a series of fuzzy flame images for detecting the temperature in a rotary kiln. However, these methods require a lot of pre-processing and manual parameter adjustment upfront.

In terms of kiln images, [15], a new deep learning-based approach is proposed, in which a deep learning model feeds flame images into a deep neural network (DNN) or convolutional neural network to predict the combustion state and heat release rate. In addition, a continuous, multistep prediction scheme based on deep neural networks is proposed in the literature [16] for detecting biomass combustion conditions. The deep learning approach proved to be able to detect the rotary kiln flame combustion status faster and more accurately. A deep learning-based rotary kiln combustion status monitoring system was proposed in the literature [17], which eliminates the tedious procedure of traditional feature extraction-based methods through an end-to-end network. In addition, the proposed convolutional recurrent neural network (CRNN) can effectively extract the flame image sequence features to predict the combustion status inside

The unsupervised approach is now the focus of the community. [18] proposes a fully unsupervised co-training variant that allows the inclusion of a second dataset with two learning strategies (splitting and recursion) for predicting the state of a machine tool based on results given by multiple sensors. [19] proposes an online unsupervised segmentation algorithm for multidimensional time series data, enhances the sliding window and bottom-up (SWAB) algorithms for the implementation of multidimensional data segmentation algorithms, and MD-SWAB (multidimensional SWAB) is proposed.

All these deep learning methods first input all existing images into the network and then train them to learn the weights, after which the images can be input for prediction; however, due to the environment in which the kiln images are taken, the visualization is poor, so this paper first performs unsupervised defogging of the images and then performs classification.UPSCA-Net constitutes a collection of UNets of different depths that partially share the same encoder, which uses feature aggregation at different scales in the decoder. Together with the attention mechanism focusing on the regions we are interested in while suppressing background regions that are not relevant to the segmentation task, this makes the defogging results more in line with our expectations.

3 Proposed Methods

In this section, we present the proposed method. In the defogging process, we follow the atmospheric scattering model, and our approach focuses on estimating the model parameters in which the fogged image is decomposed into three layers: the foggy-free map, the atmospheric map, and the transmission map. Loss estimation is performed on the three-layer network using the loss function separately to estimate the atmospheric light value and transmittance, after which the clean image layer is derived from the atmospheric scattering model equation. In the foggy-free map and the transmission map using our proposed network for parameter estimation, the atmospheric layer uses a variational self-encoder structure, which we follow [22].

3.1 Network Architecture

In this section, we present the structure of the entire network. The network is divided into three layers, corresponding to different decomposition layers, for

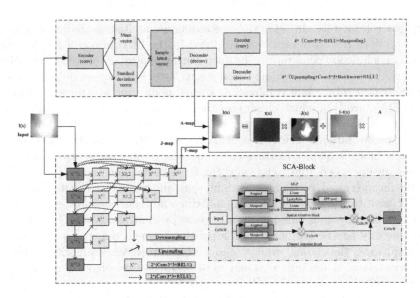

Fig. 2. The whole network framework. T-map and J-map are our proposed UPSCA network, and A-map is the traditional VAE network. A is the estimated atmospheric light image by A_map, $t(x)$ is the transmission image by T_map, and $J(x)$ is the clean image estimated by J_map.

the atmospheric light layer (A-map), the transmission layer (T-map) and the fog-free image layer (J-map) Our goal is to obtain a fog-free image of the input flame after the three decomposition layers of the network, with an emphasis on flame segmentation and edge processing. Therefore, for J-map and T-map, we propose a network form of UPSCA-Net. The focal loss is introduced to measure the reconstruction loss between the fogged original image and the reconstructed fogged image, which makes our defogged image have sharper edges and fuller chromaticity due to the parameter adjustment.

Our proposed UPSCA-Net is designed to keep the attention in the region of interest, which is the flame region instead of the background region and can learn to different levels of hair learning, making the defogging finer, as shown in Fig. 2. First, our whole network is divided into three layers. Among them, J-map and T-map are used in our proposed UPSCA-Net, which consists of encoding and decoding. Each layer is composed of 3×3 convolutional blocks, and the convolutional blocks are first passed through the SCA-block module to obtain the modules we need to focus on and then downsample, which reduces our parameters and improves the performance. Our SCA-block has a channel attention mechanism and a spatial attention mechanism fused with a channel attention mechanism for maximum pooling and average pooling, then a multilayer perceptron for fusion, then a spatial attention mechanism for maximum pooling and average pooling fusion, and a spatial pyramidal pooling of both for output features. This maximizes the retention of our desired feature values while sifting out the features we do not need. After that, the information is concatenated with the upsampled information, in which there is a skip connection, so that we can not only obtain deep information at different levels but also prevent the loss of shallow features so that our image obtains the features we want to focus on the most.

To implement A_map, we use a variant autoencoding network. It consists of a CNN-based encoder, an asymmetric decoder and an intermediate block. To obtain the latent code, we introduce KL scatter in the middle block. In this way, we completed our image defogging using a single image.

In image defogging, based on the atmospheric scattering model, to explain the causes of foggy images and the various factors included in the formation of foggy images,

$$I(x) = J(x)t(x) + A(1 - t(x)), \tag{1}$$

where $I(x)$ is the foggy image, $J(x)$ is the fog-free image, $t(x)$ is the transmission image, and A is the global atmospheric light at the pixel coordinate points.

Here, we can obtain fog-free images with a total loss of Eq. (1), after calculating loss estimates for these maps,

$$Loss = Loss_{Reconest} + Loss_A + Loss_J + Loss_{Reg}, \tag{2}$$

where $Loss_{Reconest}$ is the reconstruction loss from blurred images and reconstructed blurred images, $Loss_A$ is the estimated loss of atmospheric light, $Loss_J$ is the loss from decomposing the haze image layer into clean image layers, and $Loss_{Reg}$ is the mask regularization used for some special tasks. We perform this regularization for the A-map and T-map to increase the model stability.

One of the more noteworthy aspects is that in the reconstruction loss, the reconstruction loss is the loss between the input blurred image x and the reconstructed blurred image $I(x)$. We use focal loss, and we made changes to the original equation to adapt focal loss [23] to our needs better, as follows:

$$Loss_{Reconest} = Loss_{FFL} = FFL(I(x) - x), \tag{3}$$

$$Loss_{FFL} = \alpha(1 - p)^{\gamma} t log(p), \tag{4}$$

where $\gamma > 0$ is the adjustable factor, a is the weighting factor, $\alpha \in [0, 1]$, p is the reconstructed blurred image matrix, and t is the input blurred image matrix; thus, we can keep the loss between the reconstructed blurred image and the input blurred image increasingly smaller, after which the estimated fog-free image is closer to the ground truth.

We regularize the atmospheric light as well as t(x),

$$Loss_{Reg} = \lambda_1 ||A(x) - A||_p + \lambda_2 ||t(x)||_p, \tag{5}$$

where λ_1, λ_2 are balance factors, we follow the opinion of [7], $Loss_{Reg}$ enforces mask smoothing by minimizing the norm of the Laplace operator and additionally regularizes the atmospheric light, and A is estimated from the input image x

by our network. To recover clean images more accurately, we used a dark channel a priori algorithm for loss estimation for J-map,

$$Loss_J = ||\min_{c \in R,G,B} J^c(y)||_p, \tag{6}$$

where c represents one of the channels R, G, and B.

We use that KL divergence makes the potential variable $z \in (\mu, \sigma^2)$ of $Loss_A$ similar to the Gaussian distribution $Z \sim (0, I)$, where I represents a unit matrix. That is, we consider z as a multidimensional random variable obeying a standard multivariate Gaussian distribution. Then, this loss can be estimated.

$$Loss_A = KL(N(\mu, \sigma^2) \parallel N(0, I)) \tag{7}$$

$$= \frac{1}{2}\sum \left((N(\mu)^2 + (\sigma)^2) - 1 - log(\sigma)^2\right) \tag{8}$$

3.2   SCA-Block

Convolutional neural networks are widely used in applications such as image vision and classification, but convolutional neural networks generally rely on a large quantity of data and training sets, and a new network structure and training strategy are proposed. A U-shaped network structure is designed, and this structure can use a small number of datasets while the segmentation accuracy obtained is not very poor, as shown in Fig. 2. Therefore, UPSCA-net has been widely used in the medical image segmentation field, such as [24].

In flame images, the distribution of smoke and particulate matter in the air due to combustion is not uniform, so the weights of the thin fog region and thick fog region are not the same. If these features are treated equally, it will consume considerable time to calculate unnecessary resources and ignore some important information after the self-attention mechanism is added to the neural network, which brings good performance [25].

To better treat flame images highlighted by the flame and the color of the flame center, we add our proposed spatial and channel attention module to the original structure. Integrating the attention module in the downsampling process can reduce the number of parameters processed during feature extraction, focusing on extracting the features we need and ignoring the background features we do not need, thus improving performance and efficiency. The structure of the SCA-block is shown in Fig. 2. We add the SCA-block in the downsampling stage to combine the shallow features and deep features to obtain better image visual effects.

In the spatial module, we perform adaptive average pooling and adaptive maximum pooling before entering the multilayer perceptron. We use leakyReLU to obtain the output before entering the spatial pyramid pooling [26], which reduces overfitting; in the channel module, we perform maximum pooling and average pooling on the channels before obtaining the output.

Algorithm 1 presents the processing procedure of the proposed method.

Algorithm 1: The proposed method.

Input: The raw image: I; learning rate:0.001; epoch:$N = 500$;
Output: The Defoggy image: J;

1   Retrieve the flame data video and transform it into an image dataset in Fig. 3;
2   Input images, perform data processing, and convert to data, pass into the defogging algorithm;
3   **for** $i \in (0,N)$ **do**
4   Initial *parameters*, *loss* and optimizer;
5   Pass in parameters and learning rate to the optimizer;
6   Passing image data to J_map, T_map and A_map networks in Fig. 2;
7   Compute all losses according to Eq. (2), (4), (5), (6), and (8), gradient backpropagation, retrieve J_{out}, t_{out}, a_{out} from J_map, T_map and A_map, respectively;
8   Compute the defogging result $result = J_{out} + t_{out} + A_{out}$;
9   Update the parameters;
10   Convert the data format to the image display and retrieve the final image;

---

4 Experiment

In this section, we conduct experiments to evaluate the performance of the proposed defogging method.

4.1 Experimental Settings

Datasets. To realistically evaluate our approach, our datasets are all derived from videos of rotary kiln combustion at a steel plant in Hunan Province, China. We perform frame-by-frame extraction of a continuous sequence of images, each of 704×576 in size (color images with three channels of RGB). The dataset is shown in Fig. 3, and we divided the dataset into three categories of states, including under-combustion, normal-combustion, and over-combustion, based on the experience of the individual fire watcher. This figure shows an example of the burn state before fogging. From top to bottom, the under-combustion, normal-combustion, and over-combustion states. To better evaluate our method, we conduct comparison experiments on the parameters in Eq. (4), since the α parameter can suppress the imbalance in the number of hard and easy samples, and γ can control the imbalance in the number of hard and easy to distinguish samples, so we compare the experiments in $\gamma \in [0,5]$, $\alpha \in [0,1]$, as shown in the Fig. 4, Fig. 5, and finally, we choose $\gamma = 2$ and $\alpha = 0.1$.

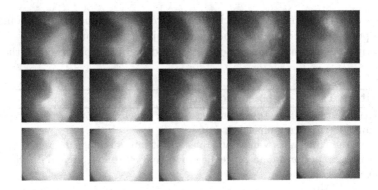

Fig. 3. Flame image dataset. From top to bottom, under-combustion, normal-combustion and over-combustion images

Experimental Environment. We run on a Google Colaboratory server based on the PyTorch framework using the Adam optimizer, with the learning rate set to 0.001.

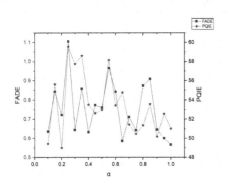

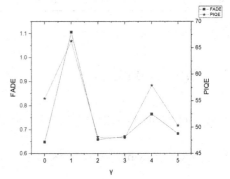

Fig. 4. Effect of different alpha on ambiguity

Fig. 5. Effect of different gamma on ambiguity

4.2   No Reference Image Quality Assessment

The rotary kiln combustion image is an image generated in real time during the production process, there is no fog-free image for reference and its composition is different from that of atmospheric fog, therefore we cannot use a reference defogging benchmark when measuring its image quality, in order to objectively and accurately assess the accuracy of the algorithm, this paper uses Reference-free (NR) QA methods, which do not require reference to no information, which is in line with the real situation of our images and with our designed zero-sample

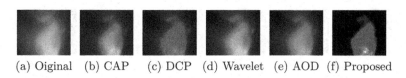

(a) Oiginal   (b) CAP   (c) DCP   (d) Wavelet   (e) AOD   (f) Proposed

Fig. 6. Comparison of defogging under-combustion conditions.

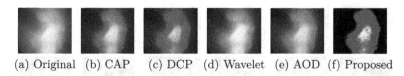

(a) Original   (b) CAP   (c) DCP   (d) Wavelet   (e) AOD   (f) Proposed

Fig. 7. Comparison of defogging under normal-combustion conditions.

defogging method, which does not require image de-fogging assistance and can be obtained directly from single image defogging.

Baseline: To obtain objective results, we compare the proposed method with five different defogging methods for validation. Validation evaluates the effectiveness using the NR method.

FADE. The absorption or scattering of light by atmospheric particles such as fog, haze or mist can significantly reduce the visibility of a scene. Factors such as the location of the kiln head, where the camera taken at the rotary kiln is mounted 15M away from the combustion area, and the combustion environment lead to problems such as deep overall haze on the rotary kiln image, as well as inconsistent local haze. Therefore wo'men used the FADE [27] metric to measure image quality, which not only predicts the perceived fog density of the entire image, but also provides an index of local fog density for each block.

PIQE. Human visual attention is highly focused on salient points or spatially active areas in an image. It is often the flame regions that require attention in rotary kiln images, and when measuring their quality, it is also desirable to estimate the quality from a perceptually meaningful space. Therefore, in this paper, image quality can be assessed using the PIQE [28] method, which generates a fine-grained block-level distortion map in the selection of features, and the local quality at the block and block level adds up to the overall quality of the image as perceived by humans, making the evaluation metric very informative.

4.3   Results

In this section, we present a comparative analysis of the results of the method proposed in Sect. 4, compare the method with different defogging algorithms, and finally prove that our method has a comparable matching excellent result for the factory flame images.

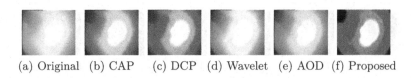

(a) Original (b) CAP   (c) DCP   (d) Wavelet (e) AOD (f) Proposed

Fig. 8. Comparison of defogging in over-combustion conditions.

(a)   (b)   (c)   (d)   (e)   (f)

Fig. 9. Raw image edge segmentation. (a) and (b) are the edge images after defogging in the under-combustion state, (c) and (d) are the edge images after defogging in the normal-combustion state, (e) and (f) are the edge images in the over-combustion state

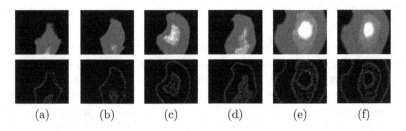

(a)   (b)   (c)   (d)   (e)   (f)

Fig. 10. Defogging image edge segmentation. (a) and (b) are the edge images after defogging in the under-combustion state, (c) and (d) are the edge images after defogging in the normal-combustion state, (e) and (f) are the edge images in the over-combustion state

Since our algorithm targets the factory flame images, we process a set of six flame images containing different combustion states, all of which are taken under real combustion conditions in the factory. Due to the existence of complex combustion conditions, large powder layer particles, the gray layer covering the camera, and other realistic interference factors in the factory flame images, there will be many cases of unsatisfactory defogging algorithm results. At the subjective level, as shown in Fig. 6, Fig. 7, and Fig. 8, we can see that the color and edge segmentation of the images defogged with our proposed method are good. Among them, the neural network-based wavelet method and the AOD method are relatively poor for fogging, they easily misestimate the blur concentration, and the flame color and current status are not restored and segmented out. Based on the image restoration CAP and DCP methods, although the effect due to the first two methods also eliminated part of the haze, the color restoration was slightly distorted, and the details of the segmentation process still existed in some fog.

At the objective level, the evaluation of the real image is more difficult because there is no exact fog-free image available, so we use two methods to evaluate the quality of the reference-free image. It should be clear that the smaller the value of FADE and PQIE means the better the image quality. From Table 1, it seems that the image blur measure of the original image is 2.1826 (FADE), 78.7028 (PQIE). Among them, the best performance in FADE is our proposed method, followed by the DCP method, while in PQIE, the DCP method is slightly higher than our proposed method, but overall our proposed method still outperforms the other methods and achieves good results.

Using our proposed method for edge extraction by The method of edge segmentation for different combustion states, as shown in Fig. 9 and Fig. 10, There is a big difference in the edge extraction before and after defogging. The edge without our method is almost invisible and it is impossible to judge the burning state, but in the Fig. 10, which has been defogged by our method, we can see that the flame shape is distinguishable, where the under-combustion state has almost no flame center, the normal-combustion state has a complete central region extracted by the red region in the center below but does not have the flame center region proposed by the yellow flame center, and the over-combustion state has a complete region in the center below, which is an edge extracted by the yellow region of the flame center. Therefore, we can clearly distinguish the burning state.

Table 1. Comparing the performance of different defogging methods

	original	Wavelet	DCP	CAP	AOD	Proposed
FADE	2.1826	1.2130	0.7462	1.0363	1.3152	0.6723
PQIE	78.7028	69.9697	48.9302	74.9233	83.5466	58.3550

4.4   Ablation Experiment

To demonstrate the superiority of our network, we select 10 images from each of the different flame states for the ablation experiments. In Table 2, the dataset for ablation experiments, we set up several different sets of network structures for the experiments, we reduce the different modular frameworks, and different parameters are designed to control the variables of its analysis according to Eq.(4), which are $\alpha = 0$ and $\gamma = 0$. From the results, we can see in the performance of our algorithm that both the channel-only attention and the see-only attention methods are numerically approximately 0.07–0.17 away from our proposed method in FADE, while PQIE is approximately 1.2–22.12 away. The lack of feature extraction in different dimensions makes the method unable to fully obtain the feature points we want, the proposed method has some advantages in the design of the structure and improves the performance.

Table 2. Performance of different methods in ablation experiments

	FADE	PQIE
ours-ca	0.8457	60.3472
ours-sa	0.7783	59.5841
$\alpha = 0$	0.7480	59.4577
$\gamma = 0$	0.7532	60.4836
Our method	0.6723	58.3550

5   Conclusion

In this paper, we propose a UPSCA-Net that incorporates preprocessing and attention mechanisms. This work solves the problem of blurred plant combustion images, and its visual effect on flame combustion images is superior to other existing methods. Next, we combine the proposed defogging method with a classification algorithm so that it becomes a complete system that can be applied to real rotary kiln coal combustion, which can make the prediction more efficient and can achieve source savings and emission reduction and reduce pollution to the environment. For the next work, we plan to investigate optimizing feature extraction, adjusting color saturation and sharpness, and improving network operation speed to better suit the kiln image environment.

References

1. Duan, M., Wang, X., et al.: Research on the temperature of cement rotary kiln burning zone based on data mining. In: 2018 3rd International Conference on Control, Automation and Artificial Intelligence (2018)
2. Shrivastava, A., Jain, S.: Single image dehazing based on one dimensional linear filtering and adoptive histogram equalization method. In: 2016 International Conference on Electrical, Electronics, and Optimization Techniques (ICEEOT) (2016)
3. Yang, H.H., Fu, Y.: Wavelet U-Net and the chromatic adaptation transform for single image dehazing. In: 2019 IEEE International Conference on Image Processing (ICIP). IEEE (2019)
4. Fattal, R.: Single image dehazing. ACM Trans. Graph. **27**(3), 1–9 (2008). https://doi.org/10.1145/1360612.1360671
5. He, K., Sun, J., Tang, X.: Single image haze removal using dark channel prior. IEEE Trans. Pattern Anal. Mach. Intell. (2011). https://doi.org/10.1109/TPAMI.2010.168

6. Cai, B., Xu, X., Jia, K., et al.: DehazeNet: an end-to-end system for single image haze removal. IEEE Trans. Image Process. **25**(11), 5187–5198 (2016). https://doi.org/10.1109/TIP.2016.2598681

7. Li, B., Gou, Y., Liu, J.Z., et al.: Zero-shot image dehazing. IEEE Trans. Image Process. **99**, 1–1 (2020). https://doi.org/10.1109/TIP.2020.3016134

8. Yang, X., Xu, Z., Luo, J.: Towards perceptual image dehazing by physics-based disentanglement and adversarial training. In: Proceedings of the AAAI Conference on Artificial Intelligence (2018)

9. Zhu, Q., Mai, J., Shao, L.: A fast single image haze removal algorithm using color attenuation prior. IEEE Trans. Image Process. **24**(11), 3522–3533 (2015). https://doi.org/10.1109/TIP.2015.2446191

10. Zhang, H., Patel, V.M.: Densely Connected Pyramid Dehazing Network. In: IEEE (2018)

11. Li, B., Peng, X., Wang, Z., Xu, J., Feng, D.: "An All-in-One Network for Dehazing and Beyond" (2017)

12. Li, W., Wang, D., Chai, T.: Burning state recognition of rotary kiln using ELMs with heterogeneous features. Neurocomputing **102**(2), 144–153 (2013)

13. Wang, J.S., Dong, X., et al.: GLCM based extraction of flame image texture features and KPCA-GLVQ recognition method for rotary kiln combustion working conditions. Int. J. Autom. Comput. **11**(1), 72–77 (2014). https://doi.org/10.1007/s11633-014-0767-8

14. Chen, H., Zhang, X., Hong, P., et al.: Recognition of the temperature condition of a rotary kiln using dynamic features of a series of blurry flame images. IEEE Trans. Industr. Inf. **12**(1), 148–157 (2016). https://doi.org/10.1109/TII.2015.2500891

15. Zhou, H., Lou, X., Xiao, J., et al.: Experimental study on image processing of flame temperature distribution in a pilot scale furnace. Proc. Chin. Soc. Electr. Eng. **15**, 295–300 (1995)

16. Wang, Z., Song, C., Chen, T.: Deep learning based monitoring of furnace combustion state and measurement of heat release. Energy **131**, 106–112 (2017)

17. Toth, P., Garami, A., Csordas, B.: Image-based deep neural network prediction of the heat output of a step-grate biomass boiler. Appl. Energy **200**, 155–169 (2017)

18. Monvoisin, M., Leray, P., Ritou, M.: Unsupervised co-training of Bayesian networks for condition prediction. In: Fujita, H., Selamat, A., Lin, J.C.-W., Ali, M. (eds.) IEA/AIE 2021. LNCS (LNAI), vol. 12799, pp. 577–588. Springer, Cham (2021). https://doi.org/10.1007/978-3-030-79463-7_49

19. Okada, S., Ishibashi, S., Nishida, T.: On-line unsupervised segmentation for multidimensional time-series data and application to spatiotemporal gesture data. In: García-Pedrajas, N., Herrera, F., Fyfe, C., Benítez, J.M., Ali, M. (eds.) IEA/AIE 2010. LNCS (LNAI), vol. 6096, pp. 337–347. Springer, Heidelberg (2010). https://doi.org/10.1007/978-3-642-13022-9_34

20. Ulyanov, D., Vedaldi, A., Lempitsky, V.: Deep image prior. In: IEEE (2017)

21. Gandelsman, Y., Shocher, A., Irani, M.: "DOUBLE-DIP": unsupervised image decomposition via coupled deep-image-priors. In: Proceedings of the IEEE/CVF Conference on Computer Vision and Pattern Recognition, 11026–11035 (2019)

22. Kingma, D.P., Welling, M.: Auto-encoding variational Bayes. In: International Conference on Learning Representations. Ithaca, NYarXiv.org (2013)

23. Lin, T.Y., Goyal, P., Girshick, R., et al.: Focal loss for dense object detection, arXiv e-prints (2017)

24. Zhou, Z., Rahman Siddiquee, M.M., Tajbakhsh, N., Liang, J.: UNet++: a nested U-net architecture for medical image segmentation. In: Stoyanov, D., et al. (eds.)

DLMIA/ML-CDS -2018. LNCS, vol. 11045, pp. 3–11. Springer, Cham (2018). https://doi.org/10.1007/978-3-030-00889-5_1

25. Trebing, K., Mehrkanoon, S.: SmaAt-UNet: precipitation nowcasting using a small attention-unet architecture (2020)

26. He, K., Zhang, X., Ren, S., Sun, J.: Spatial pyramid pooling in deep convolutional networks for visual recognition. In: Fleet, D., Pajdla, T., Schiele, B., Tuytelaars, T. (eds.) ECCV 2014. LNCS, vol. 8691, pp. 346–361. Springer, Cham (2014). https://doi.org/10.1007/978-3-319-10578-9_23

27. Choi, L.K., You, J., Bovik, A.C.: Referenceless prediction of perceptual fog density and perceptual image defogging. IEEE Trans. Image Process. **24**(11), 3888–3901 (2015)

28. Venkatanath, N., Praneeth, D., Bh, M.C., Channappayya, S.S., Medasani, S.S.: Blind image quality evaluation using perception based features. In: 2015 Twenty First National Conference on Communications (NCC), Mumbai (2015)

A Robust Document Localization Solution with Segmentation and Clustering

Hoang Dang Nguyen[1], Dinh Nguyen Vu[2], Viet Anh Nguyen[1],
Tien Dong Nguyen[2], and Phi Le Nguyen[1(✉)]

[1] School of Information and Communication Technology, Hanoi University of Science
and Technology, Hanoi, Vietnam
{dang.nh194423,anh.nv183478}@sis.hust.edu.vn, lenp@soict.hust.edu.vn
[2] CMC Applied Technology Institute, Hanoi, Vietnam
{ntdong,vdnguyen}@cmc.com.vn

Abstract. In the fields of optical character recognition and textual information extraction, document localization is recognized as a potential preprocessing step with a significant impact on accuracy. Despite numerous solutions being presented, localizing documents in images with complicated backgrounds remains an open issue. This paper offers a novel approach to document localization that may successfully handle difficult scenarios with complicated backgrounds. Our strategy blends deep learning with conventional image processing techniques. Specifically, deep learning is applied to determine a rough region of the document's boundary, while traditional image processing algorithms are exploited to identify the document's corners. Moreover, to improve model accuracy and mitigate the data-hungry drawback of the deep learning-based approach, we introduce efficient data annotation and augmentation techniques. We perform comprehensive experiments to evaluate the performance of the proposed method on the ICDAR 2015 SmartDoc challenge 1 dataset. The experimental results show that our method achieves higher accuracy while requiring less real training data. Specifically, using only 20% of the real training data, our proposal improves the Jaccard Index by 0.6% on average and by 1.7% concerning the dataset with the most complicated background.

Keywords: Document Localization · Probabilistic Hough Transform · Segmentation · K-Means Clustering

1 Introduction

The digitization of documents has been a societal trend for the past several decades. The documents will be easier to store, search, and read once they have been digitized. To accomplish this, the document must first be precisely positioned in the photos. Therefore, the document localization approach is crucial to the digitization process. The existing approaches in dealing with document localization can be categorized into three main groups: mathematical morphology-based [4,6,7], segmentation-based [2,10,11], and keypoint-based [5,18].

© The Author(s), under exclusive license to Springer Nature Switzerland AG 2023
H. Fujita et al. (Eds.): IEA/AIE 2023, LNAI 13925, pp. 167–179, 2023.
https://doi.org/10.1007/978-3-031-36819-6_15

The mathematical morphology-based inherits the concepts used in traditional image processing methods, such as Canny detector, Sobel operators, etc., to detect the contour of documents. However, this approach suffers a significant drawback as its performance relies significantly on the image's background. Recently, deep learning has emerged as a viable technique, widely applied in the field of computer vision to handle various problems, including object detection, classification, etc. The document localization problem is typically considered a segmentation task and handled by CNN models [2,10,11]. In [10], the authors proposed a model called OctHu-PageScan that is based on U-Net [14] to detect document edges and text regions in Brazilian ID Card images. By replacing the Convolutional Layers with Octave Convolutional Layers [3], their model reduces the redundancy of feature maps and obtains a lighter and faster model. Ngoc et al., in [11], represented the input image as an unordered tree of regions, which is obtained by hierarchical segmentation of the image. To extract the document, they leveraged several contrast features, including the Dahu pseudo distance and the Chi-square distance between histograms of the color sets of pixels. Nevertheless, these data-driven deep-learning models require a large amount of real training data and are vulnerable to hard samples whose background is similar to the document. In contrast to the first two approaches, the third one (i.e., keypoint-based) focuses on determining the vertices of the document [5,18]. Since there may be abundant false corners in the image, the Region Of Interest (ROI) is introduced to improve the stability of the systems. In [18], U-Net was employed to estimate ROI, and in [5], a two-stage neural network was used for this purpose. The first neural network roughly estimates the position of document corners in the input image; then, each corner is iteratively refined by a second neural network, which takes the local neighborhood of each document corner as input. The limitation of this approach is the requirement of visibility and highly contrast to the background of all document corners, which is often not possible when capturing an image with a mobile camera. In addition, they can fail if the background contains objects with corners resembling that of the document.

To overcome the aforementioned issues, we present a novel document localization method that inherits the benefits of segmentation-based and keypoint-based approaches. Our idea is comprised of two primary phases: *Region of Boundary Extraction* and *Corners Detection*. Specifically, we first leverage the segmentation-based approach to define a region of the boundary using a deep learning model. Note that by using the segmentation-based approach rather than leveraging line detectors for detecting the exact boundary lines (as in other approaches), we can better handle hard samples whose background has a similar hue to the document. Besides, to boost the accuracy and tackle the data-hungry drawback of the deep learning-based approach, we provide a method for generating synthetic data that can be used to create realistic synthetic images with diverse backgrounds. We also develop a data annotation mechanism that saves time without sacrificing training precision. In the second stage, we leverage the Probabilistic Hough Transform [9] to determine straight lines that compose the boundary region and then cluster these lines into groups using the K-Means algorithm [8]. Finally, the coordinates of the document's corners are obtained by computing the intersection of the grouped boundary lines. Compared to the conventional keypoint-based method, the use of quadrilateral corner computation on the grouped boundary lines enables more effective handling of circumstances in which objects with identical corners appear in the same image as the targeted document. Moreover, the inference speed is also boosted thanks to the elimination of the deep learning model.

The main contributions of this paper are as follows:

1. We offer a novel and robust technique for the document localization problem that employs a deep learning model to detect the document's boundary region and then combines the Probabilistic Hough Transform and K-Means algorithm to precisely calculate the document's corners. Our proposed solution can successfully handle hard samples, e.g., the image's background has a comparable color to the document; the image includes objects whose corners are similar to those of the document.
2. We propose a training data annotation method that helps to save costs without sacrificing accuracy.
3. We provide a data augmentation mechanism that generates synthetic data with diverse backgrounds, achieving high performance without requiring a huge amount of real training data.
4. We conduct comprehensive experiments and thorough ablation studies to demonstrate the efficacy of our approach and get insight into its behavior.

The remainder of the paper is organized as follows. In Sect. 2, we briefly summarize state-of-the-art methods relative to document localization. Section 3 presents our proposed method. We evaluate our method and compare it with the state-of-the-art in Sect. 4, and conclude the paper in Sect. 5.

2   Related Works

Localization of documents has been in development for decades. The early works concentrate on developing flatbed scanners, followed by OCR implementation. The document should be positioned in a restricted area with a plain background. With a transparent background, traditional threshold-based segmentation approaches [12,15] may quickly locate the document.

However, as technology advances, we want the models to localize and automatically distinguish text from any background. Thus, document boundary-detection-based approaches [4,6,7] transform the original problem into a line detection problem. The image is first subjected to edge extraction techniques like the Canny detector and Sobel operator. Then, the edges that pertain to the document border are extracted using the line detector, and false positives are filtered away. However, these techniques typically call for a document with distinct bounds. Thus, the performance of these approaches is considerably affected by occlusions, changes in illumination, and complicated images.

In recent years, the development of deep learning models has revolution-ized the field of computer vision and produced remarkable results in various image analysis tasks. Document localization is one such task that has seen significant advances with the use of deep learning. Specifically, two popular approaches for solving this problem are segmentation-based and key-point-based. With segmentation-based, authors in [2,10,11] consider the document a specific object and produce pixel-wise predictions of document or non-document. [2] simply uses U-Net [14] for segment the document. In [10], the authors used a fully octave convolutional neural network (FO-CNN) for document image seg-mentation. The FO-CNN is a modified version of the U-Net [14] architecture that uses Octave convolutional layers [3] instead of regular convolutional layers. Octave convolutional layers [3] can capture features at different scales, which is particularly useful for document image segmentation. In [11], Ngoc et al. use the Itti-Koch saliency model, which computes the saliency map by combining multi-ple feature maps, including color, intensity, and orientation. Next, the saliency map is thresholded to extract the candidate document regions. The authors use a threshold value that is adaptively determined based on the local maximum of the saliency map. This approach helps to ensure that the detected regions are salient and distinct from the background. The extracted candidate regions are then further refined using a template-matching technique. The authors use pre-defined document templates to match against the candidate regions and select the best match. The templates are designed to cover a range of document types and orientations.

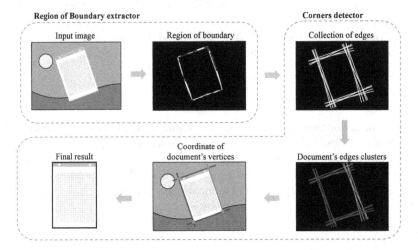

Fig. 1. Overview of the proposed document localization pipeline, which consists of two stages. The first one is to define a rough region of boundary, while the second helps to determine the exact corners of the document.

On the other hand, keypoint-based methods are also widely used. [5,18] consider the document localization problem as a four-corner detection problem.

Thus, they used keypoint-based models to predict four-corner of the document directly. The method proposed in [5] consists of two main stages: keypoint and region extraction and recursive corner detection. In the first stage, a CNN is utilized to detect keypoints of the document in the input image and region containing the corresponding keypoint. In the second stage, each region in the following stage goes through the same CNN recursively to detect a corner point in a region containing exactly one corner. In [18] by Zhu et al., the approach is similar to [5] with two stages: keypoint localization and recursive corner refinement. Firstly, the four corners of the document are roughly predicted through a "Joint Corner Detector" (JCD), which is a CNN-based model with attention mechanism. In the next stage, they also divide the image into four parts corresponding to four corners and apply four CNNs to refine corner detection results iteratively.

3   Methodology

In this section, the details of our proposed document localization solution will be introduced. We start by providing an overview of our solution in Sect. 3.1. We then describe the Boundary Extractor and Corner Detector in Sect. 3.2 and 3.3, respectively.

3.1   Overview

Figure 1 illustrates the proposed solution, which comprises two stages: *Region of Boundary Extractor* and *Corners Detector*. As previously discussed in Sect. 1, traditional approaches based on mathematical morphology [4,6,7] are hindered by complex backgrounds. To address this limitation, the first stage of our method employs a deep learning-based segmentation model to extract the region of the document's boundary. Subsequently, in the second stage, we utilize the Probabilistic Hough Transform [9], and K-Means clustering [8] techniques to compute the four corners of the document.

3.2   Region of Boundary Extractor

Model Selection. To address the limitations of the contour-based methods for document boundary extraction, we explore deep learning-based approach that can automatically detect the boundary region. Various models have been evaluated, including SegFormer [16], U^2-Net [13], etc. Through empirical analysis, we select U^2-Net [13] due to its high accuracy and compact size. The most significant contribution of U^2-Net [13] is the introduction of residual U-blocks, which have been proved to improve the model's performance through ablation studies. Their intuition is that the residual connections inside each U-Net [14] block allows for a concentration on local details, while the overall residual U-Net [14] architecture allows for the fusion of these small details with global (multi-scale) contextual information. Thanks to the use of the U-Net [14] blocks as the backbone instead of full pre-trained models, we can reduce our model size to only 5 MB.

Training Data Annotation. Accurate annotation of data is essential for deep learning models to utilize information effectively. However, it is well-known that annotating the exact mask for training a segmentation task is time-consuming. To this end, we provide an annotation method that leverages the provided coordinates of the four corners to define the document's rough boundary region. Specifically, we define the four edges of the document from the coordinates of the four corners. We then create the boundary region by expanding each boundary edge to a strip with the width of α pixels, where α is a tunable hyper-parameter. Notably, selecting a suitable value for α is critical, as an excessively large value would produce an overwhelming number of lines from the Probabilistic Hough Transform [9] (described in Sect. 3.3), leading to decreased accuracy and performance. Conversely, a value that is too small may hinder the segmentation model's ability to learn and predict the boundary region. Through an empirical study, we found that setting α to 3 pixels provides the highest accuracy.

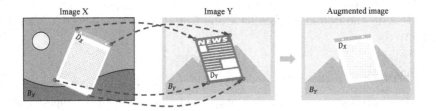

Fig. 2. From a real image X consists of a document D_X and a corresponding background B_X and an image Y containing a document D_Y and a distinct background B_Y, we generate an augmented image with document D_X and background B_Y.

Data Augmentation. The data augmentation has been widely studied in the field of computer vision and image processing. With the document localization problem, we discover that other approaches simply augmented data by placing a document on an arbitrary synthetic background. This approach, however, would not provide significant effect as the generated synthetic images are unrealistic. To this end, we propose a novel augmentation approach aiming to create more realistic synthetic images by utilizing real documents and backgrounds provided in the real training dataset. Figure 2 illustrates our augmentation method. Let X and Y be two arbitrary real images in the training dataset, whose background and documents are (B_X, D_X) and (B_Y, D_Y), respectively. Our idea is to generate an augmented image with the background B_Y of Y and the document D_X from X. To accomplish this, we crop D_Y from Y, use a perspective transformation to transform D_Y to the shape of D_X, and then place it on the position of D_X in X. This approach of augmentation enables us to enhance the diversity of the training data, thereby allowing us to achieve a high level of accuracy without a massive amount of real data.

3.3   Corner Detector

Overview. The corner detection process consists of two main steps: boundary line determination using the Probabilistic Hough Transform [9] and corner clustering using the K-Means algorithm [8]. Initially, the Probabilistic Hough Transform [9] is applied to draw straight lines within the boundary region that was determined in the previous stage. Subsequently, the lines are grouped into two clusters, namely horizontal and vertical clusters, using the K-Means algorithm [8]. The metric used in this K-Means algorithm is the lines' slope against the x-axis. Intuitively, the horizontal cluster consists of lines that are closer to the x-axis, while the vertical cluster is comprised of lines near the y-axis. Then, each cluster is further divided into two subsets to obtain four subsets, each of which consists of lines belonging to a side of the document. To this end, we apply the K-Means algorithm [8] again with the metric of the distance from the line to the coordinate system's origin. Specifically, the horizontal set is now split into an upper and a lower subset, while the vertical set is divided into a left and a right subset. Finally, we select four representative lines, each of which is the median line of a subset, and determine their intersection to obtain the document's corners.

Algorithm 1: Boundary Lines Clustering Algorithm

Input   : A set of boundary lines E, each represented as a pair of points (x_1, y_1) and (x_2, y_2).
Output   : A set of four clusters U, L, R, L, each containing a subset of boundary lines from E.
Parameter: k: the number of clusters to use in the K-means algorithm.
Function K-Means(X, k):
  Initialize k centroids $C_1, C_2, \ldots, C_k$ randomly.
  repeat
    Assign each data point x_i to the nearest centroid C_j.
    for $j \leftarrow 1$ **to** k **do**
     | $C_j \leftarrow$ mean of all points assigned to C_j.
    end
  until C *no longer changes*
  return C
Function *BoundaryLineClustering(E)*:
  for *each boundary lines* $e = \{(x_1, y_1), (x_2, y_2)\} \in E$ **do**
    Compute the slope $m = (y_2 - y_1)/(x_2 - x_1)$
    Compute the y-intercept $b = y_1 - mx_1$; Compute the distance from the boundary line to the origin $\rho = 1/\sqrt{(m/b)^2 + (1/b)^2}$
    Store the slope m and ρ of e.
  end
  $E_h \leftarrow$ K-Means$(m_E, 2)$; $E_v \leftarrow E \setminus E_h$
  $U, L \leftarrow$ K-Means$(\rho_{E_h}, 2)$; $R, L \leftarrow$ K-Means$(\rho_{E_v}, 2)$
  return U, L, R, L

Boundary Lines Extraction and Clustering. Given a binary image that represents the document's boundary region, we apply the Probabilistic Hough Transform [9] to determine straight lines forming the boundary (we name these lines as boundary lines).

Let $E = \{e_1, e_2, ..., e_n\}$ be the set of n boundary lines obtained by the Probabilistic Hough Transform [9] algorithm, for each line e_i, we calculate its angle to the x-axis (denoted by m_i), and its distance to the origin of the coordinate system (denoted by ρ_i). Now, we apply the K-Means algorithm [8] on the set $M = \{m_1, m_2, ..., m_n\}$ to divide E into two clusters, namely the horizontal cluster E_h, and the vertical cluster E_v. Subsequently, we perform K-Means on E_h and E_v using the distance ρ_i to divide them into four subsets, namely upper, lower, right, and left groups. The Algorithm 1 describes the pseudocode of our clustering process.

Corner Determination. We select from the upper, lower, right, and left groups four representative lines. Each representative line is the one with the median slope m and median y-intercept b. Using these four representative lines, we now determine their intersections to obtain the four corners of the document. Finally, we crop the document from the original image and perform the perspective transformation on the extracted document.

4   Experiments

In this section, we conduct comprehensive experiments to evaluate our proposed approach. We carefully compare it to the state-of-the-art (SOTA) document localization methods [5,18,19] under the same experimental settings. We then perform an ablation study to analyze the contribution of our proposed data augmentation method.

4.1   Dataset and Experimental Setup

To perform the evaluation, we use the ICDAR 2015 SmartDoc challenge 1 dataset [1]. This dataset contains 150 videos taken by a Google Nexus 7 tablet. From the original videos, we extracted a total of 25K frames with a resolution of 1920 × 1080 on six types of documents that are placed over five different backgrounds, as shown in Fig. 3a. The documents are entirely placed inside the images (and never hit the image's boundary). This dataset is challenging with various lighting conditions, heterogeneous backgrounds, motion blur, and out-of-focus blur. Especially the fifth background is the most complicated, with many objects (e.g., pen, cable, computer mouse, etc.) placed near to or even overlapping with the document. The sample of the fifth background is presented in Fig. 3b.

Evaluation Metrics. To evaluate the performance of the method, the Jaccard Index (JI) between the detected document A and the ground truth G is used:

$$JI = area(G \cap A)/area(G \cup A) \tag{1}$$

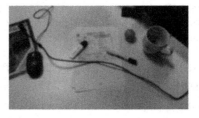

| (a) Dataset overview | (b) Sample image from the fifth background |

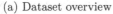

Fig. 3. Representative examples from the ICDAR 2015 SmartDoc challenge 1 dataset [1].

Training Details. In our implementation, we train the U^2-Net model [13] with the batch size of 8 and the input image size of 480×480 pixels. With the dataset, we convert all videos to get 25000 images. We used only 20% data for training, 20% for validating, and 60% for testing. From the training data, we apply our data augmentation method to generate 15000 synthetic images. Especially for the most challenging background, i.e., background 5, we increase the number of augmented images to 7500.

All implementations of U^2-Net model [13] are performed using the PyTorch framework, and the training process is conducted on a machine with an NVIDIA Tesla P100. The Probabilistic Hough Transform [9] and K-Means algorithm [8] are deployed using OpenCV and Pyclustering libraries.

4.2 Experimental Results

Quantitative results on the ICDAR 2015 SmartDoc challenge 1 dataset [1] are shown in Table 1. As shown, our method outperforms all of the others, with an overall accuracy of 98.8%. Compared with the second best method, i.e., [18], our proposal improves the accuracy by 0.6% in average, and 1.7% in the best case (background 5). In addition, our proposed method also reduces the run-time significantly compared to SOTA with compatible accuracy. For example, the per-image runtime of the third-best method was 1 min, while that of our approach is only 0.5 s. Notably, our proposal achieves the highest performance gap compared to the others when applied to the dataset with the most challenging backgrounds (background 5). To be more specific, for this setting, our proposed method improves the accuracy by 1.7% on average compared to the SOTA. In addition, thanks to the proposed augmentation method, we can reduce the amount of real training to only 20% of the dataset, compared to 50% or 70% like other methods.

Table 1. Performance comparison on the ICDAR 2015 SmartDoc challenge 1 dataset [1]. The red (resp. blue) color denotes the best (resp. second) result in each background. Our method gets the highest overall score

Method	Bg 1	Bg 2	Bg 3	Bg 4	Bg 5	Overall	Runtime
ISPL-CVML	0.987	0.965	0.985	0.977	0.856	0.966	N/A
LRDE [17]	0.987	0.978	0.989	0.984	0.861	0.972	1min
NetEase	0.962	0.955	0.962	0.951	0.222	0.882	N/A
SEECS-NUST-2 [5]	0.983	0.972	0.983	0.970	0.948	0.9743	N/A
SmartEngines [19]	0.989	0.983	0.990	0.979	0.688	0.955	N/A
L. R. S. Leal	0.961	0.944	0.965	0.930	0.412	0.895	0.43s
LRDE-2	0.905	0.936	0.859	0.903	N/A	N/A	0.04s
Zhu et al. [18]	0.988	0.984	0.983	0.984	0.961	0.982	0.6s
Ours	0.991	0.987	0.992	0.989	0.978	0.988	**0.5s**

In order to facilitate a more comprehensive comparison, we present a visualization of the outcomes derived from the ICDAR 2015 SmartDoc Challenge 1 dataset in Fig. 4, showcasing our proposed technique alongside two state-of-the-art models: SEECS-NUST-2 [5] and Zhu et al. [18]. A close examination reveals that the performance is identical for backgrounds 1, 2, and 3. However, when considering backgrounds 4 and 5, our proposed method demonstrates a superior ability to accurately localize documents in relation to the other two techniques. This finding indicates that our approach is capable of localizing documents within complex and challenging backgrounds, such as those characterized by low contrast, occlusion, and clustering. Furthermore, an analysis of detection results for the fourth image (background 4) underscores the robustness of our method in localizing documents subject to arbitrary rotation.

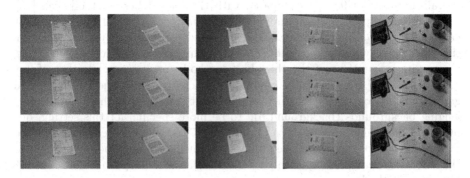

Fig. 4. Localization results for the ICDAR 2015 SmartDoc Challenge 1 dataset [1] using three methods: SEECS-NUST-2 [5], Zhu et al. [18], and our proposed method. The results are color-coded as follows: green, blue, and red represent SEECS-NUST-2, Zhu et al., and our method, respectively.

4.3   Ablation Studies

In this section, we validate the contribution of key components of our proposed method to the performance. Table 2 verifies the effectiveness of the augmentation method under different settings.

Table 2. The effectiveness of our proposed data augmentation method.

Settings	Bg 1	Bg 2	Bg 3	Bg 4	Bg 5	Overall
Baseline (Experiment 1)	0.972	0.968	0.951	0.971	0.956	0.964
Baseline (Experiment 2)	0.903	0.896	0.889	0.916	0.881	0.897
Baseline + Augmentation	**0.991**	**0.987**	**0.992**	**0.989**	**0.978**	**0.988**

Experiments 1. In this experiment, we use 60% data for training and 40% for testing. It is evident that our method continues to yield a quite good result, as shown in Table 2, with overall accuracy is 96.4%, even better than the majority of the submissions that participated in the ICDAR 2015 SmartDoc challenge 1 [1].

Experiments 2. A total of 60% of the data is used for the actual testing, while the remaining 40% is used for training and validation. However, we did not use augmentation for this experiment. We can observe that our proposed method still provides a fairly good result of 89.6% overall, and there is no background with low results. This demonstrates that we can get good results with relatively little data using our strategy.

Experiments 3. The data are split up exactly like they were in experiment 2. In contrast, our augmentation method was used for this experiment, and we produced an additional 15000 synthetic photos, of which half were fifth background images. And the effectiveness has been proved by the Table 2 above. As can be seen in Table 1, the model performed well across all backgrounds, outperforming any and all other models with 98.8% accuracy. During the process of augmenting, more difficult backgrounds, such as background 5, are included in the training data. This is one of the reasons why our method is so effective.

5   Conclusion

This paper proposed a novel approach to document localization that combines deep learning and classical image processing methods to achieve high accuracy and robustness. The proposed method was evaluated on the ICDAR 2015 Smart-Doc Challenge 1 dataset [1], which includes challenging scenarios such as complex backgrounds and varying illumination. Our approach achieved an overall accuracy of 98.8%, outperforming state-of-the-art models on this benchmark. Notably, our method obtained an accuracy of 97.8% on the most challenging background cases (Background 5), surpassing the current state-of-the-art model by 1.7% while using only 20% of the dataset.

Acknowledgement. This research is funded by CMC Applied Technology Institute (CATI).

References

1. Burie, J., et al.: ICDAR2015 competition on smartphone document capture and OCR (smartdoc). In: 2015 13th International Conference on Document Analysis and Recognition (ICDAR), pp. 1161–1165 (2015). https://doi.org/10.1109/ICDAR. 2015.7333943
2. Castelblanco, A., Solano, J., Lopez, C., Rivera, E., Tengana, L., Ochoa, M.: Machine learning techniques for identity document verification in uncontrolled environments: a case study. Pattern Recogn. **12088**, 271–281 (2020)
3. Chen, Y., et al.: Drop an octave: reducing spatial redundancy in convolutional neural networks with octave convolution. In: Proceedings of the IEEE/CVF International Conference on Computer Vision (ICCV) (2019)
4. Guillou, E., Méneveaux, D., Maisel, E., Bouatouch, K.: Using vanishing points for camera calibration and coarse 3d reconstruction from a single image. Vis. Comput. **16**, 396–410 (2000)
5. Javed, K., Shafait, F.: Real-time document localization in natural images by recursive application of a CNN. In: 2017 14th IAPR International Conference on Document Analysis and Recognition (ICDAR), vol. 01, pp. 105–110 (2017). https://doi. org/10.1109/ICDAR.2017.26
6. Kofler, C., Keysers, D., Keysers, D., Koetsier, D.A., Laagland, J., Breuel, T.M.: Gestural interaction for an automatic document capture system (2007)
7. Lampert, C.H., Braun, T., Ulges, A., Keysers, D., Breuel, T.M.: Oblivious document capture and real-time retrieval (2005)
8. MacQueen, J.B.: Some methods for classification and analysis of multivariate observations. In: Cam, L.M.L., Neyman, J. (eds.) Proceedings of the Fifth Berkeley Symposium on Mathematical Statistics and Probability, vol. 1, pp. 281–297. University of California Press (1967)
9. Matas, J., Galambos, C., Kittler, J.: Robust detection of lines using the progressive probabilistic hough transform. Comput. Vis. Image Underst. **78**(1), 119–137 (2000). https://doi.org/10.1006/cviu.1999.0831. https://www.sciencedirect.com/ science/article/pii/S1077314299908317
10. das Neves, R.B., Verccosa, L.F., Macêdo, D., Bezerra, B.L.D., Zanchettin, C.: A fast fully octave convolutional neural network for document image segmentation. In: 2020 International Joint Conference on Neural Networks (IJCNN), pp. 1–6 (2020)
11. Ngoc, M.O.V., Fabrizio, J., Géraud, T.: Document detection in videos captured by smartphones using a saliency-based method. In: 2019 International Conference on Document Analysis and Recognition Workshops (ICDARW), vol. 4, pp. 19–24 (2019)
12. Qiao, Y., Hu, Q., Qian, G., Luo, S., Nowinski, W.L.: Thresholding based on variance and intensity contrast. Pattern Recognit. **40**(2), 596–608 (2007). https://doi. org/10.1016/j.patcog.2006.04.027. https://www.sciencedirect.com/science/article/ pii/S0031320306001841
13. Qin, X., Zhang, Z., Huang, C., Dehghan, M., Zaiane, O., Jagersand, M.: U2-net: Going deeper with nested u-structure for salient object detection, vol. 106, p. 107404 (2020)

14. Ronneberger, O., Fischer, P., Brox, T.: U-Net: convolutional networks for biomedical image segmentation. In: Navab, N., Hornegger, J., Wells, W.M., Frangi, A.F. (eds.) MICCAI 2015. LNCS, vol. 9351, pp. 234–241. Springer, Cham (2015). https://doi.org/10.1007/978-3-319-24574-4_28

15. Tobias, O., Seara, R.: Image segmentation by histogram thresholding using fuzzy sets. IEEE Trans. Image Process. **11**(12), 1457–1465 (2002). https://doi.org/10.1109/TIP.2002.806231

16. Xie, E., Wang, W., Yu, Z., Anandkumar, A., Alvarez, J.M., Luo, P.: Segformer: Simple and efficient design for semantic segmentation with transformers. In: Ranzato, M., Beygelzimer, A., Dauphin, Y., Liang, P., Vaughan, J.W. (eds.) Advances in Neural Information Processing Systems, vol. 34, pp. 12077–12090. Curran Associates, Inc. (2021). https://proceedings.neurips.cc/paper_files/paper/2021/file/64f1f27bf1b4ec22924fd0acb550c235-Paper.pdf

17. Xu, Y., Carlinet, E., Géraud, T., Najman, L.: Hierarchical segmentation using tree-based shape spaces. IEEE Trans. Pattern Anal. Mach. Intell. **39**(3), 457–469 (2017). https://doi.org/10.1109/TPAMI.2016.2554550

18. Zhu, A., Zhang, C., Li, Z., Xiong, S.: Coarse-to-fine document localization in natural scene image with regional attention and recursive corner refinement. Int. J. Doc. Anal. Recogn. (IJDAR) **22**(3), 351–360 (2019). https://doi.org/10.1007/s10032-019-00341-0

19. Zhukovsky, A., et al.: Segments graph-based approach for document capture in a smartphone video stream. In: 2017 14th IAPR International Conference on Document Analysis and Recognition (ICDAR), vol. 01, pp. 337–342 (2017). https://doi.org/10.1109/ICDAR.2017.63

Decision Making

A Group Decision-Making Method Based on Reciprocal Preference Relations Created from Sentiment Analysis

José Ramón Trillo$^{(\boxtimes)}$ [ID], Ignacio Javier Pérez [ID], Enrique Herrera-Viedma [ID], Juan Antonio Morente-Molinera [ID], and Francisco Javier Cabrerizo [ID]

Department of Computer Science and Artificial Intelligence, Andalusian Research Institute in Data Science and Computational Intelligence (DASCI), University of Granada, Granada 18071, Spain
jrtrillo@ugr.es, {ijperez,viedma,jamoren,cabrerizo}@decsai.ugr.es

Abstract. Group decision-making is an event in which a group of experts have to decide between a limited set of alternatives. To share their opinions and ideas, this group of experts conducts a debate where they compare the alternatives with each other. Nevertheless, once the debate is over, the experts must provide their assessments by using reciprocal preference relations. This can be a problem, as an expert may not be consistent between what he expresses and his assessments. To create such consistency, in this work a group decision-making method is developed, which automatically creates the experts' reciprocal preference relations from the comments they make in the debate. These comments are classified into positive and negative by using sentiment analysis techniques, specifically employing the majority membership in the bag of words of a given class. To calculate each value of the reciprocal preference relation, a new operator has been developed that uses the ranked comments and weights them. Nonetheless, the method offers the possibility to modify a reciprocal preference relation if the expert wishes to do so. Finally, this new group decision-making method develops a second operator that also uses the number of comments to adjust the weight of each expert. This operator quantifies the number of comments that an expert makes during the debate and gives him or her more weight based on the number of comments he or she makes. Consequently, the more comments the expert makes, the higher the weight he or she gets.

Keywords: Reciprocal Preference Relations · Group Decision-Making · Natural Language Processing · Sentiment Analysis · Classification

1 Introduction

Group decision-making is an event in which a group of experts has to decide between a limited set of alternatives. To help experts to choose from this limited set of alternatives, Group Decision-Making methods (GDM) were developed

© The Author(s), under exclusive license to Springer Nature Switzerland AG 2023
H. Fujita et al. (Eds.): IEA/AIE 2023, LNAI 13925, pp. 183–194, 2023.
https://doi.org/10.1007/978-3-031-36819-6_16

[1]. Nonetheless, access to the Internet has increased the number of experts and alternatives available in decision-making processes. This is a challenge for traditional GDM methods, as traditionally experts did not discuss a large number of elements, held face-to-face meetings and only have to manage the information they provide [13, 19]. Nevertheless, today's world has become more complex and the number of options to be discussed has increased. Hence, GDM methods need to adapt to new technologies and new ways of providing information.

In a GDM process, experts are given the possibility to discuss to present their opinions and ideas through the use of comments. This information they generate is ambiguous and difficult for the systems to understand, as they only understand a precise language, such as binary language. Consequently, in many GDM methods, the information generated by the experts during the debate is discarded, but to take advantage of the information generated by the experts during the debate, such as whether the comment made is positive or negative or which alternatives are being compared, it is possible to use Natural Language Processing (NLP), in particular, sentiment analysis [2].

Some attempts to apply sentiment analysis to GDM methods can be found in the current literature, e.g. [4, 8]. Nonetheless, none of those methods indicates the importance that each expert must have on the decision based on his/her participation. To solve the problem of the limited set of linguistic labels [11], in this paper, we propose a novel method that uses sentiment analysis to detect, through the comments made by experts, which alternatives they are talking about. The method also detects whether the comment is positive or negative. With this double detection, a novel developed operator is used to assign a preference value to the comparison between two alternatives. Afterwards, we analyse whether there is a consensus among the experts and we calculate the weight of each of them. For this purpose, the number of comments made by the experts during the debate is used again, the greater the number of comments, the greater the weight they have in the decision. Finally, with the weight and values of each expert, the ranking of alternatives is calculated. In cases where the consensus is low, another GDM round is performed.

This document is composed of six sections. In Sect. 2, basic concepts related to Group Decision-Making and sentiment analysis will be explained. In Sect. 3, the Group Decision-Making method that uses sentiment analysis in comments to obtain their reciprocal preference relations and adjust the weight of experts is developed. Then, in Sect. 4, a theoretical example where the method proposed in this paper is applied is illustrated. In Sect. 5, the disadvantages and advantages of the method are discussed. Finally, in Sect. 6, conclusions are drawn.

2   Preliminaries

The basic concepts related to the method proposed in the document will be developed in this section. Therefore, this section has been divided into two parts: in Sect. 2.1 you can see the concepts associated with Group Decision-Making problems, such as the definition of the concept of the expert set. Section 2.2 will show the concepts related to sentiment analysis and the creation of the bag of words that will allow the classification of the comments.

2.1   Group Decision-Making Problems

Group decision-making problems it is a process where a finite and limited set of experts have to choose between a finite set of alternatives. For this purpose, the experts have to provide information and from that information, a method is developed to obtain the option or set of alternatives preferred by the experts [7]. To obtain a formal definition of these methods that solve a Group Decision-Making problem, the set of experts is defined as $E = \{e_1, \ldots, e_n\}$, where $n \in \mathbb{N}$ is the number of experts participating in the process. Afterwards, we define the set of alternatives $X = \{x_1, \ldots, x_m\}$, where $m \in \mathbb{N}$ is the total number of options available to the experts [15, 18].

When the set of experts and alternatives have been developed, we develop the process by which the experts will present their ideas. Although there are several ways to represent the information, such as the use of linguistic label sets by using numerical sets to show opinions, which can be comparisons between alternatives or a general assessment. For this paper, reciprocal preference relations using numerical sets are used to represent the information. Reciprocal preference relations are matrices of dimension $m \times m$ and have an empty main diagonal where each element is the comparison between two different alternatives. This matrix, denoted as M_s; $s = 1 \ldots, n$ is defined as $M_s = (q_s^{ij}; i \neq j = 1, \ldots, n)$, where q_s^{ij} is the comparison between alternative x_i over alternative x_j. This comparison is defined by an operator, defined as follows: $\mu_s : X \times X \rightarrow [0, 1]$. Consequently each element of the matrix can be defined as $q_s^{ij} = \mu_s(x_i, x_j)$; $x_i, x_j \in X$, verifying that $q_s^{ij} + q_s^{ji} = 1$. Once these concepts have been defined, the different steps that make up a GDM method are developed. These steps are as follows:

– Providing the opinions: during this first step, the experts discuss by comparing the alternatives with each other and providing their ideas and opinions. At the end of the debate, the values of the alternatives are obtained and these values are represented by employing reciprocal preference relations.
– Consensus analysis: this second step is an optional element where we check whether the opinions among the experts are similar enough to be able to affirm that there is a consensus among them. For this purpose, a threshold called the consensus threshold and denoted as $\alpha \in [0, 1]$, is set. To consider that there is agreement among the experts participating in the process, the threshold must be exceeded by the consensus value, denoted as $cnsus[0, 1]$. Nevertheless, the consensus value may be lower than the consensus threshold and if this happens, a feedback process will be carried out and the experts will be advised to bring their opinions and ideas closer together. This process may be cyclical and infinite, as the process threshold may never be exceeded, but to avoid this problem, some rounds are previously established, denoted as $\rho \in \mathbb{N}$, where in the case of reaching this number of rounds the ranking

of alternatives will be provided, specifying that there is no consensus among the experts.

- Aggregation of information: after this optional step, the information is aggregated to obtain a single list of preferences. This collective reciprocal preference relation, denoted as C, is a matrix of dimension $m \times m$ that contains all the information generated by the experts. To aggregate the information, it is necessary to use an aggregation operator, for this paper we will proceed to use the weighted average (WA) operator.
- Obtaining the ranking of alternatives: finally, in this step, the C matrix is used to calculate the ranking of alternatives and consequently, to obtain the experts' preferred option. To obtain this objective, it is necessary to apply to the collective reciprocal preference relation an operator that allows giving value to each alternative. There are different operators, such as the VlseKriterijumska Optimizacija I Kompromisno Resenje operator (VIKOR) or the Quantifier-Guided Degree of Dominance (QGDD) operator. For this method, we proceed by using the latter operator.

Nowadays, the number of methods that propose a solution to a GDM problem has increased. In [16], a multi-criteria GDM method is presented that is adaptable to different scenarios and uses a multi-language approach to create an adaptable solution to different problems. In [5], a multi-attribute GDM method that presents a solution to a concrete problem using a fuzzy hesitant environment is presented. Finally, in [3], a GDM model based on the granular computing paradigm is created to increase consensus.

2.2 Sentiment Analysis

Sentiment analysis is a part of NLP that aims to extract behaviours from, in this case, comments made by experts. Nonetheless, sometimes the comments made by experts can be ambiguous, which makes it more complex to extract information. To solve this problem, we are going to use a bag-of-words approach based on a ranked dataset [17] to classify comments according to their positivity. In this way, relevant information can be obtained and applied to the GDM process. The process of creating a bag of words starts with a dataset of comments previously classified into the classes to be detected, in this case, positive and negative. From these comments, the following steps are carried out:

- Obtaining relevant information: in this first step, the relevant information has to be obtained to ensure that our bag of words does not contain words that do not contribute information to the classification. Therefore, two steps will be carried out: in the first step, irrelevant information such as numbers, articles or symbols will be eliminated. To carry this out, the **stopped function** is used, which detects and eliminates this information from a dictionary with irrelevant words. This function contains a set of words considered irrelevant. So if a word in a comment is in the set of the function, it is deleted because the function considers it irrelevant. The second step is to simplify words that are written differently. For this purpose, the **stemmer function** is used, which rewrites the words and puts them in their root form.

- Splitting sentences: with the comments rewritten and simplified, they are then split into words or sets of words. Each part into which the commentary is split is called an n-gram where n stands for the number of words contained in each part. Consequently, in this paper, the comments are divided into words and as each part contains a single word, i.e. n equals one, they are called unigrams.
- Creation of a bag of words: in this last step, each of the unigrams obtained in the previous step is taken. These unigrams are placed according to the label of the comment and for this paper, two different sets are needed, one for the positive and one for the negative. The unigrams are added only once in the set, therefore, if the comment has a negative label, all the unigrams of the comment will go into the negative set. Finally, each of these sets will contain all the unigrams associated with each of the classes, it can build all comments of each class from unigrams belonging to its set.

The variety of papers related to sentiment analysis has increased in recent years. In [20], an algorithm based on a convolutional network is developed that detects sentiment and applies it to e-commerce. In [9], a GDM method is created that obtains extra information from the comments made during the debate and by using dictionaries. Finally, in [12], an algorithm is created to eliminate the noise that can generate incorrect information in a classifier that uses sentiment analysis.

3   GDM Method Based on Reciprocal Preference Relations Created from Sentiment Analysis

This section presents the GDM method proposed in this paper. This method is composed of the following parts:

- Debate between experts and reciprocal preference relation: in this first part, experts discuss opinions and ideas. Once finished, they wait for the algorithm to tell them their reciprocal preference relations and adjust the parameters if they want to.
- Consensus analysis: once the reciprocal preference relations are available, a consensus analysis is carried out to determine whether there is a similarity of opinion. To determine that this similarity exists, a consensus threshold must be exceeded.
- Calculation of the experts' weights: if the consensus threshold is exceeded, the weight of each expert is determined according to his or her participation in the debate.
- Computation of the collective reciprocal preference relation: using the weights and reciprocal preference relations obtained, the collective reciprocal preference relation is calculated using the WA operator.
- Obtaining the ranking of alternatives: finally, from the collective reciprocal preference relation and using the QGDD operator with the mean operator, the ranking of alternatives is determined.

3.1   Debate and Reciprocal Preference Relations Calculation

In this first part, the experts discuss and comment on their opinions. For this, the definitions from Sect. 2.1 are used to define the set of experts and the set of alternatives. To be able to know which alternatives are presented in each comment, a dictionary is created for each alternative, containing the name of the alternative and the ordinal and cardinal position. In case two alternatives are being compared, and these dictionaries detect this, it will be the first alternative over the second. It may also be the case that only one alternative is mentioned and therefore the comment will be reflected in the other alternatives. Finally, it may be the case that the dictionaries do not detect any word, which means that it will be taken into account for all options, i.e. the comment will have no value. Once the different dictionaries are obtained for each alternative, each comment made by the expert is made in the first two steps developed in Sect. 2.2. Once the comments are decomposed, they are compared word by word to find which alternatives are being compared. In this way, if matches are found with two different dictionaries associated with each alternative, the comparison will be made between the alternative associated with the first match with a dictionary, with the second alternative of the second dictionary, i.e., in the comment "the first alternative I like better than the fourth alternative". The first dictionary match is "first", which will refer to the first alternative and the second match will be "fourth" which will refer to the fourth option. This assumes that the comment will be made by comparing the first alternative to the fourth.

Once it is known for which alternatives each comment is compared, the classifier is used using the two bags of words created in Sect. 2.2. To create the bag of words it is necessary to use a training dataset, this training dataset is [17], where two different datasets are used and one of them has the classification of the comments as positive/negative. Once we have the bags we apply to the training set all the procedures developed in Sect. 2.2. For each comment made by the experts, the first two steps developed in Sect. 2.2 are performed, as was done to detect which alternatives were being compared. Once a comment is broken down into unigrams, we look for which of the two bags of words has the most unigrams that make up the comment. If the comment's unigrams are mostly in the negative bag of words, the comment is considered negative; otherwise, it is considered positive. Consequently, one can define the number of positive comments made by an expert e_s of alternative x_i on x_j as $cmp_s^{ij} \in \mathbb{N} \cup \{0\}$ and the number of negative comments as $cmn_s^{ij} \in \mathbb{N} \cup \{0\}$. Moreover, it is verified that $cmp_s^{ij} = cmn_s^{ji}$ and that $cmn_s^{ij} = cmp_s^{ji}$, obtaining the value of the reciprocal preference relation as follows:

$$q_s^{ij} = \frac{1 + \frac{cmp_s^{ij} - cmn_s^{ij}}{cmp_s^{ij} + cmn_s^{ij}}}{2}$$

This equation contains the positive minus the negative comments divided by the sum of the two. So if the expert only makes positive comments, the result will be equal to 1, if he/she only makes negative comments it will be equal to

−1. With that information, the interval of this part of the formula would be $[−1, 1]$. To have preference relations to be in the interval $[0, 1]$. It is necessary to move the interval, hence a $+1$ is added, leaving the interval at $[0, 2]$ and then it is normalised by dividing by 2 so that the interval of the values of the reciprocal preference relations is $[0, 1]$. Finally, in case no comment is made on the comparison of the two alternatives the value of q_s^{ij} is equal to 0.5. Once the reciprocal preference relations are obtained, the experts can alter them if they wish.

3.2   Consensus Analysis

Once the reciprocal preference relationships are obtained, the consensus analysis is carried out. The objective of this analysis is to seek a degree of acceptance among the experts participating in the process. For this purpose, a threshold is set, which varies according to the problem at hand, called the consensus threshold and denoted as $\alpha \in [0, 1]$. This threshold must be exceeded by the consensus value, denoted as $cnsus \in [0, 1]$. Nevertheless, it may be the case that the threshold is not exceeded, in which case a feedback process is necessary where experts have to be recommended to seek consensus by modifying their preferences if necessary. Nonetheless, this process can be cyclical and infinite and to avoid this process, a limited number of rounds, denoted as ρ is established, which for this document will be $\rho = 10$. Finally, the consensus value is calculated by applying the Euclidean distance:

$$cnsus = 1 - \frac{2 \cdot \sum_{s=1}^{n-1} \sum_{k=1; s>k}^{n} \frac{\sqrt{\sum_{i=1}^{m} \sum_{j=1; i\neq j}^{m} (q_s^{ij} - q_k^{ij})^2}}{m \cdot m - m}}{(n-1) \cdot n}$$

3.3   Calculation of the Experts' Weights

If the consensus threshold is exceeded, the weight of each expert is calculated for each element of their preferences. In this part of the process, the ranked comments from Sect. 3.1 are used again. Consequently, a matrix of weights is obtained, defined as $W_s = (w_s^{ij}; i \neq j = 1, \ldots, n)$, where each element of the matrix, w_s^{ij} is defined as follows:

$$w_s^{ij} = \frac{cmp_s^{ij} + cmn_s^{ij}}{\sum_{k=1}^{n} cmp_k^{ij} + cmn_k^{ij}}$$

In case the denominator is equal to 0 then the weight of each expert will be equal to $w_s^{ij} = \frac{1}{n}; s = 1, \ldots, n$.

3.4   Computation of the Collective Reciprocal Preference Relation

Once the weights of each expert and their reciprocal preference relations are obtained, we proceed to calculate the collective reciprocal preference relation. This reciprocal preference relation is a matrix $m \times m$ with an empty diagonal, containing all the information generated by the experts and defined as $C = (c^{ij}; i \neq j = 1, \dots, m)$. For this paper, the information generated by the experts has been chosen to be weighted and therefore, the WA operator is used to assign a weight to each of the values. Each element of the C matrix is calculated as follows:

$$c^{ij} = \sum_{s=1}^{n} q_s^{ij} * w_s^{ij}$$

When the values of the collective reciprocal preference relation have been obtained, the ranking of alternatives can be calculated.

3.5   Obtaining the Ranking of Alternatives

In this last stage, we proceed to calculate the ranking of alternatives. To obtain it, we proceed, on the one hand, to use the collective reciprocal preference relation, C, and on the other hand, the Quantifier-Guided Degree of Dominance (QGDD) operator with the mean operator. This operator defines the degree of dominance of an alternative x_i over the others. This operator is denoted $QGDD_i$ and is calculated as follows:

$$QGDD_i = \frac{\displaystyle\sum_{j=1; i \neq j}^{m} c^{ij}}{m - 1}$$

After using this operator with the mean operator, it is possible to determine which alternative is preferred by the experts and consequently, it is possible to determine the ranking of alternatives as:

$$X_{QGDD} = \{x_i \in X \mid QGDD_i = \sup_{x_j \in X} QGDD_j\}$$

The preferred alternative will be equal to the first value that gives X_{QGDD}.

4   Illustrative Example

In this section, an illustrative example is developed to demonstrate the usefulness of the method. Therefore, we define the set of three experts who have to choose where to invest their capital. These experts have four options in which to invest: in stocks, x_1, in real estate, x_2, in start-ups, x_3, or in currency purchases, x_4. During the debate, the experts made several comments, some of them from expert e_1 are the following:

- Stocks are safer than start-ups. The unigrams are "Stocks", "safe" (the root word of safer), and "start-ups". Using the dictionaries it can be seen that the first alternative is compared to the third alternative. Finally, only the unigram "safe" is in the bag of positive words and therefore the comment is considered positive.
- The fourth alternative is worse than the first option. The unigrams are "fourth", "alternative", "bad" (the root word of worse), "first", "option". The largest number of unigrams is found in the negative bag of words. Consequently, this comment made by the expert is considered negative.

Once the discussion is over, and all the sentences of all the experts have been analysed, the method shows the following reciprocal preference relations:

$$
M_1 = \begin{pmatrix} - & 0.6 & 0.8 & 0.9 \\ 0.4 & - & 0.5 & 0.6 \\ 0.2 & 0.5 & - & 0.7 \\ 0.1 & 0.4 & 0.3 & - \end{pmatrix} \quad M_2 = \begin{pmatrix} - & 0.7 & 0.9 & 0.8 \\ 0.3 & - & 0.7 & 0.7 \\ 0.1 & 0.3 & - & 0.5 \\ 0.2 & 0.3 & 0.5 & - \end{pmatrix} \quad M_3 = \begin{pmatrix} - & 0.8 & 0.9 & 0.9 \\ 0.2 & - & 0.7 & 0.5 \\ 0.1 & 0.3 & - & 0.7 \\ 0.1 & 0.5 & 0.3 & - \end{pmatrix}
$$

When the reciprocal preference relations have been visualised, the experts agree. So the method proceeds to calculate the consensus. In this paper, a consensus threshold of $\alpha = 0.9$ is set. As the consensus value is equal to $cnsus = 0,9615$, we proceed to calculate the weight that each expert has for each comparison, obtaining the following result:

$$
W_1 = \begin{pmatrix} - & 0.33 & 0.50 & 0.50 \\ 0.33 & - & 0.10 & 0.20 \\ 0.50 & 0.10 & - & 0.33 \\ 0.50 & 0.20 & 0.33 & - \end{pmatrix} \quad W_2 = \begin{pmatrix} - & 0.33 & 0.25 & 0.30 \\ 0.33 & - & 0.40 & 0.60 \\ 0.25 & 0.40 & - & 0.33 \\ 0.30 & 0.60 & 0.33 & - \end{pmatrix} \quad W_3 = \begin{pmatrix} - & 0.33 & 0.25 & 0.20 \\ 0.33 & - & 0.50 & 0.20 \\ 0.25 & 0.50 & - & 0.33 \\ 0.20 & 0.20 & 0.33 & - \end{pmatrix}
$$

With the weights and reciprocal preference relations, it is possible to calculate the collective reciprocal preference relation, C, as:

$$
C = \begin{pmatrix} - & 0.700 & 0.850 & 0.870 \\ 0.300 & - & 0.680 & 0.640 \\ 0.150 & 0.320 & - & 0.633 \\ 0.130 & 0.360 & 0.366 & - \end{pmatrix}
$$

With the calculated collective reciprocal preference relation, C, it is possible to determine the ranking of alternatives using the QGDD (Table 1):

Table 1. QGDD results

	x_1	x_2	x_3	x_4
QGDD	0.8067	0.5400	0.3678	0.2855

To verify that the process is correct, Trillo's theorem [14] is used. This theorem allows us to check to employ a count that the calculations in the process are correct. As the theorem is verified, then it can be seen that the supremum of Table 1 corresponds to the alternative x_1, being the one chosen among the experts.

5   Discussion

This section will discuss the advantages of the new GDM method developed. This method uses sentiment analysis to detect positivity and negativity in comments and it detects through dictionaries whether two alternatives are being compared or the comment is concerning one. Consequently, in this way, it is possible to get more out of the debate as the experts through their comments obtain their reciprocal preference relations. Furthermore, this novel method has other advantages:

- Reciprocal preference relations are adjustable: the method determines employing a sentiment analysis classifier and the operator developed in this paper a reciprocal preference relation for each expert. Nevertheless, the experts have the opportunity to adjust their preferences if they find that they do not like them. Consequently, the classifier helps the experts and does not impose a fixed reciprocal preference relation on them.
- Participation in the debate directly affects the experts: the debate gains relevance as it affects the GDM method in two parts of the process. In the first part, it affects the reciprocal preference relations, though they are obtained directly from the debate without forcing the experts to add their preferences. The second affects the weighting because participation in the debate will determine what weight each reciprocal preference relation of an expert has.

This method also has advantages compared to other GDM methods in the current literature. On the one hand, in [10], a method that employs sentiment analysis in a GDM process is created. Nonetheless, unlike this work, this method does not use a limited dictionary to obtain the sentiments of a comment made by experts but uses an already classified dataset and creates bags of words. Furthermore, our method uses a dictionary to detect which alternatives are being compared. On the other hand, in [6], a GDM method is created that detects false comments during the debate. Nevertheless, our method seeks to analyze the positive and negative comments and applies them directly to the system through the reciprocal preference relations of each expert. Moreover, unlike [6] which solves a specific problem, our method can be applied to any GDM problem.

6   Conclusions

In this paper, we have presented a novel GDM method that creates reciprocal preference relations from the comments made by the experts. Moreover, the comments are not only used for the above-mentioned purpose, they are also used to adjust the weight of each expert according to the comments made, giving more importance to those experts who have participated more in the debate.

The GDM method proposed in this paper uses a dictionary to detect which alternatives are being discussed, while bags of words is used to detect sentiment. Therefore, future research should investigate other procedures to detect which alternatives are being compared without the use of dictionaries, which can sometimes be limited.

Finally, with this novel method, matrices of reciprocal preference relations are automatically obtained from the transcripts of the debates. Therefore, the amount of information that experts have to provide to the system is reduced, as it is not necessary to provide opinions and ratings separately, as with this GDM method the comments already convey both together.

Acknowledgments. This work was supported by the project PID2019-103880RB-I00 funded by MCIN/AEI/10.13039/501100011033, by FEDER/Junta de Andalucía-Consejería de Transformación Económica, Industria, Conocimiento y Universidades/Proyecto B-TIC-590-UGR20, and by the Andalusian Government through the project P20_00673.

References

1. Bellman, R.E., Zadeh, L.A.: Decision-making in a fuzzy environment. Manage. Sci. **17**(4), B-141 (1970)
2. Bueno, I., Carrasco, R.A., Ureña, R., Herrera-Viedma, E.: A business context aware decision-making approach for selecting the most appropriate sentiment analysis technique in e-marketing situations, vol. 589, pp. 300–320. Elsevier (2022)
3. Cabrerizo, F.J., Trillo, J.R., Alonso, S., Morente-Molinera, J.A.: Adaptive multi-criteria group decision-making model based on consistency and consensus with intuitionistic reciprocal preference relations: a case study in energy storage technology selection. J. Smart Environ. Green Comput. **2**(2), 58–75 (2022)
4. Cabrerizo, F.J., Trillo, J.R., Morente-Molinera, J.A., Alonso, S., Herrera-Viedma, E.: A granular consensus model based on intuitionistic reciprocal preference relations and minimum adjustment for multi-criteria group decision making. In: 19th World Congress of the International Fuzzy Systems Association (IFSA), 12th Conference of the European Society for Fuzzy Logic and Technology (EUSFLAT), and 11th International Summer School on Aggregation Operators (AGOP), pp. 298–305. Atlantis Press (2021)
5. Hu, Y., Pang, Z.: A novel similarity-based multi-attribute group decision-making method in a probabilistic hesitant fuzzy environment. IEEE Access **10**, 110410–110425 (2022)
6. Kauffmann, E., Peral, J., Gil, D., Ferrández, A., Sellers, R., Mora, H.: A framework for big data analytics in commercial social networks: a case study on sentiment analysis and fake review detection for marketing decision-making. Ind. Mark. Manage. **90**, 523–537 (2020)
7. Liu, S., He, X., Chan, F.T., Wang, Z.: An extended multi-criteria group decision-making method with psychological factors and bidirectional influence relation for emergency medical supplier selection. Expert Syst. Appl. **202**, 117414 (2022)

8. Morente-Molinera, J.A., Cabrerizo, F., Trillo, J., Pérez, I., Herrera-Viedma, E.: Managing group decision making criteria values using fuzzy ontologies. Procedia Comput. Sci. **199**, 166–173 (2022)
9. Morente-Molinera, J.A., Cabrerizo, F.J., Mezei, J., Carlsson, C., Herrera-Viedma, E.: A dynamic group decision making process for high number of alternatives using hesitant fuzzy ontologies and sentiment analysis. Knowl.-Based Syst. **195**, 105657 (2020)
10. Morente-Molinera, J.A., Kou, G., Samuylov, K., Ureña, R., Herrera-Viedma, E.: Carrying out consensual group decision making processes under social networks using sentiment analysis over comparative expressions. Knowl.-Based Syst. **165**, 335–345 (2019)
11. Morente-Molinera, J.A., Pérez, I.J., Ureña, M.R., Herrera-Viedma, E.: On multi-granular fuzzy linguistic modeling in group decision making problems: a systematic review and future trends. Knowl.-Based Syst. **74**, 49–60 (2015)
12. Naseem, U., Razzak, I., Musial, K., Imran, M.: Transformer based deep intelligent contextual embedding for twitter sentiment analysis. Futur. Gener. Comput. Syst. **113**, 58–69 (2020)
13. Pérez, I.J., Cabrerizo, F.J., Alonso, S., Herrera-Viedma, E.: A new consensus model for group decision making problems with non-homogeneous experts. IEEE Trans. Syst. Man Cybern.: Syst. **44**(4), 494–498 (2013)
14. Trillo, J.R., Cabrerizo, F.J., Chiclana, F., Martínez, M.Á., Mata, F., Herrera-Viedma, E.: Theorem verification of the quantifier-guided dominance degree with the mean operator for additive preference relations. Mathematics **10**(12), 2035 (2022)
15. Trillo, J.R., Cabrerizo, F.J., Morente-Molinera, J.A., Herrera-Viedma, E., Zadrożny, S., Kacprzyk, J.: Large-scale group decision-making method based on trust clustering among experts. In: 2022 IEEE 11th International Conference on Intelligent Systems (IS), pp. 1–8. IEEE (2022)
16. Trillo, J.R., Herrera-Viedma, E., Cabrerizo, F.J., Morente-Molinera, J.A.: A multi-criteria group decision making procedure based on a multi-granular linguistic approach for changeable scenarios. In: Fujita, H., Selamat, A., Lin, J.C.-W., Ali, M. (eds.) IEA/AIE 2021. LNCS (LNAI), vol. 12799, pp. 284–295. Springer, Cham (2021). https://doi.org/10.1007/978-3-030-79463-7_24
17. Trillo, J.R., Herrera-Viedma, E., Morente-Molinera, J.A., Cabrerizo, F.J.: A large scale group decision making system based on sentiment analysis cluster. Inf. Fusion **91**, 633–643 (2023)
18. Trillo, J.R., Pérez, I.J., Herrera-Viedma, E., Morente-Molinera, J.A., Cabrerizo, F.J.: Multi-granular large scale group decision-making method with a new consensus measure based on clustering of alternatives in modifiable scenarios. In: Fujita, H., Fournier-Viger, P., Ali, M., Wang, Y. (eds.) IEA/AIE 2022. Lecture Notes in Computer Science, vol. 13343, pp. 747–758. Springer, Cham (2022). https://doi.org/10.1007/978-3-031-08530-7_63
19. Urena, R., Cabrerizo, F.J., Morente-Molinera, J.A., Herrera-Viedma, E.: GDM-R: a new framework in R to support fuzzy group decision making processes. Inf. Sci. **357**, 161–181 (2016)
20. Yang, L., Li, Y., Wang, J., Sherratt, R.S.: Sentiment analysis for e-commerce product reviews in Chinese based on sentiment lexicon and deep learning. IEEE access **8**, 23522–23530 (2020)

Automatically Generated Weight Methods for Human and Machine Decision-Making

Sebastian Lakmayer[1], Mats Danielson[1,2][✉] [ID], and Love Ekenberg[1,2] [ID]

[1] Department of Computer and Systems Sciences, Stockholm University, PO Box 7003, SE-164 07 Kista, Sweden
mats.danielson@su.se

[2] International Institute for Applied Systems Analysis, IIASA, Schlossplatz 1, AT-2361 Laxenburg, Austria

Abstract. In real-life decision analysis, whether in human-deliberated situations or non-human (real-time semi-intelligent machine/agent) situations, there are well-documented problems regarding the elicitation of probabilities, utilities, and criteria weights. In this paper, we investigate automatic multi-criteria weight-generating methods with a detailed investigation method not seen before. The results confirm that the Sum Rank method for the ordinal case, and the corresponding Cardinal Sum Rank method for the cardinal case, outperform all other methods regarding robustness. New findings include that there is no indication that the difference in the results in the weight generation is diminished as the number of degrees of freedom grows which was previously thought to be true. Further, as expected the cardinal models outperform the ordinal models. More unexpectedly, though, the performance of the dominance intensity-based weight models is at most mediocre for some combinations and not even suitable for other combinations. Another insight from the investigation in this paper is that previous literature is not homogeneous in the modelling of the attribute values, resulting in not all methods considered in this investigation can be directly compared.

Keywords: Multi-criteria decision analysis · Criteria weights · Criteria ranking · Rank order · Automatic weight generation · Large criteria sets

1 Introduction

One very common approach within decision analysis is multi-criteria decision-making (MCDM) leading to multi-criteria decision analysis. Therein, the most widely used method of measurement is multi-criteria value theory, also known as multi-attribute value/utility theory (MAVT/MAUT). In MAVT, the additive model is the most commonly used representational model [1]. In that model, the value of an alternative is evaluated as

$$V(a) = \sum_{i=1}^{n} w_i v_i(a)$$

© The Author(s), under exclusive license to Springer Nature Switzerland AG 2023
H. Fujita et al. (Eds.): IEA/AIE 2023, LNAI 13925, pp. 195–206, 2023.
https://doi.org/10.1007/978-3-031-36819-6_17

where $V(a)$ is the total value of alternative a, w_i is the weight of criterion i, and v_i is the alternative's value under criterion i (attribute value i). In the model, alternatives are evaluated by calculating the sum of products of attribute values and the corresponding criteria weights, resulting in a utility value for each alternative. The alternative with the highest utility is chosen as the preferred alternative.

A problem with the evaluation of many MCDM models is that there is a lack of numerically precise information actually available on the criteria weights in the decision situation, not least when there is a large number of criteria to consider [2, 3]. There have been a large number of specialised models suggested in the literature, such as second-order methods [4–6] and modifications of classical decision rules [7, 8]. Other models focus on preference intensities [9], ROC approaches [10], or Simos's method [11]. Nevertheless, most often the decision-maker (human or machine in the form of a semi-intelligent program) is not able to assign precise numbers to the criteria weights, but only ordinal information (a pure ranking) or preference strength (a ranking with varying distances between elements) of the criteria. For these cases, different approaches to weight generation were developed. One is the use of automatically generated weights (often called surrogate weights) and the other is the use of dominance intensity measures. This paper compares those two approaches. Additionally, the elicitation of the criteria weights can be done in several ways; one of them is based on the principle of point allocation; another one is based on the principle of direct rating, see below. These two different approaches result in criteria weights with different degrees of freedom.

There exist a research gap here which this paper tries to fill. For surrogate weights, different performances of the models depending on the degrees of freedom are known in the literature. For dominance intensity models, though, such a comparison has never, to the authors' knowledge, been carried out before. The behaviour of the models independent of different degrees of freedom is called robustness and is investigated in this paper. The primary cause of the differences between these classes of methods are described below, where the more traditional ranking methods are explored in the beginning of Sect. 2 (ordinal methods in Subsect. 2.1 and cardinal ones in Subsect. 2.2). Ensuing that, the dominance-based methods are explored in Subsect. 2.3. The method of comparison is explained in Subsect. 2.4, whereafter Sect. 3 is devoted to the performance differences between the approaches.

2 Rank Ordering Methods

Often, precise weights are not known to the decision-maker (DM), or the DM prefers not to use precise numbers. For such cases, several methods have been developed. One method which can be used when only the order of criteria weights is known, but not their precise values, are automatically generated surrogate weights. Surrogate weight methods transform imprecise information given by the DM into so-called surrogate weights that represents the DM's assessments of the decision situation, which can be used to evaluate the utility in the additive model [12–16].

Within the class of surrogate weights, two important concepts are ordinal ranking and preference strength ranking, where preference strength is an extension of the ordinal approach. In ordinal ranking, the criteria weights are ordered according to their importance to the DM, but without any information about the distance (relative importance) between different weights. In the preference strength method, in addition to the ranking of the criteria weights, some information about the relative importance between the weights is incorporated, e.g., criterion 1 is much more important than criterion 2, criterion 2 is a little bit more important than criterion 3, and so on.

Another approach to cope with incomplete information is the use of dominance measuring methods (DMMs). These are based on the computation of a dominance matrix D, including pairwise dominance values. From this matrix, different dominance intensities are constructed, which can be used to evaluate the dominating alternative, according to the corresponding dominance measuring method [1].

In this paper, the classic automatic generation methods are considered: rank sum weights (RS) [17], rank reciprocal weights (RR) [17], and centroid (ROC) weights [18]. They are compared to the more modern sum rank weights [19] from the same family of methods. Further, all of these ranking methods are compared to the leading DMM methods: DIM [1], DIM1 and DIM2 [20]. Of these, DIM1 is not qualified for further consideration in this paper since DIM2 outperforms DIM1 and, as noted by Mateos et al., DIM1 is also unsuitable because it is not independent of irrelevant alternatives [20].

2.1 Ordinal Ranking

The classic methods RS and RR for ordinal ranking have been described extensively in [17]. ROC is a function based on the average of the corners in the polytope defined by a simplex $S_w = w_1 > w_2 > \ldots > w_N$, $\Sigma w_i = 1$, and $0 \le w_i$, where w_i are variables representing the criteria weights. The ROC weights are then given by

$$w_i^{ROC} = 1/N \sum_{j=i}^{N} \frac{1}{j}$$

for the ranking number i among N items to rank [18]. The sum rank (SR) method was proposed in [19], a linear combination of the RS and RR methods to reduce the extreme behaviours of both methods. The SR method allocates the weights according to the formula

$$w_i^{SR} = \frac{1/i + \frac{N+1-i}{N}}{\sum_{j=1}^{N}(1/j + \frac{N+1-j}{N})}, i = 1, \ldots, N; \sum w_i = 1; 0 \le w_i.$$

Since much has already been written about the classic ordinal methods, we refer to [13−19] for more in-depth discussions. This paper uses ordinal methods as a baseline but does not strive for developing this particular range of methods any further.

2.2 Cardinal Ranking

A refinement to ordinal ranking methods is the concept of preference strength (cardinal ranking). In this concept, the use of additional information regarding the strength of each ranking between each criterion is employed. The preference strength could be considered as a measure of the distance in importance between criteria. Criteria that are closer are more equal in importance than those that are farther apart. Danielson and Ekenberg [21] use four different preference strengths in their paper, ranging from "equally important" to "much more important". This paper uses a different approach, based on the assumption that a DM does not know its precise inner assessments, and, since the range of assessments is continuous, the case "equally important" is less likely to occur, even with the concept broadly interpreted, especially in non-human decision-makers (semi-intelligent computer programs) since the actual probability that two points have precisely the same weight is zero on a continuous scale.

The assignment of preference strength information to a weight scale, see an example in Fig. 1, results in a total number Q of scale positions and a position $p(i)$ for each criterion i. In the left part of Fig. 1, $Q = 9$. Here, position 1 corresponds to the most important position (leftmost), and position Q corresponds to the least important position (rightmost). Using this approach, the ordinal methods RS, RR, ROC, and SR can be transformed into their cardinal counterparts. The extension is straightforward and we only show it for CSR, the cardinal version of the SR method. The CSR method allocates the weights according to the formula

$$w_i^{CSR} = \frac{1/p(i) + \frac{Q+1-p(i)}{Q}}{\sum_{j=1}^{N}(1/p(j) + \frac{Q+1-p(j)}{Q})}$$

where, as above, Q is the total number of scale positions and $p(i)$ is the particular position of criterion i. Figure 1 illustrates six ranked weights A to F where A is ranked the highest (most important). To the right in the figure, the weights are ordered with equal space between them (ordinal ranking) while to the left, there is a cardinal ranking since there could be more or less than one equally sized step between the weights and ties are allowed as opposed to the ordinal case which enforces a total ordering.

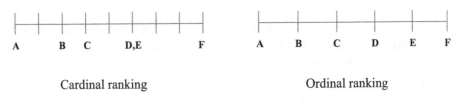

Cardinal ranking   Ordinal ranking

Fig. 1. Cardinal and ordinal ranking of six criteria A–F

The ΔROC method is a cardinal ranking method that differs from the preference strength methods above. However, since it also focuses on the distance between alternatives, it is considered a preference strength method that measures some distance between alternatives. In the original ΔROC method proposed by Sarabando and Dias [10], the imprecise information considered is not in weights but in attribute values. The attribute values are first ranked, and then subsequently the DM is asked to provide a ranking of the distances between the attribute values. Over these distances, the original ROC method is applied. Originally, ΔROC was included in this paper but since it normalises the alternative values, it did not ultimately fit into the final comparisons and since no clear-cut conclusions can then be drawn, it had to be omitted from further study in this paper.

2.3 Dominance Intensity Methods

A different approach to handling missing precise information about weights is the use of dominance intensity (DI) based methods. These methods incorporate some measure of dominance to build a dominance intensity measure, which is used to evaluate the alternatives. We will discuss two of the most prevalent ones below.

2.3.1 DIM2

The DIM2 method suggested by Mateos et al. is based on the use of the pairwise dominance matrix [20]. The DM orders the criteria weights ordinally from most important to least important criteria:

$$w = ((w_1 w_2 \ldots w_n) \mid w_1 \geq w_2 \geq \ldots \geq w_n \geq 0), \sum_i^n w_i = 1.$$

For each combination of alternatives k and l, the minimum alternative value is calculated by evaluating D_{kj} according to $D_{kj} = \min(v(A_k) - v(A_l))$, where $v(A_i)$ is the value of the respective alternative A_i. The results of these combinations are collected in a pairwise dominance matrix. If $D_{kj} \geq 0$ and if there exists at least one combination of w, v_k, and v_l in such a way that a_k is strictly greater than a_l, it is said that alternative a_k dominates alternative a_l. These values D_{kj} are calculated and form the pairwise dominance matrix. This matrix is then used to calculate a dominance intensity measure matrix. The alternative with the largest row sum of these dominance intensity measures is the selected alternative.

2.3.2 DIM

The DIM method, suggested by Aguayo et al., uses a different measure v_{kl} instead of the pairwise dominance values D_{kl} of the pairwise dominance matrix [1]. However, DIM estimates the criteria weights using the ROC method. The attribute values are estimated by using the preference strength, i.e. the ranking of the distances between alternatives. To avoid all information being concentrated at the centroid, a measure based on triangular fuzzy numbers is calculated. This measure is then used to construct a dominance intensity, which is used to evaluate the different alternatives.

All described dominance intensity-based methods were simulated based on the sampling procedure of Jia et al. [22], which results in N−1 DoF. Neither Mateos et al. [20] nor Aguayo et al. [1] differentiate between the different dimensions of generators which is a large problem when determining efficiency as well as robustness. As in Sarabando and Dias [10] and Mateos et al. [20], the attribute values are normalised, which makes the method incompatible for comparison within the framework of this study. Only DIM2 of Mateos et al. [20] can be evaluated using the standard method.

2.4 Weight Elicitation

The elicitation of the weights can be conducted in several ways. In this study, the two main branches of elicitation used are the methods based on scoring points and the direct rating (DR) method. For the case of scoring points, the point allocation (PA) method is considered in this study [21]. In PA, an overall point sum (e.g., 100 or 1000) is distributed among all criteria which are considered. Hence, each criterion gets a number of points, and the more points, the higher the corresponding weight. All distributed points sum up to the overall point sum. Since the overall point sum is limited, for N weights, the points for the endmost weight are dependent on the points which were allocated to the $N-1$ previous weights. Therefore, for the PA method, there are $N-1$ degrees of freedom (DoF). In DR, each criterion can get arbitrary points or similar measures. Then the weights are normalised by dividing each allocated point sum by the overall distributed point sum. Thus, the weights of all criteria add up to 1 and are not dependent on each other, resulting in N degrees of freedom.

2.4.1 The Generators

An N-generator is an algorithm that generates weights depending on N DoF, whereas an $N-1$-generator is an algorithm that generates weights depending on $N-1$ DoF. An intermediate combination of DoF is important in studying the respective surrogate methods' robustness. While the effects of the generator on ordinary surrogate weights have been studied, the effect on dominance measuring methods has not been studied in the literature. Hence, this knowledge gap is one of the aims of this paper.

Two different kinds of generators are defined. The first is the generator for ordinal rankings only, and the other one is used to simulate the preference strength information. The generator for ordinal information only is a mix of N-generator, using N independent samples from a uniform distribution that are normalised so that the overall sum of the weights is 1. The $N-1$-generator uses a Dirichlet distribution. The generator which includes preference strengths uses the same procedure for the combination matrix, but instead of using the number N of criteria, the number Q of total steps is used. Then the ranked matrix of the combination matrix is calculated. Next, a type matrix of the ranked matrix, i.e., a matrix that allocates the entries of the ranked matrix, which entry is a w_i and which is a $p(i)$ is evaluated. The first and last entries are always w_i's and the other steps are allocated by random (draw without replacement). The w_i are coded as 1, and the $p(i)$ are coded as 0. Then the ranked matrix is multiplied row-wise by the corresponding row of the type matrix. The remaining weights are normalised and the original ranks are stored. This information is necessary for the evaluation of the surrogate weights. By using $Q > N$ preference steps and modelling them as random weights, the simulation takes into account that a DM who uses surrogate weights has no precise knowledge about its true inner criteria weights. Hence the distances between the preference steps are not equal but rather sampled randomly. There can be some distortions, e.g. if one sampled preference step is larger than the next few preference steps together, but this could also happen in real decision situations where a DM is not completely aware of its true inner weights. Note that using this approach, no limitation in the number of intermediate preference steps exists, which can be helpful not least for non-human decision-making by machines that readily can consider more information at the same time. In [19], there are only three intermediate preference steps as the maximum.

For DIM2, criteria weights are sampled using $N-1$ DoF, referring to Jia et al. [22]), and M attribute values are sampled using M DoF, but normalising the values, so that the largest attribute value for each criterion is 1 and the smallest criterion value is 0. Nevertheless, using the method described in Aguayo et al. [1] in Sect. 4 of that paper, a pairwise dominance matrix can also be calculated with the sampled alternative values from the framework in this study. Of course, this could lead to some distortion from the original method, but it makes DIM2 comparable to the ordinal and preference strength weights methods. For the calculation of the pairwise dominance matrix, the procedure described in Aguayo et al. [1] was used in this study. This is a well-established method and will this lead to validated and comparable results. Based on this, we will now proceed to the results section in which all the results of the comparative study are shown and discussed.

3 Results

The simulation study uses different settings regarding the following parameters: Number of alternatives, number of criteria, split of N-/$N-1$-generator, type of weight generator (ordinal only vs. preference steps), and number of preference steps. For each of the tested settings, 20 alternative scenarios, each with 5000 runs, were created. The combinations for the standard settings of the number of criteria and the number of alternatives tested adhere to the combinations used by Danielson and Ekenberg [19] while the number of alternative scenarios and the number of runs are different, allowing for a higher diversification in alternative values but lowering the stability slightly. While space does not permit a thorough discussion of the experimental workbench, details of the implementations and the precise algorithms used are available on request. In this exposé, we instead focus on the main general observations and results of the study.

3.1 Comparison of Standard Settings

In the following, combinations of the number of alternatives and the number of criteria as used by Danielson and Ekenberg [19] in order to achieve comparability. Results are shown for the ordinal and cardinal (preference weight) generation methods. All results are in percentages rounded to one decimal point. The mean column shows the mean of the hit ratios over all splits and the st.dev. Column the standard deviations of the hit ratios over the N-/$N-1$-split. Both measures give information about the robustness of the studied methods. The higher the mean and the smaller the standard deviation, the better the method is regarding robustness. M is the number of alternatives, and N is the number of criteria. Q is the number of total preference steps for the preference strength model. The standard setting is $Q = 3 \cdot M$. A split of 1.0 means that only the N-generator was used and a split of 0.0 corresponds to the use of only the $N-1$-generator, see Table 1.

Table 1. Comparing standard settings.

m=3, n=3, ordinal method

DoF	0.0	0.1	0.2	0.3	0.4	0.5	0.6	0.7	0.8	0.9	1.0	Mean	St.dev
ROC	88.7	88.2	94.6	91.6	88.0	87.6	90.0	87.0	85.9	89.4	88.4	89.0	2.3
RS	87.2	86.7	94.1	91.0	87.1	87.3	91.7	88.3	88.2	90.2	89.9	89.2	2.2
RR	87.3	87.2	94.4	91.4	87.8	87.0	91.5	87.7	87.4	89.0	87.9	89.0	2.3
SR	87.5	86.8	94.6	91.4	87.7	87.7	91.5	88.3	88.3	90.1	89.3	89.4	2.2
DIM	86.9	86.7	94.5	90.1	86.7	84.2	89.0	85.8	83.6	88.8	84.3	87.3	3.0

m=3, n = 3, Q=9, preference method

DoF	0.0	0.1	0.2	0.3	0.4	0.5	0.6	0.7	0.8	0.9	1.0	Mean	St.dev
ROC	86.9	90.0	90.6	86.8	89.2	91.1	87.6	90.0	86.9	94.1	89.0	89.3	2.1
RS	81.6	84.4	85.3	78.7	84.2	88.1	81.2	83.5	84.1	93.4	86.3	84.6	3.7
RR	86.1	85.8	89.1	82.6	86.1	88.2	83.7	83.8	83.4	92.7	87.5	86.3	2.9
SR	84.9	85.4	86.9	80.6	86.0	88.3	82.1	84.0	84.8	93.1	86.9	85.7	3.2
CRS	90.2	91.4	92.5	90.3	92.4	93.4	91.9	93.0	92.4	96.2	94.2	92.5	1.6
CRR	94.2	93.1	93.1	89.6	91.1	92.1	88.5	88.9	86.1	92.5	86.5	90.5	2.6
CRC	95.2	94.7	94.4	92.7	93.1	93.6	90.7	90.8	89.6	93.9	88.8	92.5	2.1
CSR	93.6	93.9	93.5	92.2	93.2	94.1	91.8	92.4	91.5	95.3	92.1	93.1	1.1
DIM	87.3	90.0	90.6	86.2	89.5	91.1	88.0	89.5	85.2	93.6	87.7	89.0	2.3

m=9, n=9, ordinal method

DoF	0.0	0.1	0.2	0.3	0.4	0.5	0.6	0.7	0.8	0.9	1.0	Mean	St.dev
ROC	83.6	84.1	81.7	81.1	80.2	78.9	81.4	77.4	80.8	76.2	77.7	80.3	2.4
RS	75.9	78.7	77.8	78.9	80.1	80.7	84.9	83.0	87.2	85.2	88.7	81.9	4.0
RR	79.5	80.1	77.3	76.9	74.8	73.5	76.8	70.8	75.8	69.9	71.7	75.2	3.2
SR	81.7	82.7	81.3	81.5	81.5	81.5	84.6	81.4	85.5	81.7	85.1	82.6	1.6
DIM	75.6	74.1	71.4	70.3	69.5	66.9	67.4	64.6	66.2	62.7	62.1	68.3	4.2

m=9, n=9, Q=27, preference method

DoF	0.0	0.1	0.2	0.3	0.4	0.5	0.6	0.7	0.8	0.9	1.0	Mean	St.dev
ROC	83.8	81.8	81.3	79.9	80.9	80.5	78.6	78.3	81.9	77.6	80.0	80.4	1.7
RS	70.9	70.2	71.2	72.0	75.9	77.6	77.7	79.8	85.3	83.6	86.9	77.4	5.7
RR	81.9	78.8	78.5	75.8	76.9	75.8	72.8	71.7	76.3	69.8	72.8	75.6	3.4
SR	77.7	76.4	76.8	76.6	79.0	79.7	79.0	79.8	84.3	81.3	84.4	79.5	2.7
CRS	75.0	74.3	76.0	77.3	80.8	82.7	83.6	85.9	90.0	90.0	93.1	82.6	6.3
CRR	76.7	72.6	70.9	66.9	66.7	65.3	61.8	59.6	61.3	54.4	56.1	64.7	6.6
CRC	90.0	87.3	85.5	82.9	82.7	81.0	78.0	76.4	78.1	72.9	73.8	80.8	5.3
CSR	86.1	84.1	83.9	82.7	83.6	83.3	81.4	81.1	84.4	80.6	82.7	83.1	1.5
DIM	80.4	76.8	75.2	73.2	73.3	72.2	68.5	67.4	69.4	64.5	64.6	71.4	4.8

The ordinal methods show different hit ratios for the same combinations due to the different generators. It is not surprising that ordinal methods do worse in the face of cardinal input information. In the preference strength setting, the preference strength information was removed for the ordinal methods in order to leave only ordinal information. We can see that SR performs the best when only ordinal information is available. In the case that cardinal (preference strength) information is available, the cardinal versions of the ranking methods are often, but not always, able to make use of the additional information provided. The DI-based method also performs differently, depending on the DoF. As a general conclusion, DI methods (represented by DIM2) are not able to perform even close to the more classic surrogate weight methods based on ranking.

3.2 Behaviour as the Number of Criteria Grows Large

Next, it was investigated whether the gap between the N- and N−1-generators can be closed as the number of criteria grows significantly large, i.e. whether the effect of the last degree of freedom is diminishing if there are more DoF in general. For clarity, only ordinal methods were compared in this step, see Table 2.

Table 2. Comparing gaps between generators.

25 criteria

DoF	3 alternatives				6 alternatives				9 alternatives			
	0.0	0.5	1.0	Range	0.0	0.5	1.0	Range	0.0	0.5	1.0	Range
ROC	92.2	87.1	84.0	8.1	87.9	82.1	75.9	12.0	86.3	79.7	71.9	14.4
RS	82.9	88.6	95.6	12.7	74.8	84.4	92.7	17.9	71.5	82.3	91.4	19.9
RR	81.7	74.4	68.9	12.8	74.0	65.9	57.1	16.9	70.8	62.3	51.9	18.9
SR	89.1	88.9	90.5	1.6	84.3	84.8	84.3	0.5	82.0	82.6	82.1	0.6

50 criteria

DoF	3 alternatives				6 alternatives				9 alternatives			
	0.0	0.5	1.0	Range	0.0	0.5	1.0	Range	0.0	0.5	1.0	Range
ROC	94.5	87.3	81.7	12.8	91.0	82.5	75.0	15.9	89.4	79.5	74.4	15.0
RS	85.4	88.6	96.4	11.0	75.3	84.7	95.1	19.8	71.5	82.0	95.4	23.9
RR	77.0	68.0	61.6	15.4	67.4	57.3	48.9	18.6	62.5	52.2	46.4	16.1
SR	90.0	89.0	90.2	1.2	83.9	84.7	86.5	2.6	80.6	81.9	87.4	6.8

100 criteria

DoF	3 alternatives				6 alternatives				9 alternatives			
	0.0	0.5	1.0	Range	0.0	0.5	1.0	Range	0.0	0.5	1.0	Range
ROC	94.9	88.8	83.7	11.2	92.3	83.4	74.4	17.9	91.3	80.7	70.3	21.0
RS	82.1	90.1	97.9	15.7	73.6	85.3	96.5	22.9	70.5	82.6	95.8	25.3
RR	69.6	63.8	58.1	11.5	58.7	50.5	41.7	17.0	54.3	45.1	35.6	18.7
SR	87.4	90.1	92.7	5.4	81.4	85.0	88.2	6.8	79.3	82.2	86.4	7.1

It can be clearly seen that the gap between the two generators does not close as the number of criteria increases. This is clear evidence that the two modes of automatic (surrogate) weight generations are indeed very different cases that must be accounted for, rather than being a phenomenon present in smaller-scale decision situations (in the criteria sense). Further, it emphasises the importance of the property of robustness even if the number of criteria is large, such as in non-human (semi-intelligent computer program) DM situations.

4 Concluding Remarks

4.1 Main Results

The results from the investigation show that for the ordinal case, the SR method, and for the preference case, the CSR method, clearly outperform the others with regard to robustness. This is in accordance with previous literature [19]. In some tested settings, other methods sometimes show good performance, but only SR and CSR constantly show good robustness. The other methods also have their strengths in special settings, but not over all tested cases. This verifies earlier research results.

The two major new results in the paper are that i) DI-based methods cannot be seen as viable alternatives to the family of classic surrogate weight methods since they underperform considerably. Thus, more research in that direction does not seem fruitful. Further, ii) the difference in hit ratios between the two weight generation scenarios (N/N−1 DoF) does not decrease with an increase in the number of criteria considered, i.e., the difference between N/N−1 DoF is not necessarily smaller for larger N compared to smaller N. This has implications for DM situations where naturally a large set of criteria occurs. It has hitherto been assumed that as the number of criteria grows, the difference between N/N−1 DoF should be of diminishing importance, but that has turned out not to be the case.

4.2 Discussion

This study looked at both surrogate weight methods and methods based on dominance intensity measures. In the following, the general properties of the methods will be discussed first. Then, the results of this study will be discussed. Surrogate weight models offer a good possibility for the DM to express its preferences in a comprehensible manner. Even if one assumes that there exists at a special point in time something like true inner weights, it is unreasonable to assume that the DM can estimate all preferences correctly. Therefore, it is also not reasonable to assume that there exists an ideal method for estimating the true inner weights. Also, the true inner weights could change over time. One weakness of some surrogate weight models is to put too much emphasis on the largest weight with a relatively big distance to the next weight (most famously the ROC method for a small number of criteria). Then there exists the possibility of overestimating the influence of the distances between the largest weights. If one assumes that in real decision situations, there exists the possibility that the DM is not able to express its true inner preferences exactly and that the DM gives criterion 2 a slightly higher rank order, this could confound the result even more.

Dominance intensity-based methods (DIM) do not require stating the DM's preference strengths but rather only ordinal information regarding the weights. However, these are not straightforward to calculate. Therefore, there is an inherent problem in that the

DM does not trust the method if it is not easy to be retraced in an easy manner, i.e. the classic problem of transparency and traceability. Again, as for the ΔROC method by Sarabando and Dias [10], the dominance intensity method incorporating fuzzy numbers by Aguayo et al. [1] uses the same normalised alternative values, limiting its applicability in real decision problems tremendously. Only the dominance intensity methods by Mateos et al. [20] can take unrestricted alternative values into account, but it is generally outperformed by methods that are easier to use. This leads to the final conclusion that the added complexity of DIM methods are not outweighed by additional performance, yielding them a less attractive category or class of weights for employment in the search for better automatically generated criteria weight methods, both for humans and machines aiming for making decisions using computerised decision support.

5 Further Research

This study shows that the gap between N/N−1 DoF cannot be closed by increasing the number of criteria. Hence, robustness is a general issue for the weights based on imprecise information. It would be interesting to see, since as described in [21] for N DoF the weights are somewhat clustered close to the weight space centre, if discarding extreme weights in the N−1 case would close the gap between N and N−1 DoF to some extent, e.g. by using filters as described in [21]. Also, it would be interesting if the clustering of weights for N DoF can be weakened by using alternative distributions, e.g., the lognormal distribution, which also takes non-negative values and allows for more extreme values compared to the uniform distribution.

Acknowledgement. This paper is dedicated to the co-author, dear friend, and esteemed colleague Professor Love Ekenberg, who passed away in September 2022 during the research and writing leading up to the paper.

References

1. Aguayo, E.A., Mateos, A., Jiménez, A.: A new dominance intensity method to deal with ordinal information about a DM's preferences within MAVT. Knowl. Based Syst. **69**, 159–169 (2014)
2. Park, K.S.: Mathematical programming models for characterizing dominance and potential optimality when multicriteria alternative values and weights are simultaneously incomplete. IEEE Trans. Syst. Man Cybern. - Part A: Syst. Hum. **34**(5), 601–614 (2004)
3. Larsson, A., Riabacke, M., Danielson M., Ekenberg, L.: Cardinal and rank ordering of criteria – addressing prescription within weight elicitation. Int. J. Inf. Technol. Decis. Making **13** (2014)
4. Danielson, M., Ekenberg, L.: Computing upper and lower bounds in interval decision trees. Eur. J. Oper. Res. **181**(2), 808–816 (2007)
5. Danielson, M., Ekenberg, L.: An improvement to swing techniques for elicitation in MCDM methods. Knowl.-Based Syst. **168**, 70–79 (2019)
6. Ekenberg, L., Danielson, M., Larsson, A., Sundgren, D.: Second-order risk constraints in decision analysis. Axioms **3**, 31–45 (2014)

7. Ahn, B.S., Park, K.S.: Comparing methods for multiattribute decision making with ordinal weights. Comput. Oper. Res. **35**(5), 1660–1670 (2008)
8. Sarabando, P., Dias, L.: Multi-attribute choice with ordinal information: a comparison of different decision rules. IEEE Trans. Syst. Man Cybern. Part A **39**, 545–554 (2009)
9. Bana e Costa, C.A., Correa, E.C., De Corte, J.M., Vansnick, J.C.: Facilitating bid evaluation in public call for tenders: a socio-technical approach. Omega **30**, 227 – 242 (2002)
10. Sarabando, P., Dias, L.: Simple procedures of choice in multicriteria problems without precise information about the alternatives' values. Comput. Oper. Res. **37**, 2239–2247 (2010)
11. Figueira, J., Roy, B.: Determining the weights of criteria in the ELECTRE type methods with a revised Simos' procedure. Eur. J. Oper. Res. **139**, 317–326 (2002)
12. Arbel, A., Vargas, L.G.: Preference simulation and preference programming: robustness issues in priority derivation. Eur. J. Oper. Res. **69**, 200–209 (1993)
13. Barron, F., Barrett, B.: The efficacy of SMARTER: simple multi-attribute rating technique extended to ranking. Acta Psychol. **93**(1–3), 23–36 (1996)
14. Barron, F., Barrett, B.: Decision quality using ranked attribute weights. Manage. Sci. **42**(11), 1515–1523 (1996)
15. Katsikopoulos, K., Fasolo, B.: New tools for decision analysis. IEEE Trans. Syst. Man Cybern. – Part A: Syst. Hum. **36**(5), 960–967 (2006)
16. Stewart, T.J.: Use of piecewise linear value functions in interactive multicriteria decision support: a Monte Carlo study. Manage. Sci. **39**(11), 1369–1381 (1993)
17. Stillwell, W., Seaver, D., Edwards, W.: A comparison of weight approximation techniques in multiattribute utility decision making. Organ. Behav. Hum. Perform. **28**(1), 62–77 (1981)
18. Barron, F.H.: Selecting a best multiattribute alternative with partial information about attribute weights. Acta Psychol. **80**(1–3), 91–103 (1992)
19. Danielson, M., Ekenberg, L.: Rank ordering methods for multi-criteria decisions. In: Zaraté, P., Kersten, G.E., Hernández, J.E. (eds.) GDN 2014. Lecture Notes in Business Information Processing, vol. 180, pp. 128–135. Springer, Cham (2014). https://doi.org/10.1007/978-3-319-07179-4_14
20. Mateos, A., Jiménez-Martín, A., Aguayo, E.A., Sabio, P.: Dominance intensity measuring methods in MCDM with ordinal relations regarding weights. Knowl. Based Syst. **70**, 26–32 (2014)
21. Danielson, M., Ekenberg, L.: A robustness study of state-of-the-art surrogate weights for MCDM. Group Decis. Negot. **26**(4), 677–691 (2016). https://doi.org/10.1007/s10726-016-9494-6
22. Jia, J., Fischer, G.W., Dyer, J.S.: Attribute weighting methods and decision quality in the presence of response error: a simulation study. J. Behav. Decis. Making **11**(2), 85–105 (1998)

Reconciling Inconsistent Preference Information in Group Multicriteria Decision Support with Reference Sets

Andrzej M. J. Skulimowski[1,2(✉)]

[1] AGH University of Science and Technology, Decision Science Laboratory, 30 Mickiewicza ave., 30-059 Kraków, Poland
[2] International Centre for Decision Sciences and Forecasting, Progress and Business Foundation, 12B J. Lea Street, 30-048 Kraków, Poland
ams@agh.edu.pl

Abstract. This article proposes an algorithm to reconcile inconsistent recommendations of experts involved in a multicriteria decision support procedure. The algorithm yields a consistent set of reference points transformed from an arbitrary collection. By assumption, experts $S_1,...,S_n$ are agents independently involved in a decision making process of other agents termed decision makers. Experts formulate recommendations as reference points in the criteria space and simultaneously communicate them to decision makers. The above decision-making process corresponds to the schemes 'one decision maker – multiple recommending experts' (group decision support) or 'multiple decision makers – multiple experts' (group decision making and support). The assumed independence of expert judgments may provide different types of recommendation inconsistency. We define several variants of the internal and mutual inconsistency, which may occur simultaneously in the same decision-making problem. We will also assume that expert recommendations may belong to four predefined characteristic reference sets. The proposed new preference aggregation procedure regularizes the set of reference values pointed out by multiple experts. The aggregation-regularization operations include recommendation merging, reference point averaging, splitting of reference classes, moving a reference point between classes, or removing it from a class. A real-life example displaying the implementation of content-based multimedia retrieval from a knowledge repository will illustrate the above approach. In the final section, we will discuss the dependence of aggregation-regularization process outcomes on the sequence of reference classes, with reference points within each class checked for inconsistencies.

Keywords: Information inconsistency · Group recommendation · Multicriteria decision making · Reference set method · Preference aggregation

1 Introduction

This article considers a situation where multiple experts involved in decision support provide independent hints to one or more decision makers. Expert recommendations are formulated as reference points of different kinds. By definition, these are elements of the criteria space $E := IR^N$ that are assigned a special meaning to a single decision maker or to a group of them in the multicriteria optimization problem

© The Author(s), under exclusive license to Springer Nature Switzerland AG 2023
H. Fujita et al. (Eds.): IEA/AIE 2023, LNAI 13925, pp. 207–220, 2023.
https://doi.org/10.1007/978-3-031-36819-6_18

$$[F := (F_1, \ldots, F_N) : U \to E] \to min(\theta), \tag{1}$$

where θ is a convex cone in E, usually the positive orthant $\mathbf{R}_+^N$ that defines a partial order in E in the natural way as $x \leq_\theta y \Leftrightarrow y - x \in \theta$. The set of solutions to (1) is defined as

$$P(U, F, \theta) := \{u \in U : \forall z \in U[F(z) \leq_\theta F(u) \Rightarrow F(z) = F(u)]\} \tag{2}$$

and termed *Pareto-minimal* or *nondominated* set. We assume that the ultimate goal of the decision maker responsible for solving problem (1) is to acquire and apply additional preference information to select a compromise solution out of $P(U, F, \theta)$.

As such, the aforementioned reference points serve as additional preference information in the extended TOPSIS [11], bipolar [16], reference set (RefSet, [5]) methods or in risk analysis [6, 7] and marketing [4]. A method of preference aggregation in problem (1) with multiple reference points was proposed in [12]. The multicriteria decision making approaches, based on reference sets, have been widely used to solve real-life decision problems by selecting a compromise technology in advanced software design [14], building composite sustainability indicators [8, 10], and autonomous decision models [13]. These methods can also generate multicriteria rankings in various problems, for example when ranking robot team action plans or in preference- and content-based image retrieval (CBIR) [9].

The search for a compromise solution to (1) with an incremental inclusion of supplementary preference information, where interim solutions are presented sequentially to decision makers, can be regarded as a supervised learning procedure. The classes of reference points, initially proposed by experts, serve as learning ensembles. However, when multiple reference points are defined by independent agents, inconsistency problems often arise, namely, individual recommendations that are close to each other but defined by different agents may be assigned a contradictory meaning. Moreover, ensembles with the same meaning may contain elements dominated by another element of the same class. For example, an optimistic expert may propose ambitious financial indicator values to be included in a business plan, while another expert is more skeptical and defines target values which are lower than those of the first expert. The management of the company does not a priori know which expert is more credible that may lead to a confusion. This issue has hindered a wider application of group recommendations and decision support that is based on the provision of multiple reference points.

In this article, we provide a solution to the above recommendation consistency problem with a combined verification-regularization procedure of reference points. The background and related work are presented in Sect. 2, while the consistency problem is formulated in Sect. 3. The regularization algorithm is provided in Sect. 4. We assume that the verification operator, applied at a certain step of the procedure, to a single class or to a pair of reference classes, does not alter the remaining classes. The internal and mutual consistencies are both checked. The internal consistency of a reference class must be verified after each instance of mutual consistency verification involving this class. The outcomes of the regularization procedure depend on the sequence of points taken into account, and they are assumed to have equal importance to decision makers. This assumption allowed us to aggregate the results of regularization processes by constructing the union of reference classes generated by each process. If the reference set constructed is inconsistent, the entire procedure is repeated. Referring to the preference aggregation theory [1, 18, 20], it turns out that this process is convergent to the unique consistent reference set. In Sect. 5, we will present an example where human supervisors $S_1,\ldots,S_n$ provide reference values to a team of autonomous robotic agents $D_1,\ldots,D_k$, which jointly perform multicriteria multimedia retrieval from a knowledge repository. Finally, we will discuss the regularization approach as compared with other information aggregation methods such as the ordinal regression-based UTA family [15].

2 Basic Definitions and Related Work

An expert decision recommendation procedure with multiple reference points consists of defining several – usually three or more – classes of reference points, while the elements of each class are characterized by the same utility value. Reference points and sets can also be defined by the decision maker, who plays the role of one of the experts, or by multiple decision makers within group decision making problems [20, 21]. The classes of reference points to be defined by agents involved in decision support procedures will be denoted by $A_0, A_1, A_2,\ldots$ starting from the class containing the best points with respect to the partial order $\leq_\theta$ in the criteria space E. Each class can be further split into subclasses and may evolve during an interactive decision making process. Below we recall the definitions of four basic classes of reference points [12, 13] that are motivated by the type of additional preference information provided by experts in real-life applications most frequently and used in earlier approaches such as TOPSIS:

A_0 - *Bounds of optimality* - the reference points which determine the lower bound of the region Q where optimization of criteria makes sense. The set A_0 can be specified e.g. in multicriteria optimization problems with criteria space constraints.
A_1 - *Target points* - the elements of the criteria space that model ideal solutions desired by the decision maker. These are also termed aspiration levels or ideal points.
A_2 - *Status-quo solutions* - attainable criteria values which should be outperformed during the decision-making process and must not dominate the final compromise solution. Otherwise termed reservation levels, lower aspiration levels, or pre-decisions.
A_3 - *Anti-ideal reference points* - elements of the criteria space which correspond to the wrong choice. Therefore, they should be avoided during decision making, e.g. by choosing a solution most distant to A_3. Other notation: failure or avoidance levels.

Reference points serve to estimate an underlying utility (or value) function v according to the assumption that the elements of A_i are assigned the same deterministic utility value $\alpha_i > 0$ such that $\alpha_i < \alpha_j$ when $j < i$. Hence, by the same assumption, $v(A_i) \cong \alpha_i$, which means that $v(A_i)$ equals approximately to a_i with a given accuracy, and v can be maximized on U as a scoring function for the problem (1).

In some real-life decision problems, a finer classification of reference points is necessary. For example, one can distinguish between more and less desired target points and split the class A_1 into two or more subclasses, as shown in Fig. 1.

A similar operation may also be applied to other reference classes. Depending on the decision making context, reference points may be updated, filtered, re-classified, or aggregated during an interactive procedure. Based on the utility values assigned to each class, a new utility-estimating function v is constructed as an extension of α to a certain subset of E including all A_i and $F(U)$. The function v is applied to find a compromise

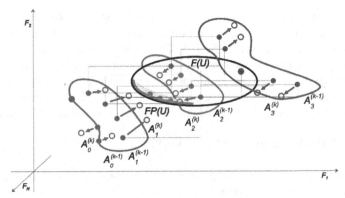

Fig. 1. An example of four evolving classes of reference sets, $A_0,...,A_3$, in generations $(k$-$1)$st (bold points) and k-th (circles), used as additional preference information within an interactive procedure of selecting a compromise solution to the multicriteria optimization problem $(F : U \to IR^N) \to \min(\theta := \mathbf{R}_+^N, N = 3)$ with multiple expert recommendations.

solution to the multicriteria optimization problem (1) or to rank all decisions if the set U is discrete.

The background of the multiple reference points (MREF) and the reference set (RefSet) methods has been given in [5, 12], while its updated description is provided in [13]. In the RefSet method, neighboring classes (i-th and $(i + 1)$th, for $i = 0,1,2$) of reference points are aggregated pairwise into reference sets with the algorithms provided in [5, 12]. In the most common RefSet variant [5], the pairs of reference classes (A_0,A_1) and (A_2,A_3) are aggregated into two subsets of the criteria space, the first one to be approached and the other one to be avoided. This aggregation consists of two steps: first, the construction of convex hulls for the sets $A_i + \mathbf{R}_+^N$ and $A_{i+1} - \mathbf{R}_+^N$, $i = 0,1,2$, $\mathbf{R}_+^N := [0, \infty)^N$, followed by the construction of the polyhedra Q_i:

$$Q_i := \text{env}\left(A_i + \mathbf{R}_+^N\right) \cap \text{env}\left(A_{i+1} - \mathbf{R}_+^N\right), \text{ for } i = 0, 1, 2, \tag{3}$$

where env(X) denotes the convex hull of X. The scoring function q is defined as

$$q(u) := \text{d}(u, Q_0) - \lambda\text{d}(u, Q_2), \tag{4}$$

where $\lambda > 0$ and $\text{d}(u, X) := \inf\{\|u - x\| : x \in X\}$. Observe that so-defined q is to be minimized. The set Q_1 is considered as a criteria space constraint on compromise solutions to (1).

The above construction of the sets Q_i (3) and the function q (4), as well as other procedures of estimating a utility function from the information contained in reference points, is only possible if the reference classes satisfy certain regularity conditions, such as those ensuring that the sets Q_i are non-empty. The next section is devoted to the study of reference point consistency in cases where multiple experts independently formulate their recommendations. We will provide the rules and operations to convert inconsistent reference classes into the preference structure that complies with the utility modelling principles, i.e. ensures that v is monotonically increasing with respect to the order $\leq_\theta$.

3 The Expert Information Fusion Problem

As stated in Sect. 2, the utility function estimation with reference points requires decision support experts to consistently assign utility values α_i to reference points. The utility function v must comply with the monotonicity principle, which follows from two distinct properties of reference points, namely their internal and mutual consistency. This will be explained further. Additionally, the situation of A_i with respect to the attainable set $F(U) \subset E$ must conform to the above presented common-sense meaning of reference points. This additional property, which is termed the *plausibility consistency with respect to the problem (1)*, is analyzed in Table 1 further in this section.

Let us recall that the main idea of the multiple reference points approach presumes that all elements of the class A_i correspond to the same value of the estimated utility function v. It is easy to see that to comply with the monotonicity assumption, it is necessary that no different elements of A_i are mutually comparable with respect to $\leq_\theta$. We will call this property *internal consistency* of the class A_i.

Definition 1. *The set of reference points A_i is internally consistent iff*

$$\forall q_1, q_2 \in A_i, q_1 \neq q_2 : q_1 \text{ and } q_2 \text{ are non} - \text{comparable.} \tag{5}$$

∎

If a reference set A_i results from aggregation of different expert judgments, then it may be internally inconsistent. However, applying any nondominated subset selection algorithm, it is easy to find a subset V of A_i consisting of non-comparable points. As V, one can take either the subset of Pareto-minimal points $P(A_i, \theta)$ or Pareto-maximal points $P(A_i, (-\theta))$ of $A_i (F \equiv id_{A_i})$ and use it instead of A_i. Moreover, each of the sets $A_i, 0 \leq i \leq K - 1$, where K is the number of classes of reference points, should be well-defined with respect to all other reference points. This requirement is equivalent to the condition that each element of A_{i-1} should be dominated by an element of A_i, for $1 \leq i \leq K$, i.e.

$$\forall x \in A_i \exists y \in A_{i+1} : x \leq_\theta y. \tag{6}$$

In order to obtain the desired properties of the level sets of v, we imposed an additional condition (7), symmetric to (6), which allowed us (cf. [12]) to formulate the definition of mutual consistency,

$$\forall y \in A_{i+1} \exists x \in A_i : x \leq_\theta y. \tag{7}$$

Definition 2. *The reference classes A_j and A_{j+1} satisfying the conditions (6)–(7) will be termed mutually consistent.* ∎

Along with consistency, rationality is a fundamental property of multicriteria decision-making methods, which should be verified in the first order of importance.

Definition 3. *A multicriteria decision selection procedure is termed rational if its ultimate outcome is nondominated in (1).* ∎

Checking and correcting mutual consistency is an essential part of multicriteria decision-making algorithms based on reference sets. For example, if d is a distance in

E, the construction of reference sets provided in [12] yields for any $w > 0$ and the appropriately situated $x \in E$ (cf. Theorem 1) the function v defined in a similar way as q (4):

$$v(x) := d(x, A_i) - wd(x, A_{i+1}). \tag{8}$$

For $i = 1$ v is also similar to the scoring function used in the TOPSIS method [11]. The definition (8) of v is justified by the following fact [12]:

Theorem 1. *If all classes of reference points $A_i, i = 0,...,K\text{-}1$, for the problem (1) are both internally and mutually consistent and the function $v : E \to IR$ is such that A_i are contained in the level sets of v, the values of $v(x)$ are interpolated for x that fulfill the condition*

$$\exists y_1 \in A_i,\ y_2 \in A_{i+1} : y_2 \leq_\theta x \leq_\theta y_1 \tag{9}$$

and extrapolated for $x \in (A_0 - \theta) \cup (A_{K-1} + \theta)$, then the decision process based on maximizing v as a scoring function is rational. ∎

The proof of Theorem 1 follows directly from the monotonicity property of v, namely so defined v is monotonically increasing with respect to $\leq_\theta$ which is a sufficient condition that its maximum is admitted at a nondominated value of F. Observe that in the construction of v the consistency conditions play a crucial role as they guarantee the existence of reference points needed to fulfill the interpolation condition (9) in Theorem 1.

Moreover, the reference points in the classes A_i, $i = 0, 1, 2, 3$, may have a predetermined interpretation referring to the attainable set $F(U)$. This interpretation is already contained in their verbal description in Sect. 2. A characterization of an ideal situation, where the initial decision maker's judgments concerning A_i fully comply with the actual situation of attainable values in $F(U)$, is given in Table 1 below.

Definition 4. *Table 1 defines the plausibility consistency conditions for A_i with respect to the set of criteria values $F(U)$. The strong conditions exactly model the real life meaning of reference points, while the relaxed conditions refer to the situation where an estimation of the utility v with reference points yields a monotonically increasing function, but the real-life intuition of v may be disturbed.* ∎

4   The Reference Point Aggregation-Regularization Procedure

After estimating the attainable set $F(U)$ in (1), the actual situation of reference points may differ from that presented in Table 1 below. It is then necessary to reformulate the expert' or decision maker judgments, according to the general rule that the rationality of the compromise solution selection procedure is superior to the intuitive interpretation of reference points defined by experts $S_1,...,S_n$. The suitable regularization will be accomplished by applying operations defined further in this section. Thus we will get a *posterior* set of consistent reference points. The redefinition process is combined with averaging and may be performed automatically. Alternatively, the decision maker may interactively intervene in manipulating reference points.

Table 1. Conditions that define plausibility consistency of reference sets with respect to $F(U)$.

Reference class	Strong plausibility condition	Relaxed plausibility condition
A_0	The lower limits of optimality should dominate at least one nondominated point [11]	Elements of A_0 should be non-comparable with FP(U,θ): $= F(P(U,F,\theta))$
A_1	The target points should intersect the set of strictly dominating points [3]	The target reference points A_1 should dominate at least one nondominated point
A_2	The status quo solutions should be attainable and better than the nadir point n^* [17]	A_1 should be noncomparable with a certain attainable point, better than nadir point n^*
A_3	The anti-ideal points should be dominated by at least one attainable point	A_2 should be non-comparable with the set FP(U,θ)

Each operation will be applied either to a single class of reference points or to a pair of them. Experts are assigned initial credibility coefficients $c_1,...,c_n$ that are decreased when a reference value recommended by an expert is modified or rejected. The operations used and the parameters of the regularization procedure are assessed *ex-ante* w.r.t. two or more criteria: the total losses of experts' credibility and the quality of the resulting set of reference points. The latter criterion may be defined by the number of inconsistencies that remained after the procedure and/or weak consistency conditions satisfied by the aggregated reference set. Other plausible measures of *ex-ante* regularization process quality are the number of regularizing operations and the sum of the Hausdorff distances between the original and transformed classes of reference points. Consequently, we can formulate a multicriteria optimization problem where decisions are sequences of admissible aggregation-regularization operations. They are optimized with a selection of at least two indicators from the above proposed optimization criteria. The constraints concern the number, the total time, or the total cost of all operations. The initial set of reference points is fixed.

In another variant of the regularization process that integrates interactive decision support, experts are first notified about inconsistencies and have an opportunity to modify them before the aggregation-regularization operations are applied to the inconsistent classes of reference points. In addition, the overall process can be assessed *ex-post*, taking into account the quality of the compromise solution admitted with the regularized reference set, from the perspective of the decision maker(s). This feedback is used to assess the regularization parameters within a semi-supervised learning procedure. The *ex-ante* assessments are most suitable for cases where the experts and/or decision maker(s) are artificial autonomous decision agents.

The purpose of aggregating operations and the aggregation-regularization algorithm is to correct the classes of reference points A_0,A_1,A_2,A_3 in a way that ensures their internal and mutual consistency. The initial credibility coefficients $c_j > 0$ of experts $S_1,...,S_n$ are transferred to the corresponding reference points. If no information about credibility is given, we can assume $c_j = 1$ for all $1 \leq j \leq n$. Each expert may define any number of points of each type. By assumption, reference points are defined independently by each expert, so that the process may yield overlapping reference point recommendations with the credibility summed up over all the agents who defined them.

The concept of optimality of our algorithm is to regularize the set of inconsistently defined reference points with operations $O_1, \ldots, O_p$ to yield a minimum deviation δ from initial recommendations with minimum loss Δc of total expert credibility. The deviation δ is calculated as the sum of partial deviations δ_j assigned to each performed operation. Similarly, replacing or removing a reference point defined by the k-th expert in the j-th operation results in a decrease in the credibility of this expert on $\Delta c_{k,j}$. The permitted regularization methods $O_1, \ldots, O_p$ (here $p = 7$) are defined as follows:

O_1 - Averaging nearby points with expert credibility coefficients as averaging weights; the result replaces the averaged points in the next step of the procedure,

O_2 - Re-defining the meaning of a reference point (transfer to another class),

O_3 - Splitting the class of reference points into two subclasses,

O_4 - Merging two classes of reference points,

O_5 - Removing a reference point.

O_6 - Finding the Pareto-minimal (nondominated) points of a reference point class and removing the dominated reference points from this class.

O_7 - Finding the Pareto-maximal points of a reference point class and removing all other reference points from this class.

The list of operations $O_1–O_7$ has been derived from the real-life observations of multicriteria decision problems solving with multiple reference points. These operations were performed so far manually either by decision makers or by the facilitator of the decision making process. The operations are chosen at each step of the following Algorithm 1, according to certain decision rules $R_1, \ldots, R_M$ selected from a knowledge base.

The graphical illustration of the Algorithm 1 is presented in Fig. 2 below.

In the example shown in Fig. 2, there are internal as well as mutual inconsistencies of reference points. Specifically, A_1 in its $(k-1)$st iteration includes a point $a_{1,2}(k-1)$, which is simultaneously internally inconsistent within the class $A_1(k-1)$ and makes the classes $A_0(k-1)$ and $A_1(k-1)$ mutually inconsistent. In the k-th iteration of Algorithm 1, $a_{1,2}(k-1)$ is assimilated to the class $A_0(k)$ as $a_{0,2}(k)$. Furthermore, the class $A_2(k-1)$ was split into two subclasses, $A_2(k)$ and $A_3(k)$, so that a new class $A_4(k)$ replaced the $A_3(k-1)$. One reference point in the k-th iteration of Algorithm 1, namely $a_{4,3}(k)$, results from the averaging operation on $a_{3,3}(k-1)$ and $a_{3,4}(k-1)$.

This section concludes with the following:

Theorem 2. *The regularization process provided in Algorithm 1 is convergent in a finite number of steps to the unique consistent reference set A, with all classes of reference points A_i being both internally and mutually consistent.* ∎

Corollary. *From Theorems 1 and 2, it follows that the reference set method applied to the classes $A_0, \ldots, A_3$ regularized with Algorithm 1, yields a Pareto minimal compromise solution.* ∎

Algorithm 1. Reference set regularization

Input data : Reference point matrix $A := [A_0, A_1, A_2, A_3] \in M_{n0+n1+n2+n3,N}$, where nj is the number of points in A_j, $j=0,1,2,3$; expert credibility vector $c \in \mathbb{R}^r$,
Lists of indices of reference points in A proposed by each expert S_j, $B_j := [b_{j,1},...,b_{j,k(j)}]$, $j=1,...,n$, where $k(j)$ is the number of reference points proposed by the j-th expert.
Decision rules $R_1,...,R_M$ and their activity status s_m for internal and mutual consistency check.
Output: Corrected A, final values of δ, Δc

1 :	**Initialize** $\delta := 0$, $\Delta c := 0$, inconsistency:= "**true**"
2 :	**while** inconsistency **do**
3 :	**for** $i=0,...,3$ **do**
4 :	Check the internal consistency of the class A_i
5 :	**if** A_i is consistent **then** break **else**
6 :	Select the operations $O_{j(i)}$ with active rules from $R_{1,...,}R_M$ and perform them
7 :	Update A,B and the values of δ, Δc with the coefficients of $O_{j(i)}$.
8 :	**end if**
9 :	**end for**
10 :	**for** each pair of classes A_i, A_{i+1} ($i=0,...,2$) **do**
11 :	Check the mutual consistency of A_i and A_{i+1}.
12 :	**if** A_i and A_{i+1} are mutually inconsistent **then**
13 :	Perform the operations $O_{j(i,i+1)}$ selected with active rules from $R_{1,...,}R_M$
14 :	Update A,B. Update δ, Δc with the coefficients describing $O_{j(i,i+1)}$.
15 :	**end if**
16 :	**end for**
17 :	**for** $i=0,...,3$ **do**
18 :	Check the internal consistency of A_i. ‖ '*internal consistency re-check*'
19 :	**if** A_i is inconsistent **then** inconsistency='**true**', **break** (for)
20 :	**else** inconsistency='**false**'
21 :	**end if**
22 :	**end for**
23 :	**end while**
24 :	**return** A, B, the values of δ, Δc
25 :	**end** (Reference set regularization)

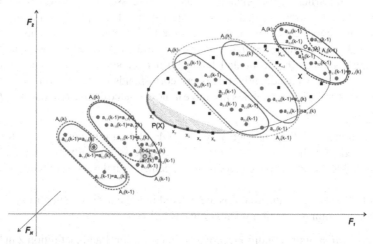

Fig. 2. An illustration of action of Algorithm 1 on four incorrectly defined initial classes of reference sets $A_0,...,A_3$ in the $(k-1)$st and k-th iterations. Dotted lines surround the reference classes in the next (k-th) iteration of Algorithm 1. Black squared dots denote the elements of the decision set $X := F(U)$, $P(X)$ is its Pareto-optimal subset. The order in the criteria space E is defined by $\mathbf{R}_+^N$.

5   An Application Example

As an application example of the above group decision support approach, we present a procedure of recommending videos, massive online courses (MOOCs), other multimedia courses and teaching material to the users of the AI-based learning repository (AILP), developed within a recent Horizon 2020 research project [14]. Instructors served as principal recommending experts, while students and young researchers involved in various adult education forms are the decision makers (DMs) who select the learning material according to the criteria G related to the achievement of learning goals, learning efficiency and comfort. The qualitative criteria G are expressed as preference-preserving functions of certain observable quantitative pre-criteria F.

To illustrate the recommendation fusion preceded by the consistency checking and regularization process, let us consider the following simple decision problem.

Example. Assume that two instructors S_1 and S_2, with the same trust coefficients of 0.8, recommend multimedia courses according to the qualitative criteria $G = (G_1, G_2)$, where G_1 is the correctness and clarity of presentation and G_2 is the presence of specific adequate real-life cases. The numerical values assigned to G can be regarded as deviations from characteristics of a certain ideal course and are to be minimized. There are three observable pre-criteria $F = (F_1, F_2, F_3)$, with F_1 defined as the coverage of the obligatory and auxiliary material (in %) to be determined by text mining from course annotations. F_2 is the average quality of graphics and videos, to be determined by checking the resolution and provenience of images and videos. F_3 is defined as the availability of supplementary material, which can be derived from the availability of source codes, data, and other files, normalized to the scale [0,1]. The dependence of G on F is disclosed initially in an explicit form for the reference set A only. However, it can be learned with adaptive regression techniques from earlier recommendation-selection processes that involved other experts and users. Thus, G is represented as $G = \varphi(F) + \eta$, where η is an estimation error, while current recommendations update the hitherto determined coefficients of φ. The learning goals can be made explicit as a query that defines a preliminary selection of the learning content to be accounted for in further recommendation and multimedia selection processes. Consequently, this query corresponds to the constraints U. In our example, we assume that U contains just three nondominated courses such that $G(F((U))$ = {(2,4),(3,3),(4,2)}.

The reference points in the set $A := A_1 \cup A_2 \cup A_3$ are provided as vectors with coordinates equal to the quantified values of criteria G. Additionally, we assume that A_0 = {(0,0)}. Table 2 presents the elements of A together with the corresponding values of criteria.

After the expert recommendations are entered into the decision support system, the verification – fusion – selection process runs as follows:

1. The *verification* of the conditions provided in Definition 1 and Definition 2 in Sect. 3 discovers an internal inconsistency in the class A_2, while all other classes and their mutual situations are correct.
2. The *regularization* procedure starting from $a_{2,3}$ and $a_{2,4}$ replaces this pair with their average $a_{2,5} = (5,7)$. This new reference point turns out to still be comparable with $a_{2,2}$, so in the second step of this run, both are replaced with $a_{2,6} = (5,6.5)$ that

Table 2. The reference points defined by experts within the course selection process.

A	Expert	G_1	G_2	F_1	F_2	F_3
$a_{1,1}$	S_1	2	1	1	0.8	0.9
$a_{1,2}$	S_2	1	3	1	0.9	0.7
$a_{2,1}$	S_1	7	3	0.8	0.6	0.6
$a_{2,2}$	S_2	5	6	0.7	0.7	0.7
$a_{2,3}$	S_2	4	7	0.6	0.7	0.9
$a_{2,4}$	S_2	6	7	0.6	0.5	0.7
$a_{3,1}$	S_1	8	4	0.6	0.4	0.5
$a_{3,2}$	S_1	7	7	0.5	0.6	0.4

together with $a_{2,1}$ yield a correct class A_2'. The next run of averaging takes into account the second potential expert recommendation fusion, namely the pair $a_{2,2}$ and $a_{2,4}$ is compared first, so that a different average is calculated, $a_{2,8} = (5.5,6.5)$, that is non-comparable with $a_{2,1} = (7,3)$ and with $a_{2,3} = (4,7)$. The class A_2'' consists of the latter three points. Both runs yield correct classes A_2 and there are no further inconsistencies, so to calculate the utility, the procedure averages the results of all runs and retains the class $A_2^c = \{(7,3),(5.25,6.5),(4,7)\}$ as final.

3. When replacing comparable reference elements of the same class, the *trust coefficients* of experts S_1 and S_2 are decreased proportionally to the distance between the final averaged point and the replaced values proposed by experts.

4. The *recommendation fusion* procedure inter- or extrapolates the utility v_c of criteria G values from its level sets constructed as triangulations of reference points of each class according to the formula (8) presented in Sect. 3. The utility v as a function of decisions $u \in U$ is then expressed as $v := v_c^\circ \varphi^\circ F$ (for clarity reasons, the estimation error of φ is omitted).

5. The functions v_c and φ are updated based on A and F, respectively. This unsupervised learning procedure yields the course $u_3 := (2,4)$ with the highest utility value and presents it as the *compromise recommendation* to the user.

6. The overall procedure stops when the proposed course is accepted, otherwise the above steps 1–5 are repeated with new expert recommendations and/or user-preferred course parameters included into the class A_1.

Let us observe that the elements of each reference class are non-comparable with respect to F, although the regularization procedure was necessary when considering the criteria G. This explains the source of potential inconsistencies of expert judgments, which based on the analysis of the course features F but experts presented user-oriented assessments G. Consequently, when fusing reference sets with other preference information such as trade-off constraints, experts should take into account the pre-criteria F rather than the qualitative criteria G (Fig. 3).

The criteria of individual learners f may be different from G and not disclosed to the instructors. We assume that they serve as user preferences when selecting compromise courses if expert recommendations do not indicate a unique course. Moreover, the design

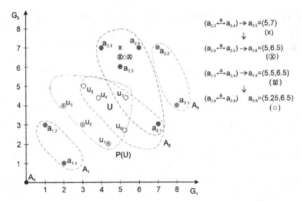

Fig. 3. An illustration of the course selection example. The operation "$\overset{a}{\leftrightarrow}$" denotes aggregation of two reference points, for example $a_{2,5}$ is the average of $a_{2,3}$ and $a_{2,4}$. The sequence of aggregation results is indicated by arrows.

of this repository course selection mechanism allows the users to provide mutual (social) recommendations and to use adaptive learning-support tools [14].   ∎

The instructors' recommendations analyzed in the above example allowed the learners to select the nondominated course taking into account all expert information in a most objective way, i.e. without any bias resulting from preferring one expert to another. Checking mutual consistencies did not indicate in this case a need to apply regularization operations to the pairs of reference classes. However, in the general case it may be necessary to eliminate the impact of order of mutual consistency check by averaging the results of all feasible permutations of pairwise consistency checks.

To conclude this section, let us note that the above presented reference-set based decision process can also be applied to defining the parameters of future group learning scenarios, resulting from an assessment of learning needs with user surveys, expert Delphi exercises, or elicited from autonomous learning system supervisors.

6   Discussion and Conclusions

As observed in Sect. 4, the output of Algorithm 1 depends on the order in which the reference points and classes are taken into account. This is why the results of performing it for every permutation of points in each class can be averaged, so that the result is order-independent. It can be shown that to check internal inconsistency merely permutations of non-comparable points inside classes A_i, $i = 0, \ldots, 3$, are relevant. In addition, it suffices to investigate the mutual consistency of neighboring classes only. Numerical experiments showed that if the number of experts in a decision problem is smaller than 10, and each of them defines no more than 10 reference points, which can be regarded as standard in real life problems, the above averaging is computationally feasible. Further decision problem consistency conditions follow from general rational multi-agent properties [2].

The aggregation of different regularization outcomes cannot be identified with the aggregation of experts' judgments [1]. Such an aggregation would be performed in one step and would yield a unique system of reference points. As a consequence, experts' credibility could not be modified during this process and the information to which extent particular expert judgments required modification would be lost. Moreover, in another approach, the process described by Algorithm 1 can be regarded as interactive and performed as long as the output indices δ and Δc reach satisfactory values. Thus, a kind of scalability of the regularization could be defined that is impossible in one-time expert judgment aggregation.

Another variant of the above procedure can also be performed, namely, the modified Algorithm 1 may independently apply the selected operations in each step to all classes of reference points. Thus, this new algorithm will create a 'next generation' of reference points as an output of a parallel procedure, similar to the next generation of cells in classical synchronous cellular automata. When comparing their numerical results, both approaches were convergent to certain sets of reference points, which need not be the same. This problem will be a subject of further studies.

In Sect. 5 we have shown how the above regularization method could be applied to filter inconsistent reference criteria values defined by sponsors or stakeholders of the knowledge repository [14] as model use scenarios. However, educational recommendations do not exhaust the area of potential applications of our approach. We claim that most applications of preference structures with multiple reference points to select compromise solutions to multicriteria decision problems of type (1) may encounter expert inconsistency problems. In addition, autonomous decision making procedures that acquire preference information automatically from data streams or expert systems are particularly vulnerable to import inconsistencies to their decision-making engines.

Finally, let us note that the terms *"multiple reference vectors"*, or *"reference sets"* are often used in other meaning than in the present article, namely as certain auxiliary dominating points in the criteria space E computed directly from the sets $F(U)$ and used predominantly in evolutionary multicriteria optimization [3, 19] to decompose the problem of approximating the Pareto set (2). Since these reference values are not defined by experts, the inconsistency problems described in this article do not affect them.

References

1. Beliakov, G., Pradera, A., Calvo, T.: Aggregation Functions: A Guide for Practitioners. Studies in Fuzziness and Soft Computing, vol. 221, p. 361. Springer, Heidelberg (2007). https://doi.org/10.1007/978-3-540-73721-6
2. Dorri, A., Kanhere, S.S., Jurdak, R.: Multi-agent systems: a survey. IEEE. Access **6**, 28573–28593 (2018). https://doi.org/10.1109/ACCESS.2018.2831228
3. Gholamnezhad, P., Broumandnia, A., Seydi, V.: A model-based many-objective evolutionary algorithm with multiple reference vectors. Prog. Artif. Intell. **11**, 251–268 (2022). https://doi.org/10.1007/s13748-022-00283-5
4. Ghoshal, T., Yorkston, E., Nunes, J.C., Boatwright, P.: Multiple reference points in sequential hedonic evaluation: an empirical analysis. J. Mark. Res. **51**(5), 563–577 (2014). https://doi.org/10.1509/jmr.12.0075
5. Górecki, H., Skulimowski, A.M.J.: A joint consideration of multiple reference points in multicriteria decision making. Found. Control Eng. **11**(2), 81–94 (1986)
6. Harris, C., Wu, C.: Using tri-reference point theory to evaluate risk attitude and the effects of financial incentives in a gamified crowdsourcing task. J. Bus. Econ. **84**(3), 281–302 (2014). https://doi.org/10.1007/s11573-014-0718-4

7. Koop, G.J., Johnson, J.G.: The use of multiple reference points in risky decision making. J. Behav. Decis. Mak. **25**, 49–62 (2012). https://doi.org/10.1002/bdm.713

8. Ricciolini, E., et al.: Assessing progress towards SDGs implementation using multiple reference point based multicriteria methods: the case study of the European countries. Soc. Indic. Res. **162**, 1233–1260 (2022). https://doi.org/10.1007/s11205-022-02886-w

9. Rotter, P.: Relevance feedback based on n-tuplewise comparison and the ELECTRE methodology and an application in content-based image retrieval. Multimed. Tools. Appl. **72**(1), 667–685 (2013). https://doi.org/10.1007/s11042-013-1384-1

10. Ruiz, F., Gibari, S.E., Cabello, J.M., Gómez, T.: MRP-WSCI: multiple reference point based weak and strong composite indicators. Omega **95**, 102060 (2020). https://doi.org/10.1016/j.omega.2019.04.003

11. Shih, H.-S., Olson, D.L.: TOPSIS and Its Extensions: A Distance-Based MCDM Approach. In: Studies in Systems, Decision and Control, vol. 447, p. 221. Springer, Cham (2022). https://doi.org/10.1007/978-3-031-09577-1

12. Skulimowski, A.M.J.: Methods of multicriteria decision support based on reference sets. In: Caballero, R., Ruiz, F., Steuer, R.E. (eds.) Advances in Multiple Objective and Goal Programming, Lecture Notes in Economics and Mathematical Systems, vol. 455, pp. 282–290, Springer, Heidelberg (1997). https://doi.org/10.1007/978-3-642-46854-4_31

13. Skulimowski, A.M.J.: Freedom of choice and creativity in multicriteria decision making. In: Theeramunkong, T., Kunifuji, S., Sornlertlamvanich, V., Nattee, C. (eds.) Knowledge, Information, and Creativity Support Systems. Lecture Notes in Computer Science (Lecture Notes in Artificial Intelligence), vol. 6746, pp. 190–203. Springer, Heidelberg (2011). https://doi.org/10.1007/978-3-642-24788-0_18

14. Skulimowski, A.M.J., Köhler, T.: A future-oriented approach to the selection of artificial intelligence technologies for knowledge platforms. J. Assoc. Inf. Sci. Technol. **74**(8), 905–922 (2023). https://doi.org/10.1002/asi.24763

15. Sobrie, O., Gillis, N., Mousseau, V., Pirlot, M.: UTA-poly and UTA-splines: additive value functions with polynomial marginals. Eur. J. Oper. Res. **264**(2), 405–418 (2018). https://doi.org/10.1016/j.ejor.2017.03.021

16. Trzaskalik, T.: Bipolar sorting and ranking of multistage alternatives. Cent. Eur. J. Oper. Res. **29**(3), 933–955 (2021). https://doi.org/10.1007/s10100-020-00733-2

17. Wang, H., He, S., Yao, X.: Nadir point estimation for many-objective optimization problems based on emphasized critical regions. Soft. Comput. **21**(9), 2283–2295 (2015). https://doi.org/10.1007/s00500-015-1940-x

18. Yu, D.: A scientometrics review on aggregation operator research. Scientometrics **105**(1), 115–133 (2015). https://doi.org/10.1007/s11192-015-1695-2

19. Zhang, L., Wang, L., Pan, X., Qiu, Q.: A reference vector adaptive strategy for balancing diversity and convergence in many-objective evolutionary algorithms. Appl. Intell. **53**, 7423–7438 (2023). https://doi.org/10.1007/s10489-022-03545-w

20. Zhang, Q., Wang, R., Yang, J., Ding, K., Li, Y., Hu, J.: Collective decision optimization algorithm: a new heuristic optimization method. Neurocomputing **221**, 123–137 (2017). https://doi.org/10.1016/j.neucom.2016.09.068

21. Zhang, Y., Bouadi, T., Wang, Y., Arnaud, M.: A distance for evidential preferences with application to group decision making. Inf. Sci. **568**, 113–132 (2021). https://doi.org/10.1016/j.ins.2021.03.011

E-Learning

A Design Method for an Intelligent Tutoring System with Algorithms Visualization

Hien D. Nguyen[1,2(✉)], Hieu Hoang[1,2], Triet Nguyen[1,2], Khai Truong[1,2], Anh T. Huynh[1,2], Trong T. Le[1,2], and Sang Vu[1,2]

[1] University of Information Technology, Ho Chi Minh city, Vietnam
{21520232,21520497,21520274}@gm.uit.edu.vn,
{anhht,tronglt,sangvm,hiennd}@uit.edu.vn
[2] Vietnam National University, Ho Chi Minh city, Vietnam

Abstract. Nowadays, learning has become more efficient via active learning methods. Active learning methods bring excitement and engagement to students. The proposed method in this paper suggests the utilization of graphical and dynamic web-based tools for visualization, as it is one of the most common and straightforward approaches. The objective of this method is to design an intelligent system for learning algorithms that can display the developed algorithm visually. This method proposes a model for representing the knowledge of an algorithm, called *AI-Algo model*, and solving problems about algorithm visualizing. The application of this method involves the development of an intelligent learning system focused on algorithms in a data structures and algorithms course. Additionally, it can support the knowledge engineer in creating and updating the content of visualization.

Keywords: Intelligent system · Knowledge engineering · Visualization · Data Strucutre and Algorithms

1 Introduction

Intelligent Tutoring System (ITS) is an effective instrument for enhancing students' learning [21,26]. Active learning techniques, particularly when it comes to acquiring new programming skills and learning algorithms, have been found to generate excitement about learning [3,5]. The incorporation of graphical and dynamic web-based tools, such as visualization, into the learning process of these courses has been shown to help learners reduce their study time [8,10]. The visualization of algorithms helps learners to understand the step-by-step process of those algorithms.

The course of Data Structure and Algorithms is an important course in the Information Technology (IT) curriculum [6,27]. In this course, students learn about the foundation of algorithms [27]. The problem is that there are still many students who do not understand the steps of an algorithm, making it

H. Fujita et al. (Eds.): IEA/AIE 2023, LNAI 13925, pp. 223–234, 2023.
https://doi.org/10.1007/978-3-031-36819-6_19

difficult for them to write a program. The possible cause of this problem is there are no learning media to visualize abstract actions of algorithms which make it easier for students to understand. Through [11,16,18], the following are some explanations of the requirements for an algorithm learning system:

- For users as learners: Algorithms are described by a programming language or pseudo code. The system can help learners to understand the running of algorithms through the visualization of their processing [18]. Users can input an example of the algorithm and the system will envisage with that example.
- For the user as a knowledge engineer: The system is designed for the knowledge engineer can define and create a new algorithm [14,16]. The system will automatically check whether the overall of inputted code are correct. Besides, it also permits to update/modify the algorithm for the engineer.

In this paper, a methodology for creating an ITS for algorithm learning is proposed. This method constructs a model for representation the knowledge of an algorithm, called *AI-Algo model*. The AI-Algo model is created based on the execution steps involved in the algorithm's processing, also known as tasks. This model comprises the task structure and a specification language that represents the components of the algorithm. The proposed method is capable of visualizing the changes occurring during the algorithm's execution process. The visualization process synchronizes three components, which include displaying the algorithm's current state, exhibiting its variables, and presenting the current state within a graphical environment.

Using the proposed method, an Intelligent Learning System focused on Sorting Algorithms has been developed for university-level education. This system assists the knowledge engineer in creating and updating algorithmic content that interacts with the learner step-by-step by utilizing visualizations of the algorithms.

2 Related Work

Active learning techniques, such as the utilization of graphical and dynamic web-based tools for visualization, have been shown to assist students in learning these courses [11,15]. There are many programs for supporting the learning of algorithms. However, they only can represent and visualize algorithms had been specified discretely. They have not yet proposed the general method to represent, create or modify algorithms for the knowledge engineer in a determined course.

SAS (Starting with Algorithmic Structures) is a program designed for teaching the concepts and structures of algorithms [13]. This system enables the learner to track the execution of the algorithm based on their input data. Additionally, a sorting algorithm learning system has been developed in [14]. However, these systems only visualize specific algorithms, and their architectures lack the capability to support the creation of new content for knowledge engineers.

The primary focus of the Artificial Intelligent Teaching System (AITS) is to educate students about searching algorithms in the context of an AI course [10]. This system provides step-by-step visualizations of the algorithms being taught to enhance the learning experience. PATHFINDER is a tutoring system to learn Dijkstra's algorithm [28]. The animation algorithm visualization panel is shown here. It can display the current coding step that the student is running. Both systems are able to visualize algorithms dynamically. Nonetheless, those programs only represent a part of knowledge in a course, and they also cannot permit the knowledge engineer to update the content of algorithms.

Authors in [7] established an Intelligent Educational software for learning of Graph Theory and Discrete Mathematics. This system is built based on the knowledge model E-COKB. It can support to solve common exercises of those courses automatically. However, it only shows solutions, it cannot tutor and visualize algorithms in those courses. Hence, the learner is difficult to understand the processing of algorithms.

The studies in [19, 20] presented the algorithms for computing the semantic of logic programming by linear algebra. However, the students are very difficult to catch those algorithms without their visualization.

Knowledge models for relations and operators have been studied and employed to create Intelligent Problem Solvers in mathematical courses, such as Geometry [24] and Linear Algebra [17]. However, these models have limitations when it comes to representing the knowledge of algorithms and are incapable of solving problems that pertain to visualizing an algorithm's execution process.

Algorithm Visualizer is an interactive online platform that visualizes algorithms from code [1, 9]. This system can visualize the code of algorithms in many programming language, such as: JavaScript, C++, Java. However, examples in this system are fixed, the user cannot modify the input data of algorithms. VisualAlgo is a website visualizing of algorithms in courses about Data Structure, Graph Theory, Sorting and Searching algorithms [2]. This system only supports algorithms which were set up, it has not yet had a completely knowledge base to support the studying.

3 The Frame for Representing the Knowledge of Algorithms

3.1 Tasks of an Algorithm

When visualizing the processing of a algorithm, the system has to show each running step of it. The visualization has been made on five environments synchronously: the acronym, textual content, tasks, and graphical environment of the algorithm. In order to better explain how an algorithm operates, it is helpful to visually represent the performance process.

A task is a specific phase that demonstrates a state of an algorithm's process. In algorithms, a task is a simple statement or a collection of statements. Tasks that show the execution of the statement will be included if it is a conditional or loop statement.

Each task in the algorithm displays the state of the current execution phase. In fact, the task is set up manually. It is synonymous to visualize every changes which happen on the graphic and the results of data in the algorithm.

A statement or group statements is a task. There are two categories of statements, ordinary statements and controller statements, which are used for visualization in the learning of algorithms. A controller statement is a conditional or looping statement, whereas an ordinary statement is an assign statement.

Definition 3.1: *The specification of a task*

1. **Specification of an ordinary statement:**

ordi-statement	::= ordi-statement+
ordi-statement	::= assignment-state
assignment-state	::= name:=express
express	::= express | rel-express
express	::= express $\oplus$ term | term
term	::= $\otimes$ term | element $\wedge$ term | element
element	::= (express) | name | number
rel-express	::= express rel-operator express

$\oplus$ and $\otimes$ are binary and unary operators, respectively.

2. **Specification of a control statement:**

ordi-primary	::= ordi-statement | ordi-statement+
control-statement	::= condi-statement | condi-statement+ | loop-statement| loop-statement+
condi-statement	::= IF logic-express THEN ordi-primary+ ENDIF; | IF logic-express THEN ordi-primary+ ELSE ordi-primary+ ENDIF
loop-statement	::= FOR variable IN [range] DO ordi-primary+ ENDFOR; | WHILE logic-express DO ordi-primary+ ENDWHILE
logic-express	::= logic-express OR logic-term | logic-express AND logic-term | NOT logic-term | logic-term
logic-term	::= express | rel-express | quantify-express | TRUE | FALSE
quantify-expr	::= FORALL(name<,name>*), logic-express | EXISTS(name), logic-express

3. **Specification of a task:**

task	::= task-primary+
task-primary	::= ordi-statement | control-statement

3.2 Structure of a Frame Representing the Knowledge of an Algorithm

The knowledge of an algorithm includes list of tasks, which consist of statements to excute that algorithm. The kinds of statements are classified as Definition 3.1.

Definition 3.2: *(Frame of an algorithm).* The structure of a frame representing an algorithm, called *Algo-AI* model, includes five elements:

$$(Name, Content, Code, Tasks, Visual)$$

In which:

- *Name*: identify the name of the corresponding algorithm
- *Content*: describe content of the algorithm
- *Code*: The algorithm as pseudo-code.
- *Tasks*: It is a list of tasks of the algorithm. Those tasks are set up by the knowledge engineer based on specification language of statements in Definition 3.1.
- *Visual*: The technique for visualizing the algorithm. It is a list of actions to be taken:

$$Visual = \{s_1, ..., s_k\}$$

Each $s_j \in Visual$ is a result of the task in *Tasks* $(1 \leq j \leq k)$. Each s_j has the structure *(sol-text, sol-graph)*, in which, *sol-text* contains the output presented as text or a string, and *sol-graph* contains the output presented as graphic elements like pictures, charts, or graphs.

Example 2: The structure of frame for visualizing of Bubble Sort algorithm is described as Table 1.

4 Design an Intelligent Tutoring System in Learning of Algorithms

4.1 The Architecture of an Intelligent Tutoring System

There are two kinds of users interacting with an ITS in learning of algorithms: the knowledge engineer and commonly users. The knowledge engineer plays as an administrator of this system. He/She can create a new algorithm for its visualizing or modify the performing content. Commonly users are students who are learning of algorithms; thus they need to obverse the actions of an algorithm with an inputted data by them. Through that, the architecture of this system includes two processes for two kinds of users as Fig. 1.

The Function for the Knowledge Engineer: The engineer requests the system to create/modify an algorithm. This action is worked through the verifying of the knowledge manager component. After that, the results will be updated to the knowledge base of the system.

The Function for the Commonly Users: When the user inputs a data for an algorithm. The knowledge manager will analysis and select the algorithm being suitable that requirement. Using the structure representing this algorithm, the system visualizes it through the user-interface.

4.2 The Function for the Knowledge Engineer

The platform is an interactive tool that allows for the visualization of algorithms from code. Therefore, it is necessary for the system to enable knowledge engineers to program on its platform

Table 1. The frame of Bubble Sort algorithm

Component	Content
Name	Bubble Sort
Content	The Bubble Sort algorithm compares every pair of adjacent elements, and if they are not in the correct order, swaps them out.

Code	```
	for (i = n − 1; i ≥ 1; i − −)
	    for (j = 0; j ≤ i − 1; j + +)
	        if (a[j] > a[j + 1])
	        {
	            temp = a[j];
	            a[j] = a[j + 1];
	            a[j + 1] = temp;
	        }
	``

Tasks	Task 1: $\boxed{\text{for } (i = n − 1; i ≥ 1; i − −)}$ Task 2: $\boxed{\text{for } (j = 0; j ≤ i − 1; j + +)}$ Task 3: $\boxed{\text{if } (a[j] > a[j + 1])}$ Task 4: $\boxed{\begin{array}{l}\text{temp} = a[j]; \\ a[j] = a[j + 1]; \\ a[j + 1] = \text{temp};\end{array}}$

Visual	Example $A = [1, -4, 5, 2]$ then the list of execution steps: $s = [s_1, s_2, ..., s_{10}]$ as follows :
	Step s_1 :
	    sol-text: With $i = 3$ and $j = 0$
	    sol-graph: 1 -4 5 2
	Step s_2 :
	    sol-text: $j = 0, a[0] = 1, a[1] = -4, a[j] > a[j + 1]$, Swapping $a[j]$ and $a[j + 1]$
	    sol-graph: -4 1 5 2
	Step s_3 :
	    sol-text: $j = 1, a[1] = 1, a[2] = 5, a[j] < a[j + 1]$
	    sol-graph: -4 1 5 2
	Step s_4 :
	    sol-text: $j = 2, a[2] = 5, a[3] = 2, a[j] > a[j + 1]$, Swapping $a[j]$ and $a[j + 1]$
	    sol-graph: -4 1 2 5
	Step s_5 :
	    sol-text: With $i = 2$ and $j = 0$
	    sol-graph: -4 1 2 5
	Step s_6 :
	    sol-text: $j = 0, a[0] = -4, a[1] = 1, a[j] < a[j + 1]$
	    sol-graph: -4 1 2 5
	Step s_7 :
	    sol-text: $j = 1, a[1] = 1, a[2] = 2, a[j] < a[j + 1]$
	    sol-graph: -4 1 2 5
	Step s_8 :
	    sol-text: With $i = 1$ and $j = 0$
	    sol-graph: -4 1 2 5
	Step s_9 :
	    sol-text: $j = 0, a[0] = -4, a[1] = 1, a[j] < a[j + 1]$
	    sol-graph: -4 1 2 5
	Step s_{10} :
	    sol-text: $i = 0 < 1$. Finish the algorithm
	    sol-graph: -4 1 2 5

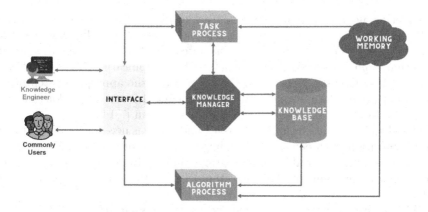

Fig. 1. The architecture of an Intelligent tutoring system.

The Creating or Editing of an Algorithm: The basic information of an algorithm can be updated manually. The primary function of this feature is to create or edit tasks within the algorithm. This process is carried out by classifying the task as either an ordinary statement or a control statement.

At first,the task type is selected, the engineer inputs its content. The knowledge manager component then verifies the content for logical programming. The validation process consists of two steps:

1. *Submission:* During the submission phase, the submitted code is compiled, if needed, and verified if it can be successfully executed in the homogeneous evaluation environment.
2. *Evaluation:* the aggregate score for the submission is calculated based on the results of all the considered test cases. If the test cases are executable and their results can be visualized, they will be outputted.

4.3   The Function for Tutoring the Learning of Algorithms

For learning of students, they require the system could animate execution steps of algorithms. With inputted data, Three contents are synchronized by the system for visualization: displaying the algorithm's state, results of variables in algorithms at this state, and performing the current state on the graphical environment. For doing this tutoring function, there are three problems to visualize an algorithm [9,14]:

Problem 4.1: Enables monitoring a current state and displaying variables results in the algorithm.

Problem 4.2: Make a graph to perform the outcomes of each step in the algorithm.

Problem 4.3: The visualization is synchronized across three contents: highlight the current state of the algorithm, the outcomes of variables at this state, and perform the current state on the graphical environment.

Given an algorithm *Algo*. The tasks tracking of the algorithm *Algo* is resolved in Problem 4.1 so that its processing may be observed. It will bring attention to task $t \in Algo.Tasks$ and compute the outcomes there. The animation of the algorithm *Algo* is resolved by Problem 4.2. The graphical visualization of each task $t \in Algo.Tasks$ is recorded in the *sol-graph* of the appropriate step in the list *Algo.Visual*. Both Problem 4.1 and Problem 4.2 are also belongs to the method of front-end programming, those are solved in [7,14].

Based on the results from Problems 4.1 and 4.2, it is necessary to synchronize the visualization of three contents: highlight the current state of the algorithm, show the results of variables at this stage, and perform the current state on the graphical environment. The algorithm to solve Problem 4.3 is presented as follows.

Algorithm 4.1: *Synchronize outcomes of the visualization.*

Input: An algorithm $Algo = (Name, Content, Code, Tasks, Visual)$ as $AI -$ *Algo* model, and an example *data* for visualization of *Algo*.
Output: Visualize the algorithm *Algo* via the example *data*.

Step 1: Calculate the outcomes of example *data* using algorithm *Algo*, then store those results in *Algo.Visual*.
Step 2: For each task $t \in Algo.Tasks$ do:
- Highlight the task t via its pseudo code in *Algo.Code*.
- Display the results of *sol-text* as text.
- Perform the results of *sol-graph* as graphical objects.

4.4   Testing and Experimental Results

The Data Structure and Algorithms course is a fundamental course in the undergraduate Information Technology (IT) curriculum. The course content includes a collection of algorithms used for testing purposes. The knowledge domain about Data Structures and Algorithms is gathered from [6,12]. The knowledge of collected algorithms is organized by $AI - Algo$ model.

The system can display a variety of linked list and sorting algorithms, including interchange, bubble, shell, selection, and insertion sorts as well as the ability to add or remove elements from linked lists. The user can input a random array of numbers for each algorithm. The system will then provide guidance on the functioning of the algorithm to help the user understand it better.

Example 3: The visualization of Bubble sorting algorithm:
　　　　Input: Array $A = [-6, -2, -8, 6, 1, 3, 7, -2, 8, 9]$
　　　　Output: Ascending sort of A by Bubble sorting algorithm.

The visualization of Bubble sorting for this example is presented in[1] as Fig. 2:

- The number of columns in a visualization frame of the system is the number of elements in the array being considered, and the height of the columns represents the value of each element in the array.

---

[1]　https://youtu.be/fAs-2sRTnbc.

- The column in pink represents the current element being processed by the algorithm.
- The columns in blue represent the elements that have not yet been processed by the algorithm.
- The values on the horizontal axis represent the positions of the elements in the array, and the values on the vertical axis represent the values of the elements in the array.
- The Access variable in the top left corner of the frame indicates the number of steps taken by the algorithm so far.

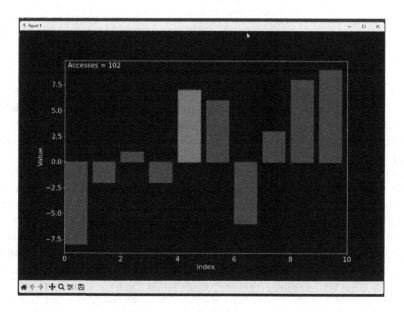

Fig. 2. The interface for visualizing an algorithm.

The outcomes are user-friendly and provide step-by-step instructions. The student has the option to manually forward or retrace their steps on each step. Along with performance steps, the algorithm's pseudo-code is also displayed. Table 2 shows the experimental results of the designed system.

The designed system can implement sorting and searching algorithms appropriately. For algorithms in data structures, some actions are not correct because there are still special cases affecting to the visualization as graphic.

Table 2. The experimental results

Kinds	Algorithms	Number of test data	Results
Sorting algorithms	Bubble Sort Insertion Sort Interchange Sort Selection Sort	24	24
Searching algorithms	Linear search Binary Search	24	24
Data Structures	Single Linked List Queue and Stack Doubly Linked List Binary Search Tree	40	36

5   Conclusion and Future Work

In this study, a design methodology for an ITS for algorithm learning is proposed. The method built an intellectual model for representing the knowledge of an algorithm, called *AI-Algo* model. This model depicts the organization of tasks that are execution actions in the processing of the algorithm. It also has a specification language to represent kinds of tasks in algorithms.

The proposed method can support the knowledge engineer to create and update the content of an algorithm for interacting to the learner step by step based on the visualizations of algorithms. The engineer can set up an algorithm through specification language. Moreover, the designed system also visualizes the happen change in an algorithm's running for commonly users who are students.

Besides, the designed method is applied to build an Intelligent Tutoring System in the course of Data Structures and Algorithms. The purpose of this system is helping students to understand how algorithms works.

In the future, the method will improve to visualize complex algorithms, such as algorithms in Graph Theory course [7]. Besides, the function for creating an algorithm could be expanded to commonly users. They can add more necessary algorithms for visualization by themselves. Moreover, the studying on ontology can combine the Intelligent Tutoring System in algorithms visualization and the intelligent Intelligent Querying System in Education [23]. Those results will build an ontology-based complete system for studying of a course [25,29]. That system can helps learners to querying the intellectual content and visualize algorithms in the course [4,22]. It makes interest on studies and bring enthusiasm for studying of students.

Acknowledgment. This research was supported by The VNUHCM-University of Information Technology's Scientific Research Support Fund.

References

1. Algorithm visualizer (2023). https://algorithm-visualizer.org/

2. Visualgo (2023). https://visualgo.net/
3. Baradac, V., Kostolányová, K.: Intelligent tutoring systems. J. Intell. Syst. **26**, 717–727 (2016)
4. Bende, I.: Data visualization in programming education. Acta Didactica Napocensia **15**(1), 52–60 (2022)
5. Casanovas, M.M., Ruíz-Munzón, N., Buil-Fabregá, M.: Higher education: the best practices for fostering competences for sustainable development through the use of active learning methodologies. Int. J. Sustain. High. Educ. **23**(3), 703–727 (2021)
6. Cormen, T.H., Leiserson, C.E., Rivest, R.L., Stein, C.: Introduction to Algorithms. MIT press, Cambridge (2022)
7. Do, N.V., Nguyen, H.D., Mai, T.T.: Intelligent educational software in discrete mathematics and graph theory. In: New Trends in Intelligent Software Methodologies, Tools and Techniques, pp. 925–938. IOS Press (2018)
8. Gan, W., Sun, Y., Sun, Y.: Knowledge interaction enhanced sequential modeling for interpretable learner knowledge diagnosis in intelligent tutoring systems. Neurocomputing **488**, 36–53 (2022)
9. Goswami, B., et al.: Algorithm visualizer: its features and working. In: 2021 IEEE 8th Uttar Pradesh Section International Conference on Electrical, Electronics and Computer Engineering (UPCON), Dehradun, India, pp. 1–5. IEEE (2021)
10. Grivokostopoulou, F., Perikos, I., Hatzilygeroudis, I.: An educational system for learning search algorithms and automatically assessing student performance. Int. J. Artif. Intell. Educ. **27**(1), 207–240 (2017)
11. Hatzilygeroudis, I., Prentzas, J.: Knowledge representation in intelligent educational systems. In: Web-Based Intelligent E-Learning Systems: Technologies and Applications. IGI Global (2006)
12. Lambert, K.: Fundamentals of Python Data Strucutres, 2nd edn. Cengage, Boston (2019)
13. Lau, W., Yuen, A.: Promoting conceptual change of learning sorting algorithm through the diagnosis of mental models: the effects of gender and learning styles. Comput. Educ. **54**, 275–288 (2010)
14. Le, T.T., et al.: Knowledge representation for designing an intelligent tutoring system in learning of courses about algorithms. In: 2019 25th Asia-Pacific Conference on Communications (APCC), Ho Chi Minh, Vietnam, pp. 310–315. IEEE (2019)
15. Mystakidis, S., Christopoulos, A., Pellas, N.: A systematic mapping review of augmented reality applications to support stem learning in higher education. Educ. Inf. Technol. **27**(2), 1883–1927 (2022)
16. Nguyen, H.D., Do, N.V., Pham, V.T.: A methodology for designing knowledge-based systems and applications. In: Applications of Computational Intelligence in Multi-Disciplinary Research, pp. 159–185. Elsevier (2022)
17. Nguyen, H.D., Do, N.V., Pham, V.T., et al.: A method for knowledge representation to design intelligent problems solver in mathematics based on Rela-Ops model. IEEE Access **8**, 76991–77012 (2020)
18. Nguyen, H.D., Do, N.V., Tran, N.P., et al.: Some criteria of the knowledge representation method for an intelligent problem solver in STEM education. Appl. Comput. Intell. Soft Comput. **2020**, 9834218 (2020)
19. Nguyen, H.D., Sakama, C., Sato, T., Inoue, K.: Computing logic programming semantics in linear algebra. In: Kaenampornpan, M., Malaka, R., Nguyen, D.D., Schwind, N. (eds.) MIWAI 2018. LNCS (LNAI), vol. 11248, pp. 32–48. Springer, Cham (2018). https://doi.org/10.1007/978-3-030-03014-8_3

20. Nguyen, T., Inoue, K., Sakama, C.: Linear algebraic abduction with partial evaluation. In: Hanus, M., Inclezan, D. (eds.) PADL 2023. Lecture Notes in Computer Science, vol. 13880, pp. 197–215. Springer, Cham (2023). https://doi.org/10.1007/978-3-031-24841-2_13

21. Noy, N., et al.: Final report on the 2013 NSF workshop on research challenges and opportunities in knowledge representation (2013)

22. Pham, M.T., Nguyen, K., et al.: An intelligent searching system for academic courses of programming based on ontology query-onto. Int. J. of Intell. Syst. Des. Comput. (IJISDC) (2022). https://doi.org/10.1504/IJISDC.2022.10048574

23. Pham, X.T., Tran, T.V., Nguyen-Le, V.T., et al.: Build a search engine for the knowledge of the course about introduction to programming based on ontology Rela-model. In: 2020 12th International Conference on Knowledge and Systems Engineering (KSE), Can Tho, Vietnam, pp. 207–212. IEEE (2020)

24. Phan, M.N., et al.: Design an intelligent problem solver in geometry based on knowledge model of relations. Eng. Lett. **28**, 1108–1117 (2020)

25. Phan, T.T., Pham, V.Q., Nguyen, H.D., Huynh, A.T., Tran, D.A., Pham, V.T.: Ontology-based resume searching system for job applicants in information technology. In: Fujita, H., Selamat, A., Lin, J.C.-W., Ali, M. (eds.) IEA/AIE 2021. LNCS (LNAI), vol. 12798, pp. 261–273. Springer, Cham (2021). https://doi.org/10.1007/978-3-030-79457-6_23

26. Shipunova, O.D., Berezovskaya, I.P., Kedich, S.I., Popova, N.V., Kvashenko, N.Y.: Intelligent human information behavior in e-learning system. In: 2021 2nd International Conference on Artificial Intelligence and Information Systems, pp. 1–4 (2021)

27. Steingartner, W., Eged, J., Radaković, D., Novitzká, V.: Some innovations of teaching the course on data structures and algorithms. In: 2019 IEEE 15th International Scientific Conference on Informatics, pp. 389–396. IEEE (2019)

28. Sánchez-Torrubia, M., Torres-Blanc, C., López-Martínez, M.: Pathfinder: a visualization emathteacher for actively learning dijkstra's algorithm. In: 2009 Fifth Program Visualization Workshop, pp. 151–158 (2009)

29. Truong, D., et al.: Construct an intelligent querying system in education based on ontology integration. In: 2nd IEEE International Conference on Computing (ICOCO 2022), Kota Kinabalu, Malaysia. IEEE (2022)

Course Recommendation Based on Graph Convolutional Neural Network

An Cong Tran[(✉)], Duc-Thien Tran, Nguyen Thai-Nghe, Tran Thanh Dien, and Hai Thanh Nguyen

Can Tho University, Can Tho, Vietnam
{tcan,ntnghe}@cit.ctu.edu.vn, {thanhdien,nthai.cit}@ctu.edu.vn

Abstract. Selecting the right learning content according to learners' learning abilities and interests is the first and most important factor in achieving good learning performance. Based on the similarity between the course rating data in the Collaborative Filtering format (user, item, rating), and along with the development of Graph Neural Networks (GNN) in developing recommendation systems, we tried to develop a Collaborative Filtering (CF) model based on GNN architecture to recommend suitable courses to the learners. In this study, two CF models based on GNN, including Neural Graph Collaborative Filtering (NGCF) and Light Graph Convolutional Neural Networks (LightGCN), were experimentally compared with some traditional CF models such as Regularized Matrix Factorization (RMF), Light Matrix Factorization (LMF), and Neural Collaborative Filtering (NCF). The experimental results on the Coursera Course Review dataset using LightGCN give promising results in the precision, recall, and RMSE metrics.

Keywords: Course Recommendation · Graph Neural Network · Collaborative Filtering · LightGCN · NGCF

1 Introduction

After the recent Covid 19 pandemic, self-study and self-knowledge have become a learning trend for many people, and Massive Open Online Courses (MOOC) have become popular in many countries around the world. It is a great difficulty for learners to choose a suitable course on Coursera, EdX, Udemy, etc., among hundreds of courses in many different fields. Selecting learning content that matches learning abilities and personal preferences is the most important factor in achieving a good academic outcome. Recommender systems (RS) are widely used for online services such as e-commerce, entertainment, and social networks to increase sales and user experience. The effectiveness and importance of recommender systems that help students select appropriate courses have been confirmed in practice.

So far, there are many types of research and development of the system that suggests learners personalized courses using different methods. One widely

H. Fujita et al. (Eds.): IEA/AIE 2023, LNAI 13925, pp. 235–240, 2023.
https://doi.org/10.1007/978-3-031-36819-6_20

used approach is to build predictive models of learner outcomes and, based on these outcomes, suggest courses in which the learner can achieve good grades. Approaches based on the CF method are commonly used in suggestive systems because of their simplicity and efficiency. However, the sparsity of data can limit the efficiency of these algorithms. The authors in [1] presented several methods (e.g., matrix factorization, User-Based Collaborative Filtering) that can be used to build course recommendation systems. Another work in [2] analyzed students' interest in the courses to indicate the similarity between the students and course goals using methods based on random forest and decision trees.

Deep Learning has also been used to develop recommendation systems for education. In [3], the authors presented a deep learning approach using Convolutional Neural Network on 1D data (CN1D) and Long Short Term Memory (LSTM) to build a model to predict students' learning outcomes in the next semester based on the learning results of previous semesters. In [4], Xiang Wang et al. introduced a recommender system based on a new GNN model called Neural Graph Collaborative Filtering (NGCF), which explicitly encodes signal collaboration through higher-order connections in the user-item interaction graph by representing vector propagation between nodes. LightGCN was introduced as a model that simplifies the design of the GCN to make it simpler and more suitable for the addition filtering problem work [5].

In this study, we propose an approach based on NGCF and LightGCN to recommend courses to learners that provides the most benefits to their study plans. In addition, we investigate the performance according to the number of network layer(s) and the learning rates. We indicate that these hyper-parameters of NGCF and LightGCN are sensitive to their efficiency.

2   Methods

2.1   Dataset and Data Pre-processing

The Coursera Course Reviews dataset includes 1.45 billion reviews on 622 courses on the Coursera online learning platform collected and publicly published by the author on Kaggle[1]. Properties of the dataset include the content of the review, the name of the reviewer, the date of the review, the rating, and the course ID.

Before using the dataset for the experiments, we performed several steps to pre-process data, such as removing unused properties (the reviews and review_date fields), removing duplicate data rows, and filtering out users whose number of interactions with courses is less than or equal to 5. Then, the rating between the learner and the course is used to build the interactive graph. In this case, the interaction between the user and the course means that the user can learn the course well. To recommend courses that are suitable for the learners, one should experimentally remove data rows with a rating less than three from the dataset, i.e., use only positive interactions between the user and course. After the data pre-processing steps, the dataset includes 10,371 users, 598 courses, and 114,849 ratings (interactions).

---

[1] https://www.kaggle.com/datasets/imuhammad/course-reviews-on-coursera.

2.2   Graphical Representation for Learner-Course Interaction

User-item interaction data in CF models can be modeled as a Bilateral Graph where nodes represent users and products, and edges between nodes representing the interaction between users and products (ratings, purchases, clicks, etc.) are illustrated in Fig. 1 with the application to student-course interaction.

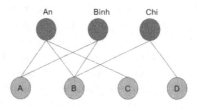

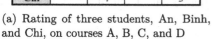

	A	B	C	D
An	4	5	3	
Binh	3	4		
Chi		4		5

(a) Rating of three students, An, Binh, and Chi, on courses A, B, C, and D

(b) Academic results can be represented graphically

Fig. 1. An illustration of user-course interactions using a graph.

Suppose we have the ratings of three students, An, Binh, and Chi, on four courses, A, B, C, and D, as described in Fig. 1a. These ratings are represented in the form of a graph as illustrated in Fig. 1b. We see that An and Chi are considered similar users of Binh, i.e., people with the same learning ability as Binh, because all three are good at course B. Therefore, Binh can do well in course C (like An) and D (like Chi), so these two courses are suggested to Binh, in which the probability of Binh doing well in course C will be higher because the similarity between An and Binh is higher because they all studied well on both courses A and B. The problem of predicting products that students might interact with in the future can be viewed as a link prediction problem in a graph, in which case the recommendation task is transformed into a prediction problem whether there is an edge between the student node and the course node.

GNN applies the representation vector propagation technique and aggregates the representations of neighboring nodes. By stacking multiple propagation layers, each node can access the information of its higher-order neighbors instead of just directly connected nodes. With its advantages in graph data processing and structure discovery, GNN-based methods have become the most advanced approach in recommender systems.

2.3   Graph Neural Networks for Course Recommendation

Neural Graph Collaborative Filtering. NGCF consisted of 3 main components [4]. The first one aims to generate vector representation of nodes to provide and initialize vector representation of users (learners) and products (courses). The representation vector propagation layers are to refine the representation vectors. By using multiple propagation layers, it can capture the cooperation signals from higher-order connections. The last one, the prediction layer, aims to aggregate representation vectors from propagation layers and estimate the likelihood of users interacting with a particular product.

Light Graph Convolutional Neural Network. LightGCN is a model that simplifies the design of Graph Convolution Network (GCN) to make it simpler and more relevant to the collaborative filtering problem [6]. The LightGCN is designed to include only the most necessary component in the GCN for a collaborative filtering problem, which is a neighbor aggregation (Neighborhood aggregation), which learns vector representations of users and products by propagating them on an interactive graph user-item display, using a weighted sum to synthesize the learned representations into the final representation vector. Because of its simple design, the model is easy to deploy and train in recommendation systems.

3   Experimental Results

3.1   Environmental Settings

The experimental dataset was randomly divided into two parts: 80% of the interactions were used to train the model, and the remaining 20% were used to evaluate the model. First, the experiment hides some edges of the initial interaction graph and is used to train the model. Then, the trained model is used to predict the missing edges and evaluate the model based on the interactions included in the test set.

For each user/learner, the experiment produces a recommendation list consisting of K positive courses (courses that the user will probably learn well in the future). K must be much smaller than the total number of courses for an effective recommender system, which was set by default to 10 in this experiment. The work determines the accuracy of the recommendations through Precision@K, Recall@K, and Root Mean Square Error (RMSE).

3.2   Investigation on Various Hyper-parameters

During the training of the NGCF and LightGCN models, the work has experimentally investigated two hyper-parameters: the learning rate lr = {0.0001, 0.0005, 0.001, 0.005} and the number of propagation layers L = {1, 2, 3, 4}, to find values that gives the best performance of the model. The model that gives the best results is the LightGCN model (lr = 0.005, L = 4), which has a precision@10 index of 0.077 and a recall@10 of 0.318. The training time of the NGCF model increases with the number of propagation layers, while the LightGCN model remains stable and has only a slight difference when the number of layers is one, and the number of layers is 4. The training time of the model LightGCN model is always faster than NGCF at all parameter sets.

Simultaneously observe the change of two indicators recall, precision corresponding to different learning rates, the remaining parameters are set by default: the size of vector representation latent dim of 64, batch training with a batch size of 1024, and number of epochs of 50.

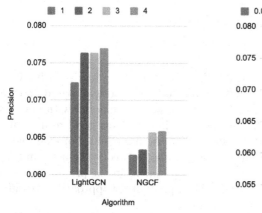

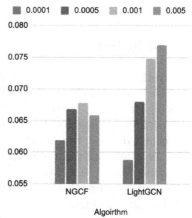

(a) The number of layers with a learning rate of 0.05

(b) Learning rate values with four layers

Fig. 2. Performance Comparison in Precision between LightGCN and NGCF.

Figure 2 shows the comparison results of how changing the number of layers and learning rate can affect the accuracy of the recommendation. Both Light-GCN and NGCF increase performance when increasing the number of layers, but it seems that the increase of NGCF is larger, as illustrated in Fig. 2a. However, for learning rate values, NGCF reveals fluctuations where it peaks at the learning rate of 0.001, while LightGCN shows a dependent on the learning rate with an increase according to the magnitude of the learning rate as illustrated in Fig. 2b.

3.3 Result Comparison

Table 1 shows the comparison results of the LightGCN model with other approaches, including RMF [7], LightFM [8], and NCF [9]. As could be observed, the results of LightGCN and NGCF showed the superiority of RMF, NCF, and LightFM algorithms in Precision@10 and Recall@10 measurements. The result of NCF was the lowest, slightly better than LightFM. RMF is better than NCF and LightFM, but is far behind LightGCN and NGCF. In addition, we also evaluated the methods using a measure commonly used in the recommender system community, namely Root Mean Square Error (RMSE). The experimental result in Table 1 shows that LightGCN also achieved the best result on this dataset.

Table 1. The results comparison of LightGCN with different methods

	RMF	NCF	LightFM	NGCF	**LightGCN**
Precision@10	0.0585	0.0439	0.0482	0.0688	**0.0770**
Recall@10	0.2540	0.1982	0.2178	0.2837	**0.3181**
RMSE	3.288	4.412	9.175	4.456	**3.132**

4 Conclusion

In this work, we trained two powerful collaborative filtering models using Graph
Neural Networks NGCF and LightGCN, to recommend courses based on course
ratings on MOOC platforms. In addition, we also experimented with many collaborative filtering models. Although the experiment yields good results on the
experimental dataset, the research still needs to be improved. For example, the
LightGCN model only uses positive interactions between the user and item
(learner and course). Therefore, negativity may appear in the proposed method.
The development direction may continue to explore other approaches to address
the above shortcomings.

References

1. Thanh-Nhan, H.L., Nguyen, H.H., Thai-Nghe, N.: Methods for building course recommendation systems. In: 2016 Eighth International Conference on Knowledge and
   Systems Engineering (KSE), pp. 163–168 (2016)
2. Anupama, V., Elayidom, M.S.: Course recommendation system: collaborative filtering, machine learning and topic modelling. In: 2022 8th International Conference
   on Advanced Computing and Communication Systems (ICACCS), vol. 1, pp. 1459–
   1462 (2022)
3. Dien, T.T., Hoai, S., Thanh-Hai, N., Thai-Nghe, N.: Deep learning with data transformation and factor analysis for student performance prediction. Int. J. Adv. Comput. Sci. Appli. **11**(8) (2020)
4. Wang, X., He, X., Wang, M., Feng, F., Chua, T.S.: Neural graph collaborative filtering. In: Proceedings of the 42nd International ACM SIGIR Conference on Research
   and Development in Information Retrieval. ACM (2019)
5. Zhu, P., et al.: SI-news: integrating social information for news recommendation with
   attention-based graph convolutional network. Neurocomputing **494**, 33–42 (2022)
6. He, X., Deng, K., Wang, X., Li, Y., Zhang, Y., Wang, M.: LightGCN. In: Proceedings
   of the 43rd International ACM SIGIR Conference on Research and Development in
   Information Retrieval. ACM (2020)
7. Feng, L., Huang, J., Shu, S., An, B.: Regularized matrix factorization for multilabel
   learning with missing labels. IEEE Trans. Cybern. **52**(5), 3710–3721 (2022)
8. Kula, M.: Metadata embeddings for user and item cold-start recommendations.
   arXiv preprint arXiv:1507.08439 (2015)
9. He, X., Liao, L., Zhang, H., Nie, L., Hu, X., Chua, T.S.: Neural collaborative filtering. In: Proceedings of the 26th International Conference on World Wide Web.
   International World Wide Web Conferences Steering Committee (2017)

Collaborative Filtering Based on Non-Negative Matrix Factorization for Programming Problem Recommendation

Daniel M. Muepu[1(✉)], Yutaka Watanobe[1], and Md. Mostafizer Rahman[1,2]

[1] The University of Aizu, Aizuwakamatsu, Japan
mdaniel108@gmail.com, yutaka@u-aizu.ac.jp
[2] Dhaka University of Engineering and Technology, Gazipur, Bangladesh
mostafiz@duet.ac.bd

Abstract. This paper explores the use of Non-Negative Factorization for adapting collaborative filtering to programming exercises. Traditional collaborative filtering uses user preferences as ratings, but user feedback is expressed differently in programming exercises. The proposed approach captures user satisfaction based on the number of attempts and the final verdict. The NMF algorithm is used to factorize a non-negative input matrix into two non-negative matrices, and user-based collaborative filtering is implemented to make recommendations. The proposed model achieved an Mean Absolute Error of 0.06, Root Mean Squared Error of 0.2, a Recall of 51%, and a Precision of 54%, demonstrating its capability to make accurate and relevant recommendations for programming exercises.

Keywords: Recommendation System · Collaborative Filtering · Matrix Factorization · Programming Education · Online Judge

1 Introduction

The importance of programming as a valuable skill for a long-term career in the digital world is increasing, and the demand for programming skills is predicted to rise [1]. In addition, programming helps students to develop critical thinking, problem-solving skills, and logical reasoning [2,3], which are helpful beyond programming. Practice is key to developing proficiency and understanding programming [4], as it allows individuals to build skills, solidify their perception of concepts, and identify and correct errors, which prepares them for real-world programming tasks [5].

Nowadays, Online judges offer platforms for users to practice and apply programming skills and concepts by providing a wide range of problems and challenges of varying difficulty levels [6]. These platforms allow instant feedback on the correctness of the submitted code. However, the availability of numerous problems can make it difficult for users to find relevant problems to solve, leading

H. Fujita et al. (Eds.): IEA/AIE 2023, LNAI 13925, pp. 241–250, 2023.
https://doi.org/10.1007/978-3-031-36819-6_21

to frustration and decreased motivation, known as choice overload [7,8]. Recommendation systems can help reduce the time spent searching for problems to solve and increase students' engagement by providing personalized and relevant recommendations [9]. This tailored recommendation can be based on a student's learning history, interests, and goals, resulting in a more personalized experience that introduces new and diverse exercises and expands student knowledge [10]. Additionally, a recommendation system can adapt recommendations based on a student's progress and strengths and weaknesses.

Recommendation systems were initially designed for business applications. However, their adaptations in the educational context present more significant challenges because it involves pedagogical principles, domain ontology, and a diverse range of knowledge and learning processes [11]. In the case of programming exercises, traditional collaborative filtering may not be effortlessly applicable as users do not assign ratings to problems. Furthermore, while positive opinions are used to make recommendations in business, in programming exercises, the goal is for users to solve all problems, requiring a recommendation system that can dynamically adjust to a user's progress and adapt recommendations based on their strengths and weaknesses. As such, users may demand access to easy-to-solve tasks or those that are slightly more challenging to facilitate their progression.

In this study, we have created a collaborative filtering model using nonnegative matrix factorization. The model is designed to generate precise and pertinent recommendations for programming problems while estimating the number of trials required for problem-solving. By leveraging this model, students can practice the most relevant and efficient exercises, enabling them to develop their skills and enhance their coding proficiency. Additionally, the model can boost motivation and engagement while supporting personalized and adaptive learning. Ultimately, our model can improve learning outcomes for students and increase satisfaction with programming education.

The remainder of this paper is organized as follows. Section 2 presents related work. Section 3 describes Collaborative filtering for programming problems, and Sect. 4 presents the implementation of the model. In Sect. 5, the results are discussed, and finally, Sect. 7 concludes with suggestions for future work.

2   Related Work

In [12], the authors conducted a systematic literature review of 16 papers related to educational recommender systems in education. The increasing use of ICT in education and the resulting increase in data have led to the growth of recommendation systems for learning experience improvement. The authors identified and discussed research trends, limitations, and future opportunities. In [13], the authors surveyed intelligent academic recommendation systems based on "traditional intelligent recommendation algorithms" and deep learning algorithms.

It is possible to recommend different learning materials for courses. In [14], the authors propose an online education course recommendation algorithm based on path factors to find and recommend similar courses more reasonably. For exercises, in [15], authors analyze learners' historical log data in a computer network course to find the similarities between a learner's knowledge and the required knowledge to solve exercises and make recommendations.

Concerning programming exercises, various approaches have been used to support learners. Some researchers have adopted content-based filtering to recommend programming problems, as in the case of [16], where authors proposed a method to provide programming problems with similar content and answer source code similar to a target assignment. Other researchers have adapted collaborative filtering to the reality of online judge systems, as seen [7], where the authors proposed a three-level collaborative filtering recommendation method for online judge systems to present alternative problems to users that they may be interested in potentially.

This study presents a novel approach to programming exercise recommendations by capturing user satisfaction levels and implementing a collaborative filtering model based on Non-negative Matrix Factorization. To our knowledge, this is the first study to incorporate user satisfaction in the recommendation process.

3 Collaborative Filtering for Programming Problems

Collaborative Filtering is a recommendation technique that involves making recommendations based on the preferences and behaviors of other users with similar tastes and interests [17].

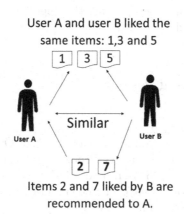

User A and user B liked the
same items: 1,3 and 5

Items 2 and 7 liked by B are
recommended to A.

Fig. 1. Collaborative filtering based on user ratings

Collaborative filtering leverages user preferences, usually ratings, to identify other users with similar tastes (see Fig. 1). The recommendation list is then compiled from items that have received positive reviews from similar users but have not yet been tried by the targeted user [18].

In programming exercises, user feedback is not usually given in the form of ratings. While a simple adaptation of collaborative filtering could involve treating the completion of an exercise as a binary value (1 = solved, 0 = attempted but unsolved), this approach fails to capture the nuanced levels of user satisfaction that are typically expressed through explicit ratings (e.g., 5/5 or 3/5) in traditional recommendation settings.

Table 1. Final verdicts on submitted solution codes from different users, that are evaluated by an online judging system

User_ID	Problem_Id	Verdict
1	1	Wrong Answer
1	1	Wrong Answer
1	1	Accepted
2	1	Accepted
2	2	Wrong Answer
2	2	Accepted
3	2	Runtime error
4	2	Compiler error
4	2	Runtime error

In Table 1, which shows a submission log for programming exercises, we can see that both *user* 1 and *user* 2 solved problem 1, but *user* 1 required three attempts while *user* 2 only needed one, this highlights the importance of the number of trials required by a user to solve a problem, which can be used to express the user's preference.

4   Model Implementation

4.1   Data

The submission logs dataset obtained from the Aizu Online Judge (AOJ) system contains information on User_ID, Problem_ID, and Verdict. We used submission logs related to 27,143 users and 1,352 problems, collected from AOJ (launched in 2004) and containing over 3,000 programming problems and 120,000 users, supporting 20 programming languages [6].

4.2   Data Preprocessing

To capture users' satisfaction with a problem, we adopt an approach that requires converting submission log data into ratings. Specifically, for each user 'u' and each problem 'p', we record the number of trials 'n' used by 'u' when attempting to solve 'p'. We also record the final verdict 'v', which is 1 if the problem was solved successfully (accepted) and 0 otherwise.

Table 2. Mapping the user attempts and verdicts

(a) User-Problem-Verdict

user_ID	Problem_Id	Verdict
1	1	Wrong Answer
1	1	Wrong Answer
1	1	Accepted
2	1	Accepted
2	2	Wrong Answer
2	2	Accepted
3	2	Runtime error
4	2	Compiler error
4	2	Runtime error

$\Longrightarrow$

(b) User-Problem-number of attempts-Final verdict

u	p	n	v
1	1	3	1
2	1	1	1
3	2	1	0
4	2	2	0

Table 2a illustrates examples of user attempts to solve programming problems. For instance, User 1 attempted to solve Problem 1 three times and ultimately succeeded (with $n = 3, v = 1$); in contrast, User 2 solved the same Problem on the first attempt (with $n = 1, v = 1$). However, User 3 could not solve Problem 2 in their only attempt (with $n = 1, v = 0$), while User 4 tried twice with the same unsuccessful result (with $n = 2, v = 0$).

To capture the user's preference, we assumed that the low number of trials required to solve a problem implies higher satisfaction. Thus, we converted the number of attempts and verdicts into ratings (r) using Algorithm 1, as shown in Table 3.

Table 3. Conversion of attempts and verdicts into ratings

(a) User-Problem-number of attempts-Final verdict

u	p	n	v
1	1	3	1
2	1	1	1
3	2	1	0
4	2	2	0

$\Longrightarrow$

(b) User-Problem-Rating

u	p	r
1	1	4
2	1	5
3	2	2
4	2	2

The rating can be used to tailor the collaborative filtering technique to programming exercises, resulting in more personalized and proper recommendations for users.

Algorithm 1: Rating generation from the attempts and verdicts

---

Input: Attempt (n), and Verdict (v)
Output: Rating (r)
if *v=1* **then**
 │ **if** $n \geq 1$ && $n \leq 2$ **then**
 │ │ $r \longleftarrow 5$
 │ **end**
 │ **if** $n > 2$ && $n \leq 5$ **then**
 │ │ $r \longleftarrow 4$
 │ **end**
 │ **else**
 │ │ $r \longleftarrow 3$
 │ **end**
end
else
 │ **if** $n < 5$ **then**
 │ │ $r \longleftarrow 2$
 │ **end**
 │ **else**
 │ │ $r \longleftarrow 1$
 │ **end**
end

4.3   Non-Negative Matrix Factorization Implementation

The non-negative matrix factorization (NMF) is a matrix factorization variant in which all the values in the matrices must be non-negative. This constraint is effective in recommendation systems where the ratings have naturally non-negative values [19]. In our approach, we first converted the dataset into a user-problem matrix (V), as shown in Table 4. All the empty cells representing non-attempted problems were rated 0.

Table 4. Conversion of the dataset into user-problem matrix

(a) User-Problem-Rating

u	p	r
1	1	4
2	1	5
3	2	2
4	2	2

$\Longrightarrow$

(b) User-Problem matrix

u/p	1	2
1	4	0
2	5	0
3	0	2
4	0	2

Then, we factorized V into two non-negative matrices W and H such that:

$$V \approx WH \tag{1}$$

We optimized the model by factorizing matrix V into two non-negative matrices, W and H, where W is a $m \times k$ matrix, H is a $k \times n$ matrix, and k is the number of latent features. To achieve this, we used the Multiplicative Update Rule, an iterative algorithm that updates the factorization matrices by repeatedly multiplying the elements of the matrices until convergence or a maximum number of iterations is reached [20]. The factorization matrices are updated as follows:

$$W_{ij} = W_{ij} \frac{(VH^\top)ij}{(WHH^\top)ij} \tag{2}$$

$$H_{ij} = H_{ij} \frac{(W^\top V)ij}{(W^\top WH)ij} \tag{3}$$

where i and j are indices for the elements, and the operations between the matrices are element-wise multiplication, also known as the Hadamard product[1]. Element-wise multiplication is an operation that multiplies two matrices by multiplying each element in the first matrix with the corresponding component in the second matrix. The resulting matrix has similar dimensions as the input matrices [21].

We used the Frobenius norm to quantify the discrepancy between the original and reconstructed matrices. This norm (also known as the Euclidean norm for matrices) calculates the magnitude of a matrix as the square root of the sum of the squares of the matrix elements [22]. The formula for the Frobenius norm of a matrix A is as follows:

$$||A||_F = \sqrt{\sum_{i,j} A_{ij}^2} \tag{4}$$

To make predictions, we first compute the Pearson correlation to find similarities between users as follow:

$$sim(u,v) = \frac{\sum_{i \in P} (r_{u,i} - \bar{r}_u)(r_{v,i} - \bar{r}_v)}{\sqrt{\sum_{i \in P} (r_{u,i} - \bar{r}_u)^2} \sqrt{\sum_{i \in P} (r_{v,i} - \bar{r}_v)^2}} \tag{5}$$

Here, $r_{u,i}$ is the rating of user u for item i, $\bar{r}_u$ is the average rating of user u across all rated items, $r_{v,i}$ is the rating that user v has given to item i, $\bar{r}_v$ is the average rating of user v across all the rated items, and P is the set of items that are rated by both users. To predict the rating of user u for item i:

$$\hat{r}_{u,i} = \bar{r}_u + \frac{\sum_{v \in N(u)} sim(u,v) \times (r_{v,i} - \bar{r}_v)}{\sum_{v \in N(u)} sim(u,v)} \tag{6}$$

---

[1] https://en.wikipedia.org/wiki/Hadamard_product_(matrices).

In the above equation, $\bar{r}_u$ represents the average rating assigned by user u, $N(u)$ denotes the set of users similar to user u, $sim(u, v)$ is the similarity between users u and v, $r_{v,i}$ is the rating that user v gave to the item i, and $\bar{r}_v$ represents the average rating assigned by user v.

5   Results

We split the matrix into a training matrix and a test matrix with respectively 80% and 20% of the total size. To measure the discrepancy between the predicted ratings and the actual ratings, we computed the Mean Absolute Error (MAE) and the Root Mean Squared Error (RMSE). The model achieved an MAE of 0.04 and an RMSE of 0.12 for the training matrix and an MAE of 0.06 and an RMSE of 0.2 for the test matrix. To gain further insight into the performance of the recommendation system, we calculated the precision and recall metrics for the top 10 recommended problems for the individual user. Precision measures the proportion of recommended items that are relevant, while recall measures the ratio of the recommended items that are relevant.

$$Recall = \frac{\text{Number of recommended items that are relevant}}{\text{Number of relevant items}} \tag{7}$$

$$Precision = \frac{\text{Number of recommended items that are relevant}}{\text{Total number of recommended items}} \tag{8}$$

The model has achieved a Recall of 0.60 and a Precision of 0.63 for the training matrix and a Recall of 0.51 and a Precision of 0.54 for the test matrix.

6   Discussion

The achieved MAE and RMSE values indicate that the model can make accurate predictions with little difference between the predicted and actual ratings, as provided by users. The recall values suggest that the model can recommend about half of the relevant problems for the users in the dataset, which indicates that the model can identify and recommend a significant portion of the problem that users are likely to be interested in. The precision values imply that the model's recommendations are correct for more than half of the time, indicating a relatively high probability that users will be interested in the suggested problem.

The diverse metrics described above suggest that the model is proficient at identifying and analyzing the underlying patterns in the user-problems interaction matrix and can generate precise predictions for new problems. The findings are encouraging and suggest that a collaborative model based on NMF could be a viable option for implementation in a practical recommendation system.

However, to any collaborative filtering model, this approach is susceptible to the cold-start problem, which implies that the model may struggle to provide accurate recommendations for new users or problems with limited historical interaction data. Additionally, as the dataset grows in size, the computational demands of the model can become prohibitively high, making it difficult to scale to countless datasets. In cases where several potential user-item interactions are missing from the dataset, the model may struggle to make accurate predictions due to the lack of information. Furthermore, since the model solely relies on user-problem interactions, it does not consider other types of data, such as problem content, user demographics, or temporal information, which limit its ability to provide more precise recommendations.

7   Conclusion and Future Work

This study proposed a model that adapts collaborative filtering to programming exercises. The model captures the user's satisfaction with practice problems through an algorithm that converts the number of trials and the final verdict into ratings, which allows us to generate personalized recommendation lists for each user and estimate the required number of trials to solve the recommended exercises. Additionally, the model can adapt the recommendation criteria based on the user's needs, suggesting either easy or challenging problems. Our results are valuable to educators and learners. These results allow for better personalization of programming exercise recommendations based on the student's context. The model can suggest affordable exercises to learners who require additional support or more complicated problems to advanced learners to encourage progress. In the future, we plan to develop a hybrid recommendation system that considers both the learner's ability to solve programming exercises and the similarity of the instructions needed to solve these exercises.

References

1. Li, Z., Jie, Z., Daming, H.: Design and implementation of student programming profile-based teaching aids solution in introductory programming course. In: 2020 15th International Conference on Computer Science and Education (ICCSE), pp. 383–390. IEEE (2020)
2. Amin, M.F.I., Rahman, M.M., Watanobe, Y., Daniel, M.M.: Impact of programming language skills in programming learning. In: 2022 IEEE 15th International Symposium on Embedded Multicore/Many-Core Systems-on-Chip (MCSoC), pp. 271–277. IEEE (2022)
3. Salau, L., Hamada, M., Prasad, R., Hassan, M., Mahendran, A., Watanobe, Y.: State-of-the-art survey on deep learning-based recommender systems for e-learning. Appl. Sci. **12**(23), 11996 (2022)
4. Wakatani, A., Maeda, T.: Automatic generation of programming exercises for learning programming language. In: 2015 IEEE/ACIS 14th International Conference on Computer and Information Science (ICIS), pp. 461–465 (2015)
5. Saha, A.K.: A real-time simulation-based practical on overcurrent protection for undergraduate electrical engineering students. IEEE Access **10**, 52537–52550 (2022)
6. Watanobe, Y., Rahman, M.M., Amin, M.F.I., Kabir, R.: Identifying algorithm in program code based on structural features using CNN classification model. Appl. Intell. **53**, 12210–12236 (2023)

7. Yu, X., Chen, W.: Research on three-layer collaborative filtering recommendation for online judge. In: 2016 Seventh International Green and Sustainable Computing Conference (IGSC), pp. 1–4. IEEE (2016)
8. Scheibehenne, B., Greifeneder, R., Todd, P.M.: Can there ever be too many options? A meta-analytic review of choice overload. J. Consum. Res. **37**(3), 409–425 (2010)
9. Qian, Z., Jie, L., Guangquan, Z.: Recommender systems in e-learning. J. Smart Environ. Green Comput. (2022)
10. Gulzar, Z., Leema, A.A.: Towards recommending courses in a learner centered system using query classification approach. In: 2017 4th International Conference on Advanced Computing and Communication Systems (ICACCS), pp. 1–5. IEEE (2017)
11. Torres, N.: Recommender systems for education: a case of study using formative assessments. In: 2022 41st International Conference of the Chilean Computer Science Society (SCCC), pp. 1–6. IEEE (2022)
12. da Silva, F.L., Slodkowski, B.K., da Silva, K.K.A., Cazella, S.C.: A systematic literature review on educational recommender systems for teaching and learning: research trends, limitations and opportunities. Educ. Inf. Technol. **28**(3), 3289–3328 (2023)
13. Yang, H., Zhou, H., Li, Y.: A review of academic recommendation systems based on intelligent recommendation algorithms. In: 2022 7th International Conference on Image, Vision and Computing (ICIVC), pp. 958–962. IEEE (2022)
14. Shen, Y., Li, H., Liao, Z.: Online education course recommendation algorithm based on path factors. In: 2022 IEEE 5th International Conference on Information Systems and Computer Aided Education (ICISCAE), pp. 257–260. IEEE (2022)
15. Zhu, L., et al.: A study on exercise recommendation method using knowledge graph for computer network course. In: 2020 International Conference on Networking and Network Applications (NaNA), pp. 436–442. IEEE (2020)
16. Yoshimura, R., Sakamoto, K., Washizaki, H., Fukazawa, Y.: Recommendation system providing similar problems instead of model answers to programming assignments. In: 2022 IEEE 5th Eurasian Conference on Educational Innovation (ECEI), pp. 229–232. IEEE (2022)
17. Shrivastava, N., Gupta, S.: Analysis on item-based and user-based collaborative filtering for movie recommendation system. In: 2021 5th International Conference on Electrical, Electronics, Communication, Computer Technologies and Optimization Techniques (ICEECCOT), pp. 654–656. IEEE (2021)
18. Sammut, C., Webb, G.I. (eds.): Collaborative Filtering, p. 189. Springer, Boston (2010)
19. Aghdam, M.H., Analoui, M., Kabiri, P.: Collaborative filtering using non-negative matrix factorisation. J. Inf. Sci. **43**(4), 567–579 (2017)
20. Zoidi, O., Tefas, A., Pitas, I.: Multiplicative update rules for concurrent nonnegative matrix factorization and maximum margin classification. IEEE Trans. Neural Netw. Learn. Syst. **24**(3), 422–434 (2013)
21. Styan, G.P.: Hadamard products and multivariate statistical analysis. Linear Algebra Appl. **6**, 217–240 (1973)
22. Meyer, C.D.: Matrix Analysis and Applied Linear Algebra. Society for Industrial and Applied Mathematics, Philadelphia, PA (2000)

Information Fusion

MAF: Multimodal Auto Attention Fusion for Video Classification

Chengjie Zheng[1]($\boxtimes$) (ID), Wei Ding[1], Shiqian Shen[2], and Ping Chen[1]

[1] Department of Computer Science, University of Massachusetts Boston, Boston, USA
{chengjie.zheng001,wei.ding,ping.chen}@umb.edu
[2] Department of Anesthesia, Critical Care and Pain Medicine, Massachusetts General Hospital, Boston, USA
sshen2@mgh.harvard.edu

Abstract. Video classification is a complex task that involves analyzing audio and video signals using deep neural models. To reliably classify these signals, researchers have developed multimodal fusion techniques that combine audio and video data into compact, quickly processed representations. However, previous approaches to multimodal data fusion have relied heavily on manually designed attention mechanisms. To address these limitations, we propose the Multimodal Auto Attention Fusion (MAF) model, which uses Neural Architecture Search (NAS) to automatically identify effective attentional representations for a wide range of tasks. Our approach includes a custom-designed search space that allows for the automatic generation of attention representations. Using automated Key, Query, and Value representation design, the MAF model enhances its self-attentiveness, allowing for the creation of highly effective attention representation designs. Compared to other multimodal fusion methods, our approach exhibits competitive performance in detecting modality interactions. We conducted experiments on three large datasets (UCF101, ActivityNet, and YouTube-8M), which confirmed the effectiveness of our approach and demonstrated its superior performance compared to other popular models. Furthermore, our approach exhibits robust generalizability across diverse datasets.

Keywords: Multimodal · Auto Attention · video classification

1 Introduction

Video understanding is a fundamental human capability developed from infancy, as babies begin to identify and comprehend events through still images, motion, and sound. Despite advances in computer vision and machine learning, video classification remains challenging, with considerable room for improvement. Unlike image classification, video classification employs multiple cues, including image, motion, and sound, to make decisions. This multimodal nature adds complexity, as appearance alone may not be sufficient to differentiate objects.

H. Fujita et al. (Eds.): IEA/AIE 2023, LNAI 13925, pp. 253–264, 2023.
https://doi.org/10.1007/978-3-031-36819-6_22

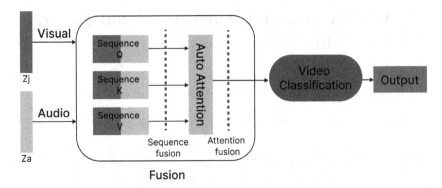

Fig. 1. Overview of the proposed Multimodal Auto Attention Fusion (MAF) Model The Multimodal Auto Attention Fusion (MAF) model is a novel multimodal fusion approach that takes unimodal representations z_j and z_a as inputs and processes them through three feature sequence fusions: Q, K, and V. These fusions generate new unimodal representations Q', K', and V' using auto attention. Subsequently, attention fusion is performed on Q', K', and V' to produce an output representation, which serves as the attention representation for the model. This attention representation can then be utilized for classification tasks.

For example, musical instruments may look similar but sound different, necessitating the use of acoustic features to improve classification accuracy.

Deep Convolutional Neural Networks (CNNs) [19] have demonstrated effectiveness in video classification and other computer vision tasks. However, their focus on local patterns results in limited improvement compared to image classification. Multimodal networks, which capture longer-range temporal patterns and relationships, are employed to harness complementary information from multiple modalities. Current end-to-end multimodal approaches, however, are limited to small datasets. Joint end-to-end training of large datasets combining video and audio signals (e.g., ActivityNet [7] and YouTube-8M [6]) remains a challenge.

A solution involves using pre-trained models or training unimodal CNN models separately, followed by extracting multimodal features [11] from new videos. This approach offers several benefits: 1) enabling transfer learning, such as from image and audio classification to video classification or between datasets; 2) producing smaller extracted features compared to original RGB frames and audio data; 3) facilitating the easier and faster study of large datasets like YouTube-8M, which often provide pre-extracted features.

Attention mechanisms have achieved success in various domains. End-to-end training of CNNs using attention mechanisms, combined with state-of-the-art feed-forward network architectures, has been demonstrated in [5]. Applications include a fine-grained attention mechanism for neural machine translation [15], a leveraged attention mechanism for video action recognition [19], and the integration of attention mechanisms into deep recurrent neural networks for speech emotion recognition [26]. However, none of these prior works focus on applying attention mechanisms to multimodal fusion.

Typically, each extracted feature represents a specific local period in a video. The sequence of ordered local features forms a comprehensive description of the video. Tensor representations modeling interactions between patterns can be used to predict the video's output class distribution. To achieve this goal more effectively and efficiently, we propose Auto Attention, a refined attention mechanism.

We introduce a novel multimodal fusion model with an auto-attention mechanism for an efficient and globally relevant fusion of multiple modalities. Our model employs a low-rank weight tensor with an attention mechanism to improve performance on two public dataset tasks. Figure 1 depicts our model's framework. We compare our results with state-of-the-art models, assessing not just classification accuracy but also model applicability and stability. This is the first application of an auto-attentive mechanism to low-rank multimodal factor fusion, yielding superior results compared to other tensor-based models in terms of generality and performance.

We can summarize the main contributions of this paper as follows:

- Our proposed Multimodal Auto Attention Fusion (MAF) model employs a combination of feature and attention fusion to effectively integrate audio and video signals, enabling the extraction and aggregation of the most pertinent information from any given input video.
- We introduce a versatile auto-attention mechanism that significantly enhances global correlation and adaptability while maintaining comparable levels of parameter complexity and computational efficiency. This mechanism can be employed for a wide range of tasks and datasets.
- The proposed Multimodal Auto Attention Fusion (MAF) model exhibits outstanding performance across various video classification tasks, surpassing previous benchmarks on the UCF-101, ActivityNet, and YouTube-8M datasets. The MAF model has been thoroughly evaluated using both trimmed and untrimmed video inputs and excels in both single-label and multi-label classification contexts.

2   Background and Related Work

2.1   Video Classification

The remarkable success of Convolutional Neural Networks (CNNs) in image classification tasks [26] has spurred their application in video classification domains [27]. Initially, 2D CNNs were employed directly on the RGB frames of videos. Karpathy et al. investigated various approaches to extend the connectivity of a CNN across the temporal dimension, thereby capturing local spatiotemporal information through techniques such as single, late, early, or slow fusion pooling [28]. However, these rudimentary pooling methods did not yield substantial improvements when compared to the single-frame baseline.

To address the shortcomings of 2D CNNs and more effectively integrate spatiotemporal information, the optical flow method was developed to capture variations across adjacent frames. [2] proposed a technique that utilizes RGB frames and stacked optical flow frames to represent appearance and motion signals, respectively [3]. [1] revealed that action recognition accuracy markedly increased by merely aggregating probability scores, signifying the valuable motion information provided by optical flow. However, the intrinsic limitations of the optical flow method confine its capacity to capture solely temporally local information.

An alternative approach to obtaining motion information is using C3D [5], which extends 2D CNNs with 3D convolution kernels. [13] found that extending the temporal length of inputs for 3D CNNs led to better results and that using optical flows as inputs outperformed RGB inputs [10]. [13] incorporated the Inception architecture [12] into 3D CNNs [11].

While CNNs excel at detecting short-term patterns in short, fixed-length videos, capturing long-term interactions in long, variable-length videos remains a challenge. In order to tackle this issue, Recurrent Neural Networks (RNNs), specifically Long Short-Term Memory (LSTM) networks, are utilized to represent long-range temporal relationships in the domain of video classification. These pre-trained LSTMs are then applied to video classification tasks. However, the accuracy and efficiency of self-attention video classification methods have been limited, and the fusion of multi-modal information has not been extensively explored.

2.2   Self-Attention Representation

The self-attention mechanism was initially introduced to enable models to selectively focus on relevant parts of source sentences when generating the next word in translations [4]. Since then, the concept of attention has been generalized beyond text alignment and is now widely used in various fields, with the Key, Query, and Value information flow being manually designed for self-attention.

Designing an effective self-attention mechanism involves two critical steps: 1) Key, Query, and Value representation and 2) self-attention calculation. While recent research has focused on the latter step, the former step is equally important but has received limited attention. This work aims to automate the first step for sequential recommendation using self-attention. [15] pioneered the idea of self-attention, employing an encoder-decoder mechanism to enhance LSTM's ability to align source and target sentences during translation. However, only the final layer of the decoder is allowed to attend to the final layer of the encoder, leaving information from other layers unused. The encoder-decoder attention has been refined and applied to various research areas, such as [11,14], which utilize self-attention to improve multi-modal fusion by introducing cross-modal co-self-attention. Nguyen and Okatani model the relationships between the encoder and decoder by densely stacking co-attention layers. [16] further investigates various representation design approaches. Despite the power of self-attention, these self-attention representations require careful design and expert knowledge to be effective for a specific task and may suffer from human bias, leading to sub-optimal results.

2.3   Neural Architecture Search

Neural architecture search (NAS) [13] is an increasingly popular technique to identify the best neural network architectures for a given task. Various search algorithms have been developed to solve the NAS problem, including reinforcement learning, evolutionary algorithms, gradient-based algorithms, and Bayesian Optimization. These algorithms are combined with different search space designs to find the optimal deep architectures for various applications, such as computer vision, natural language processing, and graph representation learning.

To improve search efficiencies, techniques such as parameter-sharing, one-shot formulation with supernets, and soft-relaxation of the search space have been introduced [12]. Parameter-sharing, in particular, speeds up the training process by sharing parameters, which can lead to a reduction in the difference in operations. However, this can also make it challenging to model the relationships between different operation choices, especially when those choices are highly relevant to the context.

In this work, we aim to achieve better performance for video classification by automating the attention representation design using NAS with context-aware parameter sharing [13]. This approach considers the relationships between different operation choices and the context in which they are being used, allowing for more accurate predictions and improved performance.

Our proposed MAF model addresses existing models' limitations by combining feature fusion, attention fusion, and auto-attention mechanisms. The feature and attention fusion components gather the most significant signals, while the auto-attention mechanism enhances global correlation and adaptability. The MAF model stands out as an illustrious solution that strikes a balance between performance and efficiency, delivering optimal results in various applications.

3   Multimodal Auto Attention Fusion

This section outlines our proposed Multimodal Auto Attention Fusion (MAF) approach for video classification. The architecture of the model is depicted in Fig. 1. We introduce our innovative auto-attention mechanism and then provide a comprehensive explanation of the attention-based multimodal fusion.

3.1   Auto Attention Representation by Neural Architecture Search (NAS)

Self-attention is a mechanism used in deep learning models, particularly in natural language processing. The model is trained to focus on specific parts of an input sequence by assigning significance scores to each element. This enables the model to weigh the importance of each input element and make decisions accordingly, resulting in a more nuanced understanding of the data. In traditional attention mechanisms, the input source and output target are different. For instance, in recommendation systems, the source is a historical click item,

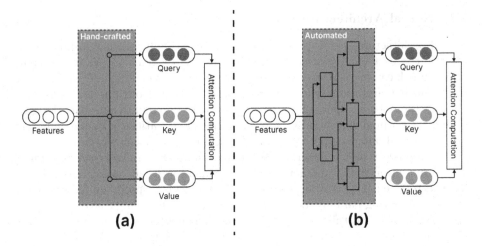

Fig. 2. Self-Attention and Auto-Attention The design of attention representation in self-attention is illustrated as follows [28]: (a) Traditional hand-designed attention representation with Key, Query, and Value derived manually from computation paths. (b) Our novel auto-attention representation, where Key, Query, and Value are automatically obtained from the input using NAS-discovered computation paths.

while the target is a potential future click item. However, in self-attention, the model calculates attention scores between elements within the input sequence rather than solely relying on predetermined, hand-engineered features. It can be considered an attention mechanism in the special case where the target is equal to the source (Fig. 2).

We now face a new challenge: How can we obtain the most effective customized attention mechanisms? Currently, most existing approaches heavily rely on manual designs of key attention components to attain top performance. However, this method fails to automatically find the optimal design for different data in various scenarios. To address this issue, we introduce our innovative auto-attention mechanism.

To achieve an optimal attention representation, it is crucial to explore both the attention representation and other neural network components, thus extending the traditional search space of Neural Architecture Search (NAS) to encompass attention representation [13]. NAS is an automated technique for designing neural networks, capable of generating high-performance structures using algorithms based on sample sets, surpassing human experts in specific tasks, and even unveiling novel network configurations. This reduces the costs associated with neural network deployment and utilization.

The three fundamental components of NAS are the search space, search strategy, and performance evaluation strategy [10]. The search space delineates the range of network structures available for exploration, the search strategy describes the approach for identifying the optimal structure, and the performance evaluation strategy establishes the method for assessing the performance of the discovered structures. Consequently, various NAS algorithms arise from distinct implementations of these components. This challenge can be framed as a bi-level optimization problem [28].

$$t^* = argmin_{t \in \mathbf{T}} L(t, m^*(t))$$
$$w.s.m^*(t) = argmin_{m \in M(t)} L_{input}(t, m) \tag{1}$$

The bi-level optimization problem presented in Eq. 1 can be computationally demanding, as identifying the ideal architecture t^* necessitates solving the internal optimization problem by training the architecture from scratch. To streamline the search process, we divide the problem into two separate optimizations: (1) determining the optimal parameters $m^*(t)$ for a fixed architecture t within the parameter space $M(t)$, and (2) discovering the best architecture t^* within the search space T. As a result, Eq. 1 can be reformulated into Eq. 2 in the following manner:

$$t^* = argmin_{t \in \mathbf{T}} L(t, m^*(t))$$
$$w.s.m^*(t) = argmin_{m \in M} \mathbf{E}_{t \hookrightarrow \Gamma(T)} L_{input}(t, m) \tag{2}$$

This method introduces $\mathbf{\Gamma}(T)$, the prior architecture distribution for $t \in T$, and m as the weight of the supernet, which encompasses all architectures within the search space T. Consequently, each architecture becomes a sub-architecture of the supernet, sharing the same parameters. This results in a significant reduction in time cost, as optimizing the supernet is more efficient than optimizing each architecture individually from scratch.

We then shift our focus to the macro search space design, which excels at capturing the global information flow within the architecture and is well-suited for video classification tasks. A deep neural network can be depicted as a collection of layers, with optional connections between any two layers to represent information flow. Each connection signifies a unary transform operation selected from a predefined set of primitive operations, taking the feature map of the source layer as input and producing a feature map for the target layer's use. The layers function as information aggregators, merely summing the received outputs from connections directed towards them. Additionally, we restrict the number of connections a single layer can receive to two.

It is crucial to acknowledge that the hyperparameters linked to each layer are dependent on the operation type, resulting in a conditional space for parameterizing the search space rather than a fixed length. Within this framework, attention can be perceived as the interplay between features of the same layer or different layers.

Thus, we formulate the following equations as the source layer and operation selection process:

$$Q, K, V = O_Q(S_Q), O_Q(S_K), O_Q(S_V) \tag{3}$$

where S_Q, S_K, and S_V represent the selected source layers for the query, key, and value, respectively, and O_Q, O_K, and O_V represent the single action selected from the predefined operation library for each input connection. By introducing the "attention layer," we automate the design of attention representations in deep neural networks. The attention layer takes in three input connections, with each connection corresponding to the source layers S_Q, S_K, and S_V, and the operations chosen for each connection are O_Q, O_K, and O_V. The attention layer then calculates the attention based on the inputs Q, K, and V.

3.2 Multimodal Fusion

In order to fully leverage the multimodal nature of videos, it is crucial to incorporate multiple modalities for optimal results. We examine two methods of multimodal fusion, feature fusion, and attention fusion, that correspond to different integration points in the overall architecture.

Feature Fusion. An efficient feature-level fusion is an intuitive approach that combines features from the same temporal segment to create a more comprehensive representation. Given multiple feature sequences, we can achieve this fusion by concatenating the features into a single sequence $(x_1, ..., x_T)$ and then classifying the video in the same way as for a single feature sequence.

Attention Fusion. In contrast to feature fusion, attention fusion operates on the video level. First, a bidirectional LSTM and individual Attention models are used to obtain the global representation $g^{(i)}$ for each input sequence. The global representations are then fused as $g = [g^{(1)}, ..., g^{(K)}]$, and the final class predictions are made through subsequent layers. It's worth mentioning that this fusion method doesn't impose a requirement for equal sequence lengths among the feature sequences.

3.3 Training Loss

Our model employs Mean Absolute Error (MAE) as its loss function. MAE calculates the average of absolute differences, providing a clearer representation of classification errors and the performance of the proposed MAF model.

$$L_{MAE} = \frac{\sum\limits_{i=1}^{m} |y_i - y_i^q|}{m} \tag{4}$$

In this expression, y_i is the output tensor obtained from the model and y_i^q is the corresponding classification value. m represents the total number of training samples. By incorporating multiple modalities and utilizing both feature fusion and attention fusion, our proposed Multimodal Auto Attention Fusion (MAF) model can efficiently handle video classification tasks. By employing MAE as the loss function, the model provides a clear representation of classification errors and performance. Overall, the MAF model presents a powerful and flexible solution for video classification across diverse applications.

4   Experimental

In this section, we proceed to evaluate and compare our proposed methods in terms of their classification accuracy (Tables 1, 2 and 3).

Table 1. YouTube-8M GAP@20 on the 60 K validation and test set

Method		Test (%)
VLAD (Xu, Yang, and Hauptmann 2020)		80.4
Video Level (Zhong et al. 2021)		78.6
LSTM + MoE (Wang et al. 2021)		80.2
Ours	RGB Self-Attention	77.3
	Feature Average	81.5
	Auto Attention Fusion	82.2

Table 2. ActivityNet results on the validation set

Method		mAP (%)
Ada3D (Li et al. 2020)		84.0
SMART (Gowda et al. 2020)		83.9
DSANet (Tran et al. 2021)		88.1
Ours	RGB Self-Attention	75.0
	Feature Average	87.5
	Auto Attention Fusion	89.5

Table 3. Mean classification accuracy on UCF-101

Method		mAP (%)
ViCC (Toering et al. 2021)		82.8
R2+1D RGB (Lin et al. 2021)		84.8
VideoMAE (Tong et al. 2022)		91.3
Ours	RGB Self-Attention	86.2
	Feature Average	90.1
	Auto Attention Fusion	92.6

4.1   Implementation Details

For the UCF101 dataset, we utilized a ResNet-152 model to extract RGB and flow features. To balance recognition performance and computational demands, we fine-tuned the model using three segments for UCF101 and seven segments for ActivityNet. We max-pooled frame-level features to 5 segment-level features for UCF101 and 20 for ActivityNet. Unlike previous methods that used trimmed videos for training, we trained our model using the whole untrimmed videos from ActivityNet for a more realistic input scenario. For YouTube-8M, we directly used the pre-extracted RGB and audio features as segment-level features with a maximum of 300 segments. The LSTM used 512 hidden units for UCF101 and ActivityNet, which is a standard choice, and 1024 for YouTube-8M to handle longer videos. We used the RMSPROP algorithm with a learning rate of 0.0001 to update parameters for improved convergence.

4.2 Experiment Results

In this section, we assess the effectiveness of the proposed Auto Attention mechanism by conducting experiments on a single RGB feature sequence. This eliminates any interference between modalities. Our model with Auto Attention is detailed in section. We compare our approach to two deep neural network-based classification methods: RGB Attention and Fusion Average. The first method involves concatenating the final hidden states of a bidirectional LSTM and using the subsequent layers for classification. The second method averages the outputs of the LSTM and classifies the averaged state vector.

Our method is compared with popular traditional methods (ViCC [20] and R2+1D RGB [21]) and self-attention approaches (VideoMAE [22]) on UCF101 and achieves competitive results. On ActivityNet, it outperforms existing published methods (Ada3D [24], SMART [23], and DSANet [25]) and achieves strong results in comparison to VLAD[21], Video Level[20], and LSTM + MoE[22] on YouTube-8M. Our model demonstrates robust performance across various datasets, including both small and large training sets and trimmed and untrimmed videos, outperforming recent publications.

5   Conclusion

We have developed a novel Auto Attention mechanism to address the sequential and multimodal nature of videos. This approach enables fast and effective learning in multimode deep neural networks. We evaluate different options for multimodal fusion in recurrent neural networks and find that the proposed attention-based fusion provides the best results. Our experiments cover three widely used datasets, including untrimmed and trimmed videos, single-label and multi-label classification settings, and small and large datasets. Our results are highly competitive in all these settings, demonstrating the robustness of our Multimodal Auto Attention Fusion (MAF) model for video classification tasks.

In future work, we aim to integrate this fusion approach into end-to-end trained CNN architectures for further improvements.

Acknowledgement. This material is based upon work partially supported by the National Science Foundation under NSF grants IIS 1914489 and IIS 2008202. Any opinion, findings, and conclusions or recommendations expressed in this material are those of the author(s) and do not necessarily reflect the views of the National Science Foundation.

References

1. Jenni, S., Jin, H.: Time-equivariant contrastive video representation learning. In: Proceedings of the IEEE/CVF International Conference on Computer Vision, pp. 9970–9980 (2021)
2. Astrid, M., Zaheer, M.Z., Lee, S.I.: Synthetic temporal anomaly guided end-to-end video anomaly detection. In: Proceedings of the IEEE/CVF International Conference on Computer Vision, pp. 207–214 (2021)
3. Sankarapandian, S., et al.: A pathology deep learning system capable of triage of melanoma specimens utilizing dermatopathologist consensus as ground truth. In: Proceedings of the IEEE/CVF International Conference on Computer Vision, pp. 629–638 (2021)
4. Rao, A., Park, J., Woo, S., Lee, J.Y., Aalami, O.: Studying the effects of self-attention for medical image analysis. In: Proceedings of the IEEE/CVF International Conference on Computer Vision, pp. 3416–3425 (2021)
5. Zhang, K., Peng, J., Fu, J., Liu, D.: Exploiting optical flow guidance for transformer-based video inpainting. arXiv preprint arXiv:2301.10048 (2023)
6. Abu-El-Haija, S., et al.: Youtube-8m: a large-scale video classification benchmark. arXiv preprint arXiv:1609.08675 (2016)
7. Ghanem, B., et al.: The activitynet large-scale activity recognition challenge 2018 summary. arXiv preprint arXiv:1808.03766 (2018)
8. Soomro, K., Zamir, A.R., Shah, M.: UCF101: a dataset of 101 human actions classes from videos in the wild. arXiv preprint arXiv:1212.0402 (2012)
9. Saxena, N., Wu, R., Jain, R.: Towards one shot search space poisoning in neural architecture search. arXiv preprint arXiv:2111.07138 (2021)
10. Shen, Y., et al.: ProxyBO: accelerating neural architecture search via Bayesian optimization with zero-cost proxies. arXiv preprint arXiv:2110.10423 (2021)
11. Yin, Y., Huang, S., Zhang, X.: BM-NAS: bilevel multimodal neural architecture search. In: Proceedings of the AAAI Conference on Artificial Intelligence, vol. 36, no. 8, pp. 8901–8909 (2022)
12. Xu, Z., So, D.R., Dai, A.M.: MUFASA: multimodal fusion architecture search for electronic health records. In: Proceedings of the AAAI Conference on Artificial Intelligence, vol. 35, no. 12, pp. 10532–10540 (2021)
13. Sato, R., Sakuma, J., Akimoto, Y.: AdvantageNAS: efficient neural architecture search with credit assignment. In: Proceedings of the AAAI Conference on Artificial Intelligence, vol. 35, no. 11, pp. 9489–9496 (2021)
14. White, C., Neiswanger, W., Savani, Y.: BANANAS: Bayesian optimization with neural architectures for neural architecture search. In: Proceedings of the AAAI Conference on Artificial Intelligence, vol. 35, no. 12, pp. 10293–10301 (2021)
15. Zhang, W., et al.: Transformer-based multimodal information fusion for facial expression analysis. In: Proceedings of the IEEE/CVF Conference on Computer Vision and Pattern Recognition, pp. 2428–2437 (2022)

16. Kong, C., Zheng, K., Liu, Y., Wang, S., Rocha, A., Li, H.: M3FAS: an accurate and robust multimodal mobile face anti-spoofing system. arXiv preprint arXiv:2301.12831 (2023)
17. Huang, R., et al.: Make-an-audio: text-to-audio generation with prompt-enhanced diffusion models. arXiv preprint arXiv:2301.12661 (2023)
18. Xu, M., Yuan, X., Miret, S., Tang, J.: ProtST: multi-modality learning of protein sequences and biomedical texts. arXiv preprint arXiv:2301.12040 (2023)
19. Wang, L., Koniusz, P., Huynh, D.Q.: Hallucinating IDT descriptors and I3D optical flow features for action recognition with CNNs. In: Proceedings of the IEEE/CVF International Conference on Computer Vision, pp. 8698–8708 (2019)
20. Toering, M., Gatopoulos, I., Stol, M., Hu, V.T.: Self-supervised video representation learning with cross-stream prototypical contrasting. In: Proceedings of the IEEE/CVF Winter Conference on Applications of Computer Vision, pp. 108–118 (2022)
21. Lin, Y., Guo, X., Lu, Y.: Self-supervised video representation learning with meta-contrastive network. In: Proceedings of the IEEE/CVF International Conference on Computer Vision, pp. 8239–8249 (2021)
22. Tong, Z., Song, Y., Wang, J., Wang, L.: VideoMAE: masked autoencoders are data-efficient learners for self-supervised video pre-training. arXiv preprint arXiv:2203.12602 (2022)
23. Gowda, S.N., Rohrbach, M., Sevilla-Lara, L.: SMART frame selection for action recognition. In: Proceedings of the AAAI Conference on Artificial Intelligence, vol. 35, no. 2, pp. 1451–1459 (2021)
24. Li, H., Wu, Z., Shrivastava, A., Davis, L.S.: 2D or not 2D? Adaptive 3D convolution selection for efficient video recognition. In: Proceedings of the IEEE/CVF Conference on Computer Vision and Pattern Recognition, pp. 6155–6164 (2021)
25. Wu, W., et al.: DSANet: dynamic segment aggregation network for video-level representation learning. In: Proceedings of the 29th ACM International Conference on Multimedia, pp. 1903–1911 (2021)
26. Zhu, H., Wang, Z., Shi, Y., Hua, Y., Xu, G., Deng, L.: Multimodal fusion method based on self-attention mechanism. Wirel. Commun. Mob. Comput. **2020**, 1–8 (2020)
27. Long, X., et al.: Multimodal keyless attention fusion for video classification. In: Proceedings of the AAAI Conference on Artificial Intelligence, vol. 32, no. 1 (2018)
28. Guan, C., Wang, X., Zhu, W.: AutoAttend: automated attention representation search. In: International Conference on Machine Learning, pp. 3864–3874. PMLR (2021)

Engineering Drawing Text Detection via Better Feature Fusion

Hainan Wang[✉][iD], Hua Shan[iD], Yu Song[iD], Yue Meng[iD], and Mei Wu[iD]

Jiangsu Frontier Electric Technology Co., Ltd., Nanjing, Jiangsu, China
jsntwhn@foxmail.com

Abstract. In recent years, text detection technology has advanced significantly. However, research on text detection of engineering drawings is lacking. The challenges faced by engineering drawing text detection are the degradation of partial occlusion and adhesion within texts, as well as the complex background noise. To address this problem, we propose an end-to-end text detection framework for degraded drawings based on multiscale feature fusion and instance segmentation, which adopts pluggable and stackable multiscale feature fusion modules to enhance the accuracy of the degraded text. We conduct experiments on several benchmarks to demonstrate the effectiveness of the proposed method on degraded drawing text and natural scene text.

Keywords: Engineering Drawing Text Detection · Attention Mechanism · Multi-Scale Feature Fusion · Instance Segmentation

1 Introduction

In recent years, natural scene image-based text spotting has made extraordinary progress, but much less effort was spent on special manually-generated documents such as engineering drawing text detection tasks. Engineering drawings mainly include lines, graphic symbols and text annotations. The text annotations determine the requirements and constraints of graphic elements, which convey rich semantic information and are vital for downstream applications. However, engineering drawings' text detection task has more degradation challenges, such as text adhesion and overlapping, as shown in Fig. 1.

Here, we take a deeper look at the engineering drawing text detection. The core of this task is to better distinguish different text instances and backgrounds. Motivated by the CBAM [8], we propose an end-to-end text detection framework based on a more efficient feature fusion mechanism. Compared with existing methods, our approach is able to achieve competitive performance on both engineering drawing text detection and public scene text detection benchmarks.

Our main contributions are summarized as follows: (1) We propose an efficient and promising end-to-end drawing text detector based on instance segmentation, which is the first to support arbitrary drawing text detection. (2) We propose a novel attention-based multi-scale feature fusion module, which is

H. Fujita et al. (Eds.): IEA/AIE 2023, LNAI 13925, pp. 265–270, 2023.
https://doi.org/10.1007/978-3-031-36819-6_23

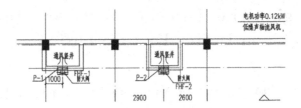

Fig. 1. Example of engineering drawings.

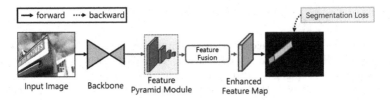

Fig. 2. Overall pipeline of the proposed method

flexible and stackable. The feature fusion module can obviously improve drawing text detection accuracy. (3) The proposed method effectively alleviates the difficulty of text detection caused by text degradation in engineering drawings and achieves competitive performance on several public text benchmarks.

2   Methods

2.1   Overall Architecture

This paper proposes a text detection algorithm based on instance segmentation and multi-scale feature fusion. The model structure is shown in Fig. 2. Our framework consists of four modules, which are the backbone network ResNet50, the lightweight stackable multi-scale feature pyramid FPM (i.e., Feature Pyramid Module), the attention-based feature fusion module FF, and a lightweight instance segmentation head. The input images are first fed into the backbone to extract the multi-scale feature maps. Then the multi-scale feature maps are sent into a set of FPM, where the output feature maps of each layer of the pyramids are fused by the attention module on the feature channel separately to finally obtain the enhanced feature maps. Then FF fuses local features and global features at different scales, so that the network can extract more discriminative features. Finally, the instance segmentation head takes the enhanced feature map as input and then outputs the text detetion results.

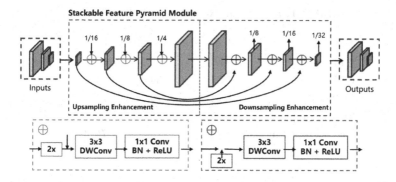

Fig. 3. Details of the stackable Feature Pyramid Module

2.2 Stackable Feature Pyramid Module

The FPM is a set of U-shaped modules, which contains two structures, downsampling enhancement and upsampling enhancement. The structure of single FPM unit is shown in Fig. 3, where downsmapling enhancement is performed layer by layer from $1/4$ of the original input image to $1/32$. And the upsampling enhancement is applied in reverse order, which is advanced from $1/32$ of the original image resolution to $1/4$. For each set of stacked pyramids, the final output is the result of downsampling, and between neighbouring $1/32$-scale feature maps. We use a combination of 3×3 depth separable convolution and 1×1convolution instead of normal convolution operations.

2.3 Attention-Based Feature Fusion Module

FF (Feature Fusion) is a module used to generate enhanced feature maps by fusing the output feature maps of stacked pyramids with attention weights. The feature maps are enhanced by sequential feature channel attention and spatial attention fusion. FF explores the implicit connection between different feature channels through the attention mechanism. By introducing contextual information with FF, the model can achieve more accurate text detection performance.

The computation process of FF is as follows. Given the output feature map F of the stackable multi-scale feature pyramid FPM ($F \in R^{c \times H \times W}$), where c denotes the number of feature channels and H, W are the feature map height and width, respectively. FF first computes the 1-D channel attention map $M^c(F)$ based on $F \in R^{c \times 1 \times 1}$, and then the 2-D spatial attention map $M^s(F) \in R^{1 \times H \times W}$, and then combine these two attention maps to perform a weighted attention operation on the feature map F.

$$F^{'} = M^c(F) \otimes F \tag{1}$$

$$F^{''} = M^s(F^{'}) \otimes F^{'} \tag{2}$$

Table 1. Experiment Results on SCUT-CTW1500

Methods	Percision %	Recall %	F1-Score %
CTD [10]	74.3	65.2	69.5
CTD+TLOC [10]	77.4	69.8	73.4
SLPR [11]	80.1	70.1	74.8
TextSnake [3]	67.9	85.3	75.6
The proposed method	80.5	78.2	**79.3**

where $\otimes$ denotes the pixel-by-pixel multiplication operation. Subsequently, the output F'' of the FF is smoothed by a 3×3 convolution operation, and the enhanced feature map F^e is produced for instance segmentation. To generate the attention graph M^c on the feature channels, we first apply average pooling and max pooling to aggregate spatial information and then a shared set of MLP networks. To generate spatial attention maps M^s, we apply the average pooling and max pooling performed along the feature channels and feed the connected feature maps into a 3×3 convolution for smoothing.

2.4 Segmentation Map Generation

Based on the above-enhanced feature map F_e, we further generate a text instance segmentation map. We apply the Dice Coefficient Loss and Online Hard Example Mining (OHEM) in the supervised process to better deal with complex text degradation situations. Suppose there are S positive text pixel samples, OHEM will pick $r \times S$ maximum loss negative samples as hard samples to train together. r is a hyperparameter, which is fixed to 3 in our experiments.

3   Experiments

Due to the current small collective of engineering drawing text data, we choose to conduct experiments on existing public benchmark to verify the effectiveness of the proposed method in this paper in order to be able to compare us more fairly with other methods. We conducted experiments on three typical and commonly used scene text datasets, namely SCUT-CTW1500, ICDAR2015 and ICDAR2017 MLT. Some results on public benchmarks are shown in Fig. 4.

3.1 Results and Analysis

The comparison results on SCUT-CTW1500 are shown in Table 1, where the F-Score reaches 79.3%, which shows the competitive performance of our method for the detection of curved text. Through contextual, multi-scale feature fusion, our proposed method is able to better discriminate text pixels from non-text pixels, thus generating better text localization results. Compared with other methods, some of the methods give more importance to precision metrics or recall values,

Fig. 4. Results on public benchmarks.

Table 2. Experiment Results on ICDAR 2015 and ICDAR 2017 MLT

Methods	ICDAR 2015			ICDAR 2017 MLT		
	Precision %	Recall %	F1-Score %	Precision %	Recall %	F1-Score %
MCLAB FCN [2]	70.8	43.0	53.6	–	–	–
CTPN [7]	74.2	51.5	60.9	–	–	–
Yao [9]	72.3	58.7	64.8	–	–	–
SegLink [6]	85.5	82.0	75.0	–	–	–
PixelLink [1]	80.5	78.2	80.7	–	–	–
Lyu et al. [4]	94.1	70.7	80.7	–	–	–
YY AI OCR Group [5]	–	–	–	64.8	44.3	52.6
SARI-FDU-RRPN-V0 [5]	–	–	–	74.2	51.5	60.9
SARI-FDU-RRPN-V1 [5]	–	–	–	71.2	55.5	62.4
The proposed method	86.1	83.0	**84.5**	76.8	55.9	**64.7**

thus achieving higher results in a single metric of precision or recall. However, from the results of the more comprehensive evaluation criterion F1-score, our proposed method has a more balanced and stable performance. We aslo compare the performance of the ICDAR 2015 and ICDAR 2017 MLT datasets with other methods, and the results are shown in Table 2. From the results, we can see that our method is able to achieve competitive results, achieving an F1-score of 84.5% on ICDAR 2015 and 64.7% on ICDAR 2017 MLT, respectively. It should be noted that Lyu [4]'s method was able to achieve 94.1% in accuracy, which is higher than the 86% achieved by our method. The reason for the higher accuracy of Lyu's method is that they were pre-trained on a larger autogenerated dataset containing 800,000 autogenerated natural scene text images. In addition, they performed finer parameter filtering on the ICDAR dataset. Unlike their more accuracy-oriented choice, our approach chooses a more balanced performance, and we use smaller training data, which is relatively less difficult to train, while still achieving a competitive performance compared to Lyu et al.

4 Conclusions

In this paper, we propose an end-to-end instance segmentation network to detect degraded text in both complex engineering drawing environments and natural scenes. We design a stackable multi-scale feature pyramid modules that can fully extract and fuse multi-scale image features with text features. We also introduce an attention-based feature fusion module. Experiments show that our proposed method can obtain better text detection and recognition accuracy and works well in engineering drawings.

References

1. Deng, D., Liu, H., Li, X., Cai, D.: Pixellink: detecting scene text via instance segmentation. In: AAAI Conference on Artificial Intelligence (2018). https://doi.org/10.1609/aaai.v32i1.12269
2. Lin, T.Y., Dollár, P., Girshick, R., He, K., Hariharan, B., Belongie, S.: Feature pyramid networks for object detection. In: Proceedings of the IEEE Conference on Computer Vision and Pattern Recognition, pp. 2117–2125 (2017)
3. Long, S., Ruan, J., Zhang, W., He, X., Wu, W., Yao, C.: Textsnake: a flexible representation for detecting text of arbitrary shapes. In: Proceedings of the European Conference on Computer Vision (ECCV), pp. 20–36 (2018). https://doi.org/10.1007/978-3-030-01216-8_2
4. Lyu, P., Yao, C., Wu, W., Yan, S., Bai, X.: Multi-oriented scene text detection via corner localization and region segmentation. In: Proceedings of the IEEE Conference on Computer Vision and Pattern Recognition, pp. 7553–7563 (2018). https://doi.org/10.1109/CVPR.2018.00788
5. Nayef, N., et al.: ICDAR 2017 robust reading challenge on multi-lingual scene text detection and script identification-RRC-MLT. In: 2017 14th IAPR International Conference on Document Analysis and Recognition (ICDAR), vol. 1, pp. 1454–1459. IEEE (2017). https://doi.org/10.1109/ICDAR.2017.237
6. Shi, B., Bai, X., Belongie, S.: Detecting oriented text in natural images by linking segments. In: Proceedings of the IEEE Conference on Computer Vision and Pattern Recognition, pp. 2550–2558 (2017). https://doi.org/10.1109/CVPR.2017.371
7. Tian, Z., Huang, W., He, T., He, P., Qiao, Yu.: Detecting text in natural image with connectionist text proposal network. In: Leibe, B., Matas, J., Sebe, N., Welling, M. (eds.) ECCV 2016. LNCS, vol. 9912, pp. 56–72. Springer, Cham (2016). https://doi.org/10.1007/978-3-319-46484-8_4
8. Woo, S., Park, J., Lee, J.-Y., Kweon, I.S.: CBAM: convolutional block attention module. In: Ferrari, V., Hebert, M., Sminchisescu, C., Weiss, Y. (eds.) ECCV 2018. LNCS, vol. 11211, pp. 3–19. Springer, Cham (2018). https://doi.org/10.1007/978-3-030-01234-2_1
9. Yao, C., Bai, X., Sang, N., Zhou, X., Zhou, S., Cao, Z.: Scene text detection via holistic, multi-channel prediction. arXiv preprint arXiv:1606.09002 (2016)
10. Yuliang, L., Lianwen, J., Shuaitao, Z., Sheng, Z.: Detecting curve text in the wild: new dataset and new solution. arXiv preprint arXiv:1712.02170 (2017)
11. Zhu, Y., Du, J.: Sliding line point regression for shape robust scene text detection. In: 2018 24th International Conference on Pattern Recognition (ICPR), pp. 3735–3740. IEEE (2018). https://doi.org/10.1109/ICPR.2018.8545067

A Transformer Based Multimodal Fine-Fusion Model for False Information Detection

Bai-Ning Xu[1] (ID), Yu-Bo Cao[1] (ID), Jie Meng[2] (ID), Zi-Jian He[2] (ID), and Li Wang[2](✉) (ID)

[1] School of Software, Taiyuan University of Technology, Jinzhong, Shanxi, China
xubaining5600@link.tyut.edu.cn, 1914719673@qq.com
[2] Data Science College, Taiyuan University of Technology, Jinzhong, Shanxi, China
{mengjie0488,hezijian1549}@link.tyut.edu.cn, wangli@tyut.edu.cn

Abstract. With the development and the popularity of internet, WWW is becoming the main platform of exchanging information and accessing information for people. For the openness and free, the information published on it may be not true. The spread of false information has a serious impact on social stability and detecting false information has become an urgent task. Text and image are two main information modals and some work proposed to combine them to enhance the detection accuracy. However, in almost these work, the granularity of information fusion is not refined enough to get the complete representation from multimodal information at the same time. Inspired by this, we propose a Multimodal, fine-grained Fusion false information detection model based on Transformer,namely TMF. First, a feature extraction module is used to extract the representation of each word in the text and the representation of each region in the image, respectively, to obtain a multi-modal, fine-grained representation. Then, a Transformer based multimodal fusion module, Transformer-MF, is designed to learn the interaction between words and words, words and regions, and regions and regions simultaneously from both global and local levels, and obtain global and local multimodal representations. Finally, raw representations of text and images are combined with global and local multi-modal representations for false information detection. Experimental results show that our model performs better than the baseline models in terms of false information detection accuracy.

Keywords: False information detection · multi-mode fusion · transformer · attention mechanism · fine-grained

1 Introduction

Social media has brought convenience to people, but it has also promoted the spread of false information and poses a huge threat to social stability. It is urgently need to detect false information automatically.Earlier research primarily relied on linguistic features for detecting fake news, while the use of multimodal data has now become an effective method for improving accuracy. Jin et al. [1] proposed a recurrent neural network with an attention mechanism for rumor detection, while Khattar et al. [3] used variational autoencoder to discover the correlation between various modalities in tweets. However,

© The Author(s), under exclusive license to Springer Nature Switzerland AG 2023
H. Fujita et al. (Eds.): IEA/AIE 2023, LNAI 13925, pp. 271–277, 2023.
https://doi.org/10.1007/978-3-031-36819-6_24

there are still two aspects that need improvement. Firstly, during the feature extraction stage, the different representations of various regions in images have been ignored, which prevents the capture of the correspondence between words and image regions. Secondly, the influence of intra-modal relationships on multimodal representations cannot be fully considered during the learning of multimodal representations.

To address these issues, we propose a Transformer based multi-mode fine-fusion model for false information detection, namely TMF. Our main contributions can be summarized as follows:

1) We established fine-grained representations for text and images, which makes the basic for discovering the relationship between small different cells.
2) We applied Transformer to fake news detection, which offer a framework for learning the interactive relationships between words, regions, and regions, and merge multimodal information from both a global and local perspective.
3) The experimental results show that our proposed TMF model outperforms the state-of-the-art multimodal fake news detection model.

2 Related Work

The task of detecting fake news typically involves different types of information, such as images, text, and videos, each representing a different modality. These methods can be divided into two categories: single-modal and multimodal-based.

Single-modal methods use a single modality to detect fake news. Wang et al. [4] proposed a graph neural network model that could capture the interaction between sentences, achieving good results. In addition to text information, visual have also been proven to play a crucial role in detecting fake news. Qi et al. [5] proposed an end-to-end model, which used a CNN-based network to capture complex patterns in images, as well as extract visual features of different semantic levels from the pixel domain. However, single modality may result in limited utilization of information and ineffective capture of complete news information. Multimodal-based methods employ both text and image content to detect fake news. Khattar et al. [3] proposed a multimodal variational autoencoder (MVAE), which learn shared representations of text and visual information, discover the correlation between different modalities, and combine the variational autoencoder with a classifier to detect fake news. Although these methods have achieved some success, there is still significant room for improvement.

3 Model

3.1 Problem Definition

Let $P = \{p_1, p_2, \cdots, p_m\}$ be a information set, where p_i is the i th post and m is the number of posts in the dataset. For any post $p = \{T, V\}$, T and V represent its text and picture respectively. The false information detection task can be described as learning a function $f : f(T, V) \rightarrow y$, Where the tag value $y \in \{0,1\}$, 0 represents real information and 1 represents false information.

3.2 TMF Model

The proposed model TMF is mainly composed of four parts: image-text semantic feature extraction module, Transformer-MF input module, Transformer-MF module and false information detection module, as shown in Fig. 1.

Image-Text Semantic Feature Extraction Module. The function of this module is to extract semantic features from text and images to obtain the original representations.

The text in each post can be represented as $T = \{e_1, e_2, \cdots e_n\}$. The bidirectional semantic dependencies of sentences are captured by the Bi-LSTM, and $H_T \in \mathbb{R}^d$ represents the original representation of the text.

$$H_T = BiLSTM(T) \tag{1}$$

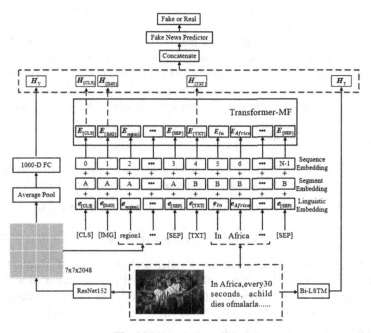

Fig. 1. The overview of TMF.

After passing through the ResNet152 network, the output image corresponds to a size of $7 \times 7 \times 2048$. Then it is passed through an average pool and full connected layers to obtain the original representation $H_V \in \mathbb{R}^d$ of the image. And then it is reshaped into a representation of size 49×2048 and is transformed into d dimensions by a fully connected layer. That is, the image semantic representation can be expressed as $V = \{e_{region1}, e_{region2}, \cdots e_{region49}\}$, $e_{region} \in \mathbb{R}^d$ is the representation of each region.

Transformer-MF Input Module. As shown in Fig. 1, to accommodate multimodal inputs, the input representation of each token comprises three components: the semantic representation (Linguistic Embedding) used for word or image region meaning, the segment representation (Segment Embedding) used to differentiate between different modality information, and the sequence representation (Sequence Embedding) employed to indicate the order of the input sequence.

$$E_{[CLS]}E_{[IMG]}E_{[region1]} \cdots E_{[region49]}E_{[SEP]}E_{[TXT]}E_{w_1} \cdots E_{w_n}E_{[SEP]} \qquad (2)$$

where [CLS] represents a global multimodal token, [SEP] denotes a delimiter between visual and textual features, [region] denotes a visual feature region token, w denotes a textual subword sequence token, [IMG] denotes a visual modality token, and [TXT] denotes a textual modality token.

Transformer-MF Module. We have introduced a mask matrix into the input structure of Transformer and proposed the Transformer-MF module can learn multimodal representations from both global and local levels. The computation process is as follows:

$$Attention(Q, K, V) = softmax(\frac{QK^T}{\sqrt{d_k}} + M)V \qquad (3)$$

where $\mathbf{M} \in \mathbb{R}^{l \times l}$ represents the mask matrix, is used to restrict the receptive field and mask certain positional information during the interaction of text and image. The horizontal and vertical axes of the mask matrix correspond to the positional encoding in the input sequence. The yellow squares indicate visible position information, while the black squares indicate the opposite. The mask matrix can be defined as follows:

$$\mathbf{M}_{i,j} = \begin{cases} 0 & (i, j) \in yellow\ square \\ -\infty & (i, j) \in gray\ square \end{cases} \qquad (4)$$

After the multi head attention layer, the residual network is used to strengthen the role of the input matrix X. The detailed calculation process is as follows:

$$\mathbf{F} = LayerNorm(\mathbf{X} + \mathbf{A}), \mathbf{FF} = Relu((\mathbf{FW}_1 + \mathbf{b}_1)\mathbf{W}_2 + \mathbf{b}_2) \qquad (5)$$

$$\mathbf{Output} = LayerNorm(\mathbf{F} + \mathbf{FF}) \qquad (6)$$

A represents result of input matrix *X* after multiple heads of attention calculation. Each row of **Output** matrix represents the final representation of a token. We extracted global multimodal representation $H_{[CLS]} \in \mathbb{R}^d$, image- and text-centered local multimodal representation $H_{[IMG]} \in \mathbb{R}^d$ and $H_{[TXT]} \in \mathbb{R}^d$, respectively.

False Information Detection Module. Considering that in the process of multimodal information fusion, the original information of both images and text may be lost, in this section, the representations from each modality are concatenated and then passed through a softmax layer for final classification. The fake information detector is defined as follows:

$$\hat{y} = softmax(\mathbf{W} \times [\mathbf{H}_{[CLS]}, \mathbf{H}_{[IMG]}, \mathbf{H}_{[TXT]}, \mathbf{H}_V, \mathbf{H}_T] + b) \qquad (7)$$

where, $\hat{y} = [\hat{y}_0, \hat{y}_1]$, $\hat{y}_0$ and $\hat{y}_1$ respectively represent the probability that the post is true information and false information. The loss function $L(\theta)$ is defined as follows:

$$L(\theta) = -y\ log(\hat{y}_1) - (1 - y)\ log(\hat{y}_0) \qquad (8)$$

4 Experiments

Dataset. We use two public real social media datasets. One is Weibo dataset that was collected from Chinese news websits and its number of false, true information and images are 4749,4779 and 9528 respectively. CCF Competition dataset comes from the competition held by the China Computer Federation (CCF), and its number of false, true information and images are 4324,5521 and 9845 respectively.

Experiment Analysis. We compare our model with eight other fake news detection methods, including two single-modality methods and six multi-modality methods. Table 1 presents the results of the benchmark models and our proposed model on two datasets. Bold indicates the highest performing model. Our model outperformed the benchmark models across all evaluation metrics on both datasets.

The accuracy of the text model was higher than that of the visual model on both datasets. This may be attributed to the fact that images posted by users are often unrelated to the content they express, leading to decreased performance of visual models.

Table 1. Experimental results on two datasets

Datasets	Model	Acc	False Information			True Information		
			Precision	Recall	F1	Precision	Recall	F1
CCF Competition	Text	0.767	0.870	0.701	0.776	0.681	0.857	0.757
	Visual	0.733	0.756	0.862	0.805	0.687	0.559	0.615
	VQA [7]	0.839	0.888	0.751	0.812	0.782	0.905	0.841
	NeuralTalk [8]	0.822	0.867	0.737	0.796	0.792	0.903	0.844
	att-RNN [1]	0.889	0.884	0.899	0.894	0.892	0.877	0.883
	EANN [2]	0.909	0.949	0.865	0.912	0.852	0.931	0.895
	MVAE [3]	0.915	0.933	0.901	0.921	0.904	0.929	0.917
	CARMN [6]	0.928	0.939	0.875	0.906	0.918	0.942	0.930
	TMF	**0.953**	**0.962**	**0.942**	**0.951**	**0.946**	**0.962**	**0.953**
Weibo	Text	0.643	0.662	0.578	0.617	0.609	0.685	0.647
	Visual	0.608	0.610	0.605	0.607	0.607	0.611	0.609
	VQA [7]	0.736	0.797	0.634	0.706	0.695	0.838	0.760
	NeuralTalk [8]	0.726	0.794	0.713	0.692	0.684	0.840	0.754
	att-RNN [1]	0.772	0.854	0.656	0.742	0.720	0.889	0.795
	EANN [2]	0.789	0.792	0.802	0.799	0.785	0.776	0.781
	MVAE [3]	0.814	0.725	0.894	0.853	0.833	0.704	0.755

(continued)

Table 1. (*continued*)

Datasets	Model	Acc	False Information			True Information		
			Precision	Recall	F1	Precision	Recall	F1
	CARMN [6]	0.831	0.824	0.881	0.836	**0.844**	0.824	0.831
	TMF	**0.856**	**0.866**	**0.901**	**0.875**	0.843	**0.895**	**0.863**

In contrast, VQA and NeuralTalk outperformed both Text and Visual models. This indicates that relying on a single modality can lead to incomplete information extraction.

In multimodal models, att-RNN introduced an attention mechanism that effectively integrated text and visual features, thereby improving the model's performance. MVAE,by learning shared multimodal representations of text and visual patterns, discovered correlations between these patterns, achieving higher accuracy than att-RNN and EANN. CARMN introduced residual networks, selectively extracting information from the source modality relevant to the target. In comparison to CARMN, the TMF model not only has a more fine-grained multimodal fusion method, but also adopts a dual-layer Transformer-MF that more deeply explores the semantic relationship between text and visual information, resulting in better detection performance.

5   Conclusion

This study proposes a transformer based multimodal fine-grained fusion model, TMF, for false information detection. The proposed model can capture the interactive relationships among text, image regions, and their interdependence simultaneously. Experiments results demonstrate that the detection accuracy of the proposed model is better than that of the benchmark model. Future work will consider the effect of multiple images on false information detection performance.

References

1. Jin, Z., Cao, J., Guo, H., et al.: Multimodal fusion with recurrent neural networks for rumor detection on microblogs. In: Proceedings of the 25th ACM International Conference on Multimedia, pp. 795–816 (2017)
2. Wang, Y., Ma, F., Jin, Z., et al.: Eann: event adversarial neural networks for multi-mode fake news detection. In: Proceedings of the 24th ACM SIGKDD International Conference on Knowledge Discovery & Data Mining, pp. 849–857 (2018)
3. Khattar, D., Goud, J.S., Gupta, M., et al.: Mvae: multimodal variational autoencoder for fake news detection. In: The World Wide Web Conference, pp. 2915–2921 (2019)
4. Wang, Y., Wang, L., Yang, Y., Lian, T.: SemSeq4FD: Integrating global semantic relationship and local sequential order to enhance text representation for fake news detection. Expert Syst. Appl. **166**, 114090 (2020)
5. Qi, P., Cao, J., Yang, T., et al.: Exploiting multi-domain visual information for fake news detection. In: 2019 IEEE International Conference on Data Mining (ICDM), pp. 518–527. IEEE (2019)

6. Song, C., Ning, N., Zhang, Y., et al.: A multimodal fake news detection model based on crossmodal attention residual and multichannel convolutional neural networks. Inf. Process. Manage. **58**(1), 102437 (2021)
7. Antol, S., Agrawal, A., Lu, J., et al.: Vqa: visual question answering. In: Proceedings of the IEEE International Conference on Computer Vision, pp. 2425–2433 (2015)
8. Vinyals, O., Toshev, A., Bengio, S., et al.: Show and tell: a neural image caption generator. In: Proceedings of the IEEE Conference on Computer Vision and Pattern Recognition, pp. 3156–3164 (2015)

Knowledge Graph and Link Prediction

Domain-Specific Knowledge Graph Adaption with Industrial Text Data

Felix Hamann$^{(\boxtimes)}$ and Adrian Ulges

RheinMain University of Applied Sciences, Wiesbaden, Germany
{felix.hamann,adrian.ulges}@hs-rm.de

Abstract. We suggest an interactive approach towards knowledge acquisition based on neural text mining. Our method enables experts to extend a given knowledge graph-which is general and scarce-with knowledge discovered in a text collection covering a particular customer or subdomain. Our tool suggests text passages that contain new concepts and links, which the domain expert inspects and adds to the graph. The underlying discovery model combines a transformer-based contextualized text encoder with a knowledge graph completion model. End-to-end training of both components is bootstrapped by sampling mentions of the given knowledge graph's concepts from the text collection. We evaluate our approach quantitatively based on manual annotations of model predictions, including a comparison with fastText. Furthermore, we conducted an expert annotation session using the tool and a subsequent interview. The resulting observations show the potential of the approach for knowledge engineering in the wild.

Keywords: Data Mining · Knowledge Acquisition · Artificial Intelligence

1 Introduction

Knowledge graphs (KG) are known to be powerful tools for modern web search, where formal knowledge is available at large scale [7]. This raises the question whether specific business domains can benefit from knowledge graphs as well, for example, the handling of technical issues in machine manufacturing. Here, given the rapid development of technology paired with a scarce and increasingly fluctuating workforce, experience management becomes vital, and formalizing knowledge enables domain experts and service technicians to do the job even when inexperienced or when facing outdated technology. For providers of semantic search in such specific domains, knowledge reuse and knowledge acquisition are key challenges: Given a domain's *world knowledge* $\mathcal{G}$ – which includes general symptoms (tearing, squeaking, ...), component types (belts, saw blades, ...), solutions (cleaning, oiling, ...) – the goal is to bootstrap a KG for a specific customer in a particular subdomain *(gas turbine production, wood-processing machine manufacturing, ...)* that describes the subdomain's terminology.

H. Fujita et al. (Eds.): IEA/AIE 2023, LNAI 13925, pp. 281–293, 2023.
https://doi.org/10.1007/978-3-031-36819-6_25

Such knowledge engineering is costly since it involves both the domain expert and the knowledge engineer. On the one hand, KGs are built proactively, but not data-driven, i.e. the knowledge engineers ponder and decide which problems are reasonable and add them based on these assumptions. On the other hand, if an issue occurs repeatedly, the domain expert informs the knowledge engineer, who again extends the KG. In consequence, these KGs are usually incomplete, do not necessarily model the most pressing issues of the subdomain, and are not linked with any actual issue reports in natural language to serve as grounding.

In this paper, we investigate whether a proactive knowledge acquisition approach can be established using neural NLP

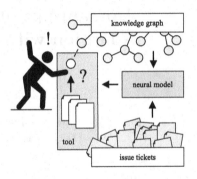

Fig. 1. The approach: A neural model learns to connect knowledge graph (KG) vertices and edges with unlabelled issue reports. An interactive tool employs this model to show interesting tickets to an expert, who decides whether to put the information into the KG.

(Fig. 1). Besides the generic graph $\mathcal{G}$, we assume a collection of tickets to be given, in which customer-specific issues are described. We present an interactive tool enabling the knowledge engineer to explore the ticket collection. To do so, a neural NLP model points him/her to interesting text passages that contain new concepts and links. The knowledge engineer can then annotate key phrases and add them to the graph *"the machine burns off way too much gas"* and reject or blacklist irrelevant phrases *"Mr. Burns"* ordered some gas as backup fuel. Our underlying ML model features three components (see the orange boxes in Fig. 3)[1]:

(1) **Scoring**: Overall, our model acts as an embedding-based knowledge graph completion (KGC) triple scorer: Given a concept/node v in the graph, a relation r (such as *hypernym*, *solution*, *affected-part*) and a text passage that describes another vertex v', the model estimates the probability that the text passage *contains* a mention of a concept v which is in relation r with concept v'.

(2) **Encoder**: Text contexts are encoded with a transformer to utilise the strengths of modern language modelling (LM) regarding learning language structure, and to achieve contextualization of tokens (e.g., the German word lager can either refer to a warehouse or a bearing).

(3) **Text Sampler**: The key challenge with our setup is how to bootstrap a weakly supervised learning process from graph $\mathcal{G}$ and the ticket collection. To this end, we utilise a rule-based text sampler that discovers mentions of $\mathcal{G}$'s concepts in the ticket collection. Based on these mentions, we train our encoder and KGC scorer.

---

[1] The implementation can be found here: https://github.com/lavis-nlp/iea23-hamann.

To our knowledge, our contribution is the first application of state-of-the-art LMs and KGC models for domain-specific knowledge acquisition. We cover the entire pipeline, from data preparation and learning process to the integration into a practical tool. We challenge the utility of our approach in a case study on a German collection of 1.15 million tickets of a woodworking machine manufacturer and a KG of 249 general concepts of the machine domain, provided by an application partner that offers knowledge services. We compare our models to fastText [1], and in an expert evaluation, we collect actionable insights regarding the practical applicability of the approach.

2   Related Work

We tackle an open-world knowledge graph completion (OW-KGC) scenario which aims to enable geometric reasoning in graphs through the alignment of dense graph- and text representations. This combines KGC [11,19,22]—which aims at the prediction of missing links between existing KG entities—with language modelling (LM) [1,3,10] which produces dense vector representations for a vocabulary.

One of the earliest attempts is NTN [17]. They learn to estimate the plausibility that two entity descriptions *belong* together through a relationship that is observed in the KG. Later approaches extend this idea: DKRL [21], ConMask [16] and MIA [4], introduce models that jointly learn the connection between entity and graph representations. In an attempt to decouple the KGC scorer and text encoder, [14,15,24] present approaches where a KGC scorer is trained independently and in a separate step, a projection of entity descriptions to their associated KG-embeddings is learned. Daza et al. [2] present BLP, a model where all entities are representations of their associated text contexts and the KGC objective is trained end-to-end while fine-tuning the encoder. All these approaches can work with out-of-knowledge base entities but assume a single concise entity description to be given. In contrast, we tackle a scenario where we encounter many weak entity descriptions. This is studied using the IRT datasets proposed by Hamann et al. [5,6]. The model presented in this paper is the precursor of the end-to-end models studied in those works.

Apart from KGC inspired approaches, relation extraction (RE) likewise aims to extract new entities and relations from text. Here, weakly supervised approaches exist [13,18]; however, it is assumed that both relation and involved entities are expressed in a single text context. This is rarely the case for taxonomic relations such as hyponomy.

3   Problem Description

We assume a customer-independent KG to be given, which is a directed graph $\mathcal{G} = (\mathcal{V}, \mathcal{R}, \mathcal{T}, \mathcal{P})$. $\mathcal{V}$ is a set of vertices, with each $v \in \mathcal{V}$ representing a certain *thing* (e.g. a machine malfunction) associated with a set of synonymous phrases $\mathcal{P}(v)$, e.g. {device crashes, system crash, ... }. $\mathcal{R}$ denotes a set of edge types, such as {*synonym, hypernym, ...* }. Finally, $\mathcal{T}$ is the set of all triples $(v, r, v') \in \mathcal{V} \times$

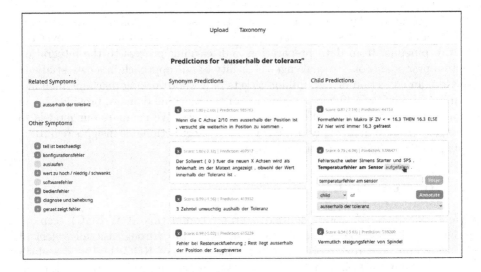

Fig. 2. Screenshot of the annotation page-on the left side the KG neighbourhood of the current prediction can be browsed. Below, all other KG vertices can be selected. For each vertex, predictions are presented in two lists. Upon clicking any token of the proposals, an interactive annotation form opens up. This form is pre-filled with the current prediction and respective relation. The selected token phrase can be freely changed, used to filter out undesired predictions containing the same phrase, or sent to the server as a new phrase for the KG.

$\mathcal{R} \times \mathcal{V}$ that connect the graph's concepts via typed edges. We define the synonym property as a reflexive property of the graph: $\forall v \in \mathcal{V} : (v, synonym, v) \in \mathcal{T}$.

Additionally, we assume a large, unstructured, non-curated, unlabelled corpus of textual tickets to be given. We associate each of a nodes' phrases p (e.g., does not boot) with a set of textual contexts $C(p)$:

e.g. *"The machine does not always boot up correctly."*. These contexts are mined from the corpus using a self-implemented text sampler (see Sect. 4.1). The *training corpus* $\mathcal{C}$ is the set of all text contexts associated with any known concept. All other text contexts form the *query corpus* $\mathcal{Q}$.

Model Objective. The purpose of our model is to discover text contexts in the query corpus $\mathcal{Q}$ that describe previously unknown concepts/symptoms and link them to the existing graph $\mathcal{G}$. To do so, given a vertex v' and a relation of interest r, the model retrieves a ranked list of textual contexts $(q, q', \dots)$ from the query corpus, which is supposed to contain phrases of concepts v in relation r with concept v'. For example, the query $(?, r = hypernym, v' = \text{configuration error})$ searches for new hyponyms of configuration error and returns proposals such as (*"Cables are not correctly laid."*, *"Box not reachable due to incorrect routing."*, ...)

Annotation Tool. Second, proposals are presented to a domain expert for annotation (see Fig. 2). The expert's task is to identify whether the text context includes a mention of a concept of interest, annotate the precise phrase in the context, and link the phrase to the KG. An important requirement for the tool is to ease the annotation procedure, e.g. by easy token selection or by filtering noise and redundant predictions.

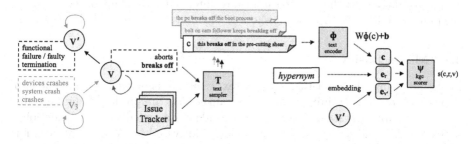

Fig. 3. Overview of the system while training. Each vertex v (left) is associated with a set of synonymous phrases, such as aborts, breaks off. The text sampler **T** identifies text contexts c containing v's phrases, which are encoded by the text encoder ϕ and mapped into an embedding space by a simple feed-forward layer. Finally, a KGC scorer combines the embeddings of text passages, relation type and vertex v'. Based on the resulting score, we discover a text passage which likely contains a description of a concept v' which stands in the given relation with v.

4   Approach

We propose a tool-aided approach to support the knowledge engineer with KG building. Our tool is designed to lower the technical barrier for a knowledge engineer to explore a new customer's pile of unstructured text, and to ease the expert's work by offering shortcuts and removing redundant activities. The tool offers easy access to the top text proposals for any concept and relation and allows for easy annotation of texts such that phrases can be defined and adjusted. We have implemented a dynamic web app with the following features:

Fig. 4. The annotation dialogue. Given a context (top), the input fields are pre-filled with the model's prediction. The free-text input field is dynamically filled with the tokens that are selected with a simple click on the respective words of the sentence.

(1) KG Maintenance and Exploration: A given KG can be modified, which includes adding and removing nodes, assigning or deleting phrases to/from nodes, and browsing the texts the text sampler associates with the phrases.

(2) Guided Annotation: When a node is selected, the associated predictions are shown as ranked lists of text passages per relation (see Fig. 2). Undesired predictions are discardable and redundant proposals can be filtered out. The knowledge engineer selects a phrase by marking tokens in a context. If necessary, he/she can change the predicted vertex or relation if necessary. The text sampler is run instantly with the selected phrase to filter out redundant proposals from the prediction list. Example screenshots of the interface are given in Fig. 4 and 2.

4.1   Model Basics

In the following, the model for scoring text contexts is defined. We outline two approaches towards training, define how ranked lists are produced and describe the text sampling system. We pick up the ideas presented in [21,23] for joint text encoding and graph reasoning models. Motivated by recent advances for OW-KGC models [15] our approach combines a transformer model [3] for text encoding and a triple scorer [19].

Figure 3 offers a high-level overview. First, a text encoder ϕ maps an input context c to a d'-dimensional representation $\phi(c)$ (we use BERT's CLS token). Second, given the text context, a target relation $r \in \mathcal{R}$, and a concept $v \in \mathcal{V}$, a triple scorer ψ produces a plausibility score:

$$s(c, r, v) = \psi(\, W{\cdot}\phi(c){+}\mathbf{b},\ \mathbf{e}_r,\ \mathbf{e}_v\,) \tag{1}$$

where $\mathbf{e}_r, \mathbf{e}_v \in \mathbb{R}^d$ are learned embeddings representing relation and vertex, and the affine projection with $W \in \mathbb{R}^{d \times d'}$, $\mathbf{b} \in \mathbb{R}^d$ maps the d'-dimensional text vector to the d-dimensional embedding space.

Note that, in principle, arbitrary triple scorers ψ based on dense vector representations are applicable (we use ComplEx [19] in this work). Also, the above model is generally capable of extending the graph with new vertices and relations by simply introducing additional vertex- and relation embeddings. We focus on tail prediction for a head-vertex mention encoding. If head-prediction is required, this can easily be done by either reversing the head and tail parameters or introducing an inverted relation in the graph.

In the following, we outline two training loss functions based on this setup: (1) using a cross entropy loss (CE-Loss), and (2) adding negative sampling and applying a binary cross entropy loss (BCE-Loss).

Model 1: Cross Entropy (CE) Our first model maps the raw scores from Eq. (1) to probabilities using a softmax over all concepts:

$$\sigma(c, r, v) = \frac{\exp\big(s(c, r, v)\big)}{\sum\limits_{v' \in \mathcal{V}} \exp\big(s(c, r, v')\big)} \tag{2}$$

To learn our model parameters (i.e. embeddings $\mathbf{e}_r, \mathbf{e}_v$, mapping $W, \mathbf{b}$, text encoder ϕ), we iteratively sample triples (c, r, v) from the existing knowledge graph, run a forward pass to obtain probabilities $\sigma(c, r, v')$ for all $v' \in \mathcal{V}$, and enforce the output probabilities to be high iff. $v = v'$ using a cross-entropy loss:

$$\mathcal{L}_{\text{CE}} = -log(\sigma(c, r, v)) \tag{3}$$

The details of sampling a context-relation-concept triple (c, r, v) are as follows: First, we draw a random concept-relation-concept triple (v', r, v) from the existing graph's triple set $\mathcal{T}$. Then, we draw a random phrase p from $\mathcal{P}(v')$. We use our text sampler (see Sect. 4.1) to robustly detect mentions of known concepts' phrases in the ticket collection, including p's textual contexts $C(p)$. Finally, we sample a random context c from $C(p)$ and define our training sample as (c, r, v). We draw 6K such triples per epoch, which corresponds to an oversampling of the actual knowledge graph.

Model 2: Negative Sampling (NS) A potential limitation of Model 1 (CE) is that the model is only confronted with text samples in training which contain at least one concept v. In contrast, our final ranker is supposed to mine a large ticket collection, featuring a lot of irrelevant text. Therefore, our second model version utilises the same sampling process as outlined above, but for each sample (c, r, v), we also draw additional negative samples (c', r, v), where a different, *wrong* text context c' replaces the correct context. c' is randomly drawn from the query corpus $\mathcal{Q}$. Since the training data now contains samples for which no concept is appropriate, we replace the softmax from Eq. (2) with a sigmoid

$$\sigma(c, r, v) = \Big(1 + \exp\big(-s(c, r, v)\big)\Big)^{-1} \tag{4}$$

and the cross entropy loss from Eq. (3) with a binary cross entropy loss:

$$\begin{aligned} \mathcal{L}_{\text{BCE}} = -\sum_{v' \in \mathcal{V}} \Big(&\mathbf{1}_{v'=v} \cdot log(\sigma(c, r, v')) \\ &+ (1 - \mathbf{1}_{v'=v}) \cdot log(1 - \sigma(c, r, v')) \\ &+ log(1 - \sigma(c', r, v')) \Big) \end{aligned} \tag{5}$$

Hyperparameters: Both models are trained for $5 \cdot 10^5$ steps with the Adam optimizer [9] and a learning rate of 10^{-5}. The vertex and relation embeddings are initialized randomly from $\mathcal{N}(0, 1)$ (for CE) and $\mathcal{N}(0, 0.5)$ (for NS) respectively. We use a BERT-Encoder pre-trained for German (bert-base-german-cased[2]). We selected these hyperparameters by observing a proxy validation loss, for which we set aside 15% of all text samples assigned to a vertex. We then test the capability of the model to predict the correct known vertex using these held-back samples. The final model checkpoints selected are based on the best validation hits@10 performance. We use PyTorch[3] and the transformer implementation provided by Hugging Face[4].

---

[2] https://www.deepset.ai/german-bert.
[3] https://pytorch.org/.
[4] https://huggingface.co.

Ranking: Given a trained model of either version, a concept v, and relation r, we rank all target contexts c in the query corpus $\mathcal{Q}$ by descending score $s(c, r, v)$. Optionally, we also *filter* the result list, keeping only those contexts c for which the concept v is the top-scored one, i.e.

$$\{ c \in \mathcal{Q} \mid v = \arg\max_{v' \in \mathcal{V}} s(c, r, v') \} \qquad (6)$$

Text Sampling. A key challenge for training is the lack of labels describing which concepts and relations appear in which text passages. To bootstrap our training set, we connect the knowledge graph's known concepts with texts using a self-implemented keyphrase matcher that handles scattered and overlapping phrases. For example, *"On Mondays the stuttering machine does not reliably boot or initialize"* matches does not boot, does not initialize and stutters. To do so, the tickets of the corpus are filtered, and their content is split into sentences using SoMaJo [12] as the sentencizer and a set of hand-crafted rules for filtering undesired text such as email headings. Each phrase of the KG is expanded based on a rule set to achieve robustness against word order. For example: bad quality expands to $\{quality\ bad, bad\ quality\ q\}$ based on the simple rule $(?, bad) \mapsto \{(?, bad), (bad, ?)\}$. In total, we define 10 such domain-specific rules that expand phrases. These patterns are then reduced to their lemma tokens and stem tokens and matched against the tokenized, stemmed, and lemmatized sentences. We use spaCy [8][5] for tokenization in conjunction with a German stemmer [20] in an implementation with linear runtime in regard to total token count[6]. The text collection is split into TRAIN (for model development and parameter tuning) and TEST (for a later expert evaluation). Some key figures of the matcher's performance are enumerated in Table 1.

Table 1. Key figures of the matcher's performance. The knowledge graph offers 370 phrases in total, which are not all matched, as it also contains vertices that do not apply to woodworking machinery. The *found mentions*-row shows the number of deduplicated variations found in the text corpus (e.g. geht nicht aus, nicht aus gegangen, nicht aus geht, nicht aus ging—which are variants of does not turn off). Overall, our training corpus $\mathcal{C}$ consists of $\sim$ 293K text contexts containing 4190 distinct mentions.

	TRAIN	TEST
Total Contexts	2,677,322	2,677,321
Matched Contexts	293,473	251,016
Matched Phrases	335	336
Found Mentions	4,190	4,795

---

[5] https://spacy.io with the base model de_core_news_lg.
[6] We offer the spaCy component here: https://github.com/lavis-nlp/scaphra.

5 Evaluation

We evaluate the system on a German woodworking machine manufacturer's ticket corpus of 1.15 million tickets, which we split into 5.3 million sentences. We emphasize the challenge involved in working with this type of data: These tickets do not necessarily contain any information of interest for the task at hand. Other intents expressed include spare part orderings and status updates on repair progress. Moreover, most text is written by non-native-speaking mechanical repair personnel, resulting in many orthographic and grammatical errors.

An initial annotation of 800 random text samples indicates that around 18% of all sentences contain phrases of interest. The given knowledge graph describes general symptom phrases used to classify problems in the machine manufacturing domain. It comprises 249 vertices, 370 associated phrases, and only two relations *synonym* and *hypernym*. The average number of known synonyms per entity is ≈ 1.49 (around 28% of all entities have at least one additional synonym). We measure performance by the rate and noise-to-positives ratio of newly identified symptoms.

5.1 FastText Baseline

We use fastText [1] to assess the quality of a non-contextualized embedding model in contrast to our approach. We train the skipgram variant from scratch using all text contexts of the TRAIN data for five epochs. The embedding size is 100, the learning rate $5 \cdot 10^2$ and the char n-grams span from 3 to 6. For each phrase of the knowledge graph, synonym proposals are produced by a nearest neighbour search $\mathrm{NN}(\cdot)$ of the phrase's centroid $G(\mathrm{phrase})$. For hyponym predictions, we adapt

Table 2. Baseline experiment evaluating the **accuracy** of the **top-20 predictions** using fastText and our models. In total, we annotated 1600 samples for each model (800 *synonym*, 800 *hyponym*). In contrast: drawing randomly from the tickets yields 18% **viable** results.

	fastText	NS (our)	CE (our)
	synomym		
correct	13.00%	15.38%	13.63%
viable	20.63%	37.25%	28.63%
	hyponym		
correct	9.63%	5.88%	6.25%
viable	14.75%	37.38%	25.50%

the analogy task by calculating the average offset $\mathbf{h}$ over all child-parent pairs $\mathcal{H}$ and searching the vicinity of the added query vertex representation: $\mathrm{NN}(\mathbf{h} + G(\mathrm{phrase}))$:

$$\mathbf{h} = 1 \setminus |\mathcal{H}| \left(\sum_{(c,p) \in \mathcal{H}} (c - p) \right) \tag{7}$$

We randomly select 40 concepts and annotate the top 20 predictions (without removing redundancy) for both relations of the fastText model, as well as our model trained with negative sampling (NS) and cross-entropy (CE). Predictions are annotated as either **correct** or **viable** (the latter describing predictions better placed somewhere else in the knowledge graph). An example for a correct *hyponym* prediction for falsch angeschlossen (connected wrongly), a configuration error, is falsch verdrahtet (wired wrongly). A viable prediction would be falsch gespeichert (save error) which is no configuration error but functional failure and must be put in a different place of the graph.

Table 2 describes the model's performance quantitatively. Prediction correctness is quite low, which is understandable given the weak training signal. Encouragingly, the overall recall (i.e. viable samples) is greatly increased compared to random drawing (18%) such that around every third retrieved text sample contains valuable information to extend the KG with. Using negative samples (NS) from the query corpus is an important addition to increasing recall substantially.

Qualitatively, we found the predictions made by the models to be very different. For compounds – which are common in German – fastText yields good results: e.g. given Faltenbildung (wrinkling), the model easily proposes similar compounds such as Rillenbildung (grooving), Klumpenbildung (lump formation), etc. However, fastText struggles with multi-token phrases such as does not boot as its centroid will not be influenced much by "does" and "not" (words occurring in many other contexts). Also, the nearest neighbour search will only return single-token phrases as proposals, which limits recall. Other approaches, such as frequency-based models for discovering simple terms that occur more frequently in the domain-specific ticket collection are determined by the same challenge. However, it is crucial for our model to correctly discern text sequences such as *"X fällt auf, dass ..."* (*"X notices that"*) and *"X fällt ab, weil ..."* (*"X falls off because"*) where the former is irrelevant and the latter an important phrase to be added to the graph. In contrast, our models (CE, NS) yield entire sentences containing multi-token phrases, e.g. Achse bewegt sich nicht (axis does not move) as a *hyponym* for keine Bewegung (no movement).

5.2 Domain Expert Evaluation

In our evaluation session, a domain expert used the tool for both the NS and CE models for 45 minutes each. The expert was instructed to explore the text collection at will and to link as many new entities of practical relevance to the graph as possible. Prediction lists have not been capped to allow for a free and unbiased exploration process. In total, the expert first retrieved 52 phrases (20 synonyms, 32 children) using the NS model. He then switched to the CE model, with which he retrieved 42 additional phrases (11 synonyms, 32 children) (Table 3).

We conducted a 1-hour interview immediately after the annotation process, assessing (1) whether

Table 3. Expert annotation results. In total, the expert retrieved around 95 phrases from both model predictions.

	NS	CE
synonyms	20	11
children	32	32
correct concept	48%	70%
correct relation	35%	37%
both correct	17%	18%

the expert sees potential in the current proof-of-concept as a permanent addition to the knowledge engineer's tool belt and (2) how valuable the rankings of the models are found to be.

User Experience and Information Access: The current process of KG-refinement is based on customer interviews and guesswork. The expert emphasises that unveiling the information in the issue tracker corpus in itself is a crucial aspect to improving setting up a customer-specific KG. The presentation through the tool is considered favourably, including that our models yield entire text contexts. Those were vital to assess a problem's nature and severity and quickly identify whether a particular result list was interesting enough to dig into the annotation. Clicking on the (scattered) tokens to mark phrases was appreciated for a quick and easy phrase acquisition. This greatly aids the rate of exploration, and the expert deems a day of work would easily yield a few hundred new phrases for the graph.

Prediction Quality: The expert's impression is that correct, viable, and useless predictions balance each other. The found phrases, however, are very customer-specific: finding them is usually associated with much work without the aid of the model predictions. It needs to be noted that the models struggle to deviate from the known phrases and tend to rank text with considerable sub-word overlap or misspelt phrases highly (e.g. Druckschwankungen (pressure fluctuation). The expert notes that these misspellings are still valuable to link more text for downstream applications. However, we also encounter very promising proposals such as Spindel-schwingung (spindle vibration) as a child of vibriert (vibrates). We observe that in the final annotation set are multi-token phrases that cannot easily be retrieved using fastText or comparable approaches.

6   Conclusion

We have proposed a tool-assisted approach towards early-stage KG building from unstructured text and scarce, general KGs. To this end, we built an interactive web application for domain experts to explore a corpus of technical issue reports driven by a neural engine that links text contexts to KG vertices and edges. The tool reveals promising text contexts and allows for a quick and easy domain exploration. The expert interview results emphasise the approach's potential to become an effective instrument of a knowledge engineer's tool belt.

Models: The models show promising results, as they can hint at relevant multi-word phrases for nearly every third proposed text context. However, this first proof-of-concept also reveals two expandable research questions: (1) How can the models better discern irrelevant noise from texts with relevant phrases? (2) How can the ranking be improved upon? An important future step is establishing a human-in-the-loop process, where the expert's feedback is fed into an instant retraining cycle. We hope this eliminates redundancy and substantially improves our model's suggestions, mainly because the KG we bootstrap from is scarce.

Tooling: Building a knowledge model is an iterative and creative process. Such a model is constantly adjusted to meet formal, technical and downstream application requirements. As such, there is no single correct way to set up these graphs, and asking a model to build a domain-specific graph semi-automatically is asking too much. It follows that adequate tool support should not try to make the most correct prediction for a single entity of the graph but give the most viable hints for a specific thematic area (i.e. a subgraph). This not only allows to *add* information but, when presented with new information, *update* the current knowledge model as well. How these subgraphs and thematic areas can be discovered, discerned and presented remains open for future work.

References

1. Bojanowski, P., Grave, E., Joulin, A., Mikolov, T.: Enriching word vectors with subword information. corr abs/1607.04606. http://arxiv.org/abs/1607.04606 (2016)
2. Daza, D., Cochez, M., Groth, P.: Inductive entity representations from text via link prediction. In: Proceedings of the Web Conference 2021, pp. 798–808 (2021)
3. Devlin, J., Chang, M.W., Lee, K., Toutanova, K.: BERT: pre-training of deep bidirectional transformers for language understanding. arXiv preprint arXiv:1810.04805 (2018)
4. Fu, C., et al.: Multiple interaction attention model for open-world knowledge graph completion. In: Cheng, R., Mamoulis, N., Sun, Y., Huang, X. (eds.) WISE 2020. LNCS, vol. 11881, pp. 630–644. Springer, Cham (2019). https://doi.org/10.1007/978-3-030-34223-4_40
5. Hamann, F., Ulges, A., Falk, M.: IRT2: inductive linking and ranking in knowledge graphs of varying scale. arXiv preprint arXiv:2301.00716 (2023)
6. Hamann, F., Ulges, A., Krechel, D., Bergmann, R.: Open-world knowledge graph completion benchmarks for knowledge discovery. In: Fujita, H., Selamat, A., Lin, J.C.-W., Ali, M. (eds.) IEA/AIE 2021. LNCS (LNAI), vol. 12799, pp. 252–264. Springer, Cham (2021). https://doi.org/10.1007/978-3-030-79463-7_21
7. Hogan, A., et al.: Knowledge graphs. Synth. Lect. Data Semant. Knowl. **12**(2), 1–257 (2021)
8. Honnibal, M., Montani, I., Van Landeghem, S., Boyd, A.: spaCy: Industrial-strength Natural Language Processing in Python (2020). https://doi.org/10.5281/zenodo.1212303
9. Kingma, D.P., Ba, J.: Adam: a method for stochastic optimization. arXiv preprint arXiv:1412.6980 (2014)
10. Mikolov, T., Sutskever, I., Chen, K., Corrado, G.S., Dean, J.: Distributed representations of words and phrases and their compositionality. In: Advances in Neural Information Processing Systems, pp. 3111–3119 (2013)
11. Nathani, D., Chauhan, J., Sharma, C., Kaul, M.: Learning attention-based embeddings for relation prediction in knowledge graphs. arXiv preprint arXiv:1906.01195 (2019)
12. Proisl, T., Uhrig, P.: SoMaJo: state-of-the-art tokenization for German web and social media texts. In: Proceedings of the 10th Web as Corpus Workshop (WAC-X) and the EmpiriST Shared Task, pp. 57–62. Association for Computational Linguistics (ACL), Berlin (2016). http://aclweb.org/anthology/W16-2607
13. Riedel, S., Yao, L., McCallum, A.: Modeling relations and their mentions without labeled text. In: Balcázar, J.L., Bonchi, F., Gionis, A., Sebag, M. (eds.) ECML PKDD 2010. LNCS (LNAI), vol. 6323, pp. 148–163. Springer, Heidelberg (2010). https://doi.org/10.1007/978-3-642-15939-8_10

14. Shah, H., Villmow, J., Ulges, A.: Relation specific transformations for open world knowledge graph completion. In: Proceedings of the Graph-based Methods for Natural Language Processing (TextGraphs), pp. 79–84. Association for Computational Linguistics, Barcelona, Spain (2020). https://www.aclweb.org/anthology/2020.textgraphs-1.9
15. Shah, H., Villmow, J., Ulges, A., Schwanecke, U., Shafait, F.: An open-world extension to knowledge graph completion models. In: Thirty-Third AAAI Conference on Artificial Intelligence (2019)
16. Shi, B., Weninger, T.: Open-world knowledge graph completion. arXiv preprint arXiv:1711.03438 (2017)
17. Socher, R., Chen, D., Manning, C.D., Ng, A.: Reasoning with neural tensor networks for knowledge base completion. In: Advances in Neural Information Processing Systems, pp. 926–934 (2013)
18. Toutanova, K., Chen, D., Pantel, P., Poon, H., Choudhury, P., Gamon, M.: Representing text for joint embedding of text and knowledge bases. In: Proceedings of the 2015 Conference on Empirical Methods in Natural Language Processing, pp. 1499–1509 (2015)
19. Trouillon, T., Welbl, J., Riedel, S., Gaussier, É., Bouchard, G.: Complex embeddings for simple link prediction. In: International Conference on Machine Learning, pp. 2071–2080 (2016)
20. Weissweiler, L., Fraser, A.: Developing a stemmer for German based on a comparative analysis of publicly available stemmers. In: Rehm, G., Declerck, T. (eds.) GSCL 2017. LNCS (LNAI), vol. 10713, pp. 81–94. Springer, Cham (2018). https://doi.org/10.1007/978-3-319-73706-5_8
21. Xie, R., Liu, Z., Jia, J., Luan, H., Sun, M.: Representation learning of knowledge graphs with entity descriptions. In: Thirtieth AAAI Conference on Artificial Intelligence (2016)
22. Yang, B., Yih, W.T., He, X., Gao, J., Deng, L.: Embedding entities and relations for learning and inference in knowledge bases. arXiv preprint arXiv:1412.6575 (2014)
23. Zhong, H., Zhang, J., Wang, Z., Wan, H., Chen, Z.: Aligning knowledge and text embeddings by entity descriptions. In: Proceedings of the 2015 Conference on Empirical Methods in Natural Language Processing, pp. 267–272 (2015)
24. Zhou, Y., Shi, S., Huang, H.: Weighted aggregator for the open-world knowledge graph completion. In: Zeng, J., Jing, W., Song, X., Lu, Z. (eds.) ICPCSEE 2020. CCIS, vol. 1257, pp. 283–291. Springer, Singapore (2020). https://doi.org/10.1007/978-981-15-7981-3_19

Towards Knowledge Graph Creation from Greek Governmental Documents

Amalia Georgoudi[1]([⊠]), Nikolaos Stylianou[1][iD], Ioannis Konstantinidis[2][iD],
Georgios Meditskos[1][iD], Thanassis Mavropoulos[3][iD], Stefanos Vrochidis[3][iD],
and Nick Bassiliades[1][iD]

[1] School of Informatics, Aristotle University of Thessaloniki,
54124 Thessaloniki, Greece
ageorgoudi@csd.auth.gr
[2] School of Science and Technology, International Hellenic University,
57001 Thessaloniki, Greece
[3] Information Technologies Institute, Centre for Research and Technology Hellas,
57001 Thessaloniki, Greece

Abstract. Documents contain textual information, which is of the utmost importance for all the organizations. Document management systems have been used to store vast amounts of unstructured textual data described with minimal metadata, a method that has several limitations. In order to convert hidden knowledge into machine-readable data with rich connections, this paper presents work in progress on the development of the first end-to-end guided approach to construct a Knowledge Graph from Greek governmental documents from the Greek open government portal. The resulted Knowledge graph constitutes a proof-of-concept graph, that illustrates the beneficial semantic relationships between the textual data.

Keywords: Knowledge Graph Construction · RDF Triples · Ontologies · Natural Language Processing · Knowledge Representation · Government Documents

1 Introduction

With the rise of the terms open government and open data, several public sector Document Management Systems are publishing their documents to the Web as open data to increase transparency and accessibility. Yet, the problem with those document management systems are that their information is not machine-readable and they do not support data interconnection and linking. This is the situation with the Greek web portal, known as DIAVGEIA (in English: Clarity), which publishes all public sector administrative decisions and acts, as required by the law, resulting in a massive and rapidly growing collection of over 43 million documents.

Knowledge Graphs (KGs) [1] are a way of representing data in graphs, through which it is possible to describe the significance of the data as well

© The Author(s), under exclusive license to Springer Nature Switzerland AG 2023
H. Fujita et al. (Eds.): IEA/AIE 2023, LNAI 13925, pp. 294–299, 2023.
https://doi.org/10.1007/978-3-031-36819-6_26

as the relationships between them. In order to utilize the advantages of using a KG, this paper has focused on transforming the retrieved information from the governmental documents in DIAVGEIA to Resource Description Framework (RDF) [2] triples in order to construct a KG.

In this paper, we present our findings, challenges faced and approaches used, as part of an ongoing work, focusing on guided triple exaction from Greek governmental documents. By organizing the retrieved information in a Knowledge Graph, semantic relationships and links interconnect the data, giving them a machine-readable form, which easily could lead to drawing conclusions and extract new information. Yet, Greek is a low-resource language with very limited available NLP tools and many open challenges. Our approach addresses these issues and constructs a Knowledge Graph, based on a widely used ontology schema, populated with the extracted triples.

The remainder of the paper is organized as follows. Section 2 presents the related work. In Sect. 3 the proposed method is introduced, while in Sect. 4 the resulted proof-of-concept KG is presented. Section 5 concludes and gives directions for future work.

2   Related Work

Our work was based on a previous study [8], in which the authors proposed a theoretical framework for KG construction in DIAVGEIA. In this paper, the problem will be analyzed in a more technical way, by taking into account the technical difficulties and the limited number of available NLP tools for the Greek language.

A very limited number of works have focused on end-to-end knowledge graph construction from a document repository. The majority of the studies concentrate on particular subtasks, such as entity recognition, entity disambiguation, entity linking, and relation extraction. T2KG [3] presents a hybrid method for mapping predicates in an existing KG that combines a rule-based approach with a similarity-based approach. Other methods approach Knowledge Graph Construction as a multi-label sequence labeling task and uses a deep learning neural network architecture to jointly learn to produce and extract triples from text [4].

Knowledge graph construction is a task that has been applied in text with different types of domains [5] and languages [6]. Regarding the Greek language, there is no other work for Knowledge Graph construction from Greek unstructured documents, except [7]. In [7] they proposed to utilize transformer models for machine translation from Greek to English and backwards, in order to apply existing triple extraction tools for English texts. Yet, this approach do not achieve satisfactory results with the domain-specific vocabulary of government documents.

3   Proposed Method

The proposed approach uses a guided triple extraction algorithm, that searches for pre-determined triples and relations. After a systematic analysis of the documents by domain experts, the approach is focused only on obtaining triples that contain the most important information.

The proposed guided triple extraction method consists of three phases. Figure 1 presents the architecture of the proposed approach. In the first phase, the PDF file is parsed into different machine-readable formats (text, HTML) in order to apply NLP techniques to extract the important information. In the second phase, a reusable ontology is created based on a widely-used schema (Party in Role), while in the third phase, the extracted information is transformed into RDF triples to construct the Knowledge Graph.

Information Extraction. In the first phase, our method focuses on extracting the important information from the documents. To extract those triples, first, the PDF was parsed into a machine-readable form. More specifically, during this phase, the PDF was initially parsed into a textual form. From the text was possible to extract information such as the unique ADA number of the document, which is a unique Internet Uploading Number that every uploaded document in Diavgeia has, using regular expressions. Then the PDF was parsed also into HTML, in order to obtain additional information, such as the location or the number of words of a part of the PDF.

The next step was to detect the main body of the document. The main text is usually located in document's text body and has the highest number of words, compared to other parts of texts. As already described, the documents

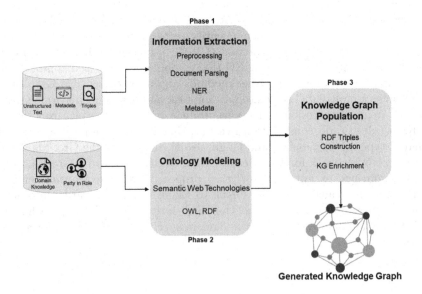

Fig. 1. Architecture Overview

in DIAVGEIA usually contain a lot of noise. There are many numbers, symbols, words' initials, abbreviations, multiple tabs, etc. Furthermore, text inside parenthesis and quotation marks adds extra "noise" to text data since they usually contain alphanumeric numbers of laws and decisions. For those reasons, a pipeline for text cleaning and normalization needed to be applied. As such, the text inside parentheses, quotation marks, numbers, punctuation, and multiple spaces were deleted so as to facilitate parsing the content. The cleaned text was then machine-readable and easier to parse. A Named Entity Recognition tool was then utilized to find the name of the individual who was appointed to the position.

Structural information was taken into account, i.e., the position of the text in the PDF. Finally, the GreekBERT-based NER tagger [10] was used to locate and classify named entities, such as the names of the signer and the organization. Based on preliminary experiments, on benchmark datasets and intrinsically on documents originating from DIAVGEIA, we found GreekBERT [9] to have the best performance in Greek language tasks.

Ontology Modelling. During the second phase, a readable, scalable and reusable schema that describes the documents and the various parties (person, organization), was created. The ontology schema was based on the logic of a "Party in Role", which is a very common schema used by large organizations to describe people in different roles (someone may now be appointed in a position but later in another document, he could be the signatory). This pattern is also used in very large ontologies, such as FIBO (Financial Industry Business Ontology) [11]. Figure 2 shows the ontology's class hierarchy.

The class Document describes the Greek government documents from DIAVGEIA. The class Party represents all the participants/entities and has two subclasses: Person and Organization. The class Party_in_Role represents a participant who has a specific role. The class Role describes the roles that a person or an organization could have. In this case, the possible roles are the publisher, the signer and the appointee. These roles are declared as instances of the class Role.

Knowledge Graph Population. The next step was to transform the extracted triples and their relationships into RDF triples, to populate the Knowledge Graph. RDF stores information in the form of semantic triples. Each triple

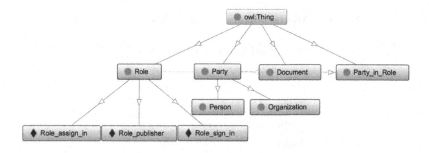

Fig. 2. Ontology: Party in Role

consists of a subject, a predicate, and an object. Each element in the triple is denoted by a unique Web URI.

The resulted triples were parsed into an RDF file following the Turtle (Terse RDF Triple Language) format [12].

4   Produced Knowledge Graph

The produced Knowledge graph constitutes a proof-of-concept graph, that converts the textual data into machine-readable data and illustrates the beneficial semantic relationships between them.

Currently, there isn't any annotated dataset that could be used to test and validate the proposed approach. For this reason, the approach was tested on a manually annotated dataset consisting of 30 documents, created by domain experts. Table 1 illustrates the accuracy scores for the extracted information. The ADA number has the highest accuracy score, while the organization has the lowest. This was anticipated since the unique ADA number has a uniform format and a specific position in a document. On the other hand, extracting the organization from a document could be very challenging since sometimes it can be represented in different ways, such as pictures or logos. The results were also evaluated by humans, working in the public sector, who were very satisfied with the performance of the method.

5   Discussion and Conclusion

This paper presents an end-to-end guided approach to construct a Knowledge Graph from the Greek government documents, by extracting specific triples from the hidden textual data. Organizing and semantically linking the textual information in a Knowledge graph, which is included among the state-of-the-art technologies and has been acknowledged as the most efficient way of organizing and describing data as well as retrieving information, will enable and substantially improved semantically-based searching, transparency, and reusability.

Some limitations of our work that could encourage for future research are that we focused only on a specific type of decision while our approach only works for documents that follow a widely-accepted format. In future work, we

Table 1. Accuracy scores for the retrieved information.

Extracted Information	Accuracy
Organization	0.70
ADA	1.00
Referred ADA	0.80
Appointed Person	0.85
Signer	0.80

plan to focus more on the triple extraction task for the Greek language and scale our method to larger datasets, including more types of decisions and document formats. Yet, there is a lot of room for contributions regarding NLP tools for low resource languages, such as Greek. Having at our disposal more NLP tools would benefit the Knowledge Graph construction task.

Acknowledgements. The research for this paper is partially funded by the Horizon Europe project ENCRYPT (Grant Agreement no. 101070670).

References

1. Fensel, D., et al.: Introduction: what is a knowledge graph? Knowl. Graph. 1–10 (2020)
2. Miller, E.: An introduction to the resource description framework. J. Libr. Adm. **34**, 245–255 (2001)
3. Kertkeidkachorn, N., Ichise, R.: T2kg: an end-to-end system for creating knowledge graph from unstructured text. In: Workshops At The Thirty-First AAAI Conference On Artificial Intelligence (2017)
4. Stewart, M., Liu, W.: Seq2KG: an end-to-end neural model for domain agnostic knowledge graph (not text graph) construction from text. In: International Conference On Principles Of Knowledge Representation And Reasoning, vol. 17, pp. 748–757 (2020)
5. Rossanez, A., Dos Reis, J., Silva Torres, R., Ribaupierre, H.: KGen: a knowledge graph generator from biomedical scientific literature. BMC Med. Inform. Decis. Mak. **20**, 1–24 (2020)
6. To, H., Do, P.: Extracting triples from Vietnamese text to create knowledge graph. In: 12th International Conference On Knowledge and Systems Engineering (KSE), pp. 219–223 (2020)
7. Papadopoulos, D., Papadakis, N., Matsatsinis, N.: PENELOPIE: enabling open information extraction for the Greek language through machine translation. ArXiv Preprint ArXiv:2103.15075 (2021)
8. Stylianou, N., Vlachava, D., Konstantinidis, I., Bassiliades, N., Peristeras, V.: Doc2KG: transforming document repositories to knowledge graphs. Int. J. Semant. Web Inf. Syst. (IJSWIS) **18**, 1–20 (2022)
9. Koutsikakis, J., Chalkidis, I., Malakasiotis, P., Androutsopoulos, I.: GREEK-BERT: the Greeks visiting sesame street. In: 11th Hellenic Conference On Artificial Intelligence, pp. 110–117 (2020)
10. Smyrnioudis, N., Koutsikakis, J.: A transformer-based natural language processing Toolkit for Greek-named entity recognition and multi-task learning (2021)
11. Bennett, M.: The financial industry business ontology: best practice for big data. J. Bank. Regul. **14**, 255–268 (2013)
12. Consortium, W., et al.: RDF 1.1 Turtle: terse RDF triple language. In: World Wide Web Consortium, 2014 (2014)

Information Retrieval from Legal Documents with Ontology and Graph Embeddings Approach

Dung V. Dang[1,2], Hien D. Nguyen[1,2(✉)], Hung Ngo[3], Vuong T. Pham[2,4,5], and Diem Nguyen[1,2]

[1] University of Information Technology, Ho Chi Minh city, Vietnam
{dungdv,hiennd,diemntn}@uit.edu.vn
[2] Vietnam National University, Ho Chi Minh city, Vietnam
[3] Technological University Dublin, Dublin, Ireland
hung.ngo@tudublin.ie
[4] Faculty of Mathematics and Computer Science, University of Science, Ho Chi Minh city, Vietnam
[5] Sai Gon University, Ho Chi Minh city, Vietnam
vuong.pham@sgu.edu.vn

Abstract. The legal search has great demand and a role in society. Ontology is a useful solution to represent the legal domain. This paper introduces a method to extract knowledge from law documents for building a legal knowledge base as the Legal-Onto Ontology. The method also proposes a solution to extract concepts and their relationships to create a knowledge graph. This is the foundation for solving the semantic query problem and returning the correct answer to meet the user's needs. The experimental results show that it is possible to build a law lookup application, which meets the practical requirements of users.

Keywords: Knowledge Representation · Knowledge graph · Graph embedding · Legal document

1 Introduction

In recent times, artificial intelligence (AI) has been used to help people in legal fields [23,28]. It can help humans predict legal outcomes through the provision of legal documents, and has even suggested court decisions [6,25]. The potential benefits of AI in law are real and we should go into deep research and development. It has assisted people in many areas of law, helping to reduce human time and effort in this area [26].

The legal search always has a great demand and role for society [6,10]. However, the current legal query systems have limitations, which cannot give the most accurate answers to users. It is difficult to extract the meaning of the query from legal documents and retrieve appropriate law information.

In the legal domain, the knowledge base needs to be organized to reason and retrieve in this domain [10,15]. Ontology Legal-Onto is a suitable method

© The Author(s), under exclusive license to Springer Nature Switzerland AG 2023
H. Fujita et al. (Eds.): IEA/AIE 2023, LNAI 13925, pp. 300–312, 2023.
https://doi.org/10.1007/978-3-031-36819-6_27

for representing the legal domains with those requirements [19, 21]. It is developed from the intellectual model of relations, Rela-model [9]. This ontology was applied to organize the knowledge base for Vietnamese Land Law.

In this paper, we propose a method to extract knowledge from law documents. The extracted knowledge can be used to build a legal knowledge base by ontology Legal-Onto. The proposed method is constructed to establish key phrases along with the relationships between them. The semantics of relations between key phrases is based on graph embedding. In addition, the research proposes a method for optimizing the organization and storage of knowledge bases in the form of knowledge graphs to enhance performance and reduce query time. This is achieved through the use of star decomposition for subgraph matching, which also improves the ability to extract knowledge from different data sources. These methods can significantly contribute to the development of modern knowledge technology and improve the quality and accuracy of knowledge-based applications. Additionally, the study addresses the query problem based on legal document expressions and discusses the use of word transformers to convert keywords on the graph into vectors, supporting the matching process for keywords and relationships across two graphs.

The next section reviews related work in the field of AI and law. Section 2 presents the process for building knowledge graphs from legal documents, including the structure of the legal system, the design of knowledge representations, and building knowledge graphs. We describe the experimental process to validate the proposed model based on the knowledge repository on road traffic law in Sect. 4. Finally, the article will be concluded and will give several future research directions in Sect. 5.

2   Related Work

Nowadays, there are many research topics and systems have been built to apply artificial intelligence to the management of legal documents [12, 29]. It supports the need of searching, and answering questions about law, it can even assist in judicial decision-making. These works use modern technologies, such as Natural Language Processing (NLP) [20, 30] or knowledge mapping, to solve problems [8, 27].

Ontology is an effective method for representing the knowledge in multiple domains for information searching [16, 22], especially in the law domain [23–25]. LIDO is an ontology for legal informatics documents [24]. This ontology can represent legal actions that affect the document, legal temporal events, the structure of the legal resource, and the semantic structure of the organization of legal documents. The Legal Knowledge Graph and ontology are organized and connected by the Lynx Service Platform using a data model [25]. It allows for the adaptable orchestration of a number of NLP and information retrieval services that handle legal document processing.

The authors in [13] proposed a method to measure the similarity between legal court case documents, which can help match the results of the current case with the results of other legal documents. The case has happened before to draw conclusions. However, this approach only processes with determined cases in its repository and it does not work well when a new and unprecedented case occurs.

The study in [7] presented a deep learning technique in law when early adaptation and legal word embeddings were trained on large corpora. The authors have applied deep learning to classify documents, and extract and query legal knowledge information. Nevertheless, the method does not give highly accurate results for semantic legal questions, and this method is costly in terms of training. In another study, Zhong et al. summarized the benefit of NLP in Legal Artificial Intelligence [30]. Those systems have built a good solution to apply artificial intelligence in the legal field. They can assist users in predicting legal judgments or comparing past representative similar cases and answering legal questions. However, the knowledge modeling and knowledge base building for the system is still done manually, requiring the knowledge builder for the system to have legal knowledge, so these things take a lot of work human time and effort.

Maftuhah et al. proposed an ontology model on legal documents in Indonesia [12]. Knowledge representation by this method can find inconsistent regulations and can perform a search for concepts in regulations in the legal documents of this country.

As mentioned, there are now a lot of useful research projects born to help people access and understand more about the law in a convenient, fast, and easy way [28]. However, current methods of building knowledge bases are not suitable or labor intensive to implement. This paper is intended to build a platform to support users in organizing legal document knowledge based on the knowledge representation model according to the ontology approach. This ontology can be used to construct a key phrase graph that represents the content of the extracted legal documents.

3   Building a Knowledge Graph

3.1   Legal Structure

In Vietnam, the current system of legal documents is specified in the Law on Promulgation of Legal Documents [3]. Although legal documents change continuously according to economic and social development, Vietnam's system of legal documents has the following levels [18]:

- *The Constitution* is the basic law of the Socialist Republic of Vietnam. Promulgated by the National Assembly and is the document with the highest legal effect.
- *The Code and the law* are legal documents promulgated by the National Assembly to concretize the Constitution to regulate various types of social relations in the fields of activities of the society.
- *Sub-law documents* are documents promulgated by competent authorities in accordance with the order and procedures prescribed by law. Sub-law documents are promulgated to provide specific, detailed, and guiding documents for legal documents and must not be contrary to the provisions of legal documents.

Depending on the content, the structure of a document can be arranged as a group of sections, chapters, subsections, articles, clauses, and points [2]. To represent the knowledge of a particular legal document, the Rela-model is a useful and suitable ontology to represent knowledge about the relations in this domain [9,19]. This model includes conceptual components and relations between concepts [21]. Concepts are concepts or entities mentioned in legal documents. The relations between the concepts are acts or events, so that with each relationship, it is possible to fully determine the content and meaning of the behavior or event in legal documents.

3.2   Knowledge Structure Design

In general, the ontology structure consists of concepts and the relations of concepts. This structure fully expresses the meaning of the legal document [24]. It is suitable to represent knowledge of current legal documents of the Vietnamese legal system. Ontology Rela-model is a knowledge model of relations [9]. It consists of concepts, relations, and inference rules. Based on Rela-model, ontology Legal-Onto and its improvement have been constructed to apply for representing the knowledge of Land Law [19] and Road Traffic Law [21]. The full structure of ontology Legal-Onto is as Defintion 3.1:

Definition 3.1: Ontology Legal-Onto consists of followed elements:

$$K = (C, \ R, \ Rules) + (Conc, \ Rel) \tag{1}$$

where:

- *(C, R, Rules)* is a structure of Rela-model, which **C** is a set of concepts, each concept in **C** has been improved its internal structure to organize its law information; **R** is a set of relations, those relations are between concepts, key phrases and database storing the content of the law document; and **Rules** is a set of inference rules of the knowledge domain.
- *(Conc, Rel)* is a knowledge graph, which represents the relations between key phrases of legal documents. In which, **Conc** is a set of terms representing concepts in the law document; **Rel** is the set of arcs, each arc is always directed and represents a semantic relation between two concepts.

The structure of ontology Legal-Onto is shown in Fig. 1. In this model, the knowledge graph is used to represent the key phrases that have been extracted through the concept in the document and the relationship between these key phrases through the relation for easy organization and knowledge management. Using knowledge graphs can link fragmented data, turning data into knowledge. In addition, it also supports users to solve semantic queries.

3.3   Building Knowledge Graphs

Building a knowledge graph is the process of converting user-inputted legal documents into knowledge graphs to represent the content of legal documents (Fig. 2).

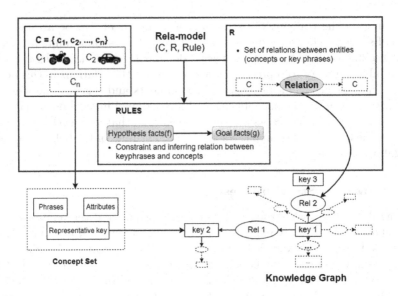

Fig. 1. Structure of Legal Rela-model.

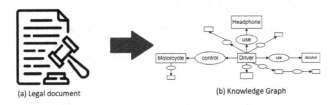

(a) Legal document   (b) Knowledge Graph

Fig. 2. Illustrating the construction of a knowledge graph

The knowledge graph represents the set of concepts and relations between them. Each concept represented by the knowledge graph has the structure as Definition 3.2.

Definition 3.2: *(Structure of concept)* - Each concept $c \in \mathbf{C}$ is a tube as follows:

$$c = (Name, Meaning, Attrs, Keyphrases, Similar) \tag{2}$$

In which, *Name* is the identifying name of the concept, *Meaning* presents the meaning of the concept, *Attrs* contains a list of attributes of the concept, *Keyphrases* is a set of key phrases determined or related to the concept. These key phrases have been declared in a list with type = "N". Finally, *Similar* includes different representations of the corresponding concept. It is usually the most popular key phrase when talking about this concept.

Definition 3.3: *(The structure of relation)* Each relation $r \in \mathbf{R}$ is a tube as follows:

$$r = (Name, Meaning, ConckeyS, ConckeyO, Prop, Keywords) \tag{3}$$

In which, *Name* is the name or symbol of the identification of the relation, *Meaning* presents the meaning of the relation. *ConckeyS* and *ConckeyO* are concepts in the relation, where *ConckeyS* is used for the subject and *ConckeyO* is used for the object. *Prop* presents a set of properties of the relation. This study only mentions two main properties as a binary relation, including transitive and symmetric. *Keywords* contains a set of keywords for the relation.

There are two stages to build the knowledge graph for representing the legal document. Stage 1 is the process to build ontology representing the content of this document according to the structure of Legal-Onto. Stage 2 constructs the knowledge graph from the built ontology.

Stage 1: *Build ontology representing the content of the law document based on Legal-Onto.* This stage is carried out in two steps as follows:
Step 1.1: Extract key phrases from the law document
- Collect and extract a set of key phrases.
- Classify extracted keyhrases into two kinds: the kind of representing concepts in the document (type "C") and the kind of representing relations between concepts (type "R")

Example 3.1: In the road traffic law, there are 3 legal documents in the field of road that regulate acts [1,4,5]. These documents are scanned to extract key phrases about concepts and relations, such as *"motorcycle"*, *"phone"* as concepts, and *"control"* as a relation. Figure 3 shows several key phrases and their types.

Step 1.2: Building ontology for the law document
- Construct a set **C** which is the set of concepts extracted from legal documents.
- Construct a set **R** which is the set of relations between concepts in set **C**.

Example 3.2: With extracted key phrase in Example 3.1:

- The concept "motorcycle" is used to mean "two- or three-wheeled motor vehicles and similar vehicles, driven by engines with a cylinder capacity of 50 cm3 or more, with a vehicle weight not exceeding 400 kg". This is a road vehicle, and is specified in Section 3.39, Article 3 of [5]. The list of key phrases used to represent this concept contains "Mopeds", "motorcycles", and key phrases, that are used to represent the concept "motorcycle". Table 1 shows the structure of the relation "use".
- The relation *"use"* is extracted from articles in [4]. This relation performs the use of the tool when a person is participating in traffic (shown in Table 2).

Key phrase	Vietnamese	Type
People	Người	C
Use	Sử dụng	R
Control	Điều khiển	R
Motorcycle	Xe máy	C
Headphone	Tai nghe	C
Phone	Điện thoại	C
Umbrella	Ô, dù	C
Drug	Ma túy	C
Banners	Băng rôn	C

Fig. 3. List of key phrases

Stage 2: *Build the knowledge graph to serve as the knowledge base for the system.* This stage includes three steps as follows:

Step 2.1: Store legal documents in the database

- Build relational tables to store full information in the legal document (including chapters, articles, clauses, and points) in the database.
- Use foreign keys to link tables.

Table 1. Example of concept "motorbike"

Element	Type	Meaning
Name	Text	motorbike
Meaning	Text	"two- or three-wheeled motor vehicles and similar vehicles, driven by engines with a cylinder capacity of 50 cm3 or more, with a vehicle weight not exceeding 400 kg"
Attrs	Dict	**-kind**: road traffic vehicle **-legal**: Section 3.39, Article 3 of National Technical Regulation QCVN 41:2016/BGTVT
Keyphrases	Set	Mopeds, motorcycles
Similar	Word	motorbike

Table 2. Example of relation "use"

Element	Type	Meaning
Name	Text	use
Meaning	Text	Person uses one of the objects in the ConcKeyO list as a vehicle to serve a certain need or purpose when participating in traffic
ConcKeyS	Key phrase	person
ConcKeyO	List	Headphone, phone, umbrella
Prop	Set	transitive: 0, symmetric: 0
Keywords	Set	Use, control, do, make

Step 2.2: Determine nodes of the knowledge graph by extracted key phrases

- Perform extracted keyphrases which were declared in the *KeyPhrase* table.
- For each key phrase, the concept containing this key phrase is determined by the set of key phrases in the *KeyPhrase* column of the *Concept* table.
- Proceed to retrieve similar words of each concept.

Other key phrases if their concepts cannot be found will remain the same. After standardizing the list of key phrases, duplicate keyword phrases will be removed.

Step 2.3: Create arcs of the graph through relations between keyphrases.

- From the extracted key phrases, determine the relations declared in the *Relation* table by matching the key phrases with the values in the columns *ConcKeyS*, *RepresentativeKey* and *ConcKeyO* columns (for the *ConcKeyO* column, match a value in the declared list).
- Identify specific relations between key phrases. For each relation, *Subject-Relationship-Object* and the position in the document to express the knowledge of the sentence can be determined.

Example 3.3: The relation *(person-use-umbrella)* between two key phrases *"person"* and *"umbrella"* at Article 30, Clause 3, Point c of Vietnam Road Traffic Law [1] (Fig. 4):

Fig. 4. Graphical illustration of the "person-use-umbrella" relational knowledge triple

Step 2.4: Graph optimization.
Graph optimization is the process of reducing the size of graphs and improving the accuracy of data analysis results.

- From the existing graph, we remove meaningless triples that do not reflect the characteristic meaning of the document item.
- Duplicate or semantically equivalent triples are also reduced.

From the built knowledge triads, the knowledge graph is formed. This is the knowledge base of the knowledge domain to be represented.

4   Experiments and Testing Results

Searching on Road Traffic law is very necessary for residents. In Vietnam, the foundation of Road Traffic Law is in [1, 4, 5]. This section presents the application of the proposed solution to retrieve information from those legal documents. The knowledge base in this domain is built semi-automatically. Firstly, the information about concepts, relations, and rules in those documents will be automatically extracted and built into a triad, then the knowledge engineer. will check and edit it according to the expert's opinion. Secondly, the process of constructing the knowledge graph is utilized to create a graph representing the extracted knowledge. This is also verified by the knowledge engineer

4.1   Setup the Knowledge Base in Road Traffic Law

A collection of legal documents related to the area studied has been built from legal documents [1, 4, 5], with a total of 28 chapters, 265 articles, 1,003 clauses, and 2,503 points. From this collection, we have built 1,398 concepts and 1,091 relationships between concepts in the road traffic law document. This process is carried out in Step 1.1 of Stage 1 of Sect. 3.3.

Based on these concepts and relationships, knowledge graphs are built to represent the semantics of documents and store them in the form of triples. Next, the graph will be optimized by removing meaningless or duplicate triples to reduce the size of the graph. The process of completing the knowledge graph is shown in Stage 2 in Sect. 3.3.

In the next step, the foundation is built to organize the knowledge base. This platform will represent the content of legal documents entered by users to create knowledge graphs showing the meaning of legal documents. The knowledge representation process will proceed semiautomatically and according to the researched and designed method of organization and the model of knowledge representation. The platform also allows system administrators to examine and modify the knowledge base of the system from their point of view. After that, the key phrases and relations are extracted from its knowledge base. Those are resources to create a knowledge graph representing the content of road traffic law.

Figure 5 shows a part of the built graph. This is a knowledge graph consisting of circles representing concepts in the road traffic law and arrows to represent directional relationships between them. Each circle has the concept's name written inside. The arrows indicate the direction of the relationship between the concepts. The relationships between concepts are described by phrases indicated on the arrows. This knowledge graph makes it easy for readers to understand the relationships between concepts and to explain complex concepts in an intuitive and easy-to-understand manner.

For example, pursuant to point e, point g, and point h of Clause 4, Article 6 of Decree No. 100/2019/ND-CP, the following rules are stipulated:

A fine of between VND 600,000 and VND 1,000,000 shall be imposed on motorcyclists who commit one of the following violations: e) Failure to obey traffic signal signals; g) Failure to obey orders and instructions of traffic controllers or traffic controllers; h) The person driving the vehicle using an umbrella (umbrella), mobile phone. These rules will be represented with a model that includes:

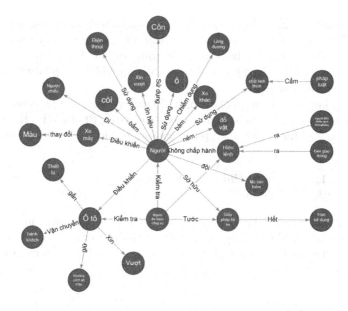

Fig. 5. A part of knowledge graph representing Vietnam Road Traffic Law.

Concepts including: "Driver", "Motorbike", "Phone", "Umbrella", "Command", "Traffic controller", and "Traffic light" are represented as circles in the knowledge graph. The relationships "control", "use", "disregard", and "signal" are represented by arrows to indicate relationships between concepts. For example, an arrow from "Driver" to "Phone" with the phrase "use" describes the driver's behavior of using a phone (Fig. 6).

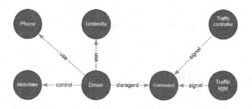

Fig. 6. A small part of the road traffic law.

By this method, the knowledge representation is built quickly, saving a lot of time and effort. Administrators need to verify the returned results and correct them if their results are not appropriate.

4.2   Searching on the Knowledge Graph

After transforming legal documents in Vietnam Road Traffic Law to the knowledge base, a retrieval system is built to perform the lookup on the organized knowledge base [19, 21]. This system extracts important key phrases from input queries. Then, those key phrases are standardized into similar key phrases, which are stored in the knowledge base. Next, a graph of key phrases for the inputted query is built. Finally, this process uses graph embedding to predict the missing component in the triple.

With the key phrase graph of an inputted query, the system searches the most similar subgraphs inside the knowledge base by using PhoBERT's transformer[1]. It converts key phrases on the graph to vectors to aid in matching between two graphs.

Example 4.1: The query *"How are the penalties for a person who controls a motorbike with using alcohol?"*

Figure 7 illustrates the matching process to answer this query in Vietnamese. Figure 7b is the key phrase graph of this query. From that, the system will match this graph with the knowledge graph representing the law content in Fig. 7a.

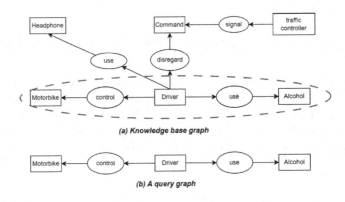

(a) Knowledge base graph

(b) A query graph

Fig. 7. Illustrates the searching to answer a query in Vietnamese.

5   Conclusion and Future Work

This paper designed a solution to extract knowledge from legal documents and organize it as a knowledge base through the structure of ontology Legal-Onto. This study also proposed a method to create a knowledge graph that represents concepts and their relations. This graph is used to search for and query legal knowledge based on the built knowledge base.

In addition, this study also constructed a platform to support the query of legal knowledge and application in the field of road traffic law to evaluate the effectiveness of the proposed method. The system can support the lookup of concepts, violations as well as corresponding penalties in accordance with provisions of the legal documents in the road traffic law.

---

[1] https://github.com/VinAIResearch/PhoBERT.

In the future, the study will focus on building ontology automatically with the verification from a knowledge engineer [17]. Concepts and relations in the ontology for the knowledge domain are generated automatically from the legal documents. In addition, NLP techniques will be studied to handle more complex natural questions to be able to handle a wide variety of user-entered questions [11,14].

Acknowledgement. This research is funded by Vietnam National University Ho Chi Minh City (VNU-HCM) under grant number DS2023-26-04.

Dung V. Dang is funded a part from VNUHCM - University of Information Technology (UIT) under grant number D1-2023-04.

References

1. Law on Road Traffic. Law No. 23/2008/QH12. Vietnam National Assembly (2008)
2. Circular of the Minister about the formats, and techniques for legal documents of the Government, the Prime Minister, Ministers, and joint legal documents. No. 25/2011/TT-BTP. Vietnam Ministry of Justice (2011)
3. Law on Promulgation of Legislative Documents. No. 80/2015/QH13. Vietnam National Assembly (2015)
4. Decree on Administrative penalties for road traffic and rail transport offences. No. 100/2019/ND-CP. Vietnam Government (2019)
5. National Technical Regulation on Traffic Signs and Signals. QCVN 41:2019/BGTVT. Vietnam Ministry of Transport (2019)
6. Ashley, K.D.: Artificial intelligence and legal analytics: new tools for law practice in the digital age. Cambridge University Press (2017)
7. Chalkidis, I., Kampas, D.: Deep learning in law: early adaptation and legal word embeddings trained on large corpora. Artif. Intell. Law **27**(2), 171–198 (2019)
8. Choi, B., Ko, Y.: Knowledge graph extension with a pre-trained language model via unified learning method. Knowl.-Based Syst. **262**, 110245 (2023)
9. Do, N.V., Nguyen, H.D., Selamat, A.: Knowledge-based model of expert systems using rela-model. Int. J. Softw. Eng. Knowl. Eng. **28**, 1047–1090 (2018)
10. Governatori, G., Bench-Capon, T., Verheij, B., et al.: Thirty years of artificial intelligence and law: the first decade. Artif. Intell. Law **30**(4), 481–519 (2022)
11. Hoang, S.N., Nguyen, B., Nguyen, N.P., et al.: Enhanced task-based knowledge for lexicon-based approach in Vietnamese hate speech detection. In: Proceedings of 14th International Conference on Knowledge and Systems Engineering (KSE 2022), pp. 1–5. IEEE (2022)
12. Maftuhah, T., Purwarianti, A., Asnar, Y.: Ontology modelling on legal document: case study: legal document of Indonesian republic. In: Journal of Physics: Conference Series, vol. 1201, p. 012061. IOP Publishing (2019)
13. Mandal, A., Chaki, R., Saha, S., et al.: Measuring similarity among legal court case documents. In: Proceedings of the 10th Annual ACM India Compute Conference, pp. 1–9 (2017)
14. Nguyen, D.H., Huynh, T., Hoang, S.N., et al.: Language-oriented sentiment analysis based on the grammar structure and improved self-attention network. In: Proceedings of 15th International Conference on Evaluation of Novel Approaches to Software Engineering (ENASE 2020), pp. 339–346 (2020)

15. Nguyen, D.H., Sakama, C., Sato, T., Inoue, K.: An efficient reasoning method on logic programming using partial evaluation in vector spaces. J. Log. Comput. **31**(5), 1298–1316 (2021)

16. Nguyen, H.D., Tran, T.V., Pham, X.T., Huynh, A.T.: Ontology-based integration of knowledge base for building an intelligent searching chatbot. Sens. Mater. **33**(9), 3101–3123 (2021)

17. Nguyen, H.D., Do, N.V., Pham, V.T.: A methodology for designing knowledge-based systems and applications. In: Applications of Computational Intelligence in Multi-Disciplinary Research, pp. 159–185. Elsevier (2022)

18. Nguyen, P.K.: How to conduct research in Vietnamese law: overview of the legal system of the socialist republic of Vietnam. Int. J. Leg. Inf. **27**(3), 307–331 (1999)

19. Nguyen, T., Nguyen, H., Pham, V., et al.: Legal-onto: an ontology-based model for representing the knowledge of a legal document. In: Proceedings of 17th International Conference on Evaluation of Novel Approaches to Software Engineering (ENASE 2022), Online streaming, pp. 426–434 (2022)

20. Nguyen, T.-S., Nguyen, L.-M., Tojo, S., Satoh, K., Shimazu, A.: Recurrent neural network-based models for recognizing requisite and effectuation parts in legal texts. Artif. Intell. Law **26**(2), 169–199 (2018). https://doi.org/10.1007/s10506-018-9225-1

21. Pham, V.T., Nguyen, H.D., Le, T., et al.: Ontology-based solution for building an intelligent searching system on traffic law documents. In: Proceedings of 15th International Conference on Agents and Artificial Intelligence (ICAART 2023), Lisbon, Portugal, pp. 217–224 (2023)

22. Phan, T.T., Pham, V.Q., Nguyen, H.D., Huynh, A.T., Tran, D.A., Pham, V.T.: Ontology-based resume searching system for job applicants in information technology. In: Fujita, H., Selamat, A., Lin, J.C.-W., Ali, M. (eds.) IEA/AIE 2021. LNCS (LNAI), vol. 12798, pp. 261–273. Springer, Cham (2021). https://doi.org/10.1007/978-3-030-79457-6_23

23. Sartor, G., Araszkiewicz, M., Atkinson, K., et al.: Thirty years of artificial intelligence and law: the second decade. Artif. Intell. Law **30**, 521–557 (2022)

24. Sartor, G., Casanovas, P., Biasiotti, M., Fernández-Barrera, M.: Approaches to Legal Ontologies. Springer, Dordrecht (2019). https://doi.org/10.1007/978-94-007-0120-5

25. Schneider, J.M., Rehm, G., Montiel-Ponsoda, E., et al.: Lynx: a knowledge-based AI service platform for content processing, enrichment and analysis for the legal domain. Inf. Syst. **106**, 101966 (2022)

26. Szostek, D., Zalucki, M.: Legal tech: information technology tools in the administration of justice. Nomos (2021)

27. Tiddi, I., Schlobach, S.: Knowledge graphs as tools for explainable machine learning: a survey. Artif. Intell. **302**, 103627 (2022)

28. Villata, S., Araszkiewicz, M., Ashley, K., et al.: Thirty years of artificial intelligence and law: the third decade. Artif. Intell. Law **30**, 561–591 (2022)

29. Zhang, H., Dou, Z., Zhu, Y., Wen, J.R.: Contrastive learning for legal judgment prediction. ACM Trans. Inf. Syst. **41**(4), 113 (2023)

30. Zhong, H., Xiao, C., Tu, C., et al.: How does NLP benefit legal system: a summary of legal artificial intelligence. In: Proceedings of the 58th Annual Meeting of the Association for Computational Linguistics, pp. 5218–5230 (2020)

Recommendations Based on Reinforcement Learning and Knowledge Graph

Wei Song[1]([✉]) [ID], Tichang Wang[1], and Zihan Zhang[2]

[1] School of Information Science and Technology, North China University of Technology, Beijing 100144, China
songwei@ncut.edu.cn
[2] Brunel London School, North China University of Technology, Beijing 100144, China

Abstract. Reinforcement learning is playing an increasingly important role in the field of recommender systems. In this paper, we enhance the performance of a reinforcement learning-based recommender system by incorporating a knowledge graph, which serves as the embedding method for translating entities and relationships into vectors. To recommend diverse items, we define an explorative reward function for the Markov decision process that determines the recommendation. We also describe an action space pruning strategy that narrows down the reasoning space, and present a target for policy gradient optimization. Our experimental results show that the proposed method improves the recommendation performance and provides rational explanations.

Keywords: Recommender system · Reinforcement learning · Knowledge graph · Markov decision process · Explorative reward function

1 Introduction

With the rapid increase of internet and mobile information resources, recommender systems (RSs) are an important means of providing suggestions for items that are of interest to a user. From their emergence to the present day, several intelligent techniques have been successfully applied in RSs, such as clustering [10], matrix factorization [9], and multi-criteria decision-making [12]. However, interpreting the recommendation results properly remains a challenging problem.

One possible solution for improving interpretability is to introduce knowledge graphs (KG) into RSs. KGs capture the semantics of a domain using a set of definitions of concepts, their properties, the relations between them, and any logical constraints that are expected to hold. Through the use of KGs, information from disparate data sources can be linked and made accessible to answer questions that the user may not even have thought of.

There are two main methods of applying KGs in RSs. Several approaches focus on using KG embedding models to make recommendations [2]. These methods align the KGs in a regularized vector space and account for the similarity between entities by computing their representation distance. However, embedding methods cannot exploit the multi-hop relational paths of KGs. The second category makes recommendations from the paths in KGs [13]. This technique improves the recommendation performance, but it is generally not possible to explore all paths for each user–item pair in a large-scale KG.

Our motivation is to use KGs as a representation method, and model the RS problem through reinforcement learning (RL). RL is concerned with how intelligent agents ought to take actions in an environment to maximize the cumulative reward. From this point of view, the KG can be regarded as the environment of the agent, storing knowledge on the users, items, and their relationships. Starting from the user, the agent conducts explicit multi-step path reasoning on the graph to find suitable items to recommend. If the agent draws conclusions based on an explicit reasoning path, it is easy to explain the reasoning process for each recommendation result. Our goal is not only to pick out a set of items for recommendation, but also to provide corresponding reasoning paths for explanation.

In this paper, we first represent the entities and relationships of KGs using the TransD embedding method [6]. We then describe a model of the recommendation problem as a deterministic Markov decision process (MDP) on a KG. For the recommendation process, the agent learns to explore items that the user may be interested in with RL, and explains the recommendation results through the reasoning process. To recommend more items, we define an explorative reward function. Furthermore, we describe action space pruning and optimization strategies. Experiments on real-world datasets show the superiority of the proposed method.

2 Related Work

Incorporating more related information, such as historical information [11], visual appearance [4], and review text [7], is effective in improving the recommendation performance. For example, the Joint Representation Learning framework [15] integrates review text, product images, and numerical ratings to learn the corresponding user and item representations. The main problem for these methods is that the additional information is not easy to collect.

KGs contain a large amount of information about the relationships between entities and can be used as a convenient way to enrich user and item information. Thus, the problem of sparse data interactions between users and items faced by traditional RSs could be solved by constructing a KG. The node2vec framework [2] learns continuous feature representations for the nodes in a network. The main idea of node2vec is to learn a mapping of nodes to a low-dimensional space of features that maximizes the likelihood of preserving network neighborhoods of nodes. However, this method does not consider the multi-hop relation path. By taking account of the semantics of both entities and relations, Wang et al. proposed a KG-aware model for recommendations [13]. Their model executes reasoning on paths to allow the underlying rationale of a user–item interaction to be inferred. However, the computational cost for enumerating all paths between each user and each item is high.

Since its success in learning to play AlphaGo, RL has been widely applied in various fields, including RSs [16]. Xian et al. proposed the policy-guided path reasoning (PGPR) method [14], which couples recommendations and interpretability by providing the actual paths in a KG. PGPR uses TransE [1] as the KG embedding technique, whereas we use TransD [6] instead. Thus, besides one-to-one relations, our method can also handle one-to-N, N-to-one, and N-to-N relations. Furthermore, TransD solves the problem that TransE treats entities and relations equally in the same vector space.

3 Problem Description

A KG $\mathcal{G}$ is a set of triplets, each composed of a head entity e_h, a tail entity e_t, and the relationship from e_h, to e_t. Specifically, $\mathcal{G} = \{(e_h, e_t, r)|e_h, e_t \in \varepsilon, r \in \mathcal{R}\}$, where ε is the entity set and $\mathcal{R}$ is the relation set.

The *k-hop path* is used in our recommendation method to provide an explanation of the reasoning. A k-hop path from entity e_0 to entity e_k is defined as a sequence of $k + 1$ entities connected by k relations, denoted by $p_k(e_0, e_k) = \{e_0 \overset{r_1}{\leftrightarrow} e_1 \overset{r_2}{\leftrightarrow} \cdots \overset{r_{k-1}}{\leftrightarrow} e_{k-1} \overset{r_k}{\leftrightarrow} e_k\}$, where $e_{i-1} \overset{r_i}{\leftrightarrow} e_i$ represents $(e_{i-1}, e_i, r_i) \in \mathcal{G}$ or $(e_i, e_{i-1}, r_i) \in \mathcal{G}$.

In this paper, we consider a special type of KG for recommendations, denoted by $\mathcal{G}_{\mathcal{R}}$. This KG contains a subset of user entities $\mathcal{U}$ and a subset of item entities $\mathcal{I}$, where $\mathcal{U}, \mathcal{I} \subseteq \varepsilon$ and $\mathcal{U} \cap \mathcal{I} = \emptyset$. Correspondingly, the relationship between user u and item i is denoted by r_{ui}.

Let $u \in \mathcal{U}$ be the target user, $\mathcal{G}_{\mathcal{R}}$ be a KG, N be the number of recommended items, and K be the maximal number of relations between a recommended item and user u. The recommendation goal is to find a set of items $\{i_j \mid 1 \leq j \leq N, (u, i_j)$ is associated with one reasoning path $p_k(u, i_j)$ $(2 \leq k \leq K)\}$, where $p_k(u, i_j)$ is a k-hop path from u to i_j.

4 Proposed Method

The proposed method is composed of four parts: KG embedding, MDP modeling, action space pruning, and policy gradient. These parts are now explained in turn.

4.1 KG Embedding

KG embeddings are low-dimensional representations of the entities and relations in a KG. They provide a generalizable context about the overall KG that can be used to infer relations.

In the proposed method, TransD [6] is used for KG embedding. In TransD, each entity and relation are transformed into a relation vector space by two vectors. These two vectors are used to construct mapping matrices: the first one captures the meaning of an entity (relation) and the second one constructs the mapping matrices.

Specifically, for a triplet (e_h, e_t, r_{ht}), we have the vectors $\mathbf{h}, \mathbf{h}_p, \mathbf{t}, \mathbf{t}_p, \mathbf{r}, \mathbf{r}_p$, where $\mathbf{h}$, $\mathbf{t}, \mathbf{r}$ are entity/relation vectors and $\mathbf{h}_p, \mathbf{t}_p, \mathbf{r}_p$ are projection vectors, with $\mathbf{h}, \mathbf{h}_p, \mathbf{t}, \mathbf{t}_p \in \mathbb{R}^n$ and $\mathbf{r}, \mathbf{r}_p \in \mathbb{R}^m$. For each triplet (e_h, e_t, r_{ht}), two mapping matrices $\mathbf{M}_{rh}, \mathbf{M}_{rt} \in \mathbb{R}^{m \times n}$ are used to project users/items from the entity space to the relation space. These matrices are defined as:

$$\mathbf{M}_{rh} = \mathbf{r}_p \mathbf{h}_p^{\mathrm{T}} + \mathbf{I}^{m \times n}, \tag{1}$$

$$M_{rt} = \mathbf{r}_p \mathbf{t}_p^T + \mathbf{I}^{m \times n}, \tag{2}$$

where $\mathbf{h}_p^T$ and $\mathbf{t}_p^T$ are the transpose matrices of $\mathbf{h}_p$ and $\mathbf{t}_p$, and $\mathbf{I}^{m \times n}$ is the $m \times n$ identity matrix. With these mapping matrices, the projected vectors are defined as:

$$\mathbf{h}_\perp = M_{rh}\mathbf{h}, \tag{3}$$

$$\mathbf{t}_\perp = M_{rt}\mathbf{t}. \tag{4}$$

The score function of TransD is:

$$f_r(\mathbf{h}, \mathbf{t}) = -\|\mathbf{h}_\perp + \mathbf{r} - \mathbf{t}_\perp\|_2^2, \tag{5}$$

and the loss function of TransD is defined as:

$$L = \sum_{\zeta \in \Delta} \sum_{\zeta' \in \Delta'} \left[\gamma + f_r(\zeta') - f_r(\zeta) \right]_+, \tag{6}$$

Where $\Delta = \{(e_h, e_t, r_{ht}) \mid y = 1\}$ is the set of positive training triplets, $\Delta' = \{(e_h, e_t, r_{ht}) \mid y = 0\}$ is the set of negative triplets, γ is the margin separating positive triplets and negative triplet, $[x]_+ = max(0, x)$. Positive training triplets are the real entity–relationship pairs in $\mathcal{G}_\mathcal{R}$ while negative triplets are constructed by:

$$\Delta' = \{((e_m, e_t, r_{ht})) \mid e_m \neq e_h \wedge y = 1\} \cup \{(e_h, e_n, r_{ht}) \mid e_n \neq e_t \wedge y = 1\} \tag{7}$$

4.2 MDP Modeling

Given a KG, the paths between target user u and recommended item i can be used to explain the recommendation results. However, if there are several paths between u and i, it is important to determine which path is used for explanation. Namely, the path used for explanation may be inconsistent with the actual path from which u selected i. To address this issue, we use MDP for modeling the recommendation process. With KG as the environment, the strategy to be learned by the agent during the training phase is to navigate from the target user to potential items of interest. If the correct item is reached, the agent receives a higher reward from the environment.

The MDP is a mathematical model of sequential decisions and a dynamic optimization method. An MDP is defined as $M = \{\mathcal{S}, \mathcal{A}, \mathcal{P}, \mathcal{R}\}$, where $\mathcal{S}$ is the set of all possible states, $\mathcal{A}$ is the set of all possible actions, $\mathcal{P}$ is the set of state transition probabilities, and $\mathcal{R}$ is the set of real-valued reward functions. We describe these four sets in detail for the proposed method.

The State Set $\mathcal{S}$. State s_t at step t is defined as a tuple (u, e_t, h_t), where $u \in \mathcal{U}$ is the starting user entity, e_t is the entity the agent has reached at step t, and h_t is the history prior to step t. The k-step history is the combination of all entities and relations in the past k steps, i.e., $\{e_{t-k}, r_{t-k+1}, \ldots, e_{t-1}, r_t\}$. For a user u, the initial state is $s_0 = (u, u, \emptyset)$. If we define T as the maximal length of paths, then the terminal state is $s_T = (u, e_T, h_T)$.

The Action Set $\mathcal{A}$. The complete action space A_t of states t is defined as all possible outgoing edges of entity e_t excluding history entities and relations. Formally, $A_t = \{(r, e)|(e_t, r, e) \in G_R, e \notin \{e_0, \ldots, e_{t-1}\}\}$.

The Probability Set $\mathcal{P}$. Given state s_t and action $a_t = (r, e)$, the transition probability to the next state s_{t+1} is $\sum_{s_{t+1} \in \mathcal{S}} p(s_{t+1}|(s_t, a_t)) = 1$.

The Reward Set $\mathcal{R}$. Let T be the maximal length of paths. Only the terminal states are considered to give a reward, $T = (u, e_T, h_T)$. The basic idea is to identify whether the items interacted with by u are found by the agent. Specifically, let r be the relationship between u and e_T, and let $\mathbf{u}$, $\mathbf{e}_T$, $\mathbf{r}$ be vectors for u, e_T, and r transformed by TransD. The *explorative reward function* (ERF) is defined as:

$$R_T = \begin{cases} 1, & \text{if } e_T \in \mathcal{I}, u \text{ interacted with } e_T \\ f((r, e_T)|u), & \text{if } e_T \in \mathcal{I}, u \text{ did not interact with } e_T, \\ -1, & \text{if } e_T \notin \mathcal{I} \end{cases} \tag{8}$$

where

$$f((r, e_T)|u) = <\mathbf{u} + \mathbf{r}, \mathbf{e}_T> /N_f, \tag{9}$$

in which $<, >$ is the dot product operation and N_f is a normalization term, which ensures the value of $f((r, e_T)|u)$ is in the range $(0, 1)$.

With the ERF, those items that did not interact with target user u in the KG still have a chance of being recommended according to their relationship with u. This improves the diversity of the recommendation results.

4.3   Action Space Pruning

The out-degree of nodes in a KG obeys a long-tail distribution, i.e., most nodes have a very low out-degree and a few nodes have a very high out-degree. As a result, maintaining the size of the action space based on the largest out-degree is very inefficient. Thus, we use a scoring function to retain the promising edges for the target user.

Specifically, the scoring function $s((r, e)|u)$ maps any edge (r, e) $(\forall r \in \mathcal{R}, \forall e \in \varepsilon)$ to a real-valued score conditioned on user u. This function is defined as:

$$s((r, e)|u) = s\left((u, e)|\tilde{r}_{k,j}\right) = <\mathbf{u} + \sum_{l=1}^{j} \mathbf{r}_l, \mathbf{e} + \sum_{l=j+1}^{k} \mathbf{r}_l> +b, \tag{10}$$

where $\tilde{r}_{k,j} = \{r_1, r_2, \ldots, r_j, r_{j+1}, \ldots, r_k\}$ when the current path is $\{u \xrightarrow{r_1} e_1 \xrightarrow{r_2} \cdots \xrightarrow{r_j} e_j \xleftarrow{r_{j+1}} e_{j+1} \xleftarrow{r_{j+2}} \cdots \xleftarrow{r_k} e_k\}$, $\mathbf{u}, \mathbf{e}, \mathbf{r} \in \mathbb{R}^d$ are d-dimensional vector representations of user u, entity e, and relation r, and $b \in \mathbb{R}$ is the bias for e.

The pruned action space of state s_t is then defined as:

$$A_t(u) = \{(r, e)|rank(s((r, e)|u)) \leq \alpha, (r, e) \in A_t\}, \tag{11}$$

where α is a pre-defined integer that upper-bounds the size of the action space, and $rank()$ is a function that returns the rank of users according to their scoring function values.

4.4 Policy Gradient

The goal of RL is to find the optimal behavior strategy by which the agent obtains the optimal reward. Policy gradient methods model and optimize the policy directly. Based on the abovementioned MDP formulation, our goal is to learn a stochastic policy π that maximizes the expected cumulative reward for any initial user u:

$$J = \mathbb{E}_\pi \left[\sum_{t=0}^{T-1} \gamma^t R_{t+1} | s_0 = (u, u, \emptyset) \right], \tag{12}$$

where $\gamma \in [0, 1]$ is a discount factor.

The problem is solved with REINFORCE as a baseline [8] by designing a policy network and a value network that share the same feature layers. Let $\mathbf{s}$ be the state vector, represented as the concatenation of the embeddings u, e_t, and h_t, and let $\mathbf{A}_u$ be the binarized vector of the pruned action space $A(u)$. For the binarized pruned action space $\mathbf{A}_u \in \{0, 1\}^{d_A}$, d_A is set as the maximum size among all pruned action spaces. The policy network $\pi(\cdot|\mathbf{s}, \mathbf{A}_u)$ outputs the probability of each action, with all actions not in $A(u)$ assigned a probability of zero. The value network $v(\mathbf{s})$ maps the state vectors to real values, which are used as the baseline in REINFORCE. The structures of the two networks are defined as:

$$\pi(\cdot|\mathbf{s}, \mathbf{A}_u) = \text{softmax}(\mathbf{A}_u \odot (\mathbf{x}\mathbf{W}_p)), \tag{13}$$

$$v(\mathbf{s}) = \mathbf{x}\mathbf{W}_v, \tag{14}$$

where $\odot$ is the Hadamard product to mask invalid actions and $\mathbf{X} \in \mathbb{R}^{d_f}$ is the vector composed of the learned hidden features of the state, defined as:

$$\mathbf{X} = \text{dropout}(\sigma(\text{dropout}(\sigma(\mathbf{s}\mathbf{W}_1))\mathbf{W}_2)), \tag{15}$$

in which σ is the exponential linear unit activation function and $\mathbf{W}_1, \mathbf{W}_2, \mathbf{W}_p, \mathbf{W}_v$ consist of the model parameters for both networks, i.e., $\Theta = \{\mathbf{W}_1, \mathbf{W}_2, \mathbf{W}_p, \mathbf{W}_v\}$. The policy gradient is defined as:

$$\nabla_\Theta J(\Theta) = \mathbb{E}_\pi \left[\nabla_\Theta \log \pi_\Theta(\cdot|\mathbf{s}, \mathbf{A}_u) \left(\sum_{t=0}^{T-1} \gamma^t R_{t+1} - v(\mathbf{s}) \right) \right]. \tag{16}$$

4.5 General Recommendation Roadmap

The general routine of the proposed hybrid RS based on KG and RL (HR-RL-KG) method is as follows.

Step 1. Perform KG embedding using TransD.

Step 2. Construct the MDP model.

Step 3. Prune the action space.

Step 4. Optimize with policy gradient.

Step 5. Recommend N items in descending order of their ERF values to the target user.

5 Experimental Results

We compare the performance of our HR-RL-KG method with that of five existing methods. BPR-HFT [7] is a hidden factors and topics model that incorporates topic distributions to learn latent factors from reviews of users or items. VBPR [4] builds upon the Bayesian personalized ranking model by incorporating visual product knowledge. TransRec [3] invokes translation-based embeddings for sequential recommendations. It learns to map both user and item representations in a shared embedding space through personalized translation vectors. JRL [15] is a joint RL model that combines multimodal information including images, text, and ratings into a neural network. PGPR [14] incorporates both RL and KG to produce recommendations, and provides the actual reasoning paths for the interpretation of the recommendation results.

5.1 Datasets and Parameter Settings

All experiments were conducted on the Amazon e-commerce datasets collection [5], consisting of product reviews and meta information from Amazon.com. The datasets include four categories: Beauty, Cell Phones, Clothing and CDs. Each category constitutes a KG containing five types of entities and seven types of relations. Table 1 presents the characteristics of the datasets used in the experiments. The datasets were randomly divided into two parts, with 70% used as the training set and 30% used as the testing set.

Table 1. Characteristics of the datasets

Dataset	User	Item	Feature	Brand	Category	Interaction
Beauty	22,363	12,101	22,564	2,077	248	198,502
Cell Phones	27,879	10,429	22,493	955	206	194,439
Clothing	39,387	23,033	21,366	1,182	1,193	278,677
CDs	75,258	64,421	202,959	1,414	770	1,097,592

Following Xian et al. [14], the maximum path length was set to 3 and the maximum size of the pruned action space was set to 250. The HR-RL-KG model was trained for 40 epochs, with an initial learning rate of 0.1 that was gradually decreased to facilitate model convergence. The state's history sequence length was set to 1. Namely, the history vector $\mathbf{h}_t$ was represented by the concatenation of the embeddings of e_{t-1} and r_t.

5.2 Evaluation Metrics

All models are evaluated in terms of four representative top-N recommendation measures.

Precision is one of the most popular evaluation metrics used in RSs, and is defined as:

$$Prec = \frac{|ES \cap AS|}{|ES|} \times 100\%, \tag{17}$$

where ES is the set of items recommended to a user and AS is the set of items selected by that user. Precision measures how many of the recommended items are selected by the user.

In contrast, recall is the ratio of successfully recommended items to all accessed items, defined as:

$$Rec = \frac{|ES \cap AS|}{|AS|} \times 100\%. \tag{18}$$

Hit ratio (HR) is the fraction of users for which the correct answer is included in the recommendation list of length N:

$$HR = \frac{|U_h|}{|U|} \times 100\%, \tag{19}$$

where $|U_h|$ is the number of users for which the correct answer is included in the top-N recommendation list and $|U|$ is the total number of users.

Normalized discounted cumulative gain (NDCG) is another metric for measuring ranking quality, and is defined as:

$$NDCG = \frac{1}{|U|} \times \sum_{u \in U} NDCG(u) \times 100\%, \tag{20}$$

where $NDCG(u)$ is the NDCG of user u, which is defined as:

$$NDCG(u) = Z_N \times \sum_{k=1}^{N} \frac{2^{r(k,u)} - 1}{\log_2(k + 1)}, \tag{21}$$

in which Z_N is a normalizer used to guarantee that the perfect recommendation score is 1 and $r(k, u)$ is an indicator that represents whether the kth item is relevant to u ($r(k, u)$ = 1) or not ($r(k, u) = 0$).

Equations 17–20 indicate that higher values represent better recommendation results. For all experiments, these ranking metrics were computed based on the top-10 predictions for every user in the test set.

5.3 Comparison Results

A comparison of the results given by the different methods is presented in Table 2. For each dataset, the underlined value in each row represents the optimal value of that measure.

Table 2 demonstrates that the proposed HR-RL-KG method obtains the best results with respect to the four evaluation parameters on the four datasets. HR-RL-KG outperforms BPR-HFT, VBPR, TransRec, and JRL significantly. This verifies that RL and KG are effective in forming high-quality recommendations. Furthermore, HR-RL-KG is clearly superior to the similar PGPR method. There are two main reasons for this. One is that the TransD method is used to vectorize the entities and relationships of the KG, making the embedding more effective. The other reason is that the ERF enables the agent to explore more diverse paths, resulting in better performance.

Table 2. Comparison of the recommendation results given by different algorithms

Dataset	Measure (%)	BPR-HFT	VBPR	TransRec	JRL	PGPR	HR-RL-KG
Beauty	Prec	1.132	0.902	1.285	1.546	1.707	1.947
	Rec	4.459	2.786	4.853	6.949	8.324	8.734
	HR	8.268	5.961	0.867	12.776	14.401	14.788
	NDCG	2.934	1.901	3.218	4.396	5.449	5.834
Cell Phones	Prec	0.860	0.507	0.962	1.096	1.274	1.365
	Rec	5.307	3.489	6.279	7.510	8.416	8.934
	HR	8.125	5.002	8.725	10.940	11.904	12.503
	NDCG	3.151	1.797	3.361	4.364	5.042	5.431
Clothing	Prec	0.297	0.166	0.312	0.442	0.728	0.876
	Rec	1.819	0.968	2.078	2.989	4.834	5.112
	HR	2.872	1.557	3.116	4.634	7.020	7.398
	NDCG	1.067	0.560	1.245	1.735	2.858	3.143
CDs	Prec	1.268	0.328	1.837	2.085	2.157	2.201
	Rec	3.570	0.845	5.283	7.545	7.569	7.590
	HR	9.926	2.930	11.956	16.774	16.886	16.947
	NDCG	2.661	0.631	3.372	5.378	5.590	5.702

5.4 Explanation of the Recommendation Results

We demonstrate the explanation effects of HR-RL-KG with two randomly selected recommendation cases on the Amazon e-commerce datasets.

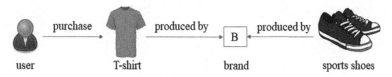

Fig. 1. A recommendation case with only one reasoning path

As shown in Fig. 1, a user purchased a T-shirt produced by brand "B." Thus, the HR-RL-KG model recommends sports shoes produced by the same brand to this user.

Figure 2 shows a more general case in which dumbbells were recommended to the target user from two reasoning paths. First, another user who mentioned the feature "fitness" has purchased dumbbells. Second, dumbbells could be recommended to the target user because she/he has previously bought sports shoes described by the feature "sports". The average reasoning path per item varies across the four datasets: 1.73 for Amazon Beauty, 2.16 for Cell Phones, 1.65 for Clothing, and 1.63 for CDs.

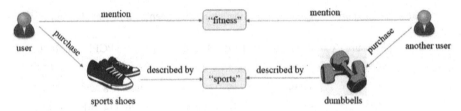

Fig. 2. A recommendation case with two reasoning paths

5.5   Ablation Study

In this section, we introduced a variant of the HR-RL-KG method, denoted as HR-RL-KG*, which employs the basic embedding method TransE [1] to embed the KG into a continuous vector space. We compare the performance of the two methods to demonstrate the impact of different KG embedding methods on recommendation performance, and show the results in Fig. 3. Our results indicate that the HR-RL-KG method outperforms the variant in most cases. This suggests that the choice of embedding method has a significant impact on recommendation performance, and an appropriate embedding method can better represent the entities and relations in the KG, thus demonstrating the effectiveness of our proposed method.

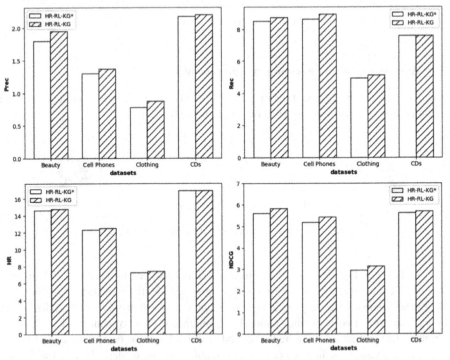

Fig. 3. Comparison of performance of HR-RL-KG and HR-RL-KG* on different datasets

6 Conclusions

We have developed an RS by integrating RL and KG. We used RL to reason potential items for recommendation, and employed a KG to provide accurate vector embedding. We proposed a new reward function to calculate a flexible reward, and explained the proposed method in detail. The experimental results show that incorporating both RL and KG not only improves the recommendation performance, but also provides reasonable explanations.

Acknowledgments. This work was partially supported by the National Natural Science Foundation of China (61977001), and Great Wall Scholar Program (CIT&TCD20190305).

References

1. Bordes, A., Usunier, N., García-Durán, A., Weston, J., Yakhnenko, O.: Translating embeddings for modeling multi-relational data. In: Proceedings of the 27th Annual Conference on Neural Information Processing Systems, pp. 2787–2795 (2013)
2. Grover, A., Leskovec, J.: node2vec: scalable feature learning for networks. In: Proceedings of the 22nd ACM SIGKDD International Conference on Knowledge Discovery and Data Mining, pp. 855–864 (2016)
3. He, R., Kang, W.-C., McAuley, J.J.: Translation-based recommendation. In: Proceedings of the Eleventh ACM Conference on Recommender Systems, pp.161–169 (2017)
4. He, R., McAuley, J.J.: VBPR: visual Bayesian personalized ranking from implicit feedback. In: Proceedings of the Thirtieth AAAI Conference on Artificial Intelligence, pp.144–150 (2016)
5. He, R., McAuley, J.J.: Ups and downs: modeling the visual evolution of fashion trends with one-class collaborative filtering. In: Proceedings of the 25th International Conference on World Wide Web, pp. 507–517 (2016)
6. Ji, G., He, S., Xu, L., Liu, K., Zhao. J.: Knowledge graph embedding via dynamic mapping matrix. In: Proceedings of the 53rd Annual Meeting of the Association for Computational Linguistics, pp. 687–696 (2015)
7. McAuley, J.J., Leskovec, J.: Hidden factors and hidden topics: understanding rating dimensions with review text. In: Proceedings of the Seventh ACM Conference on Recommender Systems, pp. 165–172 (2013)
8. Sutton, R.S., Barto, A.G.: Reinforcement Learning: An Introduction. MIT Press, Cambridge (2018)
9. Song, W., Li, X.: A non-negative matrix factorization for recommender systems based on dynamic bias. In: Torra, V., Narukawa, Y., Pasi, G., Viviani, M. (eds.) MDAI 2019. LNCS (LNAI), vol. 11676, pp. 151–163. Springer, Cham (2019). https://doi.org/10.1007/978-3-030-26773-5_14
10. Song, W., Liu, S.: Optimal user categorization from a hierarchical clustering tree for recommendation. In: Fujita, H., Fournier-Viger, P., Ali, M., Wang, Y. (eds.) Advances and Trends in Artificial Intelligence. Theory and Practices in Artificial Intelligence. IEA/AIE 2022. LNCS, vol. 13343, pp. 759–770. Springer, Cham (2022). https://doi.org/10.1007/978-3-031-08530-7_64
11. Song, W., Yang, K.: Personalized recommendation based on weighted sequence similarity. In: Wen, Z., Li, T. (eds.) Practical Applications of Intelligent Systems. AISC, vol. 279, pp. 657–666. Springer, Heidelberg (2014). https://doi.org/10.1007/978-3-642-54927-4_62

12. Tejaswi, S., Sastry, V. N., Bhavani, S. D.: MCMARS: hybrid multi-criteria decision-making algorithm for recommender systems of mobile applications. In: Molla, A.R., Sharma, G., Kumar, P., Rawat, S. (eds.) Distributed Computing and Intelligent Technology. ICDCIT 2023. ICDCIT 2023. LNCS, vol. 13776, pp. 107–124. Springer, Cham (2023). https://doi.org/10.1007/978-3-031-24848-1_8

13. Wang, X.: Explainable reasoning over knowledge graphs for recommendation. In: Proceedings of the Thirty-Third AAAI Conference on Artificial Intelligence, pp. 5329–5336 (2019)

14. Xian, Y., Fu, Z., Muthukrishnan, S., de Melo, G., Zhang, Y.: Reinforcement knowledge graph reasoning for explainable recommendation. In: Proceedings of the 42nd International ACM SIGIR Conference on Research and Development in Information Retrieval, pp. 285–294 (2019)

15. Zhang, Y., Ai, Q., Chen, X., Croft, W. B.: Joint representation learning for top-n recommendation with heterogeneous information sources. In: Proceedings of the 2017 ACM on Conference on Information and Knowledge Management, pp.1449–1458 (2017)

16. Zheng, G., et al: DRN: a deep reinforcement learning framework for news recommendation. In: Proceedings of the 2018 World Wide Web Conference on World Wide Web, pp. 167–176 (2018)

Link-Aware Link Prediction over Temporal Graph by Pattern Recognition

Bingqing Liu[1,2(✉)] and Xikun Huang[1,2]

[1] Academy of Mathematics and Systems Science, Chinese Academy of Sciences, Beijing 100190, China
huangxikun@amss.ac.cn
[2] School of Mathematical Sciences, University of Chinese Academy of Sciences, Beijing 100049, China
liubingqing20@mails.ucas.ac.cn

Abstract. A temporal graph can be considered as a stream of links, each of which represents an interaction between two nodes at a certain time. On temporal graphs, link prediction is a common task, which aims to answer whether the query link is true or not. To do this task, previous methods usually focus on the learning of representations of the two nodes in the query link. We point out that the learned representation by their models may encode too much information with side effects for link prediction because they have not utilized the information of the query link, i.e., they are link-unaware. Based on this observation, we propose a link-aware model: historical links and the query link are input together into the following model layers to distinguish whether this input implies a reasonable pattern that ends with the query link. During this process, we focus on the modeling of link evolution patterns rather than node representations. Experiments on six datasets show that our model achieves strong performances compared with state-of-the-art baselines, and the results of link prediction are interpretable. The code and datasets are available on the project website: https://github.com/lbq8942/TGACN.

Keywords: Temporal graph · Link prediction · Sampling · Transductive learning · Inductive learning · Interpretability

1 Introduction

Temporal graphs are powerful mathematical abstractions to describe complex dynamic networks and have a wide range of applications in various areas of network science, such as citation networks, communication networks, social networks, biological networks, and the World Wide Web [4]. In temporal graph, there are many insightful patterns (usually refers to small and induced temporal subgraph, which is also called motif or graphlet [13]) which summarize the evolution laws of links. To evaluate whether our model captures these patterns,

© The Author(s), under exclusive license to Springer Nature Switzerland AG 2023
H. Fujita et al. (Eds.): IEA/AIE 2023, LNAI 13925, pp. 325–337, 2023.
https://doi.org/10.1007/978-3-031-36819-6_29

link prediction is a widely used task [9], which is defined in dynamic graphs as, given all historical links before t, determine whether link $e = (s, o)$ will happen at timestamp t, where s and o are the source and destination nodes respectively. In previous studies, a standard paradigm of link prediction is centered on learning of the temporal node representations of s and o, and then the two representations are concatenated and fed into an MLP for link prediction, in which, representation learning is typically operated by the message passing mechanism, i.e., aggregating information from neighborhoods [2,17,18,21]. We note that this is suboptimal for link prediction cause they do not use the information $e = (s, o)$ when learning temporal representations. In other words, the prior methods are (query) link-unaware for link prediction.

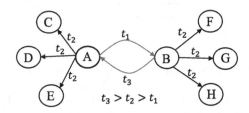

Fig. 1. An example temporal graph. Temporal subgraph with red links shows an example pattern, i.e., $\{(A,B,t_1),(B,A,t_3)\}$, which means that B will interact with A after A interacts with B. (Color figure online)

Figure 1 shows a temporal graph and the temporal subgraph with red links shows an example pattern. The perspective of pattern gives us inspiration for link prediction. For example, the pattern in Fig. 1 tells us that, given the link (B,A,t_3) to be predicted, we only need to look for the existence of the link from A to B in the history (we name this kind of links as target links). Notice that only by first considering (B,A,t_3), can we directly check the target links and ignore the other noisy links. However, this is not the case for previous methods. To predict (B,A,t_3), previous methods first learn the representations of A and B from historical links. Without taking the query link (B,A,t_3) into account, they can easily absorb noisy messages such as (A,C,t_2) and (B,F,t_2) into their node representations, though we only need the message from (A,B,t_1). As a result, much of their aggregated information is not necessary and often has side effects for link prediction because the important information may be diluted by the noisy links. Based on this, we propose a link-aware method, where historical links and the query link are input together into the following model layers to distinguish whether this input implies a reasonable pattern that ends with the query link. Under the instruction of the query link, our model can directly check the target links.

Although we have methodological differences for link prediction, for graph learning, we share the following challenges. **First, how to make sampling more efficient?** Given the query link, we usually need sample links from the history due to the huge size of the temporal graph. However, previous sampling

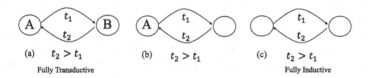

Fig. 2. Patterns of different granularity. Pattern (a) shows that B will respond to A after A interacts with B, pattern (b) describes that no matter whom A interacts with, afterwards this person will response to A, whereas pattern (c) reveals that such sequence holds for any two arbitrary nodes.

techniques are usually heuristic methods [10,18,19,21] and thus not flexible. In order to recall the target links, sometimes they need very long sampling lengths, which significantly increases the number of noisy links. **Second, how to learn patterns of different granularity?** Figure 2 shows three patterns of different granularity. Though they are equally important, previous models usually focus only on the extremes, i.e., either fully transductive [7,9,15] or fully inductive [19,21]. **Third, how to make our results for link prediction interpretable?** Interpretability for link prediction is rarely studied in previous work. APAN [18] has discussed interpretability, however, it can only tell the importance of historical links to the node representation, which can not be used to interpret the results for link prediction. In fact, the reason why the previous models are not interpretable can be attributed once again to the fact that they are link-unaware.

To meet the above challenges, here, (1) we develop a link-aware model for link prediction over temporal graphs, which can make full use of the query link when doing link prediction. (2) we propose a sampling method called parametric sampling to recall historical links that are useful but distant from the query link, which makes our sampling more efficient. (3) To capture patterns of different granularity, two kinds of attention are proposed to perform transductive and inductive learning simultaneously. (4) By equipping our model with technique class activation mapping (CAM) [22], interpretability is easily accessed, which tells us which historical links promote our decision for link prediction.

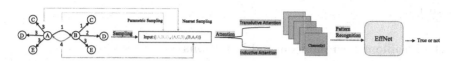

Fig. 3. The overall pipeline of the proposed Temporal Graph Attention Convolution Network (TGACN). Given the query link (the link from B to A with purple color), TGACN first uses nearest sampling and parametric sampling to recall historical links that may help to predict the query link. Then we encode the input links by two kinds of attention: transductive attention and inductive attention, where node identities information and the inductive structural information are preserved. Finally, a convolutional neural network EffNet is utilized to recognize whether the input implies a reasonable pattern that ends with the query link.

2   Related Work

Prior work for link prediction over temporal graph mainly focuses on the learning of nodes' representation [1,12]. Early models are mainly snapshot-based methods, which learns temporal graphs in discrete time space. This kind of method divides the temporal graph into snapshots where links in one snapshot are assumed to take place at the same time and links in different snapshots still maintain the chronological order [5,8,11]. Within snapshots, they usually utilize static graph neural networks (GNN) [2,6,17] to encode structural features. Between snapshots, they use RNNs or Transformer [16] to model the temporal dynamics. The main drawback of these approaches is that they need to predetermine a time granularity for snapshot partition and thus hard to learn structural and temporal dynamics in different time scales.

Learning on temporal graphs in continuous time space recently gained attention. These methods can be broadly classified into two categories, streaming methods and non-streaming methods. Streaming methods maintain a chronologically changing table for representations of all nodes and chronologically predict the links. Each time a new link appears, they use RNNs or Transformer to update that table, i.e., update representations of the source and destination node (and their neighbors) in that new link [7,10,15,18]. With the updated representations, they can predict the future link. Given a query link, streaming methods need to first digest all the previous historical links, while non-streaming methods do not [19–21]. It samples only a few historical links and uses GNN or Transformer to aggregate their information to obtain the representations of the two nodes in the query link. Commonly used sampling techniques include nearest sampling [10] and probabilistic sampling [19].

3   The TGACN Model

In this section, we introduce the proposed model, Temporal Graph Attention Convolution Network (TGACN). We first formally give the problem formulation and notations of the link prediction task over a temporal graph, then we introduce our model, which includes three parts: sampling, attention, and pattern recognition.

3.1   Problem Formulation and Notations

A temporal graph can be represented as a stream of links that come in over time, i.e., $E = \{e_1, \cdots, e_i, \cdots\}$, where link e_i is defined as a triplet (s_i, o_i, t_i). Link e_i shows that source node s_i interacted with destination node o_i at timestamp t_i. Link prediction requires our model to distinguish the ground truth triplet (s_g, o_g, t_g) and the corrupted triplet (s_g, o_{neg}, t_g), where o_{neg} is sampled from the nodes set V. That is, link prediction can be described as: given historical links $e_h = (s_h, o_h, t_h), t_h < t_q$, tell whether query link $e_q = (s_q, o_q, t_q)$ is a ground truth or not.

A sequence with l links in chronological order is denoted as $ES = \{e^1, \cdots, e^l\}$ and we use $ES(\cdot) \in \mathbb{R}^l$ denotes the corresponding sequence of $\cdot$, for example, $ES(t) = \{t^1, \cdots, t^l\}$. Specially, we use $ES(e) \in \mathbb{R}^{l \times d}$ denotes the vector representations of all links, where boldface $\mathbf{e} \in \mathbb{R}^d$ denotes the vector representation of link e. We use matrix $H \in \mathbb{R}^{|V| \times d}$ denotes the trainable representations of all nodes and $H(\cdot) \in \mathbb{R}^d$ denotes the representation of node $\cdot$.

3.2   Method

Sampling. Given a query link, we first need sampling due to the large scale of historical links. Without domain knowledge, a widely used sampling technique is neighborhood sampling [17,21], i.e., links that are close to the query link should be sampled with higher priority. However, nearest sampling alone may sometimes fail, for example, in Fig. 3, when we sample $N = 3$ nearest links, the target link (A,B,1) will be missed and it is not ideal to simply increase the sampling length because it will introduce more noisy links. Based on this consideration, for nearest sampling, we still keep N small and propose parametric sampling for those useful but more distant links. Parametric sampling locates valuable historical link e_h by computing its "closeness" to the query link e_q as follows:

$$\text{closeness}(e_q, e_h) = \mathbf{e_q} \circ \mathbf{e_h} \tag{1}$$

In which, $\circ$ denotes the dot product between two vectors, $\mathbf{e_q}$ and $\mathbf{e_h}$ are computed as follows:

$$\mathbf{e_q} = \phi(0) + H(s_q) + H(o_q) \tag{2}$$

$$\mathbf{e_h} = \phi(t_q - t_h) + H(s_h) + H(o_h) \tag{3}$$

$$\phi(t) = [cos(\omega_1 t + b_1), \cdots, cos(\omega_d t + b_d)] \tag{4}$$

where $\phi(\cdot) \in \mathbb{R}^d$ is a time encoding proposed in TGAT [21] and $[\omega_1, b_1, \cdots, \omega_d, b_d] \in \mathbb{R}^{2d}$ are all trainable parameters. We calculate the "closeness" of M (usually much larger than N) nearest historical links, and select P (usually very small) links with the largest "closeness". Note that despite its potential of recalling useful links that are distant, parametric sampling practically consumes more time than nearest sampling, so we need a trade-off to achieve the best performance.

By nearest sampling and parametric sampling, we sampled a total of $N + P$ historical links, which with the query event together form our input with $l = (N + P + 1)$ links $ES = \{e^1, \cdots, e^l\}$.

Attention. In order to determine whether there is a reasonable pattern that ends with the query link in the input links, we first need to encode these input links. During the encoding, we should provide enough convenience for the query link to directly check the target links while preserving as much of the original information as possible. In this paper, the attention mechanism is utilized, specifically includes transductive attention and inductive attention. Compared with traditional attention mechanism [16], we differ in two ways. First, the traditional attention mechanism is based on vector representation and dot-product, while inductive attention is not. Second, we use only the attention values computed by the "query" and "key", which we believe encode rich pattern information. In the following, we first introduce the transductive attention, and then the inductive attention.

Transductive Attention. Transductive attention tries to extract the pattern information from the representation of input links. Since it is representation-based, the attention values carry rich information of nodes and edges, and thus can be used to capture fine-grained patterns. We first calculate the vector representations for each link in the input links by Eq. 2 – Eq. 4. As a result, we get $ES(\mathbf{e}) \in \mathbb{R}^{l \times d}$. Then we compute the attention values between every two input links using dot product, i.e., we get

$$\begin{bmatrix} \mathbf{e}^1 \circ \mathbf{e}^1 & \dots & \mathbf{e}^1 \circ \mathbf{e}^l \\ \vdots & \ddots & \vdots \\ \mathbf{e}^l \circ \mathbf{e}^1 & \dots & \mathbf{e}^l \circ \mathbf{e}^l \end{bmatrix}_{l \times l}$$

We denote the above attention result as $channel(\mathbf{e}) \in \mathbb{R}^{l \times l}$

Inductive Attention. Inductive attention operates directly on node identities and link timestamps rather than vector representations. The goal of this attention is to remove node identities while still preserving the structure of the pattern so that they can be generalized to nodes and links that have not been seen before (see Fig. 2(c)). In order to do this, new attention functions are required.

The timestamps of the input links $ES(t)$ not only reflect the order of occurrence of the links, but the time interval itself carries a wealth of information. To encode this, we use the following attention functions:

$$attn_1(x, y) = \exp(-\alpha |x - y|) \tag{5}$$

where time decaying coefficient $\alpha > 0$ is a hyperparameter. We first pair the elements in $ES(t)$ and then the above attention function is utilized, i.e., the attention result is:

$$\begin{bmatrix} attn_1(t^1, t^1) & \dots & attn_1(t^1, t^l) \\ \vdots & \ddots & \vdots \\ attn_1(t^l, t^1) & \dots & attn_1(t^l, t^l) \end{bmatrix}_{l \times l}$$

We denote the above attention result as $channel(t) \in \mathbb{R}^{l \times l}$.

To remove the node identities while still maintain the original pattern topology, we propose to use the following attention function:

$$attn_2(x, y) = \begin{cases} 1 & x = y \\ 0 & else \end{cases} \tag{6}$$

Like handling $ES(t)$ with Eq. 5, we handle $ES(s)$ and $ES(o)$ with Eq. 6. Similarly, we can get $channel(s) \in \mathbb{R}^{l \times l}$ and $channel(o) \in \mathbb{R}^{l \times l}$. Note that

$ES(s)$ and $ES(o)$ may share the same nodes, while this kind of information is not yet reflected in the above two channels $ES(s)$ and $ES(o)$. To reserve this information, we perform mutual attention between $ES(s)$ and $ES(o)$ and get $channel(s,o)$, i.e.,

$$\begin{bmatrix} attn_2(s^1,o^1) \dots attn_2(s^1,o^l) \\ \vdots \quad \ddots \quad \vdots \\ attn_2(s^l,o^1) \dots attn_2(s^l,o^l) \end{bmatrix}_{l \times l}$$

It is easy to find that the above three channels retain the original pattern structure and do not lose any structural information. That is, given the channels, we can reverse back to the original pattern structure.

The above five channels are finally stacked to form an "image" with shape of $5 \times l \times l$, which encodes rich pattern information of these input links, including both nodes identities information and pattern structure information, which helps us capture patterns of different granularity. Note that the above attention functions are all symmetric, without losing any information, we set half of the "image" being zero.

Pattern Recognition. Given the "image", we decide in this part whether it contains a reasonable pattern that ends with the query link. Like in computer vision, a convolutional neural network (CNN) is utilized to carry out this pattern recognition. Here, we directly use the existing CNN architecture, which has already achieved excellent performance in the image classification task. In this paper, EfficientNetV2-S [14] is selected. Since our "image" ($5 \times l \times l$) (l is usually less than 20) is much smaller than images ($3 \times 224 \times 224$) in the real world, without harming the performance, we further simplify EfficientNetV2-S as EffNet by simply removing the last few stages and tune the number of layers in the left stages. The architecture of EffNet is shown in Table 1. Besides, to be explainable, a technique called Class Activation Mapping (CAM) [22] is utilized, which is able to identify the discriminative regions. For the architecture, CAM requests the utilization of the global average pooling layer before the last classification layer, which is already satisfied by EffNet.

To sum up, to be link-aware, TGACN makes use of the query link at two points. First and most importantly, the sampled historical links and the query link are put together as input. Under the instruction of the query link, it is possible for subsequent model layers to directly check the target links. Secondly, we use the vector representation of the query link to conduct parametric sampling, so as to recall historical links that may help to predict the query link.

4 Experiment

4.1 Experimental Setup

Datasets. We evaluate our method on six widely used datasets, UCI [19], Social Evolution [15,19], Enron [11,19], Wikipedia [7], Lastfm [7] and MOOC [7]. UCI is a network between online posts made by students, Social Evolution is a network recording the physical proximity between students. Enron is an email communication network. Wikipedia is a network between wiki pages and human editors. Lastfm is a music listening network between users and songs. MOOC is a network of students and online course content units. Table 2 briefly shows the statistics of the datasets used in our experiments, more details are referred to [9]. For all these datasets, we split them into training, validation, and testing data by chronological order, with the number of links in three datasets scaled to 70%, 10%, and 20% respectively.

Baseline Methods. Various kinds of approaches are chosen as benchmark models. DySAT [11] and Evolve-GCN [8] are snapshot-based methods. Dyrep [15], JODIE [7], APAN [18] and TGN [10] are streaming methods. For the non-streaming methods, we compared with TGAT [21] and CAW-N [19]. All of these models had the best performance in their papers. In addtion, we also selected the memory-based method EdgeBank [9], which predicts the query link by simply checking if (s_q, o_q) have ever shown up in the history. Since EdgeBank has not any parameters to learn, thus can help us to check whether our models have learned something. For all baselines, we follow the parameter settings in their papers.

Table 1. The architecture of EffNet, which is simplified from EfficientNetV2-S [14].

Stage	#Layers	Operator	Channel(in/out)
0	1	Conv(k3*3)	4/64
1	3	Fused-MBConv1(k3*3)	64/64
2	7	Fused-MBConv4(k3*3)	64/64
3	1	Conv(k1*1)	64/1280
4	1	Average Pooling & FC	1280/2

Table 2. Statistics of the datasets used in our experiments.

	UCI	Social Evo.	Enron	Wikepdia	Lastfm	MOOC
Number of Links	59835	66898	125235	157474	250000	411749
Number of Nodes	1899	66	184	9227	1297	7144

4.2   Results

In this part, we report the performance of link prediction, which can be seen in Table 3. By comparing with the memory-based approach Edgebank, we find that there are some models with worse performance, suggesting that these models are actually not learned well for link prediction (similar conclusion with [9]). Results show that we outperform all baselines consistently and significantly on six datasets. We attribute it to that the proposed model is link-aware, thus more

Table 3. AUC performance (in percentage) for link prediction on six datasets. The best results are typeset in bold and the second bests are highlighted with underline. All the results are averaged over 10 runs and values in brackets represent the standard deviations.

Model	UCI	Social Evo.	Enron	Wikipedia	Lastfm	MOOC
EdgeBank	81.2(0.02)	63.2(0.03)	82.8(0.03)	94.3(0.02)	83.2(0.04)	47.1(0.10)
DyREP	69.6(1.50)	70.6(0.02)	67.2(0.44)	93.2(1.26)	70.1(1.11)	63.8(1.88)
JODIE	82.3(0.75)	85.8(0.12)	85.6(1.35)	94.6(0.60)	80.5(1.09)	89.9(0.28)
DySAT	81.0(0.74)	85.5(0.52)	85.0(0.31)	93.2(0.12)	81.3(1.07)	69.1(1.22)
EvolveGCN	81.2(0.32)	83.5(0.78)	83.9(0.54)	93.4(0.13)	82.9(1.02)	71.7(1.78)
TGAT	81.4(0.98)	90.1(0.17)	75.3(0.98)	95.3(0.22)	75.9(1.52)	82.5(1.21)
APAN	90.3(0.72)	83.9(1.20)	83.3(1.62)	98.1(0.09)	85.3(0.52)	88.4(0.45)
TGN	92.2(0.54)	92.8(0.43)	85.5(0.76)	98.5(0.05)	83.2(1.47)	90.6(0.39)
CAW-N	94.3(0.41)	87.2(0.55)	91.5(0.73)	**99.0(0.04)**	88.0(1.27)	85.6(0.72)
TGACN	**96.0(0.13)**	**94.5(0.23)**	**92.6(0.58)**	**99.0(0.04)**	**92.3(0.53)**	**91.9(0.64)**

Table 4. Efficiency comparison between TGACN and CAW-N on the convergence speed. The results report the number of epochs required to get the best performance.

	UCI	Social Evo.	Enron	Wikipedia	Lastfm	MOOC
CAW-N	7	6	16	4	10	20
TGACN	**4**	**3**	**2**	**2**	**4**	**13**

Table 5. Efficiency comparison between TGACN and CAW-N on training speed. The results report the required training time (minutes per epoch).

	UCI	Social Evo.	Enron	Wikipedia	Lastfm	MOOC
CAW-N	30.3	34.9	66.7	83.7	167.3	186.3
TGACN	**14.0**	**17.3**	**66.5**	**82.5**	**152.6**	**77.4**

Table 6. Ablation study on the sampling methods, two kinds of attention and the architecture of CNN.

ablation	UCI	Social Evo.	Enron	Wikipedia	Lastfm	MOOC
remove parametric sampling	96.0	94.5	90.0	98.6	90.3	91.9
remove nearest sampling	94.9	93.6	92.8	98.8	91.3	81.4
remove transduction attention	96.4	94.4	92.4	99.1	87.9	79.8
remove inductive attention	92.0	92.9	90.9	85.7	91.5	77.7
use EfficientNetV2-S	95.6	94.6	92.7	98.8	92.2	91.1
use ResNet18	95.8	94.4	92.4	99.0	92.1	90.3
remove stage 1 and 2 in EffNet	93.6	93.4	92.0	98.9	90.0	86.7

Table 7. Hyperparameter investigation on nearest sampling length N, parametric sampling length P and time decaying coefficient α.

	UCI	Social Evo.	Enron	Wikipedia	Lastfm	MOOC
$N=2$	94.0	92.6	92.4	98.9	91.3	90.7
$N=12$	96.0	94.5	92.6	99.1	92.3	89.9
$N=24$	95.4	94.3	91.7	99.1	92.3	92.5
$P=0$	96.0	94.5	91.7	98.6	89.9	91.9
$P=6$	96.4	92.4	92.2	99.0	92.3	89.5
$P=10$	96.3	92.4	92.6	99.1	92.2	89.6
$\alpha=1$	95.9	94.4	92.4	98.9	92.2	88.9
$\alpha=5$	96.0	94.5	92.6	99.0	92.3	91.9
$\alpha=10$	96.0	94.6	92.3	99.1	92.3	89.2

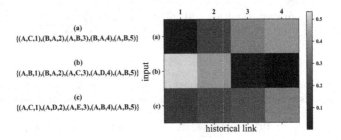

Fig. 4. Illustration of our model's interpretability. On the left of this Figure, we present three ground truth query links and sample four historical links for each (the end of input is the query link). On the right, by CAM, we show the importance of four historical links to the query link for each input.

advantageous for link prediction. CAW-N, a fully inductive method, generally speaking, achieves the second-best performance. However, CAW-N falls down on some datasets, such as MOOC, a possible reason is that the fully inductive CAW-N can not capture the fine-grained patterns, which harms their performance. In contrast, we consider both transductive learning and inductive learning, which remarkably boosts our performance. In addition, compared with previous SOTA model CAW-N, TGACN has faster convergence speed and training speed. As presented in Table 4, we usually get the best performance within a few epochs. Table 5 shows that we also have fewer training time per epoch than CAW-N.

4.3   Ablation Study

Impact of the Sampling Method. We explore this by using only the nearest sampling or parametric sampling. As shown in Table 6, generally speaking, these two kind of removals both see a decline in performance, which verifies the effectiveness of our proposed parametric sampling. **Impact of two kinds of attention.** Table 6 shows that remove transductive or inductive attention both brings about a decline in model performance, especially for MOOC, which demonstrates the importance of learning patterns of different granularity. **Impact of the CNN architecture.** We first replace EffNet with ResNet18 [3] and EfficientNetV2-S [14] respectively. Table 6 shows the robustness of the architecture of CNN, we can see that comparable results are obtained but our EffNet has much fewer parameters. Second, we further simplify EffNet by removing stage 1 and 2, with only a few convolutional layers left. The results show that performance drops but not much. A reasonable conjecture is that the attention values have already encoded high-level information and thus do not require a very deep neural network to extract. This validates the effectiveness of our proposed attention mechanism for link prediction.

4.4 Hyperparameter Investigation

In this part, we investigate how nearest sampling length N, parametric sampling length P and time decaying coefficient α in Eq. 5 affect the model performance. As shown in Table 7, generally speaking, model's performance increases with length N and then stabilizes, similar observation can be made for parametric sampling length P. Table 7 also shows that the proposed model is robust with respect to time decaying coefficient α for most of the datasets.

4.5 Interpretability

In this part, we take the model learned from dataset UCI as an example to conduct a case study about interpretability. Interpretability requires us to get the impact of historical links on the query link. However, CAM only outputs an "image" with shape of $1 \times l \times l$, which marks the importance of each pixel. To translate this importance of pixels to that of links, we sum the values of ith row and column in that "image" as the importance of the ith historical link to the query link. Figure 4 shows three examples for link prediction and illustrates our interpretation for the results of link prediction, i.e., showing the importance of the historical links to the query link. From the heatmap in this Figure, we can see that the query link can directly notice the target links, which verifies the TGACN's effectiveness of being link-aware.

5 Conclusion

In this paper, we propose a model named Temporal Graph Attention Convolution Neural Network (TGACN), which is specially designed for link prediction on temporal graphs. TGACN is as far as we know the first link-aware method and predict the query link from the perspective of pattern recognition rather than learning the node representations. The empirical results demonstrated that the proposed model has achieved the best performance. We believe that our work provides an alternative, effective way for link prediction. In the future, we will explore more opportunities for our proposed method. A promising direction is to apply our method to the link prediction of static graph, we leave this for future work.

References

1. Chen, F., Wang, Y.C., Wang, B., Kuo, C.C.J.: Graph representation learning: a survey. APSIPA Trans. Signal Inf. Process. **9** (2020)
2. Hamilton, W., Ying, Z., Leskovec, J.: Inductive representation learning on large graphs. Adv. Neural Inf. Process. Syst. **30** (2017)
3. He, K., Zhang, X., Ren, S., Sun, J.: Deep residual learning for image recognition. In: Proceedings of the IEEE Conference on Computer Vision and Pattern Recognition, pp. 770–778 (2016)
4. Ji, S., Pan, S., Cambria, E., Marttinen, P., Philip, S.Y.: A survey on knowledge graphs: representation, acquisition, and applications. IEEE Trans. Neural Netw. Learn. Syst. **33**(2), 494–514 (2021)
5. Kazemi, S.M., et al.: Representation learning for dynamic graphs: a survey. J. Mach. Learn. Res. **21**(70), 1–73 (2020)
6. Kipf, T.N., Welling, M.: Semi-supervised classification with graph convolutional networks. arXiv preprint arXiv:1609.02907 (2016)
7. Kumar, S., Zhang, X., Leskovec, J.: Predicting dynamic embedding trajectory in temporal interaction networks. In: Proceedings of the 25th ACM SIGKDD International Conference on Knowledge Discovery & Data Mining (2019)
8. Pareja, A., et al.: EvolveGCN: evolving graph convolutional networks for dynamic graphs. In: AAAI (2020)
9. Poursafaei, F., Huang, S., Pelrine, K., Rabbany, R.: Towards better evaluation for dynamic link prediction. ArXiv abs/2207.10128 (2022)
10. Rossi, E., Chamberlain, B.P., Frasca, F., Eynard, D., Monti, F., Bronstein, M.M.: Temporal graph networks for deep learning on dynamic graphs. ArXiv abs/2006.10637 (2020)
11. Sankar, A., Wu, Y., Gou, L., Zhang, W., Yang, H.: DySAT: deep neural representation learning on dynamic graphs via self-attention networks. In: Proceedings of the 13th International Conference on Web Search and Data Mining (2020)
12. Skarding, J., Gabrys, B., Musial, K.: Foundations and modeling of dynamic networks using dynamic graph neural networks: a survey. IEEE Access **9**, 79143–79168 (2021)
13. Sun, X., Tan, Y., Wu, Q., Wang, J., Shen, C.: New algorithms for counting temporal graph pattern. Symmetry **11**(10), 1188 (2019)
14. Tan, M., Le, Q.: Efficientnetv2: smaller models and faster training. In: International Conference on Machine Learning, pp. 10096–10106. PMLR (2021)
15. Trivedi, R.S., Farajtabar, M., Biswal, P., Zha, H.: DyRep: learning representations over dynamic graphs. In: ICLR (2019)
16. Vaswani, A., et al.: Attention is all you need. ArXiv abs/1706.03762 (2017)
17. Velickovic, P., Cucurull, G., Casanova, A., Romero, A., Lio', P., Bengio, Y.: Graph attention networks. ArXiv abs/1710.10903 (2018)
18. Wang, X., et al.: APAN: asynchronous propagation attention network for real-time temporal graph embedding. In: Proceedings of the 2021 International Conference on Management of Data (2021)
19. Wang, Y., Chang, Y.Y., Liu, Y., Leskovec, J., Li, P.: Inductive representation learning in temporal networks via causal anonymous walks. ArXiv abs/2101.05974 (2021)
20. Wen, Z., Fang, Y.: TREND: temporal event and node dynamics for graph representation learning. In: Proceedings of the ACM Web Conference 2022 (2022)

21. Xu, D., Ruan, C., Körpeoglu, E., Kumar, S., Achan, K.: Inductive representation learning on temporal graphs. ArXiv abs/2002.07962 (2020)
22. Zhou, B., Khosla, A., Lapedriza, À., Oliva, A., Torralba, A.: Learning deep features for discriminative localization. In: 2016 IEEE Conference on Computer Vision and Pattern Recognition (CVPR), pp. 2921–2929 (2016)

Machine Learning Theory

Unsupervised Disentanglement Learning via Dirichlet Variational Autoencoder

Kunxiong Xu[1], Wentao Fan[2,3]([✉]) [iD], and Xin Liu[1]

[1] Department of Computer Science and Technology, Huaqiao University, Quanzhou, China
[2] Department of Computer Science, Beijing Normal University-Hong Kong Baptist University United International College (BNU-HKBU UIC), Zhuhai, China
wentaofan@uic.edu.cn
[3] Guangdong Provincial Key Laboratory of Interdisciplinary Research and Application for Data Science, BNU-HKBU United International College, Zhuhai, China

Abstract. Unsupervised disentanglement learning is the process of discovering factorized variables that include interpretable semantic information and encode separate factors of variations in the data. It is a critical learning problem and has been applied in various tasks and domains. Most of the existing unsupervised disentanglement learning methods are based on the variational autoencoder (VAE) and adopt Gaussian distribution as the prior over the latent space. However, these methods suffer from a collapse of the decoder weights, which leads to degraded disentangling ability, due to the Gaussian prior. To address this issue, in this paper we propose a novel unsupervised disentanglement learning method based on a VAE framework in which the Dirichlet distribution is deployed as the prior over latent space. In our method, the interpretable factorised latent representations can be obtained by balancing the capacity of the latent information channel and the learning of statistically independent latent factors. The effectiveness of our method is validated through experiments on several publicly available datasets.

Keywords: Disentanglement learning · Variational autoencoder · Dirichlet distribution

1 Introduction

The process of discovering factorized variables in the latent space that include interpretable semantic information and encode separate factors of variations in the data is known as unsupervised disentanglement learning [4]. It is an important learning problem that continuously draws significant attention and has been applied in various tasks and domains [6,25,27–29].

In the past, unsupervised disentanglement learning methods based on (variational autoencoder) VAE [19] have shown promising performance [4,13,17]. In these methods, disentanglement can be defined as the latent variables generated

H. Fujita et al. (Eds.): IEA/AIE 2023, LNAI 13925, pp. 341–352, 2023.
https://doi.org/10.1007/978-3-031-36819-6_30

by the encoder-decoder structure, and a single latent variable is only sensitive to a single factor of the data. That is, it is only influenced by a single factor, but not by other factors [2]. It has been shown that, if a learning method can learn to disentangle different factors, it can get better generalization ability from unlabeled data more effectively, so as to better guide downstream tasks [12]. In [13], β-VAE was proposed to construct latent variables as independent Gaussian distributions, and disentangled individual factors of the data with each independent Gaussian distribution. β-tcvae [4] and factor-vae [17] decompose the Kullback-Leibler Divergence (KL) of VAE and only focus on the total correlation item in it, make latent variables more independent by penalizing the total correlation. Similar to other VAE-based methods [7,16,18,23,31], these aforementioned unsupervised disentanglement learning methods assume that the latent variables follow a Gaussian prior. Although effective, these VAE-based methods have a major limit due to their Gaussian assumption for the latent space, which causes these methods suffer from a collapse of the decoder weights and leads to degraded disentangling ability [15], decoder weight collapse is when latent variables to the next decoder have a large number of decoder weights close to zero in the neural network. If these weights are close to zero, the value of the latent variable has a weaker influence on the next decoder.

There is another part that is based on the disentangling research of (Generative adversarial network)GAN [10], such as infoGAN [5], IB-GAN [14], infoGAN-CR [21], VPGAN [30] and PS-SC GAN [32]. These models all tend to get data variation through a single latent variable in a vector space.

In this work, we propose a novel unsupervised disentanglement learning method based on a VAE framework in which the Dirichlet distribution is deployed as the prior over latent space. The motivation of using Dirichlet distributions as the prior of latent variables is that, in comparison with the Gaussian distribution which only allows symmetric mode, the Dirichlet distribution permits multiple symmetric and asymmetric modes, leading to more flexibility in data modeling. Recently, the Dirichlet distribution has shown better performance than the Gaussian for modeling proportional data which naturally appear in various applications. Thus, the latent variables in this framework consist of multiple Dirichlet distributions, each of which is used to disentanglement a single factor of the data. In our method, the interpretable factorised latent representations can be obtained by balancing the capacity of the latent information channel and the learning of statistically independent latent factors. We demonstrate the effectiveness of the proposed unsupervised disentanglement learning method by conducting experiments on several publicly available datasets.

2   Background

VAE is a model based on the encoder-decoder structure. It does not directly estimate the maximum likelihood of the marginal log-likelihood, but trains by optimizing the variational lower bound(ELBO). The VAE takes the standard Gaussian distribution as a prior and makes the encoder generate the parameters

μ and σ of the Gaussian distribution, and then generates the latent variable z through the reparameterization trick $z = \mu + \sigma \epsilon$ (ϵ is a Gaussian distribution random variable), making it in the latent variables generate Gaussian-distributed data for disentanglement. The variational lower bound of VAE is

$$\mathcal{L} = E_{q_\phi(z|x)}[log p_\theta(x|z)] - KL(q_\phi(z|x)||p_\theta(z)), \qquad (1)$$

where E is the expectation and KL is the KL divergence, $log p_\theta(x|z)$ is the generative network(decoder), $q_\phi(z|x)$ is the variational posterior(encoder), θ is the generative parameters, ϕ is the variational parameters, $p_\theta(z)$ is the prior, and $\mathcal{L}$ is the variational lower bound.

β-vae makes some modifications to VAE. By assigning the $KL(q_\phi(z|x)||p_\theta(z))$ of VAE with a heavier penalty (i.e. set $\beta > 1$) to make it demonstrate stronger disentangling ability. Its variational lower bound is shown below:

$$\mathcal{L} = E_{q_\phi(z|x)}[log p_\theta(x|z)] - \beta KL(q_\phi(z|x)||p_\theta(z)), \qquad (2)$$

where β is a constant. Varying β changes the weights of the KL divergence during training, thus encouraging different representations.

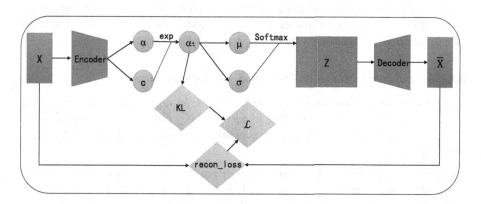

Fig. 1. The overall structure of our proposed model.

3   Unsupervised Learning Disentanglement Based on Dirichlet Distribution

In this section, we propose a model for unsupervised disentanglement based on VAE and the Dirichlet distribution (namely Dir-βkl). The overall structure of the proposed model can be viewed in Fig. 1. The input data passes through the Encoder to obtain temporary parameters α and c, and obtains the parameter α_t of the Dirichlet distribution through $e^{(\alpha \times c)}$, and the parameters μ and σ are obtained by using Laplace approximation, the parameters of the Gaussian distribution are obtained the reparameterization trick obtains an approximate Dirichlet distribution, which is finally input into the Decoder to reconstruct the data. KL is the KL divergence between the model prior and the variational posterior, recon_loss is the reconstruction loss, $\mathcal{L}$ is the total loss.

3.1 Overview of Our Model

In this part, we provide details on how to use the Dirichlet distribution for unsupervised disentanglement learning. The probability density function of the Dirichlet distribution is

$$Dir(X|\alpha) = \frac{\Gamma(\alpha_0)}{\prod_{d=1}^{D} \Gamma(\alpha_d)} \prod_{d=1}^{D} X_d^{\alpha_d-1}, \tag{3}$$

where $0 \le X_d \le 1$, $\sum_{d=1}^{D} X_d = 1$, Γ denotes the gamma function, D denotes dimensionality of the Dirichlet distribution and $D \ge 2$, α denotes the parameter of the Dirichlet distribution and $\alpha_d \ge 0$, $\alpha_0 = \sum_{d=1}^{D} \alpha_d$.

Given the input data, we obtain parameters α and c through the encoder, where the activation function Tanh is adopted for obtaining α, and Softplus is used to obtain c. Then, we obtain the parameter α_t of the Dirichlet distribution through $e^{(\alpha \times c)}$. The parameters μ and σ can be inferred by adopting the Laplace approximation method to the parameter α_t. Then, we apply the reparameterization trick and use the Softmax function on the reparameterized result to obtain an approximate Dirichlet representation z, which is used to generate the reconstructed data $\bar{X}$ through the decoder. In our model, we adopt the cross-entropy loss function with sigmoid as the reconstruction loss of our model.

3.2 Reparameterization Trick and KL Divergence

Here, we introduce the reparameterization trick in our method, as well as the regularization term during training in terms of KL divergence. In our case, we use the Laplace approximation as the reparameterization trick for the Dirichlet distribution.

Reparameterization via Laplace Approximation. Inspired by [11], we apply the reparameterization through Laplace approximation for the Dirichlet distribution to obtain parameters μ and σ as

$$\mu_d = \log \alpha_d - \frac{1}{D} \sum_{d=1}^{D} \log \alpha_d, \tag{4}$$

$$\sigma_d = \frac{1}{\alpha_d}(1 - \frac{2}{D}) + \frac{1}{D^2} \sum_{d=1}^{D} \frac{1}{\alpha_d}, \tag{5}$$

where D denotes the dimensionality of the Dirichlet distribution. Then, the result is approximated by the Softmax function: $softmax(\mu + \varepsilon\sigma) = Dirichlet(\alpha)$, where ϵ is a random Gaussian sample.

Compared with other reparameterization tricks such as Inverse CDF Approximation [15], Generalized Reparameterization Gradients [26], Rejection Sampling Variational Inference (RSVI) [24] and Implicit Reparameterization Gradients [9], the Laplace approximation trick in our model can achieve fast training, better disentangling effect, and no model collapse while training.

KL Divergence. Motivated by [8], we can define the KL divergence between two Dirichlet distributions as

$$kl(Dir(\alpha_1)\|Dir(\alpha_2)) = \log \Gamma(\sum_{d=1}^{D} \alpha_{1,d}) - \log \Gamma(\sum_{d=1}^{D} \alpha_{2,d}) - \sum_{d=1}^{D} \log \Gamma(\alpha_{1,d})$$

$$+ \sum_{d=1}^{D} log\Gamma(\alpha_{2,d}) + \sum_{d=1}^{D}(\alpha_{1,d} - \alpha_{2,d})(\Psi(\alpha_{1,d}) - \Psi(\sum_{j=1}^{D} \alpha_{1,j})), \tag{6}$$

where Γ denotes the gamma function and Ψ denotes the digamma function.

Algorithm 1. The training process of our model

Data: Random minibatch of Ndatapoints $\{X_k\}_{k=1}^{N}$
1: **for all** $k \in \{1,...,N\}$ **do**
2:   $\alpha, c = Encoder(X_k)$
3:   $\alpha_t = e^{\alpha \times c}$
4:   $\mu_d = log\alpha_{t,d} - \frac{1}{D}\sum_{d=1}^{D} \log \alpha_{t,d}$
   $\sigma_d = \frac{1}{\alpha_{t,d}}(1 - \frac{2}{D}) + \frac{1}{D^2}\sum_{d=1}^{D} \frac{1}{\alpha_{t,d}}$
5:   $z = softmax(\mu_d + \sigma_d\epsilon)$,
   where ϵ is a Gaussian random sample
6:   $\bar{X} = Decoder(z)$
7:   compute $reconstrcution\_loss$
8:   compute $kl(Dir(\alpha_t)\|Dir(\frac{1}{D}))$
9:   $\mathcal{L} = reconstrcution\_loss + kl(Dir(\alpha_t)\|Dir(\frac{1}{D}))$
10:   update Encoder and Decoder to maximize $\mathcal{L}$
11: **end for**

Following [20], we set the parameter of the Dirichlet prior to $1/D$, so the KL divergence can be simplified as

$$kl(Dir(\alpha_1)\|Dir(\frac{1}{D})) = \log \Gamma(\sum_{d=1}^{D} \alpha_{1,d}) - \sum_{d=1}^{D} log\Gamma(\alpha_{1,d})$$

$$+ \sum_{d=1}^{D} log\Gamma(\frac{1}{D}) + \sum_{d=1}^{D} \alpha_{1,d}\Psi(\alpha_{1,d})$$

$$- \sum_{d=1}^{D} \alpha_{1,d}\Psi(\sum_{j=1}^{D} \alpha_{1,j})$$

$$- \frac{1}{D}\sum_{d=1}^{D}(\Psi(\alpha_{1,d}) - \Psi(\sum_{j=1}^{D} \alpha_{1,j})). \tag{7}$$

Lastly, the variational lower bound of our model can be obtained by

$$\mathcal{L}_d = E_{q\phi(z|x)}[logp_\theta(x|z)] - \beta(log\Gamma(\sum_{d=1}^{D}\alpha_{1,d})$$

$$- \sum_{d=1}^{D}log\Gamma(\alpha_{1,d}) + \sum_{d=1}^{D}log\Gamma(\frac{1}{D})$$

$$+ \sum_{d=1}^{D}\alpha_{1,d}\Psi(\alpha_{1,d}) - \sum_{d=1}^{D}\alpha_{1,d}\Psi(\sum_{j=1}^{D}\alpha_{1,j})$$

$$- \frac{1}{D}\sum_{d=1}^{D}(\Psi(\alpha_{1,d}) - \Psi(\sum_{j=1}^{D}\alpha_{1,j}))).$$

$$(8)$$

The training process of our model is shown in Algorithm 1.

Table 1. Detailed information of each dataset.

Dataset	Ground truth factors	sample size
dsprites	shape(3), scale(6), rotation(40), posX(32), posY(32)	737280
3dshapes	floor hue(10), wall hue(10), object hue(10), scale(8), shape(4), orientation(15)	480000
chair	–	86366

4   Experimental Results

In this section, we validate the effectiveness of the proposed method by conducting experiments and comparing it with three state-of-the-art unsupervised disentanglement learning methods that are based on VAE.

4.1   Datasets and Experimental Settings

We adopt three datasets for testing the performance of our method: 3dshapes [3], dsprites [22] and chair [1]. The resolutions of the three datasets are all 64×64, of which the dsprites dataset is one-channel, and the 3dshapes and chair dataset are three-channel data. We show the ground truth factors and sample size of each dataset in Table 1. The values in the parentheses is the number of quantized values for each factor.

In our experiments, our proposed model is trained using the Adam optimizer with an epoch of 50, a learning rate of 1e-3, and batch normalization (BN) is adopted to prevent overfitting. For the 3dshapes and chair dataset, the encoder we used is a 5-layer convolutional neural network with 4×4 kernels, stride 2, padding 1, and the number of channels 3-32-32-64-64-512. The decoder we used is 5 transposed convolutional neural networks with opposite number of channels. For the dsprites dataset, we use a linear neural network of 4096-1200-1200 for the encoder and a linear neural network of 1200-1200-4096 for the decoder.

Table 2. Unsupervised disentanglement comparison on the 3dshapes dataset.

Model	3dshapes
lie-group vae [31]	$0.86_{\pm0.56}$
β-vae [13]	$0.52_{\pm0.21}$
β-tcvae [4]	$0.96_{\pm0.43}$
ours(Dir-βkl,$\beta = 1$)	$0.87_{\pm0.26}$
ours(Dir-βkl,$\beta = 5$)	$\mathbf{0.98}_{\pm0.45}$

4.2 Disentangled Comparison

We adopt the Mutual Information Gap (MIG) [4] metric to show the performance of our model, which measures the gap between the latent variable with the most information and the one with the second most information about the factor. Thus, the higher the MIG score, the better disentanglement performance of the model. We compare our model with three state-of-the-art unsupervised disentanglement learning methods based on VAE: lie-group vae [31], β-vae [13] and β-tcvae [4]. The results obtained by different methods are shown in Table 2 on the 3dshapes dataset. As shown in this table, our method is able to outperform other methods in terms of the highest MIG scores. These results demonstrate the advantages of our method. We also show the experimental results for adjusting β in the lower part of Table 2, and it can be clearly seen that when $\beta = 5$, the model has a higher MIG score, so the parameter β in Eq. 8 is necessary.

4.3 Disentangled Comparison of Different Dimension Numbers

We also set the number of dimensions of the Dirichlet distribution as a hyperparameter for experiments to test the MIG score of our model under different numbers of dimensions. According to Fig. 2, we can clearly see that as the number of dimensions of our model increases, the MIG score generally shows a trend of first increasing and then decreasing. When $\beta = 5$, the model achieves the maximum MIG score at dim $= 4$, and when $\beta = 1$, the model achieves the maximum MIG score at dim $= 18$.

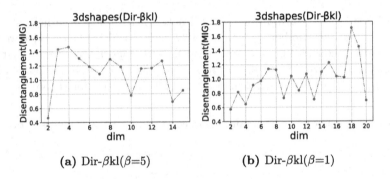

Fig. 2. The MIG scores with different dimensions on the 3dshapes dataset.

Although the MIG score of the model increases with increasing dimensionality, this is not entirely favorable. We control $\beta = 5$, and reconstruct the latent variables of the two models with dim = 3 and dim = 4 into images. According to Fig. 3, we can see that when dim=3 is selected, the model can disentanglement 5 different factors. When dim = 4 is selected, the model only has three latent variables to disentanglement factors, and there are different factor embeddings the same latent variable. That is, the increase in the number of dimensions is usually accompanied by multiple factors embedded in the same latent variable, which rarely or does not appear when the number of dimensions is low. Therefore, all our experimental results take both into account. For example, in Sect. 4.2, when $\beta = 5$, we use the dim = 3 model for disentangling comparison, and when $\beta = 1$, we use the dim = 5 model for disentangling Comparison.

4.4   Qualitative Comparison

We compare the qualitative performance of our method with β-tcvae by showing the disentangled latent factors. We conduct multiple random sampling and then perform softmax on a single latent variable to find the factors disentangled from this latent variable. In other case, we traverse five numbers, from left to right to −2, −1, 0, 1 and 2, respectively.

Figure 4 demonstrates the disentangling results on the 3dshapes dataset. As shown in this figure, β-tcvae repeatedly disentanglements the same factors. In contrast, the proposed Dir-βkl model only disentangles different factors. Therefore, the disentanglement performance of our model is better. Figure 5 shows the disentangling results on the dsprites dataset. As shown in this figure, β-tcvae can only disentangle four factors, while our model (Dir-βkl) is able to disentangle up to five factors. This results verifies the merit of using VAE with a Dirichlet prior for disentangling latent factors.

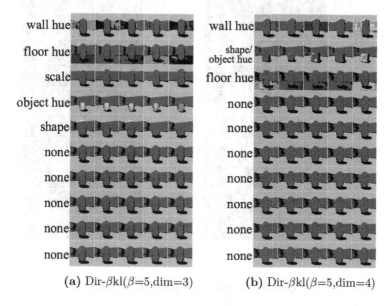

(a) Dir-βkl(β=5,dim=3)   (b) Dir-βkl(β=5,dim=4)

Fig. 3. Latent traversals for our models with different numbers of dimensions.

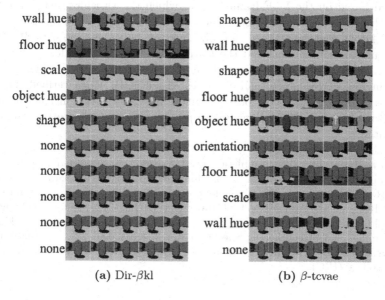

(a) Dir-βkl   (b) β-tcvae

Fig. 4. Latent traversals of the two models on the 3dshapes dataset.

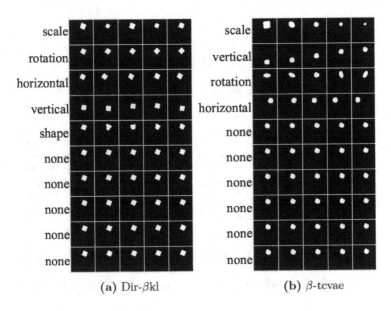

(a) Dir-βkl	(b) β-tcvae

Fig. 5. Latent traversals of the two models on the dsprites dataset.

5   Conclusion

In this paper, a novel unsupervised disentanglement learning method was propoed based on the VAE framework in which the Dirichlet distribution was adopted as the prior over latent space. In our method, the interpretable factorised latent representations were obtained by balancing the capacity of the latent information channel and the learning of statistically independent latent factors. Experimental results showed that the proposed method achieved better disentangling performance than other tested methods, which verified the effectiveness of our method. One possible future direction is to consider the latent space with hierarchical relationships to provide more representative latent representations.

Acknowledgements. The completion of this work was supported in part by the National Natural Science Foundation of China (62276106), the UIC Start-up Research Fund (UICR0700056-23), the Guangdong Provincial Key Laboratory of Interdisciplinary Research and Application for Data Science (2022B1212010006), the Guangdong Higher Education Upgrading Plan (2021–2025) of "Rushing to the Top, Making Up Shortcomings and Strengthening Special Features" (R0400001-22), and the Artificial Intelligence and Data Science Research Hub (AIRH) of BNU-HKBU United International College (UIC).

References

1. Aubry, M., Maturana, D., Efros, A.A., Russell, B.C., Sivic, J.: Seeing 3D chairs: exemplar part-based 2D–3D alignment using a large dataset of cad models. In: Proceedings of the IEEE Conference on Computer Vision and Pattern Recognition, pp. 3762–3769 (2014)
2. Bengio, Y., Courville, A., Vincent, P.: Representation learning: a review and new perspectives. IEEE Trans. Pattern Anal. Mach. Intell. **35**(8), 1798–1828 (2013)
3. Burgess, C., Kim, H.: 3D shapes dataset (2018). https://github.com/deepmind/3dshapes-dataset/
4. Chen, R.T., Li, X., Grosse, R.B., Duvenaud, D.K.: Isolating sources of disentanglement in variational autoencoders. Adv. Neural Inf. Process. Syst. **31** (2018)
5. Chen, X., Duan, Y., Houthooft, R., Schulman, J., Sutskever, I., Abbeel, P.: Infogan: interpretable representation learning by information maximizing generative adversarial nets. Adv. Neural Inf. Process. Syst. **29** (2016)
6. Chen, X., et al.: Unpaired deep image dehazing using contrastive disentanglement learning. In: Avidan, S., Brostow, G., Cisse, M., Farinella, G.M., Hassner, T. (eds.) Computer Vision – ECCV 2022. ECCV 2022. LNCS, vol. 13677, pp. 632–648. Springer, Cham (2022). https://doi.org/10.1007/978-3-031-19790-1_38
7. Ding, Z., et al.: Guided variational autoencoder for disentanglement learning. In: Proceedings of the IEEE/CVF Conference on Computer Vision and Pattern Recognition, pp. 7920–7929 (2020)
8. Epaillard, E., Bouguila, N.: Data-free metrics for Dirichlet and generalized Dirichlet mixture-based HMMs-a practical study. Pattern Recogn. **85**, 207–219 (2019)
9. Figurnov, M., Mohamed, S., Mnih, A.: Implicit reparameterization gradients. Adv. Neural Inf. Process. Syst. **31** (2018)
10. Goodfellow, I., et al.: Generative adversarial networks. Commun. ACM **63**(11), 139–144 (2020)
11. Hennig, P., Stern, D., Herbrich, R., Graepel, T.: Kernel topic models. In: Artificial Intelligence and Statistics, pp. 511–519. PMLR (2012)
12. Higgins, I., et al.: Early visual concept learning with unsupervised deep learning. arXiv preprint arXiv:1606.05579 (2016)
13. Higgins, I., et al.: Beta-VAE: learning basic visual concepts with a constrained variational framework. In: International Conference on Learning Representations (2017)
14. Jeon, I., Lee, W., Pyeon, M., Kim, G.: IB-GAN: disentangled representation learning with information bottleneck generative adversarial networks. In: Proceedings of the AAAI Conference on Artificial Intelligence, vol. 35, pp. 7926–7934 (2021)
15. Joo, W., Lee, W., Park, S., Moon, I.C.: Dirichlet variational autoencoder. Pattern Recogn. **107**, 107514 (2020)
16. Khemakhem, I., Kingma, D., Monti, R., Hyvarinen, A.: Variational autoencoders and nonlinear ICA: a unifying framework. In: International Conference on Artificial Intelligence and Statistics, pp. 2207–2217. PMLR (2020)
17. Kim, H., Mnih, A.: Disentangling by factorising. In: International Conference on Machine Learning, pp. 2649–2658. PMLR (2018)
18. Kim, M., Wang, Y., Sahu, P., Pavlovic, V.: Relevance factor VAE: learning and identifying disentangled factors. arXiv preprint arXiv:1902.01568 (2019)
19. Kingma, D.P., Welling, M.: Auto-encoding variational bayes. arXiv preprint arXiv:1312.6114 (2013)

20. Kurihara, K., Welling, M., Teh, Y.W.: Collapsed variational dirichlet process mixture models. In: IJCAI, vol. 7, pp. 2796–2801 (2007)
21. Lin, Z., Thekumparampil, K.K., Fanti, G., Oh, S.: InfoGAN-CR: disentangling generative adversarial networks with contrastive regularizers, p. 60 (2019). arXiv preprint arXiv:1906.06034
22. Matthey, L., Higgins, I., Hassabis, D., Lerchner, A.: dSprites: disentanglement testing sprites dataset (2017). https://github.com/deepmind/dsprites-dataset/
23. Mita, G., Filippone, M., Michiardi, P.: An identifiable double VAE for disentangled representations. In: International Conference on Machine Learning, pp. 7769–7779. PMLR (2021)
24. Naesseth, C., Ruiz, F., Linderman, S., Blei, D.: Reparameterization gradients through acceptance-rejection sampling algorithms. In: Artificial Intelligence and Statistics, pp. 489–498. PMLR (2017)
25. Peri, R., Parthasarathy, S., Bradshaw, C., Sundaram, S.: Disentanglement for audio-visual emotion recognition using multitask setup. In: ICASSP 2021–2021 IEEE International Conference on Acoustics, Speech and Signal Processing (ICASSP), pp. 6344–6348. IEEE (2021)
26. Ruiz, F.R., Aueb, T.R., Blei, D., et al.: The generalized reparameterization gradient. Adv. Neural Inf. Process. Syst. **29** (2016)
27. Wang, C.: Lip movements information disentanglement for lip sync. arXiv preprint arXiv:2202.06198 (2022)
28. Wang, Z., et al.: Unsupervised feature disentanglement for video retrieval in minimally invasive surgery. Med. Image Anal. **75**, 102296 (2022)
29. Yang, K., Zhou, T., Zhang, Y., Tian, X., Tao, D.: Class-disentanglement and applications in adversarial detection and defense. Adv. Neural. Inf. Process. Syst. **34**, 16051–16063 (2021)
30. Zhu, X., Xu, C., Tao, D.: Learning disentangled representations with latent variation predictability. In: Vedaldi, A., Bischof, H., Brox, T., Frahm, J.-M. (eds.) ECCV 2020. LNCS, vol. 12355, pp. 684–700. Springer, Cham (2020). https://doi.org/10.1007/978-3-030-58607-2_40
31. Zhu, X., Xu, C., Tao, D.: Commutative lie group VAE for disentanglement learning. In: International Conference on Machine Learning, pp. 12924–12934. PMLR (2021)
32. Zhu, X., Xu, C., Tao, D.: Where and what? Examining interpretable disentangled representations. In: Proceedings of the IEEE/CVF Conference on Computer Vision and Pattern Recognition, pp. 5861–5870 (2021)

Spiking Generative Networks in Lifelong Learning Environment

Jie Zhang[1], Wentao Fan[2,3]($\boxtimes$) (iD), and Xin Liu[1]

[1] Department of Computer Science and Technology, Huaqiao University,
Quanzhou, China
[2] Department of Computer Science, Beijing Normal University-Hong Kong Baptist
University United International College (BNU-HKBU UIC), Zhuhai, China
wentaofan@uic.edu.cn
[3] Guangdong Provincial Key Laboratory of Interdisciplinary Research
and Application for Data Science, BNU-HKBU United International College,
Zhuhai, China

Abstract. Spiking neural networks (SNNs) have gained popularity due
to their ability to operate at ultra-high speed and ultra-low power consumption, making them suitable for energy-efficient applications in various fields. However, current SNNs lack the capability to generate high-
quality images, and SNN-based generative models often confront the
issue of catastrophic forgetting when dealing with sequential probabilistic representations of multiple datasets. In this work, we propose a novel
SNN-based generative framework called Lifelong-SGN, which consists of
three components: Teacher, Student, and Assistant. To overcome the
issue of catastrophic forgetting, we utilize the Teacher module based on
Generative Adversarial Network (GAN), to store and replay probabilistic representations from previously learned knowledge. For the Student
module, we utilize an SNN-based VAE implementation to learn probabilistic representations from both the output obtained by the Teacher
module and the new dataset. Moreover, we introduce the Discriminator
module as an Assistant to train the SNN-based generative model using
adversarial training principles, which helps generate high-quality images.
Our experiments on Lifelong-SGN demonstrate its effectiveness in image
classification and generation in lifelong learning environment.

Keywords: Spiking neural networks · Lifelong learning · Image
generation · Image classification

1 Introduction

The relentless pursuit of accuracy has spurred the advancement of machine
learning and artificial intelligence systems, resulting in the proliferation of various Artificial neural networks (ANNs) with heterogeneous architectures that
have demonstrated remarkable success in domains such as computer vision and
natural language processing [14,18]. However, the execution of these resource-
intensive pattern recognition algorithms entails substantial energy consumption, presenting a formidable challenge for devices with limited computational

H. Fujita et al. (Eds.): IEA/AIE 2023, LNAI 13925, pp. 353–364, 2023.
https://doi.org/10.1007/978-3-031-36819-6_31

resources. In contrast, Spiking Neural Networks (SNNs) - the third generation of neural networks - offer a promising solution by virtue of their binary event-driven nature and neuron dynamics. SNNs can be implemented on neuromorphic hardware devices [3,6], offering ultra-high-speed performance at ultra-low power consumption, rendering them a formidable candidate for energy-efficient applications in diverse domains [12].

Many studies have shown that Spiking Neural Networks (SNNs) surpass traditional Artificial neural networks (ANNs) in both information representation and computational efficiency [2]. As a result, SNNs are expected to have a wide range of applications, including running generative models on edge devices to produce high-quality images. While image generation models have been thoroughly explored in ANNs and can generate superior images, recent pioneering works such as Spiking-GAN [11] and FSVAE [9] demonstrate the potential of generating images entirely using SNNs. Nevertheless, the performance of SNN-based generative models is substantially inferior to that of ANN-based models [10,17] owing to the lack of a suitable training paradigm.

Moreover, deep generative models often experience the challenge of catastrophic forgetting [5] when working with sequential probabilistic representations from multiple databases. This occurs because deep learning models that are initially trained on a specific database tend to lose their prior knowledge when being retrained on a new dataset for a different task. While there have been various attempts to mitigate this issue in ANN-based generative models [15,19], there currently does not exist a framework for addressing catastrophic forgetting in SNNs. In this study, we propose a comprehensive framework for spiking generative models, known as Lifelong-SGN, which not only produces high-quality images but also addresses the issue of catastrophic forgetting when processing sequential probabilistic representations from multiple databases. The model utilizes fully-integrated SNNs for both image generation and classification tasks, and its design enables future implementation on neuromorphic edge devices, which is expected to bring significant improvements in terms of speed and energy efficiency. Our key contributions are summarized as follows:

- We explore the utilization of SNNs for lifelong learning, which holds great promise in the realm of edge Artificial Intelligence.
- We propose a comprehensive SNN generation framework, named LifeLong-SGN, which integrates a Teacher module, a Student module, and an Assistant module to effectively tackle the issue of catastrophic forgetting in learning sequential probabilistic representations from multiple datasets.
- We conduct evaluations on the performance of our proposed Lifelong-SGN in both image generation and classification tasks. Furthermore, we extend the model to a semi-supervised setting. Our experimental results demonstrate the robustness and effectiveness of our proposed model.

2 Lifelong Spking Generative Networks

2.1 Overview of Our Model

In the field of deep learning, generative models, including those based on SNNs, learn a single probability distribution and utilize maximum marginal likelihood to model the underlying data. However, in practical applications, the model often needs to learn a series of data tasks, each represented by a unique probability distribution. Conventional models can only retain knowledge from the current task and are unable to preserve previously acquired knowledge while adapting to newly arrived tasks. To address this challenge, we propose a lifelong learning model that combines both ANN and SNN to facilitate the adaptation of SNNs to the context of lifelong learning, allowing the model to preserve all previously learned knowledge while still being able to perform the learning of newly arrived tasks. Figure 1 illustrates the proposed Spiking Generative Network framework, which is capable of not only learning a single dataset to generate high-quality images but also mitigating catastrophic forgetting when presented with multiple sequential datasets. The framework comprises three key components: a Teacher, a Student, and an Assistant. The Teacher module utilizes a generative model with strong generalization performance for images, and is fulfilled with Wasserstein GAN (WGAN) [7] in this work. The role of the Teacher module is to preserve and replay prior knowledge. The Student module is composed of a SNN-based VAE that includes three encoders and one decoder, which can be deployed on edge devices for performing tasks once learning is completed. The Assistant module, which is an ANN-based discriminator, trains the SNN model via adversarial training, leading to greatly improved image generation quality by the SNN.

2.2 The Teacher Module

The Teacher module is designed to store and replay past knowledge. This module can be implemented with any generative model that is robust to image information learning, such as the ANN-based WGAN. The objective function of WGAN is given by:

$$\min_{G} \max_{D} E_{x_r \sim p_{real}}[D(x_r)] - E_{z \sim p_\varepsilon}[D(G(z))]$$
$$+ \lambda E_{\tilde{x} \sim p_{\tilde{x}}}[((\| \nabla_{\tilde{x}} D(\tilde{x}) \|_2 - 1)^2] \tag{1}$$

where G and D are the generator and discriminator, respectively. p_{real} is the probability distribution of the real image, z is a random noise vector sampled from p_ε, which is generally uses the standard Gaussian distribution. G generates the fake image based on z, and the discriminator is trained to minimize the probability distribution of the real image and the fake image. $\tilde{x}$ is the interpolated result by $\tilde{x} = \eta x_r + (1 - \eta)G(z)$ where η is a random value provided by a uniform distribution. The last term is gradient penalty, used to avoid mode collapse.

To further explain the illustration, we give the following definition, where we define the probability of the data for K tasks as $p(x^1), p(x^2), ..., p(x^K)$, the

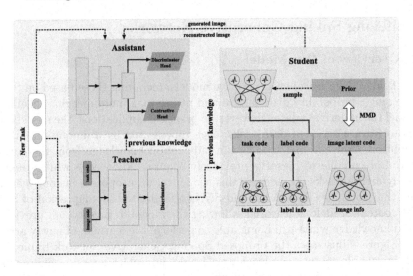

Fig. 1. Overview of the model.

current learning task probability definition $p(x^k)$ and all previous past knowledge $p(x^{1\sim k-1})$, and we train the Teacher module by generative replay mechanism since the Teacher itself has strong learning capability. So the objective function of the Teacher module is as follows:

$$\min_{G} \max_{D} E_{x\sim p(\hat{x}_{1:k-1},x_k)}[D(x)] - E_{\hat{x}\sim G(z,\varsigma)}[D(\hat{x}_k)]$$
$$+ \lambda E_{\tilde{x}\sim p_{\tilde{x}}}[(\|\nabla_{\tilde{x}}D(\tilde{x})\|_2 - 1)^2] \quad (2)$$

where x is sample from $p(\hat{x}_{1:k-1})$ and $p(x_k)$, the ratio is dependent on the importance of the new task, and in our experiments we set it to 0.5. The input to G consists of a continuous random variable z which is used to represent the image information, and the discrete domain variable ς, which will encode the specific task information characteristic obtained during the lifelong learning process.

2.3   The Student Module

For the design of the student module, we consider two crucial keys: 1) the network is composed using SNNs; 2)the model with inference mechanisms. Therefore, we use the SNN-based VAE(Variational Autoencoder) model FSVAE [9], which integrates the concept of VRNN into SNN. For the problem that floating point computation is not possible in SNN, FSVAE uses autoregressive SNN to construct prior and posterior. The latent variables are sampled from the output of the autoregressive SNN through a Bernoulli process, so that the sampling process does not require floating-point computation and can be implemented on neuromorphic devices. In addition, the model does not use the traditional KL as a distribution metric distance but uses MMD (Maximum Mean Discrepancy) because it is considered more suitable in the SNN [1], so the Evidence Lower Bound (ELBO) of SNN-based VAE as:

$$\mathcal{L}_{ELBO}(\theta, \phi; x) = - E_{z_{1:T} \sim q_\phi(z_{1:T}|x_{1:T})}[\log(p_\theta(x_{1:T}|z_{1:T}))] \\ + MMD[q_\phi(z_{1:T}|x_{1:T})\|p(z_{1:T})], \tag{3}$$

where T indicates time step, in our experiments, we set $T = 16$, p denotes the prior which is composed of SNN and can be used for binary time series output. $q_\phi(z_{1:T}|x_{1:T})$ is a SNN-based encoder and $p_\theta(x_{1:T}|z_{1:T})$ is a SNN-based decoder.

To encourage the encoders to learn a meaningful representation of the data, we introduce two additional encoders for learning tasks information and categories information. In the subsequent sections, for simplicity, variables with time in SNNs such as $x_{1:T}$ or $z_{1:T}$ are simplified to x and z, leading to the following lose functions:

$$\mathcal{L}_{Stu}^{cate} = E_{x \sim p(\hat{x}_{1:k-1}, x_k), y \sim p(\hat{y}_{1:k-1}, y_k)} ce(E_1(x), y) \tag{4}$$

$$\mathcal{L}_{Stu}^{task} = E_{x \sim p(\hat{x}_{1:k-1}, x_k), \varsigma \sim p(\varsigma)} ce(E_2(x), \varsigma) \tag{5}$$

where E_1, E_2 are the categories and tasks information encoders, respectively, x is sampled in a certain ratio from the Teacher module $p(\hat{x}_{1:k-1})$, and the new task $p(x_k)$, which we set equal ratio in our experiments, $p(\hat{y}_{1:k-1}, y_k)$ is the distribution of the dataset labels, $\hat{x}_{1:k-1}$ from the Teacher module is passed through E_1 to obtain $\hat{y}_{1:k-1}$, $p(\varsigma)$ is the distribution of the tasks, and in our experiments we set ς to the one-hot vector, and ce is the cross-entropy loss.

In practice, there are often incomplete data, such as some of the labels are missing, so we provide a more general objective function for the Student module, which consists of four terms $\mathcal{L}_{Stu}^1$, $\mathcal{L}_{Stu}^2$, $\mathcal{L}_{Stu}^{cate}$ and $\mathcal{L}_{Stu}^{task}$. $\mathcal{L}_{Stu}^1$ is the case where the label is considered to exist, $\mathcal{L}_{Stu}^2$ describes the objective function when the label is missing, when the label training is inferred by the category encoder, and two remaining items are the cross-entropy losses of the category and the task

$$\mathcal{L}_{Stu} = \alpha_1 \mathcal{L}_{Stu}^1 + \alpha_2 \mathcal{L}_{Stu}^2 + \alpha_3 \mathcal{L}_{Stu}^{cate} + \alpha_4 \mathcal{L}_{Stu}^{task} \tag{6}$$

where α_1 and α_2 are to control the magnitude of unsupervised or supervised, and α_3 and α_4 are used to control the encoder cross-entropy loss.

The detailed equations for $\mathcal{L}_{Stu}^1$ and $\mathcal{L}_{Stu}^2$ are given:

$$\mathcal{L}_{Stu}^1 = - E_{z, \varsigma \sim q_\phi(z, \varsigma|x), y \sim p(y)}[\log(p_\theta(x \mid z, y, \varsigma))] \\ + MMD[q_\phi(z \mid x) \| p(z)] \tag{7}$$

where we consider the learning process with labeled data, x is sampled from $p(\hat{x}_{1:k-1}, x_k)$, y is category labels from $p(y)$, which encourage the separation of category attributes from other variables and ς is inferred by the encoder, for the case of missing labels, the main learning objective of the Student model is given below:

$$\mathcal{L}_{Stu}^2 = - E_{z, y, \varsigma \sim q_\phi(z, y, \varsigma|x)}[\log(p_\theta(x \mid z, y, \varsigma))] \\ + MMD[q_\phi(z \mid x) \| p(z)] \tag{8}$$

where y is obtained by inferring from the encoder.

2.4   The Assistant Module

SNNs often perform poorly for image learning, so we use the ANN-based discriminator as an Assistant module to help the Student module learn past knowledge passed on by the Teacher and new data from the new task. Several research works [8,21] have applied the concept of contrastive learning to generative models, and inspired by this we use contrastive feature reconstruction loss as the reconstruction error, so $\mathcal{L}^1_{Stu}$ and $\mathcal{L}^2_{Stu}$ are rewritten as

$$\mathcal{L}^1_{Stu} = - E_{z,\varsigma \sim q_\phi(z,\varsigma|x), y \sim p(y)}[\log \frac{e^{critic(x_i, f_\theta(z,y,\varsigma))}}{\sum_{j=1}^n e^{critic(x_j, f_\theta(z,y,\varsigma))}}]$$
$$+ MMD[q_\phi(z \mid x) \parallel p(z)] \qquad (9)$$

$$\mathcal{L}^2_{Stu} = - E_{z,y,\varsigma \sim q_\phi(z,y,\varsigma|x)}[\log \frac{e^{critic(x_i, f_\theta(z,y,\varsigma))}}{\sum_{j=1}^n e^{critic(x_j, f_\theta(z,y,\varsigma))}}]$$
$$+ MMD[q_\phi(z \mid x) \parallel p(z)] \qquad (10)$$

where i represents the index for training samples and $\{x_j\}$ denotes the set of positive and negative samples, f_θ is the SNN-based decoder parameterized by θ and D_Φ indicates the discriminator parameterized by Φ. The critic function $critic(x, y)$ measures the compatibility between samples x and y using cosine similarity.

We extract the features by the discriminator to calculate the contrastive loss.

$$critic(x, y) = \frac{D_\Phi(x)^T D_\Phi(y)}{||D_\Phi(x)||_2 ||D_\Phi(y)||_2}, \qquad (11)$$

Then the adversarial loss of the Assistant module is given as follows

$$\mathcal{L}_{Ass}(\theta, \phi, D_\Phi; x) = \log D_\Phi(x_{previous}) + \log D_\Phi(x_{new})$$
$$+ E_{z \sim p(z)} \log(1 - D_\Phi(f_\theta(z_{p,1:T})))$$
$$+ E_{z \sim q_\phi(z|x)} \log(1 - D_\Phi(f_\theta(z_{1:T}))), \qquad (12)$$

where $x_{previous}$ is from Teacher, x_{new} is from latest task, $f_\theta(z_p)$ is obtained by decoding the spikng signal sampled from prior and $f_\theta(z)$ is reconstructed image. Finally, the total loss for the proposed Lifelong-SGN is

$$\mathcal{L}_{total} = \mathcal{L}_{Tea} + \mathcal{L}_{Stu} + \beta \mathcal{L}_{Ass} \qquad (13)$$

3   Experimental Results

In this section, we assess the performance of our proposed Lifelong-SGN on three publicly available datasets: MNIST [4], Fashion-MNIST [20], and SVHN [13]. Our evaluation includes assessing the image generation and classification capabilities of our model on multiple datasets. We also explore the effectiveness of our model in a semi-supervised lifelong learning setting. Finally, we compare our proposed SNN-based Lifelong-SGN model with ANN-based lifelong learning models, highlighting the benefits of using SNNs in terms of model performance and computational efficiency. In our experiments, we set the number of timesteps to 16. The model was trained for 50 epochs using a learning rate of 0.001. The MNIST and Fashion-MNIST datasets consisted of 60,000 training images and 10,000 testing images, while the SVHN dataset consisted of 73,257 training images and 26,032 testing images. In the lifelong learning setting, each task was trained for 50 epochs. When gray images were trained alongside color images, all images were resized to $32 \times 32 \times 3$ pixels.

3.1   Image Classification and Image Generation in Lifelong Learning

In this subsection, we evaluate the image generation and classification performance of Lifelong-SGN. The process of the model learning MNIST first and then Fashion MNIST dataset is referred to as M-F. For the hyperparameters setting, we set $\alpha_1, \alpha_3, \alpha_4$ all equal to 0, $\alpha_2 = 1$ and $\beta = 1$ during the image generation task and $\alpha_1, \alpha_3, \alpha_4$ all equal to 1, $\alpha_2 = 0$ and $\beta = 1$ during the classification and condition generation tasks. We train the model on two different sets of data: completely different datasets (MNIST and Fashion MNIST) and similar datasets (MNIST and SVHN).

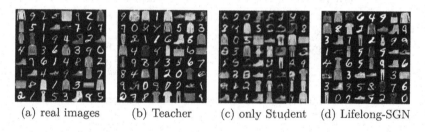

| (a) real images | (b) Teacher | (c) only Student | (d) Lifelong-SGN |

Fig. 2. Generation and reconstruction results for Lifelong-SGN when considering unsupervised training with M-F.

For completely different datasets, as presented in Table 1, the Lifelong-SGM model demonstrates improved classification accuracy when compared to the optimal value achieved through joint training. This improvement is attributed to the incorporation of both the Assistant and Teacher modules. In the M-F task, the model demonstrates higher classification accuracy for the MNIST dataset due to its prior training on the same. Additionally, the image generation performance of the Lifelong-SGN model has also been evaluated, with the generation replay mechanism being utilized in the absence of the Teacher module. With the integration of the ANN-based Teacher and Assistant modules, the SNN exhibits a stable ability to generate images for diverse tasks without forgetting previous knowledge. Visualization results of the generated images are presented in Fig. 2, demonstrating the improved quality of the Lifelong-SGN image generation after the addition of the Assistant and Teacher modules. The images generated exhibit high comparability to real images, owing to the robust learning capability of the Teacher module.

MNIST and SVHN have the similar representation and our model performs well on these data sets. The average classification accuracy for MNIST and SVHN is nearly as good as the joint training accuracy, as presented in Table 2.

Table 1. Generation Performance and Classification accuracy on the M-F and F-M under the lifelong learning setting.

Tasks	Method	Dadaset	FID	Acc
	joint-traing	MNIST	/	93.13
		Fashion		94.88
M-F	w/o Ass	MNIST	121.6	93.16
	w/o Tea	Fashion	116.5	80.22
	w/ Ass	MNIST	102.35	95.37
	w/o Tea	Fashion	95.26	80.92
	Lifelong-SGN	MNIST	**74.67**	**98.38**
		Fashion	**90.51**	**82.54**
F-M	w/o Ass	MNIST	97.67	88.74
	w/o Tea	Fashion	128.5	86.42
	w/ Ass	MNIST	81.67	88.61
	w/o Tea	Fashion	118.6	88.82
	Lifelong-SGN	MNIST	**82.29**	**88.94**
		Fashion	**82.92**	**90.25**

Table 2. Classification accuracy and Average Classification accuracy on the M-S and S-M under the lifelong learning setting.

Tasks	Method	Dataset	Acc	Average
	joint-traing	MNIST	98.92	93.54
		SVHN	88.16	
M-S	w/o Ass	MNIST	95.02	90.68
	w/o Tea	SVHN	86.35	
	w/ Ass	MNIST	96.82	92.01
	w/o Tea	SVHN	87.19	
	Lifelong-SGN	MNIST	98.38	**92.76**
		SVHN	87.13	
S-M	w/o Ass	MNIST	98.47	91.96
	w/o Tea	SVHN	85.45	
	w/ Ass	MNIST	98.26	92.49
	w/o Tea	SVHN	86.72	
	Lifelong-SGN	MNIST	98.50	**92.93**
		SVHN	87.36	

3.2 Lifelong Semi-supervised Learning

In this subsection, we evaluate the performance of Lifelong-SGN in a semi-supervised learning scenario, which is a more general case. We set hyperparameters $\alpha_1, \alpha_2, \alpha_3, \alpha_4 = 1$ and $\beta = 1$, and assume that data is incomplete in a lifelong learning environment with most data in the M-F task being unlabeled. Specifically, we use only 5% of the labeled data, with each class of the labeled data having the same number of images. After training on MNIST, we assign class labels to all generated data after inference by the model due to the strong generative power of the Teacher module. We observe that the accuracy does not decrease significantly after incorporating the Fashion MNIST dataset for training, as shown in Fig. 3. However, we find that the model's performance degrades substantially after the Teacher and Assistant modules are removed. The results demonstrate the robustness and effectiveness of Lifelong-SGN in semi-supervised learning scenarios with incomplete data.

3.3 ANN and SNN

In this subsection, we compare the performance of Lifelong-SGN with ANN-based lifelong learning models, both of which use the same network structure, in order to ensure fairness of the evaluation. Table 3 shows the results of the classification task. Our evaluation reveals that Lifelong-SGN outperforms the ANN model in the M-S task. However, in the M-F-S task, Continual Unsupervised Representation Learning (CURL) [16] produces better results, as a result of its mixture model that can more effectively capture image information from different domains. Despite a slight accuracy loss in the three sequential tasks, Lifelong-SGN offers the advantage of being deployable and executable on edge AI. In future research, we will further explore more advanced SNN-based lifelong learning methods.

SNNs possess the advantage of low energy consumption and high speed resulting from their event-driven nature. This experiment assesses the complexity of the SNN model and compares it with Lifelong-SGN using LGM, a method based on ANN [15]. Results indicate that, when generating a MNIST image, SNNs exhibit a higher number of addition operations in comparison to Artificial neural networks (ANNs), but significantly fewer multiplication operations. Given that multiplication operations are deemed more computationally expensive, this highlights the efficacy of SNNs in edge AI applications. Furthermore, the Lifelong-SGN model affords the capability of lifelong learning, making it a desirable choice for deployment in resource-limited edge devices (Table 4).

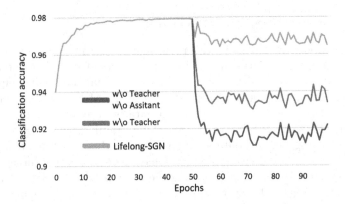

Fig. 3. Classification accuracy curve under semi-supervised of MNIST in M-F tasks.

Table 3. Average Classification accuracy on the M-S and M-F-S under the lifelong learning setting between Lifelong-SGN and ANN-based model.

Tasks	Network	Method	Average
M-S	ANN	LGM [15]	88.72
		CURL [16]	91.68
	SNN	Lifelong-SGM	**92.76**
M-F-S	ANN	LGM [15]	78.63
		CURL [16]	**84.29**
	SNN	Lifelong-SGM	80.06

Table 4. Compare the amount of computations required to generate an image from the MNIST dataset.

Model	#Additions	#Multiplications
LGM [15]	$\mathbf{2.4 \times 10^7}$	2.4×10^7
Lifelong-SGN	1.6×10^8	$\mathbf{8.5 \times 10^5}$

4   Conclusion

In this work, we proposed Lifelong-SGN, a spiking generative network model capable of lifelong learning. Lifelong-SGN is composed of three modules: Teacher, Student, and Assistant. The Teacher module generates knowledge from previous learning using an ANN-based generative model. The Student module is an SNN-based VAE that is trained with knowledge from the Teacher and the latest task. The Assistant module, an ANN-based discriminator, facilitates the Student's learning process. By incorporating SNN, Lifelong-SGN generates high-quality images while mitigating catastrophic forgetting in the presence of multiple datasets. Our work demonstrates the effectiveness of Lifelong-SGN in unsupervised, supervised, and semi-supervised settings. Moreover, as SNNs can operate at high speeds on neuromorphic devices, this work provides a framework for future deployment of image applications in edge AI.

Acknowledgements. The completion of this work was supported in part by the National Natural Science Foundation of China (62276106), the UIC Start-up Research Fund (UICR0700056-23), the Guangdong Provincial Key Laboratory of Interdisciplinary Research and Application for Data Science (2022B1212010006), the Guangdong Higher Education Upgrading Plan (2021–2025) of "Rushing to the Top, Making Up Shortcomings and Strengthening Special Features" (R0400001-22), and the Artificial Intelligence and Data Science Research Hub (AIRH) of BNU-HKBU United International College (UIC).

References

1. Arribas, D., Zhao, Y., Park, I.M.: Rescuing neural spike train models from bad MLE. Adv. Neural. Inf. Process. Syst. **33**, 2293–2303 (2020)
2. Cassidy, A.S., et al.: Real-time scalable cortical computing at 46 giga-synaptic ops/watt with~ 100× speedup in time-to-solution and~ 100,000× reduction in energy-to-solution. In: SC 2014: Proceedings of the International Conference for High Performance Computing, Networking, Storage and Analysis, pp. 27–38. IEEE (2014)
3. Davies, M., et al.: Loihi: a neuromorphic manycore processor with on-chip learning. IEEE Micro **38**(1), 82–99 (2018)
4. Deng, L.: The MNIST database of handwritten digit images for machine learning research [best of the web]. IEEE Sig. Process. Mag. **29**(6), 141–142 (2012)
5. French, R.M.: Catastrophic forgetting in connectionist networks. Trends Cogn. Sci. **3**(4), 128–135 (1999)
6. Furber, S.B., Galluppi, F., Temple, S., Plana, L.A.: The spinnaker project. Proc. IEEE **102**(5), 652–665 (2014)
7. Gulrajani, I., Ahmed, F., Arjovsky, M., Dumoulin, V., Courville, A.C.: Improved training of Wasserstein GANs. In: Advances in Neural Information Processing Systems, vol. 30 (2017)
8. Jeong, J., Shin, J.: Training GANs with stronger augmentations via contrastive discriminator (2021)
9. Kamata, H., Mukuta, Y., Harada, T.: Fully spiking variational autoencoder. In: Proceedings of the AAAI Conference on Artificial Intelligence, vol. 36, pp. 7059–7067 (2022)
10. Karras, T., Laine, S., Aila, T.: A style-based generator architecture for generative adversarial networks. In: Proceedings of the IEEE/CVF Conference on Computer Vision and Pattern Recognition, pp. 4401–4410 (2019)
11. Kotariya, V., Ganguly, U.: Spiking-GAN: a spiking generative adversarial network using time-to-first-spike coding. In: 2022 International Joint Conference on Neural Networks (IJCNN), pp. 1–7. IEEE (2022)
12. Maass, W.: Networks of spiking neurons: the third generation of neural network models. Neural Netw. **10**(9), 1659–1671 (1997)
13. Netzer, Y., Wang, T., Coates, A., Bissacco, A., Wu, B., Ng, A.Y.: Reading digits in natural images with unsupervised feature learning (2011)
14. Otter, D.W., Medina, J.R., Kalita, J.K.: A survey of the usages of deep learning for natural language processing. IEEE Trans. Neural Netw. Learn. Syst. **32**(2), 604–624 (2020)

15. Ramapuram, J., Gregorova, M., Kalousis, A.: Lifelong generative modeling. Neurocomputing **404**, 381–400 (2020)
16. Rao, D., Visin, F., Rusu, A., Pascanu, R., Teh, Y.W., Hadsell, R.: Continual unsupervised representation learning. In: Advances in Neural Information Processing Systems, vol. 32 (2019)
17. Vahdat, A., Kautz, J.: NVAE: A deep hierarchical variational autoencoder. Adv. Neural. Inf. Process. Syst. **33**, 19667–19679 (2020)
18. Voulodimos, A., Doulamis, N., Doulamis, A., Protopapadakis, E.: Deep learning for computer vision: a brief review. Comput. Intell. Neurosci. **2018**, 13 (2018)
19. Wu, C., Herranz, L., Liu, X., van de Weijer, J., Raducanu, B., et al.: Memory replay GANs: learning to generate new categories without forgetting. In: Advances in Neural Information Processing Systems, vol. 31 (2018)
20. Xiao, H., Rasul, K., Vollgraf, R.: Fashion-MNIST: a novel image dataset for benchmarking machine learning algorithms. arXiv preprint arXiv:1708.07747 (2017)
21. Yu, N., et al.: Dual contrastive loss and attention for GANs (2021)

A Contrastive Method for Continual Generalized Zero-Shot Learning

Chen Liang[1], Wentao Fan[2,3]($\boxtimes$) (iD), Xin Liu[1], and Shu-Juan Peng[1]

[1] Department of Computer Science and Technology, Huaqiao University,
Quanzhou, China
[2] Department of Computer Science, Beijing Normal University-Hong Kong Baptist
University United International College (BNU-HKBU UIC), Zhuhai, China
wentaofan@uic.edu.cn
[3] Guangdong Provincial Key Laboratory of Interdisciplinary Research
and Application for Data Science, BNU-HKBU United International College,
Zhuhai, China

Abstract. Generalized zero-shot learning (GZSL) aims to train a model
that can classify seen and unseen samples based on semantic information.
Continual learning, as one of the factors distinguishing artificial intelligence, has received more and more attention in recent years. In this
paper, we propose a deep learning model based on a conditional generative model and a contrastive learning framework that can continuously
learn from incoming data. In the training phase, knowledge distillation
and generative replay mechanisms are used to accumulate past knowledge. In the testing phase, the test samples are mapped to the embedding
space to perform generalized zero-shot classification task. Our model not
only does not require additional buffers to store data so that it will not
cause data leakage problems, but also through experiments show that our
model can achieve state-of-the-art results on three benchmark datasets.
The source code of the proposed model is available at: https://github.
com/liangchen976/CCGZSL.

Keywords: Generalized Zero-shot learning · Generative Adversarial
Networks · Contrastive Learning · Continuous Learning · Deep
Learning

1 Introduction

Deep learning technology has made great achievements in image processing and
representation learning. However, training a model with promising generalization performance often reacquires a larger amount of labeled training samples.
In recent years, some works have proposed the concept of zero-shot learning
[27,43], which allows the model to recognize samples that had never been seen
before. This framework can solve the problem of missing data to a certain extent.
At present, zero-shot learning can be attributed to two methods, namely the

H. Fujita et al. (Eds.): IEA/AIE 2023, LNAI 13925, pp. 365–376, 2023.
https://doi.org/10.1007/978-3-031-36819-6_32

method based on the embedding method and the generative method [33]. The former method often encounters more problems such as *bias towards the seen classes* and *hubness* problems. Therefore, in recent years, methods based on conditional generative models have received great attention [2,6,43]. However, these methods cannot cope with the situation when the training data comes in a flow-like sequence. If the training method is not changed, it will inevitably lead to the catastrophic forgetting problem [30].

Recent works [13–15,25,37] focus on the combination of continual learning and generalized zero-shot learning, mostly using rehearsal mechanisms to accumulate past knowledge to the current model, thereby alleviating the problem of catastrophic forgetting. However, there are some disadvantages. For example, for the model [25] that only uses the rehearsal mechanism to generate data of previous tasks, when the task sequence is long or the new task only contains small batches of data, a large amount of past data still needs to be synthesized, which will not only greatly increase the computational burden, and once the generation module at a certain moment does not learn the current data well, it will have a bad impact on the subsequent task learning. For models [14,15] that use the rehearsal mechanism to store data of previous tasks, not only will they encounter the problem of capacity setting when setting the buffer and the update of stored data, but also corresponding to a specific environment, saving data will have the risk of data leakage to a certain extent.

Given the above problems, we propose a continual generalized zero-shot learning model based on bidirectional knowledge distillation in a contrastive learning framework. In the training phase, knowledge distillation and generative replay mechanisms are used to accumulate past knowledge. In the testing phase, the test samples are mapped to the embedding space to perform a generalized zero-shot classification task. Our contributions can be summarized as follows.

1. We propose a continual generalized zero-shot learning method for inductive semantics, which not only requires no semantic information of unseen classes during model training but also does not require additional buffers to store visual-semantic feature sample pairs.
2. We propose a bidirectional knowledge distillation method based on a conditional generative module and a feature learning module, which can accumulate knowledge from old models to new models.
3. We evaluate the performance of our model on 3 standard datasets through extensive experiments and achieve very competitive results.

2   Related Work

2.1   Generalized Zero-Shot Learning

Zero-shot learning refers to giving the model the data to identify unseen classes by learning from the data of the seen classes. In recent years, based on generative models such as Variational Autoencoder (VAE) [22], Generative Adversarial Networks (GAN) [16] and FLOW [7] gradually dominates, because this generative approach can well alleviate the *bias towards the seen classes* [10,21] and *hubness* problems [44] that exist based on embedding methods. The authors of [41] used Wasserstern GAN (WGAN) conditioned on semantic information to generate unseen visual features. [11] combines VAE and GAN to generate higher-quality unseen visual features. [32] introduces a feedback mechanism to constrain the generator to generate more discriminative features. CADA-VAE [35] uses two VAEs to align the latent space of different modal data to complete the transformation from semantic features to visual features. However, the zero-shot learning method mentioned above can only be used when all the training data can be obtained. When the data arrives in sequence, the above models cannot retain past knowledge. There are some recent works [13,14,25] dedicated to solving the zero-shot learning problem under continuous learning conditions. But these methods either use a buffer to store past data or use a replay mechanism to generate a large amount of past data to transform the continuous learning problem into an ordinary zero-shot learning problem. Although it can alleviate the problem of catastrophic forgetting to a certain extent, this learning method is very time-consuming, requires storage capacity, and has the problem of leakage of private data.

2.2   Continual Learning

Work on continuous learning can be roughly divided into Rehearsal-based methods, Regularization-based [23,28,43] methods and Parameter isolation-based methods. [34] stores a portion of samples for each class as an exemplar, and in the testing phase, the class mean is calculated based on all samples for the nearest neighbor mean classification. [36] applies GAN to continuous learning conditions through knowledge distillation [20] and replay. [29] realizes the ability to learn new knowledge by changing the mask of learnable parameters when a new task comes. [42] propose to only activate and select sparse neurons for learning current and past tasks at any stage in order to make the model capacity can be reserved for future tasks. [9] proposes a method for self-supervised learning to complete continuous class incremental learning. However, few articles discuss generalized zero-shot learning under continuous learning conditions. Inspired by [1], contrastively learned representations are more robust against catastrophic forgetting than ones trained with the cross-entropy objective. Contrastingly learned representations suffer less from forgetting than the ones trained with cross-entropy loss.

2.3   Contrastive Learning

Contrastive learning started as a self-supervised representation learning method based on identifying similarities and differences between objects. The goal of contrastive learning is to make the distance between positive samples (similar samples) as close as possible, and the distance between negative samples as far as possible. InstDisc [39] proposed a memory bank to store the representation of all the images in the dataset. CPC [38] proposes a new idea to construct positive sample pairs in contrastive learning to process information from different perspectives/modalities. MoCo [5,18] increases the number of negatives and maintains a long queue to provide a large number of negatives by using the momentum contrast mechanism of the forced query encoder. SimCLR [3] uses more data augmentation(e.g. Grayscale, Random Resized Cropping) and an additional MLP prediction layer, resulting in a huge improvement in unsupervised classification.

In generalized zero-shot learning, many articles [2,6,17,24] pointed out that classification in visual space is not the best choice. To further achieve better classification results, CE-GZSL [17] learns a new embedding space by establishing instance-level and class-level contrast losses, so that downstream classification tasks can be better completed. [24] introduces a self-supervised teacher-student model based on [17], which learns a more discriminative embedding space by constructing representation distillation loss and standard logistic distillation loss. Similarly, our model also uses a similar approach to learn a new embedding space to generalize the zero-shot classification task.

3 Approach

3.1 Problem Definition

We follow the setting of Proposed Split (PS) [40] to split all classes on each datasets into seen and unseen classes, where are recorded as $\{\mathcal{X}^s, \mathcal{Y}^s, \mathcal{A}^s\}$ and $\{\mathcal{X}^u, \mathcal{Y}^u, \mathcal{A}^u\}$, where $\mathcal{X}$ represents visual features, $\mathcal{Y}$ represents the label of the sample, $\mathcal{A}$ represents the semantic information of the sample, s represents the seen class, and u represents the unseen class. The intersection of seen and unseen categories of each modality data is empty. Our model are different from [25], in the training phase, the semantic information of the unseen class samples after the current moment t is unknowable. In the process of data division of continual learning, we divide the training data into N_t parts according to the number of tasks N_t on average, namely $D_{tr} = \{D_{tr}^1, \ldots, D_{tr}^{N_t}\}$, which $D_{tr}^t = \{(x_i^s, a_i^s, y_i^s)_{i=1}^{N_s^t} \mid x_i^s \in X_s^t, a_i^s \in A_s^t, y_i^t \in Y_s^t\}$; $D_{te} = \{D_{te}^1, \ldots, D_{te}^{N_t}\}$, where $D_{te}^t = \{(x_i, a_i)_{i=1}^{N^t} \mid x_i \in (X_s^{\leq t} \cup X_u^{\leq t}), a_i \in (A_s^{\leq t} \cup A_u^{\leq t})\}$ where $X_s^{\leq t}$ and $A_s^{\leq t}$ denote the visual representations and attributes of all the seen classes encountered so far, respectively.

3.2 Conditional Generation Module

Following [41], we embed the conditional CGAN model [31] into our model as the generation part. Our feature generation module is mainly composed of two parts, the conditional generator network G parameterized by θ and the conditional discriminator network Dis parameterized by ω. The input of the generator is noise $\epsilon \sim \mathcal{N}(0, 1)$ and semantic information a^s. The input of the discriminator is the real semantic condition information a, the real sample x_s and the generated sample $(x, a), (\tilde{x}, a)$. The discriminator and the generator compete against each other. For the discriminator, it can train itself to continuously improve its ability to judge the true and false samples; for the generator, it can continuously improve the ability of its own synthesized samples to fool the discriminator. After such a game, the generator will finally have a better ability to generate enough real samples. The generated adversarial loss function is given by

$$\mathcal{L}_{WGAN} = \mathbb{E}[Dis_\omega(x, a)] - \mathbb{E}[Dis_\omega(\tilde{x}, a)]$$
$$- \lambda \mathbb{E}\left[\left(\|\nabla_{\hat{x}} Dis_\omega(\hat{x}, a)\|_2 - 1\right)^2\right], \tag{1}$$

where $\mathbb{E}[\cdot]$ is the calculation of expectation, $\tilde{x} = G_\theta(\epsilon, a^s)$ denotes the generation of fake samples. $\hat{x} = \alpha x + (1 - \alpha)\tilde{x}$ and $\alpha \sim U(0, 1)$, λ is the penalty coefficient.

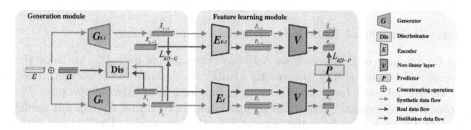

Fig. 1. The framework of our contrastive continual generative zero-shot learning model.

3.3 Feature Learning Module

Because contrastive learning has powerful feature learning ability [1,2,6,17], we take supervised contrastive learning as our feature learning module.

The training method of supervised contrastive learning is as follows: give a batch of training data $\{(x_i, y_i)\}_{i=1}^N$, first map the visual features to the embedding space via E. $p = E_\varphi(x)$, where φ denotes the parameter of the encoder E. and then maps p to a unit sphere of d dimension through a nonlinear layer V, that is, $z = V_\vartheta(p)$, where ϑ denotes the parameter of V. Here we follow the strategy of [4], adding a nonlinear layer V before the unit z vector to deal with our downstream classification task. By taking the data of the same label as a positive sample pair and the data of different labels as a negative sample pair, this brings about a contrastive loss. In a minibatch consisting of $z_1, z_2, \ldots, z_N$, for the sample z^+, select its same class $z^\top$ as a positive sample, other K samples of different categories from z^+ are used as its negative samples z_k^- ($k = 1 \ldots K$). So, we have

$$\ell_{con}(z_i, z^+) = -\log \frac{\exp\left(z_i^\top z^+/\tau\right)}{\exp\left(z_i^\top z^+/\tau\right) + \sum_{k=1}^K \exp\left(z_i^\top z_k^-/\tau\right)} \tag{2}$$

$$\mathcal{L}_{CON} = \mathbb{E}_{z_i, z^+}\left[\ell_{con}(z_i, z^+)\right] \tag{3}$$

where $\tau > 0$ represents the temperature parameter in our instance-level contrastive supervision.

Table 1. Comparison with results from other methods.

Methods	AWA1			AWA2			APY		
	mSA	mUA	mH	mSA	mUA	mH	mSA	mUA	mH
A-CZSL [14]	78.03	35.38	52.51	82.91	42.19	57.74	64.06	16.82	24.46
Tf-GCZSL [13]	61.79	57.77	59.72	67.42	58.08	62.41	72.12	19.66	30.90
DVGR-CZSL [15]	76.90	42.04	53.38	78.17	40.44	50.89	69.67	31.58	43.44
NM-ZSL [37]	75.59	60.87	67.44	**89.22**	51.38	63.41	**79.60**	22.29	32.61
UCLT* [25]	76.82	68.11	71.61	78.23	68.91	72.32	34.68	23.82	20.71
UCLT [25]	**79.51**	69.13	73.49	79.19	70.71	74.09	74.92	33.94	46.26
CCGZSL(Ours)	76.70	**71.36**	**73.69**	80.64	**72.04**	**75.84**	52.65	**44.03**	**47.17**

3.4 Bidirectional Knowledge Distillation Mechanism

At the moment of t, although we only have the training data D_{tr}^t, we hope the model still has the ability to correctly identify the samples of the previous task, so the model must have the ability to accumulate knowledge in the past. We propose a bidirectional knowledge accumulation method that enables our model to transfer knowledge from the old model to the new model. The forward stage takes place in the conditional generation module. When the parameters of G^{t-1} are frozen, the semantic condition information at t-1 moment is concatenated with the random Gaussian noise ϵ to the old and new generators G^t and G^{t-1} respectively, expect them to generate the same output, as shown in the following equation

$$\mathcal{L}_{\text{KD-G}} = \mathcal{L}\left(\tilde{x}_i^{t-1}, \tilde{x}_i^t\right) \tag{4}$$

The forward stage enables the generative model at time t to have the generative ability of the old model. In the backward stage, we design a prediction head P parameterized by η to complete the knowledge accumulation of the feature learning module. By inputting the training data at time t to the new and old feature extractors $V_\vartheta^t(E_\varphi^t(x_i^t))$ and $V_\vartheta^{t-1}(E_\varphi^{t-1}(x_i^t))$. Unlike previous work which directly constrains the similarity between the two outputs above, a predictor network P parameterized by ρ is used to map the new feature space to the old feature space, such as the following equation

$$\mathcal{L}_{\text{KD-P}} = \mathcal{L}\left(P_\rho\left(V_\vartheta^t\left(E_\varphi^t(x_i^t)\right)\right), V_\vartheta^{t-1}\left(E_\varphi^{t-1}(x_i^t)\right)\right) \tag{5}$$

If the new feature space can predict the old feature space well, it means that the feature learning ability of the new feature extractor is at least as good as the old feature extractor [9].

3.5 Generate Replay Mechanism

To alleviate the catastrophic forgetting problem that occurs during model training, we can generate visual features of previously seen classes by passing the concatenation of semantic attributes and noise vectors as input to the generative network

$$D_{rp}^t = G\left(\epsilon, A_s^{<t}\right) \tag{6}$$

Then, the training data at time t is $D_{rp}^t \cup D_{tr}^t$.

In summary, the overall structure of the proposed model can be viewed in Fig. 1 which consists of four parts: a conditional generation module, a feature learning module, a bidirectional distillation mechanism and a generative replay mechanism. The total loss of our model is given by

$$\mathcal{L}_{total} = \mathcal{L}_{WGAN}^s + \mathcal{L}_{CON} + \lambda_1 \mathcal{L}_{KD-G} + \lambda_2 \mathcal{L}_{KD-P} \tag{7}$$

where λ_1 and λ_2 are the weights of the corresponding loss.

4 Experimental Results

4.1 Datasets and Experimental Settings

We evaluate our model on three benchmark datasets. Animals with Attributes 1&2 (AWA1&AWA2) [26,40] and APY [8]. The 2048-dimensional visual features of all datasets are extracted by the ResNet-101 network [19] pre-trained on the Imagenet dataset. To compare the results fairly, we follow the division method of [12,15], the AWA1&2 datasets are divided into 5 tasks. The APY dataset is divided into 4 tasks. On the measure of classification effect, we extend the scheme proposed by [40] to the case of continual learning using an evaluation method similar to [12,13].

All modules in our model use a fully connected neural network, the activation function is LeakyReLU, and the parameters are updated using the Adam optimizer with optimizer parameters of 0.5 and 0.999. The learning rates are all 0.0001. We perform one update for generator parameters after five discriminator updates. We take L_1 loss as our bidirectional knowledge distillation loss.

4.2 Comparison with State-of-the-Arts

The results of our model on the three datasets are shown in Table 1. Note that the result with * is the result of removing the semantic information related modules of the unseen class in the training phase. From the table, we can find that our model achieves state-of-the-art results on mUA and mH metrics on all datasets. In particular, our results are better than UCLT's results using unseen class semantic information without using unseen class semantic features during training.

4.3 Ablation Experiment

To analyze the impact of different modules or mechanisms of our model, we evaluate our experimental results in the absence of different modules or mechanisms, as shown in Table 2. 'Seq-CCGZSL' indicates our model without any replay and distillation mechanism, which means training our model sequentially. 'CCGZSL

Table 2. The influence of each module/mechanism on the model classification effect.

Methods	AWA1			AWA2			APY		
	mSA	mUA	mH	mSA	mUA	mH	mSA	mUA	mH
Seq-CCGZSL	32.89	31.26	31.45	33.72	33.30	33.06	26.63	28.73	27.27
CCGZSL w/o kd	60.20	62.16	60.70	68.72	65.96	66.94	47.98	40.13	42.97
CCGZSL w/o kd-g	64.48	63.50	63.76	71.30	61.16	65.37	46.43	40.63	42.89
CCGZSL w/o kd-p	75.06	62.28	69.60	75.62	70.38	72.73	51.23	42.85	45.89
CCGZSL w/o replay	**80.40**	60.94	68.02	67.22	61.62	63.85	40.33	36.73	37.72
CCGZSL(Ours)	76.70	**71.36**	**73.69**	**80.64**	**72.04**	**75.84**	**52.65**	**44.03**	**47.17**

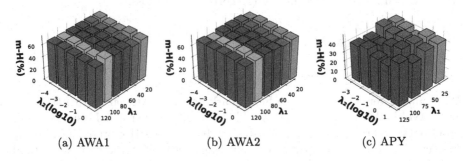

(a) AWA1   (b) AWA2   (c) APY

Fig. 2. The CGZSL performance of our approach with different knowledge distillation weights for different datasets.

w/o kd' represents our approach without a bidirectional knowledge distillation mechanism. 'CCGZSL w/o kd-g' and 'CCGZSL w/o kd-p' indicates the methods without forward and backward distillation mechanism, respectively. 'CCGZSL w/o replay' represents our model without generative replay in the training stage. From the table, we can find that all modules and mechanisms in our model mitigate the problem of catastrophic forgetting to a certain extent.

4.4   Hyperparameter Analysis and Visualization

In this subsection, to explore the effect of the weight of bidirectional knowledge distillation mechanisms in our model, we did a lot of experiments. For AWA1 and AWA2 datasets, we set $\lambda_1 \in [20, 40, 60, 80, 100, 120]$, $\lambda_2 \in [1e-4, 1e-3, 1e-2, 1e-1, 1]$; for the APY dataset we set $\lambda_1 \in [20, 50, 80, 110]$, $\lambda_2 \in [1e-3, 1e-2, 1e-1, 1, 10]$, the results are shown in Fig. 2. As we may notice from this figure, the variation of m-H values is not significant for each dataset, which indicates that our approach is robust to knowledge distillation weights. Our approach obtains the best continual GZSL performance on AWA1 when $\lambda_1 = 60$ and $\lambda_2 = 1e-1$. For AWA2 dataset, $\lambda_1 = 100$ and $\lambda_2 = 1e-2$. For APY dataset, $\lambda_1 = 110$ and $\lambda_2 = 1e-2$.

To verify that the feature learning module can effectively extract features under the condition of continuous learning, we use T-SNE to visualize the result

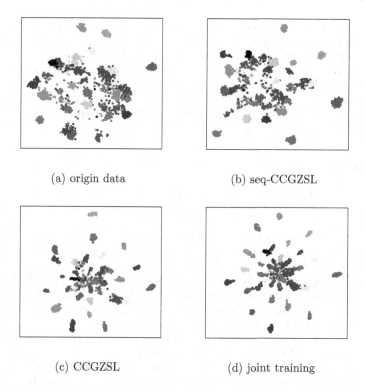

(a) origin data   (b) seq-CCGZSL

(c) CCGZSL   (d) joint training

Fig. 3. A visualization of the features learned by our CCGZSL model in a different setting.

of inputting the test data of the AWA2 dataset to the feature learning module E, as shown in Fig. 3. We can find that our model can learn the features of the seen class samples well, which proves the effectiveness of our model's feature learning module and distillation mechanism.

5   Conclusion and Future Works

In this work, we proposed a continual generalized zero-shot learning method for inductive semantics GZSL, which not only requires no semantic information of unseen classes during model training but also does not require additional buffers to store visual-semantic feature sample pairs. We also proposed a bidirectional knowledge distillation mechanism based on a conditional generative module and a feature learning module, which can accumulate knowledge from old models to new models. The proposed method was validated through experiments on several benchmark datasets. One possible future work is to adopt more advanced generative modules (such as flow-based generative models or more sophisticated GAN-based generative models) in our approach to improve its generation ability, which may enhance of the GZSL performance.

Acknowledgements. The completion of this work was supported in part by the National Natural Science Foundation of China (62276106), the UIC Start-up Research Fund (UICR0700056-23), the Guangdong Provincial Key Laboratory of Interdisciplinary Research and Application for Data Science (2022B1212010006), the Guangdong Higher Education Upgrading Plan (2021–2025) of "Rushing to the Top, Making Up Shortcomings and Strengthening Special Features" (R0400001-22), and the Artificial Intelligence and Data Science Research Hub (AIRH) of BNU-HKBU United International College (UIC).

References

1. Cha, H., Lee, J., Shin, J.: Co2l: contrastive continual learning. In: Proceedings of the IEEE/CVF International Conference on Computer Vision (ICCV), pp. 9516–9525 (2021)
2. Chen, S., et al.: Free: feature refinement for generalized zero-shot learning. In: Proceedings of the IEEE/CVF International Conference on Computer Vision (ICCV), pp. 122–131 (2021)
3. Chen, T., Kornblith, S., Norouzi, M., Hinton, G.: A simple framework for contrastive learning of visual representations. In: Proceedings of the 37th International Conference on Machine Learning. In: Proceedings of Machine Learning Research, vol. 119, pp. 1597–1607. PMLR, 13–18 July 2020
4. Chen, T., Kornblith, S., Norouzi, M., Hinton, G.: A simple framework for contrastive learning of visual representations (2020)
5. Chen, X., Fan, H., Girshick, R.B., He, K.: Improved baselines with momentum contrastive learning. CoRR abs/2003.04297 (2020). https://arxiv.org/abs/2003.04297
6. Chen, Z., et al.: Semantics disentangling for generalized zero-shot learning. In: Proceedings of the IEEE/CVF International Conference on Computer Vision (ICCV), pp. 8712–8720 (2021)
7. Dinh, L., Krueger, D., Bengio, Y.: Nice: non-linear independent components estimation (2014). https://doi.org/10.48550/ARXIV.1410.8516, https://arxiv.org/abs/1410.8516
8. Farhadi, A., Endres, I., Hoiem, D., Forsyth, D.: Describing objects by their attributes. In: 2009 IEEE Conference on Computer Vision and Pattern Recognition, pp. 1778–1785. IEEE (2009)
9. Fini, E., da Costa, V.G.T., Alameda-Pineda, X., Ricci, E., Alahari, K., Mairal, J.: Self-supervised models are continual learners. In: Proceedings of the IEEE/CVF Conference on Computer Vision and Pattern Recognition (CVPR), pp. 9621–9630 (2022)
10. Fu, Y., Hospedales, T.M., Xiang, T., Gong, S.: Transductive multi-view zero-shot learning. IEEE Trans. Pattern Anal. Mach. Intell. **37**(11), 2332–2345 (2015). https://doi.org/10.1109/TPAMI.2015.2408354
11. Gao, R., et al.: Zero-VAE-GAN: Generating unseen features for generalized and transductive zero-shot learning. IEEE Trans. Image Process. **29**, 3665–3680 (2020)
12. Gautam, C., Parameswaran, S., Mishra, A., Sundaram, S.: Generalized continual zero-shot learning. CoRR abs/2011.08508 (2020). https://arxiv.org/abs/2011.08508
13. Gautam, C., Parameswaran, S., Mishra, A., Sundaram, S.: Tf-GCZSL: task-free generalized continual zero-shot learning. Neural Netw. **155**, 487–497 (2022). https://doi.org/10.1016/j.neunet.2022.08.034, https://www.sciencedirect.com/science/article/pii/S0893608022003343

14. Ghosh, S.: Adversarial training of variational auto-encoders for continual zero-shot learning(A-CZSL). In: 2021 International Joint Conference on Neural Networks (IJCNN), pp. 1–8 (2021). https://doi.org/10.1109/IJCNN52387.2021.9534367

15. Ghosh, S.: Dynamic VAEs with generative replay for continual zero-shot learning. arXiv preprint arXiv:2104.12468 (2021)

16. Goodfellow, I.J., et al.: Generative adversarial networks (2014)

17. Han, Z., Fu, Z., Chen, S., Yang, J.: Contrastive embedding for generalized zero-shot learning. In: Proceedings of the IEEE/CVF Conference on Computer Vision and Pattern Recognition (CVPR), pp. 2371–2381 (2021)

18. He, K., Fan, H., Wu, Y., Xie, S., Girshick, R.: Momentum contrast for unsupervised visual representation learning. In: Proceedings of the IEEE/CVF Conference on Computer Vision and Pattern Recognition (CVPR) (2020)

19. He, K., Zhang, X., Ren, S., Sun, J.: Deep residual learning for image recognition (2015)

20. Hinton, G., Vinyals, O., Dean, J., et al.: Distilling the knowledge in a neural network. arXiv preprint arXiv:1503.02531 2(7) (2015)

21. Jia, Z., Zhang, Z., Wang, L., Shan, C., Tan, T.: Deep unbiased embedding transfer for zero-shot learning. IEEE Trans. Image Process. **29**, 1958–1971 (2020). https://doi.org/10.1109/TIP.2019.2947780

22. Kingma, D.P., Welling, M.: Auto-encoding variational Bayes (2013). https://doi.org/10.48550/ARXIV.1312.6114, https://arxiv.org/abs/1312.6114

23. Kirkpatrick, J., et al.: Overcoming catastrophic forgetting in neural networks. Proc. Nat. Acad. Sci. **114**, 3521–3526 (2016). https://doi.org/10.1073/pnas.1611835114

24. Kong, X., et al.: En-compactness: self-distillation embedding & contrastive generation for generalized zero-shot learning. In: Proceedings of the IEEE/CVF Conference on Computer Vision and Pattern Recognition (CVPR), pp. 9306–9315 (2022)

25. Kuchibhotla, H.C., Malagi, S.S., Chandhok, S., Balasubramanian, V.N.: Unseen classes at a later time? No problem. In: Proceedings of the IEEE/CVF Conference on Computer Vision and Pattern Recognition (CVPR), pp. 9245–9254 (2022)

26. Lampert, C.H., Nickisch, H., Harmeling, S.: Learning to detect unseen object classes by between-class attribute transfer. In: 2009 IEEE Conference on Computer Vision and Pattern Recognition, pp. 951–958. IEEE (2009)

27. Larochelle, H., Erhan, D., Bengio, Y.: Zero-data learning of new tasks. In: AAAI, vol. 1, p. 3 (2008)

28. Li, Z., Hoiem, D.: Learning without forgetting. IEEE Trans. Pattern Anal. Mach. Intell. **40**(12), 2935–2947 (2018). https://doi.org/10.1109/TPAMI.2017.2773081

29. Mallya, A., Lazebnik, S.: PackNet: adding multiple tasks to a single network by iterative pruning. In: Proceedings of the IEEE Conference on Computer Vision and Pattern Recognition (CVPR) (2018)

30. McCloskey, M., Cohen, N.J.: Catastrophic interference in connectionist networks: the sequential learning problem. In: Psychology of Learning and Motivation, vol. 24, pp. 109–165. Academic Press (1989). https://doi.org/10.1016/S0079-7421(08)60536-8, https://www.sciencedirect.com/science/article/pii/S0079742108605368

31. Mirza, M., Osindero, S.: Conditional generative adversarial nets (2014)

32. Narayan, S., Gupta, A., Khan, F.S., Snoek, C.G.M., Shao, L.: Latent embedding feedback and discriminative features for zero-shot classification. In: Vedaldi, A., Bischof, H., Brox, T., Frahm, J.-M. (eds.) ECCV 2020. LNCS, vol. 12367, pp. 479–495. Springer, Cham (2020). https://doi.org/10.1007/978-3-030-58542-6_29

33. Pourpanah, F., et al.: A review of generalized zero-shot learning methods (2021)

34. Rebuffi, S.A., Kolesnikov, A., Sperl, G., Lampert, C.H.: iCaRL: incremental classifier and representation learning. In: Proceedings of the IEEE Conference on Computer Vision and Pattern Recognition (CVPR) (2017)
35. Schonfeld, E., Ebrahimi, S., Sinha, S., Darrell, T., Akata, Z.: Generalized zero- and few-shot learning via aligned variational autoencoders. In: Proceedings of the IEEE/CVF Conference on Computer Vision and Pattern Recognition, pp. 8247–8255 (2019)
36. Shin, H., Lee, J.K., Kim, J., Kim, J.: Continual learning with deep generative replay. In: Guyon, I., et al. (eds.) Advances in Neural Information Processing Systems, vol. 30. Curran Associates, Inc. (2017). https://proceedings.neurips.cc/paper/2017/file/0efbe98067c6c73dba1250d2beaa81f9-Paper.pdf
37. Skorokhodov, I., Elhoseiny, M.: Class normalization for (continual)? Generalized zero-shot learning. In: International Conference on Learning Representations (2021). https://openreview.net/forum?id=7pgFL2Dkyyy
38. Tian, Y., Krishnan, D., Isola, P.: Contrastive Multiview coding. In: Vedaldi, A., Bischof, H., Brox, T., Frahm, J.-M. (eds.) ECCV 2020. LNCS, vol. 12356, pp. 776–794. Springer, Cham (2020). https://doi.org/10.1007/978-3-030-58621-8_45
39. Wu, Z., Xiong, Y., Yu, S.X., Lin, D.: Unsupervised feature learning via nonparametric instance discrimination. In: Proceedings of the IEEE Conference on Computer Vision and Pattern Recognition (CVPR) (2018)
40. Xian, Y., Lampert, C.H., Schiele, B., Akata, Z.: Zero-shot learning-a comprehensive evaluation of the good, the bad and the ugly. IEEE Trans. Pattern Anal. Mach. Intell. **41**(9), 2251–2265 (2018)
41. Xian, Y., Lorenz, T., Schiele, B., Akata, Z.: Feature generating networks for zero-shot learning. In: Proceedings of the IEEE Conference on Computer Vision and Pattern Recognition, pp. 5542–5551 (2018)
42. Yan, Q., Gong, D., Liu, Y., van den Hengel, A., Shi, J.Q.: Learning Bayesian sparse networks with full experience replay for continual learning. In: Proceedings of the IEEE/CVF Conference on Computer Vision and Pattern Recognition (CVPR), pp. 109–118 (2022)
43. Yu, Y., Ji, Z., Han, J., Zhang, Z.: Episode-based prototype generating network for zero-shot learning. In: Proceedings of the IEEE/CVF Conference on Computer Vision and Pattern Recognition (CVPR) (2020)
44. Zhang, L., Xiang, T., Gong, S.: Learning a deep embedding model for zero-shot learning. In: Proceedings of the IEEE Conference on Computer Vision and Pattern Recognition (CVPR) (2017)

Active Learning Based Labeling Method for Fault Disposal Pre-plans

Sichi Zhou[1]*, Shouyu Liang[2]*, Qun Yang[1]([✉]), Huafeng Zhou[2], Wei Jiang[2], Yubin He[2], and Yingchen Li[2]

[1] College of Computer Science and Technology, Nanjing University of Aeronautics and Astronautics, Nanjing, China
qun.yang@nuaa.edu.cn
[2] Dispatching and Control Center China Southern Power Grid, Guangzhou, China

Abstract. Power grid companies have vast quantities of data that can be mined for valuable information. However, there is a limited quantity of labeled pre-plans data due to the high labeling cost. This paper proposes an active learning-based sequence labeling method, aiming at achieving good deep learning model performance with only a small amount of labeled data. It proposes a sample selection strategy based on uncertainty and slot, in which the uncertainty and slot respectively represent the informativeness and representativeness of the sample. Meanwhile, to avoid getting into local details in each round of model training, a method for evaluating the performance of data labeling is proposed. Based on these two works, the active learning and data labeling processes are also present. We use four strategies as comparative methods in our experiment, and the results demonstrate that our method outperforms other active learning methods. We conclude that our method is efficient and applicable to tasks involving the labeling of textual data in other contexts.

Keywords: Active learning · Sample selection strategy · Informativeness · Representativeness

1 Introduction

As the volume of industrial data grows, data mining is able to extract increasingly valuable information. The power industry has data on power grid operation, including grid fault disposal pre-plans, referred to in this paper as pre-plans. These pre-plans are textual data that record the dispatcher's disposal method when a fault occurs, and the analysis of these data can play a crucial role in guiding dispatchers in their daily handling of grid faults [1,2]. Recently, natural language processing has been applied to extract information from textual data [3]. However, it typically requires a large amount of labeled data [4,5], whereas

---

S. Zhou and S. Liang—These two authors contributed equally to this work.

H. Fujita et al. (Eds.): IEA/AIE 2023, LNAI 13925, pp. 377–382, 2023.
https://doi.org/10.1007/978-3-031-36819-6_33

only a small amount of pre-plans data has been labeled, as pre-plans are typically utilized only by power grid companies. This paper proposes a new active learning-based labeling method that aims to achieve good performance with a small amount of labeled data for deep neural networks. In general, the texts in the pre-plans exhibit two characteristics: (1) the repetition of certain phrases in multiple sentences; and (2) the high degree of syntactic similarity between the sentences. The primary objective of active learning is to devise a reasonable sample selection strategy [6,7]. Inspired by [8–10], this paper employs an uncertainty and slot-based strategy to select samples for labeling, taking into account the aforementioned characteristics. In addition, this paper proposes an evaluation method suitable for text sequence labeling of the pre-plans to test the performance of our method. The process of learning and data labeling is also described.

2   Text Sequence Labeling Method of Pre-plans Based on Active Learning

The procedure for the text sequence labeling method based on active learning is as follows: (1) Load all data first, then construct the seed set using selection strategy in Sect. 2.1. After that, manually label the samples in seed set to form the training set. (2) Train the LSTM model with the training set and assign a score to the unlabeled data using the sample selection strategy described in Sect. 2.2. (3) Sort all unlabeled data and manually label a specified number of samples. (4) Incorporate the labeled data into the current training set. Repeat steps two through four until the termination condition is satisfied.

2.1   Construction of the Seed Set

Typically, random sampling is used to construct the seed set; however, random sampling tends to lead to unstable model performance and does not fit the overall sample distribution well [11]. In the pre-plans, a cluster is defined as a collection of sentences that belong to the same category. We propose a new strategy for constructing seed sets that assigns a deterministic number of slots to each cluster, with the number of slots corresponding to the maximum number of samples that cluster can hold. The construction of seed sets is thoroughly described in Algorithm 1.

2.2   Selection Strategy for the Training Set

Once the seed set is constructed, it can be used to train a basic classifier that will be used to label the remaining data. During the training process, the LSTM model uses Eqs. (1) and (2) to calculate the uncertainty, and the unlabeled samples are ranked in descending order according to the calculated uncertainty value. After that, as a rule, the top 10% of the ranked samples are selected and manually labeled by experts. The top 10% of the ranked samples are then

---

Algorithm 1. Seed set construction algorithm

Input: Q: A training set with **0** samples; **D**: A dataset with **N** samples, where **N** is the number of total samples
Output: Q: A training set with **n**(deterministic number for seeds set) samples
1: **if** the sample in **D** contains the unincluded words (that are not included in the bag of words): **then**
2:    Sort decreasingly by the number of the unincluded words in the sample
3: **else**
4:    Sort decreasingly by the number of words in the sample
5: **end if**
6: Update **D**
7: **while** sample in **D** && **Q** not full **do**
8:    **if** there are empty slots in the sample cluster **then**
9:       Add the sample to **Q**;
10:      Add the unincluded words to the bag of words;
11:      Number of empty slots **-1**;
12:   **end if**
13: **end while**

---

typically selected and manually labeled by experts. These samples are then re-added to the training set and utilized to train the LSTM model. This process, i.e., selecting new samples for manual labeling and adding them to the training set to train the LSTM model, will be repeated multiple times. In each iteration, 2% of the data is selected, and the iteration ends when the number of samples reaches 80% of the total training set. We propose a sample selection strategy that combines uncertainty and representativeness criteria to avoid duplicate labeling. To measure the degree of uncertainty, we employ the maximum normalized log probability (MNLP) method [12]. It can be stated as follows:

$$MNLP = \max_{y_1,\dots,y_n} \frac{1}{m} \sum_{j=1}^{m} \log P\left[y_i \mid y_1,\dots,y_{n-1},x_j\right] \qquad (1)$$

$$Uncertainty = 1 - MNLP \qquad (2)$$

where x_j denotes the j-th token in the sentence, $P[y_i|y_1,\cdots,y_{n-1};x_j]$ denotes the probability that the model gives the labeled value y_i if given a token x_j, and m represents the length of the sentence.

The above sample selection strategy is described in Algorithm 2.

3 Experiments

3.1 Datasets

We use fault disposal pre-plans as data set. It is provided by the power grid companies and contains 18770 sentences. It is divided into 10 categories, i.e., 10 clusters, according to the fault type and disposal type. In the experiment, the data set is randomly divided into a training set and a test set with a 9:1 ratio.

Algorithm 2. Training set construction algorithm

Input: Q: A training set with **0** samples; **D**: A dataset with **N** samples, where **N** is the number of total samples

Output: Q: A training set with **n** samples, where **n** is the deterministic number for seeds set

1: **for** sample in **D do**
2:     Calculates sample uncertainty according to Eq. (2)
3: **end for**
4: Sort decreasingly according to uncertainty
5: Updates **D**
6: **while** sample in **D** && **Q** not full **do**
7:     **if** there are empty slots in the sample cluster **then**
8:         Add the sample to **Q**;
9:         Number of empty slots **-1**;
10:     **end if**
11: **end while**

3.2   Experimental Settings

This paper employs four distinct active learning strategies for its experiments: random (abbreviated as random), random pick-and-slot (abbreviated as random slot), uncertainty (abbreviated as lc), and uncertainty-and-slot (abbreviated as lc slot). The lc strategy has been utilized extensively among them. 10% of the overall training set is used as the seed set in the experiments. Specifically, in experiments employing random slot, lc, and lc slot strategies, the method described in Sect. 2.1 is used to construct the seed set, whereas 10% of the data are randomly selected as the seed set in experiments employing random strategies. For each experimental strategy, the entire data set is divided into 10 equal parts and 10-fold cross-validation experiments are conducted. In each cross-validation experiment, a subset of the data is used as the test set (denoted test_random), and the remaining samples are used as the training set. Since 10% of the final training set remains unlabeled, this portion is used as a test set and is referred to as test_rest.

3.3   Evaluation Method

Following prior work, we assess the performance of sequence labeling using the F1 score. In addition, we use the pass-through scale to evaluate the model's performance for data labeling. The pass-through scale is the amount of data required for the model to reach the pass-through threshold in the training set, where the pass-through threshold is a specific F1 score.

4   Results and Analysis

Experiments were conducted out on the test_random and test_rest test sets, as shown in Figs. 1 and 2, respectively. On the test_random test set, the proposed lc_slot strategy consistently outperforms the lc, random, and random_slot strategies in terms of F1 score, with final F1 scores of 62, 57, 57, and 58 for the four, respectively. The lc_slot strategy improves by nearly 6.9%. On the test_rest test set, the final F1 scores for these four strategies are 78, 57, 56, and 58, respectively. The lc_slot strategy improves by 34.5%.

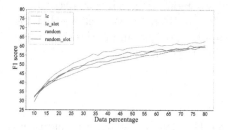

Fig. 1. The result on test_random.

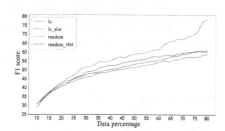

Fig. 2. The result on test_rest.

When the pass-through threshold is set to 60, the pass-through scale of the method with the lc_slot policy is 58%, which is better than the methods using the other three strategies, while the methods using the lc and random_slot strategies have a pass-through scales of 78% and 80%, and the method using the random strategy fails to reach the pass-through threshold even when 80% of the overall data is labeled. When the pass-through threshold is set to 65, the pass-through scale of the method with the lc_slot policy is 64%, whereas the method with the other three policies fails to reach the pass-through threshold even when 80% of the overall data is labeled. The preceding results indicate that the significance of representative and informative samples increases with the oversampling threshold (Figs. 3 and 4).

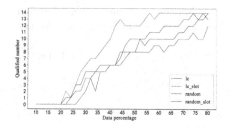

Fig. 3. Set the pass-through threshold to 60.

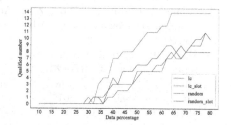

Fig. 4. Set the pass-through threshold to 65.

5 Conclusion

To solve the problems of insufficient labeled data and high labeling cost for pre-plans data, this paper proposes a sequence labeling method based on active learning. Meanwhile, it provides the evaluation method. To test the effectiveness of the proposed methods, comparative experiments are conducted by using four selection strategies. The experimental results demonstrate that our method can achieve good performance on metrics described in Sect. 3.3. We believe that the method proposed in this paper can also be applied to other industries other than the power grid where sequence labeling tasks are costly.

References

1. Chai, E., Zeng, P., Ma, S., Xing, H., Zhao, B.: Artificial intelligence approaches to fault diagnosis in power grids: a review. In: 2019 Chinese Control Conference (CCC), pp. 7346–7353 (2019)
2. Stock, S., Babazadeh, D., Becker, C.: Applications of artificial intelligence in distribution power system operation. IEEE Access **9**, 150098–150119 (2021)
3. Chowdhary, K., Chowdhary, K.: Natural language processing. In: Fundamentals of Artificial Intelligence, pp. 603–649. Springer, New Delhi (2020). https://doi.org/10.1007/978-81-322-3972-7_19
4. Zhao, Y., Prosperi, M., Lyu, T., Guo, Y., Zhou, L., Bian, J.: Integrating crowd-sourcing and active learning for classification of work-life events from tweets. In: Fujita, H., Fournier-Viger, P., Ali, M., Sasaki, J. (eds.) IEA/AIE 2020. LNCS (LNAI), vol. 12144, pp. 333–344. Springer, Cham (2020). https://doi.org/10.1007/978-3-030-55789-8_30
5. Yadav, V., Bethard, S.: A survey on recent advances in named entity recognition from deep learning models. arXiv preprint arXiv:1910.11470 (2019)
6. Shelmanov, A., et al.: Active learning with deep pre-trained models for sequence tagging of clinical and biomedical texts. In: 2019 IEEE International Conference on Bioinformatics and Biomedicine (BIBM), pp. 482–489. IEEE (2019)
7. Zhan, X., Wang, Q., Huang, K.h., Xiong, H., Dou, D., Chan, A.B.: A comparative survey of deep active learning. arXiv preprint arXiv:2203.13450 (2022)
8. Huang, S.J., Jin, R., Zhou, Z.H.: Active learning by querying informative and representative examples. In: Advances in Neural Information Processing Systems, vol. 23 (2010)
9. Hazra, R., Gupta, S., Dukkipati, A.: Active learning with Siamese twins for sequence tagging. CoRR (2019)
10. Huang, S.J., Gao, N., Chen, S.: Multi-instance multi-label active learning. In: IJCAI, pp. 1886–1892 (2017)
11. Huang, H., Wang, H., Jin, D.: A low-cost named entity recognition research based on active learning. Sci. Program. **2018**, 1–10 (2018)
12. Shen, Y., Yun, H., Lipton, Z.C., Kronrod, Y., Anandkumar, A.: Deep active learning for named entity recognition. arXiv preprint arXiv:1707.05928 (2017)

Pattern Recognition

Global Spatial Representation: EEG Correcting for Subject-Independent Emotion Recognition

Jing Zhang[✉], Yixin Wang, and Guiyan Wei

School of Computer and Information Technology, University of Liaoning Normal,
Dalian, China
zhangjing_0412@lnnu.edu.cn

Abstract. Subject-independent emotion recognitions take full advantage of existing EEG signals to construct intelligent models, and generalize to other subjects for detecting, differentiating and predicting. However, objective differences originating from different subjects strength the difficulties of constructing models, which are summarized as both of challenges: 1) the physiological difference products incorrect EEG signals, and 2) the psychological difference may be generated the early or late response signals to induce the local semantic invalidation. Aiming to above problems, we propose a novel EEG subject-independent model (termed of Unbiased Global Spatial Representation). First, present the self-incremental Auto-encoder network to obtain latent unified features to correct the physiological deviation. Second, leverage gramian angular fields (GAF) to transfer from one-dimension time sequences to two-dimension spatial images to remedy the local semantic invalidation. Finally, attention-CNN is constructed to extract more discriminate global features to enhance performances. The proposed model is verified in popular datasets for subject-independent emotion recognitions, and compare with classical models achieving satisfactory performances.

Keywords: Emotion recognition · EEG · Subject-independent recognition · Convolutional neural network

1 Introduction

Psychologists presented that emotions play the important role in human living, such as, environmental perception, interpersonal communication, decision-making process and so on. Emotion recognition based on machine learning sampling various of body signals to construct intelligent models achieving emotion detection, analysis and prediction. Emotion data usually are derived from physiological and behavioral signals, where behavioral signals, including facial expression, voice, action and posture, are extremely easy disturbed by the surrounding environment, therefore, it is difficult to obtain stable and effective emotion information. Physiological signals are obtained by specific equipment including EEG sampling machines, magnetic resonance imaging, eye movement instruments,

H. Fujita et al. (Eds.): IEA/AIE 2023, LNAI 13925, pp. 385–396, 2023.
https://doi.org/10.1007/978-3-031-36819-6_34

which are more objective and accurate than behavioral signals. Hence, it is widely applied in emotion tracking, automatic driving, disease diagnosis and so on, which mainly contain EEG, ECG, EOG, and GSR. EEG as a kind of non-intrusion signal is excited by the electric current originated from neurons located in the cerebral cortex according to time sequence, which provide the effective method for researching emotion activities.

According to different targets, EEG emotion recognition models are divided into subject-dependence and subject-independence. For subject-dependence models, the training and testing dataset sampling from the same source, which avoid the negative effect originated from the innate biological differences. Hence, it is a kind of popular EEG emotion recognition methods, moreover, the related works more focus on extraction and optimization of features [1,2]. However, subject-dependence models product the strong dependence for training subjects in testing process, which greatly reduce the generalization and limit promotion and utilization of models. Subject-independence models leverage all of subjects to construct models, and separate between training and testing targets to enhance the generalization. [3] minimizes the difference between source and target of human brain. But this method needs a large of training samples and meet the prerequisite that all of subjects follow the normal distribution. Aiming to above problem, [4] proposed convolutional recurrent attention model based on EEG to integrate recognition models from all subjects and focus on some time-clips with discriminate. Meanwhile, [5] presented graph-embedded convolutional neural network to extract local convolution features and leverage LSTM incremental learning of model [6]. However, above methods are difficult to solve the local semantic invalidation. Based on this, we summarize two challenges for subject-independence EEG emotion recognition: 1) How to obtain unbiased EEG signals. 2) How to ensure the semantic consistency of local features from different subjects.

Aiming to above challenges, we propose a novel subject-independent emotion recognition model (termed of Unbiased Global Spatial Representation-UGSR). First, present self-incremental Auto-encoder network to obtain the unified latent representation of EEG without classification labels. And then, utilize GAF to transfer from one-dimension time sequences to global two-dimension spatial-features, meanwhile, leverage the attention-CNN network to strength discriminability of features. Contributions are summarized as follows:

1) We propose the self-incremental Auto-encoder network to obtain the unified representation of all subjects without labels, which avoid errors that originated from physiological difference of different subjects.
2) We leverage GAF to achieve the global spatial representation of each subject to solve the problem of losing local semantics resulting from psychological difference of different subjects. And, utilize the attention-CNN network to obtain more discriminative features.
3) The proposed model improve the accuracy of subject-independent emotion recognition in three popular datasets including SEED, DEAP, DREAMER, and this model provide inspiring for constructing subject-independent models.

2   Related Works

Auto-Encoder Network. Rum et al. [7] proposed the auto-encoder network (AE) with the help of the neural network architecture, and build up the optimization goal of minimizing the restoration error to mining data nonlinearity features. The network structure of single hidden layer Auto-encoder network includes an input layer, a hidden layer, and an output layer. The calculation process maps input samples to features of the hidden layer through the encoder, and the decoder reconstructs the features of the hidden layer into the output layer. In the signal hidden Auto-encoder network, the encoder $g\left(\cdot\right)$ receives the input samples $X \in \Re^{N \times d}$ with d-dimension, and construct mapping $g : \Re^d \rightarrow \Re^h$ to achieve encoding of data and obtain the output of hidden level $Z = \sigma(W^T X + b)$, where W is the linear projection matrix, b is the encoder bias vector, and σ is the nonlinear activation function. The decoder $f\left(\cdot\right)$ accepts the samples processed by the encoder, that is, the output of hidden layer Z, decodes it as the original sample, constructs the map $f : \Re^h \rightarrow \Re^d$, and obtains the reconstruction $\hat{X} = f\left(g\left(X\right)\right)$ of the input samples as the prediction of X. The squared error function is used to minimize the sample reconstruction error between $X = \left\{x_i \in \Re^N\right\}_{i=1}^{N}$ and the reconstructed sample set $\hat{X} = \left\{\hat{x}_i \in \Re^N\right\}_{i=1}^{N}$.

At the same time, the model is solved by using gradient descent and back-propagating errors. In unsupervised learning, samples can obtain more discriminative potential nonlinear features after passing the autoencoder network.

Spatial Representation of Samples and Global Feature Extraction. In order to transfer from one-dimension time-sequences to two-dimension spatial images, Wang et al. based on the Gram matrix proposed GAF [8], which generate polar coordinates by taking the time-stamp as the arc cosine of the radius and scale value, and the polar coordinate angle value is provided. Both time-sequences are represented by the polar coordinate system instead of the cartesian coordinate system. Since GAF can well preserve the dependencies and correlations of time series, it can avoid the loss of information during processing signals. Therefore, this method can be used as retaining the characteristics of EEG time-sequences, and convers signals to two-dimensional images.

At the same time, the deep convolutional neural network (CNN) effectively improves the recognition accuracy of two-dimensional images by extracting nonlinear high-dimensional features of samples. The biological receptive field mechanism inspires the model establishment. Based on this, CNN is composed of convolutional layers, pooling layers, and fully connected layers. The convolutional layer regularly scans the input samples, and the pooling layer reduces the dimension of features and maintains the scale invariance of features to a certain extent. Moreover, CNN has the advantages of local connection, weight sharing, and aggregation in the structure. Each neure located on the current convolute layer connect with some neures located on the adjacent layer, and the size of domain is decided by the size of convolutional kernel. In training, samples as the input of network with regularly.

3   Proposed Model

Aiming at above problems for subject-independence EEG emotion recognition that result from data deviation and local semantic failure caused by the heterogeneity of subjects, we propose the unbiased global spatial representation model. The framework is shown in Fig. 1.

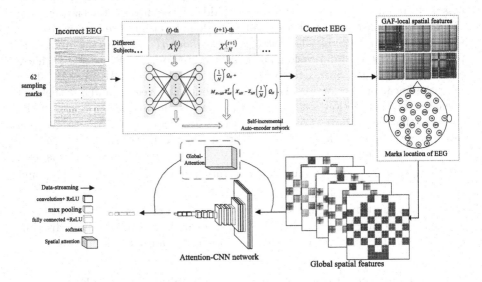

Fig. 1. The framework of the proposed mode.

3.1   Self-incremental Unbiased Subject-Independent Correction

EEG signals are highly susceptible facing to psychological influences of subjects, which result in non-stationary, heterogeneous, and other characteristics. In the paper, propose an unbiased incremental subject-independent correction method to adequately leverage the EEG database and ensure the accuracy of emotion recognition. The dataset $X^{(t)} \in \Re^{N \times 62}$ is collected by N subjects at the time $t = 1, 2, \ldots T$ original from 62 electrodes. According to the auto-encoding network, we can obtain the features of hidden layer of all subjects $Z_N^{(t)} = \mathrm{g}\left(X_N^{(t)}\right)$ and $Z^{(t)} \in \Re^{N \times 62}$, where g $(\cdot)$ is the encoding network. In this paper, the single-hidden layer autoencoder network can better represent EEG at each time due to the number of neurons in the auto-encoding network is a fixed value of 62 from the collecting method of EEG. Moreover, in order to enhance the solving efficiency and avoid the problem of the local optimal solutions, we are inspired by Hunag et al. [9] that proposed and proved the effectiveness and feasibility of extreme learning machine for solving the single hidden layer network. In this work, the decoder model $f(\cdot)$ can be solved by the linear formula system.

Therefore, based on the solution process of the paper [9], we can obtain the decoder (the weighted matrix of network output):

$$\hat{Q} = (Z^T Z)^{-1} Z^T \hat{X}. \tag{1}$$

However, EEG as time-sequences how to improve the learning efficiency while ensuring the accuracy of the model has become an essential issue. This paper is inspired by Scardapane et al. [10], combining with the single-hidden layer autoencoder network structure, the self-incremental unified feature correction model is proposed for the unlabeled EEG. The model only learns $X_N^{(t+1)}$ at the current time $t + 1$, and does not need to repeat train the existing all of samples to achieve knowledge accumulation.

For samples $X_N^{(t)}$ at time t including training samples and testing samples, we expect to achieve correcting without the help of label information. According to the Eq. (1), we can solve the weight matrix of the decoder in the single hidden layer autoencoder network $\hat{Q}_N$. The collected samples $X_{N+\Delta N}^{(t+1)}$ at time $t + 1$ from the terminal. In order to ensure that the model is updated from the new information and the old knowledge is not forgotten, we get the new output matrix $Q_{N+\Delta N} = \begin{bmatrix} q_{N+1}^T & q_{N+2}^T & \cdots & q_{N+\Delta N}^T \end{bmatrix}^T$ after all the current samples undergo the encoding process, that is, linear transformation and nonlinear activation function calculation. At the same time, the output layer vector of decoder is $\hat{X}_{N+\Delta N} = \begin{bmatrix} \hat{x}_{N+1} & \hat{x}_{N+2} & \cdots & \hat{x}_{N+\Delta N} \end{bmatrix}^T$. Combining the new samples at the current time with the Eq. (1), and the weight matrix of output of all samples can be obtained, as shown in Eq. (2).

$$\hat{Q}_{N+\Delta N} = \left(Z_N^T Z_N + Z_{\Delta N}^T Z_{\Delta N}\right)^{-1} \left(Z_N^T \hat{X}_N + Z_{\Delta N}^T \hat{X}_{\Delta N}\right). \tag{2}$$

where $Z_{N+\Delta N}^T Z_{N+\Delta N} = Z_N^T Z_N + Z_{\Delta N}^T Z_{\Delta N}$. At this time, for the convenience of calculation, the auxiliary matrix can be set: $M_{N+\Delta N}^{-1} = M_N^{-1} + Z_{\Delta N}^T Z_{\Delta N}$. Therefor, Eq. (3) can be obtained by simultaneously inverting both sides of the above formula.

$$M_{N+\Delta N} = \left(M_N^{-1} + Z_{\Delta N}^T Z_{\Delta N}\right)^{-1}. \tag{3}$$

Therefore, combining both of the Eq. (2) and Eq. (3) can be obtained.

$$M_{N+\Delta N} = M_N - M_N Z_{\Delta N}^T \left(I_{\Delta N} + Z_{\Delta N}^T M_N Z_{\Delta N}\right)^{-1} Z_{\Delta N} M_N. \tag{4}$$

Putting the Eq. (4) into the Eq. (2), the updated output layer model at time $t + 1$ can be obtained, as shown in Eq. (5).

$$\begin{aligned} \hat{Q}_{N+\Delta N} &= M_{N+\Delta N} \left(Z_N^T \hat{X}_N + Z_{\Delta N}^T \hat{X}_{\Delta N}\right) \\ &= M_{N+\Delta N} \left(\left(M_{N+\Delta N}^{-1} - Z_{\Delta N}^T Z_{\Delta N}\right) Q_N + Z_{\Delta N}^T Z_{\Delta N}\right) \\ &= Q_N + M_{N+\Delta N} Z_{\Delta N}^T \left(\hat{X}_{\Delta N} - Z_{\Delta N} Q_N\right). \end{aligned} \tag{5}$$

The adaptive forgetting factor is introduced to weaken the influence of the last moment on the current model, and the final updated model is obtained, as shown in the Eq. (6).

$$\hat{Q}_{N+\Delta N} = \left(\frac{1}{N}\right)^r Q_N + M_{N+\Delta N} Z_{\Delta N}^T \left(X_{\Delta N} - Z_{\Delta N}\left(\frac{1}{N}\right)^r Q_N\right). \tag{6}$$

Among them, r is an integer constant, which is used to control the forgetting speed of the model for the pre-order data.

For time-sequences EEG, the new information is updated at each time t while the current information is retained. At the same time, according to the Eq. (6), the correction model at the current moment is obtained as an encoder to realize the correction and obtain a unified latent space expression:

$$X' = \hat{Q}_{N+\Delta N}^T X_{\Delta N}^{(t+1)}. \tag{7}$$

3.2   Global Spatial Representation

Psychological differences make that different subjects do not produce emotional activity signals at about same time when they receive the common stimuli. They only exist information related to emotional triggers in a few time periods, which is likely to cause local semantic invalidation in different subjects. In order to solve this problem, we propose the global spatial representation model.

First, to prevent other subjects from producing temporally different local responses to the same environment. In this paper, the GAF method is used to transfer from the one-dimension time-sequences to two-dimensional images with spatially, and then extract more robust global features. The method is aimed at the corrected EEG. To achieve numerical convenience and reduce the mean square errors, with Eq.(19), all of testing samples of each time-sequence are projected to [-1, 1], and the sequence $\tilde{x}_i = \frac{x'_i - \max X' + x'_i - \min X'}{\max X' - \min X'}$ is obtained. In order to avoid the missing information during the processing of time-sequences, each element in Cartesian coordinates is converted to the cosine value of paired time-sequence values in polar coordinates with the help of GAF, that is, transfering $\tilde{x}_i$ into an angular cosine expression. $\begin{cases} \phi = \arccos \tilde{x}_i - 1 \leq \tilde{x}_i \leq 1 \\ R = \frac{t_i}{N} t_i \in N \end{cases}$. is used to obtained expression in polar coordinates, where R is the radius. t is the timestamp and N is a constant factor normalizing the polar coordinate space. Moreover, through the Gramian Angular Summation Field (GASF) of the cosine function supplement the paired time-sequence in polar coordinates, and express the polar coordinates of the time-sequence as image features. Then define the following Eq. (7).

$$G_{GASF} = \begin{bmatrix} \cos\phi_1 + \phi_1 \cdots \cos\phi_1 + \phi_n \\ \cos\phi_2 + \phi_1 \cdots \cos\phi_2 + \phi_n \\ \vdots \\ \cos\phi_n + \phi_1 \cdots \cos\phi_n + \phi_n \end{bmatrix} = \tilde{X}^T \tilde{X} - \sqrt{I - (\tilde{X}^2)}^T \sqrt{I - (\tilde{X}^2)}. \tag{8}$$

where I is the unit row vector, and $\widetilde{X}^T$ is the transposed vector. In subject-independent scenarios, because of the variability among subjects, GAF combines temporal and spatial features by transforming the one-dimensional signal into two-dimensional feature data. In order to keep the spatial structure of consistent with electrode positions,we array the two-dimension image of each electrode according to the spatial coordinates of EEG electrodes and the relative positions between different electrodes. All of transformed two-dimension representations of time-sequences are reconstructed as a global image with a size of 9*9, and we fill the positions without values. Therefore, according to the image representation of different subjects, we can exploit a deep convolutional network model to extract more discriminative non-linear features.

The CNN network with 7-level convolutions and 4-levels pooling is constructed to extract more discriminate features. The deep network architecture through layer-by-layer convolution operations and the maximum pooling to obtain the nonlinear features of the image, and it is easier to highlight the local features of images. Moreover, we induce the global attention to strength features with semantics.

4 Experiments

This paper verifies the performances of the proposed method on three public and popular EEG datasets, including SEED, DEAP and DREAMER, and compares it with the classical recognition models, such as SVM, DBN, DGCNN and STRNN, to further illustrate the effectiveness of the proposed model in solving the problem of subject-independent emotion recognition In the experiments, we measure and compare the results by the kind of evaluation methods the accuracy (acc) value. Moreover, EEG has the following four types of expression: time domain, frequency domain, time-frequency and spatial, where frequency domain is the most common expression. Zouridakis et al. [11] used the band-pass filtering method to decompose EEG into five bands. Then, according to the method proposed by Zheng et al. [12] to achieve Differential Entropy (DE) and Power Spectrum Density in frequency. Each frequency band and the splicing features of all frequency bands in PSD are used as inputs in the process of emotion recognition model construction. PSD is the power expression method for calculating signal frequency band, and the Fourier transform method is usually used to calculate the power spectral density.

This model deploys on the PC with Intel Core I7- 11700,2.5Hz,16 cores, NVIDIA GTX 3070 graphics card and 8GB video memory with the PyCharm development platform. Open source framework Tensorflow2 under the implementation.

4.1 Analysis of Experimental Results

In this paper, the effectiveness of the proposed model is verified and compared on three popular EEG datasets including SEED, DEAP, DREAMER.

SEED. SEED consists of multi-subject collected by the BCMI Laboratory, including 15 subjects, triggered by 15 movie clips lasting about 4 min, including neutral, negative and positive emotions. In order to verify the effectiveness of the model for subject-independent emotion recognition, we obtain the average accuracy of the testing results of 14 subjects by subject-independent.

The experimental results are shown in Fig. 2. We can know that USGR can obtain the unified potential space of all samples through incremental correcting to avoid the identification error caused by the difference subjects. At the same time, the global features eliminates the influence of difference. At all frequencies, performances are better than other comparison methods. The accuracy of the frequency γ reached 86.67%, and accuracies of all frequency still reached 84.44%. In comparison methods, SVM, TCA, TKL, SA and GFKD are all aimed at improving the discriminability. However, these methods do not consider the negative influence of incorrecting data for the classification results, then have not achieved satisfactory results in all frequency. DGCNN based on the graph neural network model, and multi-channel EEG signals are used as graph-data to capture the relationship between samples, then achieve better results. STRN utilizes the framework of RNN with incremental learning for time-sequences to express continuous features of EEG. GECNN combines both of local and global features to obtain complementary emotional information to enhance recognition performances. However, above models can not solve the negative effect original from errors of different subjects.

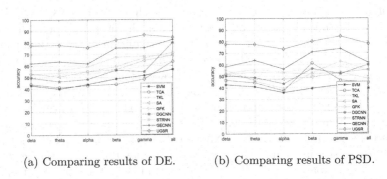

(a) Comparing results of DE.   (b) Comparing results of PSD.

Fig. 2. Experimental results in the SEED dataset

DEAP. DEAP is the multi-subject multi-modal affective state dataset from 32 subjects. EEG were generated by watching 401 min music-videos. In this paper, Valence and Arousal were labeled as positive if values were higher than 5, and vice versa. Because of the preprocessed data provided by DEAP is filtered in the 4.0–45.0Hz frequency band (the δ band is removed), we select only four frequency bands, namely θ(4-8Hz), α(8-14Hz), β(14-31Hz) and γ (31-50Hz) in DEAP, and the interval window is 2s. At the same time, the 3-second pre-experimental baseline was deleted in DE and PSD. Consistent with the SEED dataset, this paper adopted the cross-validation strategy to construct training and testing datasets to calculate the accuracy for subjects-independent emotion recognition.

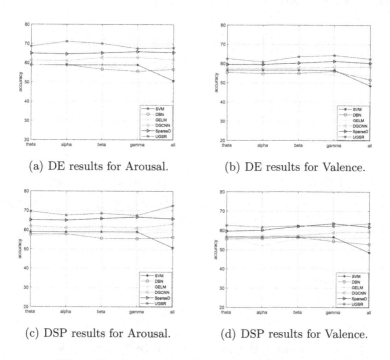

(a) DE results for Arousal.   (b) DE results for Valence.

(c) DSP results for Arousal.   (d) DSP results for Valence.

Fig. 3. Experimental results in the DEAP dataset.

As shown in Fig. 3., the comparing results of all methods in this dataset. The proposed model (USGR) eliminates the noise caused by the heterogeneity of subjects for subject-independent recognition, at the same time, fully avoids the local semantic invalidation problem from the delay of emotional features. Therefore, our method both of DE and PSD in DEAP dataset reached the highest accuracy. The full-band recognition rate of two kinds of emotions of DE reached 62.45% and 67.83%, and in PSD reached 63.57% with 72.05%. DBN is improved by integrating the discriminant results, but the influence of EEG on the model construction is not considered. At the same time, the generalization of subject-independent recognition problems is also weak. SparseD is an improved sparse DGCNN model. Although the SparseD model has made some progress in solving the problem of emotion discrimination by applying sparse optimization to the weighted graph, it fails to achieve better results facing subject-independent recognitions. In this paper, we leverage the global attention mechanism to enhance the discriminability of output features in supervised learning. In order to illustrate the effectiveness of operation, we print the comparing results between the non-attention and attention. Figure 3 shows visualization results, moreover, Fig. 3(a) and (c) are the global features without attention, and Fig. 3(b) and (c) supplement attention to strength the global features. According to figures, attention operation can strength important features under supervised of labels to enhance the discriminability (Fig. 4).

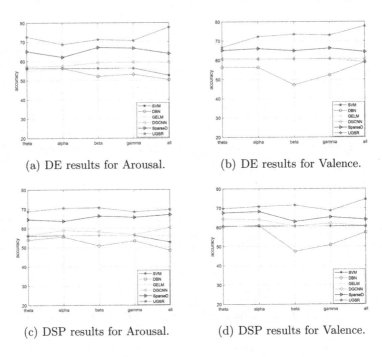

(a) DE results for Arousal.   (b) DE results for Valence.

(c) DSP results for Arousal.   (d) DSP results for Valence.

Fig. 4. Experimental results in the DREAMER dataset.

DREAMER. DREAMER is a multi-modal, multi-subject emotion dataset. It is recorded by the Emotiv EPOC system 128 Hz sampling rate. The dataset collected from 23 subjects. Consistent with DREAMER dataset, it contains four frequency bands: θ(4-8Hz), α(8-14Hz), β(14-31Hz) and γ(31-50Hz). PSD and DE were calculated for each frequency band. In the DREAMER dataset, happiness and arousal degree are larger than 3 for the positive label, and vice versa for the negative label. In order to ensure the fairness of the experiments and count the accuracy of subject-independent recognition, we also use the cross-validation strategy to build training and testing datasets and summarize the results.

Testing results are shown in Fig. 6. Compared with other methods, the proposed model in this dataset still achieved better recognition accuracy for subject-independent experiments, and for two kinds of DE and PSD, the highest recognition accuracy is 77.64 and 70.66, respectively. The latent features of different subjects can be obtained by subject-independent correcting, which effectively reduces the individual differences subjects and improves the recognition performances. At the same time, global spatial features effectively weakened the local differentiation of different subjects at time-sequences, comparing with other methods to obtain robust features, which improves performances for subject-independent recognition.

4.2 Ablation Experiments

In order to further discuss the challenges of solving the subject-independent emotion recognition problem for EEG, and the rationality and effectiveness of the proposed model, this paper conducted ablation experiments on all of datasets, and the statistical results are shown in Table 1. The ablation experimental results on SEED: 1) the original EEG dataset (no-adjust) is used to test, and results is summarized in Table 1. In all frequency bands of SEED dataset, the model does not get the satisfactory performances due to acquisition bias from individual physical differences; 2) only utilize the self-incremental auto-encoder network (no-GAF), according to results from Table 1. The proposed model corrects the original data to obtain the latent unify features, and avoid the dissimilation problems from different subjects to enhance the accuracy; 3) supplement the global spatial representation by GAF based on (2) to obtain discriminate features leveraging CNN network (no-attention), the results are shown in Table 1. In addition to the errors caused by physiological factors, subjects product reflecting signals at different time-stamp in the same environment, which cause local semantic invalidation. Aiming to above problem, in this paper, the global spatial features transfer from one-dimension time features to two-dimension image expression and exploit CNN network to achieve better discriminate features; 4) exploit the global attention mechanism (USGR) in the CNN network based on (3), the results are summarized in Table 1. We obtain more discriminate features by attention and achieve the highest accuracy in all bands. According to above results, we can verify the mainly factors of reducing performances of subject-independent are the heterogeneous problems from different subjects. Moreover, the proposed model can effectively release above problems.

Table 1. Accuracy Of Ablation Test For SEED Dataset

Feature	δ	θ	α	β	γ	all
UGSR	77.56	77.79	75.56	82.22	86.67	84.44
without attention	75.22	75.23	74.21	80.00	85.12	82.22
without GAF	73.52	73.33	72.04	77.10	84.45	80.02
without adjust	71.35	71.35	70.97	75.78	77.49	80.14

5 Conclusion

Subject-dependent EEG emotion recognitions is only utilized in the current training subject, which reduces the generalization, and the amount of EEG datasets are wasted. Aiming to above problems, we propose the novel subject-independence model to obtain the latent unbiased representation of subject according to self-incremental auto-encoder network. Furthermore, leverage GAF to avoid local semantic invalidation, and the global attention CNN network is utilized to extract the discriminative features to enhance performances. In the future, we will excavate the structure between electrodes in the collecting process of EEG to remove the negative effect of noises for constructing models.

References

1. Song, T., Zheng, W., Song, P., Cui, Z.: EEG emotion recognition using dynamical graph convolutional neural networks. IEEE Trans. Affect. Comput. **11**(3), 532–541 (2018)
2. Zhang, G., Yu, M., Liu, Y.J., Zhao, G., Zhang, D., Zheng, W.: SparseDGCNN: recognizing emotion from multichannel EEG signals. IEEE Transactions on Affective Computing (2021)
3. Li, Y., Zheng, W., Zong, Y., Cui, Z., Zhang, T., Zhou, X.: A bi-hemisphere domain adversarial neural network model for EEG emotion recognition. IEEE Trans. Affect. Comput. **12**(2), 494–504 (2018)
4. Zhang, D., Yao, L., Chen, K., Monaghan, J.: A convolutional recurrent attention model for subject-independent EEG signal analysis. IEEE Sig. Process. Lett. **26**(5), 715–719 (2019)
5. Song, T., Zheng, W., Liu, S., Zong, Y., Cui, Z., Li, Y.: Graph-embedded convolutional neural network for image-based EEG emotion recognition. IEEE Trans. Emerg. Top. Comput. **10**, 1399–1413 (2021)
6. Michieli, U., Zanuttigh, P.: Incremental learning techniques for semantic segmentation. In: Proceedings of the IEEE/CVF International Conference on Computer Vision Workshops (2019)
7. Bourlard, H., Kamp, Y.: Auto-association by multilayer perceptrons and singular value decomposition. Biol. Cybernet. **59**(4), 291–294 (1988)
8. Wang, Z., Oates, T.: Encoding time series as images for visual inspection and classification using tiled convolutional neural networks. In: Workshops at the Twenty-Ninth AAAI Conference on Artificial Intelligence (2015)
9. Huang, G.B., Zhu, Q.Y., Siew, C.K.: Extreme learning machine: theory and applications. Neurocomputing **70**(1–3), 489–501 (2006)
10. Scardapane, S., Comminiello, D., Scarpiniti, M., Uncini, A.: Online sequential extreme learning machine with kernels. IEEE Trans. Neural Netw. Learn. Syst. **26**(9), 2214–2220 (2014)
11. Zouridakis, G., Patidar, U., Padhye, N.S., Pollonini, L., Passaro, A., Papanicolaou, A.C.: Spectral power of brain activity associated with emotion-a pilot meg study. In: Supek, S., Sušac, A. (eds.) 17th International Conference on Biomagnetism Advances in Biomagnetism – Biomag 2010. IFMBE Proceedings, vol. 28, pp. 354–357. Springer, Berlin (2010). https://doi.org/10.1007/978-3-642-12197-5_83
12. Zheng, W.L., Lu, B.L.: Investigating critical frequency bands and channels for EEG-based emotion recognition with deep neural networks. IEEE Trans. Auton. Ment. Dev. **7**(3), 162–175 (2015)

Micro-expression Recognition Based on Local Optical Flow Capsule Network

Zhihua Xie[✉] and Xiaoyu Liu

Key Lab of Optic-Electronic and Communication, Jiangxi Science and Technology Normal
University, Nanchang 330013, China
xie_zhihua68@aliyun.com

Abstract. Micro-expression (ME) is a kind of facial muscle movement sponta-
neously, which can reflect people's real emotions and be widely used in psychological treatment, suspect interrogation and other fields. However, the intensity
and duration of ME pose enormous challenges to robust micro-expression recognition (MER). In this work, a capsule network based on local optical flow features
(LOFCAP) is proposed to explore efficient MER. In the MER based on LOFCAP,
the input ME images are divided into small blocks with the same size. Then, each
one is sent to residual network (ResNet) convolutional layer for feature extraction.
Finally, the fused features are sent into the capsule network for final classification.
SMIC, SAMM and CASME II databases are used to validate experimental results.
Furthermore, unweighted F1 score (UF1) and unweighted average recall (UAR)
are used as evaluation metrics. Especially, when the image is divided into 9 blocks,
UF1 and UAR reached 0.8104 and 0.8403, respectively. Experimental results from
full micro-expression datasets show that our LOFCAP model can effectively represent the local features on ME and the overall performance is successful than the
state-of-the-art methods.

Keywords: Micro-expression Recognition · Local Features · Optical Flow ·
Capsule network · Motion Feature

1 Introduction

ME (micro-expression) is a rapid and involuntary facial expression triggered to hide
people's real emotions [1]. The standard ME lasts between 1/25 and 1/3s, normally
occurs only in specific positions of face [2], which is characterized by its low intensity
and fast-moving. Although automatic MER (ME recognition) is an extremely difficult
task, it has aroused great interest of many researchers. [3]. Over the years, many methods
based on machine learning and deep learning for MER have emerged. The LBP-TOP
(Local Binary Patterns from Three Orthogonal Planes) method designed by Zhao et al.
uses the histogram of LBP-TOP to extract dynamic facial texture features [4], which is
considered as a baseline in most of studies. Liu et al. Liong et al. illustrated Bi-weighted
Oriented Optical Flow (Bi-WOOF) feature approach [5], which utilized optical flow
strain to weight features of different regions to highlight ME. Zong et al. [6] proposed

© The Author(s), under exclusive license to Springer Nature Switzerland AG 2023
H. Fujita et al. (Eds.): IEA/AIE 2023, LNAI 13925, pp. 397–406, 2023.
https://doi.org/10.1007/978-3-031-36819-6_35

a hierarchical space division scheme for spatiotemporal descriptor extraction, which assigns different weights to facial blocks and can measure each block's special contribution to MER. On this basis, they proposed a hierarchical model of kernelized Group Sparse Learning (KGSL) to enhance recognition result. Wei et al. [7] proposed a MER formula based on kernelized two-groups sparse learning model (KTGSL) that fused local space and local motion features, and achieved better recognition performance than the traditional convolutional neural network model by focusing on block regional features and efficient fusion features. The researches mentioned above all indicate that paying attention to local features is an effective way for ME task.

In recent years, methods of deep learning have emerged for MER. Quang et al. [8] firstly introduced capsule network into the research of MER, which considered the mutual position link among extracted features. However, this method only focused on the spatial characteristics of micro-expressions and ignored the temporal information of micro-expressions. The DCADAN approach conducted by Xie et al. [9] used optical flow maps as input in a capsule network and performed transfer learning on the macro expression dataset, which obtained a good effect on MER. Given that ME appears in particular position. Chen et al. [10] maintained the relationship between facial regional features by Block Division Convolutional Network (BDCNN) verifies the important role of the relationship between local features in MER task. Lei et al. developed a model based on facial graph representation learning and facial action unit fusion, which learned a representation of facial graph using node learning and edge learning and seized subtle changes of ME by learning AU relationship through GCN. This model made full use of the position relationship of ME in different facial regions and got a good recognition rate on MER [11].

To sum up, the regional and spatial location information is significant for MER and worthwhile to further be explored. In response to the diverse local features representation learning, the main contributions of this work can be summarized as following four points:

(1) We apply Farneback optical flow calculated by the apex and onset frame as input to the network rather than only employ apex frame for motion representation.
(2) We divide input images into the same size of pieces and resize them into 224*224 to explore more useful local information.
(3) Aiming to leave the extracted features more subtle and hierarchical, we feed these pieces into ResNet18 model and utilize its convolution layer for feature extraction.
(4) To focus on the relationship representation among the movement features of ME, the capsule network is built to identify the efficient and regional features.

2   Related Works

2.1   Farneback Optical Flow

Optical flow is considered as a relatively simple way for displaying the movement of image. It is the instantaneous speed of the pixel of moving objects on the imaging plane, and can capture the tiny motion of objects. In ME sequence, the magnitude and direction of optical flow can be employed to describe the movement information of facial muscles. As for the study of optical flow, it is generally classified by sparse optical flow and dense optical flow. Sparse optical flow algorithm can only process a few features of the image, which suffers limitations, while dense optical flow algorithm calculates the optical flow information of each pixel point, so as to acquire the dense optical flow field of the whole image. This paper applies the dense Farneback optical flow [12] conducted by Gunner Farneback to support our work. The key of the algorithm is to create an approximate polynomial to represent the neighborhood information of each pixel. Assuming the gradient and local optical flow are constant, image I is estimated by polynomials as follows:

$$I_1(x) = x^T A_1 x + b_1{}^T x + c_1. \tag{1}$$

where A_1 is a symmetric matrix, b is a vector, and c is a scalar. If there is a global offset with vector d between the next and the previous frames, the second frame can be estimated as follows:

$$
\begin{aligned}
I_2(x) = I_1(x - d) &= (x - d)^T A_1(x - d) + b_1^T(x - d) + c_1 \\
&= x^T A_1 x + (b_1 - 2A_1 d)^T x + d^T A_1 d - b_1^T d + c_1 = x^T A_2 x + b_2^T x + c_2
\end{aligned} \tag{2}
$$

Among them:

$$A_2 = A_1. \tag{3}$$

$$b_2 = b_1 - 2A_1 d. \tag{4}$$

$$c_2 = d^T A_1 d - b_1{}^T d + c_1. \tag{5}$$

If A_1 is a non-singular matrix, then the global offset vector d is expressed as below:

$$d = -\frac{1}{2}A_1^{-1}(b_2 - b_1). \tag{6}$$

In sense, it is too idealistic to fit an image only with one polynomial and is less rigorous to denote the motion of one image. Therefore, $A_1(x)$ and $A_2(x)$ is not equal to some extent. Consequently, $A(x)$, $\Delta b(x)$ will be estimated approximately by the average value.

$$A(x) = \frac{A_1(x) + A_2(x)}{2}. \tag{7}$$

$$\Delta b(x) = -\frac{1}{2}(b_2(x) - b_1(x)). \tag{8}$$

$$A(x)d(x) = \Delta b(x). \tag{9}$$

Obviously, if the operation is performed on each pixel point according to Eq. (9), it will inevitably impose a huge amount of calculation. Here, Weighted Least Squares (WLS) is applied to construct the objective function e(x), and the task of this function is to seek the appropriate value of d(x) to minimize the value of e(x). The e(x) is represented by Eq. (10), where $w(\Delta x)$ is the weight function of pixel point x.

$$e(x) = \Sigma_{\Delta x \in P} w(\Delta x) \big| \big| A(x + \Delta x)d(x) - \Delta d(x + \Delta x)^2 \big| \big|^2 \tag{10}$$

Through Eq. (10), d(x) and e(x) are inferred as follows:

$$d(x) = \left(\Sigma wA^TA\right)^{-1} \Sigma wA^Tb \tag{11}$$

$$e(x) = \left(\Sigma w\Delta b^T \Delta b\right) - d(x)^T \Sigma wA^T \Delta b \tag{12}$$

Under the same coordinate, the polynomial extension will change and expand errors with the with the increase of the spatial displacement. Hence, a prior displacement $\tilde{d}(x)$ is introduced to solve this problem.

$$\tilde{x} = x + \tilde{d}(x) \tag{13}$$

As a result, there are:

$$A(x) = \frac{A_1(x) + A_2\left(\tilde{x}\right)}{2} \tag{14}$$

$$\Delta b(x) = -\frac{1}{2}\left(b_2\left(\tilde{x}\right) - b_1(x)\right) + A(x)\,\tilde{d}\,(x) \tag{15}$$

2.2 Capsule Network

CNN replaced the traditional manual feature extraction methods with its ability to extract features automatically. However, Professor Hinton believes that CNN is not able to perceive the relative position relationship between local features on account of the scalar neurons. Sabour et al. [13] put forward CapsNet and introduced the concept of "capsule" where each capsule can be regarded as a vector neuron. Especially, because the vector has multiple dimensions including size and direction, a capsule can deal with the internal relationship of the image well. Thus Quang et al. [8] firstly applied the CapsuleNet to MER. CapsuleNet applies convolutional layer including initial capsule layer and fully connected layer. The initial capsule layer converts the feature map extracted from the convolutional layer into vector capsule, and then finds connection between part of the image and the whole through dynamic routing mechanism. Vector neurons of capsule network are shown in Fig. 1:

In the dynamic routing iteration of the capsule network, the digital capsule v_j is calculated from the primary capsule u_i. In the Fig. 1, u_i is denoted as the i-th (i = 1,2... N) primary capsule while v_j is called the j-th (j = 1..., n) digital capsule, and w_{ij} is the transformation matrix to encode the relationship between low-level features and high-level features. The predicting capsule vector $U_{j|i}$ is obtained when W_{ij} multiplies u_i as shown in Eq. (16):

$$U_{j|i} = W_{ij}u_i \tag{16}$$

Similarity b_{ij} is between the prediction vector $U_{j|i}$ and the output vector v_j, and it changes in the process of dynamic routing as follows:

$$b_{ij} \leftarrow b_{ij} + U_{j|i} \cdot v_j \tag{17}$$

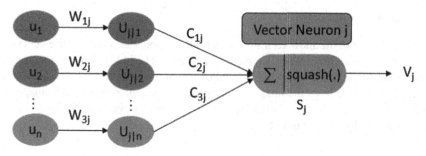

Fig. 1. Schematic diagram of vector neurons

The coupling coefficient c_{ij} is acquired through Eq. (18):

$$c_{ij} = \frac{\exp(b_{ij})}{\Sigma_j \exp(b_{ij})} \tag{18}$$

S_j is the sum input of the upper capsule layer, which is obtained as Eq. (19). v_j is defined by S_j through a nonlinear activation function called 'squash', with the vector direction unchanged and the length constrained between 0 and 1.

$$S_j = \Sigma_i c_{ij} U_{j|i} \tag{19}$$

$$v_j = \frac{||s_j||^2}{1 + ||s_j||^2} \frac{s_j}{||s_j||} \tag{20}$$

3 Proposed MER Method

Since the capsule network can well handle the position relationship between the local features of image, LOFCAP network is designed for efficient MER. The change of micro-expression is subtle, and optical flow can use the change of image sequence in the time domain to find the corresponding relationship between the previous frame and the current frame. As a result, we select the onset and apex frame to calculate motion information between them. Using only the onset frame and apex frame instead of the video sequence can reduce the computation cost while retaining most of the features. In our method, two frames are fed into method of Farneback Optical Flow. Then, the area of 120*120 in the center of the optical flow map is cropped as the input of the network. Thirdly, the input image is split into the same size of blocks, and each block is enlarged into 224*224 to get a richer receptive field. Accordingly, we further choose convolutional layers of ResNet18 to extract regional and salient features. The convolved local feature maps are fused in capsule network and the aggregated maps are used to classify the MEs. Finally, the feature maps after fusion are more discriminative when compared with the origin ones in our results as shown in Table 2.

3.1 Data Preprocessing

At first, the onset frame and apex frame of each ME sequence are obtained to calculate the optical flow feature map. Next, two pictures are resized to 144*144 to ensure complete information of pictures and possess a smaller size at the same time. After deriving the optical flow feature map, the image was cropped in the center to get a sub-image with the resolution of 120*120, and then the original image was evenly divided into a series of blocks, which is shown in Fig. 2.

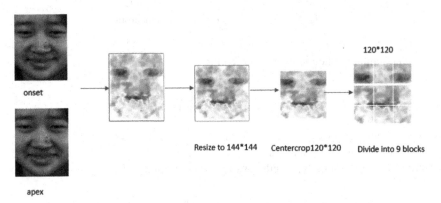

Fig. 2. The process of partitioning with 9 blocks

3.2 The Detail Architecture of LOFCAP

Based on the basic architecture of capsule network, we introduce an approach of local optical flow feature extraction to enhance the network. The detail structure of LOFCAP is shown in Fig. 3.

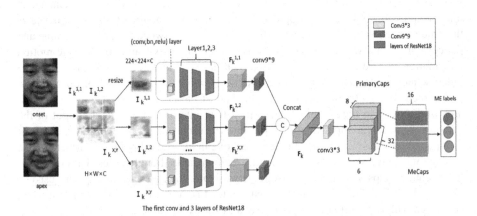

Fig. 3. The framework of LOFCAP

As visualized in Fig. 3, apex and onset frames are given to calculate the input denoted by I_K. Let $I_K \in R^{H \times W \times C}$, where H, W, and C represent the height, width and channel number of the image. In the block division module, each image is separated into blocks with a size of X $\times$ Y, where X = W/S, Y = H/S and S is the length of the single block. Finally, the image feature I_K can be expressed as:

$$I_K = \{I_K{}^{i,j} | 1 \le i \le X, 1 \le j \le Y\} \tag{21}$$

where $I_K{}^{i,j}$ corresponds to the block of i-th row and j-th column. In addition, the size of each block is S $\times$ S $\times$ C originally. Then each block resizes to 224*224 and is sent to ResNet18 model without the fourth convolutional layer. The output $F_K{}^{i,j}$ of each block after being convolved with a 9 $\times$ 9 kernel is concatenated, that is:

$$F_K = Conv_{9*9}(Concat(F_K{}^{1,1}, F_K{}^{1,2}, F_K{}^{X,Y})) \tag{22}$$

The aggerated feature F_K are next convolved with a 3 $\times$ 3 kernel and fed into the capsule network.

4 Experiments and Analysis

4.1 Evaluations

Our dataset is derived from three publicly available ME databases: SMIC [14], SAMM [15], and CASME II [16]. To evaluate the performance of MER effectively, leave-one-subject-out (LOSO)cross-validation is adopted to assess the robustness of the model on the cross-database. The comparison results are listed in Table1.

Table 1. Performance from our proposed methods and the baselines. Bold fonts indicate the best results.

Methods	UF1(Full dataset)	UAR(Full dataset)
LBP-TOP [4]	0.588	0.578
Bi-WOOF [5]	0.629	0.622
CapsuleNet [8]	0.652	0.650
DConv + ETran + AUGCN + AUFsuion [11]	0.791	0.793
DCADAN [9]	0.801	0.829
LOFCAP-4(ours)	0.769	0.815
LOFCAP-9(ours)	**0.810**	**0.840**

On account of the imbalance of sentiment samples in the database, Unweighted F1-score (UF1) and Unweighted Average Recall (UAR) are used as evaluation indicators in the experiment. Both indicators are calculated using the following formula:

$$UF1 = \frac{1}{C} \sum_i^c \frac{2TP_i}{2TP_i + FP_i + FN_i} \tag{23}$$

$$UAR = \frac{1}{C} \sum_{i}^{c} \frac{TP_i}{N_i} \tag{24}$$

where C is the number of classes and TP_i, FP_i, FN_i, and N_i denote the number of true positives, false positives, false negatives and total samples belong to class i, respectively.

It can be seen in Table 1 that our model has a good performance on MER. Especially, when the input pictures are divided into 9 pieces, the network performance is higher than CapsuleNet on UF1 by 15.8% and on UAR by 19%. In fact, we should have continued to explore whether the more blocks, the better the recognition effect, but gave up due to the limitation of the big computation complexity. However, judging from the results in the last two rows of the Table 1, our LOFCAP method is quite efficient and achieves the best recognition performance.

4.2 Ablation Study

The ablation results of different models conducted on the full dataset are listed in Table 2. First, model A omits these three modules and is set as the baseline. Model B with only the module of optical flow has a remarkable increase of 21% in UAR and 19% in UF1 when compared with model A. It can be inferred that the superiority of extracting salient motion features with optical flow. Judging from the consequence of model D and model E/F, we can indicate that our partition strategy is valid and successful. However, the performance evaluations of fused features are varied from different positions in LOFCAP.

Table 2. Ablation studies on different position of fusing separated features. Bold fonts indicate the best results.

Models	Optical flow	Block_Num	Concate_position	UAR	UF1
A	----	----	----	0.6048	0.5969
B	√	----	----	0.8141	0.7852
C	√	4	Before PrimaryCaps	0.8146	0.7688
D	√	4	After PrimaryCaps	0.8288	0.7997
E	√	9	Before PrimaryCaps	**0.8403**	**0.8104**
F	√	9	After PrimaryCaps	0.8204	0.7891

As illustrated in Table 2, model C attains a UAR of 0.8146 and a UF1 of 0.7688, and meanwhile, model D obtains a UAR of 0.8288 and a UF1 of 0.7977. Based on the available data, it can be found that when the image is separated into 4 pieces, the optimal fusion position is after the PrimaryCaps. With respect to model E and model F, the study demonstrates that the suitable fusion position is before the PrimaryCaps when the picture is divided into 9 pieces, and achieves the best results with a UAR of 0.8403 and a UF1 of 0.8104. From Table 2, the proposed model E and model F both outperform model C and model D, which reveals the fact that the partition mode with 9 blocks is more efficient than the partition mode with 4 blocks for MER based on LOFCAP.

5 Conclusion

This work takes the optical flow image processed by the onset and apex frames in ME sequence as the input of the network to capture the motion features from ME. Our capsule network is separated into different pieces and each piece is normalized to extract the local features on face images. When the ME image is chunked into 9 blocks equally, the recognition performance of our LOFCAP reaches 0.8104 and 0.8403 on UF1 and UAR respectively. Overall, the experimental results prove that proposed LOFCAP model has strong representation capability for the specific MER task.

Acknowledgements. This paper is supported by the Natural Science Foundation of Jiangxi Province of China (No.20224ACB202011), the National Nature Science Foundation of China (No.61861020) and the Jiangxi Province Graduate Innovation Special Fund Project (No. YC2022-s790).

References

1. Ekman, P., Friesen, W.V.: Nonverbal leakage and clues to deception. Psychiatry **32**(1), 88–106 (1969)
2. Yan, W.J., Wu, Q., Liang, J., et al.: How fast are the leaked facial expressions. J. Nonverbal Behav. **37**(4), 217–230 (2013)
3. Song, B., Zong, Y., Li, K., et al.: Cross-database micro-expression recognition based on a dual-stream convolutional neural network. IEEE Access **10**, 66227–66237 (2022)
4. Zhao, G., Pietikainen, M.: Dynamic texture recognition using local binary patterns with an application to facial expressions. IEEE Trans. Pattern Anal. Mach. Intell. **29**(6), 915–928 (2007)
5. Liong, S.T., See, J., Wong, K.S., et al.: Less is more: Micro-expression recognition from video using apex frame. Sign. Process. Image Commun. **62**, 82–92 (2018)
6. Zong, Y., Huang, X., Zheng, W., et al.: Learning from hierarchical spatiotemporal descriptors for micro-expression recognition. IEEE Trans. Multimed. **20**(11), 3160–3172 (2018)
7. Wei, J., Lu, G., Yan, J.: Learning two groups of discriminative features for micro-expression recognition. Neurocomputing **479**, 22–36 (2022)
8. Van Quang, N., Chun, J., Tokuyama, T.: CapsuleNet for micro-expression recognition. In: IEEE International Conference on Automatic Face & Gesture Recognition, pp. 1–7 (2019)
9. Xie, Z., Shi, L., Cheng, S., et al.: Micro-expression recognition based on deep capsule adversarial domain adaptation network. J. Electron. Imaging **31**(1), 013021 (2022)
10. Chen, B., Liu, K., Xu, Y., et al.: Block division convolutional network with implicit deep features augmentation for micro-expression recognition. IEEE Trans. Multimed. **25**, 1345–1358 (2022)
11. Lei, L., Chen, T., Li, S., et al.: Micro-expression recognition based on facial graph representation learning and facial action unit fusion. In: Proceedings of the IEEE/CVF Conference on Computer Vision and Pattern Recognition, pp. 1571–1580 (2021)
12. Farnebäck, G.: Two-frame motion estimation based on polynomial expansion. In: Bigun, J., Gustavsson, T. (eds.) Image Analysis: 13th Scandinavian Conference, SCIA 2003. Lecture Notes in Computer Science, vol. 2749, pp. 363–370. Springer, Berlin (2003). https://doi.org/10.1007/3-540-45103-X_50
13. Sabour, S., Frosst, N., Hinton, GE.: Dynamic routing between capsules. In: Advances in Neural Information Processing Systems, vol, 30 (2017)

14. Li, X., Pfister, T., Huang, X., et al.: A spontaneous micro-expression database: inducement, collection and baseline. In: IEEE International Conference and Workshops on Automatic face and gesture recognition. 1–6 (2013)

15. Davison, A.K., Lansley, C., Costen, N., et al.: SAMM: a spontaneous micro-facial movement dataset. IEEE Trans. Affect. Comput. **9**(1), 116–129 (2016)

16. Yan, W.J., Li, X., Wang, S.J., et al.: CASME II: an improved spontaneous micro-expression database and the baseline evaluation. PLoS ONE **9**(1), e86041 (2014)

Emotion Prediction Based on Conversational Context and Commonsense Knowledge Graphs

Takumi Fujimoto$^{(\boxtimes)}$ and Takayuki Ito

Department of Social Informatics, Kyoto University, Kyoto 6068317, Japan
fujimoto.takumi.68h@st.kyoto-u.ac.jp, ito@i.kyoto-u.ac.jp

Abstract. Existing studies on emotion recognition in conversations have generally analyzed and classified emotions based on a speaker's utterances from conversations. On the other hand, little research has predicted emotions without such speaker utterances. In this study, we propose an emotion prediction model that forecasts a speaker's emotion before she makes a statement utilizing conversational context and commonsense knowledge graphs. In an evaluation experiment, we rate our proposed model's performance using an emotion recognition dataset in conversations.

Keywords: Emotion Prediction · Emotion Recognition in Conversation

1 Introduction

As the proliferation of social media and chat tools continues to grow, opportunities for text-based conversations and discussions are greatly expanding. However, compared to face-to-face communication, text communication struggles to feel sympathy and effect smooth communication because it lacks such information as the facial expressions and the gestures of each participant.

In response to these problems, understanding emotions, a requirement which influences every aspect of decision-making [7], is critical in text-based communication. However, although many studies on emotion recognition have focused on analyzing and classifying emotions based on a speaker's utterances in a conversation, there is little research on predicting an emotion before an actual utterance is made [9].

Therefore, this study deals with emotion prediction in conversation and aims to predict a speaker's emotion before the actual utterance appears in a conversation. The rest of this paper is organized as follows: Sect. 2 discusses related work; Sect. 3 provides a detailed description of our model; Sect. 4 presents and discusses the experimental results, and Sect. 5 concludes our paper.

2 Related Work

Emotion recognition in conversation classifies the feelings of a given participant's utterances based on such information as those texted at the time in the conversation and previous history.

H. Fujita et al. (Eds.): IEA/AIE 2023, LNAI 13925, pp. 407–412, 2023.
https://doi.org/10.1007/978-3-031-36819-6_36

In research on emotion recognition in conversation, one study [6] focused not only on the utterance texts themselves but also on the speaker's state and the conversational context. Another study [2] tracked emotional changes outside of the context by utilizing a commonsense knowledge graph as external knowledge along with the conversation context.

Emotion prediction in conversations aims to predict the emotion of a given participant's utterance before it is made, based on such information as the previous utterance in the conversation and the conversation history. This approach differs from emotion recognition in conversation in that it does not use the speaker's utterance at the time for predicting the speaker's emotion.

In research on emotion prediction in conversation, a previous study [4] focused on two emotion characteristics, persistence, and contagiousness, to predict emotions by considering the influence of the conversation context on them. Another study [5] utilized context-independent external knowledge from a commonsense knowledge graph. Our study differs from these previous studies because it attempts emotion prediction by combining a context model, which predicts emotions by addressing the influence of bi-directional conversation context, and a commonsense model, which predicts emotions independently of context with a commonsense knowledge graph.

3 Emotion Prediction Based on Context and Commonsense

3.1 Emotion Prediction Model

As shown in Fig. 1, the proposed method combines a bi-directional context model (Sect. 3.2) and a commonsense model (Sect. 3.3) and predicts emotions.

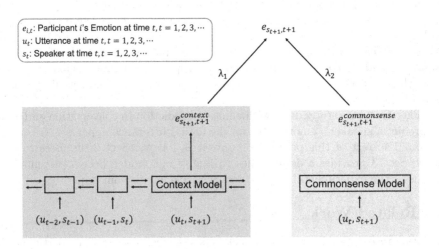

Fig. 1. Overview of proposed emotion prediction model

Emotion $e_{i,t+1}$ of participant i at time $t+1$ is calculated by Eq. (1):

$$e_{i,t+1} = \lambda_1 \cdot e_{i,t+1}^{context} + \lambda_2 \cdot e_{i,t+1}^{commonsense}, \tag{1}$$

where $e_{i,t+1}^{context}$ is the output of context model (Sect. 3.2), $e_{i,t+1}^{commonsense}$ is the output of commonsense model (Sect. 3.3), and λ_1, λ_2 are hyperparameters $0 \leq \lambda_1, \lambda_2 \leq 1$. As a result of preliminary experiments, we used the ($\lambda_1 = 1.0, \lambda_2 = 0.3$) setting in the following experiments.

3.2   Context Model

A context model, which predicts emotions based on conversation environments, consists of the following three processes (Fig. 2).

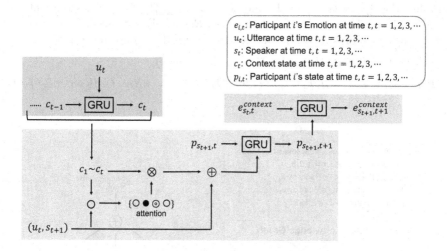

Fig. 2. Overview of context model

First, context state c_t at time t is calculated by

$$c_t = GRU(c_{t-1}, u_t), \tag{2}$$

where u_t is an utterance at time t.

Second, participant i's state $p_{i,t}$ at time $t+1$ is calculated by Eq. (3):

$$p_{i,t+1} = \lambda_i^{u_t} \cdot p_{i,t} + (1 - \lambda_i^{u_t}) \cdot GRU(p_{i,t}, (u_t \oplus Attention(u_t, [c_1, c_2, ..., c_t]))),$$

$$Attention(u_t, [c_1, c_2, ..., c_t]) = softmax(u_t^T \otimes [c_1, c_2, ..., c_t]) \otimes [c_1, c_2, ..., c_t]^T,$$

$$\lambda_i^{u_t} = \begin{cases} 0, \text{participant } i \text{ is a speaker of } u_t \\ 1, \text{participant } i \text{ is not a speaker of } u_t \end{cases}, \tag{3}$$

where $[c_1, c_2, ..., c_t]$ is all the conversation history before time t.

Finally, emotion state $e_{i,t+1}^{context}$ of participant i at time $t+1$ is calculated by

$$e_{i,t+1}^{context} = GRU(e_{i,t}^{context}, p_{i,t+1}).\tag{4}$$

3.3 Commonsense Model

In this study, as a commonsense knowledge graph, we use ATOMIC [10], which is organized as typed, if-then relations with variables $\{subject, relation, object\}$, and COMET [1], which is a commonsense generative model trained on ATOMIC, to predict emotions using commonsense for each utterance. COMET generates an $object$ from the $subject$ and the $relation$ following $object = COMET(subject, relation)$ (e.g., s = "take a nap," r = Causes, o = "have energy").

Our commonsense model predicts emotions from commonsense knowledge graphs (Fig. 3). In this model, emotion state $e_{i,t+1}^{commonsense}$ of participant i at time $t+1$ is calculated using parameters $oReact$, $oWant$, and $oEffect$, which denote others (non-speakers) obtained from COMET, following Eq. (5):

$$e_{i,t+1}^{context} = ReLu(oReact_{i,t}, oWant_{i,t}, oEffect_{i,t}),$$
$$oReact_{i,t}, oWant_{i,t}, oEffect_{i,t} = COMET(u_t, s_{t+1}, oReact, oWnat, oEffect).\tag{5}$$

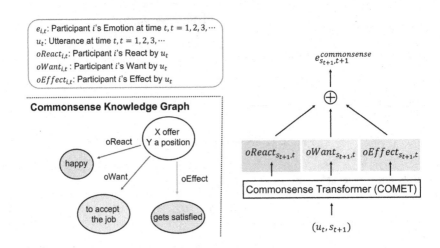

Fig. 3. Overview of commonsense model

4 Evaluation

4.1 Dataset

We evaluated the performance of our proposed method by MELD [8], a multimodal conversation dataset used in emotion recognition. This dataset is categorized into seven emotion categories: surprise, fear, sadness, joy, disgust, anger (Ekman's six basic emotions), and neutral.

4.2 Comparison Method

We evaluated the performance of our proposed method in comparison experiments with the following four existing methods. DialogueRNN [6] recognizes the speaker's emotion by utilizing the conversation context of each participant. COSMIC [2] recognizes a speaker's emotions using conversation context and commonsense knowledge graphs. DialogInfer-(S+G) [4] is an emotion prediction model that combines a sequence-based model and a graph-based model that captures short-term and long-term emotion propagation. DialogInfer-(S+G)+K [5] is a hybrid emotion prediction model that combines DialogInfer-(S+G) and a commonsense knowledge graph.

The input features for all the models were unified into 1024-dimensional input using RoBERTa-Large. We used batch size of 8, learning rate of 0.001, masking rate of 0.4 for context model, and dropout rate of 0.1 to train the models. Cross entropy was used as the optimization objective function of the model, and the optimization algorithm was Adam. All models were trained for 60 epochs and other hyperparameters were optimized using the grid search.

4.3 Results and Discussion

As shown in Table 1, the proposed method outperformed the existing methods in all emotion categories and achieved the highest score of 46.22 on MELD. There were significant improvements by about 10% or more in joy and sadness compared with other methods. Especially about disgust, though existing methods failed to detect it at all, the proposed method could predict it and achieved a score of 5.71. However, the results for negative emotions (disgust and anger) showed no difference or are lower than when the context model is used alone. One possible reason for this result is that the commonsense model cannot sufficiently identify negative emotions. To address this point, we will update a commonsense model using the ATOMIC$^{20}_{20}$ [3].

Table 1. Experimental results on MELD: Weighted-F1 is used as evaluation metric in reference to previous emotion recognition studies. DialogueRNN and COSMIC were adjusted to fit this task. Since DialogInfer-(S+G) and DialogInfer-(S+G)+K are not publicly available, we used the values previously reported in papers for this evaluation.

Method	Neutral	Surprise	Fear	Sadness	Joy	Disgust	Anger	Weighted-F1
DialogueRNN	55.39	16.22	03.77	01.84	28.57	00.00	21.37	35.75
COSMIC	60.64	07.31	00.00	06.96	15.16	00.00	29.01	36.58
DialogInfer-(S+G)	62.05	13.77	04.17	10.57	25.18	00.00	35.01	40.67
DialogInfer-(S+G)+K	62.19	15.95	00.00	07.62	25.47	00.00	36.94	40.96
Context	64.07	23.63	06.67	20.45	39.88	08.33	36.25	46.19
Commonsense	36.09	11.93	02.26	16.32	23.30	06.55	17.66	26.04
Context+Commonsense (ensemble)	63.83	23.76	00.00	21.26	39.28	02.90	37.44	45.95
Context+Commonsense (proposed)	64.07	23.69	06.78	21.38	39.94	05.71	36.25	**46.22**

5   Conclusion

We confirmed that combining a context model, which predicts emotions by recognizing conversational contexts in bi-directions, and a commonsense model, which predicts emotions using a commonsense knowledge graph, is effective for emotion prediction.

In future work, we will enhance the inference quality by a commonsense knowledge graph and improve the performance of emotion prediction by considering emotion changes that cannot be tracked just by the conversational context.

Acknowledgements. This work was supported by JST CREST Grant Number JPMJCR20D1, Japan.

References

1. Bosselut, A., Rashkin, H., Sap, M., Malaviya, C., Celikyilmaz, A., Choi, Y.: COMET: commonsense transformers for automatic knowledge graph construction. In: Proceedings of the 57th Annual Meeting of the Association for Computational Linguistics, pp. 4762–4779 (2019)
2. Ghosal, D., Majumder, N., Gelbukh, A., Mihalcea, R., Poria, S.: COSMIC: commonsense knowledge for emotion identification in conversations. In: Findings of the Association for Computational Linguistics: EMNLP 2020, pp. 2470–2481 (2020)
3. Hwang, J.D., et al.: (comet-) ATOMIC 2020: on symbolic and neural commonsense knowledge graphs. In: Proceedings of the AAAI, vol. 35, pp. 6384–6392 (2021)
4. Li, D., et al.: Emotion inference in multi-turn conversations with addressee-aware module and ensemble strategy. In: Proceedings of the 2021 Conference on Empirical Methods in Natural Language Processing, pp. 3935–3941 (2021)
5. Li, D.: Enhancing emotion inference in conversations with commonsense knowledge. Knowl.-Based Syst. **232**, 107449 (2021)
6. Majumder, N., Poria, S., Hazarika, D., Mihalcea, R., Gelbukh, A., Cambria, E.: DialogueRNN: an attentive RNN for emotion detection in conversations. In: Proceedings of the AAAI, vol. 33, pp. 6818–6825 (2019)
7. Polignano, M., Narducci, F., de Gemmis, M., Semeraro, G.: Towards emotion-aware recommender systems: an affective coherence model based on emotion-driven behaviors. Expert Syst. Appl. **170**, 114382 (2021)
8. Poria, S., Hazarika, D., Majumder, N., Naik, G., Cambria, E., Mihalcea, R.: MELD: a multimodal multi-party dataset for emotion recognition in conversations. In: Proceedings of the 57th Annual Meeting of the Association for Computational Linguistics, pp. 527–536 (2019)
9. Rong, H., Ma, T., Cao, J., Tian, Y., Al-Dhelaan, A., Al-Rodhaan, M.: Deep rolling: a novel emotion prediction model for a multi-participant communication context. Inf. Sci. **488**, 158–180 (2019)
10. Sap, M., et al.: ATOMIC: an atlas of machine commonsense for if-then reasoning. In: Proceedings of the AAAI, vol. 03, pp. 3027–3035 (2019)

Author Index

H. Fujita et al. (Eds.): IEA/AIE 2023, LNAI 13925, pp. 413–416, 2023.
https://doi.org/10.1007/978-3-031-36819-6

Printed in the United States
by Baker & Taylor Publisher Services